A Stanley Gibbons checklist
of the stamps of Great Britain

Collect British Stamps

75th Edition
2024

S T A N L E Y
GIBBONS
THE HOME OF STAMP COLLECTING

By Appointment to
Her Majesty Queen Elizabeth II
Philatelists
Stanley Gibbons Ltd
London

Published by Stanley Gibbons Ltd
Editorial, Publications Sales Offices
and Distribution Centre:
7 Parkside, Christchurch Road, Ringwood,
Hants BH24 3SH

© Stanley Gibbons Ltd 2023

British Library Cataloguing in
Publication Data.
A catalogue record for this book is available
from the British Library.

Errors and omissions excepted. The colour
reproduction of stamps is only as accurate as
the printing process will allow.

ISBN-13: 978-1-7394673-7-1

Item No. R0289-24

Printed by Sterling, Kettering

Contents

The 2024 Edition

COLLECT BRITISH STAMPS has been the standard guide for collectors of Great Britain ever since the first edition was published in September 1967.

It provides a straightforward, easy-to-use work of reference, with every stamp design illustrated in colour and clear, uncomplicated listings ideally suited to the newer collector, while at the same time providing a handy checklist for the more advanced philatelist – small wonder that over four million copies have been sold to collectors around the world.

Collect British Stamps appears in the autumn of each year: for a more detailed listing, the *Great Britain Concise Catalogue* is published in the spring, incorporating many additional features and is ideal for the collector who needs more information about GB stamps.

Scope. Collect British Stamps comprises:

- All stamps with different watermark (wmk) or perforation (perf).
- Visible plate numbers on Victorian issues.
- Graphite-lined and phosphor issues, including variations in the numbers of phosphor bands.
- First Day Covers for Definitives from 1936, Regionals and all Special Issues.
- Presentation, Gift and Souvenir Packs.
- Post Office Yearbooks, Collectors Packs and Miniature Sheet collections.
- Regional issues and War Occupation stamps of Guernsey and Jersey.
- Postage Due and Official Stamps.
- Post Office Picture Cards (PHQ cards).
- Commemorative gutter pairs and 'Traffic Light' gutter pairs listed as mint sets.
- Royal Mail Postage Labels priced as sets and on P.O. First Day Cover.
- Royal Mail Post & Go Stamps
- Royal Mail Prestige Stamp Booklets.
- Royal Mail Numismatic and Medallic covers.
- The introduction includes a Great Britain collector's glossary and articles giving helpful advice on a range of collecting topics
- A fully revised and updated design index now appears at the end of the catalogue.

Stamps of the independent postal administrations of Guernsey, Isle of Man and Jersey are contained in *Collect Channel Islands and Isle of Man Stamps.*

New for this edition

- Issues up to Christmas 2021 have been added and the listings of earlier issuesd carefully checked and updated.
- Prices have been carefully reviewed thoughout.
- Style and content brought in line with the Great Britian Concise stamp catalogue, with additional type illustrations added where needed to aid readers.

Layout

Stamps are set out chronologically by date of issue. In the catalogue lists the first numeral is the Stanley Gibbons

catalogue number; the black (boldface) numeral alongside is the type number referring to the respective illustration. A blank in this column implies that the number immediately above is repeated. The denomination and colour of the stamp are then shown. Before February 1971 British currency was:

£1 = 20s. One pound = twenty shillings and

1s = 12d. One shilling = twelve pence.

Upon decimalisation this became:

£1 = 100p.

One pound = one hundred (new) pence.

The catalogue list then shows two price columns. The left-hand is for unused stamps and the right-hand for used. Our method of indicating prices is: Numerals for pence, e.g. 10 denotes 10p. (10 pence). Numerals for pounds and pence, e.g. 4·25 denotes £4·25 (4 pounds and 25 pence). For £100 and above, prices are in whole pounds and so include the £ sign and omit the zeros for pence.

Where a stamp is described as 'As' another stamp, it means similar in appearance to that stamp, but differing in some key respect, such as gum, paper, perforation or printing method. It does not mean that it is the *same* as that stamp.

Note that stamps which only appear within miniature sheets are not seperately listed as individual items. However stamps which come from booklets are listed individually.

It should be noted that if a stamp or set is self-adhesive this is specifically noted in the set heading. If there is no reference to a stamp being self adhesive it will have ordinary gum.

Colour illustrations

The colour illustrations of stamps are intended as a guide only; they may differ in shade from the originals.

Size of illustrations

To comply with Post Office regulations stamp illustrations are three-quarters linear size, miniature sheets are further reduced to fit in the available space. Separate illustrations of surcharges, overprints and watermarks are actual size.

Prices

The prices quoted in this catalogue are the estimated selling prices of Stanley Gibbons Ltd at the time of publication. They are *unless it is specifically stated otherwise,* for examples in very fine condition for the issue concerned. Superb examples are worth more; those of a lower quality considerably less. For more details on catalogue prices, see page xiv

The unused prices for stamps of Queen Victoria to King George V are for lightly hinged examples. Unused prices for King Edward VIII to Queen Elizabeth II are for unmounted mint (though when not available unmounted, mounted stamps are often supplied at a lower price). Prices for used stamps refer to very fine postally used examples, for issues from about 1880 with a very fine circular or oval dated cancellation. For further guidance on condition, see 'The Stanley Gibbons Guide to Stamp Pricing on page xiv. All prices are subject to change without prior notice and we give no guarantee to supply all stamps priced, since it is not possible to keep every catalogued item in stock. Commemorative issues may only be available in complete sets.

In the price columns:

† = Does not exist.

(—) or blank = Exists, or may exist, but price cannot

be quoted.

* = Not normally issued (the so-called 'Abnormals' of 1862–1880).

Minimum price

The minimum price quoted is 10 pence. For individual stamps prices between 10 pence and 95 pence are provided as a guide for catalogue users. The lowest price *charged* for individual stamps or sets purchased from Stanley Gibbons is £1.

Perforations

The 'perforation' is the number of holes in a length of 2 cm, as measured by the Gibbons Instanta gauge. The stamp is viewed against a dark background with the transparent gauge put on top of it. Perforations are quoted to the nearest half. Stamps without perforation are termed 'imperforate'. From 1992 certain stamps occur with a large elliptical (oval) hole inserted in each line of vertical perforations. The £10 definitive, No. 1658, is unique in having two such holes in the horizontal perforations.

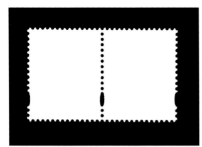

Elliptical perforations

Se-tenant combinations

Se-tenant means 'joined together'. Some sets include stamps of different design arranged *se-tenant* as blocks or strips and these are generally collected unsevered as issued. Where such combinations exist the stamps are priced both mint and used, as singles or complete sets. The set price refers to the unsevered combination plus singles of any other values in the set.

Miniature sheets sold singly include a barcode and other information in a panel at the left-hand edge. Sheets from presentation packs have this panel trimmed off. Catalogue prices are the same, either way.

First day covers

Prices for first day covers are for complete sets used on plain covers (Nos. 430/438, 453/460, 462/478*b*, 485/490, and 503/512) or on special covers (Nos. 461, 479/484, 491/502 and 513 onwards), the stamps of which are cancelled with ordinary operational postmarks (1924–1962) or by the standard 'First Day of Issue' postmarks (1963 onwards). The British Post Office did not provide 'First Day' treatment for every definitive issued after 1963. Where the stamps in a set were issued on different days, prices are for a cover from each day.

For all decimal issues (from 1971), first day cover prices are for official Royal Mail philatelic bureau products. Others may be worth more, but will frequently be worth less. If there was no official bureau first day cover service for a particular stamp or set, no price will be available.

Presentation Packs

Special packs comprising slip-in cards with printed information inside a protective covering, were introduced for the 1964 Shakespeare issue. Collectors packs, containing commemoratives from the preceding 12 months, were issued from 1967. Some packs with text in German from 1968–1969, exist as does a Japanese version of the pack for Nos. 916/917. Yearbooks, hardbound and illustrated in colour within a slip cover, joined the product range in 1984.

Many modern presentation packs include the relevant miniature sheet, however not all do so. If the miniature sheet is to be found in the presentation pack this is now noted.

It should be noted that prices given for presentation packs are for items as originally sold, including any additional inserts such as questionaire forms and publicity material.

PHQ cards

Since 1973 the Post Office has produced a series of picture cards, which can be sent through the post as postcards. Each card shows an enlarged colour reproduction of a current British stamp, either of one or more values from a set or of all values. Cards are priced here in fine mint condition for sets complete as issued. The Post Office gives each card a 'PHQ' serial number, hence the term. The cards are usually on sale shortly before the date of issue of the stamps, but there is no officially designated 'first day'. Used prices are for cards franked with the stamp depicted, on the obverse or reverse; the stamp being cancelled with an official postmark for first day of issue. For 1973–1976 issues cards with stamps on the obverse are worth about 25% more than the prices quoted.

Gutter pairs

Almost all modern Great Britain commemoratives are produced in sheets containing two panes of stamps separated by a blank horizontal or vertical margin known as a gutter. This feature first made its appearance on some supplies of the 1972 Royal Silver Wedding 3p., and marked the introduction of Harrison & Sons' new 'Jumelle' stamp-printing press. There are advantages for both the printer and the Post Office in such a layout which has now been used for nearly all commemorative issues since 1974. The term 'gutter pair' is used for a pair of stamps separated by part of the blank gutter margin. We do not list gutter pairs for self-adhesive stamps since, although the production format is the same, the stamps are separated by die-cutting.

Gutter pair

Most printers include some form of colour check device on the sheet margins, in addition to the cylinder or plate numbers. Harrison & Sons used round 'dabs' or spots of colour, resembling 'traffic lights'. For the period from the 1972 Royal Silver Wedding until the end of 1979 these colour dabs appeared in the gutter margin. Gutter pairs showing these 'traffic lights' are worth considerably more than the normal version. From the 2004 Entente Cordiale set, Walsall reintroduced traffic lights in the gutters of certain sets. Where these extend over more than one section of gutter margin on any stamp they are priced as blocks rather than pairs.

Traffic light gutter pair

No Value Indicated Stamps

From 22 August 1989 various definitive and special stamps appeared inscribed '2nd', '1st' or 'E' instead of a face value. These were sold at the current minimum rates for these services which were as follows:

Inland Postage Rate	2nd Class	1st Class
5 September 1988	14p.	19p.
2 October 1989	15p.	20p.
17 September 1990	17p.	22p.
16 September 1991	18p.	24p.
1 November 1993	19p.	25p.
8 July 1996	20p.	26p.
26 April 1999	19p.	26p.
17 April 2000	19p.	27p.
8 May 2003	20p.	28p.
1 April 2004	21p.	28p.
7 April 2005	21p.	30p.
3 April 2006	23p.	32p.
2 April 2007	24p.	34p.
7 April 2008	27p.	36p.
6 April 2009	30p.	39p.
6 April 2010	32p.	41p.
4 April 2011	36p.	46p.
30 April 2012	50p.	60p.
31 March 2014	53p.	62p.
30 March 2015	54p.	63p.
29 March 2016	55p.	64p.
27 March 2017	56p.	65p.
26 March 2018	58p.	67p.
25 March 2019	61p.	70p.
23 March 2020	65p.	76p.
1 January 2021	66p.	85p.
4 April 2022	68p.	95p.
3 April 2023	75p.	£1·10
2 October 2023	75p.	£1·25

European Airmail Rate	
26 April 1999	30p.
25 October 1999	34p.
27 April 2000	36p.
2 July 2001	37p.
27 March 2003	38p.
1 April 2004	40p.

From June 2004, European Airmail rate stamps reverted to showing a face value.

From 21 August 2006 'Large' letters were charged at a higher rate following the introduction of 'Pricing in Proportion'. Rates as follows:

Inland Postage Rate	2nd Class Large	1st Class Large
21 August 2006	37p.	44p.
2 April 2007	40p.	48p.
7 April 2008	42p.	52p.
6 April 2009	47p.	61p.
6 April 2010	51p.	66p.
4 April 2011	58p.	75p.
30 April 2012	69p.	90p.
31 March 2014	73p.	93p.
30 March 2015	74p	95p
29 March 2016	75p.	96p.
27 March 2017	76p.	98p.
26 March 2018	79p.	£1·01
25 March 2019	83p.	£1·06
23 March 2020	80p.	£1·15

1 January 2021	96p.	£1·29
4 April 2022	£1·05	£1·45
3 April 2023	£1·15	£1·60
2 October	£1·55	£1·95

Catalogue numbers used

This checklist uses the same catalogue numbers as other current Stanley Gibbons catalogues.

Latest issue date for stamps recorded in this edition is 7 December 2023.

We regret we do not give opinions as to the genuineness of stamps, nor do we identify stamps or number them by our Catalogue.

Guarantee

All stamps are guaranteed genuine originals in the following terms:

If not as described, and returned by the purchaser, we undertake to refund the price paid to us in the original transaction. If any stamp is certified as genuine by the Expert Committee of the Royal Philatelic Society, London, or by BPA Expertising Ltd, the purchaser shall not be entitled to make any claim against us for any error, omission or mistake in such certificate.

Consumers' statutory rights are not affected by the above guarantee.

The recognised Expert Committees in this country are those of the Royal Philatelic Society, London, 15 Abchurch Lane, London EC4 7BW, and B.P.A. Expertising Ltd, P.O. Box 1141, Guildford, Surrey GU5 0WR. They do not undertake valuations under any circumstances and fees are payable for their services.

Contacting the Catalogue Editor

The Editor is always interested in hearing from people who have new information which will improve or correct the Catalogue. As a general rule he must see and examine the actual stamps before they can be considered for listing; photographs or scans are insufficient evidence, although an initial email to *Thecatalogueeditor@stanleygibbons.com* will determine whether or not an item is likely to be of interest.

Where information is solicited purely for the benefit of the enquirer, the editor cannot undertake to reply if the answer is already contained in these published notes. Email communications are greatly preferred to enquiries by telephone and the editor regrets that he or his staff cannot see personal callers without a prior appointment being made. Correspondence may be subject to delay during the production period of each new edition.

Collecting Stamps – the Basics

It seems reasonable to assume, since you are reading this, that you already collect British stamps – but of course there are many ways of building on any collection and, if you are relatively new to it, we hope that the following will be of some guidance.

Traditionally, stamp collectors were introduced to the hobby with a quantity of world stamps, some still on envelopes and cards, which were then sorted and mounted in an album. In due course, many would decide to concentrate on a single country or group of countries and 'specialisation' would begin, based on the experience built up as a 'world collector'.

More recently, an alternative route has become prevalent, in which, often as a gift, collections may be built on a 'standing order' from a philatelic bureau, with stamps or covers arriving automatically, as they are issued, to be mounted in an album or stockbook. Albums are conveniently designed to meet the needs of this type of collection, with an illustrated space in which to mount every stamp.

This type of collection has much to recommend it – but one big disadvantage – it will be exactly the same as thousands of others, built up in the same way.

For this reason, many collectors are now returning to the delights of general collecting while maintaining their existing collections, and finding that the fun they had as children is very easy to recapture!

If you came to the hobby via 'the standing order' route and would like to start a second 'general collection', here are a few tips and suggestions.

Obtaining your stamps

Children were encouraged to buy – or persuade their parents to buy – the largest packet of stamps they could, as just sorting them into countries would prove enormously useful and interesting. Unfortunately large packets of world stamps are not as easy to obtain as they used to be, but you can still buy existing collections of all sorts at stamp fairs, shops or at auction, prices to suit every pocket. Just sorting and remounting such a collection will prove tremendously exciting.

Sooner or later, of course, you will identify gaps in your collection that you want to fill. It is useful to keep a note of these in a book that you can take with you when you visit a stamp shop or stamp fair – no one can remember everything and it is always annoying to discover that you have just bought a stamp you didn't need!

It is vitally important of course that you keep your 'wants' book up-to-date and cross out items as you acquire them.

As well as visiting stamp fairs, you can check out the advertisements in the press; establish a good relationship with a dealer you like and, he will be happy to receive a 'wants list' from you. He will then supply you with any items on it he has currently in stock and keep a record of anything else so that he can send it on to you if he gets one. All such items are usually 'on approval', so that if you have found them somewhere else, you are not obliged to purchase them.

More expensive items can be purchased at auction. Many of the larger auction houses do not like to sell items of lower value and therefore, in the main, offer more expensive single stamps and covers or complete collections and accumulations.

Other auctions offer single items of lower value and these can be a great way of picking up items you need and, once again, it is good to identify an auction house which regularly offers the type of material you are looking for and provides a reliable service.

Another method of buying stamps is 'kiloware'. These are stamps sold by weight and generally assumed to be 'unsorted' i.e. no one has been through them before and picked the good ones out. Many collectors enjoy this approach to stamp collecting and they will tell you of the wonderful 'finds' they have made – but inevitably you will be left with a vast majority of stamps that you do not want because they duplicate items already in your collection. Charity shops will always be happy to receive them – and they will eventually finish up in someone else's 'genuinely unsorted kiloware' – so once again, if this is your kind of collecting, establish a good relationship with a reliable supplier.

'Kiloware' is generally supplied in the form of stamps on paper, torn or cut from envelopes – so this is probably a good point at which to discuss one of the real basics of stamp collecting – soaking stamps off paper.

It is helpful to carry out some rudimentary sorting before you start. Soaking stamps is quite a time-consuming process, so you do not want to waste time on stamps you don't need or don't want, maybe because they are damaged.

Once you have sorted out the stamps you want to soak off, pour some clean water (warm but *not* hot) into a bowl; then float each stamp (face uppermost) on the surface of the water. You can float as many stamps at one time as you have room for.

Leave the stamps for 15 minutes or so to give the water time to soak the gum that is sticking the stamp to the paper. Most stamps can then be gently peeled away. If they do not come away easily do not try to tear them off the paper. Leave them for another five minutes or so and try again.

Providing your hands are clean it's better to handle the stamps with your fingers when peeling off the envelope paper. The paper of stamps is weakened when it is damp and picking them up with tweezers may damage them.

When you have peeled the stamps off the envelope there will probably be some damp gum still on the back of them. Use a soft brush dipped in water to remove this, a paint brush is ideal. Alternatively let the stamp float on the water for a few minutes – the gum will dissolve away. However, do not immerse the stamp in water. For most stamps this would be safe enough but for some it would be dangerous as the ink may run.

Then shake off any excess water and place the stamps face upwards on a sheet of clean kitchen paper towel. This is why it is so important to clean all the gum off. If you do not, your stamps will stick to the paper and you will have to float them off all over again. When all the stamps are laid out cover them with more paper towel then make a kind of sandwich by putting a few sheets of ordinary paper on top.

Place a heavy book on this sandwich. This will flatten the stamps as they dry. After half an hour open up the sandwich and carefully remove the stamps. Spread them out on another piece of clean paper and leave to dry in the air for a little while. When completely dry they are ready for mounting in your album.

Or you can just lay the stamps face down on paper towel and allow them to dry out in the air. If you use this method do not try to speed up the drying by putting the stamps in the sun or close to a hot radiator as they will curl up and you may damage them when you flatten them out to put them in your album.

There are two things which you must be very careful about when floating stamps. Firstly, many old stamps were printed in special inks which run, change colour, or even disappear completely in water. Fewer modern stamps are affected in this way but even so it is best to be safe, so avoid letting water get on the surface of the stamp when you are floating-off. Be careful when floating stamps to keep separate stamps affixed to white and coloured envelopes. Take out any stamp which are stuck to bits of coloured paper and float these separately. Floating can easily make the ink run and so damage your stamps by staining them with unwanted colours.

These days, many countries produce 'self-adhesive' stamps and these may not come away from their backing paper at all. If you believe that a stamp may be 'self-adhesive', it would be better to leave it on the paper, carefully trimming round it with scissors, making sure you do not cut into the stamp.

Finally, always think twice before tearing a stamp off an envelope. Most old stamps and some modern ones too, if they have interesting postmarks, will be more valuable if left on the envelope. If in doubt always try to ask a more experienced collector's advice.

Choosing an Album and Mounting your stamps

These are two different topics but really need to be considered together, as the way you mount your stamps will depend on the album you choose and your choice of album may depend on the way you wish to mount your stamps. Here are some of the options:

New Age album

Printed Albums

You may be used to an album printed with a space for every stamp, and these may be obtained for larger groups of countries, such as the Stanley Gibbons New Age Album, with spaces for all Commonwealth Queen Elizabeth stamps up to 1962. If this is the sort of collection you hope to build they are fine albums – but as they have a space for every stamp, filling one would be a time-consuming business!

Blank albums

These are made up of blank pages, printed with a faint quadrille (tiny squares) which help you lay your stamps out neatly. These give you freedom to lay your collection out as you wish, leaving spaces for stamps you are hoping to obtain, or a neat display of the stamps you have. The former option may mean that you have a lot of gaps on the page, the latter may mean fairly regular rearrangement of your collection – the choice is yours.

Blank albums come in a wide range of prices and binding types, from inexpensive ring binders, through traditional springbacks to high quality peg-fitting types. Again, the choice is yours.

Stockbooks

In the past, collectors used stockbooks to hold duplicates and stamps awaiting mounting in the main album, but due to their convenience and cost, many collectors are now using stockbooks to house their main collections.

They certainly make it easy to mount your stamps – you just slip them into the strips on the pages and you can move them around easily to accommodate new acquisitions too! You can even write notes regarding different stamps or sets and slip those into the strips.

Stock albums

These are loose-leaf stockbooks, which have the added benefit of being able to insert extra pages in the book. Also, because the strips come in a number of formats, they look better than a stockbook layout which is a bit restricting and does not show larger items, such as covers, blocks and miniature sheets, very well.

Mounting your stamps

Before we come on to cover albums, let's return to the matter of mounting your stamps. If you have chosen either the stockbook or stock album option, this is not really an issue as you can just slip your stamps into the strips on the page. If you have opted for a printed or blank album, on the other hand, the question of mounting is important.

The traditional stamp hinge is generally the preferred option for used stamps. Instructions for their use are generally given on the packet, so we will not repeat them here, but we must stress that the key points are to *lightly* moisten the hinge before attaching it to the stamp or album page and *not to try to remove it* until it's dry or you may damage the page – or even more important, the stamp.

For unused stamps that have been previously mounted, stamp hinges are also perfectly acceptable, but for stamps which still have 'full original gum' and show no evidence of having been previously hinged, most collectors now favour 'hingeless mounts', which allow you to attach the stamp to the page without disturbing the gum (keeping the stamp 'unmounted').

For most of the frequently encountered stamp sizes, cut-to-size mounts are available for immediate use. Less common sizes will have to be cut from larger strips, but even large blocks and miniature sheets can be mounted in this way.

Although hingeless mounts are gummed, ready for use, many collectors prefer to use hinges to attach them to the album page as this makes them easier to move around when new stamps are added.

Covers

Many collectors like to include covers in their collections – either 'first day' or 'souvenir' covers or simply envelopes that show examples of the stamps in use. This is especially desirable in the case of early covers, which might show unusual postmarks or other features.

Cover album

Covers can be mounted on blank pages using gummed photograph corners, but may also be accommodated in purpose-built cover albums. There are even albums, which are designed to hold stamp and cover pages together (and booklet pages too!).

What else?

So, that's covered the choice of album and the mounting of stamps: What else do you need? This comes under two headings: equipment and information.

Information

You can manage without background information, but it would be a bit like setting out on a journey to somewhere you've never been without a map.

The first thing is a catalogue to tell you what exists and will help you to identify what you have. The Stanley Gibbons catalogue range includes something for every collector from the beginner to the specialist.

Beyond that there are specialist handbooks on just about everything, but many are printed in quite small numbers and, once sold, are unlikely to be reprinted. However, specialist dealers and auction houses can be a useful source of out-of-print literature.

You should also try to keep up with what is going on in the philatelic world and, again, Stanley Gibbons is able to help, via its monthly magazine, *Gibbons Stamp Monthly*, recently described as 'the best magazine for stamp collectors published anywhere'. For a free sample copy and subscription details, please write to Stanley Gibbons Publications, *(the address is at the front of this checklist)*.

Of course, as with everything else, much information may also be found on the internet and you will almost certainly find it worth joining the local society in your area, other stamp collectors are always happy to help a newcomer.

Equipment

Again, what you need in the way of equipment will depend largely on what you are collecting, the degree of specialisation you intend to achieve and the type of album you use.

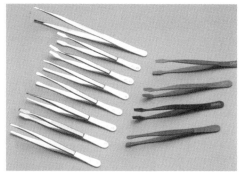

We have already discussed albums and stamp mounts, the only other item every stamp collector must have is a pair of tweezers. All stamps should be handled with tweezers; they ensure that the natural oils in our fingers do not get on to the stamps and, after a bit of practice, they are easier to use than fingers as well. They come in different lengths, with different points and made from different materials (generally stainless steel or gold-plated). Find a style that suits you and stick with it.

From then on the equipment you need is up to you. Most collectors like to have a magnifying glass so they can look at their stamps more closely. Again, they come in a wide range, from the fairly basic, offering 2 or 3× magnification to pocket microscopes giving 30× magnification, and digital microscopes that you can attach to your computer for really detailed examination of your stamps.

Another useful type of magnifier is one that incorporates a millimetre scale – ideal for measuring overprints and other features.

Even a quick look in any catalogue will show that differences in perforation, watermark and colour can make an enormous difference to the price of a stamp. So most collectors like to have the necessary equipment to measure perforations, view watermarks and identify colours and shades.

Fortunately, as far as perforations are concerned, the perforation gauge used by most of the world's top collectors and dealers is accessible to all – it's the Stanley Gibbons Instanta – which measures perforations to a decimal point and is easy to use. There is an electronic perforation measurer which is even easier to use – but it is a bit more expensive than the Instanta.

Watermark detectors also come in a variety of types and designs at different prices, so it is useful to seek the advice of an experienced collector before deciding on the one to buy.

If you are collecting older stamps, watermarks are generally clearer and can be identified simply by placing the stamps face down on a dark background or watermark tray and, if necessary, adding a few drops of lighter fluid or watermark fluid. The Morley Bright products are an excellent alternative if you do not like using fluids, which many collectors do not.

More modern stamps, especially mint ones are more difficult to sort and for these one of the electric watermark detectors will probably be the answer. The Stanley Gibbons Detectamark Spectrum and other similar products take a bit of practice to get used to, but are very effective. Their drawback is that they can only handle single stamps and cannot accommodate blocks or sheets. If you are able to, visit a shop where you can see the different products demonstrated and make your choice.

Happily, the standard colour guide for stamp collectors, the Stanley Gibbons Colour Key, is another relatively inexpensive item which will provide years of use. It features 200 different colours and will allow you to tell the difference between 'mauve', 'purple', 'lilac' and 'violet' with ease.

Finally and especially if you are collecting the modern stamps of Great Britain at a more specialised level, you will probably want an ultraviolet lamp to identify different papers and phosphor types. Again, these come in a range of designs at different prices, so it is useful to seek the advice of an experienced collector before deciding on the one to buy. If you collect Great Britain stamps, you really need a 'short wave' lamp to identify different phosphors, but some lamps incorporate both 'long' and 'short' wave bulbs, which give them wider potential use.

A lamp with a 'hood' or viewing eyepiece is generally to be recommended, firstly because direct exposure to prolonged ultraviolet light is damaging to the eyes, so you should avoid lamps which cause you to see the bulb itself while you are using it. Also, such lamps are more effective in the dark, so anything which shields the stamp being examined from other light sources, including daylight, will improve the effectiveness of the lamp.

The Stanley Gibbons Ultraviolet lamp, introduced in 2012, offers a broad spectrum light, suitable for detecting all phosphors, while the unique eyepiece makes it suitable for use wherever you are.

Philatelic accessories of all types are available from Stanley Gibbons Publications or at the SG shop in London. The current product guide is available on request. Alternatively, a host of useful information can be found here: www.stanleygibbons.com

Stanley Gibbons Numbers

When Stanley Gibbons published his first stamp catalogue in 1865 the stamps in it were simply listed by country and description. It was not long, however, before there were just too many stamps to be listed in this way and in order to simplify the way in which stamps could be ordered by customers, each was given its unique and individual number.

Nowadays, as each stamp is added to the catalogue in the supplement published in *Gibbons Stamp Monthly,* it is assigned its number; sets being listed according to the date on which they were issued and then by face value within that set. If several stamps of the same value belong to one set, usually issued in the form of a sheet or sheetlet, the numbering starts at the top left-hand stamp and runs down to the stamp at bottom right.

Long definitive series are listed together for the convenience of collectors so this often involves adding new numbers to an existing series. It can also happen that a stamp or set of stamps are discovered which were unknown at the time of issue – these also have to be inserted in their correct chronological sequence.

Easy identification

The Stanley Gibbons number appears in the left-hand column of the stamp listing and should not be confused with the bold number that often appears to its right and refers to its illustration. So, by using the country name and catalogue number, every stamp can be easily identified and, rather than having to order Great Britain 1924 10d. turquoise-blue on Block Cypher watermarked paper, all you have to do is order a Great Britain SG 428 and state whether you want it used or unused.

In order to render them immediately identifiable, certain types of stamps are given a prefix to their catalogue number thus a number prefixed with a 'D' is a postage due stamp, while an 'O' means it's an official stamp. Some countries' stamps also have a prefix to allow them to be easily identified. Thus, in this catalogue, Scotland stamp numbers are prefixed with an 'S' and those for Wales with a 'W'.

Changes

Once a number has been assigned it is not changed unless absolutely necessary. The reason, for this is that collectors often maintain their 'wants lists' using SG numbers, while auction houses around the world quote them in their descriptions, as do books and articles in the philatelic press.

Expertising bodies, including the expert committee of the Royal Philatelic Society London and the British Philatelic Association also quote SG numbers in their certificates, which generally identify scarcer or more valuable stamps, so regular changing of those numbers would render such certificates out-of-date.

Nevertheless, sometimes complete sections of the catalogue, occasionally even complete countries, have to be re-organised, and under such circumstances renumbering does take place – but this is infrequent.

Usually, new stamps added into the middle of listings have a letter suffix. This can occur in two forms. If the stamp is listable in its own right the suffix forms a part of the 'main' number in the left-hand column of the listing. Thus, when the Wilding 4½d. and 5d. values with phosphor bands appeared, in 1961 and 1967 respectively, but the 4d. and 6d., both issued in 1960, had already been given the numbers 616 and 617, the 4½d. became 616*a* and the 5d. was listed as 616*b*.

Varieties of such 'main' stamps, such as errors, booklet panes and watermark varieties are given letter suffixes in a different way, so that the phosphor version of the 1963 6d. Paris Postal Conference stamp (SG 636) has a 'p' suffix which appears in the listing itself, to differentiate it from the normal, non-phosphor stamp – so to order one, all you need to ask for is SG 636p.

Sometimes, of course, so many stamps are subsequently added to a listing that the use of suffix letters would just become too complicated and, so far as Great Britain is concerned, this has happened with the decimal Machin series, which are prefixed 'X' for the conventionally perforated series, first issued in 1971, and 'Y' for the series with elliptical perforations at each side, first issued in 1993. In 2009 a new series with additional security features began to appear and these are listed with a 'U' prefix.

Adding new numbers

Thus when new stamps are added to such series – and several are appearing each year – adding new numbers does not have to mean changing those of subsequently issued commemorative issues.

Within the 'U' series, new 'main' values are initially added with a suffix letter, so the numbers of previously issued stamps do not have to be adjusted with each new catalogue, but every four or five years the complete listing is updated to eliminate the suffix letters and maintain a 'clean' listing of numbers. When ordering stamps from these series it is as well to mention which edition of the catalogue you are using as, if your dealer is using a different one, you may not receive what you expect!

The Stanley Gibbons numbering system represents an easy-to-use and universally recognised system of stamp identification. Collectors all over the world use it to keep their collections in order and dealers sort and classify their stocks by it, so its use makes life easier for everyone.

Stanley Gibbons numbers are fully protected by copyright and, while their use is encouraged, they may not be reproduced without the prior permission of Stanley Gibbons Limited.

The Stanley Gibbons Guide to Stamp Pricing

Catalogue editor and lifelong collector, Hugh Jefferies, offers a few tips.

It is a common fallacy that the prices in this catalogue show what a stamp is 'worth', should you wish to sell it.

They are, instead, the price at which Stanley Gibbons will sell a very fine example of the stamp in question, but that price includes a lot of other factors, as well as the inherent 'value' of the stamp itself. There are costs in running any business and these are built into the price of any stamp shown in the catalogue, although the proportion of the price that relates to the stamp and that which relates to 'business overheads' will vary from stamp to stamp.

What is true is that the prices shown in this catalogue represent an accurate 'guide' to the value of the stamps listed in it. **Stanley Gibbons are now the only major philatelic publisher whose stamp catalogue is also their price list.** Naturally, if the prices are set too high, no one will buy our stamps, if they are too low, we will have difficulty replacing our stocks. It is therefore vitally important to the future of the company that the prices in this catalogue are set as accurately as possible. As a result, a great deal of care is taken over those prices – which is why they are held in such regard by collectors, dealers and stamp auction houses throughout the world.

A very accurate picture

Each year, every price in our annual catalogues is checked and amended if necessary, having regard to the prices being achieved at auction as well as the demands of our customers at 399 Strand and orders coming in via the post, email and our website. Prices are held, increased or reduced according to those factors, giving a very accurate picture of the state of the market for each and every stamp.

Can stamps be purchased for less than the prices quoted in this catalogue? Of course they can. Stanley Gibbons themselves will frequently have stamps in stock at prices lower than 'full catalogue'. Every business offers discounts and makes 'special offers' from time to time and Stanley Gibbons is no different. That apart, however, it should always be remembered that the prices quoted in this catalogue are for stamps in very fine condition. Stamps with minor defects, heavy postmarks, slight fading and other flaws will frequently be offered at lower prices, both by Stanley Gibbons and by other dealers and auction houses.

Checking condition

It is very important that, when you are thinking of buying a stamp for your collection, you carefully consider the condition of the item in question. Does it match up to the Stanley Gibbons definition of 'Very Fine'? If it doesn't, is the price at which it is being offered too high? If you believe that the price is higher that it should be, leave it alone – or if you are really desperate, haggle for a better deal.

The knowledge as to what is 'very fine' and therefore worthy of 'full catalogue' is one that you will gain with experience and will vary from stamp to stamp. Any stamp less than 100 years old should really be perfect in every way, but one can be more forgiving with older issues.

Briefly, here are a few of the things to consider.

- **Gum** – for unused stamps issued after 1936 prices are for unmounted mint – stamps never previously hinged. Modern stamps with hinge marks should be substantially discounted. For earlier stamps, heavy mounts and multiple hinges will also detract from the value, while unused stamps with the gum removed are worth considerably less.

- **Margins** – for imperforate stamps these should be clear on all sides – the design should not be cut into or even touching the edge of the stamp.

- **Perforations** – check that these are complete, that none are missing or short, especially at the stamp corners. Ideally the margin between the stamp design and the perforations should be even and well balanced – known as 'well-centred'.

- **Paper** – Check that there are no tears or thins to the paper – on the front as well as the back – and that there are no bends or creases. Again, the greater the damage the further away from 'full catalogue' the stamp is worth.

- **Postmarks** – these should be clear, clean and should not disfigure the stamp. **The prices for all British stamps issued after 1880 assume used stamps to be cancelled with a clean, clear circular datestamp. Heavy parcel, wavy line or slogan cancellations reduce stamp values significantly.** On the other hand, very lightly cancelled stamps should sometimes be viewed with suspicion. There needs to be enough of the postmark showing to prove that the stamp has really been used!

If the above notes seem complicated, don't worry. You will soon become adept at viewing every stamp in the light of its condition and deciding what proportion of catalogue you are prepared to pay. If you are not certain, ask the dealer for a guarantee that he will refund your money if you're not happy with your purchase. All good dealers will be happy to provide this.

So, buy carefully – but, above all, have fun!

It should always be remembered that the prices quoted in this catalogue are for stamps in very fine condition.

Great Britain Stamp Collector's Glossary

Adhesive A gummed stamp

Albino A design impression without colour

Aniline A fugitive (water soluble) ink or dye

Bisect Part of a stamp that has been cut in two for separate use; usually during a shortage of stamps

Blind perforation A perforation which has not been punched out

Block A group of four or more unseparated stamps

Bogus A spurious, pretend stamp

Booklet A small book containing 'panes' of stamps

Booklet pane A leaf or page of stamps from a booklet

Cachet A commemorative marking, usually applied by rubber stamp

Cancellation Any authorised defacing mark on a stamp

Centre The position of a stamp design within its perforations, e.g. 'well-centred' or 'off-centre'

Chalk-surfaced paper Stamp paper coated with a chalky solution for security purposes. Attempted removal of the postmark damages the surface of the stamp

Charity stamp One bearing a premium or surcharge for charitable purposes

Classic A country's early stamp issues, mostly up to about 1875; a choice stamp

Coil stamp One from a roll of stamps used in vending machines

Coil join A tab uniting two sections of a roll of stamps

Commemorative A stamp issued to mark a special anniversary or event

Country stamp See Regional

Cover A postally used envelope, letter-sheet or wrapper

Cylinder number Letters/numerals in sheet margins identifying printing cylinders. Normally collected in 'Cylinder block' of six stamps. Also see 'Plate number'

Die An engraved plate for impressing design etc. on softer metal

Doctor blade A steel blade which removes surplus ink from the printing cylinder in the press – faulty wiping by this blade will cause a 'Doctor blade' flaw

Embossing A form of printing in relief, now rarely used

Error A mistake in stamp design, printing or production

Essay A trial stamp design, sometimes differing from the issued stamps

Face value The denomination of a stamp, expressed on its face

Fake A genuine stamp doctored in some way to deceive collectors

First Day Cover A cover bearing stamps postmarked on their day of issue

Flaw A fortuitous blemish on a stamp; a printing fault

Forgery A fraudulent copy of a genuine postage stamp, overprint or postmark

Frama stamps See Machine label

Graphite lines Black vertical lines printed on the back of GB definitives, 1957–1959, for use with automatic letter-sorting equipment. Also see 'Phosphor' stamps

Greetings stamp Stamp intended for use on birthday or other greetings mail

Gum Mucilage on the back of adhesive stamps. Not 'glue'

Gutter The narrow space between stamps in the sheet permitting perforation

Gutter margin The blank margins dividing a sheet of stamps into panes

Handstamp A postmark or overprint applied by hand

Imperforate Stamps printed and issued without perforations, deliberately or in error

Imprint The name of the printer or issuing authority inscribed on the stamps or in the sheet margins

Imprinted stamps Stamps other than adhesives, printed direct on postal stationery items (postcards, envelopes, etc)

Jubilee line Coloured line found in the sheet margin of British stamps

Local A stamp with geographical limits of postal use and validity. These are not normally listed in the Stanley Gibbons catalogues

Machin The name given to GB definitives, first issued in 1967, bearing the Queen's head designed by Arnold Machin

Machine label Postage stamp produced by a micro-processor machine after the insertion of coins of the required value, popularly known as Frama stamps

Maltese cross Name given to the cross-shaped cancellation used on the first British stamps

Margin The unprinted edging surrounding or dividing a sheet of stamps. See also 'Gutter margin'

Maximum card A picture postcard bearing a stamp and cancellation relevant to the picture on the card

Miniature sheet A small sheet of one or several stamps, usually with decorative margins, issued as a souvenir for collectors

Mint A stamp in its original pristine state, with full gum (if so issued), when it is said to have its 'original gum' ('O.G.'). 'Unmounted mint' stamps have not been hinged. Also see 'Unused'

Mulready Envelopes and letter sheets issued by Britain in 1840 with a pictorial motif designed by William Mulready

Non Value Indicator stamp (NVI) A stamp which bears no monetary inscription, but shows the class of postage (1st, 2nd, etc) instead

Obsolete A stamp no longer sold by a post office though it may still be valid for postage

Overprint A printed addition to a stamp. Also see 'Surcharge'

Pair Two unseparated stamps, joined as originally issued

Pane A formation or group of stamps within the sheet. Also see 'Booklet pane'

Perforations Holes punched between stamps in sheets to enable easy separation

Personalised stamp Stamp with an attached non-postal label bearing an image taken from a personal photograph

Phosphor stamps Stamps overprinted or coated with phosphorescent materials recognised by high technology letter sorting machinery

Plate number Letters/numerals in sheet margins identifying printing plates. Also see 'Cylinder number' many Victorian stamps included the plate number in the design; these are listed in this catalogue

Post & Go stamp Illustrated self-adhesive label dispensed from a machine with inkjet printed indicator of the service required. This catalogue only lists Post & Go stamps available from machines within post offices, it does not include those from stamp exhibitions or non-post office establishments.

Postmark Any mark, such as a cancellation, connected with the postal service and found on items transmitted by post

Presentation pack A philatelic souvenir containing a set of stamps and descriptive text

Prestige booklet Stamp booklet devoted to a particular subject or event and containing special panes of stamps with descriptive text printed alongside

Proof A trial impression taken from an original die or printing plate

Regional Name given by collectors to stamps issued by Royal Mail (who term them Country stamps) for use in England, Scotland, Wales or Northern Ireland. Issues were also made for Guernsey and Jersey (until 1969) and the Isle of Man (until 1973)

Seahorse Name given to the high value definitive stamps of King George V

Self-adhesive Gummed stamps (with protective backing) which do not require moistening

Se-tenant Stamps of different design or face value that are joined together

Specimen Sample stamp usually with 'specimen' overprinted or perforated on it

Strip Three or more stamps joined in a row

Tête-bêche A stamp inverted in relation to the adjoining stamp in a pair

Traffic lights Collectors' term for the colour check dots found in sheet margins

Unused An uncancelled stamp, not necessarily 'mint'

Used A stamp which has been postally used and appropriately postmarked

Used abroad Stamps of one country used and postmarked in another

Used on piece Stamp kept on part of the original cover to preserve the complete postmark

Variety A stamp differing in some detail from the normal issue

Watermark A distinctive device or emblem in stamps, formed by 'thinning' of the paper during production. Watermarks illustrated in this catalogue are shown as if viewed through the front of the stamp

Wilding The name given to British definitive stamps, first issued in 1952, bearing the Queen's head from a photographic portrait by Dorothy Wilding

Wing margin Wide margin on one side of a stamp caused by central perforation of the sheet gutter margin

For other and fuller definitions, see the Stanley Gibbons book *Philatelic Terms Illustrated* by James Mackay.

How can Stanley Gibbons help you to build your collection?

Our History

Stanley Gibbons started trading in 1856 and we have been at the forefront of stamp collecting for more than 160 years, making us the world's oldest philatelic company. We can help you build your collection in a wide variety of ways – all with the backing of our unrivalled expertise.

When building a collection it helps to know what you have. You can use Collect British Stamps as a checklist to highlight all the items you currently own. You can then easily see where the gaps are that you need to fill.

Visit 399 Strand, London, UK

Our world famous stamp shop is a collector's paradise which aims to keep a full range of Great Britain stamps to sell at current catalogue price — so if there are any changes via a different catalogue, then prices will be adjusted accordingly. As well as stamps, the shop stocks albums, accessories and specialist philatelic books. Plan a visit now!

GB Specialist Department

When purchasing high value items you should definitely contact our specialist department for advice and guarantees on the items purchased. We can explain what to look for and where, and help you plan your future collection.

Auctions and Valuations

Stanley Gibbons Auctions have been running since the 1900's. They offer a range of auctions to suit all levels of collectors and dealers. You can of course also sell your collection or individual rare items through our public auctions and regular postal auctions. You can check out charges with the auction department directly.

Stanley Gibbons Publications

Our catalogues are trusted worldwide as the industry standard To keep up to date with new issues you can follow the additions to this listing in our magazine *Gibbons Stamp Monthly*. This is a must-read for all collectors and dealers. It contains news, views and insights into all things philatelic, from beginner to specialist.

Completing the set

When is it cheaper to complete your collection by buying a whole set rather than item by item? You can use the prices in *Collect British Stamps*, which lists single item values and a complete set value, to check if it is better to buy the odd items missing, or a complete set. Some of the definitive sets can be built up over time. The current definitive set is regularly augmented by Royal Mail.

Condition

Condition can make a big difference to the price you can pay for an item (see 'The Stanley Gibbons Guide to Stamp Pricing on p xiv). The prices in this catalogue are for items in very fine condition. When building your collection you do need to keep condition in mind and always buy the best condition you can find and afford. Collectors are reminded that for issues from 1936 to date, prices in the unused column are for unmounted mint. This means that the condition of the gum is the same as issued from the Post Office. If the gum is disturbed or has had an adhesion it can be classed as mounted. When buying issues prior to 1936 you should always look for the least amount of disturbance and adhesion. You do have to keep in mind the age of the issue when looking at the condition.

When buying philatelic items listed you need to make sure they are in the same condition as issued by the Post Office. This applies to Presentation Packs, were the stamps are issued on a stock card with an information card and held together in a plastic wallet and also to Year Books, which should be in a slip case with a stock card of stamps. The prices quoted are for a complete item in good condition so make sure you check this – and of course that they are complete. You will find some items may appear in different formats (e.g. language cards, different bindings, etc) which will be listed under the normal listing within this catalogue.

Ask the Experts

While you are building your collection, if you need help or guidance, you are welcome to come along to Stanley Gibbons in the Strand and ask for assistance. If you would like to have your collection appraised, you can arrange for a verbal evaluation Monday to Friday 9.00am – 4.30pm. We also provide insurance valuations should you require. Of course this up-to-date catalogue listing can assist with the valuation and may be presented to an insurance agent or company.

Guide to Entries

Ⓐ **Accession to the Throne**

Ⓑ **Illustration** – Generally all stamps illustrated. To comply with Post Office regulations illustrations are reduced to 75%, with overprints shown actual size.

Ⓒ **Illustration or Type Number** – These numbers are used to help identify stamps, in the type column.

Ⓓ **Date of Issue** – When a set of definitive stamps have been issued over several years the Year Date given is for the earliest issue, commemorative sets are set in chronological order.

Ⓔ **Phosphor Description** – Phosphorised paper is activated by ultraviolet light.

Ⓕ **Perforations** – The 'perforation' is the number of holes in a length of 2 cm, as measured by the Stanley Gibbons *Instanta* gauge. From 1992 certain stamps occur with a large elliptical (oval) hole inserted in each line of vertical perforations. From 2009 certain stamps have U-shaped die-cut slits.

Ⓖ **Stanley Gibbons Catalogue Number** – This is a unique number for each stamp to help the collector identify stamps in the listing. The Stanley Gibbons numbering system is universally recognized as definitive, where insufficient numbers have been left to provide for additional stamps listings, some stamps will have a suffix letter after the catalogue number.

Ⓗ **Catalogue Price** – Mint/Unused. Prices quoted for pre-1945 stamps are for lightly hinged examples. Prices quoted of unused King Edward VIII to Queen Elizabeth issues are for unmounted mint.

Ⓘ **Catalogue Price** – Used. Prices generally refer to very fine postally used examples.

Prices

Before February 1971 British currency was:

£1 = 20s. One pound = twenty shillings *and*
1s = 12d. One Shilling = 12 pence

Under decimalisation this became:

£1 = 100p One pound = one hundred (new) pence

Shown in Catalogue as	Explanation
10	10 pence
1·75	£1·75
15·00	£15
£150	£150
£2300	£2300

Ⓙ **Face Value** – This refers to the value of the stamp and is sold at the Post Office when issued. Some modern stamps do not have their values in figures but instead indicate the service which they cover.

Ⓚ **Type Number** – Indicates a design type on which stamp is based. These are bold figures found below each illustration. The type numbers are also given in bold in the second column of figures alongside the stamp description to indicate the design of each stamp.

Ⓛ **Colour** – Colour of stamps (if fewer than four colours, otherwise noted as 'multicoloured').

Ⓜ **Sets of Stamps** – Two or more stamps with a common theme or subject.

Ⓝ **First Day Covers** – Prices for first day covers are for complete sets used on plain covers or on special covers.

Ⓞ **Presentation Packs** – Special packs consisting of the issue and slip-in cards with printed information inside a protective covering.

Ⓟ **PHQ Cards** – Each card shows a large reproduction of a current British stamp.

Ⓠ **Sets of Gutters** – The term is used for a pair of stamps separated by part of the blank gutter margin or with Traffic Lights on the gutter margin.

Ⓡ **Footnote** – Further information on background or key facts on issues.

Ⓢ **Other Types of Stamps** – Postage Dues, Officials and Regional Issues

Ⓣ **Number Prefix** – Stamps other than definitives and commemoratives have a prefix letter before the catalogue number.

QUEEN ELIZABETH II

A Accession to
   the Throne —— • 6 February, 1952

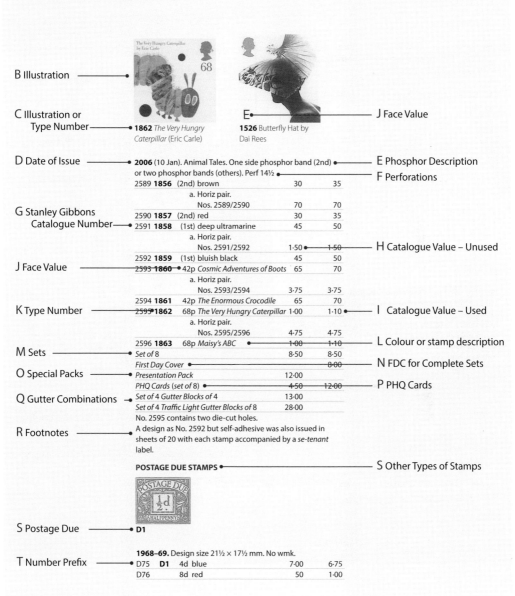

B Illustration ——

C Illustration or
   Type Number —— • **1862** *The Very Hungry Caterpillar* (Eric Carle)   **1526** Butterfly Hat by Dai Rees

E •————— J Face Value

D Date of Issue —— • **2006** (10 Jan). Animal Tales. One side phosphor band (2nd) •——— E Phosphor Description
or two phosphor bands (others). Perf 14½ •——— F Perforations

G/K		J/L	H	I
2589 **1856**	(2nd) brown		30	35
	a. Horiz pair.			
	Nos. 2589/2590		70	70
2590 **1857**	(2nd) red		30	35
2591 **1858**	(1st) deep ultramarine		45	50
	a. Horiz pair.			
	Nos. 2591/2592		1·50	1·50
2592 **1859**	(1st) bluish black		45	50
2593 **1860**	42p *Cosmic Adventures of Boots*		65	70
	a. Horiz pair.			
	Nos. 2593/2594		3·75	3·75
2594 **1861**	42p *The Enormous Crocodile*		65	70
2595 **1862**	68p *The Very Hungry Caterpillar*		1·00	1·10
	a. Horiz pair.			
	Nos. 2595/2596		4·75	4·75
2596 **1863**	68p *Maisy's ABC*		1·00	1·10
Set of 8			8·50	8·50
First Day Cover				8·00
Presentation Pack			12·00	
PHQ Cards (set of 8)			4·50	12·00
Set of 4 Gutter Blocks of 4			13·00	
Set of 4 Traffic Light Gutter Blocks of 8			28·00	

G Stanley Gibbons Catalogue Number ——

J Face Value ——

K Type Number ——

M Sets ——

O Special Packs ——

Q Gutter Combinations ——

H Catalogue Value – Unused

I Catalogue Value – Used

L Colour or stamp description

N FDC for Complete Sets

P PHQ Cards

R Footnotes —— No. 2595 contains two die-cut holes.
A design as No. 2592 but self-adhesive was also issued in sheets of 20 with each stamp accompanied by a *se-tenant* label.

POSTAGE DUE STAMPS •————— S Other Types of Stamps

S Postage Due —— • **D1**

T Number Prefix —— **1968–69.** Design size 21½ × 17½ mm. No wmk.

D75	**D1**	4d blue	7·00	6·75
D76		8d red	50	1·00

Stanley Gibbons Auctions

Lot 250 - Sold for £10,200   Lot 171 - Sold for £3600

Your trusted auction house with integrity, offering a tailored approach when selling your collection. Talk to our team about selling your collection today.

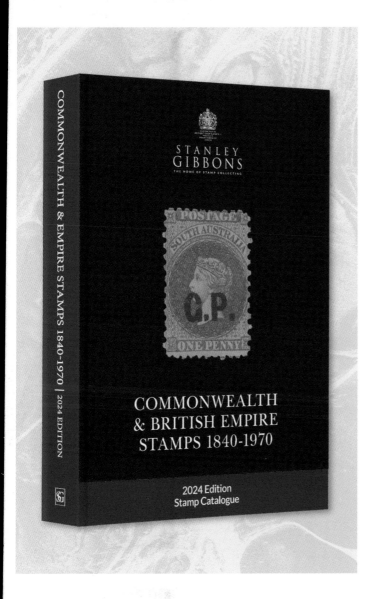

Queen Victoria

20 June 1837-22 January 1901

IDENTIFICATION. In this checklist Victorian stamps are classified firstly according to which printing method was used; line-engraving, embossing or surface-printing.

Corner letters. Numerous stamps also have letters in all four, or just the lower corners. These were an anti-forgery device and the letters differ from stamp to stamp. If present in all four corners the upper pair are the reverse of the lower. Note the importance of these corner letters in the way the catalogue is arranged.

Watermarks. Further classification depends on watermarks: these are illustrated in normal position, with stamps priced accordingly.

1. Line-engraved Issues

1   **1a**   **2** Small Crown

1840. Letters in lower corners. Wmk Small Crown, W **2**. Imperf.

2	**1**	1d. black	£12500	£375
5	**1a**	2d. blue.	£38000	£975

1b   **3** White lines
added above
and below
head

1841

8	**1b**	1d. red-brown.	£600	35·00
14	**3**	2d. blue	£5000	90·00

4 Large Crown
watermark

1854–57

		(a) Wmk Small Crown, W **2**. Perf 16.		
17	**1b**	1d. red-brown	£375	35·00
19	**3**	2d. deep blue	£4700	£100
		(b) Wmk Small Crown, W **2**. Perf 14.		
23	**3**	2d. blue	£13000	£225
24	**1b**	1d. red-brown	£700	70·00
		(c) Wmk Large Crown, W **4**. Perf 16.		
26	**1b**	1d. red-brown	£2500	£130
36*a*	**3**	2d. blue	£14500	£325
		(d) Wmk Large Crown, W **4**. Perf 14.		
40	**1b**	1d. rose-red	40·00	8·00
34	**3**	2d. blue	£2800	70·00

5

6   **7**   **8**

9 Watermark extending over three stamps

Plate Numbers. Stamps included a 'plate number' in their design and this affects the price. The cheapest plates are priced here; see complete list of plates overleaf.

1858–70. Letters in all four corners

		(a) Wmk W **9**. Perf 14.		
48	**7**	½d. rose-red	£110	30·00
		(b) Wmk Large Crown, W **4**. Perf 14.		
43	**5**	1d. rose-red	27·00	2·75
51	**8**	1½d. rose-red	£500	75·00
45	**6**	2d. blue	£350	15·00

Plate numbers on stamps 1858–1870 having letters in all four corners.

Showing position of the   Showing the plate
plate number on the 1d.   number (9) on the ½d.
and 2d. values (Plate 170   value
shown)

Position of plate
numbers (3) on the
1½d. value

Halfpenny Value (SG 48)

Plate	Un	Used
1	£325	£100
3	£250	55·00
4	£150	50·00
5	£110	30·00
6	£120	30·00
8	£600	£120
9	£5000	£700
10	£130	£700
11	£120	30·00
12	£120	30·00
13	£120	30·00

Plate	Un	Used
14	£120	30·00
15	£175	50·00
19	£300	65·00
20	£350	85·00

Penny Value (SG 43)

Plate	Un	Used
71	55·00	4·00
72	60·00	5·00
73	60·00	4·00
74	60·00	2·75
76	55·00	2·75
77	—	£600000
78	£130	2·75
79	48·00	2·75
80	65·00	2·75
81	65·00	3·00
82	£130	5·00
83	£155	9·00
84	80·00	3·00
85	60·00	4·00
86	70·00	5·00
87	48·00	2·75
88	£190	9·50
89	60·00	2·75
90	60·00	2·75
91	75·00	7·00
92	55·00	2·75
93	70·00	2·75
94	65·00	6·00
95	60·00	2·75
96	65·00	2·75
97	60·00	4·50
98	70·00	7·00
99	75·00	6·00
100	80·00	3·00
101	80·00	11·00
102	65·00	2·75
103	70·00	4·50
104	£100	6·00
105	£130	9·00
106	75·00	2·75
107	80·00	9·00
108	£110	3·00
109	£120	4·50
110	80·00	11·00
111	70·00	3·00
112	90·00	3·00
113	70·00	15·00
114	£325	15·00
115	£130	3·00
116	£100	11·00
117	65·00	2·75
118	70·00	2·75
119	65·00	2·75
120	27·00	2·75
121	60·00	11·00
122	27·00	2·75
123	60·00	2·75
124	42·00	2·75
125	60·00	2·75
127	75·00	3·00
129	60·00	10·00
130	75·00	3·00
131	85·00	20·00
132	£190	27·00
133	£160	11·00
134	27·00	2·75
135	£130	30·00
136	£130	24·00
137	42·00	3·00
138	32·00	2·75
139	80·00	20·00
140	32·00	2·75
141	£160	11·00
142	95·00	30·00
143	80·00	17·00
144	£130	25·00
145	48·00	3·00
146	60·00	7·00
147	70·00	4·00
148	60·00	4·00
149	60·00	7·00
150	27·00	2·75
151	80·00	11·00
152	80·00	7·50
153	£140	11·00
154	70·00	2·75
155	70·00	3·00

Plate	Un	Used
156	65·00	2·75
157	70·00	2·75
158	48·00	2·75
159	48·00	2·75
160	48·00	2·75
161	80·00	9·00
162	70·00	9·00
163	70·00	4·00
164	70·00	4·00
165	65·00	2·75
166	65·00	7·00
167	65·00	2·75
168	70·00	10·00
169	80·00	9·00
170	55·00	2·75
171	27·00	2·75
172	48·00	2·75
173	95·00	11·00
174	50·00	2·75
175	80·00	4·50
176	80·00	3·00
177	60·00	2·75
178	80·00	4·50
179	70·00	3·00
180	80·00	6·50
181	65·00	2·75
182	£130	6·50
183	75·00	4·00
184	48·00	3·00
185	70·00	4·00
186	90·00	3·00
187	70·00	2·75
188	95·00	12·00
189	95·00	8·50
190	70·00	7·00
191	48·00	9·00
192	70·00	2·75
193	48·00	2·75
194	70·00	10·00
195	70·00	10·00
196	70·00	6·50
197	75·00	11·00
198	60·00	7·00
199	75·00	7·00
200	80·00	2·75
201	48·00	6·00
202	80·00	10·00
203	48·00	20·00
204	75·00	3·00
205	75·00	4·00
206	75·00	11·00
207	80·00	11·00
208	75·00	18·00
209	65·00	10·00
210	90·00	15·00
211	95·00	25·00
212	80·00	13·00
213	80·00	13·00
214	90·00	23·00
215	90·00	23·00
216	95·00	23·00
217	95·00	9·00
218	90·00	10·00
219	£130	85·00
220	60·00	9·00
221	95·00	20·00
222	£110	50·00
223	£130	75·00
224	£165	65·00
225	£3000	£700

Plates 69, 70, 75, 77, 126 and 128 were prepared but rejected. No stamps therefore exist, except for a very few from Plate 77 which somehow reached the public. Plate 177 stamps, by accident or design, are sometimes passed off as the rare Plate 77.

Three-Halfpenny Value (SG 51)

Plate	Un	Used
(1)	£725	£110
3	£500	75·00

Plate 1 did not have the plate number in the design. Plate 2 was not completed and no stamps exist.

Twopenny Value (SG 45)

Plate	Un	Used
7	£2000	65·00
8	£1850	45·00

Plate		Un	Used
9		£350	15·00
12		£3000	£140
13		£375	30·00
14		£500	38·00
15		£525	38·00

Plate 10 and 11 were prepared but rejected.

2. Embossed Issues

PRICES. The prices quoted are for cut-square stamps with average to fine embossing. Stamps with exceptionally clear embossing are worth more.

10	11

12	13

1847-54. Wmk W **13** (6d.), no wmk (others). Imperf

54	**10**	1s. pale green (11.9.47)	£24000	£1000
57	**11**	10d. brown (6.11.48)	£11500	£1500
59	**12**	6d. dull lilac (1.3.54)	£19500	£1000

NOTE. Collectors are reminded that Types **10/12** were also used to print postal stationery. 6d. stamps without watermark and 10d. and 1s. values without 'silk' threads embedded in the paper come from this source and should not be confused with the listed stamps.

3. Surface-printed Issues

IDENTIFICATION. Check first whether the design includes corner letters or not, as mentioned for 'Line-engraved Issues'. The checklist is divided up according to whether any letters are small or large, also whether they are white (uncoloured) or printed in the colour of the stamp. Further identification then depends on watermark.

PREFORATIONS. All surface-printed issues of Queen Victoria are perf 14, with the exception of Nos. 126/129.

ABNORMALS. The majority of the great rarities in the surface printed group of issues are the so-called 'abnormals', whose existence is due to the practice of printing six sheets from every plate as soon as made, one of which was kept for record purposes at Somerset House, while the others were perforated and usually issued. If such plates were not used for general production or if, before they came into full use, a change of watermark or colour took place, the six sheets originally printed would differ from the main issue in plate, colour or watermark and, if issued would be extremely rare. The abnormal stamps of this class listed in this Catalogue are distinguished by an asterisk (*) before the price.

14	15 Small Garter	16 Medium Garter

17 Large Garter

18	19	20 Emblems

1855-57. No Corner letters

(i) Wmk Small Garter, W **15**.

62	**14**	4d. carmine (*shades*)	£8500	£450

(ii) Wmk Medium Garter, W **16**.

64	**14**	4d. pale carmine	£13000	£500

(iii) Wmk Large Garter, W **17**.

66	**14**	4d. rose	£1750	£150

(iv) Wmk Emblems. W **20**.

68	**18**	6d. lilac	£1350	£120
72	**19**	1s. green	£3250	£350

Plate Numbers. Stamps as Nos. 90/163 should be checked for the 'plate numbers' indicated, as this affects the price (the cheapest plates are priced here). The mark 'Pl.' shows that several numbers exist, priced in a separate list.

Plate numbers are the small numerals appearing in duplicate in some part of the frame design or adjacent to the lower corner letters (in the 5s. value a single numeral above the lower inscription).

21	22

23	24	25 Plate 2

1862-64. Small uncoloured corner letters. Wmk Large Garter, W **17** (4d.) or Emblems, W **20** (others).

76	**21**	3d. bright carmine-rose	£2700	£350
80	**22**	4d. pale red	£2000	£140
84	**23**	6d. lilac	£2250	£140
87	**24**	9d. straw	£4000	£475
90	**25**	1s. green	£3200	£300

26	27

28 (with hyphen)

29 30 31

1865–67. Large uncoloured corner letters. Wmk Large Garter, W **17** (4d.) or Emblems, W **20** (others).

92	**26**	3d. rose (Plate 4) (1.3.65)	£2500	£250
94	**22**	4d. vermilion	£575	75·00
97	**23**	6d. lilac (with hyphen)	£1200	£140
98	**29**	9d. straw (Plate 4) (25.10.65)	£4800	£600
99	**30**	10d. red-brown (Plate 1) (11.11.67)	—	£55000
101	**31**	1s. green (Plate 4) (19.1.65)	£2850	£275

The 10d. stamps, No. 99, were printed in error on paper watermarked 'Emblems' instead of on 'Spray of Rose'.

32 33 Spray of Rose 34

1867–80. Large uncoloured corner letters. Wmk Spray of Rose. W **33**.

103	**26**	3d. rose	£525	60·00
105	**28**	6d. deep lilac (with hyphen) (Plate 6)	£1900	£185
109		6d. mauve (without hyphen)	£700	90·00
111	**29**	9d. pale straw (Plate 4)	£2400	£300
112	**30**	10d. red-brown (1.7.67)	£3600	£400
117	**31**	1s. green	£800	45·00
118	**32**	2s. dull blue (1.7.67)	£4500	£225
121		2s. brown (Plate 1) (27.2.80)	£30000	£4250

1872–73. Large uncoloured corner letters. Wmk Spray of Rose, W **33**.

122b	**34**	6d. pale chestnut (Plate 11) (1872)	£800	65·00
123		6d. pale buff (18.10.72)	£1100	£140
125		6d. grey (Plate 12) (24.4.73)	£1900	£300

PLATE NUMBERS ON STAMPS OF 1862–1883

Small White Corner Letters (1862–1864)

SG No.		Unused	Used
90	Plate 2 1s. green	£3200	£300
90	Plate 3	*£35000	

Plate 2 is actually numbered as '1' and Plate 3 as '2' on the stamps.

Large White Corner Letters (1865–1883)

SG No.		Unused	Used
103	Plate 4 3d. rose	£1850	£300
103	Plate 5	£525	70·00
103	Plate 6	£550	70·00
103	Plate 7	£650	70·00
103	Plate 8	£625	60·00
103	Plate 9	£625	70·00
103	Plate 10	£875	£150
94	Plate 7 4d. vermilion	£650	£130
94	Plate 8	£600	90·00
94	Plate 9	£600	90·00
94	Plate 10	£825	£150
94	Plate 11	£625	90·00
94	Plate 12	£575	75·00
94	Plate 13	£650	75·00
94	Plate 14	£775	£110

97	Plate 5 6d. lilac	£1150	£140
97	Plate 6	£3800	£275
109	Plate 8 6d. mauve	£800	£140
109	Plate 9	£700	90·00
109	Plate 10		*£37500
122b	Plate 11 6d. pale chestnut	£700	65·00
123	Plate 12 6d. pale buff	£1100	£125
111	Plate 4 9d pale straw	£2400	£300
112	Plate 1 10d. red-brown	£3600	£400
112	Plate 2	*£50000	*£15000
117	Plate 4 1s. green	£975	65·00
117	Plate 5	£800	45·00
117	Plate 6	£1200	45·00
117	Plate 7	£1400	90·00
118	Plate 1 2s. dull blue	£4500	£225
118	Plate 3		*£16500
126	Plate 1 5s. rose	£9500	£675
126	Plate 2	£15000	£1500

Large Coloured Corner Letters (1873–1883)

SG No.		Unused	Used
139	Plate 1 2½d. rosy mauve	£650	£120
139	Plate 2	£650	£120
139	Plate 3	£1000	£175
141	Plate 3 2½d. rosy mauve	£1350	£150
141	Plate 4	£525	85·00
141	Plate 5	£525	85·00
141	Plate 6	£525	85·00
141	Plate 7	£525	85·00
141	Plate 8	£525	85·00
141	Plate 9	£525	85·00
141	Plate 10	£550	85·00
141	Plate 11	£525	85·00
141	Plate 12	£525	85·00
141	Plate 13	£525	85·00
141	Plate 14	£525	85·00
141	Plate 15	£525	85·00
141	Plate 16	£525	85·00
141	Plate 17	£1700	£300
142	Plate 17 2½d. blue	£575	75·00
142	Plate 18	£575	55·00
142	Plate 19	£575	55·00
142	Plate 20	£575	55·00
157	Plate 21 2½d.blue	£500	45·00
157	Plate 22	£450	45·00
157	Plate 23	£450	35·00
143	Plate 11 3d. red	£450	80·00
143	Plate 12	£525	80·00
143	Plate 14	£525	80·00
143	Plate 15	£450	80·00
143	Plate 16	£450	80·00
143	Plate 17	£525	80·00
143	Plate 18	£525	80·00
143	Plate 19	£450	80·00
143	Plate 20	£850	£140
158	Plate 20 3d. rose	£900	£150
158	Plate 21	£500	£100
152	Plate 15 4d. vermilion	£3000	£475
152	Plate 16		*£35000
153	Plate 15 4d. sage-green	£1600	£325
153	Plate 16	£1400	£300
153	Plate 17		*£20000
160	Plate 17 4d. grey-brown	£475	80·00
160	Plate 18	£450	75·00
147	Plate 13 6d. grey	£500	90·00
147	Plate 14	£500	90·00
147	Plate 15	£500	90·00
147	Plate 16	£500	90·00
147	Plate 17	£950	£180
161	Plate 17 6d. grey	£425	80·00
161	Plate 18	£400	80·00
150	Plate 8 1s. green	£825	£175
150	Plate 9	£825	£175
150	Plate 10	£775	£200
150	Plate 11	£775	£175
150	Plate 12	£650	£160
150	Plate 13	£650	£160
150	Plate 14		*£40000
163	Plate 13 1s. orange-brown	£875	£170
163	Plate 14	£750	£170

35 36 37

38

39 Maltese Cross   **40** Large Anchor

1867–83. Large uncoloured corner letters.

(a) Wmk Maltese Cross, W **39**. Perf 15½×15.

126	**35**	5s. rose (1.7.67)	£9500	£675
128	**36**	10s. greenish grey (Plate 1) (26.9.78)	£50000	£3000
129	**37**	£1 brown-lilac (Plate 1) (26.9.78)	£75000	£3750

(b) Wmk Large Anchor, W **40**. Perf 14.

131	**36**	10s. grey-green (Plate 1) (2.83)	£110000	£4500
132	**37**	£1 brown-lilac (Plate 1) (12.82)	£140000	£6500
134	**35**	5s. rose (Plate 4)	£28000	£3250
137	**38**	£5 orange (Plate 1)	£10000	£3500

41   **42**   **43**

44   **45**   **46**

47 Small Anchor   **48** Orb

1873–80. Large coloured corner letters.

(a) Wmk Small Anchor, W **47**.

139	**41**	2½d. rosy mauve (*white paper*)	£675	£120
		rosy mauve		

(b) Wmk Orb, W **48**.

| 141 | **41** | 2½d. rosy mauve (1.5.76) | £525 | 85·00 |
| 142 | | 2½d. blue (5.2.80) | £575 | 55·00 |

(c) Wmk Spray of Rose, W **33**.

143	**42**	3d. rose (5.7.73)	£450	80·00
145	**43**	6d. pale buff (Plate 13) (15.3.73)		*£25000
147		6d. grey.	£500	90·00
150	**44**	1s. green	£650	£160
151		1s. orange-brown (Plate 13) (14.10.80)	£4750	£550

(d) Wmk Large Garter, W **17**.

152	**45**	4d. vermilion (1.3.76)	£3000	£525
153		4d. sage-green (12.3.77)	£1400	£300
154		4d. grey-brown (Plate 17) (15.8.80)	£2800	£500
156	**46**	8d. orange (Plate 1) (11.9.76)	£1850	£350

49 Imperial Crown

3d   **6d**

(50)   (51)

Surcharges in red

1880–83. Large coloured corner letters. Wmk Imperial Crown, W **49**.

157	**41**	2½d. blue (23.3.81)	£450	35·00
158	**42**	3d. rose (3.81)	£500	£100
159		3d. on 3d. lilac (surch Type **50**) (pl. 21) (1.1.83)	£650	£160
160	**45**	4d. grey-brown (8.12.80)	£450	75·00
161	**43**	6d. grey (1.1.81)	£400	80·00
162		6d. on 6d. lilac (surch Type **51**) (pl. 18) (1.1.83)	£675	£150
163	**44**	1s. orange-brown (24.5.81)	£750	£170

52   **53**

54   **55**   **56**

1880–81. Wmk Imperial Crown, W **49**.

164	**52**	½d. deep green (14.10.80)	55·00	22·00
166	**53**	1d. Venetian red (1.1.80)	35·00	15·00
167	**54**	1½d. Venetian red (14.10.80)	£250	60·00
168	**55**	2d. pale rose (8.12.80)	£350	£120
169	**56**	5d. indigo (15.3.81)	£725	£175

57   Die I   Die II

1881. Wmk Imperial Crown, W **49**.

(a) 14 dots in each corner, Die I (12 July).

171	**57**	1d. pale lilac	£225	45·00

(b) 16 dots in each corner, Die II (13 December).

174	**57**	1d. mauve	2·75	1·70

58   **59**   **60**

1883–84. Coloured letters in the corners. Wmk Large Anchor, W **40.**

178	**58**	2s.6d. lilac	£600	£160
181	**59**	5s. crimson	£975	£250
183	**60**	10s. ultramarine	£2250	£525

61

1884 (1 Apr). Wmk Three Imperial Crowns, W **49.**

185	**61**	£1 brown-lilac	£28000	£3000

1888 (Feb). Wmk Three Orbs, W **48.**

186	**61**	£1 brown-lilac	£60000	£4500

62   63   64

65    66

1883 (1 Aug). (9d.) or **1884** (1 Apr) (others). Wmk Imperial Crown, W **49** (sideways on horiz designs).

187	**52**	½d. slate-blue	35·00	10·00
188	**62**	1½d. lilac	£125	45·00
189	**63**	2d. lilac	£230	80·00
190	**64**	2½d. lilac	95·00	20·00
191	**65**	3d. lilac	£280	£100
192	**66**	4d. dull green	£580	£210
193	**62**	5d. dull green	£580	£210
194	**63**	6d. dull green	£625	£240
195	**64**	9d. dull green	£1250	£480
196	**65**	1s. dull green	£1600	£325

The above prices are for stamps in the true dull green colour. Stamps which have been soaked, causing the colour to run, are virtually worthless.

71   72   73

74   75   76

77   78   79

80    81    82

1887 (1 Jan)–**92.** Jubilee issue. New types. The bicoloured stamps have the value tablets, or the frames including the value tablets, in the second colour. Wmk Imperial Crown, W **49** (Three Crowns on £1).

197	**71**	½d. vermilion	1·75	1·20
198	**72**	1½d. dull purple and pale green	18·00	8·00
200	**73**	2d. grey-green and carmine	35·00	15·00
201	**74**	2½d. purple/*blue*	25·00	5·00
202	**75**	3d. purple/*yellow*	25·00	5·00
205	**76**	4d. green and purple-brown	40·00	18·00
206	**77**	4½d. green and carmine (15.9.92)	11·00	4·00
207*a*	**78**	5d. dull purple and blue (Die II) (1888)	42·00	15·00
208	**79**	6d. purple/*rose-red*	40·00	15·00
209	**80**	9d. dull purple and blue	75·00	48·00
210	**81**	10d. dull purple and carmine (*shades*) (24.2.90)	60·00	45·00
211	**82**	1s. dull green	£275	80·00
212	**61**	£1 green (28.1.91)	£4000	£800

1900. Colours changed. Wmk Imperial Crown, W **49.**

213	**71**	½d. blue-green (17.4.00)	2·25	2·25
214	**82**	1s. green and carmine (11.7.00)	65·00	£140
Set of 14	(excl. £1)		£650	£380

The ½d. No. 213, in bright blue, is a colour changeling caused by a constituent of the ink used for some months in 1900.

Departmental Officials

The following Official stamps were exclusively for the use of certain government departments. Until 1882 official mail used ordinary postage stamps purchased at post offices, the cash being refunded once a quarter. Later the government departments obtained Official stamps by requisition. Official stamps may have been on sale to the public for a short time at Somerset House but they were not sold from post offices. The system of only supplying the Government departments with stamps was open to abuse so that all official stamps were withdrawn on 13 May 1904.

INLAND REVENUE

These stamps were used by revenue officials in the provinces, mail to and from Head Office passing without a stamp. The London Office used these stamps only for foreign mail.

I.R.   **I. R.**

OFFICIAL   **OFFICIAL**

(O1)   (O2)

1882–1901. Stamps of Queen Victoria. Optd with T **O1** or T **O2** (5s., 10s., £1).

O2	**52**	½d. pale green (1.11.82)	90·00	40·00
O5		½d. slate-blue (8.5.85)	£110	35·00
O13	**71**	½d. vermilion (15.5.88)	15·00	7·00
O17		½d. blue-green (4.01)	20·00	15·00
O3	**57**	1d. lilac (Die II) (1.10.82)	10·00	7·00
O6	**64**	2½d. lilac (12.3.85)	£525	£180
O14	**74**	2½d. purple/*blue* (2.92)	£175	30·00
O4	**34**	6d. grey (Plate 18) (3.11.82)	£575	£140
O18	**79**	6d. purple/*rose-red* (1.7.01)	£625	£150
O7	**65**	1s. dull green (12.3.85)	£6000	£1900
O15	**89**	1s. dull green (9.89)	£1000	£375
O19		1s. green and carmine (12.01)	£4250	£1800
O9	**59**	5s. rose (Wmk Anchor) (3.90)	£12000	£2500
O10	**60**	10s. ultramarine (Wmk Anchor) (3.90)	£11500	£3750
O11	**61**	£1 brown-lilac (Wmk Crowns) (12.3.85)	£60000	£22000
O12		£1 brown-lilac (Wmk Orbs) (3.90)	£85000	£30000
O16		£1 green (6.92)	£12500	£2500

OFFICE OF WORKS

These were issued to Head and Branch (local) offices in London and in Branch (local) offices at Birmingham, Bristol, Edinburgh, Glasgow, Leeds, Liverpool, Manchester and Southampton. The overprints on stamps of value 2d. and upwards were created later in 1902, the 2d. for registration fees and the rest for overseas mail.

O.W.

OFFICIAL
(O3)

1896 (24 Mar)–**02**. Stamps of Queen Victoria. Optd with T **O3**.

O31	71	½d. vermilion	£350	£150
O32		½d. blue-green (2.02)	£475	£225
O33	57	1d. lilac (Die II)	£500	£150
O34	78	5d. dull purple and blue (Die II) (29.4.02)	£4000	£1400
O35	81	10d. dull purple and carmine (28.5.02)	£7250	£2250

ARMY

Letters to and from the War Office in London passed without postage. The overprinted stamps were distributed to District and Station Paymasters nationwide, including Cox and Co., the Army Agents, who were paymasters to the Household Division.

ARMY ARMY

OFFICIAL OFFICIAL
(O4) (O5)

1896 (1 Sept)–**01**. Stamps of Queen Victoria optd with T **O4** (½d., 1d.) or T **O5** (2½d., 6d.).

O41		½d. vermilion	10·00	5·00
O42		½d. blue-green (6.00)	10·00	15·00
O43		1d. lilac (Die II)	8·00	7·00
O44		2½d. purple/*blue*	50·00	35·00
O45		6d. purple/*rose-red* (20.9.01)	£110	60·00

GOVERNMENT PARCELS

These stamps were issued to all departments, including Head Office, for use on parcels weighing over 3lb. Below this weight government parcels were sent by letter post to avoid the 55% of the postage paid from accuring to the railway companies, as laid down by parcel-post regulations. Most government parcels stamps suffered heavy postmarks in use.

GOVᵀ PARCELS
(O7)

1883 (1 Aug)–**1900**. Stamps of Queen Victoria. Optd with T **O7**.

O69	57	1d. lilac (Die II) (18.6.97)	£100	30·00
O61	62	1½d. lilac (1.5.86)	£400	£100
O65	72	1½d. dull purple and pale green (29.10.87)	£170	30·00
O70	73	2d. grey-green and carmine (24.10.91)	£250	50·00
O71	77	4½d. green and carmine (29.9.92)	£400	£275
O62	62	6d. dull green (1.5.86)	£3500	£1400
O66	79	6d. purple/*rose-red* (19.12.87)	£275	75·00
O63	64	9d. dull green	£2750	£1200
O67	80	9d. dull purple and blue (21.8.88)	£425	£120
O64	25	1s. orange-brown (pl. 13)	£1750	£300
O64c		1s. orange-brown (pl. 14)	£3500	£600
O68	82	1s. dull green (25.3.90)	£700	£275
O72	82	1s. green and carmine (11.00)	£650	£275

BOARD OF EDUCATION

BOARD OF EDUCATION
(O8)

1902 (19 Feb). Stamps of Queen Victoria. Optd with T **O8**.

O81	78	5d. dull purple and blue (II)	£5750	£1500
O82	82	1s. green and carmine	£12000	£6000

King Edward VII

22 January 1901–6 May 1910

83	**84**	**85**
86	**87**	**88**
89	**90**	**91**
92	**93**	**94**
95	**96**	
	97	

1902–13. Wmk Imperial Crown W **49** (½d. to 1s.); Large Anchor, W **40** (2s.6d. to 10s.), Three Crowns, W **49** (£1). P. 14.

(a) Perf 14.

215	83	½d. dull blue-green (1.1.02)	2·00	1·50
217		½d. pale yellowish green (26.11.04)	2·00	1·50
219		1d. scarlet (1.1.02)	2·00	1·50
224	84	1½d. slate-purple and bluish green (7.05)	45·00	22·00
291	85	2d. deep dull green and carmine (8.8.11)	30·00	25·00
231	86	2½d. pale ultramarine	20·00	15·00
232	87	3d. dull purple/*orange-yellow* (20.3.02)	50·00	18·00
238	88	4d. deep green and chocolate-brown (1.06)	40·00	20·00
240		4d. pale orange (12.09)	20·00	18·00
294	89	5d. deep dull reddish purple and bright blue (7.8.11)	30·00	22·00
297	83	6d. dull purple (31.10.11)	30·00	22·00
249	90	7d. grey-black (4.5.10)	15·00	22·00
307	91	9d. dull reddish purple and blue (10.11)	60·00	60·00
311	92	10d. dull reddish purple and carmine (5.12)	80·00	60·00
314	93	1s. green and carmine (15.4.12)	60·00	35·00
260	94	2s.6d. lilac (5.4.02)	£280	£150
263	95	5s. bright carmine (5.4.02)	£450	£225
265	96	10s. ultramarine (5.4.02)	£1000	£500
320	97	£1 deep green (3.9.11)	£2000	£750

(b) Perf 15×14.

279	83	½d. dull green (30.10.11)	40·00	45·00
281		1d. rose-carmine (4.11.11)	15·00	15·00
283	86	2½d. bright blue (14.10.11)	22·00	15·00
285	87	3d. purple/*lemon* (22.9.11)	45·00	15·00
286	88	4d. bright orange (11.11.11)	30·00	15·00
Set of 5			£130	90·00

Departmental Officials

INLAND REVENUE

These stamps were used by revenue officials in the provinces, mail to and from Head Office passing without a stamp. The London Office used these stamps only for foreign mail.

(O1) (O2)

1902–04. Stamps of King Edward VII. Optd with T **O1** (½d. to 1s.) or T **O2** (others)

O20	83	½d. blue-green (4.2.02)	32·00	5·00
O21		1d. scarlet (4.2.02)	22·00	5·00
O22	86	2½d. ultramarine (19.2.02)	£1000	£275
O23	83	6d. pale dull purple (14.3.04)	£500000	£300000
O24	93	1s. dull green and carmine (29.4.02)	£3750	£900
O25	95	5s. bright carmine (29.4.02)	£38000	£10000
O26	96	10s. ultramarine (29.4.02)	£85000	£45000
O27	97	£1 dull blue-green (29.4.02)	£50000	£18000

OFFICE OF WORKS

These were issued to Head and Branck (local) offices in London and to Branch (local) offices in Birmingham, Bristol, Edinburgh, Glasgow, Leeds, Liverpool, Manchester and Southampton. The overprints onj stamps of value 2d. and upwards were created later in 1902, the 2d. for registration fees and the rest for overseas mail.

(O3)

1902 (11 Feb)–**03.** Stamps of King Edward VII. Optd with T **O3**

O36	83	½d. blue-green (2.02)	£575	£180
O37		1d. scarlet	£575	£180
O38	85	2d. yellowish green and carmine-red (27.4.02)	£2000	£450
O39	86	2½d. ultramarine (29.4.02)	£3500	£675
O40	92	10d. dull purple and carmine (28.5.03)	£40000	£7000

ARMY

Letters to and from the War Office in London passed without postage. The overprinted stamps were distributed to District and Station Paymasters nationwide, including Cox and Co., the Army Agents, who were paymsters to the Household Division.

(O4)

1902–03. Stamps of King Edward VII optd with T **O4**.

O48	**83**	½d. blue-green (11.2.02)	6·00	2·50
O49		1d. scarlet (11.2.02)	6·00	2·50
O50		6d. pale dull purple (23.8.02)	£175	80·00

GOVERNMENT PARCELS

These stamps were issued to all departments, inluding Head Office, for use on parcels weighing over 3lb. Below this weight government parcels were sent by letter post to avoid the 55% of the postage paid from accuring to the railiway companies, as laid down by parcel-post regultions. Most government parcels stampsw suffered heavy postmarks in use.

GOVT PARCELS
(O7)

1902. Stamps of King Edward VII. Optd with T **O7**

O74	**83**	1d. scarlet (30.10.02)	75·00	22·00
O75	**85**	2d. yellowish green and carmine-red (29.4.02)	£225	60·00
O76	**83**	6d. pale dull purple (19.2.02)	£275	60·00
O77	**91**	9d. dull purple and ultramarine (28.8.02)	£650	£175
O78	**93**	1s. dull green and carmine (17.12.02)	£1350	£300

BOARD OF EDUCATION

BOARD OF EDUCATION
(O8)

1902 (19 Feb)–**04**. Stamps of King Edward VII. Optd with T **O8**.

O83	**83**	½d. blue-green	£180	45·00
O84		1d. scarlet	£180	45·00
O85	**86**	2½d. ultramarine	£5000	£475
O86	**89**	5d. dull purple and ultramarine (6.2.04)	£30000	£8500
O87	**93**	1s. dull green and carmine (23.12.02)	£160000	—

ROYAL HOUSEHOLD

R.H. OFFICIAL
(O9)

1902. Stamps of King Edward VII optd with T **O9**.

O91		½d. blue-green (29.4.02)	£375	£200
O92		1d. scarlet (19.2.02)	£325	£175

ADMIRALTY

ADMIRALTY OFFICIAL
(O10)

1903 (1 Apr). Stamps of King Edward VII optd with T **O10**.

O101	**83**	½d. blue-green	30·00	15·00
O102		1d. scarlet	20·00	10·00
O103	**84**	1½d. dull purple and green	£325	£150
O104	**85**	2d. yellowish green and carmine-red	£350	£160
O105	**86**	2½d. ultramarine	£475	£150
O106	**87**	3d. purple/*yellow*	£425	£160

King George V

6 May 1910-20 January 1936

98 (Hair dark)   **99** (Lion unshaded)   **100** Simple Cypher

1911–12. Wmk Imperial Crown, W **49**. Perf 15×14.

322	**98**	½d. green (22.6.11)	4·00	4·00
327	**99**	1d. carmine-red (22.6.11)	4·50	2·50

1912 (28 Sept). Booklet stamps. Wmk Royal Cypher (Simple), W **100**. Perf 15×14.

335	**98**	½d. green	45·00	40·00
336	**99**	1d. scarlet	30·00	30·00

101 (Hair light)   **102** (Lion shaded)   **103** Multiple Cypher

1912 (1 Jan). Wmk Imperial Crown, W **49**. Perf 15×14.

339	**101**	½d. green	8·00	4·00
341	**102**	1d. bright scarlet	5·00	2·00

1912 (Aug). Wmk Royal Cypher (Simple), W **100**. Perf 15×14.

344	**101**	½d. green	7·00	3·00
345	**102**	1d. scarlet	8·00	4·50

1912 (Sept–Oct). Wmk Royal Cypher (Multiple), W **103**. Perf 15×14.

346	**101**	½d. green (10.12)	12·00	8·00
350	**102**	1d. scarlet	18·00	10·00

104   **105**   **106**

107   **108**

1912–24. Wmk Royal Cypher (Simple), W **100**. (6d.). Perf 15×14.

351	**105**	½d. green (16.1.13)	1·00	1·00
357	**104**	1d. bright scarlet (8.10.12)	1·00	1·00
364	**105**	1½d. chestnut	3·00	1·00
368	**106**	2d. orange	4·00	3·00
371	**104**	2½d. cobalt-blue (18.10.12)	12·00	4·00
375	**106**	3d. violet	8·00	3·00
379		4d. grey-green	15·00	2·00
381	**107**	5d. brown (30.6.13)	15·00	5·00
385		6d. reddish purple (8.13)	15·00	7·00
		a. Perf 14	90·00	£110

387		7d. olive (1.8.13)	20·00	10·00
390		8d. black/*yellow* (1.8.13)	32·00	11·00
392	**108**	9d. agate (30.6.13)	15·00	6·00
393*a*		9d. olive-green (9.22)	£110	30·00
394		10d. turquoise-blue (1.8.13)	22·00	20·00
395		1s. bistre (1.8.13)	20·00	4·00
Set of 15			£250	95·00

1913 (Aug). Wmk Royal Cypher (Multiple), W **103**. Perf 15×14.

397	**105**	½d. bright green	£150	£180
398	**104**	1d. dull scarlet	£225	£225

See also Nos. 418/419.

109   **110**

1913–19. Wmk Cypher W **110**. Perf 11×12.

414	**109**	2s.6d. chocolate-brown (12.18)	£160	75·00
416		5s. rose-red (1.19)	£325	£135
417		10s. dull grey-blue (1.19)	£475	£175
403		£1 green (1.8.13)	£2800	£1400
Set of 4			£3500	£1500

T **109** Background around portrait consists of horizontal lines. See also Nos. 450/451.

111 Block Cypher

1924 (Feb)–**26**. Wmk Block Cypher, W **111**. Perf 15×14.

418	**105**	½d. green	1·00	1·00
419	**104**	1d. scarlet	1·00	1·00
420	**105**	1½d. red-brown	1·00	1·00
421	**106**	2d. orange (7.24)	2·50	2·50
422	**104**	2½d. blue (10.10.24)	5·00	3·00
423	**106**	3d. violet (10.10.24)	10·00	2·50
424		4d. grey-green (10.10.24)	12·00	2·50
425	**107**	5d. brown (17.10.24)	20·00	3·00
426*a*		6d. purple (6.26)	4·00	1·50
427	**108**	9d. olive-green (11.11.24)	12·00	3·50
428		10d. turquoise-blue (28.11.24)	40·00	40·00
429		1s. bistre-brown (10.24)	22·00	3·00
418/429 *Set of* 12			£110	60·00

112

1924–25. British Empire Exhibition. W **111**. Perf 14.

(a) Dated 1924 (23.4.24).

430	**112**	1d. scarlet	10·00	11·00
431	**112a**	1½d. brown	15·00	15·00
First day Cover				£450

(b) Dated 1925 (9.5.25).

432	**112**	1d. scarlet	15·00	30·00
433	**112a**	1½d. brown	40·00	70·00
First Day Cover				£1700

113   **114**   **115**

123   **123a**

123b   **123c**

1935 (7 May). Silver Jubilee. W **111**. Perf 15×14.

453	**123**	½d. green	1·00	1·00
454	**123a**	1d. scarlet	1·50	2·00
455	**123b**	1½d. red-brown	1·00	1·00
456	**123c**	2½d. blue	5·00	6·50
First Day Cover				£650

116 St George and the Dragon

117

1929 (10 May). Ninth UPU Congress, London.

(a) W **111**. Perf 15×14.

434	**113**	½d. green	2·25	2·25
435	**114**	1d. scarlet	2·25	2·25
436		1½d. purple-brown	2·25	1·75
437	**115**	2½d. blue	10·00	10·00

(b) W **117**. Perf 12.

438	**116**	£1 black	£750	£600
Set of 4 (to 2½d.)			15·00	14·50
First Day Cover (Nos. 434/437) (4 values)				£675
First Day Cover (Nos. 434/438) (5 values)				£14000

118   **119**   **120**

121   **122**

1934–36. W **111**. Perf 15×14.

439	**118**	½d. green (17.11.34)	50	50
440	**119**	1d. scarlet (24.9.34)	50	50
441	**118**	1½d. red-brown (20.8.34)	50	50
442	**120**	2d. orange (19.1.35)	75	75
443	**119**	2½d. bright blue (18.3.35)	1·50	1·25
444	**120**	3d. reddish violet (18.3.35)	1·50	1·25
445		4d. deep grey-green (2.12.35)	2·00	1·25
446	**121**	5d. yellow-brown (17.2.36)	6·50	2·75
447	**122**	9d. deep olive-green (2.12.35)	12·00	2·25
448		10d. turquoise-blue (24.2.36)	15·00	10·00
449		1s. bistre-brown (24.2.36)	15·00	1·25
439/449 *Set of* 11			50·00	20·00

1934 (16 Oct). T **109** (re-engraved). Background around portrait consists of horizontal and diagonal lines. W **110**. Perf 11×12.

450	**109**	2s.6d. chocolate-brown	80·00	40·00
451		5s. bright rose-red	£175	85·00
452		10s. indigo	£350	80·00
450/452 *Set of* 3				

King Edward VIII

20 January-10 December 1936

124   **125**

1936. W **125**. Perf 15×14.

457	**124**	½d. green (1.9.36)	30	30
458		1d. scarlet (14.9.36)	60	50
459		1½d. red-brown (1.9.36)	30	30
460		2½d. bright blue (1.9.36)	30	85

First Day Covers

1.9.36	Nos. 457, 459/460	£175
14.9.36	No. 458	£200

Collectors are reminded that for issues from 1936 to date, prices in the unused column are for unmounted mint.

King George VI

11 December 1936-6 February 1952

126 King George VI and   **127**
Queen Elizabeth

1937 (13 May). Coronation. W **127**. Perf 15×14.

461	**126**	1½d. maroon	30	30
First Day Cover				35·00

128   **129**   **130**

King George VI and National Emblems

1937–47. W **127**. Perf 15×14.

462	**128**	½d. green (10.5.37)	30	25
463		1d. scarlet (10.5.37)	30	25
464		1½d. red-brown (30.7.37)	30	25
465		2d. orange (31.1.38)	1·25	50
466		2½d. ultramarine (10.5.37)	40	25
467		3d. violet (31.1.38)	5·00	1·00
468	**129**	4d. grey-green (21.11.38)	60	75
469		5d. brown (21.11.38)	3·50	85
470		6d. purple (30.1.39)	1·50	60
471	**130**	7d. emerald-green (27.2.39)	5·00	60
472		8d. bright carmine (27.2.39)	7·50	80
473		9d. deep olive-green (1.5.39)	6·50	80
474		10d. turquoise-blue (1.5.39)	7·00	80
474*a*		11d. plum (29.12.47)	3·00	2·75
475		1s. bistre-brown (1.5.39)	9·00	75
462/475 *Set of* 15			45·00	10·00

First Day Covers

10.5.37	Nos. 462/463, 466	45·00
30.7.37	Nos. 464	45·00
31.1.38	Nos. 465, 467	£100
21.11.38	Nos. 468/469	65·00
30.1.39	No. 470	60·00
27.2.39	Nos. 471/472	85·00
1.5.39	Nos. 473/474, 475	£500
29.12.47	No. 474*a*	55·00

For later printings of the lower values in apparently lighter shades and different colours, see Nos. 485/490 and 503/508.

131   **132**

133

1939–48. W **133**. Perf 14.

476	**131**	2s.6d. brown (4.9.39)	£100	8·00
476b		2s.6d. yellow-green (9.3.42)	15·00	1·50
477		5s. red (21.8.39)	20·00	2·00
478	**132**	10s. dark blue (30.10.39)	£260	22·00
478b		10s. ultramarine (30.11.42)	45·00	5·00
478c		£1 brown (1.10.48)	25·00	26·00
476/478c Set of 6			£425	60·00

First Day Covers

21.8.39	No. 477	£875
4.9.39	No. 475	£1800
30.1039	No. 478	£3250
9.3.41	No. 476b	£1750
30.11.41	No. 478b	£3750
1.10.48	No. 478c	£375

134 Queen Victoria
and King George VI

1940 (6 May). Centenary of First Adhesive Postage Stamps. W **127**. Perf 14½×14.

479	**134**	½d. green	30	75
480		1d. scarlet	1·00	75
481		1½d. red-brown	50	1·50
482		2d. orange	1·00	75
483		2½d. ultramarine	2·25	50
484		3d. violet	3·00	3·50
First Day Cover				55·00

1941–42. Head as Nos. 462/467, but with lighter background to provide a more economic use of the printing ink. W **127**. Perf 15×14.

485	**128**	½d. pale green (1.9.41)	30	30
486		1d. pale scarlet (11.8.41)	30	30
487		1½d. pale red-brown (28.9.42)	60	80
488		2d. pale orange (6.10.41)	50	50
489		2½d. light ultramarine (21.7.41)	30	30
490		3d. pale violet (3.11.41)	2·50	1·00
485/490 Set of 6			3·50	2·75

First Day Covers

21.7.41	No. 489	45·00
11.8.41	No. 486	25·00
1.9.41	No. 485	25·00
6.10.41	No. 488	60·00
3.11.41	No. 490	£110
28.9.42	No. 487	55·00

135 Symbols of Peace and Reconstruction

136 Symbols of Peace and Reconstruction

1946 (11 June). Peace. W **127**. Perf 15×14.

491	**135**	2½d. ultramarine	20	20
492	**136**	3d. violet	20	50
Set of 2			40	50
First Day Cover				65·00

137 King George VI and Queen Elizabeth

1948 (26 Apr). Royal Silver Wedding. W **127**. Perf 15×14 (2½d.) or 14×15 (£1).

493	**137**	2½d. ultramarine	35	20
494	**138**	£1 blue	40·00	40·00
Set of 2			40·00	40·00
First Day Cover				£425

1948 (10 May). Stamps of 1d. and 2½d. showing seaweed-gathering were on sale at eight Head Post Offices in Great Britain, but were primarily for use in the Channel Islands and are listed there (see Nos. C1/C2, after Royal Mail Post & Go Stamps).

139 Globe and Laurel Wreath   **140** Speed

141 Olympic Symbol   **142** Winged Victory

1948 (29 July). Olympic Games. W **127**. Perf 15×14.

495	**139**	2½d. ultramarine	50	10
496	**140**	3d. violet	50	50
497	**141**	6d. bright purple	3·25	75
498	**142**	1s. brown	4·50	2·00
495/498 Set of 4			8·00	3·00
First Day Cover				50·00

143 Two Hemispheres   **144** UPU Monument, Bern

145 Goddess Concordia, Globe and Points of Compass   **146** Posthorn and Globe

1949 (10 Oct). 75th Anniversary of Universal Postal Union. W **127**. Perf 15×14.

499	**143**	2½d. ultramarine	25	10
500	**144**	3d. violet	25	50
501	**145**	6d. bright purple	50	75
502	**146**	1s. brown	1·00	1·25
499/502 Set of 4			1·50	2·50
First Day Cover				80·00

1950–52. 4d. as No. 468 and others as Nos. 485/489, but colours changed. W **127**. Perf 15×14.

503	**128**	½d. pale orange (3.5.51)	30	30
504	**128**	1d. light ultramarine (3.5.51)	30	30
505	**128**	1½d. pale green (3.5.51)	65	60
506	**128**	2d. pale red-brown (3.5.51)	75	40
507	**128**	2½d. pale scarlet (3.5.51)	60	40
508	**129**	4d. light ultramarine (2.10.50)	2·00	1·75
503/508 Set of 6			4·00	3·25

First Day Covers

2.10.50	No. 508	£125
3.5.51	Nos. 503/507	55·00

147 HMS *Victory*

148 White Cliffs of Dover

149 St George and the Dragon

150 Royal Coat of Arms

1951 (3 May). W **133**. Perf 11×12.

509	**147**	2s.6d. yellow-green	7·50	1·00
510	**148**	5s. red	35·00	1·00
511	**149**	10s. ultramarine	15·00	7·50
512	**150**	£1 brown	45·00	18·00
509/512	*Set of 4*		£100	25·00
First Day Cover				£950

151 Commerce and Prosperity

152 Festival Symbol

1951 (3 May). Festival of Britain. W **127**. Perf 15×14.

513	**151**	2½d. scarlet	20	15
514	**152**	4d. ultramarine	30	35
Set of 2			40	40
First Day Cover				40·00

Queen Elizabeth II

6 February 1952-8 September 2022

153 Tudor Crown   **154**

155   **156**   **157**

158   **159**   **160**

1952–54. W **153**. Perf 15×14.

515	**154**	½d. orange-red (31.8.53)	25	15
516		1d. ultramarine (31.8.53)	30	20
517		1½d. green (5.12.52)	25	20
518		2d. red-brown (31.8.53)	30	20
519	**155**	2½d. carmine-red (5.12.52)	30	15
520		3d. deep lilac (18.1.54)	1·50	90
521	**156**	4d. ultramarine (2.11.53)	3·25	1·25
522	**157**	5d. brown (6.7.53)	1·00	3·50
523		6d. reddish purple (18.1.54)	4·00	1·00
524		7d. bright green (18.1.54)	9·50	5·50
525	**158**	8d. magenta (6.7.53)	1·25	85
526		9d. bronze-green (8.2.54)	23·00	4·75
527		10d. Prussian blue (8.2.54)	18·00	4·75
528		11d. brown-purple (8.2.54)	35·00	15·00
529	**159**	1s. bistre-brown (6.7.53)	80	50
530	**160**	1s.3d. green (2.11.53)	4·50	3·25
531	**159**	1s.6d. grey-blue (2.11.53)	14·00	3·75
515/531	*Set of 17*		£100	40·00

See also Nos. 540/556, 561/566, 570/594 and 599/618a. For stamps as Types **154/155** and **157/160** with face values in decimal currency see Nos. 2031/2033, 2258/2259, **MS**2326, **MS**2367, 2378/2379 and 3329.

First Day Covers

5.12.52	Nos. 517, 519	28·00
6.7.53	Nos. 522, 525, 526	60·00
31.8.53	Nos. 515/516, 518	60·00
2.11.53	Nos. 521, 530/531	£200
18.1.54	Nos. 520, 523/524	£125
8.2.54	Nos. 526/528	£250

161   **162**

163   **164**

1953 (3 June). Coronation. W **153**. Perf 15×14.

532	**161**	2½d. carmine-red	20	20
533	**162**	4d. ultramarine	80	40
534	**163**	1s.3d. deep yellow-green	3·00	1·00
535	**164**	1s.6d. deep grey-blue	6·50	2·00
	Set of 4		10·00	3·50
	First Day Cover			75·00

165 St Edward's Crown

166 Carrickfergus Castle   **167** Caernarvon Castle

168 Edinburgh Castle   **169** Windsor Castle

1955–58. W **165**. Perf 11×12.

536	**166**	2s.6d. black-brown (23.9.55)	15·00	2·00
537	**167**	5s. rose-carmine (23.9.55)	40·00	4·00
538	**168**	10s. ultramarine (1.9.55)	90·00	14·00
539	**169**	£1 black (1.9.55)	£140	35·00
	Set of 4		£250	50·00
	First Day Cover (Nos. 538/539) (1.9.55)			£850
	First Day Cover (Nos. 536/537) (23.9.55)			£650

See also Nos. 595a/598a and 759/762. For stamps as Types **166/169** with face values in decimal currency see Nos. **MS**2530 and 3221.

1955–58. W **165**. Perf 15×14.

540	**154**	½d. orange-red (9.55)	20	15
541		1d. ultramarine (19.9.55)	30	15
542		1½d. green (8.55)	25	30
543		2d. red-brown (6.9.55)	25	35
543b		2d. light red-brown (17.10.56)	30	20
544	**155**	2½d. carmine-red (Type I) (28.9.55)	30	25
545		3d. deep lilac (17.7.56)	40	25
546	**156**	4d. ultramarine (14.11.55)	1·25	45
547	**157**	5d. brown (21.9.55)	6·00	6·00
548		6d. reddish purple (20.12.55)	4·50	1·25
549		7d. bright green (23.4.56)	50·00	10·00
550	**158**	8d. magenta (21.12.55)	7·00	1·25
551		9d. bronze-green (15.12.55)	20·00	2·75
552		10d. Prussian blue (22.9.55)	20·00	2·75
553		11d. brown-purple (28.10.55)	1·00	1·10
554	**159**	1s. bistre-brown (3.11.55)	22·00	95
555	**160**	1s.3d. green (27.3.56)	30·00	1·60
556	**159**	1s.6d. grey-blue (27.3.56)	23·00	1·60
	Set of 18		£160	27·00

170 Scout Badge and Rolling Hitch   **171** Scouts coming to Britain

172 Globe within a Compass

1957 (1 Aug). World Scout Jubilee Jamboree. W **165**. Perf 15×14.

557	**170**	2½d. carmine-red	20	20
558	**171**	4d. ultramarine	50	50
559	**172**	1s.3d. green	3·00	2·00
Set of 3			3·50	2·50
First Day Cover				25·00

173

1957 (12 Sep). 46th Inter-Parliamentary Union Conference. W **165**. Perf 15×14.

560	**173**	4d. ultramarine	40	40
First Day Cover				£150

Graphite-lined and Phosphor Issues. These are used in connection with automatic sorting machinery, originally experimentally at Southampton but now also operating elsewhere. In such areas these stamps were the normal issue, but from mid 1967 all low-value stamps bear phosphor markings.

The graphite lines were printed in black on the back, beneath the gum; two lines per stamp except for the 2d. (see below)

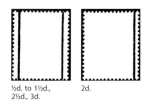

½d. to 1½d., 2d.
2½d., 3d.

Graphite line arrangements (Stamps viewed from back)

In November 1959, phosphor bands, printed on the front, replaced the graphite. They are wider than the graphite, not easy to see, but show as broad vertical bands at certain angles to the light.

Values representing the rate for printed papers (and second class mail from 1968) have one band and others have two, three or four bands according to size and format. From 1972 onwards some commemorative stamps were printed with 'all-over' phosphor.

In the small stamps the bands are on each side with the single-band at left (except where otherwise stated). In the left, centre or right varying in different issues. The bands are vertical on both horizontal and vertical designs except where otherwise stated.

See also notes above No. 881

1957 (19 Nov). Graphite-lined issue. Two graphite lines on the back, except 2d. value, which has one line. W **165**. Perf 15×14.

561	**154**	½d. orange-red	50	40
562		1d. ultramarine	70	60
563		1½d. green	2·00	1·75
564		2d. light red-brown	2·50	2·50
565	**155**	2½d. carmine-red	8·50	7·00
566		3d. deep lilac	1·40	1·25
Set of 6			14·00	12·00
First Day Cover				90·00

See also Nos. 587/594.

176 Welsh Dragon **177** Flag and Games Emblem

178 Welsh Dragon

1958 (18 July). Sixth British Empire and Commonwealth Games, Cardiff. W **165**. Perf 15×14.

567	**176**	3d. deep lilac	10	10
568	**177**	6d. reddish purple	30	30
569	**178**	1s.3d. green	1·00	1·00
Set of 3			1·20	1·20
First Day Cover				75·00

179 Multiple Crowns

WATERMARK. All the following issues to No. 755 are Watermark **179** (sideways on the vertical commemorative stamps) unless otherwise stated.

1958–65. W **179**. Perf 15×14.

570	**154**	½d. orange-red (25.11.58)	10	10
571		1d. ultramarine (11.58)	10	10
572		1½d. green (12.58)	10	15
573		2d. light red-brown (4.12.58)	10	10
574	**155**	2½d. red	10	20
575		3d. deep lilac (11.58)	20	15
576	**156**	4d. deep ultramarine (28.4.65)	15	15
577		4½d. chestnut (9.2.59)	10	25
578	**157**	5d. brown (10.11.58)	30	40
579		6d. deep claret (23.12.58)	30	25
580		7d. bright green (26.11.58)	50	45
581	**158**	8d. magenta (24.2.60)	60	40
582		9d. bronze-green (24.3.59)	60	40
583		10d. Prussian blue (18.11.58)	1·00	50
584	**159**	1s. bistre-brown (30.10.58)	75	30
585	**160**	1s.3d. green (17.6.59)	75	30
586	**159**	1s.6d. grey-blue (16.12.58)	5·00	40
Set of 17			9·00	4·25
First Day Cover (No. 577) (9.2.59)				£250

1958 (24 Nov)–**61**. Graphite-lined issue. Two graphite lines on the back, except 2d. value, which has one line. W **179**. Perf 15×14.

587	**154**	½d. orange-red (15.6.59)	9·00	9·00
588		1d. ultramarine (18.12.58)	2·00	1·50
589		1½d. green (4.8.59)	90·00	80·00
590		2d. light red-brown (24.11.58)	10·00	3·50
591	**155**	2½d. carmine-red (9.6.59)	12·00	10·00
592		3d. deep lilac (24.11.58)	90	65
593	**156**	4d. ultramarine (29.4.59)	5·50	5·00
594		4½d. chestnut (3.6.59)	6·50	5·00
Set of 8			£110	7·00

The prices quoted for Nos. 587 and 589 are for examples with inverted watermark. Stamps with upright watermark are priced at: ½d. £9 *mint*, £9 *used* and 1½d. £90 *mint*, £80 *used*.

1959–68. W **179**. Perf 11×12.

595	**166**	2s.6d. black-brown (22.7.59)	35	40
596	**167**	*167 red* (15.6.59)	1·25	50
597	**168**	10s. *Bright ultramarine* (21.7.59)	4·50	4·50
598	**169**	£1 black (30.6.59)	13·00	8·00
Set of 4			15·00	11·00

1959 (18 Nov). Phosphor-Graphite issue. Two phosphor bands on front and two graphite lines on back, except 2d. value, which has one band on front and one line on back.

(a) W **165**. Perf 15×14.

599	**154**	½d. orange-red	4·25	4·25
600		1d. ultramarine	11·00	11·00
601		1½d. green	4·50	4·50

(b) W **179**. Perf 15×14.

605	**154**	2d. light red-brown (1 band)	6·00	4·25
606	**155**	2½d. carmine-red	22·00	18·00
607		3d. deep lilac	12·00	8·00
608	**156**	4d. ultramarine	20·00	16·00
609		4½d. chestnut	30·00	20·00
Set of 8			£100	80·00

1960 (22 June)–**67**. Phosphor issue. Two phosphor bands on front, except where otherwise stated. W **179**. Perf 15×14.

610	**154**	½d. orange-red	10	15
611		1d. ultramarine	10	10
612		1½d. green	15	15
613		2d. light red-brown (1 band)	22·00	22·00
613a		2d. light red-brown (4.10.61)	10	15
614	**155**	2½d. carmine-red	40	30
614a		2½d. carmine-red (1 band)	60	75
615		3d. deep lilac	60	55
615c		3d. deep lilac (1 centre band) (8.12.66)	40	45
616	**156**	4d. ultramarine	3·50	3·50
616b		4½d. chestnut (13.9.61)	55	30
616c	**157**	5d. brown (9.6.67)	55	35
617		6d. purple	55	30
617a		7d. bright green (15.2.67)	70	50
617b	**158**	8d. magenta (28.6.67)	70	55
617c		9d. bronze-green (29.12.66)	70	65
617d		10d. Prussian blue (30.12.66)	1·00	1·00
617e	**159**	1s. bistre-brown (28.6.67)	1·00	35
618	**160**	1s.3d. green	1·90	2·50
618a	**159**	1s.6d. grey-blue (12.12.66)	2·00	2·00
Set of 17 (one of each value)			10·50	8·00

No. 615c exists with the phosphor band at left or right of the stamp.

180 Postboy of 1660   **181** Posthorn of 1660

1960 (7 July). Tercentenary of Establishment of General Letter Office. W **179** (sideways on 1s.3d.). Perf 15×14 (3d.) or 14×15 (1s.3d.).

619	**180**	3d. deep lilac	20	20
620	**181**	1s.3d. green	1·60	1·75
Set of 2			1·60	1·75
First Day Cover				50·00

182 Conference Emblem   **182a** Conference Emblem

1960 (19 Sep). First Anniversary of European Postal and Telecommunications Conference. W **179**. Perf 15×14.

621	**182**	6d. bronze-green and purple	1·00	20
622	**182a**	1s.6d. brown and blue	5·50	2·25
Set of 2			6·00	2·25
First Day Cover				50·00

183 Thrift Plant   **184** 'Growth of Savings'

185 Thrift Plant

1961 (28 Aug). Centenary of Post Office Savings Bank. W **179** (sideways on 2½d.) Perf 14×15 (2½d.) or 15×14 (others).

623A	**183**	2½d. black and red	10	10
624A	**184**	3d. orange-brown and violet	10	10
625A	**185**	1s.6d. red and blue	1·00	1·25
Set of 3			1·00	1·25
First Day Cover				45·00

186 CEPT Emblem   **187** Doves and Emblem

188 Doves and Emblem

1961 (18 Sept). European Postal and Telecommunications (CEPT) Conference, Torquay. W **179**. Perf 15×14.

626	**186**	2d. orange, pink and brown	10	10
627	**187**	4d. buff, mauve and ultramarine	10	10
628	**188**	10d. turquoise, pale green and Prussian blue	20	20
Set of 3			30	30
First Day Cover				4·00

189 Hammer Beam Roof, Westminster Hall   **190** Palace of Westminster

1961 (25 Sept). Seventh Commonwealth Parliamentary Conference. W **179** (sideways on 1s.3d.) Perf 15×14 (6d.) or 14×15 (1s.3d.).

629	**189**	6d. purple and gold	10	10
630	**190**	1s.3d. green and blue	1·25	1·25
Set of 2			1·25	1·25
First Day Cover				25·00

191 Units of Productivity   **192** National Productivity

193 Unified Productivity

1962 (14 Nov). National Productivity Year. W **179** (inverted on 2½d. and 3d.). Perf 15×14.

631	**191**	2½d. myrtle-green and carmine-red (shades)	10	10
		p. One phosphor band. Blackish olive and carmine-red	60	50
632	**192**	3d. light blue and violet (shades)	25	25
		p. Three phosphor bands	1·50	80
633	**193**	1s.3d. carmine, light blue and deep green	80	80
		p. Three phosphor bands	35·00	22·00
Set of 3 (Ordinary)			1·00	1·00
Set of 3 (Phosphor)			35·00	22·00
First Day Cover (Ordinary)				45·00
First Day Cover (Phosphor)				£125

194 Campaign Emblem and Family   **195** Children of Three Races

1963 (21 Mar). Freedom from Hunger. W **179** (inverted). Perf 15×14.

634	**194**	2½d. crimson and pink	10	10
		p. One phosphor band	3·00	1·25
635	**195**	1s.3d. bistre-brown and yellow	1·00	1·00
		p. Three phosphor bands	30·00	23·00
Set of 2 (Ordinary)			1·00	1·00
Set of 2 (Phosphor)			30·00	23·00
First Day Cover (Ordinary)				25·00
First Day Cover (Phosphor)				40·00

196 'Paris Conference'

1963 (7 May). Paris Postal Conference Centenary. W **179** (inverted). Perf 15×14.

636	**196**	6d. green and mauve	20	20
		p. Three phosphor bands	3·00	2·75
First Day Cover (Ordinary)				7·50
First Day Cover (Phosphor)				30·00

197 Posy of Flowers   **198** Woodland Life

1963 (16 May). National Nature Week. W **179**. Perf 15×14.

637	**197**	3d. yellow, green, brown and black	10	10
		p. Three phosphor bands	30	30
638	**198**	4½d. black, blue, yellow, magenta and brown-red	15	15
		p. Three phosphor bands	1·40	1·40
Set of 2 (Ordinary)			20	20
Set of 2 (Phosphor)			15·00	1·50
First Day Cover (Ordinary)				12·00
First Day Cover (Phosphor)				35·00

199 Rescue at Sea   **200** 19th-century Lifeboat

201 Lifeboatmen

1963 (31 May). Ninth International Lifeboat Conference, Edinburgh. W **179**. Perf 15×14.

639	**199**	2½d. blue, black and red	10	10
		p. One phosphor band	50	60
640	**200**	4d. red, yellow, brown, black and blue	20	20
		p. Three phosphor bands	50	60
641	**201**	1s.6d. sepia, yellow and grey-blue	1·50	1·50
		p. Three phosphor bands	48·00	28·00
Set of 3 (Ordinary)			1·50	1·50
Set of 3 (Phosphor)			48·00	28·00
First Day Cover (Ordinary)				20·00
First Day Cover (Phosphor)				55·00

202 Red Cross   **203**

204

1963 (15 Aug). Red Cross Centenary Congress. W **179**. Perf 15×14.

642	**202**	3d. red and deep lilac	25	25
		p. Three phosphor bands	1·10	1·00
643	**203**	1s.3d. red, blue and grey	1·25	1·25
		p. Three phosphor bands	35·00	30·00
644	**204**	1s.6d. red, blue and bistre	1·25	1·25
		p. Three phosphor bands	35·00	27·00
Set of 3 (Ordinary)			2·50	2·50
Set of 3 (Phosphor)			65·00	55·00
First Day Cover (Ordinary)				20·00
First Day Cover (Phosphor)				60·00

205 Commonwealth Cable

1963 (3 Dec). Opening of COMPAC (Trans-Pacific Telephone Cable). W **179**. Perf 15×14.

645	**205**	1s.6d. blue and black	1·25	1·25
		p. Three phosphor bands	7·25	7·00
First Day Cover (Ordinary)				12·00
First Day Cover (Phosphor)				35·00

206 Puck and Bottom (A Midsummer Night's Dream)   **207** Feste (Twelfth Night)

208 Balcony Scene (Romeo and Juliet)   **209** Eve of Agincourt (Henry V)

210 Hamlet contemplating Yorick's Skull (Hamlet) and Queen Elizabeth II

1964 (23 Apr). Shakespeare Festival. W **179**. Perf 11×12 (2s.6d.) or 15×14 (others).

646	**206**	3d. yellow-bistre, black and deep violet-blue (shades)	10	10
		p. Three phosphor bands	25	25
647	**207**	6d. yellow, orange, black and yellow-olive (shades)	20	20
		p. Three phosphor bands	75	75
648	**208**	1s.3d. cerise, blue-green, black and sepia (shades)	40	40
		p. Three phosphor bands	2·00	2·00

649	**209**	1s.6d. violet, turquoise, black and blue			
		(shades)	60	60	
		p. Three phosphor bands	2·50	2·50	
650	**210**	2s.6d. deep slate-purple (shades)	1·25	1·25	
Set of 5 (Ordinary)			2·00	2·00	
Set of 4 (Phosphor) (Nos. 646p/649p)			5·00	5·00	
First Day Cover (Ordinary)				5·00	
First Day Cover (Phosphor)				9·00	
Presentation Pack (Ordinary)			12·00		

PRESENTATION PACKS were first introduced by the GPO for the Shakespeare Festival issue. The packs include one set of stamps and details of the designs, the designer and the stamp printer. They were issued for almost all later definitve and special issues.

211 Flats near Richmond Park (Urban Development)

212 Shipbuilding Yards, Belfast (Industrial Activity)

213 Beddgelert Forest Park, (Snowdonia Forestry)

214 Nuclear Reactor, Dounreay (Technological Development)

1964 (1 July). 20th International Geographical Congress, London. W **179**. Perf 15×14.

651	**211**	2½d. black, olive-yellow, olive-grey and		
		turquoise-blue	10	10
		p. One phosphor band	40	50
652	**212**	4d. orange-brown, red-brown, rose,		
		black and violet	30	30
		p. Three phosphor bands	1·25	1·25
653	**213**	8d. yellow-brown, emerald, green		
		and black	80	80
		p. Three phosphor bands	2·50	3·50
654	**214**	1s.6d. yellow-brown, pale pink, black		
		and brown	1·40	1·40
		p. Three phosphor bands	28·00	22·00
Set of 4 (Ordinary)			2·00	2·00
Set of 4 (Phosphor)			30·00	25·00
First Day Cover (Ordinary)				10·00
First Day Cover (Phosphor)				35·00
Presentation Pack (Ordinary)			£100	

215 Spring Gentian

216 Dog Rose

217 Honeysuckle

218 Fringed Water Lily

1964 (5 Aug). Tenth International Botanical Congress, Edinburgh. W **179**. Perf 15×14.

655	**215**	3d. violet, blue and sage-green	25	25
		p. Three phosphor bands	40	40
656	**216**	6d. apple-green, rose, scarlet and		
		green	30	30
		p. Three phosphor bands	2·50	2·75
657	**217**	9d. lemon, green, lake and rose-red	80	80
		p. Three phosphor bands	4·50	4·50
658	**218**	1s.3d. yellow, emerald, reddish violet		
		and grey-green	1·25	1·25
		p. Three phosphor bands	25·00	20·00
Set of 4 (Ordinary)			2·00	2·00
Set of 4 (Phosphor)			30·00	25·00
First Day Cover (Ordinary)				10·00
First Day Cover (Phosphor)				35·00
Presentation Pack (Ordinary)			£125	

219 Forth Road Bridge

220 Forth Road and Railway Bridges

1964 (4 Sept). Opening of Forth Road Bridge. W **179**. Perf 15×14.

659	**219**	3d. black, blue and reddish violet	10	10
		p. Three phosphor bands	50	50
660	**220**	6d. blackish lilac, light blue and		
		carmine-red	20	20
		p. Three phosphor bands	2·25	2·25
Set of 2 (Ordinary)			25	25
Set of 2 (Phosphor)			2·50	2·50
First Day Cover (Ordinary)				3·00
First Day Cover (Phosphor)				10·00
Presentation Pack (Ordinary)			£325	

221 Sir Winston Churchill

1965 (8 Jul). Churchill Commemoration. W **179**. Perf 15×14.

661	**221**	4d. black and olive-brown	15	15
		p. Three phosphor bands	20	20
662		1s.3d. black and grey	45	45
		p. Three phosphor bands	1·00	1·00
Set of 2 (Ordinary)			60	60
Set of 2 (Phosphor)			1·10	1·10
First Day Cover (Ordinary)				4·75
First Day Cover (Phosphor)				5·00
Presentation Pack (Ordinary)			40·00	

222 Simon de Montfort's Seal

223 Parliament Buildings (after engraving by Hollar, 1647)

1965 (19 July). 700th Anniversary of Simon de Montfort's Parliament. W **179**. Perf 15×14.

663	**222**	6d. olive-green	10	10
		p. Three phosphor bands	50	50
664	**223**	2s.6d. black, grey and pale drab	40	40
Set of 2 (Ordinary)			40	40
First Day Cover (Ordinary)				6·00
First Day Cover (Phosphor)				20·00
Presentation Pack (Ordinary)			65·00	

224 Bandsmen and Banner

225 Three Salvationists

1965 (9 Aug). Salvation Army Centenary. W **179**. Perf 15×14.

665	**224**	3d. indigo, grey-blue, cerise, yellow		
		and brown	10	10
		p. One phosphor band	20	20
666	**225**	1s.6d. red, blue, yellow and brown	60	60
		p. Three phosphor bands	90	90
Set of 2 (Ordinary)			60	60
Set of 2 (Phosphor)			1·00	1·00

First Day Cover (Ordinary)				10·00
First Day Cover (Phosphor)				22·00

226 Lister's Carbolic Spray **227** Lister and Chemical Symbols

1965 (1 Sept). Centenary of Joseph Lister's Discovery of Antiseptic Surgery. W **179**. Perf 15×14.

667	**226**	4d. indigo, brown-red and grey-black	10	10
		p. Three phosphor bands	25	25
668	**227**	1s. black, purple and new blue	40	40
		p. Three phosphor bands	1·00	1·00
Set of 2 (Ordinary)			45	45
Set of 2 (Phosphor)			1·10	1·10
First Day Cover (Ordinary)				5·00
First Day Cover (Phosphor)				9·00

228 Trinidad Carnival Dancers **229** Canadian Folk Dancers

1965 (1 Sept). Commonwealth Arts Festival. W **179**. Perf 15×14.

669	**228**	6d. black and orange	10	10
		p. Three phosphor bands	40	40
670	**229**	1s.6d. black and light reddish violet	40	40
		p. Three phosphor bands	1·25	1·25
Set of 2 (Ordinary)			45	45
Set of 2 (Phosphor)			1·50	1·50
First Day Cover (Ordinary)				7·00
First Day Cover (Phosphor)				14·00

230 Flight of Supermarine Spitfires **231** Pilot in Hawker Hurricane Mk I

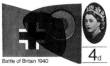 

232 Wing-tips of Supermarine Spitfire and Messerschmitt Bf 109 **233** Supermarine Spitfires attacking Heinkel He-111H Bomber

234 Supermarine Spitfire attacking Junkers Ju 87B Stuka Dive-bomber **235** Hawker Hurricanes Mk I over Wreck of Dornier Do-17Z Bomber

236 Anti-aircraft Artillery in Action **237** Air Battle over St Paul's Cathedral

1965 (13 Sept). 25th Anniversary of Battle of Britain. W **179**. Perf 15×14.

671	**230**	4d. yellow-olive and black	25	25
		a. Block of 6. Nos. 671/676	2·50	2·50

		p. Three phosphor bands	40	40
		pa. Block of 6. Nos. 671p/676p	3·75	3·75
672	**231**	4d. yellow-olive, olive-grey and black	25	25
		p. Three phosphor bands	40	40
673	**232**	4d. red, new blue, yellow-olive, olive-grey and black	25	25
		p. Three phosphor bands	40	40
674	**233**	4d. olive-grey, yellow-olive and black	25	25
		p. Three phosphor bands	40	40
675	**234**	4d. olive-grey, yellow-olive and black	25	25
		p. Three phosphor bands	40	40
676	**235**	4d. olive-grey, yellow-olive, new blue and black	25	25
		p. Three phosphor bands	40	40
677	**236**	9d. bluish violet, orange and slate purple	1·75	1·75
		p. Three phosphor bands	2·00	2·00
678	**237**	1s.3d. light grey, deep grey, black, light blue and bright blue	1·75	1·75
		p. Three phosphor bands	2·00	2·00
Set of 8 (Ordinary)			5·50	5·50
Set of 8 (Phosphor)			7·00	7·00
First Day Cover (Ordinary)				10·00
First Day Cover (Phosphor)				15·00
Presentation Pack (Ordinary)			40·00	

Nos. 671/678 were issued together *se-tenant* in blocks of six (3×2) within the sheet.

238 Tower and Georgian Buildings **239** Tower and Nash Terrace, Regent's Park

1965 (8 Oct). Opening of Post Office Tower. W **179** (sideways on 3d.). Perf 14×15 (3d.) or 15×14 (1s.3d.).

679	**238**	3d. olive-yellow, new blue and bronze-green	10	10
		p. One phosphor band at right	15	15
680	**239**	1s.3d. bronze-green, yellow-green and blue	20	20
		p. Three phosphor bands	30	30
Set of 2 (Ordinary)			25	25
Set of 2 (Phosphor)			40	40
First Day Cover (Ordinary)				2·50
First Day Cover (Phosphor)				4·75
Presentation Pack (Ordinary)			12·50	
Presentation Pack (Phosphor)			12·50	

240 UN Emblem **241** ICY Emblem

1965 (25 Oct). 20th Anniversary of UNO and International Co-operation Year. W **179**. Perf 15×14.

681	**240**	3d. black, yellow-orange and light blue	10	10
		p. One phosphor band	25	25
682	**241**	1s.6d. black, bright purple and light blue	35	35
		p. Three phosphor bands	1·00	1·00
Set of 2 (Ordinary)			40	40
Set of 2 (Phosphor)			1·10	1·10
First Day Cover (Ordinary)				5·00
First Day Cover (Phosphor)				9·00

242 Telecommunications Network **243** Radio Waves and Switchboard

1965 (15 Nov). International Telecommunications Union Centenary. W **179**. Perf 15×14.

683	**242**	9d. red, ultramarine, deep slate, violet, black and pink	20	20
		p. Three phosphor bands	75	75
684	**243**	1s.6d. red, greenish blue, indigo, black and light pink	40	40
		p. Three phosphor bands	2·00	2·00
Set of 2 (Ordinary)			50	50
Set of 2 (Phosphor)			2·50	2·50
First Day Cover (Ordinary)				8·00
First Day Cover (Phosphor)				13·00

244 Robert Burns (after Skirving chalk drawing)

245 Robert Burns (after Nasmyth portrait)

1966 (25 Jan). Burns Commemoration. W **179**. Perf 15×14.

685	**244**	4d. black, deep violet-blue and new blue	10	10
		p. Three phosphor bands	20	20
686	**245**	1s.3d. black, slate-blue and yellow-orange	20	20
		p. Three phosphor bands	90	90
Set of 2 (Ordinary)			25	25
Set of 2 (Phosphor)			1·00	1·00
First Day Cover (Ordinary)				1·25
First Day Cover (Phosphor)				3·50
Presentation Pack (Ordinary)			40·00	

246 Westminster Abbey

247 Fan Vaulting, Henry VII Chapel

1966 (28 Feb). 900th Anniversary of Westminster Abbey. (3d.). W **179**. Perf 15×14 (3d.) or 11×12 (2s.6d.).

687	**246**	3d. black, red-brown and new blue	10	10
		p. One phosphor band	10	10
688	**247**	2s.6d. black	30	30
Set of 2			30	30
First Day Cover (Ordinary)				2·50
First Day Cover (Phosphor)				8·00
Presentation Pack (Ordinary)			40·00	

248 View near Hassocks, Sussex

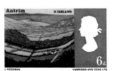

249 Antrim, Northern Ireland

250 Harlech Castle, Wales

251 Cairngorm Mountains Scotland

1966 (2 May). Landscapes. W **179**. Perf 15×14.

689	**248**	4d. black, yellow-green and new blue	10	10
		p. Three phosphor bands	10	10
690	**249**	6d. black, emerald and new blue	10	10
		p. Three phosphor bands	10	10
691	**250**	1s.3d. black, greenish yellow and greenish blue	15	15
		p. Three phosphor bands	15	15
	251	1s.6d. black, orange and Prussian blue	15	15
		p. Three phosphor bands	15	15
	·dinary)		40	40
	·sphor)		40	40

First Day Cover (Ordinary)	3·50
First Day Cover (Phosphor)	4·50

252 Players with Ball

253 Goalmouth Mêlée

254 Goalkeeper saving Goal

1966 (1 June). World Cup Football Championship. W **179** (sideways on 4d.). Perf 14×15 (4d.) or 15×14 (others).

693	**252**	4d. red, reddish purple, bright blue, flesh and black	10	10
		p. Two phosphor bands	10	10
694	**253**	6d. black, sepia, red, apple green and blue	10	10
		p. Three phosphor bands	10	10
695	**254**	1s.3d. black, blue, yellow, red and light yellow-olive	15	15
		p. Three phosphor bands	15	15
Set of 3 (Ordinary)			30	30
Set of 3 (Phosphor)			30	30
First Day Cover (Ordinary)				9·00
First Day Cover (Phosphor)				11·50
Presentation Pack (Ordinary)			30·00	

255 Black-headed Gull

256 Blue Tit

257 European Robin

258 Blackbird

1966 (8 Aug). British Birds. W **179**. Perf 15×14.

696	**255**	4d. grey, black, red, emerald-green, bright blue, greenish yellow and bistre	10	10
		a. Block of 4. Nos. 696/699	40	40
		p. Three phosphor bands	10	10
		pa. Block of 4. Nos. 696p/699p	40	40
697	**256**	4d. black, greenish yellow, grey, emerald-green, bright blue and bistre	10	10
		p. Three phosphor bands	10	10
698	**257**	4d. red, greenish yellow, black, grey, bistre, reddish brown and emerald-green	10	10
		p. Three phosphor bands	10	10
699	**258**	4d. black, reddish brown, greenish yellow, grey and bistre	10	10
		p. Three phosphor bands	10	10
Set of 4 (Ordinary)			40	40
Set of 4 (Phosphor)			40	40
First Day Cover (Ordinary)				3·50
First day Cover (Phosphor)				4·50
Presentation Pack (Ordinary)			15·00	

Nos. 696/699 were issued together *se-tenant* in blocks of four within the sheet.

259 Cup Winners

1966 (18 Aug). England's World Cup Football Victory. W **179** (sideways).
Perf 14×15.

700	**259**	4d. red, reddish purple, bright blue, flesh and black	10	10
First Day Cover				7·50

260 Jodrell Bank Radio Telescope

261 British Motor cars

262 SRN 6 Hovercraft

263 Windscale Reactor

1966 (19 Sept). British Technology. W **179**. Perf 15×14.

701	**260**	4d. black and lemon	10	10
		p. Three phosphor bands	10	10
702	**261**	6d. red, deep blue and orange	10	10
		p. Three phosphor bands	10	10
703	**262**	1s.3d. black, orange-red, slate and light greenish blue	15	15
		p. Three phosphor bands	20	20
704	**263**	1s.6d. black, yellow-green, bronze-green, lilac and deep blue	15	15
		p. Three phosphor bands	20	20
Set of 4 (Ordinary)			40	40
Set of 4 (Phosphor)			50	50
First Day Cover (Ordinary)				2·50
First Day Cover (Phosphor)				2·50
Presentation Pack			20·00	

264

265

266

267

268

269

270 Norman Ship

271 Norman Horsemen attacking Harold's Troops

1966 (14 Oct). 900th Anniversary of Battle of Hastings. W **179** (sideways on 1s.3d.). Perf 15×14.

705	**264**	4d. black, olive-green, bistre, deep blue, orange, magenta, green, blue and grey	10	10
		a. Strip of 6. Nos. 705/710	60	60
		p. Three phosphor bands	10	10
		pa. Strip of 6. Nos. 705p/710p	60	60
706	**265**	4d. black, olive-green, bistre, deep blue, orange, magenta, green, blue and grey	10	10
		p. Three phosphor bands	10	10
707	**266**	4d. black, olive-green, bistre, deep blue, orange, magenta, green, blue and grey	10	10
		p. Three phosphor bands	10	10
708	**267**	4d. black, olive-green, bistre, deep blue, magenta, green, blue and grey	10	10
		p. Three phosphor bands	10	10
709	**268**	4d. black, olive-green, bistre, deep blue, orange, magenta, green, blue and grey	10	10
		p. Three phosphor bands	10	10
710	**269**	4d. black, olive-green, bistre, deep blue, orange, magenta, green, blue and grey	10	10
		p. Three phosphor bands	10	10
711	**270**	6d. black, olive-green, violet, blue, green and gold	10	10
		p. Three phosphor bands	10	10
712	**271**	1s.3d. black, lilac, bronze-green, rosine, bistre-brown and gold	20	30
		p. Four phosphor bands	20	40
Set of 8 (Ordinary)			85	1·00
Set of 8 (Phosphor)			85	1·00
First Day Cover (Ordinary)				2·00
First Day Cover (Phosphor)				3·25
Presentation Pack (Ordinary)			8·50	

Nos. 705/710 show battle scenes and they were issued together *se-tenant* in horizontal strips of six within the sheet.

272 King of the Orient

273 Snowman

1966 (1 Dec). Christmas, Children's Paintings. W **179** (sideways on 3d.). Perf 14×15.

713	**272**	3d. black, blue, green, yellow, red and gold	10	10
		p. One phosphor band	10	10
714	**273**	1s.6d. blue, red, pink, black and gold	10	10
		p. Two phosphor bands	10	10
Set of 2 (Ordinary)			20	20
Set of 2 (Phosphor)			20	20
First Day Cover (Ordinary)				70
First Day Cover (Phosphor)				70
Presentation Pack (Ordinary)			10·00	

No. 713p exists with phosphor band at left or right.

274 Sea Freight

275 Air Freight

1967 (20 Feb). European Free Trade Association (EFTA). W **179**. Perf 15×14.

715	**274**	9d. deep blue, red, lilac, green, brown, new blue, yellow and black	10	10
		p. Three phosphor bands	10	10
716	**275**	1s.6d. violet, red, deep blue, brown, green, blue-grey, new blue, yellow and black	10	10
		p. Three phosphor bands	10	10
Set of 2 (Ordinary)			20	20
Set of 2 (Phosphor)			20	20
First Day Cover (Ordinary)				5·00
First Day Cover (Phosphor)				5·00
Presentation Pack (Ordinary)			20·00	

276 Hawthorn and Bramble   277 Larger Bindweed and
Viper's Bugloss

278 Ox-eye Daisy, Coltsfoot   279 Bluebell, Red Campion and
and Buttercup   Wood Anemone

280 Dog Violet   281 Primroses

1967 (24 Apr). British Wild Flowers. W **179**. Perf 15×14.

717	**276**	4d. grey, lemon, myrtle-green, red, agate and slate-purple	10	10
		a. Block of 4. Nos. 717/720	40	40
		p. Three phosphor bands	10	10
		pa. Block of 4. Nos. 717p/720p	40	40
718	**277**	4d. grey, lemon, myrtle-green, red, agate and violet	10	10
		p. Three phosphor bands	10	10
719	**278**	4d. grey, lemon, myrtle-green, red and agate	10	10
		p. Three phosphor bands	10	10
720	**279**	4d. grey, lemon, myrtle-green, reddish purple, agate and violet	10	10
		p. Three phosphor bands	10	10
721	**280**	9d. lavender-grey, green, reddish violet and orange-yellow	15	15
		p. Three phosphor bands	15	15
722	**281**	1s.9d. lavender-grey, green, greenish yellow and orange	15	15
		p. Three phosphor bands	15	15
Set of 6 (Ordinary)			50	50
Set of 6 (Phosphor)			50	50
F__ Day Cover (Ordinary)				1·25
__ y Cover (Phosphor)				7·00
__tion Pack (Ordinary)			20·00	
__ion Pack (Phosphor)			20·00	

__/720 were issued together *se-tenant* in blocks of four within

282

282a

I   II

Two types of the 2d.

I. Value spaced away from left side of stamp (cylinders 1 no dot and dot).

II. Value close to left side from new multipositive used for cylinders 5 no dot and dot onwards. The portrait appears in the centre, thus conforming to the other values.

1967 (5 June)–**70**. Two phosphor bands *except where otherwise stated.* No wmk. Perf 15×14.

723	**282**	½d. orange-brown (5.2.68)	10	10
724		1d. light olive (*shades*) (5.2.68)	10	10
725		1d. yellowish olive (1 centre band) (16.9.68)	45	45
726		2d. lake-brown (Type I) (5.2.68)	10	10
727		2d. lake-brown (Type II) (1969)	10	10
728		2d. lake-brown (1 centre band) (27.8.69)	35	40
729		3d. violet (*shades*) (1 centre band) (8.8.67)	10	10
730		3d. violet (6.4.68)	10	15
731		4d. deep sepia (*shades*)	10	10
732		4d. deep olive-brown (*shades*) (1 centre band) (16.9.68)	10	10
733		4d. bright vermilion (1 centre band) (6.1.69)	10	10
734		4d. bright vermilion (1 band at left) (6.1.69)	65	75
735		5d. royal blue (*shades*) (1.7.68)	10	10
736		6d. bright reddish purple (shades) (5.2.68)	10	10
737	**282a**	7d. bright emerald (1.7.68)	25	25
738		8d. bright vermilion (1.7.68)	10	15
739		8d. light turquoise-blue (6.1.69)	25	25
740		9d. myrtle-green (8.8.67)	25	25
741	**282**	10d. drab (1.7.68)	25	25
742		1s. light bluish violet (*shades*)	20	20
743		1s.6d. greenish blue and deep blue (*shades*) (8.8.67)	25	25
		c. Phosphorised paper (*Prussian blue and indigo*) (10.12.69)	30	35
744		1s.9d. dull orange and black (*shades*)	25	25
723/744 *Set of 16* (one of each value and colour)			2·00	2·25
Presentation Pack (one of each value)			7·00	
Presentation Pack (German)			90·00	

First Day Covers

5.6.67	Nos. 731, 742, 744	2·00
8.8.67	Nos. 729, 740, 743	2·00
5.2.68	Nos. 723/724, 726, 736	2·25
1.7.68	Nos. 735, 737/738, 741	3·00

No. 723 exists with phosphor band at the left or the right.

283 *Master Lambton*   284 *Mares and Foals in a*
(Sir Thomas Lawrence)   *Landscape* (George Stubbs)

285 *Children Coming Out of School (L. S. Lowry)*

1967 (10 July). British Paintings (1st series). Two phosphor bands. No wmk. Perf 14×15 (4d.) or 15×14 (others).

748	**283**	4d. rose-red, lemon, brown, black, new blue and gold	10	10
749	**284**	9d. Venetian red, ochre, grey-black, new-blue, greenish yellow and black	10	10
750	**285**	1s.6d. greenish yellow, grey, rose, new blue, grey-black and gold	10	10
Set of 3			30	30
First Day Cover				1·00
Presentation Pack			20·00	

286 *Gipsy Moth IV*

1967 (24 July). Sir Francis Chichester's World Voyage. Three phosphor bands. No wmk. Perf 15×14.

751	**286**	1s.9d. black, brown-red, light emerald and blue	10	10
First Day Cover				40

287 Radar Screen

288 *Penicillium notatum*

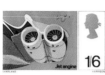

289 Vickers VC-10 Jet Engines

290 Television Equipment

1967 (19 Sept). British Discovery and Invention. Three phosphor bands (4d.) or two phosphor bands (others). W **179** (sideways on 1s.9d.). Perf 14×15 (1s.9d.) or 15×14 (others).

752	**287**	4d. greenish yellow, black and vermilion	10	10
753	**288**	1s. blue-green, light greenish blue, slate-purple and bluish violet	10	10
754	**289**	1s.6d. black, grey, royal blue, ochre and turquoise-blue	10	10
755	**290**	1s.9d. black, grey-blue, pale olive-grey, violet and orange	10	10
Set of 4			40	40
First Day Cover				70
Presentation Pack			9·00	

291 *The Adoration of the Shepherds (School of Seville)*

292 *Madonna and Child (Murillo)*

293 *The Adoration of the Shepherds (Louis le Nain)*

1967. Christmas, Paintings. One phosphor band (3d.) or two phosphor bands (others). Perf 15×14 (1s.6d.) or 14×15 (others).

756	**291**	3d. olive-yellow, rose, blue, black and gold (27.11)	10	10
757	**292**	4d. bright purple, greenish yellow, new blue, grey-black and gold (18.10)	10	10
758	**293**	1s.6d. bright purple, bistre, lemon, black, orange-red, ultramarine and gold (27.11)	15	15
Set of 3			30	30
First Day Covers (2)				3·00

Gift Pack

1967 (27 Nov). Comprises Nos. 715p/722p and 748/758

CP758c		Gift Pack	2·25

1967–68. No wmk. White paper. Perf 11×12.

759	**166**	2s.6d. black-brown (1.7.68)	10	20
760	**167**	5s. red (10.4.68)	50	50
761	**168**	10s. bright ultramarine (10.4.68)	4·50	2·00
762	**169**	£1 black (4.12.67)	6·50	2·00
Set of 4			10·00	4·25

294 Tarr Steps, Exmoor

295 Aberfeldy Bridge

296 Menai Bridge

297 M4 Viaduct

1968 (29 Apr). British Bridges. Two phosphor bands. Perf 15×14.

763	**294**	4d. black, bluish violet, turquoise-blue and gold	10	10
764	**295**	9d. red-brown, myrtle-green, ultramarine, olive-brown, black and gold	10	15
765	**296**	1s.6d. olive-brown, red-orange, bright green, turquoise-green and gold	15	20
766	**297**	1s.9d. olive-brown, greenish yellow, dull green, deep ultramarine and gold	15	25
Set of 4			45	65
First Day Cover				90
Presentation Pack			5·25	

298 'TUC' and Trades Unionists   **299** Mrs Emmeline Pankhurst (statue)

300 Sopwith Camel and English Electric Lightning Fighters   **301** Captain Cook's *Endeavour* and Signature

1968 (29 May). Anniversaries (1st series). Events described on stamps. Two phosphor bands. Perf 15×14.

767	**298**	4d. emerald, olive, blue and black	10	10
768	**299**	9d. reddish violet, bluish grey and black	10	10
769	**300**	1s. olive-brown, blue, red, slate-blue and black	15	20
770	**301**	1s.9d. yellow-ochre and blackish brown	20	25
Set of 4			50	60
First Day Cover				2·50
Presentation Pack			5·00	

302 *Queen Elizabeth I* (unknown artist)   **303** *Pinkie* (Sir Thomas Lawrence)

304 *Ruins of St Mary le Port* (John Piper)   **305** *The Hay Wain* (John Constable)

1968 (12 Aug). British Paintings (2nd series). Queen's head embossed. Two phosphor bands. Perf 15×14 (1s.9d.) or 14×15 (others).

771	**302**	4d. black, vermilion, greenish yellow, grey and gold	10	10
772	**303**	1s. mauve, new blue, greenish yellow, black, magenta and gold	10	15
773	**304**	1s.6d. slate, orange, black, mauve, greenish yellow, ultramarine and gold	15	20
774	**305**	1s.9d. greenish yellow, black, new blue, red and gold	15	20
Set of 4			45	60
First Day Cover				1·00
Presentation Pack (PO Pack No. 1)			4·50	
Presentation Pack (German)			30·00	

Collectors Pack

1968 (1 Sept). Comprises Nos. 752/758 and 763/774.

CP774e	Collectors Pack (Pack No. 3)	2·50

306 Boy and Girl with Rocking Horse

307 Girl with Doll's House   **308** Boy with Train Set

1968 (25 Nov). Christmas, Children's Toys. One centre phosphor band (4d.) or two phosphor bands (others). Perf 15×14 (4d.) or 14×15 (others).

775	**306**	4d. black, orange, vermilion, ultramarine, bistre and gold	10	10
776	**307**	9d. yellow-olive, black, brown, yellow, magenta, orange, turquoise-green and gold	15	15
777	**308**	1s.6d. ultramarine, yellow-orange, bright purple, blue-green, black and gold	15	20
Set of 3			35	40
First Day Cover				1·00
Presentation Pack (PO Pack No. 4)			9·00	
Presentation Pack (German)			30·00	

309 RMS *Queen Elizabeth 2*

310 Elizabethan Galleon   **311** East Indiaman

312 *Cutty Sark*

313 SS *Great Britain*

314 RMS *Mauretania*

1969 (15 Jan). British Ships. Two vertical phosphor bands at right (1s.), one horizontal phosphor band (5d.) or two phosphor bands (9d.). Perf 15×14.

778	309	5d. black, grey, red and turquoise	10	10
779	310	9d. red, blue, ochre, brown, black and grey	10	10
		a. Strip of 3. Nos. 779/781	40	50
780	311	9d. ochre, brown, black and grey	10	10
781	312	9d. ochre, brown, black and grey	10	10
782	313	1s. brown, black, grey, green and greenish yellow	15	15
		a. Pair. Nos. 782/783	50	60
783	314	1s. red, black, brown, carmine and grey	15	15
Set of 6			80	1·00
First Day Cover				1·50
Presentation Pack (PO Pack No. 5)			3·00	
Presentation Pack (German)			38·00	

The 9d. and 1s. values were arranged in horizontal strips of three and pairs respectively throughout the sheet.

315 Concorde in Flight

316 Plan and Elevation Views

317 Concorde's Nose and Tail

1969 (3 Mar). First Flight of Concorde. Two phosphor bands. Perf 15×14.

784	315	4d. yellow-orange, violet, greenish blue, blue-green and pale green	10	10
785	316	9d. ultramarine, emerald, red and grey-blue	15	15
786	317	1s.6d. deep blue, silver-grey and light blue	15	15
Set of 3			35	35
First Day Cover				4·00
Presentation Pack (PO Pack No. 6)			7·50	
Presentation Pack (German)			75·00	

318 Queen Elizabeth II (See also T 357)

1969 (5 Mar). Perf 12.

787	318	2s.6d. brown	20	20
788		5s. crimson-lake	85	25
789		10s. deep ultramarine	3·00	3·75
790		£1 bluish black	1·75	75
Set of 4			5·00	4·50
First Day Cover				6·50
Presentation Pack (PO Pack No. 7)			16·00	
Presentation Pack (German)			55·00	

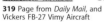

319 Page from *Daily Mail*, and Vickers FB-27 Vimy Aircraft

320 Europa and CEPT Emblems

321 ILO Emblem

322 Flags of NATO Countries

323 Vickers FB-27 Vimy Aircraft and Globe showing Flight

1969 (2 Apr). Anniversaries (2nd series). Events described on stamps. Two phosphor bands. Perf 15×14.

791	319	5d. black, pale sage-green, chestnut and new blue	10	10
792	320	9d. pale turquoise, deep blue, light emerald-green and black	10	15
793	321	1s. bright purple, deep blue and lilac	15	20
794	322	1s.6d. red, royal blue, yellow-green, black, lemon and new blue	15	20
795	323	1s.9d. yellow-olive, greenish yellow and pale turquoise-green	25	30
Set of 5			65	80
First Day Cover				1·10
Presentation Pack (PO Pack No. 9)			4·50	
Presentation Pack (German)			50·00	

324 Durham Cathedral

325 York Minster

326 St Giles, Edinburgh

327 Canterbury Cathedral

328 St Paul's Cathedral

329 Liverpool Metropolitan Cathedral

1969 (28 May). British Architecture (1st series). Cathedrals. Two phosphor bands. Perf 15×14.

796	324	5d. grey-black, orange, pale bluish violet and black	10	10
		a. Block of 4. Nos. 796/799	40	50
797	325	5d. grey-black, pale bluish violet, new blue and black	10	10
798	326	5d. grey-black, purple, green and black	10	10
799	327	5d. grey-black, green, new blue and black	10	10
800	328	9d. grey-black, ochre, pale drab, violet and black	15	20
801	329	1s.6d. grey-black, pale turquoise, pale reddish violet, pale yellow-olive and black	20	25
Set of 6			70	85
First Day Cover				1·00
Presentation Pack (PO Pack No. 10)			5·50	
Presentation Pack (German)			35·00	

Nos. 796/799 were issued together *se-tenant* in blocks of four throughout the sheet.

330 The King's Gate, Caernarvon Castle

331 The Eagle Tower, Caernarvon Castle

332 Queen Eleanor's Gate, Caernarvon Castle

333 Celtic Cross, Margam Abbey

334 HRH The Prince of Wales (after photograph by G. Argent)

1969 (1 July). Investiture of HRH The Prince of Wales. Two phosphor bands. Perf 14×15.

802	330	5d. deep olive-grey, light olive-grey, deep grey, light grey, red, pale turquoise-green, black and silver	10	10
		a. Strip of 3. Nos. 802/804	30	50
803	331	5d. deep olive-grey, light olive-grey, deep grey, light grey, red, pale turquoise-green, black and silver	10	10
804	332	5d. deep olive-grey, light olive-grey, deep grey, light grey, red, pale turquoise-green, black and silver	10	10
805	333	9d. deep grey, light grey, black and gold	15	20
806	334	1s. blackish yellow-olive and gold	15	20
Set of 5			55	80
First Day Cover				1·00
Presentation Pack (PO Pack No. 11)			3·00	
Presentation Pack (German)			35·00	
Presentation Pack (Welsh)			35·00	

Nos. 802/804 were issued together *se-tenant* in strips of three throughout the sheet.

335 Mahatma Gandhi

1969 (13 Aug). Gandhi Centenary Year. Two phosphor bands. Perf 15×14.

807	335	1s.6d. black, green, red-orange and grey	25	30
First Day Cover			3·25	

Collectors Pack

1969 (15 Sept). Comprises Nos. 775/786 and 791/807.

CP807b	Collectors Pack (Pack No. 12)	10·00	

336 National Giro 'G' Symbol

337 Telecommunications, International Subscriber Dialling

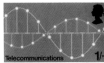
338 Telecommunications, Pulse Code Modulation

339 Postal Mechanisation, Automatic Sorting

1969 (1 Oct). Post Office Technology Commemoration. Two phosphor bands. Perf 13½×14.

808	336	5d. new blue, greenish blue, lavender and black	10	10
809	337	9d. emerald, violet-blue and black	10	10
810	338	1s. emerald, lavender and black	15	15
811	339	1s.6d. bright purple, light blue, grey-blue and black	20	20
Set of 4			50	50
First Day Cover				75
Presentation Pack (PO Pack No. 13)			5·00	

340 Herald Angel

341 The Three Shepherds

342 The Three Kings

1969 (26 Nov). Christmas, Traditional Religious Themes. Two phosphor bands (5d., 1s.6d.) or one centre band (4d.). Perf 15×14.

812	340	4d. vermilion, new blue, orange, bright purple, light green, bluish violet, blackish brown and gold	10	10
813	341	5d. magenta, light blue, royal blue, olive-brown, green, greenish yellow, red and gold	10	10
814	342	1s.6d. greenish yellow, bright purple, bluish violet, deep slate, orange, green, new blue and gold	15	15
Set of 3			30	30
First Day Cover				70
Presentation Pack (PO Pack No. 14)			3·00	

343 Fife Harling

344 Cotswold Limestone

345 Welsh Stucco

346 Ulster Thatch

1970 (11 Feb). British Rural Architecture. Two phosphor bands. Perf 15×14.

815	**343**	5d. grey, grey-black, black, lemon, greenish blue, orange-brown, ultramarine and green		10	10
816	**344**	9d. orange-brown, olive-yellow, bright green, black, grey-black and grey		15	15
817	**345**	1s. deep blue, reddish lilac, drab and new blue		15	15
818	**346**	1s.6d. greenish yellow, black, turquoise-blue and lilac		20	25
Set of 4				55	60
First Day Cover					85
Presentation Pack (PO Pack No. 15)			3·00		

347 Signing the Declaration of Arbroath

348 Florence Nightingale attending Patients

349 Signing of International Co-operative Alliance

350 Pilgrims and *Mayflower*

351 Sir William Herschel, Francis Baily, Sir John Herschel and Telescope

1970 (1 Apr). Anniversaries (3rd series). Events described on stamps. Two phosphor bands. Perf 15×14.

819	**347**	5d. black, yellow-olive, blue, emerald, greenish yellow, rose-red, gold and orange-red		10	10
820	**348**	9d. ochre, deep blue, carmine, black, blue-green, yellow-olive, gold and blue		10	10
821	**349**	1s. green, greenish yellow, brown, black, cerise, gold and light blue		15	15
822	**350**	1s.6d. greenish yellow, carmine, deep yellow-olive, emerald, black, blue, gold and sage-green		20	20
823	**351**	1s.9d. black, slate, lemon, gold and bright purple		20	20
Set of 5				70	70
First Day Cover					95
Presentation Pack (PO Pack No. 16)			4·00		

352 Mr Pickwick and Sam Weller (*Pickwick Papers*)

353 Mr and Mrs Micawber (*David Copperfield*)

354 David Copperfield and Betsy Trotwood (*David Copperfield*)

355 Oliver Asking for More (*Oliver Twist*)

356 Grasmere (from engraving by J. Farrington, RA)

1970 (3 June). Literary Anniversaries (1st series). Death Centenary of Charles Dickens (novelist) (5d.×4) and Birth Bicentenary of William Wordsworth (poet) (1s.6d.). Two phosphor bands. Perf 14×15.

824	**352**	5d. black, orange, silver, gold and magenta		10	10
		a. Block of 4. Nos. 824/827		40	60
825	**353**	5d. black, magenta, silver, gold and orange		10	10
826	**354**	5d. black, light greenish blue, silver, gold and yellow-bistre		10	10
827	**355**	5d. black, yellow-bistre, silver, gold and light greenish blue		10	10
828	**356**	1s.6d. yellow-olive, black, silver, gold and bright blue		15	20
Set of 5				50	70
First Day Cover					90
Presentation Pack (PO Pack No. 17)			4·00		

NOTE. For Nos. 829/831*b* and Types **356a** and **357** see Decimal Machin Definitive section.

358 Runners

359 Swimmers

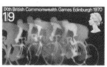

360 Cyclists

1970 (15 July). Ninth British Commonwealth Games. Two phosphor bands. Perf 13½×14.

832	**358**	5d. pink, emerald, greenish yellow and deep yellow-green		10	10
833	**359**	1s.6d. light greenish blue, lilac, bistre-brown and Prussian blue		15	15
834	**360**	1s.9d. yellow-orange, lilac, salmon and deep red-brown		15	15
Set of 3				45	45
First Day Cover					75
Presentation Pack (PO Pack No. 19)			3·00		

Collectors Pack

1970 (14 Sept). Comprises Nos. 808/828 and 832/834.

CP834*a*	Collectors Pack (Pack No. 20)	15·00

1840 first engraved issue
361 1d. Black (1840)

1847 first embossed issue
362 1s. Green (1847)

1855 first surface printed issue
363 4d. Carmine (1855)

1970 (18 Sept). Philympia 70 Stamp Exhibition. Two phosphor bands. Perf 14×14½.

835	**361**	5d. grey-black, brownish bistre, black and dull purple	10	10
836	**362**	9d. light drab, bluish green, stone, black and dull purple	15	15
837	**363**	1s.6d. carmine, light drab, black and dull purple	20	20
Set of 3			40	40
First Day Cover				75
Presentation Pack (PO Pack No. 21)			3·00	

364 Shepherds and Apparition of the Angel

365 Mary, Joseph and Christ in the Manger

366 The Wise Men bearing gifts

1970 (25 Nov). Christmas, *Robert de Lisle Psalter*. One centre phosphor band (4d.) or two phosphor bands (others). Perf 14×15.

838	**364**	4d. brown-red, turquoise-green, pale chestnut, brown, grey-black, gold and vermilion	10	10
839	**365**	5d. emerald, gold, blue, brown-red, ochre, grey-black and violet	10	10
840	**366**	1s.6d. gold, grey-black, pale turquoise-green, salmon, ultramarine, ochre and yellow-green	15	15
Set of 3			30	30
First Day Cover				40
Presentation Pack (PO Pack No. 22)			4·00	

NOTE. For 1971–1996 definitives in decimal currency with standard perforations on all sides, Nos. X841/X1058, T **367**, see Decimal Machin Definitives section.

368 *A Mountain Road* (T. P. Flanagan)

369 *Deer's Meadow* (Tom Carr)

370 *Slieve na brock* (Colin Middleton)

1971 (16 June). Ulster 1971 Paintings. Multicoloured Two phosphor bands. Perf 15×14.

881	**368**	3p. *A Mountain Road* (T. P. Flanagan)	10	10
882	**369**	7½p. *Deer's Meadow* (Tom Carr)	15	20
883	**370**	9p. *Slieve na brock* (Colin Middleton)	20	20
Set of 3			40	45
First Day Cover				75
Presentation Pack (PO Pack No. 26a)			3·00	

371 John Keats (150th Death Anniversary)

372 Thomas Gray (Death Bicentenary)

373 Sir Walter Scott (Birth Bicentenary)

1971 (28 July). Literary Anniversaries (2nd series). Multicoloured Two phosphor bands. Perf 15×14.

884	**371**	3p. John Keats	10	10
885	**372**	5p. Thomas Gray	15	20
886	**373**	7½p. Sir Walter Scott	20	20
Set of 3			40	45
First Day Cover				75
Presentation Pack (PO Pack No. 32)			3·00	

374 Servicemen and Nurse of 1921

375 Roman Centurion

376 Rugby Football, 1871

1971 (25 Aug). Anniversaries (4th series). Events described on stamps. Multicoloured Two phosphor bands. Perf 15×14.

887	**374**	3p. Servicemen and Nurse of 1921	10	10
888	**375**	7½p. Roman Centurion	15	20
889	**376**	9p. Rugby Football, 1871	20	20
Set of 3			40	45
First Day Cover				1·00
Presentation Pack (PO Pack No. 32A)			3·00	

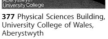

377 Physical Sciences Building, University College of Wales, Aberystwyth

378 Faraday Building, Southampton University

379 Engineering Department, Leicester University

380 Hexagon Restaurant, Essex University

1971 (22 Sept). British Architecture (2nd series). Modern University Buildings. Multicoloured Two phosphor bands. Perf 15×14.

890	**377**	3p. University College of Wales, Aberystwyth	10	10
891	**378**	5p. Southampton University	25	20
892	**379**	7½p. Leicester University	20	30
893	**380**	9p. Essex University	30	40
Set of 4			55	75
First Day Cover				80
Presentation Pack (PO Pack No. 33)			5·00	

Collectors Pack

1971 (29 Sept). Comprises Nos. 835/840 and 881/893.

CP893*a*	Collectors Pack (Pack No. 34)	20·00

381 Dream of the Wise Men

382 Adoration of the Magi

383 Ride of the Magi

1971 (13 Oct). Christmas, Stained-glass Windows. Multicoloured Ordinary paper. One centre phosphor band (2½p.) or two phosphor bands (others). Perf 15×14.

894	**381**	2½p. Dream of the Wise Men	10	10
895	**382**	3p. Adoration of the Magi	10	10
896	**383**	7½p. Ride of the Magi	20	20
Set of 3			35	35
First Day Cover				80
Presentation Pack (PO Pack No. 35)			2·25	

384 Sir James Clark Ross

385 Sir Martin Frobisher

386 Henry Hudson

387 Robert Falcon Scott

1972 (16 Feb). British Polar Explorers. Multicoloured Two phosphor bands. Perf 14×15.

897	**384**	3p. Sir James Clark Ross	10	10
898	**385**	5p. Sir Martin Frobisher	10	15
899	**386**	7½p. Henry Hudson	10	15
900	**387**	9p. Robert Falcon Scott	20	25
Set of 4			45	60
First Day Cover				85
Presentation Pack (PO Pack No. 39)			4·00	

388 Statuette of Tutankhamun

389 19th-century Coastguard

390 Ralph Vaughan Williams and Score

1972 (26 Apr). Anniversaries (5th series). Events described on stamps. Multicoloured Two phosphor bands. Perf 15×14.

901	**388**	3p. Statuette of Tutankhamun	10	10
902	**389**	7½p. 19th-century Coastguard	20	20
903	**390**	9p. Ralph Vaughan Williams	20	25
Set of 3			45	50
First Day Cover				85
Presentation Pack (PO Pack No. 40)			2·25	

391 St Andrew's, Greensted-juxta-Ongar, Essex

392 All Saints, Earls Barton, Northants

393 St Andrew's, Letheringsett, Norfolk

394 St Andrew's, Helpringham, Lincs

395 St Mary the Virgin, Huish Episcopi, Somerset

1972 (21 June). British Architecture (3rd series). Village Churches. Multicoloured Ordinary paper. Two phosphor bands. Perf 14×15.

904	**391**	3p. St Andrew's, Greensted-juxta-Ongar	10	10
905	**392**	4p. All Saints, Earls Barton	10	10
906	**393**	5p. St Andrew's, Letheringsett	10	20
907	**394**	7½p. St Andrew's, Helpringham	15	20
908	**395**	9p. St Mary the Virgin, Huish Episcopi	15	20
Set of 5			55	80
First Day Cover				1·25
Presentation Pack (PO Pack No. 41)			4·75	

Belgica 72 Souvenir Pack

1972 (24 June). Comprises Nos. 894/896 and 904/908.

CP908*b*	Souvenir Pack	3·75

396 Microphones, 1924–1969

397 Horn Loudspeaker

398 TV Camera, 1972

399 Oscillator and Spark Transmitter, 1897

1972 (13 Sept). Broadcasting Anniversaries. 75th Anniversary of Marconi and Kemp's Radio Experiments. Perf 15×14

909	**396**	3p. Microphones, 1924–1969	10	10
910	**397**	5p. Horn Loudspeaker	10	10
911	**398**	7½p. TV Camera, 1972	15	20
912	**399**	9p. Oscillator and Spark Transmitter	15	20
Set of 4			45	55
First Day Cover				1·25
Presentation Pack (PO Pack No. 43)			3·25	

400 Angel holding Trumpet

401 Angel playing Lute

402 Angel playing Harp

1972 (18 Oct). Christmas. Angels. Multicoloured One centre phosphor band (2½p.) or two phosphor bands (others). Perf 14×15.

913	**400**	2½p. Angel holding Trumpet	10	10
914	**401**	3p. Angel playing Lute	10	10
915	**402**	7½p. Angel playing Harp	20	20
Set of 3			35	35
First Day Cover				85
Presentation Pack (PO Pack No. 44)			2·00	

403 Queen Elizabeth and Duke of Edinburgh

403a Queen Elizabeth and Duke of Edinburgh

1972 (20 Nov). 'All-over' phosphor (3p.) or without phosphor (20p.).

916	**403**	3p. Queen Elizabeth and Duke of Edinburgh	20	20
917	**403a**	20p. Queen Elizabeth and Duke of Edinburgh	60	60
Set of 2			75	75
Presentation Pack (PO Pack No. 45)			2·00	
Presentation Pack (Japanese)			3·00	
Gutter Pair (3p.)			1·50	
Traffic Light Gutter Pair (3p.)			20·00	
First Day Cover (Philatelic Bureau, Edinburgh)				60
Souvenir Book			1·25	

Collectors Pack

1972 (20 Nov). Comprises Nos. 897/917.

CP918*a*	Collectors Pack (Pack No. 47)	12·00

404 Europe

404a

404b

1973 (3 Jan). Britain's Entry into European Communities. Multicoloured Two phosphor bands. Perf 14×15.

919	**404**	3p. Europe (lilac background)	10	10
920	**404a**	5p. Europe (new blue jigsaw pieces)	15	20
		a. Pair. Nos. 920/921	35	45
921	**404b**	5p. Europe (light emerald-green jigsaw pieces)	15	20
Set of 3			40	45
First Day Cover				70
Presentation Pack (PO Pack No. 48)			4·00	

Nos. 920/921 were printed horizontally *se-tenant* throughout the sheet.

405 Oak Tree

1973 (28 Feb). Tree Planting Year. British Trees (1st issue). Multicoloured Two phosphor bands. Perf 15×14.

922	**405**	9p. Oak Tree	15	15
First Day Cover				40
Presentation Pack (PO Pack No. 49)			1·25	

See also No. 949.

406 David Livingstone **407** Henry M. Stanley

408 Sir Francis Drake **409** Walter Raleigh

410 Charles Sturt

1973 (18 Apr). British Explorers. Multicoloured. 'All-over' phosphor. Perf 14×15.

923	**406**	3p. David Livingstone	10	10
		a. Pair. Nos. 923/924	20	20
924	**407**	3p. Henry M Stanley	10	10
925	**408**	5p. Sir Francis Drake	20	20
926	**409**	7½p. Walter Raleigh	20	20
927	**410**	9p. Charles Sturt	20	20
Set of 5			75	75
First Day Cover				90
Presentation Pack (PO Pack No. 50)			2·25	

Nos. 923/924 were issued horizontally *se-tenant* throughout the sheet.

411 **412**

413

1973 (16 May). County Cricket 1873–1973. 'All-over' phosphor. Perf 14×15.

928	**411**	3p. black, ochre and gold	10	10
929	**412**	7½p. black, light sage-green and gold	30	30
930	**413**	9p. black, cobalt and gold	40	40
Set of 3			75	75
First Day Cover				1·25
Presentation Pack (PO Pack No. 51)			3·25	
Souvenir Book			3·50	
PHQ Card (No. 928) (1)			35·00	£150

The PHQ Card did not become available until mid-July. The used price quoted is for an example used in July or August 1973.

414 Self-portrait **415** Self-portrait
(Reynolds) (Raeburn)

416 Nelly O'Brien **417** Reverend R.
(Reynolds) Walker (The Skater)
  (Raeburn)

1973 (4 July). British Paintings (3rd series). 250th Birth Anniversary of Sir Joshua Reynolds and 150th Death Anniversary of Sir Henry Raeburn. Multicoloured 'All-over' phosphor. Perf 14×15.

931	**414**	3p. Self-portrait (Reynolds)	10	10
932	**415**	5p. Self-portrait (Raeburn)	15	15
933	**416**	7½p. Nelly O'Brien (Reynolds)	15	15
934	**417**	9p. Reverend R. Walker (The Skater) (Raeburn)	20	20
Set of 4			50	50
First Day Cover				80
Presentation Pack (PO Pack No. 52)			1·75	

418 Court Masque Costumes **419** St Paul's Church, Covent
  Garden

420 Prince's Lodging, Newmarket

421 Court Masque Stage Scene

1973 (15 Aug). 400th Birth Anniversary of Inigo Jones (architect and designer). Multicoloured 'All-over' phosphor. Perf 15×14.

935	**418**	3p. Court Masque Costumes	10	10
		a. Pair. Nos. 935/936	20	25
936	**419**	3p. St Paul's Church, Covent Garden	10	10
937	**420**	5p. Prince's Lodging, Newmarket	15	15
		a. Pair. Nos. 937/938	30	35
938	**421**	5p. Court Masque Stage Scene	15	15
Set of 4			40	50
First Day Cover				70
Presentation Pack (PO Pack No. 53)			1·60	
PHQ Card (No. 936) (2)			95·00	95·00

The 3p. and 5p. values were printed horizontally *se-tenant* within the sheet.

422 Palace of Westminster seen from Whitehall

423 Palace of Westminster seen from Millbank

1973 (12 Sept). 19th Commonwealth Parliamentary Conference. Multicoloured 'All-over' phosphor. Perf 15×14.

939	**422**	8p. Palace of Westminster seen from Whitehall	15	15
940	**423**	10p. Palace of Westminster seen from Millbank	20	20
Set of 2			30	30
First Day Cover				55
Presentation Pack (PO Pack No. 54)			1·50	
Souvenir Book			3·50	
PHQ Card (No. 939) (3)			18·00	70·00

424 Princess Anne and Captain Mark Phillips

424a Princess Anne and Captain Mark Phillips

1973 (14 Nov). Royal Wedding. 'All-over' phosphor. Perf 15×14.

941	**424**	3½p. Princess Anne and Captain Mark Phillips	10	10
942	**424a**	20p. deep brown and silver	35	25
Set of 2			40	30
Set of 2 Gutter Pairs			80	
Set of 2 Traffic Light Gutter Pairs			65·00	
First Day Cover				40
Presentation Pack (PO Pack No. 56)			1·25	
PHQ Card (No. 941) (4)			3·75	20·00

425

426

427

428

429

430

(Types **425/430** show scenes from the carol *Good King Wenceslas*)

1973 (28 Nov). Christmas, Good King Wenceslas. Multicoloured One centre phosphor band (3p.) or 'All-over' phosphor (3½p). Perf 15×14.

943	**425**	3p. King Wenceslas sees peasant	15	15
		a. Strip of 5. Nos. 943/947	90	1·10
944	**426**	3p. Page tells king about peasant	15	15
945	**427**	3p. King and page set out	15	15
946	**428**	3p. King encourages page	15	15
947	**429**	3p. King and page give food to peasant	15	15
948	**430**	3½p. Peasant, King and page	15	15
Set of 6			95	1·10
First Day Cover				1·25
Presentation Pack (PO Pack No. 57)			1·75	

The 3p. values depict the carol *Good King Wenceslas* and were printed horizontally *se-tenant* within the sheet.

Collectors Pack

1973 (28 Nov). Comprises Nos. 919/948.

CP948*k*	Collectors Pack (Pack No. 58)	11·50

431 Horse Chestnut

1974 (27 Feb). British Trees (2nd issue). Multicoloured 'All-over' phosphor. Perf 15×14.

949	**431**	10p. Horse Chestnut	20	15
Gutter Pair			40	
Traffic Light Gutter Pair			45·00	
First Day Cover				40
Presentation Pack (PO Pack No. 59)			1·10	
PHQ Card (5)			80·00	80·00

The pack number is stated to be 58 on the reverse but the correct number is 59.

432 First Motor Fire Engine, 1904

433 Prizewinning Fire Engine, 1863

434 First Steam Fire Engine, 1830

435 Fire Engine, 1766

1974 (24 Apr). Bicentenary of the Fire Prevention (Metropolis) Act. Multicoloured 'All-over' phosphor. Perf 15×14.

950	**432**	3½p. First Motor Fire Engine, 1904	10	10
951	**433**	5½p. Prizewinning Fire Engine, 1863	10	10
952	**434**	8p. First Steam Fire Engine, 1830	15	20
953	**435**	10p. Fire Engine, 1766	20	20
Set of 4			50	55
Set of 4 Gutter Pairs			1·00	
Set of 4 Traffic Light Gutter Pairs			36·00	
First Day Cover				1·10
Presentation Pack (PO Pack No. 60)			1·50	
PHQ Card (No. 950) (6)			65·00	70·00

3 ½p P&O packet steamer Peninsular 1888   **5 ½p** First official airmail Coronation 1911

436 P & O Packet, *Peninsular*, 1888   **437** Farman HF. III Biplane, 1911

8p Airmail blue van and postbox 1930   **10p** Imperial Airways flyingboat 1937

438 Airmail-blue Van and Post Box, 1930   **439** Imperial Airways Short S.21 Flying Boat *Maia*, 1937

1974 (12 June). Centenary of Universal Postal Union. Multicoloured 'All-over' phosphor. Perf 15×14.

954	**436**	3½p. P & O Packet, *Peninsular*, 1888	10	10
955	**437**	5½p. Farman HF. III Biplane, 1911	10	10
956	**438**	8p. Airmail-blue Van and Post box, 1930	10	10
957	**439**	10p. Imperial Airways Short S.21 Flying Boat *Maia*, 1937	15	15
Set of 4			40	40
Set of 4 Gutter Pairs			80	
Set of 4 Traffic Light Gutter Pairs			28·00	
First Day Cover				60
Presentation Pack (PO Pack No. 64)			2·00	

440 Robert the Bruce   **441** Owain Glyndwr

442 Henry V   **443** The Black Prince

1974 (10 July). Medieval Warriors. Multicoloured 'All-over' phosphor. Perf 15×14.

958	**440**	4½p. Robert the Bruce	10	10
959	**441**	5½p. Owain Glyndwr	15	15
960	**442**	8p. Henry V	15	15
961	**443**	10p. The Black Prince	15	15
Set of 4			50	50
Set of 4 Gutter Pairs			1·00	
Set of 4 Traffic Light Gutter Pairs			40·00	
First Day Cover				1·25
Presentation Pack (PO Pack No. 65)			1·60	
PHQ Cards (set of 4) (7)			12·00	30·00

444 Churchill in Royal Yacht Squadron Uniform   **445** Prime Minister, 1940

446 Secretary for War and Air, 1919   **447** War Correspondent, South Africa, 1899

1974 (9 Oct). Birth Centenary of Sir Winston Churchill. Multicoloured 'All-over' phosphor. Perf 14×15.

962	**444**	4½p. Churchill in Royal Yacht Squadron Uniform	10	10
963	**445**	5½p. Prime Minister, 1940	20	15
964	**446**	8p. Secretary for War and Air, 1919	30	30
965	**447**	10p. War Correspondent, South Africa, 1899	30	30
Set of 4			80	75
Set of 4 Gutter Pairs			1·60	
Set of 4 Traffic Light Gutter Pairs			22·00	
First Day Cover				80
Presentation Pack (PO Pack No. 66)			1·75	
PHQ Card (No. 963) (8)			2·75	15·00
Souvenir Book			1·50	

448 Adoration of the Magi (York Minster, *circa* 1355)   **449** The Nativity (St Helen's Church, Norwich, *circa* 1480)

450 Virgin and Child (Ottery St Mary Church, *circa* 1350)   **451** Virgin and Child (Worcester Cathedral, *circa* 1224)

1974 (27 Nov). Christmas, Church Roof Bosses. Multicoloured. One phosphor band (3½p.) or 'All-over' phosphor (others). Perf 15×14.

966	**448**	3½p. York Minster	10	10
967	**449**	4½p. St Helen's Church, Norwich	10	10
968	**450**	8p. Ottery St Mary Church	10	10
969	**451**	10p. Worcester Cathedral	15	15
Set of 4			40	40
Set of 4 Gutter Pairs			80	
Set of 4 Traffic Light Gutter Pairs			24·00	
First Day Cover				70
Presentation Pack (PO Pack No. 67)			1·50	

Collectors Pack

1974 (27 Nov). Comprises Nos. 949/969.

CP969*a*	Collectors Pack (Pack No. 68)	4·75	

452 Invalid in Wheelchair

1975 (22 Jan). Health and Handicap Funds. 'All-over' phosphor. Perf 15×14.

970	**452**	4½p.+1½p. Invalid in Wheelchair	15	15
		Gutter Pair	30	
		Traffic Light Gutter Pair	2·25	
		First Day Cover		30

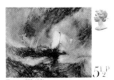

453 *Peace – Burial at Sea*

454 *Snow Storm: Steam-boat off a Harbour's Mouth*

455 *The Arsenal, Venice*

456 *St Laurent*

1975 (19 Feb). Birth Bicentenary of J. M. W. Turner (painter). Multicoloured 'All-over' phosphor. Perf 15×14.

971	**453**	4½p. *Peace – Burial at Sea*	10	10
972	**454**	5½p. *Snow Storm: Steam-boat off a Harbour's Mouth*	10	10
973	**455**	8p. *The Arsenal, Venice*	10	10
974	**456**	10p. *St Laurent*	15	15
		Set of 4	40	40
		Set of 4 Gutter Pairs	80	
		Set of 4 Traffic Light Gutter Pairs	5·50	
		First Day Cover		50
		Presentation Pack (PO Pack No. 69)	1·50	
		PHQ Card (No. 972) (9)	18·00	20·00

457 Charlotte Square, Edinburgh

458 The Rows, Chester

459 Royal Observatory, Greenwich

460 St George's Chapel, Windsor

461 National Theatre, London

1975 (23 Apr). European Architectural Heritage Year. Multicoloured 'All-over' phosphor. Perf 15×14.

975	**457**	7p. Charlotte Square, Edinburgh	10	10
		a. Pair. Nos. 975/976	20	20
976	**458**	7p. The Rows, Chester	10	10
977	**459**	8p. Royal Observatory, Greenwich	10	10
978	**460**	10p. St George's Chapel, Windsor	15	15
979	**461**	12p. National Theatre, London	20	20
		Set of 5	60	60
		Set of 5 Gutter Pairs	1·25	
		Set of 5 Traffic Light Gutter Pairs	14·00	
		First Day Cover		80
		Presentation Pack (PO Pack No. 70)	1·50	
		PHQ Cards (Nos. 975/977) (10)	4·75	10·00

Nos. 975/976 were printed horizontally *se-tenant* within the sheet.

462 Sailing Dinghies

463 Racing Keel Yachts

464 Cruising Yachts

465 Multihulls

1975 (11 June). Sailing. Multicoloured 'All-over' phosphor. Perf 15×14.

980	**462**	7p. Sailing Dinghies	10	10
981	**463**	8p. Racing Keel Yachts	10	10
982	**464**	10p. Cruising Yachts	15	15
983	**465**	12p. Multihulls	20	20
		Set of 4	50	50
		Set of 4 Gutter Pairs	1·00	
		Set of 4 Traffic Light Gutter Pairs	18·00	
		First Day Cover		70
		Presentation Pack (PO Pack No. 71)	1·25	
		PHQ Card (No. 981) (11)	2·75	8·00

A First Day of Issue handstamp was provided at Weymouth for this issue.

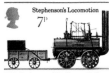

466 Stephenson's *Locomotion*, 1825

467 *Abbotsford*, 1876

468 *Caerphilly Castle*, 1923

469 High Speed Train, 1975

1975 (13 Aug). 150th Anniversary of Public Railways. Multicoloured 'All-over' phosphor. Perf 15×14.

984	**466**	7p. Stephenson's *Locomotion*, 1825	10	10
985	**467**	8p. *Abbotsford*, 1876	20	20
986	**468**	10p. *Caerphilly Castle*, 1923	20	20
987	**469**	12p. High Speed Train, 1975	30	30
		Set of 4	70	70
		Set of 4 Gutter Pairs	1·40	
		Set of 4 Traffic Light Gutter Pairs	7·50	
		First Day Cover		90
		Presentation Pack (PO Pack No. 72)	2·00	
		PHQ Cards (set of 4) (12)	30·00	30·00
		Souvenir Book	1·60	

470 Palace of Westminster

1975 (3 Sept). 62nd Inter-Parliamentary Union Conference. Multicoloured 'All-over' phosphor. Perf 15×14.

988	**470**	12p. Palace of Westminster	20	20
		Gutter Pair	40	
		Traffic Light Gutter Pair	2·25	
		First Day Cover		30
		Presentation Pack (PO Pack No. 74)	85	

471 Emma and Mr Woodhouse (*Emma*)

472 Catherine Morland (*Northanger Abbey*)

473 Mr Darcy (*Pride and Prejudice*)

474 Mary and Henry Crawford (*Mansfield Park*)

1975 (22 Oct). Birth Bicentenary of Jane Austen (novelist). Multicoloured 'All-over' phosphor. Perf 14×15.

989	**471**	8½p. Emma and Mr Woodhouse	10	10
990	**472**	10p. Catherine Morland	15	15
991	**473**	11p. Mr Darcy	15	15
992	**474**	13p. Mary and Henry Crawford	25	20
		Set of 4	60	55
		Set of 4 Gutter Pairs	1·25	
		Set of 4 Traffic Light Gutter Pairs	7·00	
		First Day Cover		75
		Presentation Pack (PO Pack No. 75)	7·00	
		PHQ Cards (set of 4) (13)	9·50	15·00

475 Angels with Harp and Lute

476 Angel with Mandolin

477 Angel with Horn

478 Angel with Trumpet

1975 (26 Nov). Christmas, Angels. Multicoloured One phosphor band (6½p.), phosphor-inked background (8½p.), 'All-over' phosphor (others). Perf 15×14.

993	**475**	6½p. Angels with Harp and Lute	10	10
994	**476**	8½p. Angel with Mandolin	10	10
995	**477**	11p. Angel with Horn	20	15
996	**478**	13p. Angel with Trumpet	20	20
		Set of 4	45	50
		Set of 4 Gutter Pairs	1·10	
		Set of 4 Traffic Light Gutter Pairs	5·00	
		First Day Cover		75
		Presentation Pack (PO Pack No. 76)	1·50	

Collectors Pack

1975 (26 Nov). Comprises Nos. 970/996.

CP996a		Collectors Pack (Pack No. 77)	4·25

479 Housewife

480 Policeman

481 District Nurse

482 Industrialist

1976 (10 Mar). Telephone Centenary. Multicoloured 'All-over' phosphor. Perf 15×14.

997	**479**	8½p. Housewife	10	10
998	**480**	10p. Policeman	15	15
999	**481**	11p. District Nurse	15	15
1000	**482**	13p. Industrialist	25	20
		Set of 4	60	55
		Set of 4 Gutter Pairs	1·25	
		Set of 4 Traffic Light Gutter Pairs	11·00	
		First Day Cover		60
		Presentation Pack (PO Pack No. 78)	1·40	

483 Hewing Coal (Thomas Hepburn)

484 Machinery (Robert Owen)

485 Chimney Cleaning (Lord Shaftesbury)

486 Hands clutching Prison Bars (Elizabeth Fry)

1976 (28 Apr). Social Reformers. Multicoloured 'All-over' phosphor. Perf 15×14.

1001	**483**	8½p. Hewing Coal (Thomas Hepburn)	10	10
1002	**484**	10p. Machinery (Robert Owen)	15	15
1003	**485**	11p. Chimney Cleaning (Lord Shaftesbury)	15	15
1004	**486**	13p. Hands clutching Prison Bars (Elizabeth Fry)	25	20
		Set of 4	60	55
		Set of 4 Gutter Pairs	1·25	
		Set of 4 Traffic Light Gutter Pairs	5·00	
		First Day Cover		60
		Presentation Pack (PO Pack No. 79)	1·25	
		PHQ Card (No. 1001) (14)	2·75	9·00

487 Benjamin Franklin (bust by Jean-Jacques Caffieri)

1976 (2 June). Bicentenary of American Revolution. Multicoloured 'All-over' phosphor. Perf 14×15.

1005	**487**	11p. Benjamin Franklin	20	20
Gutter Pair			40	
Traffic Light Gutter Pair			2·25	
First Day Cover				50
Presentation Pack (PO Pack No. 80)			65	
PHQ Card (15)			2·25	8·00

488 'Elizabeth of Glamis'

489 'Grandpa Dickson'

490 'Rosa Mundi'

491 'Sweet Briar'

1976 (30 June). Centenary of Royal National Rose Society. Multicoloured 'All-over' phosphor. Perf 14×15.

1006	**488**	8½p. 'Elizabeth of Glamis'	10	10
1007	**489**	10p. 'Grandpa Dickson'	15	15
1008	**490**	11p. 'Rosa Mundi'	15	15
1009	**491**	13p. 'Sweet Briar'	25	20
Set of 4			60	55
Set of 4 Gutter Pairs			1·25	
Set of 4 Traffic Light Gutter Pairs			6·00	
First Day Cover				60
Presentation Pack (PO Pack No. 81)			1·50	
PHQ Cards (set of 4) (16)			14·00	15·00

492 Archdruid

493 Morris Dancing

494 Scots Piper

495 Welsh Harpist

1976 (4 Aug). British Cultural Traditions. Multicoloured 'All-over' phosphor. Perf 14×15.

1010	**492**	8½p. Archdruid	10	10
1011	**493**	10p. Morris Dancing	15	15
1012	**494**	11p. Scots Piper	15	15
1013	**495**	13p. Welsh Harpist	25	20
Set of 4			60	55
Set of 4 Gutter Pairs			1·25	
Set of 4 Traffic Light Gutter Pairs			6·00	
First Day Cover				60
Presentation Pack (PO Pack No. 82)			1·25	
PHQ Cards (set of 4) (17)			7·50	12·00

496 Woodcut from *The Canterbury Tales*

497 Extract from *The Tretyse of Love*

498 Woodcut from *The Game and Playe of Chesse*

499 Early Printing Press

1976 (29 Sept). 500th Anniversary of British Printing. Multicoloured 'All-over' phosphor. Perf 14×15.

1014	**496**	8½p. Woodcut from *The Canterbury Tales*	10	10
1015	**497**	10p. Extract from *The Tretyse of Love*	15	15
1016	**498**	11p. Woodcut from *The Game and Playe of Chesse*	15	15
1017	**499**	13p. Early Printing Press	25	25
Set of 4			60	60
Set of 4 Gutter Pairs			1·25	
Set of 4 Traffic Light Gutter Pairs			6·00	
First Day Cover				65
Presentation Pack (PO Pack No. 83)			1·25	
PHQ Cards (set of 4) (18)			6·00	9·00

500 Virgin and Child

501 Angel with Crown

502 Angel appearing to Shepherds

503 The Three Kings

1976 (24 Nov). Christmas, English Medieval Embroidery. Multicoloured One phosphor band (6½p.) or 'All-over' phosphor (others). Perf 15×14.

1018	**500**	6½p. Virgin and Child	10	10
1019	**501**	8½p. Angel with Crown	15	15
1020	**502**	11p. Angel appearing to Shepherds	15	15
1021	**503**	13p. The Three Kings	20	20
Set of 4			55	55
Set of 4 Gutter Pairs			1·10	
Set of 4 Traffic Light Gutter Pairs			4·50	
First Day Cover				60
Presentation Pack (PO Pack No. 87)			1·40	
PHQ Cards (*set of 4*) (19)			1·80	5·00

Collectors Pack

1976 (24 Nov). Comprises Nos. 997/1021.

CP1021*a*	Collectors Pack (Pack No. 88)	5·50

504 Lawn Tennis

505 Table Tennis

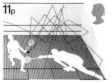

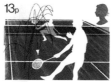

506 Squash

507 Badminton

1977 (12 Jan). Racket Sports. Multicoloured Phosphorised paper. Perf 15×14.

1022	**504**	8½p. Lawn Tennis	10	10
1023	**505**	10p. Table Tennis	15	15
1024	**506**	11p. Squash	15	15
1025	**507**	13p. Badminton	20	20
Set of 4			55	55
Set of 4 Gutter Pairs			1·10	
Set of 4 Traffic Light Gutter Pairs			5·50	
First Day Cover				60
Presentation Pack (PO Pack No. 89)			1·50	
PHQ Cards (*set of 4*) (20)			3·50	8·00

For Nos. 1026/1028 and T **508** see Decimal Machin Definitives section

509 Steroids, Conformational Analysis

510 Vitamin C, Synthesis

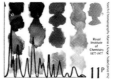

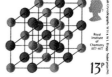

511 Starch, Chromatography

512 Salt, Crystallography

1977 (2 Mar). Royal Institute of Chemistry Centenary. Multicoloured 'All-over' phosphor. Perf 15×14.

1029	**509**	8½p. Steroids, Conformational Analysis	10	10
1030	**510**	10p. Vitamin C, Synthesis	15	15
1031	**511**	11p. Starch, Chromatography	15	15
1032	**512**	13p. Salt, Crystallography	20	20
Set of 4			55	55
Set of 4 Gutter Pairs			1·10	
Set of 4 Traffic Light Gutter Pairs			5·50	
First Day Cover				60
Presentation Pack (PO Pack No. 92)			1·50	
PHQ Cards (*set of 4*) (21)			3·50	8·00

513

1977 (11 May–15 June). Silver Jubilee. Multicoloured 'All-over' phosphor. Perf 15×14.

1033	**513**	8½p. Pale turquoise-green background	10	10
1034		9p. Lavender background (15.6.77)	20	20
1035		10p. Ochre background	10	10
1036		11p. Rose-pink background	25	30
1037		13p. Bistre-yellow background	25	30
Set of 5			80	85
Set of 5 Gutter Pairs			1·60	
Set of 5 Traffic Light Gutter Pairs			8·00	
First Day Covers (2)				90
Presentation Pack (PO Pack No. 94) (Nos. 1033, 1035/1037)			1·00	
PHQ Cards (*set of 5*) (22)			5·50	10·00
Souvenir Book			1·25	

517 Gathering of Nations

1977 (8 June). Commonwealth Heads of Government Meeting, London. Multicoloured 'All-over' phosphor. Perf 14×15.

1038	**517**	13p. Gathering of Nations	20	20
Gutter Pair			40	
Traffic Light Gutter Pair			1·75	
First Day Cover				40
Presentation Pack (PO Pack No. 95)			45	
PHQ Card (23)			1·25	1·50

518 Hedgehog

519 Brown Hare

9ᵖ

9ᵖ

520 Red Squirrel   **521** Otter

9ᵖ

522 Badger

1977 (5 Oct). British Wildlife. Multicoloured 'All-over' phosphor. Perf 14×15.

1039	**518**	9p. Hedgehog	15	20
		a. Horiz strip of 5. Nos. 1039/1043	70	95
1040	**519**	9p. Brown Hare	15	20
1041	**520**	9p. Red Squirrel	15	20
1042	**521**	9p. Otter	15	20
1043	**522**	9p. Badger	15	20
Set of 5			70	95
Gutter Strip of 10			1·40	
Traffic Light Gutter Strip of 10			5·00	
First Day Cover				1·00
Presentation Pack (PO Pack No. 96)			1·00	
PHQ Cards (set of 5) (25)			1·50	2·50

Nos. 1039/1043 were printed horizontally *se-tenant* within the sheet.

523 'Three French Hens, Two Turtle Doves and a Partridge in a Pear Tree'

524 'Six Geese-a-laying, Five Gold Rings, Four Colly Birds'

525 'Eight Maids-a-milking, Seven Swans-a-swimming'

526 'Ten Pipers piping, Nine Drummers drumming'

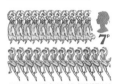

527 'Twelve Lords a-leaping, Eleven Ladies dancing'

528 'A Partridge in a Pear Tree'

1977 (23 Nov). Christmas, *The Twelve Days of Christmas*. Multicoloured One centre phosphor band (7p.) or 'All-over' phosphor (9p.). Perf 15×14.

1044	**523**	7p. 'Three French Hens, Two Turtle Doves and a Partridge in a Pear Tree'	10	10
		a. Horiz strip of 5. Nos. 1044/1048	50	50
1045	**524**	7p. 'Six Geese-a-laying, Five Gold Rings, Four Colly Birds'	10	10

1046	**525**	7p. 'Eight Maids-a-milking, Seven Swans-a-swimming'	10	10
1047	**526**	7p. 'Ten Pipers piping, Nine Drummers drumming'	10	10
1048	**527**	7p. 'Twelve Lords a-leaping, Eleven Ladies dancing'	10	10
1049	**528**	9p. 'A Partridge in a Pear Tree'	10	20
Set of 6			60	70
Set of 6 Gutter Pairs			1·25	
Traffic Light Gutter Pairs			3·75	
First Day Cover				75
Presentation Pack (PO Pack No. 97)			90	
PHQ Cards (set of 6) (26)			1·50	2·50

Nos. 1044/1048 were printed horizontally *se-tenant* within the sheet.

Collectors Pack

1977 (23 Nov). Comprises Nos. 1022/1025 and 1029/1049.

CP1049b	Collectors Pack (Pack No. 98)	3·75

529 Oil. North Sea   **530** Coal. Modern Pithead Production Platform

531 Natural Gas. Flame Rising from Sea

532 Electricity. Nuclear Power Station and Uranium Atom

1978 (25 Jan). Energy Resources. Multicoloured 'All-over' phosphor. Perf 14×15.

1050	**529**	9p. Oil	10	10
1051	**530**	10½p. Coal	15	15
1052	**531**	11p. Natural Gas	15	15
1053	**532**	13p. Electricity	20	20
Set of 4			55	55
Set of 4 Gutter Pairs			1·10	
Set of 4 Traffic Light Gutter Pairs			4·50	
First Day Cover				60
Presentation Pack (PO Pack No. 99)			85	
PHQ Cards (set of 4) (27)			1·50	2·50

533 The Tower of London   **534** Holyroodhouse

535 Caernarvon Castle   **536** Hampton Court Palace

1978 (1 Mar). British Architecture (4th series), Historic Buildings. Multicoloured 'All-over' phosphor. Perf 15×14.

1054	**533**	9p. The Tower of London	10	10
1055	**534**	10½p. Holyroodhouse	15	15
1056	**535**	11p. Caernarvon Castle	15	15
1057	**536**	13p. Hampton Court Palace	20	20
Set of 4			55	55
Set of 4 Gutter Pairs			1·10	
Set of 4 Traffic Light Gutter Pairs			4·25	
First Day Cover				60
Presentation Pack (PO Pack No. 100)			75	
PHQ Cards (set of 4) (28)			1·50	2·50
MS1058 121×89 mm. Nos. 1054/1057 (sold at 53½p.)			70	70
First Day Cover				85

The premium on No. **MS**1058 was used to support the London 1980 International Stamp Exhibition.

537 State Coach

538 St Edward's Crown

539 The Sovereign's Orb

540 Imperial State Crown

1978 (31 May). 25th Anniversary of Coronation. Multicoloured 'All-over' phosphor. Perf 14×15.

1059	**537**	9p. State Coach	15	20
1060	**538**	10½p. St Edward's Crown	20	20
1061	**539**	11p. The Sovereign's Orb	20	20
1062	**540**	13p. Imperial State Crown	25	25
Set of 4			70	75
Set of 4 Gutter Pairs			1·40	
Set of 4 Traffic Light Gutter Pairs			4·25	
First Day Cover (Philatelic Bureau, Edinburgh)				80
Presentation Pack (PO Pack No. 101)			85	
PHQ Cards (set of 4) (29)			1·50	2·25
Souvenir Book			1·25	

541 Shire Horse

542 Shetland Pony

543 Welsh Pony

544 Thoroughbred

1978 (5 July). Horses. Multicoloured 'All-over' phosphor. Perf 15×14.

1063	**541**	9p. Shire Horse	10	10
1064	**542**	10½p. Shetland Pony	15	15
1065	**543**	11p. Welsh Pony	15	15
1066	**544**	13p. Thoroughbred	20	20
Set of 4			55	55
Set of 4 Gutter Pairs			1·10	

Set of 4 Traffic Light Gutter Pairs	4·50	
First Day Cover (Philatelic Bureau, Edinburgh)		60
Presentation Pack (PO Pack No. 102)	75	
PHQ Cards (set of 4) (30)	1·00	1·75

545 Penny-farthing and 1884 Safety Bicycle

546 1920 Touring Bicycles

547 1978 Small-wheel Bicycles

548 1978 Road Racers

1978 (2 Aug). Centenaries of Cyclists' Touring Club and British Cycling Federation. Multicoloured 'All-over' phosphor. Perf 15×14.

1067	**545**	9p. Penny-farthing and 1884 Safety Bicycle	10	10
1068	**546**	10½p. 1920 Touring Bicycles	15	15
1069	**547**	11p. 1978 Small-wheel Bicycles	15	15
1070	**548**	13p. 1978 Road racers	20	20
Set of 4			55	55
Set of 4 Gutter Pairs			1·10	
Set of 4 Traffic Light Gutter Pairs			4·25	
First Day Cover (Philatelic Bureau, Edinburgh)				60
Presentation Pack (PO Pack No. 103)			75	
PHQ Cards (set of 4) (31)			1·00	1·75

549 Singing Carols round the Christmas Tree

550 The Waits

551 18th-century Carol Singers

552 The Boar's Head Carol

1978 (22 Nov). Christmas, Carol singers. Multicoloured One centre phosphor band (7p.) or 'All-over' phosphor (others). Perf 15×14.

1071	**549**	7p. Singing Carols round the Christmas Tree	10	10
1072	**550**	9p. The Waits	15	15
1073	**551**	11p. 18th-century Carol Singers	15	15
1074	**552**	13p. The Boar's Head Carol	20	20
Set of 4			55	55
Set of 4 Gutter Pairs			1·10	
Set of 4 Traffic Light Gutter Pairs			4·00	
First Day Cover				60
Presentation Pack (PO Pack No. 104)			75	
PHQ Cards (set of 4) (32)			1·00	1·75

Collectors Pack

1978 (22 Nov). Comprises Nos. 1050/1057 and 1059/1074.

CP1074a	Collectors Pack (Pack No. 105)	3·75

553 Old English Sheepdog   **554** Welsh Springer Spaniel

555 West Highland Terrier   **556** Irish Setter

1979 (7 Feb). Dogs. Multicoloured 'All-over' phosphor. Perf 15×14.

1075	**553**	9p. Old English Sheepdog	10	10
1076	**554**	10½p. Welsh Springer Spaniel	15	15
1077	**555**	11p. West Highland Terrier	15	15
1078	**556**	13p. Irish Setter	20	20
Set of 4			55	55
Set of 4 Gutter Pairs			1·10	
Set of 4 Traffic Light Gutter Pairs			4·00	
First Day Cover				60
Presentation Pack (PO Pack No. 106)			70	
PHQ Cards (set of 4) (33)			80	1·50

557 Primroses   **558** Daffodils

559 Bluebells   **560** Snowdrops

1979 (21 Mar). Spring Wild Flowers. Multicoloured 'All-over' phosphor. Perf 14×15.

1079	**557**	9p. Primroses	10	10
1080	**558**	10½p. Daffodils	15	15
1081	**559**	11p. Bluebells	15	15
1082	**560**	13p. Snowdrops	20	20
Set of 4			55	55
Set of 4 Gutter Pairs			1·10	
Set of 4 Traffic Light Gutter Pairs			4·00	
First Day Cover				60
Presentation Pack (PO Pack No. 107)			70	
PHQ Cards (set of 4) (34)			80	1·25

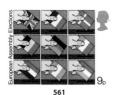
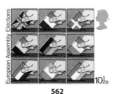

561   **562**

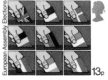

563   **564**

1979 (9 May). First Direct Elections to European Assembly. Multicoloured (colours of backgrounds to flag panels given) Phosphorised paper. Perf 15×14.

1083	**561**	9p. dull ultramarine	10	10
1084	**562**	10½p. chestnut	15	15
1085	**563**	11p. grey-green	15	15
1086	**564**	13p. brown	20	20
Set of 4			55	55
Set of 4 Gutter Pairs			1·10	
Set of 4 Traffic Light Gutter Pairs			4·00	
First Day Cover				60
Presentation Pack (PO Pack No. 108)			70	
PHQ Cards (set of 4) (35)			80	1·25

Nos. 1083/1086 show Hands placing National Flags in Ballot Boxes.

565 Saddling Mahmoud for the Derby, 1936 (Sir Alfred Munnings)   **566** The Liverpool Great National Steeple Chase, 1839 (aquatint by F. C. Turner)

567 The First Spring Meeting, Newmarket, 1793 (J. N. Sartorius)   **568** Racing at Dorsett Ferry, Windsor, 1684 (Francis Barlow)

1979 (6 June). Horse Racing Paintings Bicentenary of the Derby (9p.). Multicoloured 'All-over' phosphor. Perf 15×14.

1087	**565**	9p. Saddling Mahmoud for the Derby, 1936	10	10
1088	**566**	10½p. The Liverpool Great National Steeple Chase, 1839	15	15
1089	**567**	11p. The First Spring Meeting, Newmarket, 1793	15	15
1090	**568**	13p. Racing at Dorsett Ferry, Windsor, 1684	20	20
Set of 4			55	55
Set of 4 Gutter Pairs			1·10	
Set of 4 Traffic Light Gutter Pairs			4·50	
First Day Cover				60
Presentation Pack (PO Pack No. 109)			70	
PHQ Cards (set of 4) (36)			80	1·25

569 The Tale of Peter Rabbit (Beatrix Potter)   **570** The Wind in the Willows (Kenneth Grahame)

571 *Winnie-the-Pooh* (A. A. Milne)

572 *Alice's Adventures in Wonderland* (Lewis Carroll)

1979 (11 July). International Year of the Child. Children's Book Illustrations. Multicoloured 'All-over' phosphor. Perf 14×15.

1091	**569**	9p. *The Tale of Peter Rabbit*	15	15
1092	**570**	10½p. *The Wind in the Willows*	20	20
1093	**571**	11p. *Winnie-the-Pooh*	20	20
1094	**572**	13p. *Alice's Adventures in Wonderland*	25	25
Set of 4			75	75
Set of 4 Gutter Pairs			1·50	
Set of 4 Traffic Light Gutter Pairs			3·75	
First Day Cover				80
Presentation Pack (PO Pack No. 110)			1·00	
PHQ Cards (set of 4) (37)			80	1·40

Nos. 1091/1094 depict original illustrations from four books.

573 Sir Rowland Hill

574 Postman, *circa* 1839

575 London Postman, *circa* 1839

576 Woman and Young Girl with Letters, 1840

1979 (22 Aug–24 Oct). Death Centenary of Sir Rowland Hill. Multicoloured 'All-over' phosphor. Perf 14×15.

1095	**573**	10p. Sir Rowland Hill	15	15
1096	**574**	11½p. Postman, *circa* 1839	15	15
1097	**575**	13p. London Postman, *circa* 1839	20	20
1098	**576**	15p. Woman and Young Girl with Letters, 1840	25	25
Set of 4			70	70
Set of 4 Gutter Pairs			1·40	
Set of 4 Traffic Light Gutter Pairs			3·75	
First Day Cover				75
Presentation Pack (PO Pack No. 111)			80	
PHQ Cards (set of 4) (38)			50	1·25
MS1099 89×121 mm. Nos. 1095/1098 (*sold at 59½p.*) (24.10.79)			70	75
First Day Cover				80

The premium on No. **MS**1099 was used to support the London 1980 International Stamp Exhibition.

577 Policeman on the Beat

578 Policeman directing Traffic

579 Mounted Policewoman

580 River Patrol Boat

1979 (26 Sept). 150th Anniversary of Metropolitan Police. Multicoloured Phosphorised paper. Perf 15×14.

1100	**577**	10p. Policeman on the Beat	15	15
1101	**578**	11½p. Policeman directing Traffic	15	15
1102	**579**	13p. Mounted Policewoman	20	20
1103	**580**	15p. River Patrol Boat	25	25
Set of 4			70	70
Set of 4 Gutter Pairs			1·40	
Set of 4 Traffic Light Gutter Pairs			3·75	
First Day Cover				75
Presentation Pack (PO Pack No. 112)			80	
PHQ Cards (set of 4) (39)			50	1·25

581 The Three Kings

582 Angel appearing to the Shepherds

583 The Nativity

584 Mary and Joseph travelling to Bethlehem

585 The Annunciation

1979 (21 Nov). Christmas, Nativity Scenes. Multicoloured One centre phosphor band (8p.) or phosphorised paper (others). Perf 15×14.

1104	**581**	8p. The Three Kings	10	10
1105	**582**	10p. Angel appearing to the Shepherds	15	15
1106	**583**	11½p. The Nativity	15	15
1107	**584**	13p. Mary and Joseph travelling to Bethlehem	20	20
1108	**585**	15p. The Annunciation	20	20
Set of 5			75	75
Set of 5 Gutter Pairs			1·50	
Set of 5 Traffic Light Gutter Pairs			4·50	
First Day Cover				80
Presentation Pack (PO Pack No. 113)			80	
PHQ Cards (set of 5) (40)			50	1·25

Collectors Pack

1979 (21 Nov). Comprises Nos. 1075/1098 and 1100/1108.

CP1108*a*	Collectors Pack (Pack No. 114)	4·50

586 Common
Kingfisher

587 Dipper

588 Moorhen

589 Yellow Wagtails

1980 (16 Jan). Centenary of Wild Bird Protection Act. Multicoloured
Phosphorised paper. Perf 14×15.

1109	**586**	10p. Common Kingfisher	15	15
1110	**587**	11½p. Dipper	15	15
1111	**588**	13p. Moorhen	20	20
1112	**589**	15p. Yellow Wagtails	20	20
Set of 4			60	60
Set of 4 Gutter Pairs			1·25	
First Day Cover				65
Presentation Pack (PO Pack No. 115)			70	
PHQ Cards (set of 4) (41)			50	1·00

590 *Rocket* approaching Moorish
Arch, Liverpool

591 First and Second Class
Carriages passing through Olive
Mount Cutting

592 Third Class Carriage and
Sheep Truck crossing Chat Moss

593 Horsebox and Carriage Truck
near Bridgewater Canal

594 Goods Truck and Mail
Coach at Manchester

1980 (12 Mar). 150th Anniversary of Liverpool and Manchester Railway.
Multicoloured Phosphorised paper. Perf 15×14.

1113	**590**	12p. *Rocket*	15	10
		a. Strip of 5. Nos. 1113/1117	75	60
1114	**591**	12p. First and Second Class Carriages	15	10
1115	**592**	12p. Third Class Carriage and Sheep Truck	15	10
1116	**593**	12p. Horsebox and Carriage Truck	15	10
1117	**594**	12p. Goods Truck and Mail-Coach	15	10
Set of 5			75	60
Gutter Block of 10			1·50	

First Day Cover		70
Presentation Pack (PO Pack No. 116)	85	
PHQ Cards (set of 5) (42)	50	1·25

Nos. 1113/1117 were printed together, *se-tenant*, in horizontal strips of
five throughout the sheet.

595 Montage of London
Buildings

1980 (9 Apr–7 May). London 1980 International Stamp Exhibition.
Phosphorised paper. Perf 14½×14.

1118	**595**	50p. agate	75	70
Gutter Pair			1·50	
First Day Cover				75
Presentation Pack (PO Pack No. 117)			85	
PHQ Card (43)			20	80
MS1119 90×123 mm. No. 1118 (*sold at 75p.*) (7.5.80)			75	95
First Day Cover				95

No. **MS**1119 was sold at 75p., the premium being used for the exhibition.

596 Buckingham
Palace

597 The Albert
Memorial

598 Royal Opera
House

599 Hampton Court

600 Kensington
Palace

1980 (7 May). London Landmarks. Multicoloured Phosphorised paper.
Perf 14×15.

1120	**596**	10½p. Buckingham Palace	10	10
1121	**597**	12p. The Albert Memorial	15	15
1122	**598**	13½p. Royal Opera House	20	15
1123	**599**	15p. Hampton Court	20	20
1124	**600**	17½p. Kensington Palace	25	20
Set of 5			85	75

Set of 5 Gutter Pairs	4·25	
First Day Cover		80
Presentation Pack (PO Pack No. 118)	90	
PHQ Cards (set of 5) (43)	60	1·10

601 Charlotte Brontë (*Jane Eyre*)

602 George Eliot (*The Mill on the Floss*)

603 Emily Brontë (*Wuthering Heights*)

604 Mrs Gaskell (*North and South*)

1980 (9 July). Famous Authoresses. Multicoloured Phosphorised paper. Perf 15×14.

1125	**601**	12p. Charlotte Brontë	15	15
1126	**602**	13½p. George Eliot	15	15
1127	**603**	15p. Emily Brontë	25	25
1128	**604**	17½p. Mrs Gaskell	30	30
Set of 4			75	75
Set of 4 Gutter Pairs			1·50	
First Day Cover				80
Presentation Pack (PO Pack No. 119)			80	
PHQ Cards (set of 4) (44)			50	1·00

Nos. 1125/1128 show authoresses and scenes from novels.
Nos. 1125/1126 also include the Europa CEPT emblem.

605 Queen Elizabeth the Queen Mother

1980 (4 Aug). 80th Birthday of Queen Elizabeth the Queen Mother. Multicoloured Phosphorised paper. Perf 14×15.

1129	**605**	12p. Queen Elizabeth the Queen Mother	25	25
Gutter Pair			50	
First Day Cover				50
PHQ Card (45)			20	40

606 Sir Henry Wood

607 Sir Thomas Beecham

608 Sir Malcolm Sargent

609 Sir John Barbirolli

1980 (10 Sept). British Conductors. Multicoloured Phosphorised paper. Perf 14×15.

1130	**606**	12p. Sir Henry Wood	15	15
1131	**607**	13½p. Sir Thomas Beecham	15	15
1132	**608**	15p. Sir Malcolm Sargent	25	25
1133	**609**	17½p. Sir John Barbirolli	30	30
Set of 4			75	75
Set of 4 Gutter Pairs			1·50	
First Day Cover				80
Presentation Pack (PO Pack No. 120)			80	
PHQ Cards (set of 4) (46)			60	1·00

610 Running

611 Rugby

612 Boxing

613 Cricket

1980 (10 Oct). Sport Centenaries. Multicoloured Phosphorised paper. Perf 14×14½.

1134	**610**	12p. Running	15	15
1135	**611**	13½p. Rugby	15	15
1136	**612**	15p. Boxing	25	25
1137	**613**	17½p. Cricket	30	30
Set of 4			75	75
Set of 4 Gutter Pairs			1·50	
First Day Cover				80
Presentation Pack (PO Pack No. 121)			80	
PHQ Cards (set of 4) (47)			60	1·00

Centenaries: 12p. Amateur Athletics Association; 13½p. Welsh Rugby Union; 15p. Amateur Boxing Association; 17½p. First England–Australia Test Match.

614 Christmas Tree

615 Candles

616 Apples and Mistletoe   617 Crown, Chains and Bell

618 Holly

1980 (19 Nov). Christmas. Multicoloured One centre phosphor band (10p.) or phosphorised paper (others). Perf 15×14.

1138	614	10p. Christmas Tree	10	10
1139	615	12p. Candles	15	15
1140	616	13½p. Apples and Mistletoe	15	15
1141	617	15p. Crown, Chains and Bell	25	25
1142	618	17½p. Holly	25	25
Set of 5			80	80
Set of 5 Gutter Pairs			1·60	
First Day Cover				85
Presentation Pack (PO Pack No. 122)			85	
PHQ Cards (set of 5) (48)			75	1·00

Collectors Pack

1980 (19 Nov). Comprises Nos. 1109/1118 and 1120/1142.

CP1142a	Collectors Pack (Pack No. 123)	5·50	

619 St Valentine's Day

620 Morris Dancers

621 Lammastide

622 Medieval Mummers

1981 (6 Feb). Folklore. Multicoloured Phosphorised paper. Perf 15×14.

1143	619	14p. St Valentine's Day	20	20
1144	620	18p. Morris Dancers	20	20
1145	621	22p. Lammastide	30	35
1146	622	25p. Medieval Mummers	40	45
Set of 4			1·00	1·10
Set of 4 Gutter Pairs			2·00	
First Day Cover				1·10
Presentation Pack (PO Pack No. 124)			1·10	
PHQ Cards (set of 4) (49)			60	1·20

Nos. 1143/1144 also include the Europa CEPT emblem.

623 Blind Man with Guide Dog

624 Hands spelling 'Deaf' in Sign Language

625 Disabled Man in Wheelchair

626 Disabled Artist with Foot painting

1981 (25 Mar). International Year of the Disabled. Multicoloured. Phosphorised paper. Perf 15×14.

1147	623	14p. Blind Man with Guide Dog	20	20
1148	624	18p. Hands spelling 'Deaf'	20	20
1149	625	22p. Disabled Man in Wheelchair	35	35
1150	626	25p. Disabled Artist with Foot painting	45	45
Set of 4			1·10	1·10
Set of 4 Gutter Pairs			2·25	
First Day Cover				1·20
Presentation Pack (PO Pack No. 125)			1·25	
PHQ Cards (set of 4) (50)			60	1·25

627 Small tortoiseshell   628 Large Blue

629 Peacock   630 Chequered Skipper

1981 (13 May). Butterflies. Multicoloured Phosphorised paper. Perf 14×15.

1151	627	14p. Small tortoiseshell	20	20
1152	628	18p. Large Blue	20	20
1153	629	22p. Peacock	35	35
1154	630	25p. Chequered Skipper	45	45
Set of 4			1·10	1·10
Set of 4 Gutter Pairs			2·25	
First Day Cover				1·20
Presentation Pack (PO Pack No. 126)			1·25	
PHQ Cards (set of 4) (51)			60	1·25

631 Glenfinnan, Scotland

632 Derwentwater, England

633 Stackpole Head, Wales

634 Giant's Causeway, Northern Ireland

635 St Kilda, Scotland

1981 (24 June). 50th Anniversary of National Trust for Scotland. British Landscapes. Multicoloured Phosphorised paper. Perf 15×14.

1155	**631**	14p. Glenfinnan, Scotland	20	20
1156	**632**	18p. Derwentwater, England	20	20
1157	**633**	20p. Stackpole Head, Wales	25	25
1158	**634**	22p. Giant's Causeway, Northern Ireland	35	35
1159	**635**	25p. St Kilda, Scotland	45	45
Set of 5			1·25	1·25
Set of 5 Gutter Pairs			2·50	
First Day Cover				1·40
Presentation Pack (PO Pack No. 127)			1·40	
PHQ Cards (set of 5) (52)			75	1·40

636 Prince Charles and Lady Diana Spencer

1981 (22 July). Royal Wedding. Multicoloured Phosphorised paper. Perf 14×15.

1160	**636**	14p. Prince Charles and Lady Diana Spencer	25	20
1161		25p. Prince Charles and Lady Diana Spencer	40	35
Set of 2			60	50
Set of 2 Gutter Pairs			1·25	
First Day Cover				1·20
Presentation Pack (PO Pack No. 127a)			1·10	
Souvenir Book			1·25	
PHQ Cards (set of 2) (53)			30	70

The souvenir book is a 12 page illustrated booklet with a set of mint stamps in a sachet attached to the front cover.

637 'Expeditions'

638 'Skills'

639 'Service'

640 'Recreation'

1981 (12 Aug). 25th Anniversary of Duke of Edinburgh's Award Scheme. Multicoloured Phosphorised paper. Perf 14.

1162	**637**	14p. 'Expeditions'	20	20
1163	**638**	18p. 'Skills'	20	20
1164	**639**	22p. 'Service'	35	35
1165	**640**	25p. 'Recreation'	45	45
Set of 4			1·10	1·10
Set of 4 Gutter Pairs			2·25	
First Day Cover				1·25
Presentation Pack (PO Pack No. 128)			1·25	
PHQ Cards (set of 4) (54)			60	1·25

641 Cockle-dredging from *Linsey II*

642 Hauling in Trawl Net

643 Lobster Potting

644 Hoisting Seine Net

1981 (23 Sept). Fishing Industry. Multicoloured Phosphorised paper. Perf 15×14.

1166	**641**	14p. Cockle-dredging from *Linsey II*	20	20
1167	**642**	18p. Hauling in Trawl Net	20	20
1168	**643**	22p. Lobster Potting	35	35
1169	**644**	25p. Hoisting Seine Net	45	45
Set of 4			1·10	1·10
Set of 4 Gutter Pairs			2·25	
First Day Cover				1·25
Presentation Pack (PO Pack No. 129)			1·25	
PHQ Cards (set of 4) (55)			60	1·25

Nos. 1166/1169 were issued on the occasion of the centenary of the Royal National Mission to Deep Sea Fishermen.

645 Father Christmas

646 Jesus Christ

647 Flying Angel

648 Joseph and Mary arriving at Bethlehem

649 Three Kings approaching Bethlehem

1981 (18 Nov). Christmas. Children's Pictures. Multicoloured One phosphor band (11½p.) or phosphorised paper (others). Perf 15×14.

1170	**645**	11½p. Father Christmas	20	20
1171	**646**	14p. Jesus Christ	20	20
1172	**647**	18p. Flying Angel	20	20
1173	**648**	22p. Joseph and Mary arriving at Bethlehem	30	30
1174	**649**	25p. Three Kings approaching Bethlehem	40	40
Set of 5			1·25	1·25
Set of 5 Gutter Pairs			2·50	
First Day Cover				1·40
Presentation Pack (PO Pack No. 130)			1·25	
PHQ Cards (set of 5) (56)			75	1·40

Collectors Pack

1981 (18 Nov). Comprises Nos. 1143/1174.
CP1174a   Collectors Pack (Pack No. 131)   7·25

650 Charles Darwin and Giant Tortoises   **651** Darwin and Marine Iguanas

652 Darwin, Cactus Ground Finch and Large Ground Finch   **653** Darwin and Prehistoric Skulls

1982 (10 Feb). Death Centenary of Charles Darwin. Multicoloured Phosphorised paper. Perf 15×14.

1175	**650**	15½p. Charles Darwin and Giant Tortoises	20	20
1176	**651**	19½p. Darwin and Marine Iguanas	25	25
1177	**652**	26p. Darwin, Cactus Ground Finch and Large Ground Finch	35	35
1178	**653**	29p. Darwin and Prehistoric Skulls	50	50
Set of 4			1·25	1·25
Set of 4 Gutter Pairs			2·50	
First Day Cover				1·25
Presentation Pack (PO Pack No. 132)			1·25	
PHQ Cards (set of 4) (57)			60	1·25

654 Boys' Brigade   **655** Girls' Brigade

656 Boy Scout Movement   **657** Girl Guide Movement

1982 (24 Mar). Youth Organisations. Multicoloured Phosphorised paper. Perf 14×15.

1179	**654**	15½p. Boys' Brigade	20	20
1180	**655**	19½p. Girls' Brigade	25	25
1181	**656**	26p. Boy Scout Movement	35	35
1182	**657**	29p. Girl Guide Movement	50	50
Set of 4			1·25	1·25
Set of 4 Gutter Pairs			2·50	
First Day Cover				1·40
Presentation Pack (PO Pack No. 133)			1·40	
PHQ Cards (set of 4) (58)			60	1·40

Nos. 1179/1182 were issued on the occasion of the 75th anniversary of the Boy Scout Movement; the 125th birth anniversary of Lord Baden-Powell and the centenary of the Boys' Brigade (1983).

658 Ballerina   **659** Harlequin

660 Hamlet   **661** Opera Singer

1982 (28 Apr). Europa. British Theatre. Multicoloured Phosphorised paper. Perf 14×15.

1183	**658**	15½p. Ballerina	20	20
1184	**659**	19½p. Harlequin	25	25
1185	**660**	26p. Hamlet	35	35
1186	**661**	29p. Opera Singer	50	50
Set of 4			1·25	1·25
Set of 4 Gutter Pairs			2·50	
First Day Cover				1·40
Presentation Pack (PO Pack No. 134)			1·40	
PHQ Cards (set of 4) (59)			60	1·40

662 Henry VIII and *Mary Rose*   **663** Admiral Blake and *Triumph*

664 Lord Nelson and HMS *Victory*   **665** Lord Fisher and HMS *Dreadnought*

666 Viscount Cunningham and HMS *Warspite*

1982 (16 June). Maritime Heritage. Multicoloured Phosphorised paper. Perf 15×14.

1187	**662**	15½p. Henry VIII and *Mary Rose*	20	20
1188	**663**	19½p. Admiral Blake and *Triumph*	25	25
1189	**664**	24p. Lord Nelson and HMS *Victory*	35	35
1190	**665**	26p. Lord Fisher and HMS *Dreadnought*	40	40
1191	**666**	29p. Viscount Cunningham and HMS *Warspite*	50	50
Set of 5			1·60	1·60
Set of 5 Gutter Pairs			3·25	
First Day Cover				1·75
Presentation Pack (PO Pack No. 136)			1·75	
PHQ Cards (set of 5) (60)			75	1·75

667 'Strawberry Thief' (William Morris)

668 Untitled (Steiner and Co)

669 'Cherry Orchard' (Paul Nash)

670 'Chevron' (Andrew Foster)

1982 (23 July). British Textiles. Multicoloured Phosphorised paper. Perf 14×15.

1192	**667**	15½p. 'Strawberry Thief' (William Morris)	20	20
1193	**668**	19½p. Untitled (Steiner and Co)	25	25
1194	**669**	26p. 'Cherry Orchard' (Paul Nash)	35	35
1195	**670**	29p. 'Chevron' (Andrew Foster)	50	50
Set of 4			1·25	1·25
Set of 4 Gutter Pairs			2·50	
First Day Cover				1·40
Presentation Pack (PO Pack No. 137)			1·40	
PHQ Cards (set of 4) (61)			60	1·40

Nos. 1192/1195 were issued on the occasion of the 250th birth anniversary of Sir Richard Arkwright (inventor of spinning machine).

671 Development of Communications

672 Technological Aids

1982 (8 Sept). Information Technology. Multicoloured Phosphorised paper. Perf 14×15.

1196	**671**	15½p. Development of Communications	25	25
1197	**672**	26p. Technological Aids	35	35
Set of 2			55	55
Set of 2 Gutter Pairs			1·10	
First Day Cover				60
Presentation Pack (PO Pack No. 138)			60	
PHQ Cards (set of 2) (62)			30	60

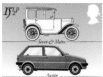

673 Austin Seven and Metro

674 Ford Model T and Escort

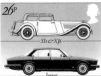

675 Jaguar SS 1 and XJ6

676 Rolls-Royce Silver Ghost and Silver Spirit

1982 (13 Oct). British Motor Cars. Multicoloured. Phosphorised paper. Perf 14½×14.

1198	**673**	15½p. Austin Seven and Metro	20	20
1199	**674**	19½p. Ford Model T and Escort	25	25
1200	**675**	26p. Jaguar SS 1 and XJ6	35	35
1201	**676**	29p. Rolls-Royce Silver Ghost and Silver Spirit	50	50
Set of 4			1·25	1·25
Set of 4 Gutter Pairs			2·50	
First Day Cover				1·40
Presentation Pack (PO Pack No. 139)			1·40	
PHQ Cards (set of 4) (63)			60	1·40

677 While Shepherds Watched

678 The Holly and the Ivy

679 I Saw Three Ships

680 We Three Kings

681 Good King Wenceslas

1982 (17 Nov). Christmas. Carols. Multicoloured One phosphor band (12½p.) or phosphorised paper (others). Perf 15×14.

1202	**677**	12½p. While Shepherds Watched	20	20
1203	**678**	15½p. The Holly and the Ivy	20	20
1204	**679**	19½p. I Saw Three Ships	25	25
1205	**680**	26p. We Three Kings	35	30
1206	**681**	29p. Good King Wenceslas	50	50
Set of 5			1·40	1·40
Set of 5 Gutter Pairs			2·75	
First Day Cover				1·50
Presentation Pack (PO Pack No. 140)			1·50	
PHQ Cards (set of 5) (64)			75	1·50

Collectors Pack

1982 (17 Nov). Comprises Nos. 1175/1206.

CP1206a		Collectors Pack (Pack No. 141)	12·00

682 Atlantic Salmon

683 Northern Pike

684 Brown Trout   **685** Eurasian Perch

1983 (26 Jan). British River Fish. Multicoloured Phosphorised paper. Perf 15×14.

1207	**682**	15½p. Atlantic Salmon	20	20
1208	**683**	19½p. Northern Pike	25	25
1209	**684**	26p. Brown Trout	35	35
1210	**685**	29p. Eurasian Perch	50	50
Set of 4			1·25	1·25
Set of 4 Gutter Pairs			2·50	
First Day Cover				1·40
Presentation Pack (PO Pack No. 142)			1·40	
PHQ Cards (set of 4) (65)			60	1·40

686 Tropical Island   **687** Desert

688 Temperate   **689** Mountain Range
Farmland

1983 (9 Mar). Commonwealth Day. Geographical Regions. Multicoloured Phosphorised paper. Perf 14×15.

1211	**686**	15½p. Tropical Island	20	20
1212	**687**	19½p. Desert	25	25
1213	**688**	26p. Temperate Farmland	35	35
1214	**689**	29p. Mountain Range	50	50
Set of 4			1·25	1·25
Set of 4 Gutter Pairs			2·50	
First Day Cover				1·40
Presentation Pack (PO Pack No. 143)			1·40	
PHQ Cards (set of 4) (66)			60	1·40

690 Humber Bridge   **691** Thames Flood Barrier

692 Iolair (oilfield emergency support vessel)

1983 (25 May). Europa. Engineering Achievements. Multicoloured Phosphorised paper. Perf 15×14.

1215	**690**	16p. Humber Bridge	20	20
1216	**691**	20½p. Thames Flood Barrier	30	30
1217	**692**	28p. Iolair	50	50
Set of 3			90	90
Set of 3 Gutter Pairs			1·75	
First Day Cover				1·00
Presentation Pack (PO Pack No. 144)			1·00	
PHQ Cards (set of 3) (67)			40	1·00

693 Musketeer and Pikeman, The Royal Scots (1633)   **694** Fusilier and Ensign, The Royal Welch Fusiliers (mid-18th-century)

695 Riflemen, 95th Rifles (The Royal Green Jackets) (1805)   **696** Sergeant (khaki service) and Guardsman (full dress), The Irish Guards (1900)

697 Paratroopers, The Parachute Regiment (1983)

1983 (6 July). British Army Uniforms. Multicoloured Phosphorised paper. Perf 14×15.

1218	**693**	16p. The Royal Scots	20	20
1219	**694**	20½p. The Royal Welch Fusiliers	25	25
1220	**695**	26p. The Royal Green Jackets	35	35
1221	**696**	28p. The Irish Guards	40	40
1222	**697**	31p. The Parachute Regiment	50	50
Set of 5			1·60	1·60
Set of 5 Gutter Pairs			3·25	
First Day Cover				1·75
Presentation Pack (PO Pack No. 145)			1·75	
PHQ Cards (set of 5) (68)			75	1·75

Nos. 1218/1222 were issued on the occasion of the 350th anniversary of the Royal Scots, the senior line regiment of the British Army.

698 20th-century Garden, Sissinghurst

699 19th-century Garden, Biddulph Grange

700 18th-century Garden, Blenheim

701 17th-century Garden, Pitmedden

1983 (24 Aug). British Gardens. Multicoloured. Phosphorised paper. Perf 14.

1223	**698**	16p. Sissinghurst	20	20
1224	**699**	20½p. Biddulph Grange	25	25
1225	**700**	28p. Blenheim	35	35
1226	**701**	31p. Pitmedden	50	50
Set of 4			1·25	1·25
Set of 4 Gutter Pairs			2·50	
First Day Cover				1·40
Presentation Pack (PO Pack No. 146)			1·40	
PHQ Cards (set of 4) (69)			60	1·40

702 Merry-go-round

703 Big Wheel, Helter-skelter and Performing Animals

704 Side Shows

705 Early Produce Fair

1983 (5 Oct). British Fairs. Multicoloured Phosphorised paper. Perf 15×14.

1227	**702**	16p. Merry-go-round	20	20
1228	**703**	20½p. Big Wheel, Helter-skelter and Performing Animals	25	25
1229	**704**	28p. Side Shows	35	35
1230	**705**	31p. Early Produce Fair	50	50
Set of 4			1·25	1·25
Set of 4 Gutter Pairs			2·50	
First Day Cover				1·40
Presentation Pack (PO Pack No. 147)			1·40	
PHQ Cards (set of 4) (70)			60	1·40

Nos. 1227/1230 were issued to mark the 850th anniversary of St Bartholomew's Fair, Smithfield, London.

706 Christmas Post (pillar box)

707 The Three Kings (chimney pots)

708 World at Peace (Dove and Blackbird)

709 Light of Christmas (street lamp)

710 Christmas Dove (hedge sculpture)

1983 (16 Nov). Christmas. Multicoloured. One phosphor band (12½p.) or phosphorised paper (others). Perf 15×14.

1231	**706**	12½p. Christmas Post (pillar box)	20	20
1232	**707**	16p. The Three Kings (chimney pots)	20	20
1233	**708**	20½p. World at Peace (Dove and Blackbird)	25	25
1234	**709**	28p. Light of Christmas (street lamp)	35	35
1235	**710**	31p. Christmas Dove (hedge sculpture)	50	50
Set of 5			1·50	1·50
Set of 5 Gutter Pairs			3·00	
First Day Cover				1·50
Presentation Pack (PO Pack No. 148)			1·50	
PHQ Cards (set of 5) (71)			75	1·50

Collectors Pack

1983 (16 Nov). Comprises Nos. 1207/1235.

CP1235a		Collectors Pack (Pack No. 149)	13·50

711 Arms of the College of Arms

712 Arms of King Richard III (founder)

713 Arms of the Earl Marshal of England

714 Arms of the City of London

1984 (17 Jan). 500th Anniversary of College of Arms. Multicoloured. Phosphorised paper. Perf 14½.

1236	**711**	16p. Arms of the College of Arms	25	25
1237	**712**	20½p. Arms of King Richard III (founder)	30	30
1238	**713**	28p. Arms of the Earl Marshal of England	40	40
1239	**714**	31p. Arms of the City of London	50	50
Set of 4			1·25	1·25

Set of 4 Gutter Pairs	2·50
First Day Cover	1·50
Presentation Pack (PO Pack No. 150)	1·50
PHQ Cards (set of 4) (72)	60 1·50

715 Highland Cow

716 Chillingham Wild Bull

717 Hereford Bull

718 Welsh Black Bull

719 Irish Moiled Cow

1984 (6 Mar). British Cattle. Multicoloured Phosphorised paper. Perf 15×14.

1240	**715**	16p. Highland Cow	25	25
1241	**716**	20½p. Chillingham Wild Bull	30	30
1242	**717**	26p. Hereford Bull	35	35
1243	**718**	28p. Welsh Black Bull	40	40
1244	**719**	31p. Irish Moiled Cow	50	50
Set of 5			1·60	1·60
Set of 5 Gutter Pairs			3·25	
First Day Cover				1·75
Presentation Pack (PO Pack No. 151)			1·75	
PHQ Cards (set of 5) (73)			75	1·75

Nos. 1240/1244 were issued on the occasion of the centenary of the Highland Cattle Society and the bicentenary of the Royal Highland and Agricultural Society of Scotland.

720 Garden Festival Hall, Liverpool

721 Milburngate Centre, Durham

722 Bush House, Bristol

723 Commercial Street Development, Perth

1984 (10 Apr). Urban Renewal. Multicoloured Phosphorised paper. Perf 15×14.

1245	**720**	16p. Garden Festival Hall, Liverpool	25	25
1246	**721**	20½p. Milburngate Centre, Durham	30	30
1247	**722**	28p. Bush House, Bristol	40	40
1248	**723**	31p. Commercial Street Development, Perth	50	50
Set of 4			1·25	1·25
Set of 4 Gutter Pairs			2·50	
First Day Cover				1·50

Presentation Pack (PO Pack No. 152)	1·50	
PHQ Cards (set of 4) (74)	60	1·50

Nos. 1245/1248 were issued on the occasion of 150th anniversaries of the Royal Institute of British Architects and the Chartered Institute of Building, and to commemorate the first International Gardens Festival, Liverpool.

724 CEPT 25th Anniversary Logo

725 Abduction of Europa

1984 (15 May). 25th Anniversary of CEPT (Europa) (T **724**) and Second Elections to European Parliament (T **725**). Multicoloured Phosphorised paper. Perf 15×14.

1249	**724**	16p. CEPT 25th Anniversary Logo	30	30
		a. Horiz pair. Nos. 1249/1250	60	60
1250	**725**	16p. Abduction of Europa	30	30
1251	**724**	20½p. CEPT 25th Anniversary Logo	35	35
		a. Horiz pair. Nos. 1251/1252	70	70
1252	**725**	20½p. Abduction of Europa	35	35
Set of 4			1·25	1·25
Set of 2 Gutter Blocks of 4			2·50	
First Day Cover				1·40
Presentation Pack (PO Pack No. 153)			1·40	
PHQ Cards (set of 4) (75)			60	1·40

Nos. 1249/1250 and 1251/1252 were each printed together, se-tenant, in horizontal pairs throughout the sheets.

726 Lancaster House

1984 (5 June). London Economic Summit Conference. Multicoloured Phosphorised paper. Perf 14×15.

1253	**726**	31p. Lancaster House	50	50
Gutter Pair			1·00	
First Day Cover				60
PHQ Card (76)			20	60

727 View of Earth from Apollo 11

728 Navigational Chart of English Channel

729 Greenwich Observatory

730 Sir George Airy's Transit Telescope

1984 (26 June). Centenary of the Greenwich Meridian. Multicoloured Phosphorised paper. Perf 14×14½.

1254	**727**	16p. View of Earth from *Apollo 11*	25	25
1255	**728**	20½p. Navigational Chart of English Channel	30	30
1256	**729**	28p. Greenwich Observatory	40	40
1257	**730**	31p. Sir George Airy's Transit Telescope	50	50
Set of 4			1·25	1·25
Set of 4 Gutter Pairs			2·50	
First Day Cover				1·50
Presentation Pack (PO Pack No. 154)			1·50	
PHQ Cards (set of 4) (77)			60	1·50

731 Bath Mail Coach, 1784

732 Attack on Exeter Mail, 1816

733 Norwich Mail in Thunderstorm, 1827

734 Holyhead and Liverpool Mails leaving London, 1828

735 Edinburgh Mail Snowbound, 1831

1984 (31 July). Bicentenary of First Mail Coach Run, Bath and Bristol to London. Multicoloured Phosphorised paper. Perf 15×14.

1258	**731**	16p. Bath Mail Coach, 1784	25	25
		a. Horiz strip of 5. Nos. 1258/1262	1·25	1·25
1259	**732**	16p. Attack on Exeter Mail, 1816	25	25
1260	**733**	16p. Norwich Mail in Thunderstorm, 1827	25	25
1261	**734**	16p. Holyhead and Liverpool Mails leaving London, 1828	25	25
1262	**735**	16p. Edinburgh Mail Snowbound, 1831	25	25
Set of 5			1·25	1·25
Gutter Block of 10			2·50	
First Day Cover				1·40
Presentation Pack (PO Pack No. 155)			1·40	
Souvenir Book			3·25	
PHQ Cards (set of 5) (78)			75	1·40

Nos. 1258/1262 were printed together, *se-tenant*, in horizontal strips of five throughout the sheet.

736 Nigerian Clinic

737 Violinist and Acropolis, Athens

738 Building Project, Sri Lanka

739 British Council Library, Middle East

1984 (25 Sept). 50th Anniversary of the British Council. Multicoloured Phosphorised paper. Perf 15×14.

1263	**736**	17p. Nigerian Clinic	25	25
1264	**737**	22p. Violinist and Acropolis, Athens	30	30
1265	**738**	31p. Building Project, Sri Lanka	40	40
1266	**739**	34p. British Council Library, Middle East	50	50
Set of 4			1·40	1·40
Set of 4 Gutter Pairs			2·75	
First Day Cover				1·50
Presentation Pack (PO Pack No. 156)			1·50	
PHQ Cards (set of 4) (79)			60	1·50

740 The Holy Family

741 Arrival in Bethlehem

742 Shepherd and Lamb

743 Virgin and Child

744 Offering of Frankincense

1984 (20 Nov). Christmas. Multicoloured One phosphor band (13p.) or phosphorised paper (others). Perf 15×14.

1267	**740**	13p. The Holy Family	25	25
1268	**741**	17p. Arrival in Bethlehem	25	25
1269	**742**	22p. Shepherd and Lamb	30	30
1270	**743**	31p. Virgin and Child	40	40
1271	**744**	34p. Offering of Frankincense	50	50
Set of 5			1·60	1·60
Set of 5 Gutter Pairs			3·25	
First Day Cover				1·75
Presentation Pack (PO Pack No. 157)			1·75	
PHQ Cards (set of 5) (80)			75	1·75

Collectors Pack

1984 (20 Nov). Comprises Nos. 1236/1271.

CP1271*a*	Collectors Pack (Pack No. 158)	16·00

Post Office Yearbook

1984 Comprises Nos. 1236/1271 in 24 page hardbound book with slip case, illustrated in colour

YB1271*a*	Yearbook	42·00

745 'Flying Scotsman'

746 'Golden Arrow'

747 'Cheltenham Flyer'

748 'Royal Scot'

749 'Cornish Riviera'

1985 (22 Jan). Famous Trains. Multicoloured Phosphorised paper. Perf 15×14.

1272	**745**	17p. 'Flying Scotsman'	25	25
1273	**746**	22p. 'Golden Arrow'	30	30
1274	**747**	29p. 'Cheltenham Flyer'	40	40
1275	**748**	31p. 'Royal Scot'	40	40
1276	**749**	34p. 'Cornish Riviera'	50	50
Set of 5			1·75	1·75
Set of 5 Gutter Pairs			3·50	
First Day Cover				1·90
Presentation Pack (PO Pack No. 159)			1·90	
PHQ Cards (set of 5) (81)			75	1·90

Nos. 1272/1276 were issued on the occasion of the 150th anniversary of the Great Western Railway Company.

750 Buff tailed bumblebee

751 Seven spotted Ladybird

752 Wart-biter bush-cricket

753 Stag Beetle

754 Emperor dragonfly

1985 (12 Mar). Insects. Multicoloured Phosphorised paper. Perf 14×15.

1277	**750**	17p. Buff tailed bumblebee	25	25
1278	**751**	22p. Seven spotted Ladybird	30	30
1279	**752**	29p. Wart-biter bush-cricket	40	40
1280	**753**	31p. Stag beetle	40	40
1281	**754**	34p. Emperor dragonfly	50	50
Set of 5			1·75	1·75
Set of 5 Gutter Pairs			3·50	
First Day Cover				1·90
Presentation Pack (PO Pack No. 160)			1·90	
PHQ Cards (set of 5) (82)			75	1·90

Nos. 1277/1281 were issued on the occasion of the centenaries of the Royal Entomological Society of London's Royal Charter, and of the Selborne Society.

755 Water Music (George Frederick Handel)

756 The Planets Suite (Gustav Holst)

757 The First Cuckoo (Frederick Delius)

758 Sea Pictures (Edward Elgar)

1985 (14 May). Europa. European Music Year. British Composers. Multicoloured Phosphorised paper. Perf 14×14½.

1282	**755**	17p. Water Music (George Frederick Handel)	25	25
1283	**756**	22p. The Planets Suite (Gustav Holst)	30	30
1284	**757**	31p. The First Cuckoo (Frederick Delius)	45	45
1285	**758**	34p. Sea Pictures (Edward Elgar)	55	55
Set of 4			1·40	1·40
Set of 4 Gutter Pairs			2·75	
First Day Cover				1·50
Presentation Pack (PO Pack No. 161)			1·50	
PHQ Cards (set of 4) (83)			60	1·50

Nos. 1282/1285 were issued on the occasion of the 300th birth anniversary of Handel.

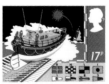

759 RNLI Lifeboat and Signal Flags

760 Beachy Head Lighthouse and Chart

761 *Marecs A* Communications Satellite and Dish Aerials

762 Buoys

769 Queen Guinevere and Sir Lancelot

770 Sir Galahad

1985 (18 June). Safety at Sea. Multicoloured Phosphorised paper. Perf 14.

1286	**759**	17p. RNLI Lifeboat and Signal Flags	25	25
1287	**760**	22p. Beachy Head Lighthouse and Chart	30	30
1288	**761**	31p. *Marecs A* Communications Satellite and Dish Aerials	45	45
1289	**762**	34p. Buoys	55	55
Set of 4			1·40	1·40
Set of 4 Gutter Pairs			2·75	
First Day Cover				1·50
Presentation Pack (PO Pack No. 162)			1·50	
PHQ Cards (set of 4) (84)			60	1·50

Nos. 1286/1289 were issued on the occasion of the bicentenary of the unimmersible lifeboat and the 50th anniversary of Radar.

1985 (3 Sept). Arthurian Legends. Multicoloured Phosphorised paper. Perf 15×14.

1294	**767**	17p. King Arthur and Merlin	25	25
1295	**768**	22p. Lady of the Lake	30	30
1296	**769**	31p. Queen Guinevere and Sir Lancelot	45	45
1297	**770**	34p. Sir Galahad	55	55
Set of 4			1·40	1·40
Set of 4 Gutter Pairs			2·75	
First Day Cover				1·50
Presentation Pack (PO Pack No. 164)			1·50	
PHQ Cards (set of 4) (86)			60	1·50

Nos. 1294/1297 were issued on the occasion of the 500th anniversary of the printing of Sir Thomas Malory's *Morte d'Arthur*.

763 Datapost Motorcyclist, City of London

764 Rural Postbus

771 Peter Sellers (from photo by Bill Brandt)

772 David Niven (from photo by Cornell Lucas)

773 Charlie Chaplin (from photo by Lord Snowdon)

774 Vivien Leigh (from photo by Angus McBean)

765 Parcel Delivery in Winter

766 Town Letter Delivery

1985 (30 July). 350 Years of Royal Mail Public Postal Service. Multicoloured Phosphorised paper. Perf 14×15.

1290	**763**	17p. Datapost Motorcyclist	25	25
1291	**764**	22p. Rural Postbus	30	30
1292	**765**	31p. Parcel Delivery in Winter	45	45
1293	**766**	34p. Town Letter Delivery	55	55
Set of 4			1·40	1·40
Set of 4 Gutter Pairs			2·75	
First Day Cover				1·50
Presentation Pack (PO Pack No. 163)			1·50	
PHQ Cards (set of 4) (85)			60	1·50

775 Alfred Hitchcock (from photo by Howard Coster)

1985 (8 Oct). British Film Year. Multicoloured Phosphorised paper. Perf 14½.

1298	**771**	17p. Peter Sellers	25	25
1299	**772**	22p. David Niven	30	30
1300	**773**	29p. Charlie Chaplin	45	45
1301	**774**	31p. Vivien Leigh	50	50
1302	**775**	34p. Alfred Hitchcock	55	55
Set of 5			1·90	1·90
Set of 5 Gutter Pairs			3·75	
First Day Cover				2·10
Presentation Pack (PO Pack No. 165)			2·10	
Souvenir Book			4·75	
PHQ Cards (set of 5) (87)			75	2·10

The souvenir book is a 24 page illustrated booklet with a set of mint stamps in a sachet attached to the front cover.

767 King Arthur and Merlin

768 Lady of the Lake

776 Principal Boy   **777** Genie

778 Dame   **779** Good Fairy

780 Pantomime Cat

1985 (19 Nov). Christmas. Pantomime Characters. Multicoloured One phosphor band (12p.) or phosphorised paper (others). Perf 15×14.

1303	776	12p. Principal Boy	20	20
1304	777	17p. Genie	25	25
1305	778	22p. Dame	30	30
1306	779	31p. Good Fairy	40	40
1307	780	34p. Pantomime Cat	50	50
Set of 5			1·40	1·40
Set of 5 Gutter Pairs			2·75	
First Day Cover				1·60
Presentation Pack (PO Pack No. 166)			1·60	
PHQ Cards (set of 5) (88)			75	1·60

Collectors Pack

1985 (19 Nov). Comprises Nos. 1272/1307.

CP1307a	Collectors Pack (Pack No. 167)	16·00

Post Office Yearbook

1985. Comprises Nos. 1272/1307 in 32 page hardbound book with slip case, illustrated in colour

YB1307a	Yearbook	30·00

17 PENCE · INDUSTRY YEAR 1986

781 Light Bulb and North Sea Oil Drilling Rig (Energy)

22 PENCE · INDUSTRY YEAR 1986

782 Thermometer and Pharmaceutical Laboratory (Health)

31 PENCE · INDUSTRY YEAR 1986

783 Garden Hoe Steelworks (Steel)

34 PENCE · INDUSTRY YEAR 1986

784 Loaf of Bread and Cornfield (Agriculture)

1986 (14 Jan). Industry Year. Multicoloured Phosphorised paper. Perf 14½×14.

1308	781	17p. Light Bulb and North Sea Oil Drilling Rig (Energy)	25	25
1309	782	22p. Thermometer and Pharmaceutical Laboratory (Health)	30	30
1310	783	31p. Garden Hoe Steelworks (Steel)	45	45

1311	784	34p. Loaf of Bread and Cornfield (Agriculture)	55	55
Set of 4			1·40	1·40
Set of 4 Gutter Pairs			2·75	
First Day Cover				1·60
Presentation Pack (PO Pack No. 168)			1·60	
PHQ Cards (set of 4) (89)			60	1·60

785 Dr Edmond Halley as Comet

786 *Giotto* Spacecraft approaching Comet

787 'Maybe Twice in a Lifetime'

788 Comet orbiting Sun and Planets

1986 (18 Feb). Appearance of Halley's Comet. Multicoloured Phosphorised paper. Perf 15×14.

1312	785	17p. Dr Edmond Halley as Comet	25	25
1313	786	22p. *Giotto* Spacecraft approaching Comet	30	30
1314	787	31p. 'Maybe Twice in a Lifetime'	45	45
1315	788	34p. Comet orbiting Sun and Planets	55	55
Set of 4			1·40	1·40
Set of 4 Gutter Pairs			2·75	
First Day Cover				1·60
Presentation Pack (PO Pack No. 168*)			1·60	
PHQ Cards (set of 4) (90)			60	1·60

* The presentation pack was incorrectly numbered 168.

789 Queen Elizabeth in 1928, 1942 and 1952

790 Queen Elizabeth in 1958, 1973 and 1982

1986 (21 Apr). 60th Birthday of Queen Elizabeth II. Phosphorised paper. Perf 15×14.

1316	789	17p. Queen Elizabeth in 1928, 1942 and 1952. Grey-black, turquoise-green, bright green, green and dull blue	30	40
		a. Pair. Nos. 1316/1317	80	1·00
1317	790	17p. Queen Elizabeth in 1958, 1973 and 1982. Grey-black, dull blue, greenish blue and indigo	30	40
1318	789	34p. Queen Elizabeth in 1928, 1942 and 1952. Grey-black, deep dull purple, yellow-orange and red	60	75
		a. Pair. Nos. 1318/1319	1·40	1·75
1319	790	34p. Queen Elizabeth in 1958, 1973 and 1982. Grey-black, olive-brown, yellow-brown, olive-grey and red	60	75
Set of 4			2·00	2·50
Set of 2 Gutter Blocks of 4			4·00	
First Day Cover				2·60
Presentation Pack (PO Pack No. 170)			2·10	
Souvenir Book			3·75	
PHQ Cards (set of 4) (91)			60	2·60

Nos. 1316/1317 and 1318/1319 were each printed together, *se-tenant*, in horizontal pairs throughout the sheet.

The souvenir book is a special booklet, fully illustrated and containing a mint set of stamps.

791 Barn Owl   **792** Pine Marten

793 Wild Cat   **794** Natterjack Toad

1986 (20 May). Europa. Nature Conservation. Endangered Species. Multicoloured Phosphorised paper. Perf 14½×14.

1320	**791**	17p. Barn Owl	25	25
1321	**792**	22p. Pine Marten	30	30
1322	**793**	31p. Wild Cat	45	45
1323	**794**	34p. Natterjack Toad	55	55
Set of 4			1·50	1·50
Set of 4 Gutter Pairs			3·00	
First Day Cover				1·60
Presentation Pack (PO Pack No. 171)			1·60	
PHQ Cards (set of 4) (92)			60	1·60

795 Peasants working in Fields   **796** Freemen working at Town Trades

797 Knight and Retainers   **798** Lord at Banquet

1986 (17 June). 900th Anniversary of *Domesday Book*. Multicoloured Phosphorised paper. Perf 15×14.

1324	**795**	17p. Peasants working in Fields	25	25
1325	**796**	22p. Freemen working at Town Trades	30	30
1326	**797**	31p. Knight and Retainers	45	45
1327	**798**	34p. Lord at Banquet	55	55
Set of 4			1·50	1·50
Set of 4 Gutter Pairs			3·00	
First Day Cover				1·60
Presentation Pack (PO Pack No. 172)			1·60	
PHQ Cards (set of 4) (93)			60	1·60

799 Athletics   **800** Rowing

801 Weightlifting   **802** Rifle Shooting

803 Hockey

1986 (15 July). 13th Commonwealth Games, Edinburgh and World Hockey Cup for Men, London (34p.). Multicoloured Phosphorised paper. Perf 15×14.

1328	**799**	17p. Athletics	25	25
1329	**800**	22p. Rowing	30	30
1330	**801**	29p. Weightlifting	45	45
1331	**802**	31p. Rifle Shooting	45	45
1332	**803**	34p. Hockey	55	55
Set of 5			1·75	1·75
Set of 5 Gutter Pairs			3·50	
First Day Cover				1·90
Presentation Pack (PO Pack No. 173)			1·90	
PHQ Cards (set of 5) (94)			75	1·90

No. 1332 also marked the centenary of the Hockey Association.

804 Prince Andrew and Miss Sarah Ferguson (from photo by Gene Nocon)   **805** Prince Andrew and Miss Sarah Ferguson (from photo by Gene Nocon)

1986 (22 July). Royal Wedding. Multicoloured. One phosphor band (12p.) or phosphorised paper (17p.). Perf 14×15.

1333	**804**	12p. Prince Andrew and Miss Sarah Ferguson	25	25
1334	**805**	17p. Prince Andrew and Miss Sarah Ferguson	40	40
Set of 2			60	60
Set of 2 Gutter Pairs			1·25	
First Day Cover				70
Presentation Pack (PO Pack No. 174)			75	
PHQ Cards (set of 2) (95)			30	75

806 Stylised Cross on Ballot Paper

1986 (19 Aug). 32nd Commonwealth Parliamentary Association Conference. Multicoloured. Phosphorised paper. Perf 14×14½.

1335	**806**	34p. Stylised Cross on Ballot Paper	50	50
Gutter Pair			1·00	
First Day Cover				55
PHQ Card (96)			15	55

807 Lord Dowding and Hawker Hurricane Mk I

808 Lord Tedder and Hawker Typhoon IB

809 Lord Trenchard and de Havilland DH.9A

810 Sir Arthur Harris and Avro Type 683 Lancaster

811 Lord Portal and de Havilland DH.98 Mosquito

1986 (16 Sept). History of the Royal Air Force. Multicoloured Phosphorised paper. Perf 14½.

1336	**807**	17p. Lord Dowding and Hawker Hurricane Mk I	25	25
1337	**808**	22p. Lord Tedder and Hawker Typhoon IB	35	35
1338	**809**	29p. Lord Trenchard and de Havilland DH.9A	45	45
1339	**810**	31p. Sir Arthur Harris and Avro Type 683 Lancaster	50	50
1340	**811**	34p. Lord Portal and de Havilland DH.98 Mosquito	55	55
Set of 5			2·00	2·00
Set of 5 Gutter Pairs			4·00	
First Day Cover				2·10
Presentation Pack (PO Pack No. 175)			2·10	
PHQ Cards (set of 5) (97)			75	2·10

Nos. 1336/1340 were issued to celebrate the 50th anniversary of the first RAF Commands.

812 The Glastonbury Thorn

813 The Tanad Valley Plygain

814 The Hebrides Tribute

815 The Dewsbury Church Knell

816 The Hereford Boy Bishop

1986 (18 Nov–2 Dec). Christmas. Folk Customs. Multicoloured One phosphor band (12p., 13p.) or phosphorised paper (others). Perf 15×14.

1341	**812**	12p. The Glastonburg Thorn	25	25
1342		13p. The Glastonburg Thorn	25	25
1343	**813**	18p. The Tanad Valley Plygain	30	30
1344	**814**	22p. The Hebrides Tribute	40	40
1345	**815**	31p. The Dewsbury Church Knell	45	45
1346	**816**	34p. The Hereford Boy Bishop	50	50
Set of 6			1·90	1·90
Set of 6 Gutter Pairs			3·75	
First Day Covers (2)				2·40
Presentation Pack (PO Pack No. 176) (Nos. 1342/1346)			2·00	
PHQ Cards (set of 5) (98) (Nos. 1342/1346)			75	1·75

Collectors Pack

1986 (18 Nov). Comprises Nos. 1308/1340 and 1342/1346.

CP1346a	Collectors Pack (Pack No. 177)	16·00

Post Office Yearbook

1986 (18 Nov). Comprises Nos. 1308/1346 in 32 page hardbound book with slip case, illustrated in colour

YB1346a	Yearbook	23·00

817 North American Blanket Flower

818 Globe Thistle

819 Echeveria

820 Autumn Crocus

1987 (20 Jan). Flower Photographs by Alfred Lammer. Multicoloured Phosphorised paper. Perf 14½×14.

1347	**817**	18p. North American Blanket Flower	25	25
1348	**818**	22p. Globe Thistle	30	30
1349	**819**	31p. Echeveria	45	45
1350	**820**	34p. Autumn Crocus	55	55
Set of 4			1·50	1·50
Set of 4 Gutter Pairs			3·00	
First Day Cover				1·60
Presentation Pack (PO Pack No. 178)			1·60	
PHQ Cards (set of 4) (99)			60	1·60

821 The Principia Mathematica

822 Motion of Bodies in Ellipses

823 *Optick Treatise*   **824** *The System of the World*

831 Volunteer with fainting Girl, 1965   **832** Transport of Transplant Organ by Air Wing, 1987

1987 (24 Mar). 300th Anniversary of *The Principia Mathematica* by Sir Isaac Newton. Multicoloured Phosphorised paper. Perf 14×15.

1351	821	18p. *The Principia Mathematica*	25	25
1352	822	22p. *Motion of Bodies in Ellipses*	30	30
1353	823	31p. *Optick Treatise*	45	45
1354	824	34p. *The System of the World*	55	55
Set of 4			1·50	1·50
Set of 4 Gutter Pairs			3·00	
First Day Cover				1·60
Presentation Pack (PO Pack No. 179)			1·60	
PHQ Cards (set of 4) (100)			60	1·60

1987 (16 June). Centenary of St John Ambulance Brigade. Multicoloured Phosphorised paper. Perf 14×14½.

1359	829	18p. Brigade Members with Ashford Litter, 1887	25	25
1360	830	22p. Bandaging Blitz Victim, 1940	30	30
1361	831	31p. Volunteer with fainting Girl, 1965	45	45
1362	832	34p. Transport of Transplant Organ by Air Wing, 1987	55	55
Set of 4			1·50	1·50
Set of 4 Gutter Pairs			3·00	
First Day Cover				1·60
Presentation Pack (PO Pack No. 181)			1·60	
PHQ Cards (set of 4) (102)			60	1·60

825 Willis Faber and Dumas Building, Ipswich   **826** Pompidou Centre, Paris

833 Arms of the Lord Lyon King of Arms   **834** Scottish Heraldic Banner of Prince Charles

827 Staatsgalerie, Stuttgart   **828** European Investment Bank, Luxembourg

835 Arms of Royal Scottish Academy of Painting, Sculpture and Architecture   **836** Arms of Royal Society of Edinburgh

1987 (12 May). Europa. British Architects in Europe. Multicoloured Phosphorised paper. Perf 15×14.

1355	825	18p. Willis Faber and Dumas Building, Ipswich	25	25
1356	826	22p. Pompidou Centre, Paris	30	30
1357	827	31p. Staatsgalerie, Stuttgart	45	45
1358	828	34p. European Investment Bank, Luxembourg	55	55
Set of 4			1·50	1·50
Set of 4 Gutter Pairs			3·00	
First Day Cover				1·60
Presentation Pack (PO Pack No. 180)			1·60	
PHQ Cards (set of 4) (101)			50	1·60

1987 (21 July). 300th Anniversary of Revival of Order of the Thistle. Multicoloured Phosphorised paper. Perf 14½.

1363	833	18p. Arms of the Lord Lyon King of Arms	25	25
1364	834	22p. Scottish Heraldic Banner of Prince Charles	30	30
1365	835	31p. Arms of Royal Scottish Academy of Painting, Sculpture and Architecture	45	45
1366	836	34p. Arms of Royal Society of Edinburgh	55	55
Set of 4			1·50	1·50
Set of 4 Gutter Pairs			3·00	
First Day Cover				1·60
Presentation Pack (PO Pack No. 182)			1·60	
PHQ Cards (set of 4) (103)			60	1·60

829 Brigade Members with Ashford Litter, 1887   **830** Bandaging Blitz Victim, 1940

837 Crystal Palace, *Monarch of the Glen* (Landseer) and Grace Darling   **838** *Great Eastern, Beeton's Book of Household Management* and Prince Albert

839 Albert Memorial, Ballot Box and Disraeli

840 Diamond Jubilee Emblem, Newspaper Placard for Relief of Mafeking and Morse Key

1987 (8 Sept). 150th Anniversary of Queen Victoria's Accession. Multicoloured Phosphorised paper. Perf 15×14.

1367	**837**	18p. Crystal Palace, *Monarch of the Glen* (Landseer) and Grace Darling	25	25
1368	**838**	22p. *Great Eastern, Beeton's Book of Household Management* and Prince Albert	30	30
1369	**839**	31p. Albert Memorial, Ballot Box and Disraeli	45	45
1370	**840**	34p. Diamond Jubilee Emblem, Newspaper Placard for Relief of Mafeking and Morse Key	55	55
Set of 4			1·50	1·50
Set of 4 Gutter Pairs			3·00	
First Day Cover				1·60
Presentation Pack (PO Pack No. 183)			1·60	
PHQ Cards (set of 4) (104)			60	1·60

841 Pot by Bernard Leach

842 Pot by Elizabeth Fritsch

843 Pot by Lucie Rie

844 Pot by Hans Coper

1987 (13 Oct). Studio Pottery. Multicoloured Phosphorised paper. Perf 14½×14.

1371	**841**	18p. Pot by Bernard Leach	25	25
1372	**842**	26p. Pot by Elizabeth Fritsch	35	35
1373	**843**	31p. Pot by Lucie Rie	45	45
1374	**844**	34p. Pot by Hans Coper	55	55
Set of 4			1·50	1·50
Set of 4 Gutter Pairs			3·00	
First Day Cover				1·60
Presentation Pack (PO Pack No. 184)			1·60	
PHQ Cards (set of 4) (105)			60	1·60

845 Decorating the Christmas Tree

846 Waiting for Father Christmas

847 Sleeping Child and Father Christmas in Sleigh

848 Child reading

849 Child playing Recorder and Snowman

1987 (17 Nov). Christmas. Multicoloured One phosphor band (13p.) or phosphorised paper (others). Perf 15×14.

1375	**845**	13p. Decorating the Christmas Tree	20	20
1376	**846**	18p. Waiting for Father Christmas	25	25
1377	**847**	26p. Sleeping Child and Father Christmas in Sleigh	30	30
1378	**848**	31p. Child reading	40	40
1379	**849**	34p. Child playing Recorder and Snowman	50	50
Set of 5			1·50	1·50
Set of 5 Gutter Pairs			3·00	
First Day Cover				1·60
Presentation Pack (PO Pack No. 185)			1·60	
PHQ Cards (set of 5) (106)			75	1·60

Collectors Pack

1987 (17 Nov). Comprises Nos. 1347/1379.

CP1379a	Collectors Pack (Pack No. 186)	16·00

Post Office Yearbook

1987 (17 Nov). Comprises Nos. 1347/1379 in 32 page hardbound book with slip case, illustrated in colour

YB1379a	Yearbook	13·00

850 Short-spined Sea scorpion ('Bull-rout') (Jonathan Couch)

851 Yellow Water Lily (Major Joshua Swatkin)

852 Whistling ('Bewick's') Swan (Edward Lear)

853 *Morchella esculenta* (James Sowerby)

1988 (19 Jan). Bicentenary of Linnean Society. Archive Illustrations. Multicoloured Phosphorised paper. Perf 15×14.

1380	**850**	18p. Short-spined Sea scorpion ('Bull-rout')	25	25
1381	**851**	26p. Yellow Water Lily	35	35
1382	**852**	31p. Whistling ('Bewick's') Swan	45	45
1383	**853**	34p. *Morchella esculenta*	60	60
Set of 4			1·50	1·50
Set of 4 Gutter Pairs			3·00	
First Day Cover				1·60
Presentation Pack (PO Pack No. 187)			1·60	
PHQ Cards (set of 4) (107)			60	1·60

854 Revd William Morgan (Bible translator, 1588)

855 William Salesbury (New Testament translator, 1567)

856 Bishop Richard Davies (New Testament translator, 1567)

857 Bishop Richard Parry (editor of Revised Welsh Bible, 1620)

1988 (1 Mar). 400th Anniversary of Welsh Bible. Multicoloured Phosphorised paper. Perf 14½×14.

1384	**854**	18p. Revd William Morgan	25	25
1385	**855**	26p. William Salesbury	35	35
1386	**856**	31p. Bishop Richard Davies	45	45
1387	**857**	34p. Bishop Richard Parry	60	60
Set of 4			1·50	1·50
Set of 4 Gutter Pairs			3·00	
First Day Cover				1·60
Presentation Pack (PO Pack No. 188)			1·60	
PHQ Cards (set of 4) (108)			60	1·60

858 Gymnastics (Centenary of British Amateur Gymnastics Association)

859 Downhill Skiing (Ski Club of Great Britain)

860 Tennis (Centenary of Lawn Tennis Association)

861 Football (Centenary of Football League)

1988 (22 Mar). Sports Organisations. Multicoloured Phosphorised paper. Perf 14½.

1388	**858**	18p. Gymnastics	25	25
		a. Imperf (pair)		
1389	**859**	26p. Downhill Skiing	35	35
1390	**860**	31p. Tennis	45	45
1391	**861**	34p. Football	60	60
Set of 4			1·50	1·50
Set of 4 Gutter Pairs			3·00	
First Day Cover				1·60
Presentation Pack (PO Pack No. 189)			1·60	
PHQ Cards (set of 4) (109)			50	1·60

862 *Mallard* and Mailbags on Pick-up Arms

863 Loading Transatlantic Mail on Liner *Queen Elizabeth*

864 Glasgow Tram No. 1173 and Pillar Box

865 Imperial Airways Handley Page HP.45 *Horatius* and Airmail Van

1988 (10 May). Europa. Transport and Mail Services in 1930s.' Multicoloured Phosphorised paper. Perf 15×14.

1392	**862**	18p. *Mallard* and Mailbags on Pick-up Arms	25	25
1393	**863**	26p. Loading Transatlantic Mail on Liner *Queen Elizabeth*	35	35
1394	**864**	31p. Glasgow Tram No. 1173 and Pillar Box	45	45
1395	**865**	34p. Imperial Airways Handley Page HP.45 *Horatius* and Airmail Van	60	60
Set of 4			1·50	1·50
Set of 4 Gutter Pairs			3·00	
First Day Cover				1·60
Presentation Pack (PO Pack No. 190)			1·60	
PHQ Cards (set of 4) (110)			60	1·60

866 Early Settler and Sailing Clipper

867 Queen Elizabeth II with British and Australian Parliament Buildings

868 W. G. Grace (cricketer) and Tennis Racquet

869 Shakespeare, John Lennon (entertainer) and Sydney Opera House

1988 (21 June). Bicentenary of Australian Settlement. Multicoloured Phosphorised paper. Perf 14½.

1396	**866**	18p. Early Settler and Sailing Clipper	25	25
		a. Horiz pair. Nos. 1396/1397	55	55
1397	**867**	18p. Queen Elizabeth II with British and Australian Parliament Buildings	25	25
1398	**868**	34p. W. G. Grace and Tennis Racquet	50	50
		a. Horiz pair. Nos. 1398/1399	1·10	1·10
1399	**869**	34p. Shakespeare, John Lennon and Sydney Opera House	50	50
Set of 4			1·50	1·50
Set of 2 Gutter Blocks of 4			3·00	
First Day Cover				1·60
Presentation Pack (PO Pack No. 191)			1·60	
Souvenir Book			6·00	
PHQ Cards (set of 4) (111)			60	1·60

Nos. 1396/397 and 1398/1399 were each printed together, *se-tenant*, in horizontal pairs throughout the sheets, each pair showing a background design of the Australian flag.

The 40 page souvenir book contains the British and Australian sets which were issued on the same day in similar designs.

870 Spanish Galeasse off The Lizard

871 English Fleet leaving Plymouth

872 Engagement off Isle of Wight

873 Attack of English Fire-ships, Calais

874 Armada in Storm, North Sea

1988 (19 July). 400th Anniversary of Spanish Armada. Multicoloured Phosphorised paper. Perf 15×14.

1400	870	18p. Spanish Galeasse off The Lizard	25	25
		a. Horiz strip of 5. Nos. 1400/1404	1·40	1·40
1401	871	18p. English Fleet leaving Plymouth	25	25
1402	872	18p. Engagement off Isle of Wight	25	25
1403	873	18p. Attack of English Fire-ships, Calais	25	25
1404	874	18p. Armada in Storm, North Sea	25	25
Set of 5			1·40	1·40
Gutter Block of 10			2·75	
First Day Cover				1·50
Presentation Pack (PO Pack No. 192)			1·50	
PHQ Cards (set of 5) (112)			75	1·50

Nos. 1400/1404 were printed together, *se-tenant*, in horizontal strips of five throughout the sheet, forming a composite design.

875 'The Owl and the Pussy-cat'

876 'Edward Lear as a Bird' (self-portrait)

877 'Cat' (from alphabet book)

878 'There was a Young Lady whose Bonnet...' (limerick)

1988 (6–27 Sept). Death Centenary of Edward Lear (artist and author). Multicoloured Phosphorised paper. Perf 15×14.

1405	875	19p. 'The Owl and the Pussy-cat'	25	25
1406	876	27p. 'Edward Lear as a Bird' (self-portrait)	35	35
1407	877	32p. 'Cat' (from alphabet book)	45	45
1408	878	35p. 'There was a Young Lady whose Bonnet...' (limerick)	60	60
Set of 4			1·50	1·50
Set of 4 Gutter Pairs			3·00	
First Day Cover				1·60
Presentation Pack (PO Pack No. 193)			1·60	
PHQ Cards (set of 4) (113)			60	1·60

MS1409 122×90 mm. Nos. 1405/1408 (*sold at* £1·35)

	(27.9.88)	3·25	3·50
First Day Cover			3·75

The premium on No. **MS**1409 was used to support the Stamp World London 90 International Stamp Exhibition.

879 Carrickfergus Castle

880 Caernarfon Castle

881 Edinburgh Castle

882 Windsor Castle

1988 (18 Oct). Ordinary paper. Perf 15×14.

1410	879	£1 Carrickfergus Castle. Bottle green	3·50	25
1411	880	£1·50 Caernarfon Castle. Maroon	3·75	50
1412	881	£2 Edinburgh Castle. Indigo	6·50	75
1413	882	£5 Windsor Castle. Deep brown	17·00	1·50
Set of 4			28·00	2·75
Set of 4 Gutter Pairs (vert or horiz)			60·00	
First Day Cover				16·00
Presentation Pack (PO Pack No. 18)			30·00	

For similar designs, but with silhouette of Queen's head see Nos. 1611/1614 and 1993/1996.

883 Journey to Bethlehem

884 Shepherds and Star

885 Three Wise Men

886 Nativity

887 The Annunciation

1988 (15 Nov). Christmas. Christmas Cards. Multicoloured One phosphor band (14p.) or phosphorised paper (others). Perf 15×14.

1414	883	14p. Journey to Bethlehem	25	25
1415	884	19p. Shepherds and Star	25	25
1416	885	27p. Three Wise Men	35	35
1417	886	32p. Nativity	40	40
1418	887	35p. The Annunciation	55	55
Set of 5			1·60	1·60
Set of 5 Gutter Pairs			3·25	
First Day Cover				1·75
Presentation Pack (PO Pack No. 194)			1·75	
PHQ Cards (set of 5) (114)			75	1·75

Collectors Pack

1988 (15 Nov). Comprises Nos. 1380/1408, 1414/1418.
CP1418a   Collectors Pack (Pack No. 195)   16·00

Post Office Yearbook

1988 (15 Nov). Comprises Nos. 1380/1404, **MS**1409, 1414/1418 in 32 page
hardbound book with slip case, illustrated in colour
YB1418a   Yearbook   13·00

888 Atlantic Puffin   **889** Avocet

890 Oystercatcher   **891** Northern Gannet

1989 (17 Jan). Centenary of Royal Society for the Protection of Birds.
Multicoloured Phosphorised paper. Perf 14×15.

1419	**888**	19p. Atlantic Puffin	25	25
1420	**889**	27p. Avocet	35	35
1421	**890**	32p. Oystercatcher	45	45
1422	**891**	35p. Northern Gannet	60	60
Set of 4			1·50	1·50
Set of 4 Gutter Pairs			3·00	
First Day Cover				1·60
Presentation Pack (PO Pack No. 196)			1·60	
PHQ Cards (*set of 4*) (115)			60	1·60

892 Rose

894 Yachts

893 Cupid

895 Fruit

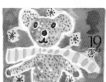

896 Teddy Bear

1989 (31 Jan). Greetings Stamps. Multicoloured Phosphorised paper. Perf
15×14.

1423	**892**	19p. Rose	50	60
		b. Horiz strip of 5. Nos. 1423/1427	10·00	12·00

1424	**893**	19p. Cupid	50	60
1425	**894**	19p. Yachts	50	60
1426	**895**	19p. Fruit	50	60
1427	**896**	19p. Teddy Bear	50	60
Set of 5			10·00	12·00
First Day Cover				12·00

Nos. 1423/1427 were printed together, *se-tenant*, in horizontal strips
of five, two such strips forming the booklet pane with 12 half stamp-
size labels.

897 Fruit and Vegetables

898 Meat Products

899 Dairy Products

900 Cereal Products

1989 (7 Mar). Food and Farming Year. Multicoloured Phosphorised paper.
Perf 14×14½.

1428	**897**	19p. Fruit and Vegetables	25	25
1429	**898**	27p. Meat Products	35	35
1430	**899**	32p. Dairy Products	45	45
1431	**900**	35p. Cereal Products	60	60
Set of 4			1·50	1·50
Set of 4 Gutter Pairs			3·00	
First Day Cover				1·60
Presentation Pack (PO Pack No. 197)			1·60	
PHQ Cards (*set of 4*) (116)			60	1·60

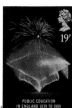

901 Mortarboard
(150th Anniversary of
Public Education in
England)

902 Cross on Ballot
Paper (Third Direct
Elections to European
Parliament)

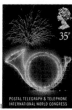

903 Posthorn (26th
Postal, Telegraph
and Telephone
International Congress,
Brighton)

904 Globe (Inter-
Parliamentary Union
Centenary Conference,
London)

1989 (11 Apr). Anniversaries. Multicoloured Phosphorised paper. Perf
14×14½.

1432	**901**	19p. Mortarboard	25	25
		a. Horiz pair. Nos. 1432/1433	60	60
1433	**902**	19p. Cross on Ballot Paper	25	25

1434	**903**	35p. Posthorn	50	50
		a. Horiz. pair. Nos. 1434/1435	1·10	1·10
1435	**904**	35p. Globe	50	50
Set of 4			1·50	1·50
Set of 2 Gutter Strips of 4			3·00	
First Day Cover				1·60
Presentation Pack (PO Pack No. 198)			1·60	
PHQ Cards (*set of 4*) (117)			60	1·60

Nos. 1432/1433 and 1434/1435 were each printed together, *se-tenant*, in horizontal pairs throughout the sheets.

905 Toy Train and Aeroplanes   **906** Building Bricks

907 Dice and Board Games   **908** Toy Robot, Boat and Doll's House

1989 (16 May). Europa. Games and Toys. Multicoloured Phosphorised paper. Perf 14×15.

1436	**905**	19p. Toy Train and Aeroplanes	25	25
1437	**906**	27p. Building Bricks	35	35
1438	**907**	32p. Dice and Board Games	45	45
1439	**908**	35p. Toy Robot, Boat and Doll's House	60	60
Set of 4			1·50	1·50
Set of 4 Gutter Strips			3·00	
First Day Cover				1·60
Presentation Pack (PO Pack No. 199)			1·60	
PHQ Cards (*set of 4*) (118)			60	1·60

909 Ironbridge, Shropshire   **910** Tin Mine, St Agnes Head, Cornwall

911 Cotton Mills, New Lanark, Strathclyde   **912** Pontcysyllte Aqueduct, Clwyd

912a Horizontal versions of Types **909/912**

1989 (4–25 July). Industrial Archaeology. Multicoloured Phosphorised paper. Perf 14×15.

1440	**909**	19p. Ironbridge, Shropshire	25	25
1441	**910**	27p. Tin Mine, St Agnes Head, Cornwall	35	35
1442	**911**	32p. Cotton Mills, New Lanark, Strathclyde	45	45
1443	**912**	35p. Pontcysyllte Aqueduct, Clwyd	60	60
Set of 4			1·50	1·50
Set of 4 Gutter Pairs			3·00	
First Day Cover				1·60
Presentation Pack (PO Pack No. 200)			1·60	
PHQ Cards (*set of 4*) (119)			50	1·60
MS1444 **912a** 122×90 mm. Horizontal versions of Types **909/912** (*sold at* £1·40) (25.7.89)			3·00	3·00
First Day Cover				3·00

The premium on No. **MS**1444 was used to support the Stamp World London 90 International Stamp Exhibition.

For Nos. 1445/1452 see Decimal Machin Definitives section.

915 Snowflake (×10)   **916** *Calliphora erythrocephala* (×5) (fly)

917 Blood Cells (×500)   **918** Microchip (×600)

1989 (5 Sept). 150th Anniversary of Royal Microscopical Society. Multicoloured Phosphorised paper. Perf 14½×14.

1453	**915**	19p. Snowflake	25	25
1454	**916**	27p. *Calliphora erythrocephala*	35	35
1455	**917**	32p. Blood Cells	45	45
1456	**918**	35p. Microchip	60	60
Set of 4			1·50	1·50
Set of 4 Gutter Pairs			3·00	
First Day Cover				1·60
Presentation Pack (PO Pack No. 201)			1·60	
PHQ Cards (*set of 4*) (120)			60	1·60

919 Royal Mail Coach

920 Escort of Blues and Royals

921 Lord Mayor's Coach

922 Passing St Paul's

923 Blues and Royals Drum Horse

1989 (17 Oct). Lord Mayor's Show, London. Multicoloured. Phosphorised paper. Perf 14×15.

1457	**919**	20p. Royal Mail Coach	25	25
		a. Horiz strip of 5. Nos. 1457/1461	1·40	1·40
1458	**920**	20p. Escort of Blues and Royals	25	25
1459	**921**	20p. Lord Mayor's Coach	25	25
1460	**922**	20p. Passing St Paul's	25	25
1461	**923**	20p. Blues and Royals Drum Horse	25	25
Set of 5			1·40	1·40
Gutter Strip of 10			2·75	
First Day Cover				1·50
Presentation Pack (PO Pack No. 202)			1·50	
PHQ Cards (set of 5) (121)			75	1·50

Nos. 1457/1461 were printed together, *se-tenant*, in horizontal strips of five throughout the sheet.

This issue commemorates the 800th anniversary of the installation of the first Lord Mayor of London.

See also No. 2957.

924 14th-century Peasants from Stained-glass Window

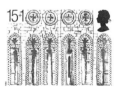

925 Arches and Roundels, West Front

926 Octagon Tower

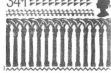

927 Arcade from West Transept

928 Triple Arch from West Front

1989 (14 Nov). Christmas. 800th Anniversary of Ely Cathedral. Multicoloured One phosphor band (15p., 15p.+1p.) or phosphorised paper (others). Perf 15×14.

1462	**924**	15p. 14th-century Peasants from Stained-glass Window	25	25
1463	**925**	15p.+1p. Arches and Roundels, West Front	25	35
1464	**926**	20p.+1p. Octagon Tower	35	35
1465	**927**	34p.+1p. Arcade from West Transept	45	45
1466	**928**	37p.+1p. Triple Arch from West Front	60	60
Set of 5			1·75	1·75
Set of 5 Gutter Pairs			3·50	
First Day Cover				1·90
Presentation Pack (PO Pack No. 203)			1·90	
PHQ Cards (set of 5) (122)			75	1·90

Collectors Pack

1989 (14 Nov). Comprises Nos. 1419/1422, 1428/1443 and 1453/1466.

CP1466a	Collectors Pack (Pack No. 204)	15·50

Post Office Yearbook

1989 (14 Nov). Comprises Nos. 1419/1422, 1428/1444 and 1453/1466 in hardbound book with slip case, illustrated in colour

YB1466a	Yearbook	14·00

929 Queen Victoria and Queen Elizabeth II

1990 (10 Jan–12 June). 150th Anniversary of the Penny Black.

(a) Photo Harrison. Perf 15×14.

1467	**929**	15p. bright blue	30	30
1468a		15p. bright blue (1 side band) (30.1.90)	1·75	1·75
1469		20p. brownish black and cream (phosphorised paper)	40	40
1470		20p. brownish black and cream (2 bands) (30.1.90)	80	80
1471		29p. deep mauve (phosphorised paper)	55	55
1472		29p. deep mauve (2 bands) (20.3.90)	3·75	3·75
1473		34p. deep bluish grey (phosphorised paper)	70	70
1474		37p. rosine (phosphorised paper)	75	75

(b) Litho Walsall. Perf 14 (from booklets).

1475	**929**	15p. bright blue (30.1.90)	50	50
1476		20p. brownish black and cream (phosphorised paper) (30.1.90)	50	50

(c) Litho Questa. Perf 15×14 (from booklets).

1477	**929**	15p. bright blue (17.4.90)	85	85
1478		20p. brownish black (phosphorised paper) (17.4.90)	85	85
Set of 5 (Nos. 1467, 1469, 1471, 1473/1474)			2·50	2·50
First Day Cover (Nos. 1467, 1469, 1471, 1473/1474)				2·75
Presentation Pack (PO Pack No. 21) (Nos. 1467, 1469, 1471, 1473/1474)			2·90	

No. 1468 exists with the phosphor band at the left or right of the stamp. For T **929** redrawn with '1st' face value see No. 2133a and 2956.

See also Nos. **MS**1501, 2133, 2955 and **MS**3965.

930 Kitten   **931** Rabbit

932 Duckling   **933** Puppy

1990 (23 Jan). 150th Anniversary of Royal Society for Prevention of Cruelty to Animals. Multicoloured Phosphorised paper. Perf 14×14½.

1479	**930**	20p. Kitten	30	30
1480	**931**	29p. Rabbit	45	45
1481	**932**	34p. Duckling	55	55
1482	**933**	37p. Puppy	65	65
Set of 4			1·75	1·75
Set of 4 Gutter Pairs			3·50	
First Day Cover				1·90
Presentation Pack (PO Pack No. 205)			1·90	
PHQ Cards (*set of 4*) (123)			80	1·90

934 Teddy Bear

935 Dennis the Menace

936 Punch

937 Cheshire Cat

938 The Man in the Moon

939 The Laughing Policeman

940 Clown

941 Mona Lisa

942 Queen of Hearts

943 Stan Laurel (comedian)

1990 (6 Feb). Greetings Stamps. Smiles. Multicoloured Two phosphor bands. Perf 15×14.

1483	**934**	20p. Teddy Bear	60	70
1484	**935**	20p. Dennis the Menace	60	70
1485	**936**	20p. Punch	60	70
1486	**937**	20p. Cheshire Cat	60	70
1487	**938**	20p. The Man in the Moon	60	70
1488	**939**	20p. The Laughing Policeman	60	70
1489	**940**	20p. Clown	60	70
1490	**941**	20p. *Mona Lisa*	60	70
1491	**942**	20p. Queen of Hearts	60	70
1492	**943**	20p. Stan Laurel	60	70
Set of 10			11·50	12·50
First Day Cover				13·00

Nos. 1483/1492 were printed together, *se-tenant*, in booklet panes of ten.

For Types **934**/**943** inscribed (1st), see Nos. 1550/1559.

SET PRICES. Please note that set prices for booklet greetings stamps are for complete panes. Sets of single stamps are worth considerably less.

944 Alexandra Palace (Stamp World London 90 Exhibition)

945 Glasgow School of Art

946 British Philatelic Bureau, Edinburgh

947 Templeton Carpet Factory, Glasgow

1990 (6 Mar). Europa (Nos. 1493 and 1495) and Glasgow 1990 European City of Culture (Nos. 1494 and 1496). Multicoloured Phosphorised paper. Perf 14×15.

1493	**944**	20p. Alexandra Palace (Stamp World London 90 Exhibition)	25	25
1494	**945**	20p. Glasgow School of Art	35	35
1495	**946**	29p. British Philatelic Bureau, Edinburgh	45	45
1496	**947**	37p. Templeton Carpet Factory, Glasgow	60	60
Set of 4			1·50	1·50
Set of 4 Gutter Pairs			3·00	
First Day Cover				1·60
Presentation Pack (PO Pack No. 206)			1·60	
PHQ Cards (*set of 4*) (124)			80	1·60

948 Export Achievement Award **949** Technological Achievement Award

1990 (10 Apr). 25th Anniversary of Queen's Awards for Export and Technology. Multicoloured Phosphorised paper. Perf 14×14½.

1497	**948**	20p. Export Achievement Award	25	25
		a. Horiz pair. Nos. 1497/1498	60	60
1498	**949**	20p. Technological Achievement Award	25	25
1499	**948**	37p. Export Achievement Award	50	50
		a. Horiz pair. Nos. 1499/1500	1·10	1·10
1500	**949**	37p. Technological Achievement Award	50	50
Set of 4			1·50	1·50
Set of 2 Gutter Strips of 4			3·00	
First Day Cover				1·60
Presentation Pack (PO Pack No. 207)			1·60	
PHQ Cards (set of 4) (125)			80	1·60

Nos. 1497/1498 and 1499/1500 were each printed together, *se-tenant*, in horizontal pairs throughout the sheets.

949a Stamp World London '90

1990 (3 May). Stamp World London '90 International Stamp Exhibition. Sheet 122×89 mm containing No. 1469. Phosphorised paper. Perf 15×14.

MS1501 **949a**	20p. brownish black and cream (*sold at £1*)	2·40	2·40
First Day Cover			2·50
Souvenir Book (Nos. 1467, 1469, 1471, 1473/1474 and **MS**1501)		8·50	

The premium on No. **MS**1501 was used to support the Stamp World London '90 International Stamp Exhibition.

KEW GARDENS 1840-1990 KEW GARDENS 1840-1990
950 Cycad and Sir Joseph Banks Building **951** Stone Pine and Princess of Wales Conservatory

KEW GARDENS 1840-1990 KEW GARDENS 1840-1990
952 Willow Tree and Palm House **953** Cedar Tree and Pagoda

1990 (5 June). 150th Anniversary of Kew Gardens. Multicoloured Phosphorised paper. Perf 14×15.

1502	**950**	20p. Cycad and Sir Joseph Banks Building	25	25
1503	**951**	29p. Stone Pine and Princess of Wales Conservatory	35	35
1504	**952**	34p. Willow Tree and Palm House	45	45
1505	**953**	37p. Cedar Tree and Pagoda	60	60
Set of 4			1·50	1 50
Set of 4 Gutter Pairs			3·00	
First Day Cover				1·60
Presentation Pack (PO Pack No. 208)			1·60	
PHQ Cards (set of 4) (126)			80	1·60

954 Thomas Hardy and Clyffe Clump, Dorset

1990 (10 July). 150th Birth Anniversary of Thomas Hardy (author). Multicoloured Phosphorised paper. Perf 14×15.

1506	**954**	20p. Thomas Hardy	30	30
Gutter Pair			60	
First Day Cover				40
Presentation Pack (PO Pack No. 209)			55	
PHQ Card (127)			20	40

955 Queen Elizabeth the Queen Mother **956** Queen Elizabeth

957 Elizabeth, Duchess of York **958** Lady Elizabeth Bowes-Lyon

1990 (2 Aug). 90th Birthday of Queen Elizabeth the Queen Mother. Multicoloured Phosphorised paper. Perf 14×15.

1507	**955**	20p. Queen Elizabeth the Queen Mother	40	40

69

1508	**956**	29p. Queen Elizabeth	60	60
1509	**957**	34p. Elizabeth, Duchess of York	90	90
1510	**958**	37p. Lady Elizabeth Bowes-Lyon	1·10	1·10
Set of 4			2·75	2·75
Set of 4 Gutter Pairs			5·50	
First Day Cover				2·90
Presentation Pack (PO Pack No. 210)			2·90	
PHQ Cards (*set of 4*) (128)			80	2·90

For these designs with Queen's head and frame in black see Nos. 2280/2283.

For Nos. 1511/1516 see Decimal Machin Definitives section.

959 Victoria Cross   **960** George Cross

961 Distinguished Service Cross and Distinguished Service Medal

962 Military Cross and Military Medal

963 Distinguished Flying Cross and Distinguished Flying Medal

1990 (11 Sept). Gallantry Awards. Multicoloured Phosphorised paper. Perf 14×15 (vert) or 15×14 (horiz).

1517	**959**	20p. Victoria Cross	35	35
1518	**960**	20p. George Cross	35	35
1519	**961**	20p. Distinguished Service Cross and Distinguished Service Medal	35	35
1520	**962**	20p. Military Cross and Military Medal	35	35
1521	**963**	20p. Distinguished Flying Cross and Distinguished Flying Medal	35	35
Set of 5			1·50	1·50
Set of 5 Gutter Pairs			3·00	
First Day Cover				1·60
Presentation Pack (PO Pack No. 211)			1·60	
PHQ Cards (*set of 5*) (129)			1·00	1·60

For T **959** with 'all-over' phosphor and Perf 14×14½ see No. 2666.

964 Armagh Observatory, Jodrell Bank Radio Telescope and La Palma Telescope

965 Newton's Moon and Tides Diagram and Early Telescopes

966 Greenwich Old Observatory and Early Astronomical Equipment

967 Stonehenge, Gyroscope and Navigation by Stars

1990 (16 Oct). Astronomy. Multicoloured Phosphorised paper. Perf 14×14½.

1522	**964**	22p. Armagh Observatory, Jodrell Bank Radio Telescope and La Palma Telescope	25	25
1523	**965**	26p. Newton's Moon and Tides Diagram and Early Telescopes	35	35
1524	**966**	31p. Greenwich Old Observatory and Early Astronomical Equipment	45	45
1525	**967**	37p. Stonehenge, Gyroscope and Navigation by Stars	60	60
Set of 4			1·50	1·50
Set of 4 Gutter Pairs			3·00	
First Day Cover				1·60
Presentation Pack (PO Pack No. 212)			1·60	
PHQ Cards (*set of 4*) (130)			80	1·60

Nos. 1522/1525 marked the centenary of the British Astronomical Association and the bicentenary of the Armagh Observatory.

968 Building a Snowman   **969** Fetching the Christmas Tree

970 Carol Singing   **971** Tobogganing

972 Ice Skating

1990 (13 Nov). Christmas. Multicoloured One phosphor band (17p.) or phosphorised paper (others). Perf 15×14.

1526	**968**	17p. Building a Snowman	25	25
1527	**969**	22p. Fetching the Christmas Tree	25	25
1528	**970**	26p. Carol Singing	35	35
1529	**971**	31p. Tobogganing	45	40
1530	**972**	37p. Ice skating	60	60
Set of 5			1·75	1·75
Set of 5 Gutter Pairs			3·50	
First Day Cover				1·90
Presentation Pack (PO Pack No. 213)			1·90	
PHQ Cards (*set of 5*) (131)			1·00	1·90

Collectors Pack

1990 (13 Nov). Comprises Nos. 1479/1482, 1493/1510 and 1517/1530.

| CP1530*a* | Collectors Pack (Pack No. 214) | 18·00 | |

Post Office Yearbook

1990 (13 Nov). Comprises Nos. 1479/1482, 1493/1500, 1502/1510, 1517/1530 in hardbound book with slip case

| YB1530*a* | Yearbook | 18·00 | |

KING CHARLES SPANIEL
GEORGE STUBBS

A POINTER
GEORGE STUBBS

973 *King Charles Spaniel*   **974** *A Pointer*

TWO HOUNDS IN A LANDSCAPE
GEORGE STUBBS

A ROUGH DOG
GEORGE STUBBS

975 *Two Hounds in a*   **976** *A Rough Dog*
Landscape

FINO AND TINY
GEORGE STUBBS

977 *Fino and Tiny*

1991 (8 Jan). Dogs. Paintings by George Stubbs. Multicoloured Phosphorised paper. Perf 14×14½.

1531	**973**	22p. *King Charles Spaniel*	25	25
1532	**974**	26p. *A Pointer*	30	30
1533	**975**	31p. *Two Hounds in a Landscape*	40	40
1534	**976**	33p. *A Rough Dog*	45	45
1535	**977**	37p. *Fino and Tiny*	60	60
Set of 5			1·75	1·75
Set of 5 Gutter Pairs			3·50	
First Day Cover				2·00
Presentation Pack (PO Pack No. 215)			2·00	
PHQ Cards (*set of 5*) (132)			1·00	2·00

978 Thrush's Nest   **979** Shooting Star and Rainbow

980 Magpies and Charm   **981** Black Cat
Bracelet

982 Common Kingfisher with   **983** Mallard and Frog
Key

984 Four-leaf Clover in Boot and   **985** Pot of Gold at End of
Match Box   Rainbow

986 Heart-shaped Butterflies   **987** Wishing Well and Sixpence

1991 (5 Feb). Greetings Stamps. Good Luck. Multicoloured Two phosphor bands. Perf 15×14.

1536	**978**	(1st) Thrush's Nest	1·20	1·00
1537	**979**	(1st) Shooting Star and Rainbow	1·20	1·00
1538	**980**	(1st) Magpies and Charm Bracelet	1·20	1·00
1539	**981**	(1st) Black Cat	1·20	1·00
1540	**982**	(1st) Common Kingfisher with Key	1·20	1·00
1541	**983**	(1st) Mallard and Frog	1·20	1·00
1542	**984**	(1st) Four-leaf clover in Boot and Match Box	1·20	1·00
1543	**985**	(1st) Pot of Gold at End of Rainbow	1·20	1·00
1544	**986**	(1st) Heart-shaped Butterflies	1·20	1·00
1545	**987**	(1st) Wishing Well and Sixpence	1·20	1·00
Set of 10			10·50	9·00
First Day Cover				9·25

Nos. 1536/1545 were printed together, *se-tenant*, in booklet panes of ten stamps and 12 half stamp-size labels.

The backgrounds of the stamps form a composite design.

Faraday – Electricity   Babbage – Computer

988 Michael Faraday   **989** Charles Babbage
(inventor of electric   (computer science
motor) (Birth   pioneer) (Birth
Bicentenary)   Bicentenary)

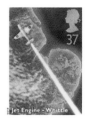

Radar – Watson Watt   Jet Engine – Whittle

990 Radar Sweep   **991** Gloster Whittle
of East Anglia (50th   E28/39 over East
Anniversary of   Anglia (50th
Operational Radar   Anniversary of First
Network)   Flight of Sir Frank
    Whittle's Jet Engine)

1991 (5 Mar). Scientific Achievements. Multicoloured Phosphorised paper. Perf 14×15.

1546	**988**	22p. Michael Faraday	35	35
1547	**989**	22p. Charles Babbage	35	35
1548	**990**	31p. Radar Sweep of East Anglia	55	55
1549	**991**	37p. Gloster Whittle E28/39 over East Anglia	65	65
Set of 4			1·75	1·75
Set of 4 Gutter Pairs			3·50	

First Day Cover		1·90
Presentation Pack (PO Pack No. 216)	1·90	
PHQ Cards (set of 4) (133)	50	1·90

992 Teddy Bear

1991 (26 Mar). Greetings Stamps. Smiles. As Nos. 1483/1492, but inscribed '1st' as T **992**. Multicoloured Two phosphor bands. Perf 15×14.

1550	992	(1st) Teddy Bear	1·20	1·00
1551	935	(1st) Dennis the Menace	1·20	1·00
1552	936	(1st) Punch	1·20	1·00
1553	937	(1st) Cheshire Cat	1·20	1·00
1554	938	(1st) The Man in the Moon	1·20	1·00
1555	939	(1st) The Laughing Policeman	1·20	1·00
1556	940	(1st) Clown	1·20	1·00
1557	941	(1st) *Mona Lisa*	1·20	1·00
1558	942	(1st) Queen of Hearts	1·20	1·00
1559	943	(1st) Stan Laurel	1·20	1·00
Set of 10			10·50	9·00
First Day Cover				9·25

Nos. 1550/1559 were originally printed together, *se-tenant,* in booklet panes of ten stamps and 12 half-size labels.

The stamps were re-issued in sheets of ten, printed in photogravure, each with *se-tenant* label on 22 May 2000 in connection with 'customised' stamps available at Stamp Show 2000. The labels show either a pattern of ribbons or a personal photograph.

A similar sheet, but printed in lithography instead of in photogravure, and perforated 14½×14 appeared on 3 July 2001 with the labels showing either greetings or personal photographs.

On 1 October 2002 three further sheets appeared printed in lithography. One contained Nos. 1550/1551 each×10 with greetings labels. Both designs were also available in sheets of 20 with personal photographs.

993 Man Looking at Space

994 Man Looking at Space

995 Space Looking at Man

996 Space Looking at Man

1991 (23 Apr). Europa. Europe in space. Multicoloured. Phosphorised paper. Perf 14½×14.

1560	993	22p. Man Looking at Space	35	35
		a. Horiz pair. Nos 1560/1561	75	75
1561	994	22p. Man Looking at Space	35	35
1562	995	37p. Space Looking at Man	65	65
		a. Horiz pair. Nos. 1562/1563	1·40	1·40
1563	996	37p. Space Looking at Man	65	65
Set of 4			1·90	1·90
Set of 2 Gutter Pairs of 4			3·75	
First Day Cover				2·10
Presentation Pack (PO Pack No. 217)			2·10	
PHQ Cards (set of 4) (134)			80	2·10

Nos. 1560/1561 and 1562/1563 were each printed together, *se-tenant,* in horizontal pairs throughout the sheets, each pair forming a composite design.

997 Fencing

998 Hurdling

999 Diving

1000 Rugby

1991 (11 June). World Student Games, Sheffield (Nos.1564/1566) and World Cup Rugby Championship, London (No. 1567). Multicoloured Phosphorised paper. Perf 14½×14.

1564	997	22p. Fencing	35	35
1565	998	26p. Hurdling	45	45
1566	999	31p. Diving	55	55
1567	1000	37p. Rugby	75	75
Set of 4			1·90	1·90
Set of 4 Gutter Pairs			3·75	
First Day Cover				2·10
Presentation Pack (PO Pack No. 218)			2·10	
PHQ Cards (set of 4) (135)			80	2·10

1001 'Silver Jubilee'

1002 'Mme Alfred Carrière'

1003 *Rosa moyesii*

1004 'Harvest Fayre'

1005 'Mutabilis'

1991 (16 July). Ninth World Congress of Roses, Belfast. Multicoloured Phosphorised paper. Perf 14½×14.

1568	1001	22p. 'Silver Jubilee'	30	30
1569	1002	26p. 'Mme Alfred Carrière'	35	35
1570	1003	31p. *Rosa moyesii*	40	40
1571	1004	33p. 'Harvest Fayre'	55	55
1572	1005	37p. 'Mutabilis'	65	65
Set of 5			2·00	2·00
Set of 5 Gutter Pairs			4·00	
First Day Cover				2·25
Presentation Pack (PO Pack No. 219)			2·25	
PHQ Cards (set of 5) (136)			60	2·25

1006 Iguanodon   **1007** Stegosaurus

1008 Tyrannosaurus   **1009** Protoceratops

1010 Triceratops

1991 (20 Aug). 150th Anniversary of Dinosaurs' Identification by Owen. Multicoloured Phosphorised paper. Perf 14½×14.

1573	**1006**	22p. Iguanodon	35	35
1574	**1007**	26p. Stegosaurus	40	40
1575	**1008**	31p. Tyrannosaurus	45	45
1576	**1009**	33p. Protoceratops	60	60
1577	**1010**	37p. Triceratops	75	75
Set of 5			2·25	2·25
Set of 5 Gutter Pairs			4·50	
First Day Cover				2·75
Presentation Pack (PO Pack No. 220)			3·00	
PHQ Cards (set of 5) (137)			1·00	2·50

1011 Map of 1816   **1012** Map of 1906

1013 Map of 1959   **1014** Map of 1991

1991 (17 Sept). Bicentenary of Ordnance Survey. Maps of Hamstreet, Kent. Multicoloured. Phosphorised paper. Perf 14½×14.

1578	**1011**	24p. Map of 1816	35	35
1579	**1012**	28p. Map of 1906	45	45
1580	**1013**	33p. Map of 1959	55	55
1581	**1014**	39p. Map of 1991	75	75
Set of 4			1·90	1·90
Set of 4 Gutter Pairs			3·75	

First Day Cover		2·00
Presentation Pack (PO Pack No. 221)	2·25	
PHQ Cards (set of 4) (138)	80	2·00

1015 Adoration of the Magi   **1016** Mary and Jesus in Stable

1017 Holy Family and Angel   **1018** The Annunciation

1019 The Flight into Egypt

1991 (12 Nov). Christmas. Illuminated Letters from Acts of Mary and Jesus Manuscript in Bodleian Library, Oxford. Multicoloured One phosphor band (18p.) or phosphorised paper (others). Perf 15×14.

1582	**1015**	18p. Adoration of the Magi	25	25
1583	**1016**	24p. Mary and Jesus in Stable	30	30
1584	**1017**	28p. Holy Family and Angel	40	40
1585	**1018**	33p. The Annunciation	55	55
1586	**1019**	39p. The Flight into Egypt	70	70
Set of 5			1·90	1·90
Set of 5 Gutter Pairs			3·75	
First Day Cover				2·00
Presentation Pack (PO Pack No. 222)			2·10	
PHQ Cards (set of 5) (139)			60	2·00

Collectors Pack

1991 (12 Nov). Comprises Nos. 1531/1535, 1546/5419 and 1560/1586.

CP1586a	Collectors Pack (Pack No. 223)	18·00

Post Office Yearbook

1991 (13 Nov). Comprises Nos. 1531/1535, 1546/1549 and 1560/1586 in hardbound book with slip case

YB1586a	Yearbook	16·00

1020 Fallow Deer in Scottish Forest   **1021** Hare on North Yorkshire Moors

1022 Fox in the Fens   **1023** Redwing and Home Counties Village

73

1024 Welsh Mountain Sheep in Snowdonia

1992 (14 Jan). The Four Seasons. Wintertime. Multicoloured One phosphor band (18p.) or phosphorised paper (others). Perf 15×14.

1587	**1020**	18p. Fallow Deer in Scottish Forest	25	25
1588	**1021**	24p. Hare on North Yorkshire Moors	30	30
1589	**1022**	28p. Fox in the Fens	45	45
1590	**1023**	33p. Redwing and Home Counties Village	55	55
1591	**1024**	39p. Welsh Mountain Sheep in Snowdonia	70	70
Set of 5			2·00	2·00
Set of 5 Gutter Pairs			4·00	
First Day Cover				2·10
Presentation Pack (PO Pack No. 224)			2·25	
PHQ Cards (set of 5) (140)			1·00	2·10

1025 Flower Spray

1026 Double Locket

1027 Key

1028 Model Car and Cigarette Cards

1029 Compass and Map

1030 Pocket Watch

1031 1854 1d. Red Stamp and Pen

1032 Pearl Necklace and Pen

1033 Marbles

1034 Bucket, Spade and Starfish

1992 (28 Jan). Greetings Stamps. Memories. Multicoloured Two phosphor bands. Perf 15×14.

1592	**1025**	(1st) Flower Spray	1·20	1·00
1593	**1026**	(1st) Double Locket	1·20	1·00
1594	**1027**	(1st) Key	1·20	1·00
1595	**1028**	(1st) Model Car and Cigarette Cards	1·20	1·00
1596	**1029**	(1st) Compass and Map	1·20	1·00
1597	**1030**	(1st) Pocket Watch	1·20	1·00
1598	**1031**	(1st) 1854 1d. Red Stamp and Pen	1·20	1·00
1599	**1032**	(1st) Pearl Necklace and Pen	1·20	1·00
1600	**1033**	(1st) Marbles	1·20	1·00
1601	**1034**	(1st) Bucket, Spade and Starfish	1·20	1·00
Set of 10			10·50	9·25
First Day Cover				9·50
Presentation Pack (PO Pack No. G1)			13·50	

Nos. 1592/1601 were originally printed together, *se-tenant*, in booklet panes of ten stamps and 12 half-size labels.

The backgrounds of the stamps form a composite design.

1035 Queen Elizabeth in Coronation Robes and Parliamentary Emblem

1036 Queen Elizabeth in Garter Robes and Archiepiscopal Arms

1037 Queen Elizabeth with Baby Prince Andrew and Royal Arms

1038 Queen Elizabeth at Trooping the Colour and Service Emblems

1039 Queen Elizabeth and Commonwealth Emblem

1992 (6 Feb). 40th Anniversary of Accession. Two phosphor bands. Perf 14½×14.

1602	**1035**	24p. Queen Elizabeth in Coronation Robes and Parliamentary Emblem	40	50
		a. Horiz strip of 5. Nos. 1602/1606	2·75	3·00
1603	**1036**	24p. Queen Elizabeth in Garter Robes and Archiepiscopal Arms	40	50
1604	**1037**	24p. Queen Elizabeth with Baby Prince Andrew and Royal Arms	40	50
1605	**1038**	24p. Queen Elizabeth at Trooping the Colour and Service Emblems	40	50
1606	**1039**	24p. Queen Elizabeth and Commonwealth Emblem	40	50
Set of 5			2·75	3·00
Gutter Block of 10			5·50	
First Day Cover				3·25
Presentation Pack (PO Pack No. 225)			3·25	
PHQ Cards (set of 5) (141)			1·00	3·25

Nos. 1602/1606 were printed together, *se-tenant*, in horizontal strips of five throughout the sheet.

1040 Tennyson in 1888 and *The Beguiling of Merlin* (Sir Edward Burne-Jones)

1041 Tennyson in 1856 and *April Love* (Arthur Hughes)

1042 Tennyson in 1864 and *I am Sick of the Shadows* (John Waterhouse)

1043 Tennyson as a Young Man and *Mariana* (Dante Gabriel Rossetti)

1992 (10 Mar). Death Centenary of Alfred, Lord Tennyson (poet). Multicoloured Phosphorised paper. Perf 14½×14.

1607	**1040**	24p. Tennyson in 1888 and *The Beguiling of Merlin*	35	35
1608	**1041**	28p. Tennyson in 1856 and *April Love*	50	50
1609	**1042**	33p. Tennyson in 1864 and *I am Sick of the Shadows*	60	60
1610	**1043**	39p. Tennyson as a Young Man and *Mariana*	75	75
Set of 4			2·00	2·00
Set of 4 Gutter Pairs			4·00	
First Day Cover				2·25
Presentation Pack (PO Pack No. 226)			2·25	
PHQ Cards (Set of 4) (142)			80	2·25

1044 Carrickfergus Castle   **1044a** Caernarfon Castle

1044b Edinburgh Castle   **1044c** Carrickfergus Castle

1044d Windsor Castle

1992 (24 Mar)–**95**. Designs as Nos. 1410/1413, but showing Queen's head in silhouette as T **1044**. Perf 15×14 (with one elliptical hole in each vertical side).

1611	**1044**	£1 Carrickfergus Castle (bottle green and gold†)	5·50	50
1612	**1044a**	£1·50 Caernarfon Castle (maroon and gold†)	6·00	75
1613	**1044b**	£2 Edinburgh Castle (indigo and gold†)	8·00	1·00
1613a	**1044c**	£3 Carrickfergus Castle (reddish violet and gold†) (22.8.95)	19·00	1·75
1614	**1044d**	£5 Windsor Castle (deep brown and gold†)	18·00	2·00
Set of 5			50·00	5·50
Set of 5 Gutter Pairs (vert or horiz)			£100	
First Day Cover (Nos. 1611/1613, 1614)				20·00
First Day Cover (No. 1613a)				6·00
Presentation Pack (PO Pack No. 27) (Nos. 1611/1613, 1614)			38·00	

Presentation Pack (PO Pack No. 33) (No. 1613a)	20·00	
PHQ Cards (D2–D5)†† (Nos. 1611/1613, 1614)	80	6·00
PHQ Card (D8) (No. 1613a)	20	2·00

† The Queen's head on these stamps is printed in optically variable ink which changes colour from gold to green when viewed from different angles.

†† The PHQ Cards for this issue did not appear until 16 February 1993.
The £1·50 (5 March 1996), £2 (2 May 1996), £3 (February 1997) and £5 (17 September 1996) subsequently appeared on PVA (white gum) instead of the tinted PVAD previously used.
See also Nos. 1410/1413 and 1993/1996.

1045 British Olympic Association Logo (Olympic Games, Barcelona)

1046 British Paralympic Association Symbol (Paralympics '92, Barcelona)

1047 *Santa Maria* (500th Anniversary of Discovery of America by Columbus)

1048 *Kaisei* (Japanese cadet brigantine) (Grand Regatta Columbus, 1992)

1049 British Pavilion, EXPO '92, Seville

1992 (7 Apr). Europa. International Events. Multicoloured Phosphorised paper. Perf 14×14½.

1615	**1045**	24p. British Olympic Association Logo	30	30
		a. Horiz pair. Nos. 1615/1616	80	80
1616	**1046**	24p. British Paralympic Association Symbol	30	30
1617	**1047**	24p. *Santa Maria*	40	40
1618	**1048**	39p. *Kaisei*	65	65
1619	**1049**	39p. British Pavilion, EXPO '92, Seville	65	65
Set of 5			2·25	2·25
Set of 3 Gutter Pairs and a Gutter Strip of 4			4·50	
First Day Cover				2·50
Presentation Pack (PO Pack No. 227)			2·50	
PHQ Cards (set of 5) (143)			1·00	2·50

Nos. 1615/1616 were printed together, *se-tenant*, in horizontal pairs throughout the sheet.

1050 Pikeman   **1051** Drummer

1052 Musketeer   **1053** Standard-bearer

1992 (16 June). 350th Anniversary of the Civil War. Multicoloured Phosphorised paper. Perf 14½×14.

1620	**1050**	24p. Pikeman	35	35
1621	**1051**	28p. Drummer	45	45
1622	**1052**	33p. Musketeer	55	55
1623	**1053**	39p. Standard-bearer	70	70
Set of 4			1·90	1·90
Set of 4 Gutter Pairs			3·75	
First Day Cover				2·00
Presentation Pack (PO Pack No. 228)			2·00	
PHQ Cards (set of 4) (144)			80	2·00

1054 *The Yeomen of the Guard*   **1055** *The Gondoliers*

1056 *The Mikado*   **1057** *The Pirates of Penzance*

1058 *Iolanthe*

1992 (21 July). 150th Birth Anniversary of Sir Arthur Sullivan (composer). Gilbert and Sullivan Operas. Multicoloured One phosphor band (18p.) or phosphorised paper (others). Perf 14½×14.

1624	**1054**	18p. *The Yeomen of the Guard*	25	25
1625	**1055**	24p. *The Gondoliers*	30	30
1626	**1056**	28p. *The Mikado*	40	40
1627	**1057**	33p. *The Pirates of Penzance*	55	55
1628	**1058**	39p. *Iolanthe*	70	70
Set of 5			2·00	2·00
Set of 5 Gutter Pairs			4·00	
First Day Cover				2·25
Presentation Pack (PO Pack No. 229)			2·25	
PHQ Cards (set of 5) (145)			1·00	2·25

1059 'Acid Rain Kills'   **1060** 'Ozone Layer'

1061 'Greenhouse Effect'   **1062** 'Bird of Hope'

1992 (15 Sept). Protection of the Environment. Children's Paintings. Multicoloured Phosphorised paper. Perf 14×14½.

1629	**1059**	24p. 'Acid Rain Kills'	35	35
1630	**1060**	28p. 'Ozone Layer'	40	40
1631	**1061**	33p. 'Greenhouse Effect'	55	55
1632	**1062**	39p. 'Bird of Hope'	70	70
Set of 4			1·75	1·75
Set of 4 Gutter Pairs			3·50	
First Day Cover				1·90
Presentation Pack (PO Pack No. 230)			2·00	
PHQ Cards (set of 4) (146)			80	1·90

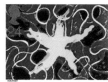

1063 European Star

1992 (13 Oct). Single European Market. Multicoloured Phosphorised paper. Perf 15×14.

1633	**1063**	24p. European Star	40	40
Gutter Pair			80	
First Day Cover				75
Presentation Pack (PO Pack No. 231)			80	
PHQ Card (147)			20	50

1064 Angel Gabriel, St James's, Pangbourne   **1065** Madonna and Child, St Mary's, Bibury

1066 King with Gold, Our Lady and St Peter, Leatherhead   **1067** Shepherds, All Saints, Porthcawl

1068 Kings with Frankincense and Myrrh, Our Lady and St Peter, Leatherhead

1992 (10 Nov). Christmas. Stained-glass Windows. Multicoloured One centre band (18p.) or phosphorised paper (others). Perf 15×14.

1634	**1064**	18p. Angel Gabriel	25	25
1635	**1065**	24p. Madonna and Child	30	30
1636	**1066**	28p. King with Gold	40	40
1637	**1067**	33p. Shepherds	55	55
1638	**1068**	39p. Kings with Frankincense and Myrrh	70	70
Set of 5			2·00	2·00
Set of 5 Gutter Pairs			4·00	
First Day Cover				2·10
Presentation Pack (PO Pack No. 232)			2·25	
PHQ Cards (*set of 5*) (148)			1·00	2·25

Collectors Pack

1992 (10 Nov). Comprises Nos. 1587/1591, 1602/1610 and 1615/1638.

CP1638*a*	Collectors Pack (Pack No. 233)	19·00

Post Office Yearbook

1992 (11 Nov). Comprises Nos. 1587/1591, 1602/1610 and 1615/1638 in hardbound book with slip case, illustrated in colour

YB1638*a*	Yearbook	19·00

1069 Mute Swan Cob and St Catherine's Chapel, Abbotsbury

1070 Cygnet and Decoy

1071 Swans and Cygnet

1072 Eggs in Nest and Tithe Barn, Abbotsbury

1073 Young Swan and the Fleet

1993 (19 Jan). 600th Anniversary of Abbotsbury Swannery. Multicoloured One phosphor band (18p.) or phosphorised paper (others). Perf 14×15.

1639	**1069**	18p. Mute Swan Cob	30	30
1640	**1070**	24p. Cygnet	50	50
1641	**1071**	28p. Swans and Cygnet	80	80
1642	**1072**	33p. Eggs in Nest	1·00	1·00
1643	**1073**	39p. Young Swan	1·40	1·40
Set of 5			3·75	3·75
Set of 5 Gutter Pairs			7·50	
First Day Cover				4·00
Presentation Pack (PO Pack No. 234)			4·00	
PHQ Cards (*set of 5*) (149)			1·00	4·00

1074 Long John Silver and Parrot (*Treasure Island*)

1075 Tweedledum and Tweedledee (*Alice Through the Looking-Glass*)

1076 William (*William* books)

1077 Mole and Toad (*The Wind in the Willows*)

1078 Teacher and Wilfrid (*The Bash Street Kids*)

1079 Peter Rabbit and Mrs Rabbit (*The Tale of Peter Rabbit*)

1080 Snowman (*The Snowman*) and Father Christmas (*Father Christmas*)

1081 The Big Friendly Giant and Sophie (*The BFG*)

1082 Bill Badger and Rupert Bear

1083 Aladdin and the Genie

1993 (2 Feb). Greetings Stamps. Gift Giving. Multicoloured Two phosphor bands. Perf 15×14 (with one elliptical hole in each horizontal side).

1644	**1074**	(1st) Long John Silver and Parrot	1·20	1·00
1645	**1075**	(1st) Tweedledum and Tweedledee	1·20	1·00
1646	**1076**	(1st) William	1·20	1·00
1647	**1077**	(1st) Mole and Toad	1·20	1·00
1648	**1078**	(1st) Teacher and Wilfrid	1·20	1·00
1649	**1079**	(1st) Peter Rabbit and Mrs Rabbit (Mrs Rabbit in blue dress)	1·20	1·00
1650	**1080**	(1st) Snowman and Father Christmas	1·20	1·00
1651	**1081**	(1st) The Big Friendly Giant and Sophie	1·20	1·00
1652	**1082**	(1st) Bill Badger and Rupert Bear	1·20	1·00
1653	**1083**	(1st) Aladdin and the Genie	1·20	1·00
Set of 10			10·50	9·25
First Day Cover				9·50
Presentation Pack (PO Pack No. G2)			13·50	
PHQ Cards (*set of 10*) (GS1)			2·00	9·50

Nos. 1644/1653 were printed together *se-tenant* in booklet panes of ten stamps and 20 half stamp-sized labels.

1084 Decorated Enamel Dial

1085 Escapement, Remontoire and Fusée

1086 Balance, Spring and Temperature Compensator

1087 Back of Movement

1993 (16 Feb). 300th Birth Anniversary of John Harrison (inventor of the marine chronometer). Details of 'H4' Clock. Multicoloured Phosphorised paper. Perf 14½×14.

1654	**1084**	24p. Decorated Enamel Dial	30	30
1655	**1085**	28p. Escapement, Remontoire and Fusée	45	45
1656	**1086**	33p. Balance, Spring and Temperature Compensator	55	55
1657	**1087**	39p. Back of Movement	70	70
Set of 4			1·75	1·75
Set of 4 Gutter Pairs			3·50	
First Day Cover				2·00
Presentation Pack (PO Pack No. 235)			2·00	
PHQ Cards (set of 4) (150)			80	2·00

1088 Britannia

1993 (2 Mar). Granite paper. Multicoloured Perf 14×14½ (with two elliptical holes in each horizontal side).

1658	**1088**	£10 Britannia	40·00	12·00
First Day Cover				18·00
Presentation Pack (PO Pack No. 28)			45·00	
PHQ Card (D1)			50	25·00

1089 Dendrobium hellwigianum

1090 Paphiopedilum Maudiae 'Magnificum'

1091 Cymbidium lowianum

1092 Vanda Rothschildiana

1093 Dendrobium vexillarius var albiviride

1993 (16 Mar). 14th World Orchid Conference, Glasgow. Multicoloured One phosphor band (18p.) or phosphorised paper (others). Perf 15×14.

1659	**1089**	18p. Dendrobium hellwigianum	30	30
1660	**1090**	24p. Paphiopedilum Maudiae 'Magnificum'	35	35
1661	**1091**	28p. Cymbidium lowianum	45	45
1662	**1092**	33p. Vanda Rothschildiana	50	50
1663	**1093**	39p. Dendrobium vexillarius var albiviride	60	60
Set of 5			2·00	2·00
Set of 5 Gutter Pairs			4·00	
First Day Cover				2·25
Presentation Pack (PO Pack No. 236)			2·25	
PHQ Cards (set of 5) (151)			1·00	2·25

1094 Family Group (bronze sculpture) (Henry Moore)

1095 Kew Gardens (lithograph) (Edward Bawden)

1096 St Francis and the Birds (Stanley Spencer)

1097 Still Life: Odyssey I (Ben Nicholson)

1993 (11 May). Europa. Contemporary Art. Multicoloured Phosphorised paper. Perf 14×14½.

1767	**1094**	24p. Family Group (bronze sculpture) (Henry Moore)	35	35
1768	**1095**	28p. Kew Gardens (lithograph) (Edward Bawden)	50	50
1769	**1096**	33p. St Francis and the Birds (Stanley Spencer)	60	60
1770	**1097**	39p. Still Life: Odyssey I (Ben Nicholson)	70	70
Set of 4			2·00	2·00
Set of 4 Gutter Pairs			4·00	
First Day Cover				2·25
Presentation Pack (PO Pack No. 237)			2·25	
PHQ Cards (set of 4) (152)			80	2·25

1098 Emperor Claudius (from gold coin)

1099 Emperor Hadrian (bronze head)

1100 Goddess Roma (from gemstone)

1101 Christ (Hinton St Mary mosaic)

1993 (15 June). Roman Britain. Multicoloured Phosphorised paper with two phosphor bands. Perf 14×14½.

1771	**1098**	24p. Emperor Claudius	35	35
1772	**1099**	28p. Emperor Hadrian	50	50
1773	**1100**	33p. Goddess Roma	60	60
1774	**1101**	39p. Christ	70	70
Set of 4			2·00	2·00
Set of 4 Gutter Pairs			4·00	
First Day Cover				2·25
Presentation Pack (PO Pack No. 238)			2·25	
PHQ Cards (set of 4) (153)			80	2·25

1102 *Midland Maid* and other Narrow Boats, Grand Junction Canal

1103 *Yorkshire Lass* and other Humber Keels, Stainforth and Keadby Canal

1104 *Valley Princess* and other Horse-drawn Barges, Brecknock and Abergavenny Canal

1105 Steam Barges, including *Pride of Scotland*, and Fishing Boats, Crinan Canal

1993 (20 July). Inland Waterways. Multicoloured Two phosphor bands. Perf 14½×14.

1775	**1102**	24p. Narrow Boats, Grand Junction Canal	35	35
1776	**1103**	28p. Humber Keels, Stainforth and Keadby Canal	50	50
1777	**1104**	33p. Horse-drawn Barges, Brecknock and Abergavenny Canal	60	60
1778	**1105**	39p. Steam Barges and Fishing Boats, Crinan Canal	70	70
Set of 4			2·00	2·00
Set of 4 Gutter Pairs			4·00	
First Day Cover				2·25
Presentation Pack (PO Pack No. 239)			2·25	
PHQ Cards (set of 4) (154)			50	2·25

Nos. 1775/1778 commemorate the bicentenary of the Acts of Parliament authorising the canals depicted.

1106 Horse Chestnut

1107 Blackberry

1108 Hazel

1109 Rowan

1110 Pear

1993 (14 Sept). The Four Seasons. Autumn. Fruits and Leaves. Multicoloured One phosphor band (18p.) or phosphorised paper (others). Perf 15×14.

1779	**1106**	18p. Horse Chestnut	30	30
1780	**1107**	24p. Blackberry	35	35
1781	**1108**	28p. Hazel	45	45
1782	**1109**	33p. Rowan	50	50
1783	**1110**	39p. Pear	60	60
Set of 5			2·00	2·00
Set of 5 Gutter Pairs			4·00	
First Day Cover				2·25
Presentation Pack (PO Pack No. 240)			2·25	
PHQ Cards (set of 5) (155)			1·00	2·25

SHERLOCK HOLMES & DR. WATSON "THE REIGATE SQUIRE"

SHERLOCK HOLMES & SIR HENRY "THE HOUND OF THE BASKERVILLES"

1111 The Reigate Squire

1112 The Hound of the Baskervilles

SHERLOCK HOLMES & LESTRADE "THE SIX NAPOLEONS"

SHERLOCK HOLMES & MYCROFT "THE GREEK INTERPRETER"

1113 The Six Napoleons

1114 The Greek Interpreter

1115 *The Final Problem*

1993 (12 Oct). Sherlock Holmes. Centenary of the Publication of *The Final Problem*. Multicoloured Phosphorised paper. Perf 14×14½.

1784	**1111**	24p. *The Reigate Squire*	30	30
		a. Horiz strip of 5. Nos. 1784/1788	1·90	2·40
1785	**1112**	24p. *The Hound of the Baskervilles*	30	30
1786	**1113**	24p. *The Six Napoleons*	30	30
1787	**1114**	24p. *The Greek Interpreter*	30	30
1788	**1115**	24p. *The Final Problem*	30	30
Set of 5			1·90	2·40
Gutter strip of 10			3·75	
First Day Cover				2·50
Presentation Pack (PO Pack No. 241)			2·75	
PHQ Cards (set of 5) (156)			1·00	2·50

Nos. 1784/1788 were printed together, *se-tenant*, in horizontal strips of five throughout the sheet.

For No. 1789, T **1116**, see Decimal Machin Definitives section.

1117 Bob Cratchit and Tiny Tim

1118 Mr and Mrs Fezziwig

1119 Scrooge

1120 The Prize Turkey

1121 Mr Scrooge's Nephew

1993 (9 Nov). Christmas. 150th Anniversary of Publication of *A Christmas Carol* by Charles Dickens. Multicoloured. One phosphor band (19p.) or phosphorised paper (others). Perf 15×14.

1790	**1117**	19p. Bob Cratchit and Tiny Tim	30	30
1791	**1118**	25p. Mr and Mrs Fezziwig	40	40
1792	**1119**	30p. Scrooge	50	50
1793	**1120**	35p. The Prize Turkey	55	55
1794	**1121**	41p. Mr Scrooge's Nephew	65	65
Set of 5			2·10	2·10
Set of 5 Gutter Pairs			4·25	
First Day Cover				2·50
Presentation Pack (PO Pack No. 242)			2·75	
PHQ Cards (set of 5) (157)			1·00	2·25

Collectors Pack

1993 (9 Nov). Comprises Nos. 1639/1643, 1654/1657, 1659/1663, 1767/1788 and 1790/1794.

CP1794*a*	Collectors Pack (Pack No. 243)	22·00

Post Office Yearbook

1993 (9 Nov). Comprises Nos. 1639/1643, 1654/1657, 1659/1663, 1767/1788 and 1790/1794 in hardbound book with slip case, illustrated in colour

YB1794*a*	Yearbook	20·00

1122 Class 5 No. 44957 and Class B1 No. 61342 on West Highland Line

1123 Class A1 No. 60149 *Amadis* at Kings Cross

1124 Class 4 No. 43000 on Turntable at Blyth North

1125 Class 4 No. 42455 near Wigan Central

1126 Class Castle No. 7002 *Devizes Castle* on Bridge crossing Worcester and Birmingham Canal

1994 (18 Jan). The Age of Steam. Railway Photographs by Colin Gifford. Multicoloured One phosphor band (19p.) or phosphorised paper with two bands (others). Perf 14½.

1795	**1122**	19p. Class 5 No. 44957 and Class B1 No. 61342	30	30
1796	**1123**	25p. Class A1 No. 60149 *Amadis*	40	40
1797	**1124**	30p. Class 4 No. 43000 on Turntable	50	50
1798	**1125**	35p. Class 4 No. 42455	60	60
1799	**1126**	41p. Class Castle No. 7002 *Devizes Castle* on Bridge	70	70
Set of 5			2·25	2·25
Set of 5 Gutter Pairs			4·50	
First Day Cover				2·50
Presentation Pack (PO Pack No. 244)			3·00	
PHQ Cards (set of 5) (158)			1·00	2·50

1127 Dan Dare and the Mekon

1128 The Three Bears

1129 Rupert Bear

1130 Alice (*Alice in Wonderland*)

1131 Noggin and the Ice Dragon

1132 Peter Rabbit posting Letter

1133 Red Riding Hood and the Wolf

1134 Orlando Marmalade Cat

1135 Biggles

1136 Paddington Bear on Station

1994 (1 Feb). Greetings Stamps. Messages. Multicoloured Two phosphor bands. Perf 15×14 (with one elliptical hole in each vertical side).

1800	**1127**	(1st) Dan Dare and the Mekon	1·20	1·00
1801	**1128**	(1st) The Three Bears	1·20	1·00
1802	**1129**	(1st) Rupert Bear	1·20	1·00
1803	**1130**	(1st) Alice (*Alice in Wonderland*)	1·20	1·00
1804	**1131**	(1st) Noggin and the Ice Dragon	1·20	1·00
1805	**1132**	(1st) Peter Rabbit posting Letter	1·20	1·00
1806	**1133**	(1st) Red Riding Hood and the Wolf	1·20	1·00
1807	**1134**	(1st) Orlando Marmalade Cat	1·20	1·00
1808	**1135**	(1st) Biggles	1·20	1·00
1809	**1136**	(1st) Paddington Bear on Station	1·20	1·00
Set of 10			10·50	9·00
First Day Cover				9·25
Presentation Pack (PO Pack No. G3)			13·50	
PHQ Cards (set of 10) (GS2)			2·00	9·25

Nos. 1800/1809 were printed together *se-tenant*, in booklet panes of ten stamps and 20 half stamp-sized labels.

1137 Castell Y Waun (Chirk Castle), Clwyd, Wales

1138 Ben Arkle, Sutherland, Scotland

1139 Mourne Mountains, County Down, Northern Ireland

1140 Dersingham, Norfolk, England

1141 Dolwyddelan, Gwynedd, Wales

1994 (1 Mar). 25th Anniversary of Investiture of the Prince of Wales. Paintings by Prince Charles. Multicoloured One phosphor band (19p.) or phosphorised paper (others). Perf 15×14.

1810	**1137**	19p. Castell Y Waun (Chirk Castle), Clwyd, Wales	30	30
1811	**1138**	25p. Ben Arkle, Sutherland, Scotland	35	35
1812	**1139**	30p. Mourne Mountains, County Down, Northern Ireland	45	45
1813	**1140**	35p. Dersingham, Norfolk, England	60	60
1814	**1141**	41p. Dolwyddelan, Gwynedd, Wales	70	70
Set of 5			2·25	2·25
Set of 5 Gutter Pairs			4·50	
First Day Cover				2·40
Presentation Pack (PO Pack No. 245)			2·50	
PHQ Cards (set of 5) (159)			1·00	2·50

1142 Bather at Blackpool

1143 Where's my Little Lad?

1144 Wish You were Here!

1145 Punch and Judy Show

1146 The Tower Crane Machine

1994 (12 Apr). Centenary of Picture Postcards. Multicoloured One side band (19p.) or two phosphor bands (others). Perf 14×14½.

1815	**1142**	19p. Bather at Blackpool	30	30
1816	**1143**	25p. Where's my Little Lad?	35	35
1817	**1144**	30p. Wish You were Here!	45	45
1818	**1145**	35p. Punch and Judy Show	60	60
1819	**1146**	41p. The Tower Crane Machine	70	70
Set of 5			2·25	2·25
Set of 5 Gutter Pairs			4·50	
First Day Cover				2·40
Presentation Pack (PO Pack No. 246)			2·40	
PHQ Cards (set of 5) (160)			1·00	2·40

1147 British Lion and French Cockerel over Tunnel

1148 Symbolic Hands over Train

1994 (3 May). Opening of Channel Tunnel. Multicoloured Phosphorised paper. Perf 14×14½

1820	**1147**	25p. British Lion and French Cockerel	30	35
		a. Horiz pair. Nos. 1820/1821	1·00	1·10
1821	**1148**	25p. Symbolic Hands over Train	30	35
1822	**1147**	41p. British Lion and French Cockerel	50	60
		a. Horiz pair. Nos. 1822/1823	1·50	1·75
1823	**1148**	41p. Symbolic Hands over Train	50	60
Set of 4			2·25	2·50
First Day Cover				2·75
First Day Covers (2) (UK and French stamps)				6·00
Presentation Pack (PO Pack No. 247)			2·75	
Presentation Pack (UK and French Stamps)			15·00	
Souvenir Book			32·00	
PHQ Cards (set of 4) (161)			60	2·50

Nos. 1820/1821 and 1822/1823 were printed together, *se-tenant*, in horizontal pairs throughout the sheets.

Stamps in similar designs were also issued by France. These are included in the joint presentation pack and souvenir book.

1149 Groundcrew replacing Smoke Canisters on Douglas Boston of 88 Sqn

1150 HMS *Warspite* (battleship) shelling Enemy Positions

1151 Commandos landing on Gold Beach

1152 Infantry regrouping on Sword Beach

1153 Tank and Infantry advancing, Ouistreham

1994 (6 June). 50th Anniversary of D-Day. Multicoloured Two phosphor bands. Perf 14½×14.

1824	**1149**	25p. Groundcrew replacing Smoke Canisters on Douglas Boston	35	30
		a. Horiz strip of 5. Nos. 1824/1828	2·10	1·75
1825	**1150**	25p. HMS *Warspite* shelling Enemy Positions	35	30
1826	**1151**	25p. Commandos landing on Gold Beach	35	30
1827	**1152**	25p. Infantry regrouping on Sword Beach	35	30
1828	**1153**	25p. Tank and Infantry advancing, Ouistreham	35	30
Set of 5			2·10	1·75
Gutter block of 10			4·25	
First Day Cover				1·90
Presentation Pack (PO Pack No. 248)			2·40	
PHQ Cards (set of 5) (162)			1·00	1·90

Nos. 1824/1828 were printed together, *se-tenant*, in horizontal strips of five throughout the sheet.

1154 The Old Course, St Andrews

1155 The 18th Hole, Muirfield

1156 The 15th Hole ('Luckyslap'), Carnoustie

1157 The 8th Hole ('The Postage Stamp'), Royal Troon

1158 The 9th Hole, Turnberry

1994 (5 July). Scottish Golf Courses. Multicoloured One phosphor band (19p.) or phosphorised paper (others). Perf 14½×14.

1829	**1154**	19p. The Old Course, St Andrews	30	30
1830	**1155**	25p. The 18th Hole, Muirfield	35	35
1831	**1156**	30p. The 15th Hole ('Luckyslap'), Carnoustie	45	45
1832	**1157**	35p. The 8th Hole ('The Postage Stamp'), Royal Troon	60	60
1833	**1158**	41p. The 9th Hole, Turnberry	70	70
Set of 5			2·10	2·10
Set of 5 Gutter Pairs			4·25	
First Day Cover				2·25
Presentation Pack (PO Pack No. 249)			2·40	
PHQ Cards (set of 5) (163)			1·00	2·25

Nos. 1829/1833 commemorate the 250th anniversary of golf's first set of rules produced by the Honourable Company of Edinburgh Golfers.

AMSER HAF/SUMMERTIME *Llanelwedd*

SUMMERTIME *Wimbledon*

1159 Royal Welsh Show, Llanelwedd

1160 All England Tennis Championships, Wimbledon

SUMMERTIME *Cowes*
1161 Cowes Week

SUMMERTIME *Lord's*
1162 Test Match, Lord's

SUMMERTIME *Braemar*
1163 Braemar Gathering

1994 (2 Aug). The Four Seasons. Summertime. Multicoloured One phosphor band (19p.) or phosphorised paper (others). Perf 15×14.

1834	**1159**	19p. Royal Welsh Show, Llanelwedd	30	30
1835	**1160**	25p. All England Tennis Championships, Wimbledon	35	35
1836	**1161**	30p. Cowes Week	45	45
1837	**1162**	35p. Test Match, Lord's	60	60
1838	**1163**	41p. Braemar Gathering	70	70
Set of 5			2·10	2·10
Set of 5 Gutter Pairs			4·25	
First Day Cover				2·25
Presentation Pack (PO Pack No. 250)			2·40	
PHQ Cards (set of 5) (164)			1·00	2·25

1164 Ultrasonic Imaging

1165 Scanning Electron Microscopy

1166 Magnetic Resonance Imaging

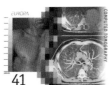

1167 Computed Tomography

1994 (27 Sept). Europa. Medical Discoveries. Multicoloured Phosphorised paper. Perf 14×14½.

1839	**1164**	25p. Ultrasonic Imaging	40	40
1840	**1165**	30p. Scanning Electron Microscopy	50	50
1841	**1166**	35p. Magnetic Resonance Imaging	60	60
1842	**1167**	41p. Computed Tomography	70	70
Set of 4			2·00	2·00
Set of 4 Gutter Pairs			4·00	
First Day Cover				2·25
Presentation Pack (PO Pack No. 251)			2·40	
PHQ Cards (set of 4) (165)			80	2·25

1168 Mary and Joseph

1169 Three Wise Men

1170 Mary with Doll

1171 Shepherds

1172 Angels

1994 (1 Nov). Christmas. Children's Nativity Plays. Multicoloured One phosphor band (19p.) or phosphorised paper (others). Perf 15×14.

1843	**1168**	19p. Mary and Joseph	30	30
1844	**1169**	25p. Three Wise Men	35	35
1845	**1170**	30p. Mary with Doll	45	45
1846	**1171**	35p. Shepherds	55	60
1847	**1172**	41p. Angels	65	70
Set of 5			2·00	2·10
Set of 5 Gutter Pairs			4·00	
First Day Cover				2·25
Presentation Pack (PO Pack No. 252)			2·25	
PHQ Cards (set of 5) (166)			1·00	2·25

Collectors Pack

1994 (14 Nov). Comprises Nos. 1795/1847.

CP1847*a*	Collectors Pack (Pack No. 253)	27·00

Post Office Yearbook

1994 (14 Nov). 1795/1799 and 1810/1847 in hardbound book with slip case, illustrated in colour

YB1847*a*	Yearbook	20·00

1173 Sophie (black cat)

1174 Puskas (Siamese) and Tigger (tabby)

1175 Chloe (ginger cat)

1176 Kikko (tortoiseshell) and Rosie (Abyssinian)

1177 Fred (black and white cat)

1995 (17 Jan). Cats. Multicoloured One phosphor band (19p.) or two phosphor bands (others). Perf 14½×14.

1848	**1173**	19p. Sophie	30	30
1849	**1174**	25p. Puskas and Tigger	40	40

1850	**1175**	30p. Chloe	50	50
1851	**1176**	35p. Kikko and Rosie	60	60
1852	**1177**	41p. Fred	70	70
Set of 5			2·25	2·25
Set of 5 Gutter Pairs			4·50	
First Day Cover				2·50
Presentation Pack (PO Pack No. 254)			2·50	
PHQ Cards (set of 5) (167)			1·00	2·50

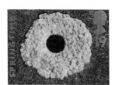

1178 Dandelions

1179 Chestnut Leaves

1180 Garlic Leaves

1181 Hazel Leaves

1182 Spring Grass

1995 (14 Mar). The Four Seasons. Springtime. Plant Sculptures by Andy Goldsworthy. Multicoloured One phosphor band (19p.) or two phosphor bands (others). Perf 15×14.

1853	**1178**	19p. Dandelions	30	30
1854	**1179**	25p. Chestnut Leaves	35	35
1855	**1180**	30p. Garlic Leaves	45	45
1856	**1181**	35p. Hazel Leaves	55	55
1857	**1182**	41p. Spring Grass	65	65
Set of 5			2·00	2·00
Set of 5 Gutter Pairs			4·00	
First Day Cover				2·25
Presentation Pack (PO Pack No. 255)			2·40	
PHQ Cards (set of 5) (168)			1·00	2·25

1183 La Danse à la Campagne (Renoir)

1184 Troilus and Criseyde (Peter Brookes)

1185 The Kiss (Rodin)

1186 Girls on the Town (Beryl Cook)

1187 Jazz (Andrew Mockett)

1188 Girls performing a Kathak Dance (Aurangzeb period)

1189 Alice Keppel with her Daughter (Alice Hughes)

1190 Children Playing (L. S. Lowry)

1191 Circus Clowns (Emily Firmin and Justin Mitchell)

1192 Decoration from All the Love Poems of Shakespeare (Eric Gill)

1995 (21 Mar). Greetings Stamps. Greetings in Art. Multicoloured Two phosphor bands. Perf 14½×14 (with one elliptical hole in each vertical side).

1858	**1183**	(1st) La Danse à la Campagne	1·20	1·00
1859	**1184**	(1st) Troilus and Criseyde	1·20	1·00
1860	**1185**	(1st) The Kiss	1·20	1·00
1861	**1186**	(1st) Girls on the Town	1·20	1·00
1862	**1187**	(1st) Jazz	1·20	1·00
1863	**1188**	(1st) Girls performing a Kathak Dance	1·20	1·00
1864	**1189**	(1st) Alice Keppel with her Daughter	1·20	1·00
1865	**1190**	(1st) Children Playing	1·20	1·00
1866	**1191**	(1st) Circus Clowns	1·20	1·00
1867	**1192**	(1st) Decoration from All the Love Poems of Shakespeare	1·20	1·00
Set of 10			10·50	9·00
First Day Cover				9·25
Presentation Pack (PO Pack No. G4)			13·50	
PHQ Cards (set of 10) (GS3)			2·00	9·25

Nos. 1858/1867 were printed together *se-tenant* in booklet panes of ten stamps and 20 half stamp-sized labels.

1193 Fireplace Decoration, Attingham Park, Shropshire

1194 Oak Seedling

1195 Carved Table Leg, Attingham Park

1196 St David's Head, Dyfed, Wales

1197 Elizabethan
Window, Little
Moreton Hall, Cheshire

1995 (11 Apr). Centenary of The National Trust. Multicoloured One phosphor band (19p.), two phosphor bands (25p., 35p.) or phosphorised paper (30p., 41p.). Perf 14×15.

1868	**1193**	19p. Fireplace Decoration	30	30
1869	**1194**	25p. Oak Seedling	35	35
1870	**1195**	30p. Carved Table Leg	45	45
1871	**1196**	35p. St David's Head	55	55
1872	**1197**	41p. Elizabethan Window	65	65
Set of 5			2·00	2·00
Set of 5 Gutter Pairs			4·00	
First Day Cover				2·25
Presentation Pack (PO Pack No. 256)			2·40	
PHQ Cards (set of 5) (169)			1·00	2·25

1198 British Troops
and French Civilians
celebrating

1199 Symbolic Hands and
Red Cross

1200 St Paul's Cathedral
and Searchlights

1201 Symbolic Hand
releasing Peace Dove

1202 Symbolic Hands

1995 (2 May). Europa. Peace and Freedom. Multicoloured One phosphor band (Nos. 1873/1874) or two phosphor bands (others). Perf 14½×14.

1873	**1198**	19p. British Troops and French Civilians celebrating	35	35
1874	**1199**	19p. Symbolic Hands and Red Cross	35	35
1875	**1200**	25p. St Paul's Cathedral and Searchlights	45	45
1876	**1201**	25p. Symbolic Hand releasing Peace Dove	45	45
1877	**1202**	30p. Symbolic Hands	60	60
Set of 5			2·00	2·00
Set of 5 Gutter Pairs			4·00	
First Day Cover				2·25
Presentation Pack (PO Pack No. 257)			2·40	
PHQ Cards (set of 5) (170)			60	2·25

Nos. 1873 and 1875 commemorate the 50th anniversary of the end of the Second World War.

No. 1874 commemorate the 125th anniversary of the British Red Cross Society.

For No. 1875 with the face value expressed as '1st' see No. **MS**2547.

Nos. 1876/1877 commemorate the 50th anniversary of the United Nations.

Nos. 1876/1877 include the EUROPA emblem.

1203 The Time Machine

1204 The First Men in the Moon

1205 The War of the Worlds

1206 The Shape of Things to Come

1995 (6 June). Science Fiction. Novels by H. G. Wells. Multicoloured Two phosphor bands. Perf 14½×14.

1878	**1203**	25p. *The Time Machine*	40	40
1879	**1204**	30p. *The First Men in the Moon*	50	50
1880	**1205**	35p. *The War of the Worlds*	60	60
1881	**1206**	41p. *The Shape of Things to Come*	70	70
Set of 4			2·00	2·00
Set of 4 Gutter Pairs			4·00	
First Day Cover				2·25
Presentation Pack (PO Pack No. 258)			2·40	
PHQ Cards (set of 4) (171)			50	2·25

Nos. 1878/1881 commemorate the centenary of publication of Wells's *The Time Machine*.

1207 The Swan, 1595

1208 The Rose, 1592

1209 The Globe, 1599

1210 The Hope, 1613

1211 The Globe, 1614

1995 (8 Aug). Reconstruction of Shakespeare's Globe Theatre. Multicoloured Two phosphor bands. Perf 14½.

1882	**1207**	25p. The Swan, 1595	40	30
		a. Horiz strip of 5. Nos. 1882/1886	2·00	2·25
1883	**1208**	25p. The Rose, 1592	40	30
1884	**1209**	25p. The Globe, 1599	40	30
1885	**1210**	25p. The Hope, 1613	40	30
1886	**1211**	25p. The Globe, 1614	40	30
Set of 5			2·00	2·25
Gutter Strip of 10			4·00	
First Day Cover				2·40
Presentation Pack (PO Pack No. 259)			2·40	
PHQ Cards (set of 5) (172)			1·00	2·40

Nos. 1882/1886 were issued together, *se-tenant*, in horizontal strips of five throughout the sheet with the backgrounds forming a composite design.

1212 Sir Rowland Hill and Uniform Penny Postage Petition

1213 Hill and Penny Black

1214 Guglielmo Marconi and Early Wireless

1215 Marconi and Sinking of *Titanic* (liner)

1995 (5 Sept). Pioneers of Communications. Multicoloured One phosphor band (19p.) or phosphorised paper (others). Perf 14½×14.

1887	**1212**	19p. Sir Rowland Hill and Uniform Penny Postage Petition	40	40
1888	**1213**	25p. Hill and Penny Black	50	50
1889	**1214**	41p. Guglielmo Marconi and Early Wireless	65	65
1890	**1215**	60p. Marconi and Sinking of *Titanic* (liner)	75	75
Set of 4			2·10	2·10
Set of 4 Gutter Pairs			4·25	
First Day Cover				2·25
Presentation Pack (PO Pack No. 260)			2·50	
PHQ Cards (set of 4) (173)			80	2·25

Nos. 1887/1888 mark the birth bicentenary of Sir Rowland Hill. Nos. 1889/1890 the centenary of the first radio transmissions.

1216 Harold Wagstaff

1217 Gus Risman

1218 Jim Sullivan

1219 Billy Batten

1220 Brian Bevan

1995 (3 Oct). Centenary of Rugby League. Multicoloured One phosphor band (19p.) or two phosphor bands (others). Perf 14½×14.

1891	**1216**	19p. Harold Wagstaff	30	30
1892	**1217**	25p. Gus Risman	35	35
1893	**1218**	30p. Jim Sullivan	45	45
1894	**1219**	35p. Billy Batten	55	55
1895	**1220**	41p. Brian Bevan	65	65
Set of 5			2·10	2·10
Set of 5 Gutter Pairs			4·25	
First Day Cover				2·25
Presentation Pack (PO Pack No. 261)			2·40	
PHQ Cards (set of 5) (174)			1·00	2·25

1221 European Robin in Mouth of Pillar Box

1222 European Robin on Railings and Holly

1223 European Robin on Snow-covered Milk Bottles

1224 European Robin on Road Sign

1225 European Robin on Door Knob and Christmas Wreath

1995 (30 Oct). Christmas. Christmas Robins. Multicoloured One phosphor band (19p.) or two phosphor bands (others). Perf 15×14.

1896	**1221**	19p. Robin in Mouth of Pillar Box	30	30
1897	**1222**	25p. Robin on Railings	35	40
1898	**1223**	30p. Robin on Milk Bottles	50	55
1899	**1224**	41p. Robin on Road Sign	60	65
1900	**1225**	60p. Robin on Door Knob	75	80
Set of 5			2·25	2·50
Set of 5 Gutter Pairs			4·50	
First Day Cover				2·75
Presentation Pack (PO Pack No. 262)			2·50	
PHQ Cards (set of 5) (175)			1·00	2·75

The 19p. value was re-issued on 3 October 2000 and 9 October 2001 in sheets of 20, each with a *se-tenant* label, in connection with 'customised' stamps available from the Philatelic Bureau. The labels show either Christmas greetings or a personal photograph.

Year Pack

1995 (30 Oct). Comprises Nos. 1848/1900.

CP1900*a*	Year Pack (Pack No. 263)	25·00

Post Office Yearbook

1995 (30 Oct). Comprises Nos. 1848/1857 and 1868/1900 in hardback book with slip case, illustrated in colour

YB1900*a*	Yearbook	20·00

1226 Opening Lines of *To a Mouse* and Fieldmouse

1227 *O my Luve's like a red, red rose* and Wild Rose

1228 *Scots, wha hae wi Wallace bled* and Sir William Wallace

1229 *Auld Lang Syne* and Highland Dancers

1996 (25 Jan). Death Bicentenary of Robert Burns (Scottish poet). Multicoloured One phosphor band (19p.) or two phosphor bands (others). Perf 14½.

1901	**1226**	19p. Opening Lines of *To a Mouse* and Fieldmouse	40	40
1902	**1227**	25p. *O my Luve's like a red, red rose* and Wild Rose	50	50
1903	**1228**	41p. *Scots, wha hae wi Wallace bled* and Sir William Wallace	65	70
1904	**1229**	60p. *Auld Lang Syne* and Highland Dancers	75	80
Set of 4			2·00	2·25
Set of 4 Gutter Pairs			4·00	
First Day Cover				2·40
Presentation Pack (PO Pack No. 264)			2·40	
PHQ Cards (set of 4) (176)			80	2·40

1230 'MORE! LOVE' (Mel Calman)

1231 'Sincerely' (Charles Barsotti)

1232 'Do you have something for the HUMAN CONDITION?' (Leo Cullum)

1233 'MENTAL FLOSS' (Mel Calman)

1234 '4.55 P.M.' (Charles Barsotti)

1235 'Dear lottery prize winner' (Larry)

1236 'I'm writing to you because....' (Mel Calman)

1237 'FETCH THIS, FETCH THAT' (Charles Barsotti)

1238 'My day starts before I'm ready for it' (Mel Calman)

1239 'THE CHEQUE IN THE POST' (Jack Ziegler)

1996 (26 Feb–11 Nov). Greetings Stamps. Cartoons. Multicoloured 'All over' phosphor. Perf 14½×14 (with one elliptical hole in each vertical side).

1905	**1230**	(1st) 'MORE! LOVE'	1·20	1·00
		p. Two phosphor bands (11.11.96)	2·50	2·50
1906	**1231**	(1st) 'Sincerely'	1·20	1·00
		p. Two phosphor bands (11.11.96)	2·50	2·50
1907	**1232**	(1st) 'Do you have something for the HUMAN CONDITION?'	1·20	1·00
		p. Two phosphor bands (11.11.96)	2·50	2·50
1908	**1233**	(1st) 'MENTAL FLOSS'	1·20	1·00
		p. Two phosphor bands (11.11.96)	2·50	2·50
1909	**1234**	(1st) '4.55 P.M.'	1·20	1·00
		p. Two phosphor bands (11.11.96)	2·50	2·50
1910	**1235**	(1st) 'Dear lottery prize winner'	1·20	1·00
		p. Two phosphor bands (11.11.96)	2·50	2·50
1911	**1236**	(1st) 'I'm writing to you because....'	1·20	1·00
		p. Two phosphor bands (11.11.96)	2·50	2·50
1912	**1237**	(1st) 'FETCH THIS, FETCH THAT'	1·20	1·00
		p. Two phosphor bands (11.11.96)	2·50	2·50
1913	**1238**	(1st) 'My day starts before I'm ready for it' (Mel Calman)	1·20	1·00
		p. Two phosphor bands (11.11.96)	2·50	2·50
1914	**1239**	(1st) 'THE CHEQUE IN THE POST' (Jack Ziegler)	1·20	1·00
		p. Two phosphor bands (11.11.96)	2·50	2·50
Set of 10 (Nos. 1905/1914)			10·50	9·00
Set of 10 (Nos. 1905p/1914p)			24·00	24·00
First Day Cover (Nos. 1905/1914)				9·50
Presentation Pack (PO Pack No. G5) (Nos. 1905/1914)			13·50	
PHQ Cards (set of 10) (GS4)			2·00	9·50

Nos. 1905/1914 were printed together, *se-tenant*, in booklet panes of ten stamps and 20 half stamp-sized labels.

These designs were re-issued on 18 December 2001 in sheets of ten, each with a *se-tenant* label showing cartoon titles. They were re-issued again on 29 July 2003 in sheets of 20 containing two of each design, each stamp accompanied by a half stamp-size label showing a crossword grid or personal photograph. Such sheets are perforated without elliptical holes.

1240 'Muscovy Duck'

1241 'Lapwing'

1242 'White-fronted Goose'

1243 'Bittern'

1244 'Whooper Swan'

1996 (12 Mar). 50th Anniversary of the Wildfowl and Wetlands Trust. Bird Paintings by C. F. Tunnicliffe. Multicoloured One phosphor band (19p.) or phosphorised paper (others). Perf 14×14½.

1915	1240	19p. 'Muscovy Duck'	30	30
1916	1241	25p. 'Lapwing'	35	35
1917	1242	30p. 'White-fronted Goose'	45	45
1918	1243	35p. 'Bittern'	55	55
1919	1244	41p. 'Whooper Swan'	65	65
Set of 5			2·10	2·10
Set of 5 Gutter Pairs			4·25	
First Day Cover				2·40
Presentation Pack (PO Pack No. 265)			2·50	
PHQ Cards (set of 5) (177)			1·00	2·40

1245 The Odeon, Harrogate

1246 Laurence Olivier and Vivien Leigh in *Lady Hamilton* (film)

1247 Old Cinema Ticket

1248 Pathé News Still

1249 Cinema Sign, The Odeon, Manchester

1996 (16 Apr). Centenary of Cinema. Multicoloured One phosphor band (19p.) or two phosphor bands (others). Perf 14×14½.

1920	1245	19p. The Odeon, Harrogate	30	30
1921	1246	25p. Laurence Olivier and Vivien Leigh in *Lady Hamilton*	35	35
1922	1247	30p. Old Cinema Ticket	45	45
1923	1248	35p. Pathé News Still	60	60
1924	1249	41p. Cinema Sign, The Odeon, Manchester	70	70
Set of 5			2·25	2·25
Set of 5 Gutter Pairs			4·50	
First Day Cover				2·40
Presentation Pack (PO Pack No. 266)			2·50	
PHQ Cards (set of 5) (178)			1·00	2·40

1250 Dixie Dean

1251 Bobby Moore

1252 Duncan Edwards

1253 Billy Wright

1254 Danny Blanchflower

1996 (14 May). European Football Championship. Multicoloured One phosphor band (19p.) or two phosphor bands (others). Perf 14½×14.

1925	1250	19p. Dixie Dean	30	30
1926	1251	25p. Bobby Moore	40	40
1927	1252	35p. Duncan Edwards	50	50
1928	1253	41p. Billy Wright	60	60
1929	1254	60p. Danny Blanchflower	90	90
Set of 5			2·50	2·50
Set of 5 Gutter Pairs			5·00	
First Day Cover				2·75
Presentation Pack (PO Pack No. 267)			2·75	
PHQ Cards (set of 5) (179)			1·00	2·75

1255 Athlete on Starting Blocks

1256 Javelin

1257 Basketball

1258 Swimming

1259 Athlete celebrating and Olympic Rings

1996 (9 July). Olympic and Paralympic Games, Atlanta. Multicoloured Two phosphor bands. Perf 14½×14.

1930	1255	26p. Athlete on Starting Blocks	30	30
		a. Horiz strip of 5. Nos. 1930/1934	2·00	2·10
1931	1256	26p. Javelin	30	30
1932	1257	26p. Basketball	30	30
1933	1258	26p. Swimming	30	30

1934	**1259**	26p. Athlete celebrating and Olympic		
		Rings	30	30
Set of 5			2·00	2·10
Gutter Strip of 10			4·00	
First Day Cover				2·50
Presentation Pack (PO Pack No. 268)			2·50	
PHQ Cards (set of 5) (180)			1·00	2·50

Nos. 1930/1934 were printed together, *se-tenant*, in horizontal strips of five throughout the sheet.

For these designs with face value expressed as '1st' see No. **MS**2554.

1260 Professor Dorothy Hodgkin (scientist)

1261 Dame Margot Fonteyn (ballerina)

1262 Dame Elisabeth Frink (sculptress)

1263 Dame Daphne du Maurier (novelist)

1264 Dame Marea Hartman (sports administrator)

1996 (6 Aug). Europa. Famous Women. Multicoloured One phosphor band (20p.) or two phosphor bands (others). Perf 14½.

1935	**1260**	20p. Professor Dorothy Hodgkin	30	30
1936	**1261**	26p. Dame Margot Fonteyn	35	35
1937	**1262**	31p. Dame Elisabeth Frink	50	50
1938	**1263**	37p. Dame Daphne du Maurier	60	60
1939	**1264**	43p. Dame Marea Hartman	70	70
Set of 5			2·25	2·25
Set of 5 Gutter Pairs			4·50	
First Day Cover				2·50
Presentation Pack (PO Pack No. 269)			2·75	
PHQ Cards (set of 5) (181)			1·00	2·50

Nos. 1936/1937 include the EUROPA emblem.

1265 *Muffin the Mule*   **1266** *Sooty*

1267 *Stingray*   **1268** *The Clangers*

1269 *Dangermouse*

1996 (3 Sept)–**97**. 50th Anniversary of Children's Television. Multicoloured One phosphor band (20p.) or two phosphor bands (others). Perf 14½×14.

1940	**1265**	20p. *Muffin the Mule*	30	30
		a. Perf 15×14 (23.9.97)	65	65
1941	**1266**	26p. *Sooty*	35	35
1942	**1267**	31p. *Stingray*	50	50
1943	**1268**	37p. *The Clangers*	60	60
1944	**1269**	43p. *Dangermouse*	70	70
Set of 5			2·25	2·25
Set of 5 Gutter Pairs			4·50	
First Day Cover				2·75
Presentation Pack (PO Pack No. 270)			3·00	
PHQ Cards (set of 5) (182)			1·00	2·75

No. 1940a was only issued in the 1997 £6·15 Celebrating 75 years of the BBC stamp booklet, No. DX19.

1270 Triumph TR3   **1271** MG TD

1272 Austin-Healey 100   **1273** Jaguar XK120

1274 Morgan Plus 4

1996 (1 Oct). Classic Sports Cars. Multicoloured One phosphor band (20p.) or two phosphor bands (others). Perf 14½.

1945	**1270**	20p. Triumph TR3	30	30
1946	**1271**	26p. MG TD	50	50
1947	**1272**	37p. Austin-Healey 100	60	65
1948	**1273**	43p. Jaguar XK120	70	75
1949	**1274**	63p. Morgan Plus 4	90	95
Set of 5			2·75	3·00
Set of 5 Gutter Pairs			5·50	
First Day Cover				3·25
Presentation Pack (PO Pack No. 271)			3·00	
PHQ Cards (set of 5) (183)			1·00	3·25

1275 The Three Kings   **1276** The Annunciation

1277 The Journey to Bethlehem

1278 The Nativity

1279 The Shepherds

1996 (28 Oct). Christmas. Multicoloured One phosphor band (2nd) or two phosphor bands (others). Perf 15×14.

1950	**1275**	(2nd) The Three Kings	60	35
1951	**1276**	(1st) The Annunciation	70	55
1952	**1277**	31p. The Journey to Bethlehem	50	65
1953	**1278**	43p. The Nativity	50	75
1954	**1279**	63p. The Shepherds	70	95
Set of 5			2·75	3·00
Set of 5 Gutter Pairs			5·50	
First Day Cover				3·25
Presentation Pack (PO Pack No. 272)			3·25	
PHQ Cards (set of 5) (184)			1·00	3·25

Year Pack

1996 (28 Oct). Comprises Nos. 1901/1954.

CP1954*a*	Year Pack (Pack No. 273)	27·50

Post Office Yearbook

1996 (28 Oct). Comprises Nos. 1901/1904 and 1915/1954 in hardback book with slip case, illustrated in colour

YB1954*a*	Yearbook	21·00

1280 *Gentiana acaulis* (Georg Ehret)

1281 *Magnolia grandiflora* (Ehret)

1282 *Camellia japonica* (Alfred Chandler)

1283 *Tulipa* (Ehret)

1284 *Fuchsia, Princess of Wales* (Augusta Withers)

1285 *Tulipa gesneriana* (Ehret)

1286 *Gazania splendens* (Charlotte Sowerby)

1287 *Iris latifolia* (Ehret)

1288 *Hippeastrum rutilum* (Pierre-Joseph Redouté)

1289 *Passiflora caerulea* (Ehret)

1997 (6 Jan). Greeting Stamps. 19th-century Flower Paintings. Multicoloured Two phosphor bands. Perf 14½×14 (with one elliptical hole in each vertical side).

1955	**1280**	(1st) *Gentiana acaulis*	1·20	1·00
1956	**1281**	(1st) *Magnolia grandiflora*	1·20	1·00
1957	**1282**	(1st) *Camellia japonica*	1·20	1·00
1958	**1283**	(1st) *Tulipa*	1·20	1·00
1959	**1284**	(1st) Fuchsia, Princess of Wales	1·20	1·00
1960	**1285**	(1st) *Tulipa gesneriana*	1·20	1·00
1961	**1286**	(1st) *Gazania splendens*	1·20	1·00
1962	**1287**	(1st) *Iris latifolia*	1·20	1·00
1963	**1288**	(1st) *Hippeastrum rutilum*	1·20	1·00
1964	**1289**	(1st) *Passiflora caerulea*	1·20	1·00
Set of 10			10·50	9·00
First Day Cover				9·50
Presentation Pack (PO Pack No. G6)			13·50	
PHQ Cards (set of 10) (GS5)			2·00	9·50

Nos. 1955/1964 were printed together, *se-tenant*, in booklet panes of ten stamps and 20 half-sized labels.

Nos. 1955/1964 were re-issued on 21 January 2003 in *se-tenant* sheets of 20, each accompanied by a label showing further flowers or personal photographs. These sheets are without elliptical holes in the perforations.

For booklet stamps in designs as Nos. 1955, 1958 and 1962 perforated 15×14 see Nos. 2463/2465.

See also Nos. 2942/2943.

1290 King Henry VIII

1291 Catherine of Aragon

1292 Anne Boleyn

1293 Jane Seymour

1294 Anne of Cleves

1295 Catherine Howard

1296 Catherine Parr

1997 (21 Jan). 450th Death Anniversary of King Henry VIII. Multicoloured Two phosphor bands. Perf 15 (No. 1965) or 14×15 (others).

1965	**1290**	26p. King Henry VIII	50	50
1966	**1291**	26p. Catherine of Aragon	50	50
		a. Horiz strip of 6. Nos. 1966/1971	3·00	3·00
1967	**1292**	26p. Anne Boleyn	50	50
1968	**1293**	26p. Jane Seymour	50	50
1969	**1294**	26p. Anne of Cleves	50	50
1970	**1295**	26p. Catherine Howard	50	50
1971	**1296**	26p. Catherine Parr	50	50
Set of 7			3·25	3·25
Set of 1 Gutter Pair and a Gutter Strip of 12			6·50	
First Day Cover				3·75
Presentation Pack (PO Pack No. 274)			4·75	
PHQ Cards (set of 7) (185)			1·40	3·75

Nos. 1966/1971 were printed together, *se-tenant*, in horizontal strips of six throughout the sheet.

1297 St Columba in Boat

1298 St Columba on Iona

1299 St Augustine with King Ethelbert

1300 St Augustine with Model of Cathedral

1997 (11 Mar). Religious Anniversaries. Multicoloured Two phosphor bands. Perf 14½.

1972	**1297**	26p. St Columba in Boat	40	40
1973	**1298**	37p. St Columba on Iona	60	60
1974	**1299**	43p. St Augustine with King Ethelbert	80	85
1975	**1300**	63p. St Augustine with Model of Cathedral	90	95
Set of 4			2·50	2·50
Set of 4 Gutter Pairs			5·00	
First Day Cover				3·00
Presentation Pack (PO Pack No. 275)			3·25	
PHQ Cards (set of 4) (186)			80	3·00

Nos. 1972/1973 commemorate the 1400th death anniversary of St Columba.

Nos. 1974/1975 the 1400th anniversary of the arrival of St Augustine of Canterbury in Kent.

For Nos. 1976/1977, Types **1301/1302**, see Decimal Machin Definitives section.

Nos. 1978/1979 are vacant.

Dracula

1303 Dracula

Frankenstein

1304 Frankenstein

Dr Jekyll and Mr Hyde

1305 Dr Jekyll and Mr Hyde

The Hound of the Baskervilles

1306 The Hound of the Baskervilles

1997 (13 May). Europa. Tales and Legends. Horror Stories. Multicoloured Two phosphor bands. Perf 14×15.

1980	**1303**	26p. Dracula	40	40
1981	**1304**	31p. Frankenstein	55	60
1982	**1305**	37p. Dr Jekyll and Mr Hyde	70	75
1983	**1306**	43p. The Hound of the Baskervilles	80	85
Set of 4			2·25	2·40
Set of 4 Gutter Pairs			4·50	
First Day Cover				2·75
Presentation Pack (PO Pack No. 276)			3·00	
PHQ Cards (set of 4) (187)			80	2·75

Nos. 1980/1983 commemorate the birth bicentenary of Mary Shelley (creator of Frankenstein) with the 26p. and 31p. values incorporating the EUROPA emblem.

1307 Reginald Mitchell and Supermarine Spitfire MkIIA

1308 Roy Chadwick and Avro Lancaster MkI

1309 Ronald Bishop and de Havilland Mosquito B MkXVI

1310 George Carter and Gloster Meteor T Mk7

1311 Sir Sydney Camm and Hawker Hunter FGA Mk9

1997 (10 June). British Aircraft Designers. Multicoloured One phosphor band (20p.) or two phosphor bands (others). Perf 15×14.

1984	**1307**	20p. Reginald Mitchell and Supermarine Spitfire MkIIA	40	40
1985	**1308**	26p. Roy Chadwick and Avro Lancaster MkI	50	50
1986	**1309**	37p. Ronald Bishop and de Havilland Mosquito B MkXVI	60	60
1987	**1310**	43p. George Carter and Gloster Meteor T Mk7	80	80
1988	**1311**	63p. Sir Sydney Camm and Hawker Hunter FGA Mk9	90	90
Set of 5			3·00	3·00
Set of 5 Gutter Pairs			6·00	
First Day Cover				3·25
Presentation Pack (PO Pack No. 277)			3·50	
PHQ Cards (set of 5) (188)			1·00	3·25

See also No. 2868.

1312 Carriage Horse and Coachman   **1313** Lifeguards Horse and Trooper

1314 Blues and Royals Drum Horse and Drummer   **1315** Duke of Edinburgh's Horse and Groom

1997 (8 July). All the Queen's Horses. 50th Anniversary of the British Horse Society. Multicoloured One phosphor band (20p.) or two phosphor bands (others). Perf 14½.

1989	**1312**	20p. Carriage Horse and Coachman	40	40
1990	**1313**	26p. Lifeguards Horse and Trooper	55	60
1991	**1314**	43p. Blues and Royals Drum Horse and Drummer	70	75
1992	**1315**	63p. Duke of Edinburgh's Horse and Groom	85	85
Set of 4			2·25	2·50
Set of 4 Gutter Pairs			4·50	
First Day Cover				2·75
Presentation Pack (PO Pack No. 278)			3·00	
PHQ Cards (set of 4) (189)			50	2·75

1315a Caernarfon Castle   **1315b** Edinburgh Castle

1315c Carrickfergus Castle   **1315d** Windsor Castle

CASTLE

Harrison plates (Nos. 1611/1614)

CASTLE

Enschedé plates (Nos. 1993/1996)

Differences between Harrison and Enschedé printings:

Harrison: 'C' has top serif and tail of letter points to right. 'A' has flat top. 'S' has top and bottom serifs.

Enschedé: 'C' has no top serif and tail of letter points upwards. 'A' has pointed top. 'S' has no serifs.

1997 (29 July). Designs as Nos. 1611/1614 with Queen's head in silhouette as T **1044**, but re-engraved with differences in inscription as shown above. Perf 15×14 (with one elliptical hole in each vertical side).

1993	**1315a**	£1·50 Caernarfon Castle (maroon and gold†)	12·00	6·00
1994	**1315b**	£2 Edinburgh Castle (indigo and gold†)	14·00	2·25
1995	**1315c**	£3 Carrickfergus Castle (violet and gold†)	30·00	3·50
1996	**1315d**	£5 Windsor Castle (deep brown and gold†)	35·00	10·00
Set of 4			80·00	18·00
Set of 4 Gutter Pairs (vert or horiz)			£175	
Presentation Pack (PO Pack No. 40)			£150	

† The Queen's head on these stamps is printed in optically variable ink which changes colour from gold to green when viewed from different angles.

There was no official Royal Mail first day cover service provided for Nos. 1993/1996.

See also Nos. 1410/1413 and 1611/1614.

1316 Haroldswick, Shetland   **1317** Painswick, Gloucestershire

1318 Beddgelert, Gwynedd   **1319** Ballyroney, County Down

1997 (12 Aug). Sub-Post Offices. Multicoloured One phosphor band (20p.) or two phosphor bands (others). Perf 14½.

1997	**1316**	20p. Haroldswick, Shetland	40	40
1998	**1317**	26p. Painswick, Gloucestershire	55	60
1999	**1318**	43p. Beddgelert, Gwynedd	70	75
2000	**1319**	63p. Ballyroney, County Down	85	85
Set of 4			2·25	2·40
Set of 4 Gutter Pairs			4·50	
First Day Cover				2·75
Presentation Pack (PO Pack No. 279)			3·00	
PHQ Cards (set of 4) (190)			80	2·75

Nos. 1997/2000 were issued on the occasion of the Centenary of the National Federation of Sub-Postmasters.

Enid Blyton's *Noddy*
1320 Noddy

Enid Blyton's *Famous Five*
1321 Famous Five

Enid Blyton's *Secret Seven*
1322 Secret Seven

Enid Blyton's *Faraway Tree*
1323 Faraway Tree

Enid Blyton's *Malory Towers*
1324 Malory Towers

1997 (9 Sept). Birth Centenary of Enid Blyton (children's author). Multicoloured One phosphor band (20p.) or two phosphor bands (others). Perf 14×14½.

2001	**1320**	20p. Noddy	30	30
2002	**1321**	26p. Famous Five	50	50
2003	**1322**	37p. Secret Seven	55	60
2004	**1323**	43p. Faraway Tree	65	70
2005	**1324**	63p. Malory Towers	75	80
Set of 5			2·50	2·75
Set of 5 Gutter Pairs			5·00	
First Day Cover				3·00
Presentation Pack (PO Pack No. 280)			3·00	
PHQ Cards (set of 5) (191)			1·00	3·00

1325 Children and Father Christmas pulling Cracker

1326 Father Christmas with Traditional Cracker

1327 Father Christmas riding Cracker

1328 Father Christmas on Snowball

1329 Father Christmas and Chimney

1997 (27 Oct). Christmas. 150th Anniversary of the Christmas Cracker. Multicoloured One phosphor band (2nd) or two phosphor bands (others). Perf 15×14.

2006	**1325**	(2nd) Children and Father Christmas pulling Cracker	90	35
2007	**1326**	(1st) Father Christmas with Traditional Cracker	1·20	55
2008	**1327**	31p. Father Christmas riding Cracker	50	60
2009	**1328**	43p. Father Christmas on Snowball	50	70
2010	**1329**	63p. Father Christmas and Chimney	70	80
Set of 5			3·25	2·75
Set of 5 Gutter Pairs			6·50	
First Day Cover				3·00
Presentation Pack (PO Pack No. 282)			4·00	
PHQ Cards (set of 5) (192)			1·00	3·00

The 1st value was re-issued on 3 October 2000 and 9 October 2001, in sheets of ten, in photogravure, each with a *se-tenant* label in connection with 'customised' service available from the Philatelic Bureau.

From 1 October 2002 the size of the sheet was increased to 20 in lithography the 1st value was again issued but perforated 14½×14. The labels show either Christmas greetings or a personal photographs.

1330 Wedding Photograph, 1947

1331 Queen Elizabeth II and Prince Philip, 1997

1997 (13 Nov). Royal Golden Wedding. One phosphor band (20p.) or two phosphor bands (others). Perf 15.

2011	**1330**	20p. Wedding Photograph, 1947. Gold, yellow-brown and grey-black	40	40
2012	**1331**	26p. Queen Elizabeth II and Prince Philip, 1997. Multicoloured	60	60
2013	**1330**	43p. Wedding Photograph, 1947. Gold, bluish green and grey-black	1·10	1·10
2014	**1331**	63p. Queen Elizabeth II and Prince Philip, 1997. Multicoloured	1·50	1·50
Set of 4			3·25	3·25
Set of 4 Gutter Pairs			6·50	
First Day Cover				3·50
Presentation Pack (PO Pack No. 281)			3·75	
Souvenir Book (contains Nos. 1668, 1989/1992 and 2011/2014)			22·00	
PHQ Cards (set of 4) (193)			80	3·50

Year Pack

1997 (13 Nov). Comprises Nos. 1965/1975, 1980/1992 and 1997/2014.

CP2014a	Year Pack (Pack No. 283)	32·00	

Post Office Yearbook

1997 (13 Nov). Comprises Nos. 1965/1975, 1980/1992 and 1997/2014 in hardback book with slip case

YB2014a	Yearbook	26·00	

20 **ENDANGERED SPECIES**
Common dormouse
Muscardinus avellanarius

1332 Common
Dormouse

26 **ENDANGERED SPECIES**
Lady's slipper orchid
Cypripedium calceolus

1333 Lady's Slipper
Orchid

31 **ENDANGERED SPECIES**
Song thrush
Turdus philomelos

1334 Song Thrush

37 **ENDANGERED SPECIES**
Shining ram's-horn snail
Segmentina nitida

1335 Shining Ram's-
horn Snail

43 **ENDANGERED SPECIES**
Mole cricket
Gryllotalpa gryllotalpa

1336 Mole Cricket

63 **ENDANGERED SPECIES**
Devil's bolete
Boletus satanas

1337 Devil's Bolete

1998 (20 Jan). Endangered Species. Multicoloured One side phosphor band (20p.) or two phosphor bands (others). Perf 14×14½.

2015	**1332**	20p. Common Dormouse	40	40
2016	**1333**	26p. Lady's Slipper Orchid	50	50
2017	**1334**	31p. Song Thrush	60	60
2018	**1335**	37p. Shining Ram's-horn Snail	70	70
2019	**1336**	43p. Mole Cricket	85	85
2020	**1337**	63p. Devil's Bolete	1·00	1·00
Set of 6			3·75	3·75
Set of 6 Gutter Pairs			7·50	
First Day Cover				4·00
Presentation Pack (PO Pack No. 284)			4·25	
PHQ Cards (set of 6) (194)			1·25	4·00

1338 Diana, Princess
of Wales (photo by
Lord Snowdon)

1339 At British Lung
Foundation Function,
April 1997 (photo by
John Stillwell)

1340 Wearing Tiara,
1991 (photo by Lord
Snowdon)

1341 On Visit to
Birmingham, October
1995 (photo by Tim
Graham)

1342 In Evening
Dress, 1987 (photo by
Terence Donovan)

1998 (3 Feb). Diana, Princess of Wales Commemoration. Multicoloured Two phosphor bands. Perf 14×15.

2021	**1338**	26p. Diana, Princess of Wales	50	30
		a. Horiz strip of 5. Nos. 2021/2025	2·00	2·00
2022	**1339**	26p. At British Lung Foundation Function, April 1997	50	30
2023	**1340**	26p. Wearing Tiara, 1991	50	30
2024	**1341**	26p. On Visit to Birmingham, October 1995	50	30
2025	**1342**	26p. In Evening Dress, 1987	50	30
Set of 5			2·00	2·00
Gutter Strip of 10			4·00	
First Day Cover				3·00
Presentation Pack (unnumbered)			8·00	
Presentation Pack (Welsh)			60·00	

Nos. 2021/2025 were printed together, *se-tenant*, in horizontal strips of five throughout the sheet.

1343 Lion of England and
Griffin of Edward III

1344 Falcon of Plantagenet
and Bull of Clarence

1345 Lion of Mortimer and
Yale of Beaufort

1346 Greyhound of Richmond
and Dragon of Wales

1347 Unicorn of Scotland and
Horse of Hanover

1998 (24 Feb). 650th Anniversary of the Order of the Garter. The Queen's Beasts. Multicoloured Two phosphor bands. Perf 15×14.

2026	**1343**	26p. Lion of England and Griffin of Edward III	50	30
		a. Horiz strip of 5. Nos. 2026/2030	2·25	2·25
2027	**1344**	26p. Falcon of Plantagenet and Bull of Clarence	50	30
2028	**1345**	26p. Lion of Mortimer and Yale of Beaufort	50	30
2029	**1346**	26p. Greyhound of Richmond and Dragon of Wales	50	30
		a. Silver (Queen's head and value omitted)	—	
2030	**1347**	26p. Unicorn of Scotland and Horse of Hanover	50	30
Set of 5			2·25	2·25
Gutter Block of 10			4·50	
First Day Cover				2·75
Presentation Pack (PO Pack No. 285)			2·50	
PHQ Cards (*set of 5*) (195)			1·00	2·75

Nos. 2026/2030 were printed together, *se-tenant*, in horizontal strips of five throughout the sheet.

The phosphor bands on Nos. 2026/2030 are only half the height of the stamps and do not cover the silver parts of the designs.

1348

1998 (10 Mar). As T **157** (Wilding Definitive of 1952–1954) but with face values in decimal currency as T **1348**. One side phosphor band (20p.) or two phosphor bands (others). Perf 14 (with one elliptical hole in each vertical side).

2031	**1348**	20p. light green	40	40
2032		26p. red-brown	50	50
2033		37p. light purple	1·10	1·10
Set of 3			1·90	1·90
First Day Cover				4·75

Nos. 2031/2033 were only issued in the 1998 £7·49 Wilding Definitives stamp booklet No. DX20.

For further Wilding designs with decimal face values and on paper watermarked W **1565** see Nos. 2258/2259, **MS**2326, **MS**2367, 2378/2379, and 3329.

1349 St John's Point Lighthouse, County Down

1350 Smalls Lighthouse, Pembrokeshire

1351 Needles Rock Lighthouse, Isle of Wight, *circa* 1900

1352 Bell Rock Lighthouse, Arbroath, mid-19th-century

1353 Original Eddystone Lighthouse, Plymouth, 1698

1998 (24 Mar). Lighthouses. Multicoloured One side phosphor band (20p.) or two phosphor bands (others). Perf 14½×14.

2034	**1349**	20p. St John's Point Lighthouse	40	40
2035	**1350**	26p. Smalls Lighthouse	50	50
2036	**1351**	37p. Needles Rock Lighthouse	60	60
2037	**1352**	43p. Bell Rock Lighthouse	80	80
2038	**1353**	63p. Original Eddystone Lighthouse	90	90
Set of 5			3·00	3·00
Set of 5 Gutter Pairs			6·00	
First Day Cover				3·25
Presentation Pack (PO Pack No. 286)			3·50	
PHQ Cards (*set of 5*) (196)			1·00	3·25

Nos. 2034/2038 commemorate the 300th anniversary of the first Eddystone Lighthouse and the final year of manned lighthouses.

For Nos. 2039/2040 see Decimal Machin Definitives section.

1354 Tommy Cooper

1355 Eric Morecambe

1356 Joyce Grenfell

1357 Les Dawson

1358 Peter Cook

1998 (23 Apr). Comedians. Multicoloured One side phosphor band (20p.) or two phosphor bands (others). Perf 14½×14.

2041	**1354**	20p. Tommy Cooper	40	40
2042	**1355**	26p. Eric Morecambe	50	50
2043	**1356**	37p. Joyce Grenfell	60	60
2044	**1357**	43p. Les Dawson	80	80
2045	**1358**	63p. Peter Cook	90	90
Set of 5			3·00	3·00
Set of 5 Gutter Pairs			6·00	
First Day Cover				3·25
Presentation Pack (PO Pack No. 287)			3·50	
PHQ Cards (*set of 5*) (197)			1·00	3·25

1359 Hands forming Heart

1360 Adult and Child holding Hands

1361 Hands forming Cradle

1362 Hand taking Pulse

1998 (23 June). 50th Anniversary of the National Health Service. Multicoloured One side phosphor band (20p.) or two phosphor bands (others). Perf 14×14½.

2046	**1359**	20p. Hands forming Heart	40	40
2047	**1360**	26p. Adult and Child holding Hands	50	50
2048	**1361**	43p. Hands forming Cradle	80	80
2049	**1362**	63p. Hand taking Pulse	90	90
Set of 4			2·25	2·25
Set of 4 Gutter Pairs			4·50	
First Day Cover				2·75
Presentation Pack (PO Pack No. 288)			2·75	
PHQ Cards (set of 4) (198)			50	2·50

1363 The Hobbit (J. R. R. Tolkien)

1364 The Lion, The Witch and the Wardrobe (C. S. Lewis)

1365 The Phoenix and the Carpet (E. Nesbit)

1366 The Borrowers (Mary Norton)

1367 Through the Looking Glass (Lewis Carroll)

1998 (21 July). Famous Children's Fantasy Novels. Multicoloured One centre phosphor band (20p.) or two phosphor bands (others). Perf 15×14.

2050	**1363**	20p. The Hobbit	35	35
2051	**1364**	26p. The Lion, The Witch and the Wardrobe	45	45
2052	**1365**	37p. The Phoenix and the Carpet	60	60
2053	**1366**	43p. The Borrowers	80	80

2054	**1367**	63p. Through the Looking Glass	90	90
Set of 5			3·00	3·00
Set of 5 Gutter Pairs			6·00	
First Day Cover				3·25
Presentation Pack (PO Pack No. 289)			3·25	
PHQ Cards (set of 5) (199)			1·00	3·25

Nos. 2050/2054 commemorate the birth centenary of C. S. Lewis and the death centenary of Lewis Carroll.

1368 Woman in Yellow Feathered Costume

1369 Woman in Blue Costume and Headdress

1370 Group of Children in White and Gold Robes

1371 Child in Tree Costume

1998 (25 Aug). Europa. Festivals. Notting Hill Carnival. Multicoloured One centre phosphor band (20p.) or two phosphor bands (others). Perf 14×14½.

2055	**1368**	20p. Woman in Yellow Feathered Costume	40	40
2056	**1369**	26p. Woman in Blue Costume and Headdress	60	60
2057	**1370**	43p. Group of Children in White and Gold Robes	75	75
2058	**1371**	63p. Child in Tree Costume	1·00	1·00
Set of 4			2·50	2·50
Set of 4 Gutter Pairs			5·00	
First Day Cover				3·00
Presentation Pack (PO Pack No. 290)			2·75	
PHQ Cards (set of 4) (200)			80	3·00

The 20p. and 26p. incorporate the EUROPA emblem.

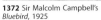

1372 Sir Malcolm Campbell's Bluebird, 1925

1373 Sir Henry Segrave's Sunbeam, 1926

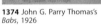

1374 John G. Parry Thomas's Babs, 1926

1375 John R. Cobb's Railton Mobil Special, 1947

1376 Donald Campbell's Bluebird CN7, 1964

1998 (29 Sept–13 Oct). British Land Speed Record Holders. Multicoloured One phosphor band (20p.) or two phosphor bands (others). Perf 15×14.

2059	**1372**	20p. Sir Malcolm Campbell's *Bluebird*	30	30
		a. Perf 14½×13½ (1 side band)		
		(13.10.98)	75	75
2060	**1373**	26p. Sir Henry Segrave's *Sunbeam*	40	40
2061	**1374**	30p. John G. Parry Thomas's *Babs*	60	60
2062	**1375**	43p. John R. Cobb's *Railton Mobil*		
		Special	80	80
2063	**1376**	63p. Donald Campbell's *Bluebird CN7*	90	90
Set of 5			2·75	2·75
Set of 5 Gutter Pairs			5·50	
First Day Cover				3·00
Presentation Pack (PO Pack No. 291)			3·25	
PHQ Cards (set of 5) (201)			1·00	3·00

Nos. 2059/2063 commemorate the 50th death anniversary of Sir Malcolm Campbell.

No. 2059a, which occurs with the phosphor band at the left or right of the stamp, was only issued in the £6·16 Breaking Barriers booklet, No. DX21.

There are minor differences between No. 2059 and No. 2059a, which also omits the copyright symbol and date.

1377 Angel with Hands raised in Blessing   **1378** Angel praying

1379 Angel playing Flute   **1380** Angel playing Lute

1381 Angel praying

1998 (2 Nov). Christmas. Angels. Multicoloured One centre phosphor band (20p.) or two phosphor bands (others). Perf 15×14.

2064	**1377**	20p. Angel with Hands raised in		
		Blessing	35	35
2065	**1378**	26p. Angel praying	45	45
2066	**1379**	30p. Angel playing Flute	60	60
2067	**1380**	43p. Angel playing Lute	80	80
2068	**1381**	63p. Angel praying	90	90
Set of 5			2·75	2·75
Set of 5 Gutter Pairs			5·50	
First Day Cover				3·00
Presentation Pack (PO Pack No. 292)			3·25	
PHQ Cards (set of 5) (202)			60	3·00

Year Pack

1998 (2 Nov). Comprises Nos. 2015/2030, 2034/2038 and 2041/2068.

CP2068*a*	Year Pack (Pack No. 293)	40·00

Post Office Yearbook

1998 (2 Nov). Comprises Nos. 2015/2030, 2034/2038 and 2041/2068 in hardback book with slip case

YB2068*a*	Yearbook	35·00

1382 Greenwich Meridian and Clock (John Harrison's chronometer)   **1383** Industrial Worker and Blast Furnace (James Watt's discovery of steam power)

 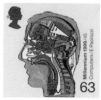

1384 Early Photos of Leaves (Henry Fox-Talbot's photographic experiments)   **1385** Computer inside Human Head (Alan Turing's work on computers)

1999 (12 Jan–21 Sept). Millennium Series. The Inventors' Tale. Multicoloured One centre phosphor band (20p.) or two phosphor bands (others). P 14×14½.

2069	**1382**	20p. Greenwich Meridian and Clock	40	40
2070	**1383**	26p. Industrial Worker and Blast		
		Furnace	60	60
2071	**1384**	43p. Early Photographs of Leaves	80	80
2072	**1385**	63p. Computer inside Human Head	1·00	1·00
		a. Perf 13½×14 (21.9.99)	1·75	1·75
Set of 4			2·50	2·50
Set of 4 Gutter Pairs			5·00	
First Day Cover (Philatelic Bureau)				4·25
Presentation Pack (PO Pack No. 294)			3·25	
PHQ Cards (set of 4) (203)			80	2·75

No. 2072a comes from the £6·99 World Changers booklet, No. DX23.

1386 Airliner hugging Globe (International air travel)   **1387** Woman on Bicycle (Development of the bicycle)

1388 Victorian Railway Station (Growth of public transport)   **1389** Captain Cook and Maori (Captain James Cook's voyages)

1999 (2 Feb). Millennium Series. The Travellers' Tale. Multicoloured One centre phosphor band (20p.) or two phosphor bands (others). Perf 14×14½.

2073	**1386**	20p. Airliner hugging Globe	40	40
2074	**1387**	26p. Woman on Bicycle	60	60
2075	**1388**	43p. Victorian Railway Station	80	80
2076	**1389**	63p. Captain Cook and Maori	1·00	1·00
Set of 4			2·50	2·50
Set of 4 Gutter Pairs			5·00	
First Day Cover (Philatelic Bureau)				3·25
Presentation Pack (PO Pack No. 295)			3·25	
PHQ Cards (set of 4) (204)			80	3·25

For Nos. 2077/2079, T **1390**, see Decimal Machins Definitive section

1391 Vaccinating Child (pattern in cow markings) (Jenner's development of smallpox vaccine)

1392 Patient on Trolley (nursing care)

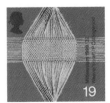

1399 Woven Threads (woollen industry)

1400 *Salts Mill, Saltaire* (worsted cloth industry)

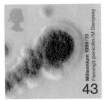

1393 Penicillin Mould (Fleming's discovery of penicillin)

1394 Sculpture of Test Tube Baby (development of in-vitro fertilisation)

1401 Hull on Slipway (shipbuilding)

1402 Lloyd's Building (City of London finance centre)

1999 (2 Mar–21 Sept). Millennium Series. The Patients' Tale. Multicoloured One centre phosphor band (20p.) or two phosphor bands (others). Perf 13½×14.

2080	**1391**	20p. Vaccinating Child	40	40
2081	**1392**	26p. Patient on Trolley	60	60
2082	**1393**	43p. Penicillin Mould	80	80
2083	**1394**	63p. Sculpture of Test-tube Baby	1·00	1·00
Set of 4			2·50	2·50
Set of 4 Gutter Pairs			5·00	
First Day Cover (Philatelic Bureau)				3·25
Presentation Pack (PO Pack No. 296)			3·25	
PHQ Cards (set of 4) (205)			80	3·25

1999 (4 May). Millennium Series. The Workers' Tale. Multicoloured One centre phosphor band (19p.) or two phosphor bands (others). Perf 14×14½.

2088	**1399**	19p. Woven Threads	40	40
2089	**1400**	26p. Salts Mill, Saltaire	60	60
2090	**1401**	44p. Hull on Slipway	80	80
2091	**1402**	64p. Lloyd's Building	1·00	1·00
Set of 4			2·50	2·50
Set of 4 Gutter Pairs			5·00	
First Day Cover (Philatelic Bureau)				3·25
Presentation Pack (PO Pack No. 298)			3·25	
PHQ Cards (set of 4) (207)			80	3·25

1395 Dove and Norman Settler (medieval migration to Scotland)

1396 Pilgrim Fathers and Native American (17th-century migration to America)

1403 Freddie Mercury (lead singer of Queen) (Popular Music)

1404 Bobby Moore with World Cup, 1966 (Sport)

1397 Sailing Ship and Aspects of Settlement (19th-century migration to Australia)

1398 Hummingbird and Superimposed Stylised Face (20th-century migration to Great Britain)

1405 Dalek from *Dr Who* (science-fiction series) (Television)

1406 Charlie Chaplin (film star) (Cinema)

1999 (6 Apr). Millennium Series. The Settlers' Tale. Multicoloured One centre phosphor band (20p.) or two phosphor bands (others). Perf 14×14½.

2084	**1395**	20p. Dove and Norman Settler	40	40
2085	**1396**	26p. Pilgrim Fathers and Native Amercian	60	60
2086	**1397**	43p. Sailing Ship and Aspects of Settlement	80	80
2087	**1398**	63p. Hummingbird and Superimposed Stylised Face	1·00	1·00
Set of 4			2·50	2·50
Set of 4 Gutter Pairs			5·00	
First Day Cover (Philatelic Bureau)				3·25
Presentation Pack (PO Pack No. 297)			3·25	
PHQ Cards (set of 4) (206)			80	3·25

1999 (1 June). Millennium Series. The Entertainers' Tale. Multicoloured One centre phosphor band (19p.) or two phosphor bands (others). Perf 14×14½.

2092	**1403**	19p. Freddie Mercury	40	40
2093	**1404**	26p. Bobby Moore with World Cup	60	60
2094	**1405**	44p. Dalek from Dr Who	80	80
2095	**1406**	64p. Charlie Chaplin	1·00	1·00
Set of 4			2·50	2·50
Set of 4 Gutter Pairs			5·00	
First Day Cover (Philatelic Bureau)				3·25
Presentation Pack (PO Pack No. 299)			3·25	
PHQ Cards (set of 4) (208)			80	3·25

1407 **1408**

Prince Edward and Miss Sophie Rhys-Jones (from photos by John Swannell)

1999 (15 June). Royal Wedding. Multicoloured Two phosphor bands. Perf 15×14.

2096	**1407**	26p. Prince Edward and Miss Sophie Rhys-Jones	40	40
2097	**1408**	64p. Prince Edward and Miss Sophie Rhys-Jones	1·00	1·00
Set of 2			1·25	1·25
Set of 2 Gutter Pairs			2·50	
First Day Cover (Philatelic Bureau)				2·00
Presentation Pack (PO Pack No. M01)			2·00	
PHQ Cards (*set of 2*) (PSM1)			40	2·00

1409 Suffragette behind Prison Window (Equal Rights for Women)

1410 Water Tap (Right to Health)

1411 Generations of School Children (Right to Education)

1412 'MAGNA CARTA' (Human Rights)

1999 (6 July). Millennium Series. The Citizens' Tale. Multicoloured One centre phosphor band (19p.) or two phosphor bands (others). Perf 14×14½.

2098	**1409**	19p. Suffragette behind Prison Window	40	40
2099	**1410**	26p. Water Tap	60	60
2100	**1411**	44p. Generations of School Children	80	80
2101	**1412**	64p. 'MAGNA CARTA'	1·00	1·00
Set of 4			2·50	2·50
Set of 4 Gutter Pairs			5·00	
First Day Cover (Philatelic Bureau)				3·25
Presentation Pack (PO Pack No. 300)			3·25	
PHQ Cards (*set of 4*) (209)			80	3·25

1413 Molecular Structures (DNA Decoding)

1414 Galapagos Finch and Fossilised Skeleton (Darwin's Theory of Evolution)

1415 Rotation of Polarised Light by Magnetism (Faraday's work on Electricity)

1416 Saturn (development of astronomical telescopes)

1999 (3 Aug–21 Sept). Millennium Series. The Scientists' Tale. Multicoloured One centre phosphor band (19p.) or two phosphor bands (others). Perf 13½×14 (19p., 64p.) or 14×14½ (26p., 44p.).

2102	**1413**	19p. Molecular Structures	40	40
2103	**1414**	26p. Galapagos Finch and Fossilised Skeleton	60	60
		b. Perf 14½×14 (21.9.99)	1·50	1·50
2104	**1415**	44p. Rotation of Polarised Light by Magnetism	80	80
		a. Perf 14½×14 (21.9.99)	1·50	1·50
2105	**1416**	64p. Saturn	1·00	1·00
Set of 4			2·50	2·50
Set of 4 Gutter Pairs			5·00	
First Day Cover (Philatelic Bureau)				3·25
Presentation Pack (PO Pack No. 301)			3·25	
PHQ Cards (*set of 4*) (210)			80	3·25

Nos. 2103b and 2104a come from the £6·99 World Changers booklet, No. DX23.

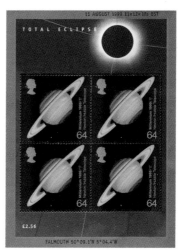

1416a Solar Eclipse

1999 (11 Aug). Solar Eclipse. Sheet 89×121 mm. Multicoloured. Two phosphor bands. Perf 14×14½.

MS2106	**1416a**	64p. Saturn×4 (*sold at* £2·56)	11·00	11·00
First Day Cover (Philatelic Bureau)				11·50

1417 Upland Landscape (Strip Farming)

1418 Horse-drawn Rotary Seed Drill (Mechanical Farming)

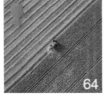

1419 Man peeling Potato (Food Imports)

1420 Aerial View of Combine-harvester (Satellite Agriculture)

1999 (7 Sept). Millennium Series. The Farmers' Tale. Multicoloured One centre phosphor band (19p.) or two phosphor bands (others). Perf 14×14½.

2107	**1417**	19p. Upland Landscape	40	40
2108	**1418**	26p. Horse-drawn Rotary Seed Drill	60	60
2109	**1419**	44p. Man peeling Potato	80	80
2110	**1420**	64p. Aerial View of Combine-harvester	1·00	1·00
Set of 4			2·50	2·50
Set of 4 Gutter Pairs			5·00	
First Day Cover (Philatelic Bureau)				3·25
Presentation Pack (PO Pack No. 302)			3·25	
PHQ Cards (set of 4) (211)			80	3·25

The 19p. includes the EUROPA emblem.

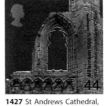
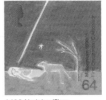

1427 St Andrews Cathedral, Fife (Pilgrimage)

1428 Nativity (First Christmas)

1999 (2 Nov). Millennium Series. The Christians' Tale. Multicoloured One centre phosphor band (19p.) or two phosphor bands (others). Perf 14×14½.

2115	**1425**	19p. 'Hark the herald angels sing' and Hymn book	40	40
2116	**1426**	26p. King James I and Bible	60	60
2117	**1427**	44p. St Andrews Cathedral, Fife	80	80
2118	**1428**	64p. Nativity	1·00	1·00
Set of 4			2·50	2·50
Set of 4 Gutter Pairs			5·00	
First Day Cover (Philatelic Bureau)				3·25
Presentation Pack (PO Pack No. 304)			3·25	
PHQ Cards (set of 4) (213)			80	3·25

1421 Robert the Bruce (Battle of Bannockburn, 1314)

1422 Cavalier and Horse (English Civil War)

1423 War Graves Cemetery, The Somme (World Wars)

1424 Soldiers with Boy (Peacekeeping)

1999 (5 Oct). Millennium Series. The Soldiers' Tale. Multicoloured. One centre phosphor band (19p.) or two phosphor bands (others). Perf 14×14½.

2111	**1421**	19p. Robert the Bruce	40	40
2112	**1422**	26p. Cavalier and Horse	60	60
2113	**1423**	44p. War Graves Cemetery, The Somme	80	80
2114	**1424**	64p. Soldiers with Boy	1·00	1·00
Set of 4			2·50	2·50
Set of 4 Gutter Pairs			5·00	
First Day Cover (Philatelic Bureau)				3·25
Presentation Pack (PO Pack No. 303*)			3·25	
PHQ Cards (set of 4) (212)			80	3·25

* The presentation pack was numbered 302 in error.

1429 'World of the Stage' (Allen Jones)

1430 'World of Music' (Bridget Riley)

1431 'World of Literature' (Lisa Milroy)

1432 'New Worlds' (Sir Howard Hodgkin)

1999 (7 Dec). Millennium Series. The Artists' Tale. Multicoloured. One centre phosphor band (19p.) or two phosphor bands (others). Perf 14×14½.

2119	**1429**	19p. 'World of the Stage'	40	40
2120	**1430**	26p. 'World of Music'	60	60
2121	**1431**	44p. 'World of Literature'	80	80
2122	**1432**	64p. 'New Worlds'	1·00	1·00
Set of 4			2·50	2·50
Set of 4 Gutter Pairs			5·00	
First Day Cover (Philatelic Bureau)				3·25
Presentation Pack (PO Pack No. 305)			3·25	
PHQ Cards (set of 4) (214)			80	3·25

Year Pack

1999 (7 Dec). Comprises Nos. 2069/2076, 2080/2105 and 2107/2122.

CP2122a	Year Pack (Pack No. 306)	65·00

Post Office Yearbook

1999 (7 Dec). Comprises Nos. 2069/2076, 2080/2105 and 2107/2122 in hardback book with slip case

YB2122a	Yearbook	50·00

1425 'Hark the herald angels sing' and Hymn book (John Wesley)

1426 King James I and Bible (Authorised Version of Bible)

1433a Millennium Timekeeper

1999 (14 Dec). Millennium Series. Millennium Timekeeper. Sheet 120×89 mm. Multicoloured Two phosphor bands. Perf 14×14½.

MS2123 **1433a** 64p. Clock face and map of North America; 64p. Clock face and map of Asia; 64p. Clock face and map of Middle East; 64p. Clock face and map of Europe		11·00	11·00
First Day Cover (Philatelic Bureau)			11·00
Presentation Pack (PO Pack No. M02)		11·00	
PHQ Cards (set of 5) (PSM02)		1·00	11·00

No. **MS**2123 also exists overprinted 'EARLS COURT, LONDON 22-28 MAY 2000 THE STAMP SHOW 2000' from Exhibition Premium Passes, costing £10, available from 1 March 2000.

The five PHQ cards show the four individual stamps and the complete miniature sheet.

For No. 2124, T **1437**, see Decimal Machin Definitives section.

1438 Barn Owl (World Owl Trust, Muncaster)

1439 Night Sky (National Space Science Centre, Leicester)

1440 River Goyt and Textile Mills (Torrs Walkway, New Mills)

1441 Gannets (Seabird Centre, North Berwick)

2000 (18 Jan–26 May). Millennium Projects (1st series). Above and Beyond. Multicoloured One centre phosphor band (19p.) or two phosphor bands (others). Perf 14×14½ (1st, 44p.) or 13½×14 (others).

2125	**1438**	19p. Barn Owl (World Owl Trust, Muncaster)	40	40
2126	**1439**	26p. Night Sky (National Space Science Centre, Leicester)	70	70
2126a		(1st) greenish yellow, magenta, pale new blue, black and silver (26.5.2000)	2·25	2·25
2127	**1440**	44p. River Goyt and Textile Mills (Torrs Walkway, New Mills)	1·00	1·00
2128	**1441**	64p. Gannets (Seabird Centre, North Berwick)	1·25	1·25
Set of 4 (ex No. 2126a)			3·00	3·00
Set of 4 Gutter Pairs			6·00	
First Day Cover (Philatelic Bureau)				4·00
Presentation Pack (PO Pack No. 307)			3·75	
PHQ Cards (set of 4) (215)			80	3·50

No. 2126a was only issued in the £2·70 Millennium booklet, No. HBA3, and on 24 September 2002 in the £6·83 Across the Universe stamp booklet, No. DX29.

1442 Millennium Beacon (Beacons across The Land)

1443 Garratt Steam Locomotive No. 143 pulling Train (Rheilffordd Eryri, Welsh Highland Railway)

1444 Lightning (Dynamic Earth Centre, Edinburgh)

1445 Multicoloured Lights (Lighting Croydon's Skyline)

2000 (1 Feb). Millennium Projects (2nd series). Fire and Light. Multicoloured One centre phosphor band (19p.) or two phosphor bands (others). Perf 14×14½.

2129	**1442**	19p. Millennium Beacon (Beacons across The Land)	40	40
2130	**1443**	26p. Garratt Steam Locomotive No. 143 pulling Train (Rheilffordd Eryri, Welsh Highland Railway)	70	70
2131	**1444**	44p. Lightning (Dynamic Earth Centre, Edinburgh)	1·00	1·00
2132	**1445**	64p. Multicoloured Lights (Lighting Croydon's Skyline)	1·25	1·25
Set of 4			3·00	3·00
Set of 4 Gutter Pairs			6·00	
First Day Cover (Philatelic Bureau)				3·50
Presentation Pack (PO Pack No. 308)			3·75	
PHQ Cards (set of 4) (216)			1·25	3·50

929 Queen Victoria and Queen Elizabeth II

1446 Queen Victoria and Queen Elizabeth II

2000 (15 Feb)–**2017**. T **929** redrawn with '1st' face value as T **1446**. Two phosphor bands. Perf 14 (No. 2133) or perf 14½×14 (both with one elliptical hole in each vertical side).

2133	**929**	20p brownish black and cream (5.6.17)	1·10	1·10
2133a	**1446**	(1st) brownish black and cream	1·10	1·10
First Day Cover (booklet pane No. 2133a×6)				9·50

No. 2133 comes from the £15·14 50th Anniversary of the Machin booklet, No. DY21.

No. 2133a was only issued in the £7·50 Special by Design booklet, No. DX24.

See also Nos. 2955/2956.

1447 Beach Pebbles (Turning the Tide, Durham Coast)

1448 Frog's Legs and Water Lilies (National Pondlife Centre, Merseyside)

1449 Cliff Boardwalk (Parc Arfordirol, Llanelli Coast)

1450 Reflections in Water (Portsmouth Harbour Development)

2000 (7 Mar). Millennium Projects (3rd series). Water and Coast. Multicoloured One centre phosphor band (19p.) or two phosphor bands (others). Perf 14×14½.

2134	**1447**	19p. Beach Pebbles (Turning the Tide, Durham Coast)	40	40
2135	**1448**	26p. Frog's Legs and Water Lilies (National Pondlife Centre, Merseyside)	70	70
2136	**1449**	44p. Cliff Boardwalk (Parc Arfordirol, Llanelli Coast)	1·00	1·00
2137	**1450**	64p. Reflections in Water (Portsmouth Harbour Development)	1·25	1·25
Set of 4			3·00	3·00
Set of 4 Gutter Pairs			6·00	
First Day Cover (Philatelic Bureau)				4·00
Presentation Pack (PO Pack No. 309)			3·75	
PHQ Cards (set of 4) (217)			1·25	4·50

1451 Reed Beds, River Braid (ECOS, Ballymena)

1452 South American Leafcutter Ants (Web of Life Exhibition, London Zoo)

1453 Solar Sensors (Earth Centre, Doncaster)

1454 Hydroponic Leaves (Project SUZY, Teesside)

2000 (4 Apr). Millennium Projects (4th series). Life and Earth. Multicoloured One centre phosphor band (2nd) or two phosphor bands (others). Perf 14×14½.

2138	**1451**	(2nd) Reed Beds, River Braid	90	90
2139	**1452**	(1st) South American Leafcutter Ants	1·00	1·00
2140	**1453**	44p. Solar Sensors	1·00	1·00
2141	**1454**	64p. Hydroponic Leaves	1·25	1·25
Set of 4			3·75	3·75
Set of 4 Gutter Pairs			7·50	
First Day Cover (Philatelic Bureau)				4·00
Presentation Pack (PO Pack No. 310)			4·25	
PHQ Cards (set of 4) (218)			1·25	4·50

1455 Pottery Glaze (Ceramica Museum, Stoke-on-Trent)

1456 Bankside Galleries (Tate Modern, London)

1457 Road Marking (Cycle Network Artworks)

1458 People of Salford (Lowry Centre, Salford)

2000 (2 May). Millennium Projects (5th series). Art and Craft. Multicoloured. One centre phosphor band (2nd) or two phosphor bands (others). Perf 14×14½.

2142	**1455**	(2nd) Pottery Glaze	90	90
2143	**1456**	(1st) Bankside Galleries	1·00	1·00
2144	**1457**	45p. Road Marking	1·00	1·00
2145	**1458**	65p. People of Salford	1·25	1·25
Set of 4			3·75	3·75
Set of 4 Gutter Pairs			7·50	
First Day Cover (Philatelic Bureau)				4·00
Presentation Pack (PO Pack No. 311)			4·25	
PHQ Cards (set of 4) (219)			1·25	4·00

For Nos. **MS2146/MS2147**, Types **1459/1459a**, see Decimal Machin Definitives section.

1460 Children playing (Millennium Greens Project)

1461 Millennium Bridge, Gateshead

1462 Daisies (Mile End Park, London)

1463 African Hut and Thatched Cottage (On the Meridian Line Project)

2000 (6 June). Millennium Projects (6th series). People and Places. Multicoloured One centre phosphor band (2nd) or two phosphor bands (others). Perf 14×14½.

2148	**1460**	(2nd) Children playing	90	90
2149	**1461**	(1st) Millennium Bridge, Gateshead	1·00	1·00
2150	**1462**	45p. Daisies	1·00	1·00
2151	**1463**	65p. African Hut and Thatched Cottage	1·25	1·25
Set of 4			3·75	3·75
Set of 4 Gutter Pairs			7·50	
First Day Cover (Philatelic Bureau)				4·00
Presentation Pack (PO Pack No. 312)			4·25	
PHQ Cards (set of 4) (220)			1·25	4·50

1464 Raising the Stone (Strangford Stone, Killyleagh)

1465 Horse's Hooves (Trans Pennine Trail, Derbyshire)

1466 Cyclist (Kingdom of Fife Cycleways, Scotland)

1467 Bluebell Wood (Groundwork's Changing Places Project)

2000 (4 July). Millennium Projects (7th series). Stone and Soil. Multicoloured One centre phosphor band (2nd) or two phosphor bands (others). Perf 14×14½

2152	**1464**	(2nd) Raising the Stone	90	90
2153	**1465**	(1st) Horse's Hooves	1·00	1·00
2154	**1466**	45p. Cyclist	90	90
2155	**1467**	65p. Bluebell Wood	1·10	1·10
Set of 4			3·50	3·50
Set of 4 Gutter Pairs			7·00	
First Day Cover (Philatelic Bureau)				4·00
Presentation Pack (PO Pack No. 313)			4·00	
PHQ Cards (*set of 4*) (221)			1·25	4·25

1468 Tree Roots (Yews for the Millennium Project)

1469 Sunflower (Eden Project, St Austell)

1470 Sycamore Seeds (Millennium Seed Bank, Wakehurst Place, West Sussex)

1471 Forest, Doire Dach (Forest for Scotland)

2000 (1 Aug). Millennium Projects (8th series). Tree and Leaf. Multicoloured One centre phosphor band (2nd) or two phosphor bands (others). Perf 14×14½.

2156	**1468**	(2nd) Tree Roots	90	90
2157	**1469**	(1st) Sunflower	1·00	1·00
2158	**1470**	45p. Sycamore Seeds	90	90
2159	**1471**	65p. Forest, Doire Dach	1·10	1·10
Set of 4			3·50	3·50
Set of 4 Gutter Pairs			7·00	
First Day Cover (Philatelic Bureau)				4·00
Presentation Pack (PO Pack No. 314)			4·00	
PHQ Cards (*set of 4*) (222)			1·25	4·25

1472 Queen Elizabeth the Queen Mother

1472a Royal Family on Queen Mother's 100th Birthday

2000 (4 Aug). Queen Elizabeth the Queen Mother's 100th Birthday. Multicoloured Phosphorised paper plus two phosphor bands. Perf 14½.

2160	**1472**	27p. Queen Elizabeth the Queen Mother	1·25	1·25
MS2161 121×89mm. **1472a** 27p.×4, Royal Family on Queen Mother's 100th Birthday			5·00	5·00
First Day Cover (booklet pane No. 2160×4)				5·25
First Day Cover (Philatelic Bureau) (No. **MS**2161)				5·25
Presentation Pack (PO Pack No. M04) (No. **MS**2161)			11·00	
PHQ Cards (*set of 5*) (PSM04)			1·50	5·50

No. 2160 was only issued in the £7·03 The Life of the Century booklet, No. DX25 and in No. **MS**2161.

The complete miniature sheet is shown on one of the PHQ cards with the others depicting individual stamps.

1473 Head of *Gigantiops destructor* (Ant) (Wildscreen at Bristol)

1474 Gathering Water Lilies on Broads (Norfolk and Norwich Project)

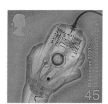

1475 X-ray of Hand holding Computer Mouse (Millennium Point, Birmingham)

1476 Tartan Wool Holder (Scottish Cultural Resources Access Network)

2000 (5 Sept). Millennium Projects (9th series). Mind and Matter. Multicoloured One centre phosphor band (2nd) or two phosphor bands (others). Perf 14×14½.

2162	**1473**	(2nd) Head of *Gigantiops destructor* (Ant)	90	90
2163	**1474**	(1st) Gathering Water Lilies on Broads	1·00	1·00
2164	**1475**	45p. X-ray of Hand holding Computer Mouse	90	90
2165	**1476**	65p. Tartan Wool Holder	1·10	1·10
Set of 4			3·50	3·50
Set of 4 Gutter Pairs			7·00	
First Day Cover (Philatelic Bureau)				4·00
Presentation Pack (PO Pack No. 315)			4·00	
PHQ Cards (*set of 4*) (223)			1·25	4·25

1477 Acrobatic Performers (Millennium Dome)

1478 Football Players (Hampden Park, Glasgow)

 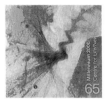

1479 Bather (Bath Spa Project)

1480 Hen's Egg under Magnification (Centre for Life, Newcastle)

2000 (3 Oct). Millennium Projects (10th series). Body and Bone. Multicoloured One centre phosphor band (2nd) or two phosphor bands (others). Perf 14×14½ (2nd) or 13½×14 (others).

2166	**1477**	(2nd) Acrobatic Performers	90	90
2167	**1478**	(1st) Football Players	1·00	1·00
2168	**1479**	45p. Bather	90	90
2169	**1480**	65p. Hen's Egg under Magnification	1·10	1·10
Set of 4			3·50	3·50
Set of 4 Gutter Pairs			7·00	
First Day Cover (Philatelic Bureau)				4·00
Presentation Pack (PO Pack No. 316)			4·00	
PHQ Cards (set of 4) (224)			1·25	4·25

1481 Virgin and Child Stained-glass Window, St Edmundsbury Cathedral (Suffolk Cathedral Millennium Project)

1482 Floodlit Church of St Peter and St Paul, Overstowey (Church Floodlighting Trust)

1483 12th-century Latin Gradual (St Patrick Centre, Downpatrick)

1484 Chapter House Ceiling, York Minster (York Millennium Mystery Plays)

2000 (7 Nov). Millennium Projects (11th series). Spirit and Faith. Multicoloured One centre phosphor band (2nd) or two phosphor bands (others). Perf 14×14½.

2170	**1481**	(2nd) Virgin and Child Stained-glass Window, St Edmundsbury Cathedral	90	90
2171	**1482**	(1st) Floodlit Church of St Peter and St Paul, Overstowey	1·00	1·00
2172	**1483**	45p. 12th-century Latin Gradual	90	90
2173	**1484**	65p. Chapter House Ceiling, York Minster	1·10	1·10
Set of 4			3·50	3·50
Set of 4 Gutter Pairs			7·00	
First Day Cover (Philatelic Bureau)				4·00
Presentation Pack (PO Pack No. 317)			4·00	
PHQ Cards (set of 4) (225)			1·25	4·25

Post Office Yearbook

2000 (7 Nov). Comprises Nos. 2125/2126, 2127/2132, 2134/2145, 2148/2159 and **MS**2161/2177 in hardback book with slip case

YB2173a	Yearbook	48·00

The last two issues in the Millennium Projects Series were supplied for insertion into the above at a later date.

1485 Church Bells (Ringing in the Millennium)

1486 Eye (Year of the Artist)

1487 Top of Harp (Canolfan Mileniwm, Cardiff)

1488 Silhouetted Figure within Latticework (TS2K Creative Enterprise Centres, London)

2000 (5 Dec). Millennium Projects (12th series). Sound and Vision. Multicoloured. One centre phosphor band (2nd) or two phosphor bands (others). Perf 14×14½.

2174	**1485**	(2nd) Church Bells	90	90
2175	**1486**	(1st) Eye	1·00	1·00
2176	**1487**	45p. Top of Harp	90	90
2177	**1488**	65p. Silhouetted Figure within Latticework	1·10	1·10
Set of 4			3·50	3·50
Set of 4 Gutter Pairs			7·00	
First Day Cover (Philatelic Bureau)				4·00
Presentation Pack (PO Pack No. 318)			4·00	
PHQ Cards (set of 4) (226)			1·25	4·25

Collectors Pack

2000 (Dec 5) Comprises Nos. 2125/216, 2127/2132, 2134/2145, 2148/2159 and **MS**2161/2177.

CP2177a	Collectors Pack (Pack No. 319)	65·00

1489 Flower (Nurture Children)

1490 Tiger (Listen to Children)

1491 Owl (Teach Children)

1492 Butterfly (Ensure Children's Freedom)

2001 (16 Jan). New Millennium. Rights of the Child. Face Paintings. Multicoloured One centre phosphor band (2nd) or two phosphor bands (others). Perf 14×14½.

2178	**1489**	(2nd) Flower (Nurture Children)	90	90
2179	**1490**	(1st) Tiger (Listen to Children)	1·00	1·00

2180	**1491**	45p. Owl (Teach Children)		1·00	1·00
2181	**1492**	65p. Butterfly (Ensure Children's Freedom)		1·25	1·25
Set of 4				3·75	3·75
Set of 4 Gutter Pairs				7·50	
First Day Cover (Philatelic Bureau)					4·00
Presentation Pack (PO Pack No. 319)				4·25	
PHQ Cards (set of 4) (227)				1·25	4·25

1493 Love   **1494** THANKS

1495 abc (New Baby)   **1496** WELCOME

1497 Cheers

2001 (6–13 Feb). Greetings Stamps. Occasions. Multicoloured Two phosphor bands. Perf 14×14½.

2182	**1493**	(1st) Love	1·20	1·00
2183	**1494**	(1st) THANKS	1·20	1·00
2184	**1495**	(1st) abc (New Baby)	1·20	1·00
2185	**1496**	(1st) WELCOME	1·20	1·00
2186	**1497**	(1st) Cheers	1·20	1·00
Set of 5			5·50	4·50
Set of 5 Gutter Pairs			11·00	
First Day Cover (Philatelic Bureau)				4·75
Presentation Pack (PO Pack No. M05) (13.2.01)			7·25	
PHQ Cards (set of 5) (PSM05)			1·50	5·00

The silver-grey backgrounds are printed in Iriodin ink which gives a shiny effect.

Further packs of Nos. 2182/2186 were sold from 3 July 2001. These comprised the listed stamps in blocks of ten (from sheets) with an insert describing the occasion (*Price £10 per pack*).

Nos. 2182/2186 were re-issued on 1 May 2001 in sheets of 20 printed in lithography instead of gravure, in connection with the 'customised' stamps scheme. Each stamp accompanied by a half stamp-sized label showing either postal symbols or a personal photographs.

1498 Dog and Owner on Bench   **1499** Dog in Bath

1500 Boxer at Dog Show   **1501** Cat in Handbag

1502 Cat on Gate   **1503** Dog in Car

1504 Cat at Window   **1505** Dog Behind Fence

1506 Cat watching Bird   **1507** Cat in Washbasin

2001 (13 Feb). Cats and Dogs. Multicoloured Self-adhesive. Two phosphor bands. Perf 15×14 die-cut.

2187	**1498**	(1st) Dog and Owner on Bench	1·20	1·00
		a. Sheet*let* of 10. Nos. 2187/2196	11·00	9·00
2188	**1499**	(1st) Dog in Bath	1·20	1·00
2189	**1500**	(1st) Boxer at Dog Show	1·20	1·00
2190	**1501**	(1st) Cat in Handbag	1·20	1·00
2191	**1502**	(1st) Cat on Gate	1·20	1·00
2192	**1503**	(1st) Dog in Car	1·20	1·00
2193	**1504**	(1st) Cat at Window	1·20	1·00
2194	**1505**	(1st) Dog Behind Fence	1·20	1·00
2195	**1506**	(1st) Cat watching Bird	1·20	1·00
2196	**1507**	(1st) Cat in Washbasin	1·20	1·00
Set of 10			11·00	9·00
First Day Cover (Philatelic Bureau)				9·75
Presentation Pack (PO Pack No. 320)			12·00	
PHQ Cards (set of 10) (228)			3·00	12·00

Nos. 2187/2196 were printed together in sheetlets of ten (5×2), with the surplus self-adhesive paper around each stamp retained. They were also issued in £3·24 booklets, the booklet pane has vertical roulettes between rows 2/3 and 4/5.

1508 'RAIN'   **1509** 'FAIR'

1510 'STORMY'   **1511** 'VERY DRY'

1511a The Weather

2001 (13 Mar). The Weather. Multicoloured One side phosphor band (19p.) or two phosphor bands (others). Perf 14½.

2197	**1508**	19p. 'RAIN'	70	70
2198	**1509**	27p. 'FAIR'	80	80
2199	**1510**	45p. 'STORMY'	95	95
2200	**1511**	65p. 'VERY DRY'	1·10	1·10
Set of 4			3·25	3·25
Set of 4 Gutter Pairs			6·50	
First Day Cover (Philatelic Bureau)				3·50
Presentation Pack (PO Pack No. 321)			9·00	
MS2201 **1511a** 105×105 mm. Nos. 2197/2200			9·25	9·25
First Day Cover (Philatelic Bureau)				10·00
PHQ Cards (set of 5) (229)			1·50	14·00

Nos. 2197/2200 show the four quadrants of a barometer dial which are combined on the miniature sheet.

The reddish violet on both the 27p. and the miniature sheet is printed in thermochromic ink which changes from reddish violet to light blue when exposed to heat.

The PHQ cards depict the four values and the miniature sheet.

1512 Vanguard Class Submarine, 1992

1513 Swiftsure Class Submarine, 1973

1514 Unity Class Submarine, 1939

1515 Holland Type Submarine, 1901

1516 White Ensign

1517 Union Jack

1518 Jolly Roger flown by HMS Proteus (submarine)

1519 Flag of Chief of Defence Staff

1519a Royal Navy Flags

2001 (10 Apr–22 Oct). Centenary of Royal Navy Submarine Service. Multicoloured One centre phosphor band (2nd) or two phosphor bands (others). Perf 15×14.

(a) Submarines. Ordinary gum.

2202	**1512**	(2nd) Vanguard Class Submarine, 1992	90	90
		a. Perf 15½×15 (22.10.01)	2·00	2·00
2203	**1513**	(1st) Swiftsure Class Submarine, 1973	1·00	1·00
		a. Perf 15½×15 (22.10.01)	1·95	1·95
2204	**1514**	45p. Unity Class Submarine, 1939	90	90
		a. Perf 15½×15 (22.10.01)	2·00	2·00
2205	**1515**	65p. Holland Type Submarine, 1901	1·10	1·10
		a. Perf 15½×15 (22.10.01)	2·00	2·00
Set of 4			3·50	3·50
Set of 4 Gutter Pairs			7·00	
First Day Cover (Philatelic Bureau)				3·75
Presentation Pack (PO Pack No. 322)			16·00	
PHQ Cards (set of 4) (230)			1·25	4·00

(b) Flags. Ordinary gum. Perf 14½.

MS2206 **1519a** 92×97 mm. (1st) White Ensign; (1st) Union Jack; (1st) Jolly Roger flown by HMS Proteus (submarine); (1st) Flag of Chief of Defence Staff (22.10.01)		5·25	5·25
First Day Cover			4·75
Presentation Pack (PO Pack No. M06)		15·00	
PHQ Cards (set of 5) (PSM07)		1·50	6·00

(c) Self-adhesive. Die-cut Perf 15½×14 (No. 2207) or 14½ (others).

2207	**1513**	(1st) Swiftsure Class Submarine, 1973 (17.4.01)	30·00	30·00
2208	**1516**	(1st) White Ensign (22.10.01)	7·00	7·00
2209	**1518**	(1st) Jolly Roger flown by HMS Proteus (submarine) (22.10.01)	7·00	7·00

Nos. 2202a/2205a were only issued in the £6·76 Unseen and Unheard booklet, No. DX27.

Nos. 2207/2209 only come from two different £1·62 self-adhesive booklets.

T **1516** was re-issued on 21 June 2005 in sheets of 20, printed in lithography instead of Gravure with half stamp-size se-tenant labels showing signal flags. (See No. 2581)

T **1517** was re-issued on 27 July 2004 in sheets of 20, printed in lithography instead of gravure with each vertical row of stamps alternated with half stamp-size labels (see No. 2805).

T **1518** was subsequently issued, printed in lithography, perf 14½ in booklet No. DX47 (see No. 2970).

The five PHQ cards depict the four designs and the complete miniature sheet, No. **MS**2206.

1520 Leyland X2 Open-top, London General B Type, Leyland Titan TD1 and AEC Regent 1

1521 AEC Regent 1, Daimler COG5, Utility Guy Arab Mk II and AEC Regent III RT Type

1522 AEC Regent III RT Type, Bristol KSW5G Open-top, AEC Routemaster and Bristol Lodekka FSF6G

1523 Bristol Lodekka FSF6G, Leyland Titan PD3/4, Leyland Atlantean PDR1/1 and Daimler Fleetline CRG6LX-33

1524 Daimler Fleetline CRG6LX-33, MCW Metrobus DR102/43, Leyland Olympian ONLXB/1R and Dennis Trident

2001 (15 May). 150th Anniversary of First Double-decker Bus. Multicoloured 'All-over' phosphor. Perf 14½×14.

2210	**1520**	(1st) Leyland X2 Open-top, London General B Type, Leyland Titan TD1 and AEC Regent 1	1·20	1·00
		a. Horiz strip of 5. Nos. 2210/2214	5·50	4·50
2211	**1521**	(1st) AEC Regent 1, Daimler COG5, Utility Guy Arab Mk II and AEC Regent III RT Type	1·20	1·00
2212	**1522**	(1st) AEC Regent III RT Type, Bristol KSW5G Open-top, AEC Routemaster and Bristol Lodekka FSF6G	1·20	1·00
2213	**1523**	(1st) Bristol Lodekka FSF6G, Leyland Titan PD3/4, Leyland Atlantean PDR1/1 and Daimler Fleetline CRG6LX-33	1·20	1·00
2214	**1524**	(1st) Daimler Fleetline CRG6LX-33, MCW Metrobus DR102/43, Leyland Olympian ONLXB/1R and Dennis Trident	1·20	1·00
Set of 5			5·50	4·50
Gutter Strip of 10			11·00	
First Day Cover (Philatelic Bureau)				4·75
Presentation Pack (PO Pack No. 323)			9·00	
PHQ Cards (set of 6) (231)			1·75	5·50
MS2215 120×105 mm. Nos. 2210/2214			6·00	6·00
First Day Cover				7·50

Nos. 2210/2214 were printed together, se-tenant, in horizontal strips of five throughout the sheet. The illustrations of the first bus on No. 2210 and the last bus on No. 2214 continue onto the sheet margins.

In No. **MS**2215 the illustrations of the AEC Regent III RT Type and the Daimler Fleetline CRG6LX-33 appear twice.

The six PHQ cards show the six stamps and No. **MS**2215.

1525 Toque Hat by Pip Hackett

1526 Butterfly Hat by Dai Rees

1527 Top Hat by Stephen Jones

1528 Spiral Hat by Philip Treacy

2001 (19 June). Fashion Hats. Multicoloured 'All-over' phosphor. Perf 14½.

2216	**1525**	(1st) Toque Hat by Pip Hackett	1·20	1·00
2217	**1526**	(E) Butterfly Hat by Dai Rees	2·25	1·50
2218	**1527**	45p. Top Hat by Stephen Jones	90	90
2219	**1528**	65p. Spiral Hat by Philip Treacy	1·10	1·10
Set of 4			4·75	4·00
Set of 4 Gutter Pairs			9·50	
First Day Cover (Tallents House)				4·25
Presentation Pack (PO Pack No. 324)			5·25	
PHQ Cards (set of 4) (232)			1·50	4·50

1529 Common Frog

1530 Great Diving Beetle

1531 Three-Spined Stickleback

1532 Southern Hawker Dragonfly

2001 (10 July). Europa. Pond Life. Multicoloured Two phosphor bands. Perf 15×14.

2220	**1529**	(1st) Common Frog	1·00	1·00
2221	**1530**	(E) Great Diving Beetle	1·75	1·50
2222	**1531**	45p. Three-Spined Stickleback	90	1·00
2223	**1532**	65p. Southern Hawker Dragonfly	1·10	1·00
Set of 4			4·25	4·00
Set of 4 Gutter Pairs			8·50	
First Day Cover (Tallents House)				4·75
Presentation Pack (PO Pack No. 325)			5·00	
PHQ Cards (set of 4) (233)			1·50	4·75

The 1st and E values incorporate the EUROPA emblem.

The bluish silver on all four values is in Iriodin ink and was used as a background for those parts of the design below the water line.

1533 Policeman

1534 Clown

1535 Mr Punch   **1536** Judy

1537 Beadle   **1538** Crocodile

2001 (4 Sept). Punch and Judy Show Puppets. Multicoloured Two phosphor bands. Perf 14×15.

(a) Gravure Walsall. Ordinary gum.

2224	**1533**	(1st) Policeman	1·20	1·00
		a. Horiz strip of 6. Nos. 2224/2229	6·50	5·50
2225	**1534**	(1st) Clown	1·20	1·00
2226	**1535**	(1st) Mr Punch	1·20	1·00
2227	**1536**	(1st) Judy	1·20	1·00
2228	**1537**	(1st) Beadle	1·20	1·00
2229	**1538**	(1st) Crocodile	1·20	1·00
Set of 6			6·50	5·50
Gutter Block of 12			13·00	
First Day Cover (Tallents House)				6·25
Presentation Pack (PO Pack No. 326)			7·00	
PHQ Cards (set of 6) (234)			1·75	6·25

(b) Gravure Questa. Self-adhesive. Die-cut Perf 14×15½.

2230	**1535**	(1st) Mr Punch	7·00	7·00
2231	**1536**	(1st) Judy	7·00	7·00

Nos. 2224/2229 were printed together, *se-tenant*, as horizontal strips of six throughout the sheet.

Nos. 2230/2231 were only issued in £1·62 stamp booklet, No. PM3.

1539 Carbon 60 Molecule (Chemistry)   **1540** Globe (Economic Sciences)

1541 Embossed Dove (Peace)   **1542** Crosses (Physiology or Medicine)

1543 Poem *The Addressing of Cats* by T. S. Eliot in Open Book (Literature)   **1544** Hologram of Boron Molecule (Physics)

2001 (2 Oct). Centenary of Nobel Prizes. Multicoloured One side phosphor band (2nd) or phosphor frame (others). Perf 14½.

2232	**1539**	(2nd) Carbon 60 Molecule (Chemistry)	90	90
2233	**1540**	(1st) Globe (Economic Sciences)	1·20	1·00
2234	**1541**	(E) Embossed Dove (Peace)	2·25	1·50
2235	**1542**	40p. Crosses (Physiology or Medicine)	1·50	1·50
2236	**1543**	45p. Poem *The Addressing of Cats* by T. S. Eliot in Open Book (Literature)	2·00	2·00
2237	**1544**	65p. Hologram of Boron Molecule (Physics)	2·50	2·50
Set of 6			8·75	8·50
Set of 6 Gutter Pairs			17·00	
First Day Cover (Tallents House)				9·00
Presentation Pack (PO Pack No. 327)			15·00	
PHQ Cards (set of 6) (235)			1·75	9·75

The grey-black on No. 2232 is printed in thermochromic ink which temporarily changes to pale grey when exposed to heat.

The centre of No. 2235 is coated with a eucalyptus scent.

1545 Robins with Snowman   **1546** Robins on Bird Table

1547 Robins skating on Bird Bath   **1548** Robins with Christmas Pudding

1549 Robins in Paper Chain Nest

2001 (6 Nov). Christmas. Robins. Self-adhesive. Multicoloured One centre phosphor band (2nd) or two phosphor bands (others). Die-cut perf 14½.

2238	**1545**	(2nd) Robins with Snowman	90	90
2239	**1546**	(1st) Robins on Bird Table	1·20	1·00
2240	**1547**	(E) Robins skating on Bird Bath	2·25	1·50
2241	**1548**	45p. Robins with Christmas Pudding	1·00	1·10
2242	**1549**	65p. Robins in Paper Chain Nest	1·10	1·25
Set of 5			6·00	5·00
First Day Cover (Tallents House)				5·50
Presentation Pack (PO Pack No. 328)			6·25	
PHQ Cards (set of 5) (236)			1·50	5·50

The 1st value was re-issued on 30 September 2003 in sheets of 20, in lithography instead of gravure, each stamp *se-tenant* with a Christmas label or personalised photograph. The sheet contained die-cut perforated stamps and labels.

The 2nd and 1st values were re-issued together on 1 November 2005 in sheets of 20 containing ten 2nd class and ten 1st class stamps, each stamp accompanied by a *se-tenant* label showing a snowman.

Year Pack

2001 (6 Nov). Comprises Nos. 2178/2200, 2202/2206, 2210/2214, 2216/2229 and 2232/2242.

CP2242a	Year Pack (Pack No. 329)	70·00

Post Office Yearbook

2001 (6 Nov) Comprises Nos. 2178/2196, **MS**2201/2206, 2210/2214, 2216/2229 and 2232/2242 in hardback book with slip case

YB2242a	Yearbook	48·00

1550 *How the Whale got his Throat* **1551** *How the Camel got his Hump*

1552 *How the Rhinoceros got his Skin* **1553** *How the Leopard got his Spots*

1554 *The Elephant's Child* **1555** *The Sing-Song of Old Man Kangaroo*

1556 *The Beginning of the Armadillos* **1557** *The Crab that played with the Sea*

1558 *The Cat that walked by Himself* **1559** *The Butterfly that stamped*

2002 (15 Jan). Centenary of Publication of Rudyard Kipling's Just So Stories. Self-adhesive. Multicoloured Two phosphor bands. Die-cut Perf 15×14.

2243	**1550**	(1st) *How the Whale got his Throat*	1·20	1·00
		a. Sheet*let* of 10. Nos. 2243/2252	11·00	9·00
2244	**1551**	(1st) *How the Camel got his Hump*	1·20	1·00
2245	**1552**	(1st) *How the Rhinoceros got his Skin*	1·20	1·00
2246	**1553**	(1st) *How the Leopard got his Spots*	1·20	1·00
2247	**1554**	(1st) *The Elephant's Child*	1·20	1·00
2248	**1555**	(1st) *The Sing-Song of Old Man Kangaroo*	1·20	1·00
2249	**1556**	(1st) *The Beginning of the Armadillos*	1·20	1·00
2250	**1557**	(1st) *The Crab that played with the Sea*	1·20	1·00
2251	**1558**	(1st) *The Cat that walked by Himself*	1·20	1·00

2252	**1559**	(1st) *The Butterfly that stamped*	1·20	1·00
Set of 10			11·00	9·00
First Day Cover (Tallents House)				9·25
Presentation Pack (PO Pack No. 330)			12·00	
PHQ Cards (*set of 10*) (237)			3·00	11·00

Nos. 2243/2252 were printed together in sheetlets of ten (5×2), with the surplus self-adhesive paper around each stamp retained.

1560 Queen Elizabeth II, 1952 (Dorothy Wilding) **1561** Queen Elizabeth II, 1968 (Cecil Beaton)

1562 Queen Elizabeth II, 1978 (Lord Snowdon) **1563** Queen Elizabeth II, 1984 (Yousuf Karsh)

1564 Queen Elizabeth II, 1996 (Tim Graham) **1565**

2002 (6 Feb). Golden Jubilee. Studio portraits of Queen Elizabeth II by photographers named. Multicoloured One centre phosphor band (2nd) or two phosphor bands (others). W **1565** (sideways). Perf 14½×14.

2253	**1560**	(2nd) Queen Elizabeth II, 1952 (Dorothy Wilding)	90	90
2254	**1561**	(1st) Queen Elizabeth II, 1968 (Cecil Beaton)	1·20	1·00
2255		Watermark upright	2·00	1·40
2256	**1563**	45p. Queen Elizabeth II, 1984 (Yousef Karsh)	1·00	1·10
2257	**1564**	65p. Queen Elizabeth II, 1996 (Tim Graham)	1·10	1·25
Set of 5			5·75	5·00
Set of 5 Gutter Pairs			11·50	
First Day Cover (Tallents House)				5·25
Presentation Pack (PO Pack No. 331)			7·00	
PHQ Cards (*set of 5*) (238)			1·50	5·75

Nos. 2253/2257 were also issued with watermark upright in the £7·29 A Glorious Accession booklet, No DX28.

1566 **1566a**

2002 (6 Feb). As Types **154/155** (Wilding definitive of 1952–1954), but with service indicator as T **1566**. One centre phosphor band (2nd) or two phosphor bands (1st). W **1565**. Uncoated paper. Perf 15×14 (with one elliptical hole in each vertical side).

2258	**1566**	(2nd) carmine-red	1·20	1·20
2259	**1566a**	(1st) green	1·25	1·25
Set of 2			2·12	2·20
First Day Cover (Philatelic Bureau Edinburgh)			8·00	

Nos. 2258/2259 were only issued in the £7·29 A Gracious Accession booklet, No. DX28.

For other Wilding designs with decimal values see Nos. 2031/2033, **MS**2326, **MS**2367, 2378/2380 and 3329.

1567 Rabbits ('a new baby')

1568 'LOVE'

1569 Aircraft Skywriting 'hello'

1570 Bear pulling Potted Topiary Tree (Moving Home)

1571 Flowers ('best wishes')

2002 (5 Mar)–2003. Greetings Stamps. Occasions. Multicoloured Two phosphor bands.

(a) Litho Questa. Ordinary gum. Perf 15×14.

2260	**1567**	(1st) Rabbits 'a new baby'	1·20	1·10
2261	**1568**	(1st) 'LOVE'	1·20	1·10
2262	**1569**	(1st) Aircraft Skywriting 'hello'	1·20	1·10
2263	**1570**	(1st) Bear pulling Potted Topiary Tree (Moving Home)	1·20	1·10
2264	**1571**	(1st) 'best wishes'	1·20	1·10
Set of 5			5·50	5·00
Set of 5 Gutter Pairs			11·00	
First Day Cover (Tallents House)				5·25
Presentation Pack (PO Pack No. M07)			5·75	
PHQ Cards (set of 5) (PSM08)			1·50	6·00

(b) Gravure Questa. Self-adhesive. Die-cut Perf 15×14.

2264a	**1569**	(1st) Aircraft Skywriting 'hello' (4.3.03)	3·00	3·00

Nos. 2260/2264 were re-issued on 23 April 2002 in sheets of 20 with half stamp-size labels, with either the five designs *se-tenant* with greetings on the labels or in sheets of one design with personal photographs on the labels. These stamps were perforated 14 instead of 15×14.

T **1569** was re-issued in sheets of 20 with half stamp-size *se-tenant* labels all printed in lithography as follows: on 30 January 2004 for Hong Kong Stamp Expo. It was issued in sheets of 20 perforated 14 with *se-tenant* labels on 21 April 2005 for Pacific Explorer 2005 World Stamp Expo, on 25 May 2006 for Washington 2006 International Stamp Exhibition, on 14 November 2006 for Belgica 2006 International Stamp Exhibition, on 5 August 2008 for Beijing 2008 Olympic Expo, on 3 August 2009 for Thaipex 09 Stamp Exhibition, on 21 October 2009 for Italia 2009 International Stamp Exhibition and on 4 December 2009 for MonacoPhil International Stamp Exhibition.

No. 2264a was only issued in £1·62 stamp booklet in which the surplus self-adhesive paper around each stamp was removed.

1574 Cliffs, Dover, Kent

1575 Padstow Harbour, Cornwall

1576 Broadstairs, Kent

1577 St Abb's Head, Scottish Borders

1578 Dunster Beach, Somerset

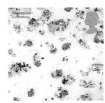

1579 Newquay Beach, Cornwall

1580 Portrush, County Antrim

1581 Sand-spit, Conwy

2002 (19 Mar). British Coastlines. Multicoloured Two phosphor bands. Perf 14½.

2265	**1572**	27p. Studland Bay, Dorset	50	50
		a. Block of 10. Nos. 2265/2274	4·50	4·50
2266	**1573**	27p. Luskentyre, South Harris	50	50
2267	**1574**	27p. Cliffs, Dover, Kent	50	50
2268	**1575**	27p. Padstow Harbour, Cornwall	50	50
2269	**1576**	27p. Broadstairs, Kent	50	50
2270	**1577**	27p. St Abb's Head, Scottish Borders	50	50
2271	**1578**	27p. Dunster Beach, Somerset	50	50
2272	**1579**	27p. Newquay Beach, Cornwall	50	50
2273	**1580**	27p. Portrush, County Antrim	50	50
2274	**1581**	27p. Sand-spit, Conwy	50	50
Set of 10			4·50	4·50
Gutter Block of 20			9·00	
First Day Cover (Tallents House)				4·75
Presentation Pack (PO Pack No. 332)			5·00	
PHQ Cards (set of 10) (239)			3·00	6·00

Nos. 2265/2274 were printed together, *se-tenant*, in blocks of ten (5×2) throughout the sheet.

1572 Studland Bay, Dorset

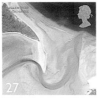

1573 Luskentyre, South Harris

1582 Slack Wire Act

1583 Lion Tamer

1584 Trick Tri-cyclists   **1585** Krazy Kar

1586 Equestrienne

2002 (10 Apr*). Europa. Circus. Multicoloured One centre phosphor band (2nd) or two phosphor bands (others). Perf 14½.

2275	**1582**	(2nd) Slack Wire Act	90	90
2276	**1583**	(1st) Lion Tamer	1·20	1·00
2277	**1584**	(E) Trick Tri-cyclists	2·25	1·50
2278	**1585**	45p. Krazy Kar	1·00	1·10
2279	**1586**	65p. Equestrienne	1·10	1·25
Set of 5			5·25	5·00
Set of 5 Gutter Pairs			11·00	
First Day Cover (Tallents House)				5·25
Presentation Pack (PO Pack No. 333)			5·75	
PHQ Cards (set of 5) (240)			1·50	5·75

*   Due to the funeral of the Queen Mother, the issue of Nos. 2275/2279 was delayed from 9 April, the date which appears on first day covers. The 1st and E values incorporate the EUROPA emblem.

1587 Queen Elizabeth the Queen Mother

1587a Queen Elizabeth

1587b Elizabeth, Duchess of York

1587c Lady Elizabeth Bowes-Lyon

2002 (25 Apr). Queen Elizabeth the Queen Mother Commemoration. Multicoloured Two phosphor bands. Perf 14×15.

2280	**1587**	(1st) Queen Elizabeth the Queen Mother	1·20	1·00
2281	**1587a**	(E) Queen Elizabeth	2·25	1·50
2282	**1587b**	45p. Elizabeth, Duchess of York	1·00	1·10
2283	**1587c**	65p. Lady Elizabeth Bowes-Lyon	1·10	1·25
Set of 4			4·75	4·25
Set of 4 Gutter Pairs			9·50	
First Day Cover (Tallents House)				4·50
Presentation Pack (PO Pack No. M08)			5·00	

1588 Airbus A340-600 (2002)

1589 Concorde (1976)

1590 Trident (1964)   **1591** VC10 (1964)

1592 Comet (1952)

2002 (2 May). 50th Anniversary of Passenger Jet Aviation. Airliners. Multicoloured One centre phosphor band (2nd) or two phosphor bands (others). Perf 14½.

(a) Gravure De La Rue. Ordinary gum.

2284	**1588**	(2nd) Airbus A340-600 (2002)	90	90
2285	**1589**	(1st) Concorde (1976)	1·20	1·00
2286	**1590**	(E) Trident (1964)	2·25	1·50
2287	**1591**	45p. VC10 (1964)	1·20	1·20
2288	**1592**	65p. Comet (1952)	1·40	1·40
Set of 5			6·25	6·00
Set of 5 Gutter Pairs			12·50	
First Day Cover (Tallents House)				6·50
Presentation Pack (PO Pack No. 334)			7·00	
MS2289 120×105 mm. Nos. 2284/2288			7·00	7·00
First Day Cover (Tallents House)				7·50
PHQ Cards (set of 6) (241)			1·75	12·00

(b) Gravure Questa. Self-adhesive. Die-cut Perf 14½.

2290	**1589**	(1st) Concorde (1976)	3·00	3·00

No. 2290 was only issued in £1·62 stamp booklets.
The complete miniature sheet is shown on one of the PHQ cards with the others depicting individual stamps.
See also No. 2897.

1593 Crowned Lion with Shield of St George

1594 Top Left Quarter of English Flag, and Football

1595 Top Right Quarter of English Flag, and Football

1596 Bottom Left Quarter of English Flag, and Football

1597 Bottom Right Quarter of English Flag, and Football

2002 (21 May). World Cup Football Championship, Japan and Korea. Multicoloured Two phosphor bands. Perf 14½×14.

(a) Ordinary gum.

2291	**1593**	(1st) Crowned Lion with Shield of St George	1·25	1·25
Gutter Pair			2·50	

MS2292 145×74 mm. No. 2291; Type **1594** (1st) Top Left Quarter of English Flag, and Football; Type **1595** (1st) Top Right Quarter of English Flag, and Football; Type **1596** (1st) Bottom Left Quarter of English Flag, and Football; Type **1597** (1st) Bottom Right Quarter of English Flag, and Football. Perf 14½ (square) or 15×14 (horiz)   5·00   5·00

First Day Cover (Tallents House) (No. **MS**2292)	5·50
Presentation Pack (PO Pack No. 335) (No. **MS**2292)	5·75
PHQ Cards (set of 6) (242)	1·75 7·50

(b) Self-adhesive. Die-cut Perf 15×14.

2293	**1594**	(1st) Top Left Quarter of English Flag, and Football	3·00	3·00
2294	**1595**	(1st) Top Right Quarter of English Flag, and Football	3·00	3·00

Stamps as T **1593** but with 'WORLD CUP 2002' inscription omitted were issued on 17 May 2007 in sheets of 20 with *se-tenant* labels showing scenes from Wembley Stadium.

Stamps as T **1597** also exist in sheets of 20 with *se-tenant* half stamp-sized labels, printed in lithography of gravure. The labels show either match scenes, supporters or personal photographs.

Nos. 2293/2294 were only issued in £1·62 stamp booklets.

The complete miniature sheet is shown on one of the PHQ cards with the others depicting individual stamps from No. **MS**2292 and No. 2291.

For Nos. 2295/2298 see Decimal Machin Definitives section.

1598 Swimming

1599 Running

1600 Cycling

1601 Long Jump

1602 Wheelchair Racing

2002 (16 July). 17th Commonwealth Games, Manchester. Multicoloured One side phosphor band (2nd) or two phosphor bands (others). Perf 14½.

2299	**1598**	(2nd) Swimming	90	90
2300	**1599**	(1st) Running	1·20	1·00
2301	**1600**	(E) Cycling	2·25	1·50
2302	**1601**	47p. Long Jump	1·10	1·25
2303	**1602**	68p. Wheelchair Racing	1·20	1·50
Set of 5			5·75	5·50
Set of 5 Gutter Pairs			11·50	
First Day Cover (Tallents House)				6·00
Presentation Pack (PO Pack No. 336)			6·00	
PHQ Cards (set of 5) (243)			1·50	6·75

1603 Tinkerbell

1604 Wendy, John and Michael Darling in front of Big Ben

1605 Crocodile and Alarm Clock

1606 Captain Hook

1607 Peter Pan

2002 (20 Aug). 150th Anniversary of Great Ormond Street Children's Hospital. *Peter Pan* by Sir James Barrie. Multicoloured One centre phosphor band (2nd) or two phosphor bands (others). Perf 15×14.

2304	**1603**	(2nd) Tinkerbell	90	90
2305	**1604**	(1st) Wendy, John and Michael Darling in front of Big Ben	1·20	1·00
2306	**1605**	(E) Crocodile and Alarm Clock	2·25	1·50
2307	**1606**	47p. Captain Hook	1·10	1·25
2308	**1607**	68p. Peter Pan	1·20	1·50
Set of 5			5·75	5·50
Set of 5 Gutter Pairs			11·50	
First Day Cover (Tallents House)				6·00
Presentation Pack (PO Pack No. 337)			6·00	
PHQ Cards (set of 5) (244)			1·50	6·75

1608 Millennium Bridge, 2001

1609 Tower Bridge, 1894

1610 Westminster Bridge, 1864

1611 Blackfriars Bridge, *circa* 1800 (William Marlow)

1612 London Bridge, *circa* 1670
(Wenceslaus Hollar)

2002 (10 Sept). Bridges of London. Multicoloured One centre phosphor
band (2nd) or two phosphor bands (others).
(a) Litho Questa. Ordinary gum. Perf 15×14.

2309	**1608**	(2nd) Millennium Bridge, 2001	90	90
2310	**1609**	(1st) Tower Bridge, 1894	1·20	1·00
2311	**1610**	(E) Westminster Bridge, 1864	2·25	1·50
2312	**1611**	47p. Blackfriars Bridge, circa 1800	1·20	1·60
2313	**1612**	68p. London Bridge, circa 1670	1·40	1·75
Set of 5			6·25	6·00
Set of 5 Gutter Pairs			12·50	
First Day Cover (Tallents House)				6·25
Presentation Pack (PO Pack No. 338)			30·00	
PHQ Cards (set of 5) (245)			1·50	7·00

(b) Gravure Questa. Self-adhesive. Die-cut Perf 15×14.

2314	**1609**	(1st) Tower Bridge, 1894	3·00	3·00

No. 2314 was only issued in £1·62 stamp booklets.

1613 Galaxies and Nebulae

2002 (24 Sept). Astronomy. Sheet 120×89 mm. Multicoloured Two
phosphor bands. Perf 14½×14.
MS2315 **1613** Galaxies and Nebulae (1st) Planetary
nebula in Aquila; (1st) Seyfert 2 galaxy in Pegasus;
(1st) Planetary nebula in Norma; (1st) Seyfert 2

galaxy in Circinus	4·80	4·80
First Day Cover (Tallents House)		5·00
Presentation Pack (PO Pack No. 339)	11·00	
PHQ Cards (set of 5) (246)	1·50	5·00

No. **MS**2315 was also issued in the £6·83 Across the Universe booklet
No. DX29.
The five PHQ cards depict the four designs and the complete miniature
sheet.

1614 Green Pillar
Box, 1857

1615 Horizontal
Aperture Box, 1874

1616 Air Mail Box,
1934

1617 Double
Aperture Box, 1939

1618 Modern Style
Box, 1980

2002 (8 Oct). 150th Anniversary of the First Pillar Box. Multicoloured One
centre phosphor band (2nd) or two phosphor bands (others). Perf
14×14½.

2316	**1614**	(2nd) Green Pillar Box, 1857	90	90
2317	**1615**	(1st) Horizontal Aperture Box, 1874	1·20	1·00
2318	**1616**	(E) Air Mail Box, 1934	2·25	1·50
2319	**1617**	47p. Double Aperture Box, 1939	1·20	1·10
2320	**1618**	68p. Modern Style Box, 1980	1·40	1·25
Set of 5			6·25	5·00
Set of 5 Gutter Pairs			12·50	
First Day Cover (Tallents House)				5·25
Presentation Pack (PO Pack No. 340)			6·75	
PHQ Cards (set of 5) (247)			1·50	5·50

1619 Blue Spruce Star

1620 Holly

1621 Ivy

1622 Mistletoe

1623 Pine Cone

2002 (5 Nov). Christmas. Self-adhesive. Multicoloured One centre
phosphor band (2nd) or two phosphor bands (others). Die-cut Perf
14½×14.

2321	**1619**	(2nd) Blue Spruce Star	90	90
2322	**1620**	(1st) Holly	1·20	1·00
2323	**1621**	(E) Ivy	2·25	1·50
2324	**1622**	47p. Mistletoe	1·25	1·25
2325	**1623**	68p. Pine Cone	1·40	1·40
Set of 5			6·00	5·00
First Day Cover (Tallents House)				5·25

Presentation Pack (PO Pack No. 341)	6·00	
PHQ Cards (set of 5) (248)	1·50	5·75

Year Pack

2002 (5 Nov). Comprises Nos. 2243/2257, 2260/2264, 2265/2288, **MS**2292, 2299/2313 and **MS**2315/2325.

CP2325a	Year Pack (Pack No. 342)	65·00

Post Office Yearbook

2002 (5 Nov). Comprises Nos. 2243/2257, 2260/2264, 2265/2288, 2291/2292, 2299/2313 and **MS**2315/2325 in hardback book with slip case

YB2325a	Yearbook	48·00

1623a Wilding Anniversary (1st issue)

2002 (5 Dec). 50th Anniversary of Wilding Definitives (1st issue). Sheet 124×70 mm, printed on pale cream. One centre phosphor band (2nd) or two phosphor bands (others). W **1565**. Perf 15×14 (with one elliptical hole in each vertical side).

MS2326 **1623a** 1p. orange-red; 2p. ultramarine; 5p. red-brown; (2nd) carmine-red; (1st) green; 33p. brown; 37p. magenta; 47p. bistre-brown; 50p. green and label showing National Emblems	5·00	5·00
First Day Cover (Tallents House)		5·25
Presentation Pack (PO Pack No. 59)	25·00	
PHQ Cards (set of 5) (D21)	1·50	5·00

The five PHQ cards depict the 1st, 2nd, 33p., 37p. and 47p. stamps.
For further Wilding designs with decimal face values, see Nos. 2031/2033, 2258/2259, **MS**2367 and 2378/2380

1624 Barn Owl landing

1625 Barn Owl with folded Wings and Legs down

1626 Barn Owl with extended Wings and Legs down

1627 Barn Owl in Flight with Wings lowered

1628 Barn Owl in Flight with Wings raised

1629 Kestrel with Wings folded

1630 Kestrel with Wings fully extended upwards

1631 Kestrel with Wings horizontal

1632 Kestrel with wings partly extended downwards

1633 Kestrel with wings fully extended downwards

2003 (14 Jan). Birds of Prey. Multicoloured Phosphor background. Perf 14½.

2327	**1624**	(1st) Barn Owl landing	1·20	1·00
		a. Block of 10. Nos. 2327/2336	10·50	9·00
2328	**1625**	(1st) Barn Owl with folded Wings and Legs down	1·20	1·00
2329	**1626**	(1st) Barn Owl with extended Wings and Legs down	1·20	1·00
2330	**1627**	(1st) Barn Owl in Flight with Wings lowered	1·20	1·00
2331	**1628**	(1st) Barn Owl in Flight with Wings raised	1·20	1·00
2332	**1629**	(1st) Kestrel with Wings folded	1·20	1·00
2333	**1630**	(1st) Kestrel with Wings fully extended upwards	1·20	1·00
2334	**1631**	(1st) Kestrel with Wings horizontal	1·20	1·00
2335	**1632**	(1st) Kestrel with wings partly extended downwards	1·20	1·00
2336	**1633**	(1st) Kestrel with wings fully extended downwards	1·20	1·00
Set of 10			10·50	9·00
Gutter Block of 20			21·00	
First Day Cover (Tallents House)				9·25
Presentation Pack (PO Pack No. 343)			11·00	
PHQ Cards (set of 10) (249)			3·00	11·00

Nos. 2327/2336 were printed together, se-tenant, in blocks of ten (5×2) throughout the sheet.

1634 'Gold star, See me, Playtime'

1635 'IU, XXXX, S.W.A.L.K.'

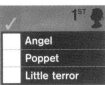
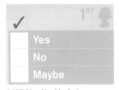

1636 'Angel, Poppet, Little terror'

1637 'Yes, No, Maybe'

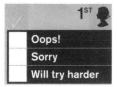

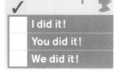

1638 'Oops!, Sorry, Will try harder'

1639 'I did it!, You did it!, We did it!'

2003 (4 Feb). Greetings Stamps. Occasions. Multicoloured Two phosphor bands. Perf 14½×14.

2337	**1634**	(1st) 'Gold star, See me, Playtime'	1·20	1·00
		a. Block of 6. Nos. 2337/2342	6·25	5·50
2338	**1635**	(1st) 'I 'heart' U, XXXX, S.W.A.L.K.'	1·20	1·00
2339	**1636**	(1st) 'Angel, Poppet, Little terror'	1·20	1·00
2340	**1637**	(1st) 'Yes, No, Maybe'	1·20	1·00
2341	**1638**	(1st) 'Oops!, Sorry, Will try harder'	1·20	1·00
2342	**1639**	(1st) 'I did it!, You did it!, We did it!'	1·20	1·00
Set of 6			6·25	5·50
Gutter Block of 12			12·50	
First Day Cover (Tallents House)				5·75
Presentation Pack (PO Pack No. M09)			6·00	
PHQ Cards (set of 6) (PSM09)			1·75	6·25

Nos. 2337/2342 were printed together, *se-tenant*, in blocks of six (3×2) throughout the sheet.

Nos. 2337/2342 were also issued in *se-tenant* sheets of 20 (containing four of Nos. 2338 and 2340 and three each of the others). The stamps are accompanied by half stamp-sized printed labels or a personalised photographs.

1640 Completing the Genome Jigsaw

1641 Ape with Moustache and Scientist

1642 DNA Snakes and Ladders

1643 Animal Scientists

1644 Genome Crystal Ball

2003 (25 Feb). 50th Anniversary of Discovery of DNA. Multicoloured One centre phosphor band (2nd) or two phosphor bands (others). Perf 14½.

2343	**1640**	(2nd) Completing the Genome Jigsaw	90	90
2344	**1641**	(1st) Ape with Moustache and Scientist	1·20	1·00
2345	**1642**	(E) DNA Snakes and Ladders	2·25	1·50
2346	**1643**	47p. Animal Scientists	1·10	1·40
2347	**1644**	68p. Genome Crystal Ball	1·25	1·60
Set of 5			6·00	5·75
Set of 5 Gutter Pairs			12·00	
First Day Cover (Tallents House)				6·25
Presentation Pack (PO Pack No. 344)			6·00	
PHQ Cards (set of 5) (250)			1·50	6·25

Nos. 2343 and 2345 come from the £6·99 Microcosmos booklet, No. DX30

1645 Strawberry   **1646** Potato

1647 Apple   **1648** Red Pepper

1649 Pear   **1650** Orange

1651 Tomato   **1652** Lemon

1653 Brussels Sprout   **1654** Aubergine

2003 (25 Mar). Fruit and Vegetables. Self-adhesive. Multicoloured Two phosphor bands. Perf 14½×14 die-cut (without teeth around protruding tops or bottoms of the designs).

2348	**1645**	(1st) Strawberry	1·20	1·00
		a. Sheet/et of 10. Nos. 2348/2357 and pane of decorative labels	10·50	
2349	**1646**	(1st) Potato	1·20	1·00
2350	**1647**	(1st) Apple	1·20	1·00
2351	**1648**	(1st) Red Pepper	1·20	1·00
2352	**1649**	(1st) Pear	1·20	1·00
2353	**1650**	(1st) Orange	1·20	1·00
2354	**1651**	(1st) Tomato	1·20	1·00
2355	**1652**	(1st) Lemon	1·20	1·00
2356	**1653**	(1st) Brussels Sprout	1·20	1·00
2357	**1654**	(1st) Aubergine	1·20	1·00
Set of 10			10·50	9·00
First Day Cover (Tallents House)				9·25
Presentation Pack (PO Pack No. 345)			12·00	
PHQ Cards (set of 10) (251)			3·00	10·50

115

Nos. 2348/2357 were re-issued on 7 March 2006 in sheets of 20, containing two of each of the ten designs accompanied by *se-tenant* labels with speech bubbles and stickers showing eyes, hats, etc. These sheets were printed in lithography instead of gravure.

Nos. 2348/2357 were printed together in sheets of ten with the surplus self-adhesive paper around each stamp retained.

The stamp pane is accompanied by a similar-sized pane of self-adhesive labels showing ears, eyes, mouths, hats, etc which are intended for the adornment of fruit and vegetables depicted. This pane is separated from the stamps by a line of roulettes.

No. 2355 was also available in sheets of 20 with personal photographs on the labels at £14·95 per sheet from Royal Mail Edinbugh.

For Nos. 2357a/2359 (Overseas Booklet Stamps), T **1655**, see Decimal Machin Definitives sections

1656 Amy Johnson (pilot) and Biplane

1657 Members of 1953 Everest Team

1658 Freya Stark (traveller and writer) and Desert

1659 Ernest Shackleton (Antarctic explorer) and Wreck of *Endurance*

1660 Francis Chichester (yachtsman) and *Gipsy Moth IV*

1661 Robert Falcon Scott (Antarctic explorer) and Norwegian Expedition at the Pole

2003 (29 Apr). Extreme Endeavours (British Explorers). Multicoloured One centre phosphor band (2nd) or two phosphor bands (others). Perf 15×14½.

		(a) Gravure Questa. Ordinary gum.		
2360	**1656**	(2nd) Amy Johnson	90	90
2361	**1657**	(1st) Members of 1953 Everest Team	1·20	1·00
2362	**1658**	(E) Freya Stark	2·25	1·50
2363	**1659**	42p. Ernest Shackleton	1·00	1·00
2364	**1660**	47p. Francis Chichester	1·10	1·25
2365	**1661**	68p. Robert Falcon Scott	1·25	1·40
Set of 6			6·75	6·25
Set of 6 Gutter Pairs			13·50	
First Day Cover (Tallents House)				7·00
Presentation Pack (PO Pack No. 346)			7·25	
PHQ Cards (set of 6) (252)			1·75	6·50

		(b) Gravure De La Rue. Self-adhesive. Die-cut Perf 14½.		
2366	**1657**	(1st) Members of 1953 Everest Team	3·00	3·00

The phosphor bands on Nos. 2361/2365 are at the centre and right of each stamp.

No. 2366 was only issued in £1·62 stamp booklets in which the surplus self-adhesive paper around each stamp was removed.

1661a Wilding Anniversary (2nd issue)

2003 (20 May). 50th Anniversary of Wilding Definitives (2nd issue). Sheet 124×70 mm, printed on pale cream. One centre phosphor band (20p.) or two phosphor bands (others). W **1565**. Perf 15×14 (with one elliptical hole in each vertical side).

MS2367 **1661a** 4p. deep lilac; 8p. ultramarine; 10p. reddish purple; 20p. bright green; 28p. bronze-green; 34p. brown-purple; (E) chestnut; 42p. Prussian blue; 68p. grey-blue and label showing National Emblems		4·50	4·75
First Day Cover (Tallents House)			5·50
Presentation Pack (PO Pack No. 61)		9·00	

1662 Guardsmen in Coronation Procession

1663 East End Children reading Coronation Party Poster

1664 Queen Elizabeth II in Coronation Chair with Bishops of Durham and Bath and Wells

1665 Children in Plymouth working on Royal Montage

1666 Queen Elizabeth II in Coronation Robes (photograph by Cecil Beaton)

1667 Children's Race at East End Street Party

1668 Coronation Coach passing through Marble Arch

1669 Children in Fancy Dress

1670 Coronation Coach outside Buckingham Palace

1671 Children eating at London Street Party

2003 (2 June). 50th Anniversary of Coronation. W **1565**. Multicoloured Two phosphor bands. Perf 14½×14.

2368	**1662**	(1st) Guardsmen in Coronation Procession	1·20	1·00
		a. Block of 10. Nos. 2368/2377	10·50	9·00
2369	**1663**	(1st) East End Children	1·20	1·00
2370	**1664**	(1st) Queen Elizabeth II in Coronation Chair	1·20	1·00
2371	**1665**	(1st) Children in Plymouth	1·20	1·00
2372	**1666**	(1st) Queen Elizabeth II in Coronation Robes	1·20	1·00
2373	**1667**	(1st) Children's Race	1·20	1·00
2374	**1668**	(1st) Coronation Coach passing through Marble Arch	1·20	1·00
2375	**1669**	(1st) Children in Fancy Dress	1·20	1·00
2376	**1670**	(1st) Coronation Coach outside Buckingham Palace	1·20	1·00
2377	**1671**	(1st) Children eating at London Street Party	1·20	1·00
Set of 10			10·50	9·00
Gutter Block of 20			21·00	
First Day Cover (Tallents House)				9·50
Presentation Pack (PO Pack No. 347)			11·00	
PHQ Cards (set of 10) (253)			3·00	10·00

Nos. 2368/2377 were printed together, se-tenant, as blocks of ten (5×2) in sheets of 60 (2 panes of 30).

No. 2372 does not show a silhouette of the Queen's head in gold as do the other nine designs.

2003 (2 June). 50th Anniversary of Coronation. Booklet stamps. W **1565**. Two phosphor bands. Perf 15×14 (with one elliptical hole in each vertical side for Nos. 2378/2379).

2378	**1671a**	47p. bistre-brown	2·00	2·00
2379	**1671b**	68p. grey-blue	2·50	2·50
2380	**1671c**	£1 deep yellow-green	26·00	26·00
Set of 3			30·00	30·00

Nos. 2378/2380 were only issued in the £7·46 A Perfect Coronation booklet, No. DX31.

Stamps as Nos. 2378/2379, but on pale cream, were also included in the Wilding miniature sheets, No. **MS**2326 or No. **MS**2367.

A £1 design as No. 2380, but on phosphorised paper, was previously included in the Stamp Show 2000 miniature sheet, No. **MS**2147.

1672 Prince William in September 2001 (Brendan Beirne)

1673 Prince William in September 2000 (Tim Graham)

1674 Prince William in September 2001 (Camera Press)

1675 Prince William in September 2001 (Tim Graham)

2003 (17 June). 21st Birthday of Prince William of Wales. Multicoloured Phosphor backgrounds. Perf 14½.

2381	**1672**	28p. Prince William in September 2001	95	95
2382	**1673**	(E) Prince William in September 2000	2·25	1·50
2383	**1674**	47p. Prince William in September 2001	1·70	1·90
2384	**1675**	68p. Prince William in September 2001	2·10	2·25
Set of 4			6·25	6·00
Set of 4 Gutter Pairs			12·50	
First Day Cover (Tallents House)				6·25
Presentation Pack (PO Pack No. 348)			8·00	
PHQ Cards (set of 4) (254)			1·25	6·75

1676 Loch Assynt, Sutherland

1677 Ben More, Isle of Mull

1678 Rothiemurchus, Cairngorms

1679 Dalveen Pass, Lowther Hills

1680 Glenfinnan Viaduct, Lochaber

1681 Papa Little, Shetland Islands

2003 (15 July). A British Journey. Scotland. Multicoloured One centre phosphor band (2nd) or two phosphor bands (others). Perf 14½.

(a) Ordinary gum.

2385	**1676**	(2nd) Loch Assynt, Sutherland	90	90
2386	**1677**	(1st) Ben More, Isle of Mull	1·20	1·00
2387	**1678**	(E) Rothiemurchus, Cairngorms	2·25	1·50
2388	**1679**	42p. Dalveen Pass, Lowther Hills	1·00	1·00
2389	**1680**	47p. Glenfinnan Viaduct, Lochaber	1·10	1·00
2390	**1681**	68p. Papa Little, Shetland Islands	1·25	1·40
Set of 6			7·00	6·25
Set of 6 Gutter Pairs			14·00	
First Day Cover (Tallents House)				6·75
Presentation Pack (PO Pack No. 349)			7·00	
PHQ Cards (set of 6) (255)			1·75	6·75

(b) Self-adhesive. Die-cut Perf 14½.

2391	**1677**	(1st) Ben More, Isle of Mull	3·00	3·00

No. 2391 was only issued in £1·68 stamp booklets in which the surplus self-adhesive paper around each stamp was removed.

1682 'The Station'
(Andrew Davidson)

1683 'Black Swan'
(Stanley Chew)

1684 'The Cross Keys'
(George Mackenney)

1685 'The Mayflower'
(Ralph Ellis)

1686 'The Barley
Sheaf' (Joy Cooper)

2003 (12 Aug). Europa. British Pub Signs. Multicoloured Two phosphor bands. Perf 14×14½.

2392	**1682**	(1st) 'The Station'	1·20	1·00
2393	**1683**	(E) 'Black Swan'	2·25	1·50
2394	**1684**	42p. 'The Cross Keys'	1·00	1·00
2395	**1685**	47p. 'The Mayflower'	1·25	1·25
2396	**1686**	68p. 'The Barley Sheaf'	1·40	1·40
Set of 5			6·25	5·50
Set of 5 Gutter Pairs			12·50	
First Day Cover (Tallents House)				5·75
Presentation Pack (PO Pack No. 350)			6·75	
PHQ Cards (set of 5) (256)			1·50	6·00

The 1st and E values include the EUROPA emblem.
No. 2392 was also issued in the £7·44 Letters by Night booklet, No. DX32.

1687 Meccano Constructor Biplane, *circa* 1931

1688 Wells-Brimtoy Clockwork Double-decker Omnibus, *circa* 1938

1689 Hornby M1 Clockwork Locomotive and Tender, *circa* 1948

1690 Dinky Toys Ford Zephyr, *circa* 1956

1691 Mettoy Friction Drive Space Ship *Eagle*, circa 1960

2003 (18 Sept). Classic Transport Toys. Multicoloured Two phosphor bands.

(a) Gravure Enschedé. Ordinary gum. Perf 14½×14.

2397	**1687**	(1st) Meccano Constructor Biplane	1·20	1·00
2398	**1688**	(E) Wells-Brimtoy Clockwork Double-decker Omnibus	2·25	1·50
2399	**1689**	42p. Hornby M1 Clockwork Locomotive and Tender	95	1·00
2400	**1690**	47p. Dinky Toys Ford Zephyr	1·25	1·25
2401	**1691**	68p. Mettoy Friction Drive Space Ship *Eagle*	1·40	1·50
Set of 5			6·25	5·50
Set of 5 Gutter Pairs			12·50	
First Day Cover (Tallents House)				5·75
Presentation Pack (PO Pack No. 351)			6·75	
PHQ Cards (set of 6) (257)			1·75	6·00
MS2402 115×105mm. Nos. 2397/2401			6·50	5·50
First Day Cover (Philatelic Bureau, Edinburgh)				6·75

(b) Gravure De La Rue. Self-adhesive. Die-cut Perf 14½×14.

2403	**1687**	(1st) Meccano Constructor Biplane	3·00	3·00

No. 2403 was only issued in £1·68 stamp booklets in which the surplus self-adhesive paper around each stamp was removed.

The complete miniature sheet is shown on one of the PHQ cards with the others depicting individual stamps.

1692 Coffin of Denytenamun, Egyptian, *circa* 900BC

1693 Alexander the Great, Greek, *circa* 200BC

1694 Sutton Hoo Helmet, Anglo-Saxon, *circa* AD600

1695 Sculpture of Parvati, South Indian, *circa* AD1550

1696 Mask of Xiuhtecuhtli, Mixtec-Aztec, *circa* AD1500

1697 Hoa Hakananai'a, Easter Island, *circa* AD1000

2003 (7 Oct). 250th Anniversary of the British Museum. Multicoloured One side phosphor band (2nd), two phosphor bands ((1st), (E), 47p.) or phosphor background at left and band at right (42p., 68p.). Perf 14×14½.

2404	**1692**	(2nd) Coffin of Denytenamun	90	90
2405	**1693**	(1st) Alexander the Great	1·20	1·00
2406	**1694**	(E) Sutton Hoo Helmet	2·25	1·50
2407	**1695**	42p. Sculpture of Parvati	90	1·00
2408	**1696**	47p. Mask of Xiuhtecuhtli	1·00	1·00
2409	**1697**	68p. Hoa Hakananai'a	1·10	1·25
Set of 6			6·25	6·00
Set of 6 Gutter Pairs			12·50	
First Day Cover (Tallents House)				6·50
Presentation Pack (PO Pack No. 352)			7·00	
PHQ Cards (set of 6) (258)			1·75	6·00

1698 Ice Spiral

1699 Icicle Star

1700 Wall of Ice Blocks

1701 Ice Ball

1702 Ice Hole

1703 Snow Pyramids

2003 (4 Nov). Christmas. Ice Sculptures by Andy Goldsworthy. Self-adhesive. Multicoloured One side phosphor band (2nd), 'all-over' phosphor (1st) or two bands (others). Die-cut Perf 14½×14.

2410	**1698**	(2nd) Ice Spiral	90	90
2411	**1699**	(1st) Icicle Star	1·20	1·00
2412	**1700**	(E) Wall of Ice Blocks	2·25	1·50
2413	**1701**	53p. Ice Ball	1·25	1·25
2414	**1702**	68p. Ice Hole	1·40	1·50
2415	**1703**	£1·12 Snow Pyramids	1·50	1·60
Set of 6			7·50	6·75
First Day Cover (Tallents House)				7·50
Presentation Pack (PO Pack No. 353)			7·25	
PHQ Cards (set of 6) (259)			1·75	7·00

Nos. 2410/2415 were each printed in sheets of 50 with the surplus backing paper around each stamp removed.

The 2nd and 1st class were also issued in separate sheets of 20 printed in lithography instead of gravure, each stamp accompanied by a half stamp-size *se-tenant* label showing either ice sculptures, animals or a personal photograph.

Year Pack

2003 (4 Nov). Comprises Nos. 2327/2357, 2360/2365, 2368/2377, 2381/2390, 2392/2401 and 2404/2415

CP2415a	Year Pack (Pack No. 354)	70·00

Post Office Yearbook

2003 (4 Nov). Comprises Nos. 2327/2357, 2360/2365, 2368/2377, 2381/2390, 2392/2401 and 2404/2415 in hardback book with slipcase

YB2415a	Yearbook	55·00

1704 Rugby Scenes

2003 (19 Dec). England's Victory in Rugby World Cup Championship, Australia. Sheet 115×85 mm. Multicoloured Two phosphor bands. Perf 14.

MS2416 **1704**	(1st) England flags and fans; (1st) England team standing in circle before match; 68p. World Cup trophy; 68p. Victorious England players after match	9·00	9·00
First Day Cover (Tallents House)			9·25
Presentation Pack (PO Pack No. M9B)		20·00	

1705 *Dolgoch*, Rheilffordd Talyllyn Railway, Gwynedd

1706 CR Class 439, Bo'ness and Kinneil Railway, West Lothian

1707 GCR Class 8K, Leicestershire

1708 GWR Manor Class *Bradley Manor*, Severn Valley Railway, Worcestershire

1709 SR West Country Class *Blackmoor Vale*, Bluebell Railway, East Sussex

1710 BR Standard Class, Keighley and Worth Valley Railway, Yorkshire

2004 (13 Jan). Classic Locomotives. Multicoloured One side phosphor band (20p.) or two phosphor bands (others). Perf 14½.

2417	**1705**	20p. *Dolgoch*, Rheilffordd Talyllyn Railway	65	65
2418	**1706**	28p. CR Class 439, Bo'ness and Kinneil Railway	75	75
2419	**1707**	(E) GCR Class 8K	2·25	1·50
2420	**1708**	42p. GWR Manor Class *Bradley Manor*, Severn Valley Railway	1·00	1·10
2421	**1709**	47p. SR West Country Class *Blackmoor Vale*, Bluebell Railway	1·10	1·25
2422	**1710**	68p. BR Standard Class, Keighley and Worth Valley Railway	1·25	1·25
Set of 6			5·75	5·50
Set of 6 Gutter Pairs			12·50	
First Day Cover (Tallents House)				6·00
Presentation Pack (PO Pack No. 355)			10·00	
PHQ Cards (set of 7) (260)			2·00	6·25
MS2423 190×67 mm. Nos. 2417/2422			14·50	14·50
First Day (Tallents House)				15·00

No. 2418/2420 were also issued in the £7·44 Letters by Night booklet, No. DX32.

The seven PHQ cards depict the six individual stamps and the miniature sheet.

1711 Postman

1712 Face

1713 Duck

1714 Baby

1715 Aircraft

2004 (3 Feb). Occasions. Multicoloured Two phosphor bands. Perf 14½×14.

2424	**1711**	(1st) Postman	1·20	1·00
		a. Horiz strip of 5. Nos. 2424/2428	5·50	4·50
2425	**1712**	(1st) Face	1·20	1·00
2426	**1713**	(1st) Duck	1·20	1·00
2427	**1714**	(1st) Baby	1·20	1·00
2428	**1715**	(1st) Aircraft	1·20	1·00
Set of 5			5·50	4·50
Gutter Block of 10			11·00	
First Day Cover (Tallents House)				5·00
Presentation Pack (PO Pack No. M10)			5·75	
PHQ Cards (set of 5) (PSM10)			1·50	6·00

Nos. 2424/2428 were also issued in sheets of 20 containing the five designs *se-tenant* with half stamp-size printed message labels. Similar sheets containing either Nos. 2424 and 2428 or Nos. 2425/2427 came with personal photographs on the label.

Nos. 2424/2428 were printed together, *se-tenant*, as horizontal strips of five in sheets of 25 (5×5).

1716 Map showing Middle Earth

1717 Forest of Lothlórien in Spring

1718 Dust Jacket for The Fellowship of the Ring

1719 Rivendell

1720 The Hall at Bag End

1721 Orthanc

1722 Doors of Durin

1723 Barad-dûr

1724 Minas Tirith

1725 Fangorn Forest

2004 (26 Feb). 50th Anniversary of Publication of *The Fellowship of the Ring* and *The Two Towers* by J. R. R. Tolkien. Multicoloured Two phosphor bands. Perf 14½.

2429	**1716**	(1st) Map showing Middle Earth	1·20	1·00
		a. Block of 10. Nos. 2429/2438	11·00	9·00
2430	**1717**	(1st) Forest of Lothlórien in Spring	1·20	1·00
2431	**1718**	(1st) Dust Jacket for *The Fellowship of the Ring*	1·20	1·00
2432	**1719**	(1st) Rivendell	1·20	1·00
2433	**1720**	(1st) The Hall at Bag End	1·20	1·00
2434	**1721**	(1st) Orthanc	1·20	1·00
2435	**1722**	(1st) Doors of Durin	1·20	1·00
2436	**1723**	(1st) Barad-dûr	1·20	1·00
2437	**1724**	(1st) Minas Tirith	1·20	1·00
2438	**1725**	(1st) Fangorn Forest	1·20	1·00
Set of 10			11·00	9·00
Gutter Block of 20			22·00	
First Day Cover (Tallents House)				9·25
Presentation Pack (PO Pack No. 356)			11·50	
PHQ Cards (set of 10) (261)			3·00	10·50

Nos. 2429/2438 were printed together, *se-tenant*, in blocks of ten (5×2) throughout the sheet.

1726 Ely Island, Lower Lough Erne

1727 Giant's Causeway, Antrim Coast

1728 Slemish, Antrim Mountains

1729 Banns Road, Mourne Mountains

1730 Glenelly Valley, Sperrins

1731 Islandmore, Strangford Lough

2004 (16 Mar). A British Journey. Northern Ireland. Multicoloured One side phosphor band (2nd) or two phosphor bands (others). Perf 14½.

(a) Ordinary gum.

2439	**1726**	(2nd) Ely Island, Lower Lough Erne	90	90
2440	**1727**	(1st) Giant's Causeway, Antrim Coast	1·20	1·00
2441	**1728**	(E) Slemish, Antrim Mountains	2·25	1·50
2442	**1729**	42p. Banns Road, Mourne Mountains	85	85
2443	**1730**	47p. Glenelly Valley, Sperrins	85	95
2444	**1731**	68p. Islandmore, Strangford Lough	1·00	1·10
Set of 6			6·25	5·50
Set of 6 Gutter Pairs			12·50	
First Day Cover (Tallents House)				5·75
Presentation Pack (PO Pack No. 357)			6·75	
PHQ Cards (set of 6) (262)			1·75	5·75

(b) Self-adhesive. Die-cut Perf 14½.

2445	**1727**	(1st) Giant's Causeway, Antrim Coast	3·25	3·25

No. 2445 was only issued in £1·68 stamp booklets in which the surplus self-adhesive paper around each stamp was removed.

1732 Lace 1 (trial proof) 1968 (Sir Terry Frost)

1733 Coccinelle (Sonia Delaunay)

2004 (6 Apr). Contemporary Paintings. Centenary of the Entente Cordiale. Multicoloured Two phosphor bands. Perf 14×14½.

2446	**1732**	28p. Lace 1 (trial proof) 1968	80	80
2447	**1733**	57p. Coccinelle	1·25	1·25
Set of 2			1·75	1·75
Set of 2 Gutter Pairs			3·50	
Set of 2 Traffic Light Gutter Blocks of 4			10·00	
First Day Cover (Tallents House)				1·90

Presentation Pack (PO Pack No. 358)	8·00	
Presentation Pack (UK and French stamps)	8·00	
PHQ Cards (set of 2) (263)	60	2·00

Stamps in similar designs were issued by France and these are included in the joint Presentation Pack.

1734 RMS Queen Mary 2, 2004 (Edward D. Walker)

1735 SS Canberra, 1961 (David Cobb)

1736 RMS Queen Mary, 1936 (Charles Pears)

1737 RMS Mauretania, 1907 (Thomas Henry)

1738 SS City of New York, 1888 (Raphael Monleaon y Torres)

1739 PS Great Western, 1838 (Joseph Walter)

1739a Ocean Liners

2004 (13 Apr). Ocean Liners. Multicoloured Two phosphor bands. Perf 14½×14.

(a) Ordinary gum.

2448	**1734**	(1st) RMS Queen Mary 2, 2004	1·20	1·00
2449	**1735**	(E) SS Canberra, 1961	2·25	1·50
2450	**1736**	42p. RMS Queen Mary, 1936	70	80
2451	**1737**	47p. RMS Mauretania, 1907	75	85
2452	**1738**	57p. SS City of New York, 1888	80	90
2453	**1739**	68p. PS Great Western, 1838	85	95
Set of 6			5·75	5·00
Set of 6 Gutter Pairs			11·50	
First Day Cover (Tallents House)				5·50
Presentation Pack (PO Pack No. 359)			6·00	
PHQ Cards (set of 7) (264)			2·00	5·25
MS2454 **1739a** 114×104mm. Nos. 2448/2453			7·25	7·25
First Day Cover (Tallents House)				7·50

(b) Self-adhesive. Die-cut Perf 14½×14.
2455   **1734**   (1st) RMS *Queen Mary 2*, 2004   3·00   3·00
Nos. 2448/2455 commemorate the introduction to service of the *Queen Mary 2*.
No. 2455 was only issued in £1·68 stamp booklets in which the surplus self-adhesive paper around each stamp was removed.
The complete miniature sheet is shown on one of the PHQ cards with the others depicting individual stamps.
See also No. 2614.

1740 *Dianthus Allwoodii*, Group   **1741** Dahlia, Garden Princess

1742 Clematis, Arabella   **1743** Miltonia, French Lake

1744 Lilium, Lemon Pixie   **1745** Delphinium, Clifford Sky

2004 (25 May). Bicentenary of the Royal Horticultural Society (1st issue). Multicoloured One side phosphor band (2nd) or 'all-over' phosphor (others). Perf 14½.

2456	**1740**	(2nd) *Dianthus Allwoodii* Group	90	90
2457	**1741**	(1st) Dahlia, Garden Princess	1·20	1·00
2458	**1742**	(E) Clematis, Arabella	2·25	1·50
2459	**1743**	42p. Miltonia, French Lake	80	85
2460	**1744**	47p. Lilium, Lemon Pixie	85	90
2461	**1745**	68p. Delphinium, Clifford Sky	90	1·00
Set of 6			6·00	5·50
Set of 6 Gutter Pairs			12·00	
First Day Cover (Tallents House)				5·75
Presentation Pack (PO Pack No. 360)			6·50	
PHQ Cards (set of 7) (265)			2·00	6·50
MS2462 115×105 mm. Nos. 2456/2461			6·50	6·50
First Day Cover (Tallents House)				7·25

Nos. 2456/2461 were also issued in the £7·23 Glory of the Garden booklet, No. DX33.
The 1st class stamp was also issued in sheets of 20, printed in lithography instead of gravure, each stamp accompanied by a *se-tenant* stamp-sized label.
The complete miniature sheet is shown on one of the PHQ cards with the others depicting individual stamps.

2004 (25 May). Bicentenary of the Royal Horticultural Society (2nd issue). Booklet stamps. Designs as Nos. 1955, 1958 and 1962 (1997 Greetings Stamps 19th-century Flower Paintings). Multicoloured Two phosphor bands. Perf 15×14 (with one elliptical hole in each vert side.)

2463	**1280**	(1st) *Gentiana acaulis* (Georg Ehret)	2·75	2·75
2464	**1283**	(1st) *Tulipa* (Ehret)	1·40	1·40
2465	**1287**	(1st) *Iris latifolia* (Ehret)	2·75	2·75
Set of 3			6·50	6·50

On Nos. 2463/2465 the phosphor bands appear at the left and centre of each stamp.
Nos. 2463/2465 were only issued in the £7·23 Glory of the Garden booklet, No. DX33.

1746 Barmouth Bridge   **1747** Hyddgen, Plynlimon

1748 Brecon Beacons   **1749** Pen-pych, Rhondda Valley

1750 Rhewl, Dee Valley   **1751** Marloes Sands

2004 (15 June). A British Journey. Wales. Multicoloured One centre phosphor band (2nd), 'all-over' phosphor (1st) or two phosphor bands (others). Perf 14½.

(a) Ordinary gum.

2466	**1746**	(2nd) Barmouth Bridge	90	90
2467	**1747**	(1st) Hyddgen, Plynlimon	1·20	1·00
2468	**1748**	40p. Brecon Beacons	70	70
2469	**1749**	43p. Pen-pych, Rhondda Valley	75	75
2470	**1750**	47p. Rhewl, Dee Valley	80	85
2471	**1751**	68p. Marloes Sands	90	95
Set of 6			4·50	4·50
Set of 6 Gutter Pairs			9·00	
First Day Cover (Tallents House)				4·75
Presentation Pack (PO Pack No. 361)			4·75	
PHQ Cards (set of 6) (266)			1·75	5·25

(b) Self-adhesive. Die-cut Perf 14½.
2472   **1747**   (1st) Hyddgen, Plynlimon   3·00   3·00
The 1st and 40p. values include the EUROPA emblem.
No. 2472 was only issued in £1·68 stamp booklets in which the surplus self-adhesive paper around each stamp was removed.

1752 Sir Rowland Hill Award   **1753** William Shipley (Founder of Royal Society of Arts)

1754 'RSA' as Typewriter Keys and Shorthand   **1755** Chimney Sweep

1756 Gill Typeface   **1757** 'Zero Waste'

2004 (10 Aug). 250th Anniversary of the Royal Society of Arts. Multicoloured Two phosphor bands. Perf 14.

2473	**1752**	(1st) Sir Rowland Hill Award	1·20	1·00
2474	**1753**	40p. William Shipley	75	75
2475	**1754**	43p. 'RSA' as Typewriter Keys and Shorthand	80	80
2476	**1755**	47p. Chimney Sweep	1·00	1·00
2477	**1756**	57p. Gill Typeface	1·25	1·25
2478	**1757**	68p. 'Zero Waste'	1·50	1·50
Set of 6			5·50	5·50
Set of 6 Gutter Pairs			11·00	
First Day Cover (Tallents House)				5·75
Presentation Pack (PO Pack No. 362)			6·00	
PHQ Cards (set of 6) (267)			1·75	6·50

1758 Pine Marten   **1759** Roe Deer

1760 Badger   **1761** Yellow-necked Mouse

1762 Wild Cat   **1763** Red Squirrel

1764 Stoat   **1765** Natterer's Bat

1766 Mole   **1767** Fox

2004 (16 Sept). Woodland Animals. Multicoloured Two phosphor bands. Perf 14½.

2479	**1758**	(1st) Pine Marten	1·20	1·00
		a. Block of 10. Nos. 2479/2488	10·50	9·00
2480	**1759**	(1st) Roe Deer	1·20	1·00
2481	**1760**	(1st) Badger	1·20	1·00
2482	**1761**	(1st) Yellow-necked Mouse	1·20	1·00
2483	**1762**	(1st) Wild Cat	1·20	1·00
2484	**1763**	(1st) Red Squirrel	1·20	1·00
2485	**1764**	(1st) Stoat	1·20	1·00
2486	**1765**	(1st) Natterer's Bat	1·20	1·00
2487	**1766**	(1st) Mole	1·20	1·00
2488	**1767**	(1st) Fox	1·20	1·00
Set of 10			10·50	9·00
Gutter Block of 20			21·00	
Traffic Light Gutter Block of 20			40·00	
First Day Cover (Tallents House)				9·25
Presentation Pack (PO Pack No. 363)			11·00	
PHQ Cards (set of 10) (268)			3·00	10·00

Nos. 2479/2488 were printed together, *se-tenant*, in blocks of ten (5×2) throughout sheets of 30.

For the miniature sheet celebrating the opening of the new Scottish Parliament Building, Edinburgh, issued 5 October 2004, see Regionals Section.

1768 Private McNamara, 5th Dragoon Guards, Heavy Brigade charge, Battle of Balaklava   **1769** Piper Muir, 42nd Regt of Foot, amphibious assault on Kerch

1770 Sergeant Major Edwards, Scots Fusilier Guards, gallant action, Battle of Inkerman   **1771** Sergeant Powell, 1st Regt of Foot Guards, Battles of Alma and Inkerman

1772 Sergeant.Major Poole, Royal Sappers and Miners, defensive line, Battle of Inkerman

1773 Sergeant Glasgow, Royal Artillery, gun battery beseiged Sevastopol

2004 (12 Oct). 150th Anniversary of the Crimean War. One centre phosphor band (2nd) or two phosphor bands (others). Perf 14.

2489	**1768**	(2nd) Private McNamara	90	90
2490	**1769**	(1st) Piper Muir	1·20	1·00
2491	**1770**	40p. Sergeant Major Edwards	1·00	1·00
2492	**1771**	57p. Sergeant Powell	1·10	1·10
2493	**1772**	68p. Sergeant Major Poole	1·25	1·25
2494	**1773**	£1·12 Sergeant Glasgow	1·60	1·60
Set of 6			6·00	6·00
Set of 6 Gutter Pairs			12·00	
Set of 6 Traffic Light Gutter Pairs			38·00	
First Day Cover (Tallents House)				6·25
Presentation Pack (PO Pack No. 364)			6·25	
PHQ Cards (set of 6) (269)			1·75	7·00

Nos. 2489/2494 show Crimean Heroes photographs taken in 1856.

1774 Father Christmas on Snowy Roof

1775 Celebrating the Sunrise

1776 On Roof in Gale

1777 With Umbrella in Rain

1778 On Edge of Roof with Torch

1779 Sheltering behind Chimney

2004 (2 Nov). Christmas. Multicoloured One centre phosphor band (2nd) or two phosphor bands (others). Perf 14½×14.

(a) Self-adhesive.

2495	**1774**	(2nd) Father Christmas on Snowy Roof	90	90
2496	**1775**	(1st) Celebrating the Sunrise	1·20	1·00
2497	**1776**	40p. On Roof in Gale	80	80
2498	**1777**	57p. With Umbrella in Rain	1·00	1·00
2499	**1778**	68p. On Edge of Roof with Torch	1·10	1·10
2500	**1779**	£1·12 Sheltering behind Chimney	1·25	1·25
Set of 6			5·50	5·50
First Day Cover (Tallents House)				5·75
Presentation Pack (PO Pack No. 365)			5·75	
PHQ Cards (set of 7) (270)			2·00	6·25

(b) Ordinary gum.

MS2501 115×105 mm. As Nos. 2495/2500	6·00	6·00
First Day Cover (Tallents House)		6·25

The 2nd and 1st class were also issued together in sheets of 20 printed in lithography instead of gravure containing ten 2nd class and ten 1st class, each stamp accompanied by a *se-tenant* half stamp-size labels showing Father Christmas.

Separate sheets of 20 2nd class and 20 1st class were available with personalised photographs.

The seven PHQ cards depict the six individual stamps and the miniature sheet.

Year Pack

2004 (2 Nov). Comprises Nos. 2417/22422, 2424/2444, 2446/2453, 2456/2461, 2466/2471 and 2473/2500.

CP2500*a*	Year Pack (Pack No. 366)	65·00

Post Office Yearbook

2004 (2 Nov). Comprises Nos. 2417/2422, 2424/2444, 2446/2453, 2456/2461, 2466/2471 and 2473/2500 in hardback book with slipcase

YB2500*a*	Yearbook	60·00

1780 British Saddleback Pigs

1781 Khaki Campbell Ducks

1782 Clydesdale Mare and Foal

1783 Dairy Shorthorn Cattle

1784 Border Collie Dog

1785 Light Sussex Chicks

1786 Suffolk Sheep

1787 Bagot Goat

1788 Norfolk Black Turkeys

1789 Embden Geese

2005 (11 Jan). Farm Animals. Multicoloured Two phosphor bands. Perf 14½.

2502	**1780**	(1st) British Saddleback Pigs	1·20	1·00
		a. Block of 10. Nos. 2502/2511	10·50	9·00
2503	**1781**	(1st) Khaki Campbell Ducks	1·20	1·00
2504	**1782**	(1st) Clydesdale Mare and Foal	1·20	1·00
2505	**1783**	(1st) Dairy Shorthorn Cattle	1·20	1·00

2506	**1784**	(1st) Border Collie Dog	1·20	1·00
2507	**1785**	(1st) Light Sussex Chicks	1·20	1·00
2508	**1786**	(1st) Suffolk Sheep	1·20	1·00
2509	**1787**	(1st) Bagot Goat	1·20	1·00
2510	**1788**	(1st) Norfolk Black Turkeys	1·20	1·00
2511	**1789**	(1st) Embden Geese	1·20	1·00
Set of 10			10·50	9·00
Gutter Block of 20			21·00	
Traffic Light Gutter Block of 20			65·00	
First Day Cover (Tallents House)				9·25
Presentation Pack (PO Pack No. 367)			11·00	
PHQ Cards (set of 10) (271)			3·00	10·50

Nos. 2502/2511 were printed together, *se-tenant*, in blocks of ten (5×2) throughout sheets of 30.

Nos. 2502/2511 were also issued in sheets of 20, printed in lithography instead of gravure, containing two of each of the ten designs, arranged in vertical strips of five alternated with printed labels.

1790 Old Harry Rocks, Studland Bay **1791** Wheal Coates, St Agnes

1792 Start Point, Start Bay **1793** Horton Down, Wiltshire

1794 Chiselcombe, Exmoor **1795** St James's Stone, Lundy

2005 (8 Feb). A British Journey. South West England. Multicoloured One centre phosphor band (2nd) or two phosphor bands (others). Perf 14½.

2512	**1790**	(2nd) Old Harry Rocks, Studland Bay	90	90
2513	**1791**	(1st) Wheal Coates, St Agnes	1·20	1·00
2514	**1792**	40p. Start Point, Start Bay	75	75
2515	**1793**	43p. Horton Down, Wiltshire	85	85
2516	**1794**	57p. Chiselcombe, Exmoor	1·00	1·00
2517	**1795**	68p. St James's Stone, Lundy	1·25	1·25
Set of 6			5·25	5·25
Set of 6 Gutter Pairs			10·50	
First Day Cover (Tallents House)				5·50
Presentation Pack (PO Pack No. 368)			5·50	
PHQ Cards (set of 6) (262)			1·75	5·75

1796 Mr Rochester **1797** Come to Me **1798** In the Comfort of her Bonnet

1799 La Ligne des Rats **1800** Refectory **1801** Inspection

2005 (24 Feb). 150th Death Anniversary of Charlotte Brontë. Illustrations of scenes from *Jane Eyre* by Paula Rego. Multicoloured One centre phosphor band (2nd), or two phosphor bands (others). Perf 14×14½.

2518	**1796**	(2nd) Mr Rochester	90	90
2519	**1797**	(1st) Come to Me	1·20	90
2520	**1798**	40p. In the Comfort of her Bonnet	1·00	1·00
2521	**1799**	57p. La Ligne des Rats	1·25	1·25
2522	**1800**	68p. Refectory	1·40	1·40
2523	**1801**	£1·12 Inspection	1·60	1·60
Set of 6			6·50	6·50
Set of 6 Gutter Pairs			13·00	
Set of 6 Traffic Light Gutter Blocks of 4			48·00	
First Day Cover (Tallents House)				6·75
Presentation Pack (PO Pack No. 369)			6·75	
PHQ Cards (set of 7) (273)			2·00	7·00
MS2524 114×105 mm. Nos. 2518/2523			6·50	6·50
First Day Cover (Tallents House)				6·75

Nos. 2518/2523 were also issued in the £7·43 The Brontë Sisters booklet, No. DX34.

The complete miniature sheet is shown on one of the PHQ cards with the others depicting individual stamps.

1802 Spinning Coin **1803** Rabbit out of Hat Trick

1804 Knotted Scarf Trick **1805** Card Trick

1806 Pyramid under Fez Trick

2005 (15 Mar). Centenary of the Magic Circle. Multicoloured Two phosphor bands. Perf 14½×14.

2525	**1802**	(1st) Spinning Coin	1·20	1·00
2526	**1803**	40p. Rabbit out of Hat Trick	1·00	1·00
2527	**1804**	47p. Knotted Scarf Trick	1·25	1·25
2528	**1805**	68p. Card Trick	1·40	1·40
2529	**1806**	£1·12 Pyramid under Fez Trick	5·50	5·50
Set of 5			5·75	5·75
Set of 5 Gutter Pairs			11·50	
First Day Cover (Philatelic Bureau, Edinburgh)				6·00
Presentation Pack (PO Pack No. 370)			6·00	
PHQ Cards (set of 5) (274)			1·50	6·00

Nos. 2525/2529 are each printed with instructions for the illusion or trick on the stamp.

No. 2525 can be rubbed with a coin to reveal the 'head' or 'tail' of a coin. The two versions, which appear identical before rubbing, are printed in alternate rows of the sheet, indicated by the letters H and T in the side margins of the sheet.

No. 2525 was also issued in sheets of 20, printed in lithography instead of gravure, with *se-tenant* half stamp-size labels illustrating magic tricks. Nos. 2526 and 2528 each show optical illusions.

The bright mauve on No. 2527 and the bright mauve, new blue, and lilac on No. 2529 are printed in thermochromic inks which fade temporarily when exposed to heat, making the pyramid under the centre fez visible.

1806a First Castles Definitives

2005 (22 Mar). 50th Anniversary of First Castles Definitives. Printed on pale cream paper. 'All-over' phosphor. Perf 11×11½.
MS2530 127×73 mm. **1806a** First Castles Definitives
50p. brownish-black; 50p. black; £1 dull vermilion;

£1 royal blue	4·50	4·50
First Day Cover (Tallents House)		5·75
Presentation Pack (PO Pack No. 69)	5·75	
PHQ Cards (set of 5) (D28)	1·50	5·75

The five PHQ cards depict the whole miniature sheet and the four stamps it contains.
See also No. 3221.

1807 Royal Wedding

2005 (9 Apr). Royal Wedding. Sheet 85×115 mm. Multicoloured 'All-over' phosphor. Perf 13½×14.
MS2531 **1807** Royal Wedding 30p.×2 Prince Charles and Mrs Camilla Parker Bowles laughing; 68p.×2 Prince Charles and Mrs Camilla Parker Bowles

smiling into camera	4·50	4·50
First Day Cover (Tallents House)		5·00
Presentation Pack (PO Pack No. M10)	8·00	

1808 Hadrian's Wall, England

1809 Uluru-Kata Tjuta National Park, Australia

1810 Stonehenge, England

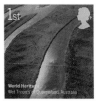

1811 Wet Tropics of Queensland, Australia

1812 Blenheim Palace, England

1813 Greater Blue Mountains Area, Australia

1814 Heart of Neolithic Orkney, Scotland

1815 Purnululu National Park, Australia

2005 (21 Apr). World Heritage Sites. Multicoloured One side phosphor band (2nd) or two phosphor bands (others). Perf 14½.

2532	**1808**	2nd Hadrian's Wall, England	90	90
		a. Horiz pair. Nos. 2532/2533	1·75	1·75
2533	**1809**	2nd Uluru-Kata Tjuta National Park, Australia	90	90
2534	**1810**	1st Stonehenge, England	1·20	1·00
		a. Horiz pair. Nos. 2534/2535	2·40	2·40
2535	**1811**	1st Wet Tropics of Queensland, Australia	1·20	1·00
2536	**1812**	47p. Blenheim Palace, England	80	80
		a. Horiz pair. Nos. 2536/2537	1·60	1·60
2537	**1813**	47p. Greater Blue Mountains Area, Australia	80	80
2538	**1814**	68p. Heart of Neolithic Orkney, Scotland	1·00	1·00
		a. Horiz pair. Nos. 2538/2539	2·00	2·00
2539	**1815**	68p. Purnululu National Park, Australia	1·00	1·00
Set of 8			6·50	6·50
Set of 4 Gutter Strips of 4			14·00	
Set of 4 Traffic Light Gutter Blocks of 8			32·00	
First Day Cover (Tallents House)				7·75
Presentation Pack (PO Pack No. 371)			7·50	
Presentation Pack (UK and Australian stamps)			11·00	
PHQ Cards (set of 8) (275)			2·50	7·50

Stamps in these designs were also issued by Australia and these are included in the joint Presentation Pack.

1816 Ensign of the Scots Guards, 2002

1817 Queen taking the salute as Colonel-in-Chief of the Grenadier Guards, 1983

1818 Trumpeter of the Household Cavalry, 2004

1819 Welsh Guardsman, 1990s

1820 Queen riding side-saddle, 1972

1821 Queen and Duke of Edinburgh in carriage, 2004

2005 (7 June). Trooping the Colour. Multicoloured One phosphor band (2nd), two phosphor bands (others). Perf 14½.

2540	**1816**	(2nd) Ensign of the Scots Guards, 2002	90	90
2541	**1817**	(1st) Queen taking the salute as Colonel-in-Chief of the Grenadier Guards, 1983	1·20	1·00
2542	**1818**	42p. Trumpeter of the Household Cavalry, 2004	85	85
2543	**1819**	60p. Welsh Guardsman, 1990s	1·00	1·00
2544	**1820**	68p. Queen riding side-saddle, 1972	1·10	1·10
2545	**1821**	£1·12 Queen and Duke of Edinburgh in carriage, 2004	1·60	1·60
Set of 6			5·75	5·75
Set of 6 Gutter Pairs			11·50	
First Day Cover (Tallents House)				6·00
Presentation Pack (PO Pack No. 372)			5·75	
PHQ Cards (set of 7) (276)			2·00	11·00
MS2546 115×105 mm. Nos. 2540/2545			5·50	5·50
First Day Cover (Tallents House)				5·75

The seven PHQ cards show the six stamps and No. **MS**2546.

1823 Norton F.1, Road Version of Race Winner (1991)

1824 BSA Rocket 3, Early Three Cylinder 'Superbike' (1969)

1825 Vincent Black Shadow, Fastest Standard Motorcycle (1949)

1826 Triumph Speed Twin, Two Cylinder Innovation (1938)

1827 Brough Superior, Bespoke Luxury Motorcycle (1930)

1828 Royal Enfield, Small Engined Motor Bicycle (1914)

2005 (19 July). Motorcycles. Multicoloured Two phosphor bands. Perf 14×14½.

2548	**1823**	(1st) Norton F.1	1·20	90
2549	**1824**	40p. BSA Rocket 3	60	60
2550	**1825**	42p. Vincent Black Shadow	65	65
2551	**1826**	47p. Triumph Speed Twin	80	80
2552	**1827**	60p. Brough Superior	1·00	1·00
2553	**1828**	68p. Royal Enfield	1·25	1·25
Set of 6			4·50	4·50
Set of 6 Gutter Pairs			9·50	
First Day Cover (Tallents House)				5·75
Presentation Pack (PO Pack No. 373)			5·25	
PHQ Cards (set of 6) (277)			1·75	5·75

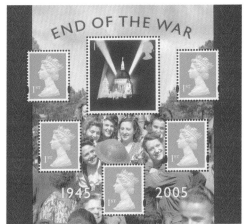

1822 End of the War

2005 (5 July). 60th Anniversary of End of the Second World War. Sheet 115×105 mm containing design as T **1200** (1995 Peace and Freedom) but with service indicator and No. 1668×5. Two phosphor bands. Perf 15×14 (with one elliptical hole in each vert side) (No. 1668) or 14½×14 (other).

MS2547 **1822** End of the War (1st) gold×5; (1st) silver, blue and grey-black		6·25	5·25
First Day Cover (Tallents House)			5·50

1829 London 2012 Host City

2005 (5 Aug). London's Successful Bid for Olympic Games, 2012. Sheet 115×105 mm containing designs as Types **1255/1259**, but with service indicator. Multicoloured Two phosphor bands. Perf 14½.

MS2554 **1829** London 2012 Host City (1st) Athlete celebrating×2; (1st) Javelin; (1st) Swimming; (1st) Athlete on starting blocks; (1st) Basketball		6·00	5·00
First Day Cover (Tallents House)			5·75
Presentation Pack (PO Pack No. M11)		6·25	

Stamps from No. **MS**2554 are all inscribed 'London 2012–Host City' and have imprint date 2005.

The design as T **1259** omits the Olympic rings.

1830 African Woman eating Rice

1831 Indian Woman drinking Tea

1832 Boy eating Sushi

1833 Woman eating Pasta

1834 Woman eating Chips

1835 Teenage Boy eating Apple

2005 (23 Aug). Europa. Gastronomy. Changing Tastes in Britain. Multicoloured. One side phosphor band (2nd) or two phosphor bands (others). Perf 14½.

2555	**1830**	(2nd) African Woman eating Rice	90	90
2556	**1831**	(1st) Indian Woman drinking Tea	1·20	1·00
2557	**1832**	42p. Boy eating Sushi	60	60
2558	**1833**	47p. Woman eating Pasta	75	75
2559	**1834**	60p. Woman eating Chips	90	90
2560	**1835**	68p. Teenage Boy eating Apple	1·10	1·25
Set of 6			4·75	4·75
Set of 6 Gutter Pairs			9·50	
First Day Cover (Tallents House)				5·00
Presentation Pack (PO Pack No. 374)			5·00	
PHQ Cards (set of 6) (278)			1·75	5·75

The 1st and 42p. values include the EUROPA emblem.

1836 *Inspector Morse*

1837 *Emmerdale*

1838 *Rising Damp*

1839 *The Avengers*

1840 *The South Bank Show*

1841 *Who Wants to be a Millionaire*

2005 (15 Sept). 50th Anniversary of Independent Television. Classic ITV Programmes. Multicoloured One side phosphor band (2nd) or two phosphor bands (others). Perf 14½×14.

2561	**1836**	(2nd) *Inspector Morse*	90	90
2562	**1837**	(1st) *Emmerdale*	1·20	1·00
2563	**1838**	42p. *Rising Damp*	60	60
2564	**1839**	47p. *The Avengers*	75	75
2565	**1840**	60p. *The South Bank Show*	90	90
2566	**1841**	68p. *Who Wants to be a Millionaire*	1·10	1·10
Set of 6			4·75	4·75
Set of 6 Gutter Pairs			9·50	
First Day Cover (Tallents House)				5·25
Presentation Pack (PO Pack No. 375)			5·00	
PHQ Cards (set of 6) (279)			1·75	5·75

The 1st class stamps were also issued in sheets of 20, printed in lithography with each stamp accompanied by a half stamp-size *se-tenant* label.

1842 *Gazania splendens* (Charlotte Sowerby)

1842a Aircraft Skywriting 'hello'

1842b 'LOVE'

1842c Union Flag

1842d Teddy Bear

1842e European Robin in Mouth of Pillar Box

2005 (4 Oct). Smilers Booklet stamps (1st series). Self-adhesive. Multicoloured Two phosphor bands. Die-cut Perf 15×14.

2567	**1842**	(1st) *Gazania splendens*	1·20	1·25
2568	**1842a**	(1st) Aircraft Skywriting 'hello'.	1·20	1·25
2569	**1842b**	(1st) 'LOVE'	1·20	1·25
2570	**1842c**	(1st) Union Jack	1·20	1·25
2571	**1842d**	(1st) Teddy Bear	1·20	1·25
2572	**1842e**	(1st) European Robin in Mouth of Pillar Box	1·20	1·25
Set of 6			9·00	9·00
First Day Cover (Tallents House) (Type K, see Introduction)				9·25

Nos. 2567/2572 were printed together, *se-tenant*, in booklet panes of six in which the surplus backing paper around each stamp was removed.

Nos. 2567/2572 were re-issued on 4 July 2006 in sheets of 20 with *se-tenant* greetings labels, printed in lithography instead of gravure.

Nos. 2568/2570 were re-issued on 15 January 2008 in sheets of 20 with circular *se-tenant* labels printed in lithography.

No. 2572 was re-issued on 28 October 2008 in sheets of ten with circular *se-tenant* Flower Fairy labels, printed in lithography.

Stamps as Nos. 2569 and 2572 but perforated with one elliptical hole on each vertical side were issued, together with Nos. 2674 and 2821/2823 and four designs from No. **MS**3024, on 8 May 2010 in sheets of 20 stamps with *se-tenant* greetings labels.

For stamp as No. 2569 with one elliptical hole in each vertical side see No. 2693.

For stamps as Nos. 2567/2568 and 2570 with one elliptical hole in each vertical side see Nos. 2819/2821.

See also Nos. 2693 and 2819/2824.

THE ASHES ENGLAND WINNERS 2005

1843 Cricket Scenes

2005 (6 Oct). England's Ashes Victory. Sheet 115×90 mm. Multicoloured Two phosphor bands. Perf 14½×14.

MS2573 **1843** Cricket Scenes (1st) England team with Ashes trophy; (1st) Kevin Pietersen, Michael Vaughan and Andrew Flintoff on opening day of First Test, Lord's; 68p. Michael Vaughan, Third Test, Old Trafford; 68p. Second Test cricket, Edgbaston ... 4·00 4·00

First Day Cover (Tallents House) ... 5·00

Presentation Pack (PO Pack No. M12) ... 4·25

1844 *Entrepreante* with dismasted British *Belle Isle*

1845 Nelson wounded on Deck of HMS *Victory*

1846 British Cutter *Entrepreante* attempting to rescue Crew of burning French *Achille*

1847 Cutter and HMS *Pickle* (schooner)

1848 British Fleet attacking in Two Columns

1849 Franco/Spanish Fleet putting to Sea from Cadiz

2005 (18 Oct). Bicentenary of the Battle of Trafalgar (1st issue). Scenes from *Panorama of the Battle of Trafalgar* by William Heath. Multicoloured Two phosphor bands. Perf 15×14½.

2574	**1844**	(1st) *Entrepreante* with dismasted British *Belle Isle*	1·20	1·00
		a. Horiz pair. Nos. 2574/2575	2·40	2·00
2575	**1845**	(1st) Nelson wounded on Deck of HMS *Victory*	1·20	1·00
2576	**1846**	42p. British Cutter *Entrepreante* attempting to rescue Crew of burning French *Achille*	70	80
		a. Horiz pair. Nos. 2576/2577	1·60	1·60
2577	**1847**	42p. Cutter and HMS *Pickle* (schooner)	70	80
2578	**1848**	68p. British Fleet attacking in Two Columns	1·00	1·10
		a. Horiz pair. Nos. 2578/2579	2·00	2·00
2579	**1849**	68p. Franco/Spanish Fleet putting to Sea from Cadiz	1·00	1·10

Set of 6 ... 5·00 5·00
Set of 3 Gutter Strips of 4 ... 10·50
First Day Cover (Tallents House) ... 5·50
Presentation Pack (PO Pack No. 376) ... 5·75
PHQ Cards (set of 7) (280) ... 2·00 11·50
MS2580 190×68 mm. Nos. 2574/2579 ... 5·25 5·50
First Day Cover (Tallents House) ... 5·75

Nos. 2574/2575, 2576/2577 and 2578/2579 were each printed together, se-tenant, in horizontal pairs throughout the sheets, each pair forming a composite design.

Nos. 2574/2575, 2576/2577 and 2578/2579 were also issued in the £7·26 Battle of Trafalgar booklet, No. DX35.

The phosphor bands are at just left of centre and at right of each stamp. The seven PHQ cards depict the six individual stamps and the miniature sheet.

2005 (18 Oct). Bicentenary of the Battle of Trafalgar (2nd issue). Booklet stamp. Design as T **1516** (2001 White Ensign from Submarine Centenary). Multicoloured Two phosphor bands. Perf 14½.

2581 **1516** (1st) White Ensign. Multicoloured ... 1·50 1·50

No. 2581 was issued in the £7·26 Bicentenary of the Battle of Trafalgar booklet, No. DX35, the £7·40 Ian Fleming's James Bond booklet, No. DX41 and the £7·93 Royal Navy Uniforms booklet, No. DX47.

1850 Black Madonna and Child from Haiti

1851 *Madonna and Child* (Marianne Stokes)

1852 The Virgin Mary with the Infant Christ

1853 *Choctaw Virgin Mother and Child* (Fr. John Giuliani)

1854 Madonna and the Infant Jesus (from India)

1855 *Come let us adore Him* (Dianne Tchumut)

2005 (1 Nov). Christmas. Madonna and Child Paintings. Multicoloured One side phosphor band (2nd) or two phosphor bands (others). Perf 14½×14.

(a) Self-adhesive.

2582	**1850**	(2nd) Black Madonna and Child from Haiti	90	90
2583	**1851**	(1st) *Madonna and Child*	1·20	1·00
2584	**1852**	42p. The Virgin Mary with the Infant Christ	90	90
2585	**1853**	60p. *Choctaw Virgin Mother and Child*	1·00	1·00
2586	**1854**	68p. Madonna and the Infant Jesus	1·25	1·25

2587	**1855**	£1·12 *Come let us adore Him*	1·40	1·40

Set of 6 — 5·75 / 5·75
First Day Cover (Tallents House) — 6·00
Presentation Pack (PO Pack No. 377) — 6·00
PHQ Cards (set of 7) (281) — 2·00 / 12·00

The seven PHQ cards depict the six individual stamps and the miniature sheet.

(b) Ordinary gum.
MS2588 115×102 mm. As Nos. 2582/2587 — 5·75 / 5·75
First Day Cover (Tallents House) — 6·00

Year Pack

2005 (1 Nov). Comprises Nos. 2502/2523, 2525/2529, **MS**2531/2545, 2548/2553, 2555/2566, 2574/2579 and 2582/2587.
CP2587*a*   Year Pack (Pack No. 378) — 65·00

Post Office Yearbook

2005 (1 Nov). Comprises Nos. 2502/2523, 2525/2529, **MS**2531/2545, 2548/2553, 2555/2566, 2574/2579 and 2582/2587.
YB2587*a*   Yearbook — 60·00

Miniature Sheet Collection

2005 (1 Nov). Comprises Nos. **MS**2524, **MS**2530/**MS**2531, **MS**2546/**MS**2547, **MS**2554, **MS**2573, **MS**2580 and **MS**2588.
MS2588*a* Miniature Sheet Collection — 45·00

2590	**1857**	(2nd) *Kipper* (Mick Inkpen)	90	90
2591	**1858**	(1st) *The Enormous Crocodile* (Roald Dahl)	1·20	1·00
		a. Horiz pair. Nos. 2591/2592	2·40	2·40
2592	**1859**	(1st) *More About Paddington* (Michael Bond)	1·20	1·00
2593	**1860**	42p. *Comic Adventures of Boots* (Satoshi Kitamura)	80	80
		a. Horiz pair. Nos. 2593/2594	1·60	1·60
2594	**1861**	42p. *Alice's Adventures in Wonderland* (Lewis Carroll)	80	80
2595	**1862**	68p. *The Very Hungry Caterpillar* (Eric Carle)	1·00	1·00
		a. Horiz pair. Nos. 2595/2596	2·00	2·00
2596	**1863**	68p. *Maisy's ABC* (Lucy Cousins)	1·00	1·00

Set of 8 — 7·00 / 6·75
Set of 4 Gutter Blocks of 4 — 14·00
Set of 4 Traffic Light Gutter Blocks of 8 — 50·00
First Day Cover (Tallents House) — 7·75
Presentation Pack (PO Pack No. 379) — 8·75
PHQ Cards (set of 8) (282) — 2·50 / 7·75

Nos. 2589/2590, 2591/2592, 2593/2594 and 2595/2596 were printed together, *se-tenant*, in horizontal pairs in sheets of 60 (2 panes 6×5).

A design as No. 2592 but self-adhesive was issued in sheets of 20, printed in lithography with each stamp accompanied by a *se-tenant* label. No. 2595 contains two die-cut holes.

1856 *The Tale of Mr Jeremy Fisher* (Beatrix Potter)   **1857** *Kipper* (Mick Inkpen)

1864 Carding Mill Valley, Shropshire   **1865** Beachy Head, Sussex

1858 *The Enormous Crocodile* (Roald Dahl)   **1859** *More About Paddington* (Michael Bond)

1866 St Paul's Cathedral, London   **1867** Brancaster, Norfolk

1860 *Comic Adventures of Boots* (Satoshi Kitamura)   **1861** *Alice's Adventures in Wonderland* (Lewis Carroll)

1868 Derwent Edge, Peak District   **1869** Robin Hood's Bay, Yorkshire

1862 *The Very Hungry Caterpillar* (Eric Carle)   **1863** *Maisy's ABC* (Lucy Cousins)

2006 (10 Jan). Animal Tales. Multicoloured One side phosphor band (2nd) or two phosphor bands (others). Perf 14½.

2589	**1856**	(2nd) *The Tale of Mr Jeremy Fisher* (Beatrix Potter)	90	90
		a. Horiz pair. Nos. 2589/2590	1·75	1·75

1870 Buttermere, Lake District   **1871** Chipping Campden, Cotswolds

1872 St Boniface Down, Isle of Wight

1873 Chamberlain Square, Birmingham

2006 (7 Feb). A British Journey. England. Multicoloured Two phosphor bands. Perf 14½.

2597	**1864**	(1st) Carding Mill Valley, Shropshire	1·20	1·00
		a. Block of 10. Nos. 2597/2606	10·50	9·00
2598	**1865**	(1st) Beachy Head, Sussex	1·20	1·00
2599	**1866**	(1st) St Paul's Cathedral, London	1·20	1·00
2600	**1867**	(1st) Brancaster, Norfolk	1·20	1·00
2601	**1868**	(1st) Derwent Edge, Peak District	1·20	1·00
2602	**1869**	(1st) Robin Hood's Bay, Yorkshire	1·20	1·00
2603	**1870**	(1st) Buttermere, Lake District	1·20	1·00
2604	**1871**	(1st) Chipping Campden, Cotswolds	1·20	1·00
2605	**1872**	(1st) St Boniface Down, Isle of Wight	1·20	1·00
2606	**1873**	(1st) Chamberlain Square, Birmingham	1·20	1·00
Set of 10			10·50	9·00
Gutter Block of 20			21·00	
First Day Cover (Tallents House)				9·50
Presentation Pack (PO Pack No. 380)			11·00	
PHQ Cards (set of 10) (283)			3·00	9·75

Nos. 2597/2606 were printed together, *se-tenant*, as blocks of ten (5×2) in sheets of 60 (2 panes of 30).

1874 Royal Albert Bridge

1875 Box Tunnel

1876 Paddington Station

1877 PSS *Great Eastern* (paddle-steamer)

1878 Clifton Suspension Bridge Design

1879 Maidenhead Bridge

2006 (23 Feb). Birth Bicentenary of Isambard Kingdom Brunel (engineer) (1st issue). Multicoloured Phosphor-coated paper (42p.) or two phosphor bands (others). Perf 14×13½.

2607	**1874**	(1st) Royal Albert Bridge	1·20	1·00
2608	**1875**	40p. Box Tunnel	60	60
2609	**1876**	42p. Paddington Station	65	65
2610	**1877**	47p. PSS *Great Eastern*	80	80
2611	**1878**	60p. Clifton Suspension Bridge	1·00	1·00
2612	**1879**	68p. Maidenhead Bridge	1·25	1·25
Set of 6			4·75	4·75
Set of 6 Gutter Pairs			9·50	
First Day Cover (Tallents House)				5·25
Presentation Pack (PO Pack No. 381)			5·75	
PHQ Cards (set of 7) (284)			2·00	11·00
MS2613 190×65 mm. Nos. 2607/2612			5·00	5·00
First Day Cover (Philatelic Bureau, Edinburgh)				5·50

The phosphor bands on Nos. 2607/2608 and 2610/2612 are at just left of centre and at right of each stamp.

Nos. 2607/2612 were also issued in the £7·40 Isambard Kingdom Brunel booklet, No. DX36.

The complete miniature sheet is shown on one of the PHQ Cards with the others depicting individual stamps.

2006 (23 Feb). Birth Bicentenary of Isambard Kingdom Brunel (2nd issue). Booklet stamp. Design as T **1739** (PSS *Great Western* from 2004 Ocean Liners). Multicoloured Two phosphor bands. Perf 14½×14.

2614	**1739**	68p. PSS *Great Western, 1838* (Joseph Walter)	2·50	2·50

No. 2614 was only issued in the £7·40 Isambard Kingdom Brunel booklet, No. DX36.

> For the miniature sheet celebrating the opening of the New Welsh Assembly, Cardiff, issued 1 March 2006, see the Regional Section.

1880 Sabre-tooth Cat

1881 Giant Deer

1882 Woolly Rhino

1883 Woolly Mammoth

1884 Cave Bear

2006 (21 Mar). Ice Age Animals. Black and silver. Two phosphor bands. Perf 14½.

2615	**1880**	(1st) Sabre-tooth Cat	1·20	1·00
2616	**1881**	42p. Giant Deer	90	90
2617	**1882**	47p. Woolly Rhino	1·00	1·00
2618	**1883**	68p. Woolly Mammoth	1·10	1·10
2619	**1884**	£1·12 Cave Bear	1·50	1·50
Set of 5			5·00	5·00
Set of 5 Gutter Pairs			10·00	
First Day Cover (Tallents House)				5·50
Presentation Pack (PO Pack No. 382)			5·50	
PHQ Cards (set of 5) (285)			1·50	5·75

1885 On *Britannia*, 1972

1886 At Royal Windsor Horse Show, 1985

1887 At Heathrow Airport, 2001

1888 As Young Princess Elizabeth with Duchess of York, 1931

1889 At State Banquet, Ottawa, 1951

1890 Queen in 1960

1891 As Princess Elizabeth, 1940

1892 With Duke of Edinburgh, 1951

2006 (18 Apr). 80th Birthday of Queen Elizabeth II. Black, turquoise-green and grey. One side phosphor band (No. 2620), one centre phosphor band (No. 2621) or two phosphor bands (others). Perf 14½.

2620	**1885**	(2nd) On *Britannia*, 1972	90	90
		a. Horiz pair. Nos. 2620/2621	1·75	1·75
2621	**1886**	(2nd) At Royal Windsor Horse Show, 1985	90	90
2622	**1887**	(1st) At Heathrow Airport, 2001	1·20	1·00
		a. Horiz pair. Nos. 2622/2623	2·40	2·00
2623	**1888**	(1st) As Young Princess Elizabeth with Duchess of York, 1931	1·20	1·00
2624	**1889**	44p. At State Banquet, Ottawa, 1951	75	75
		a. Horiz pair. Nos. 2624/2625	1·50	1·50
2625	**1890**	44p. Queen in 1960	75	75
2626	**1891**	72p. As Princess Elizabeth, 1940	1·00	1·00
		a. Horiz pair. Nos. 2626/2627	2·00	2·00
2627	**1892**	72p. With Duke of Edinburgh, 1951	1·00	1·00
Set of 8			6·75	6·50
Set of 4 Gutter Strips of 4			13·50	
First Day Cover (Tallents House)				6·75
Presentation Pack (PO Pack No. 383)			7·00	
PHQ Cards (set of 8) (286)			2·50	7·50

Nos. 2620/2621, 2622/2623, 2624/2625 and 2626/2627 were each printed together, *se-tenant*, as horizontal pairs in sheets of 60 (2 panes 6×5).

1st

1893 England (1966)

42

1894 Italy (1934, 1938, 1982)

44

1895 Argentina (1978, 1986)

50

1896 Germany (1954, 1974, 1990)

64

1897 France (1998)

72

1898 Brazil (1958, 1962, 1970, 1994, 2002)

2006 (6 June). World Cup Football Championship, Germany. World Cup Winners. Multicoloured Two phosphor bands. Perf 14½.

2628	**1893**	(1st) England	1·20	1·00
2629	**1894**	42p. Italy	80	80
2630	**1895**	44p. Argentina	85	85
2631	**1896**	50p. Germany	1·00	1·00
2632	**1897**	64p. France	1·25	1·25
2633	**1898**	72p. Brazil	1·40	1·40
Set of 6			5·50	5·50
Set of 6 Gutter Pairs			11·00	
First Day Cover (Tallents House)				5·75
Presentation Pack (PO Pack No. 384)			6·00	
PHQ Cards (set of 6) (287)			1·75	6·50

The 1st class stamp was also issued in sheets of 20 with each stamp accompanied by a *se-tenant* label showing scenes from the 1966 World Cup final

1899 30 St Mary Axe, London

1900 Maggie's Centre, Dundee

1901 Selfridges, Birmingham

1902 Downland Gridshell, Chichester

1903 An Turas, Isle of Tiree

1904 The Deep, Hull

2006 (20 June). Modern Architecture. Multicoloured Two phosphor bands. Perf 14½.

2634	**1899**	(1st) 30 St Mary Axe, London	1·20	1·00
2635	**1900**	42p. Maggie's Centre, Dundee	65	65

2636	**1901**	44p. Selfridges, Birmingham	70	70
2637	**1902**	50p. Downland Gridshell, Chichester	85	85
2638	**1903**	64p. An Turas, Isle of Tiree	1·00	1·00
2639	**1904**	72p. The Deep, Hull	1·25	1·25
Set of 6			5·00	5·00
Set of 6 Gutter Pairs			10·00	
First Day Cover (Tallents House)				5·50
Presentation Pack (PO Pack No. 385)			5·50	
PHQ Cards (set of 6) (288)			1·75	5·75

2644	**1909**	(1st) Virginia Woolf	1·20	1·00
2645	**1910**	(1st) Bust of Sir Walter Scott	1·20	1·00
2646	**1911**	(1st) Mary Seacole	1·20	1·00
2647	**1912**	(1st) William Shakespeare	1·20	1·00
2648	**1913**	(1st) Dame Cicely Saunders	1·20	1·00
2649	**1914**	(1st) Charles Darwin	1·20	1·00
Set of 10			10·50	9·00
Gutter Block of 20			21·00	
Traffic Light Gutter Block of 20			40·00	
First Day Cover (Tallents House)				9·50
Presentation Pack (PO Pack No. 386)			11·00	
PHQ Cards (set of 10) (289)			3·00	10·00

Nos. 2640/2649 were printed together, *se-tenant*, as blocks of ten (5×2) in sheets of 60 (2 panes of 30).

For Nos. 2650/2657, **MS**2658, Types **1915/1917** see Decimal Machin Definitives section.

1905 *Sir Winston Churchill* (Walter Sickert)

1906 *Sir Joshua Reynolds* (self-portrait)

1907 *I. S. Eliot* (Patrick Heron)

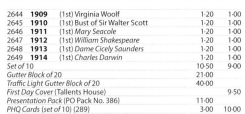

1908 *Emmeline Pankhurst* (Georgina Agnes Brackenbury)

1909 *Virginia Woolf* (photo by George Charles Beresford)

1910 *Bust of Sir Walter Scott* (Sir Francis Leggatt Chantry)

1918 Corporal Agansing Rai   **1919** Boy Seaman Jack Cornwell

1911 *Mary Seacole* (Albert Charles Challen)

1912 *William Shakespeare*

1913 *Dame Cicely Saunders*

1920 Midshipman Charles Lucas   **1921** Captain Noel Chavasse

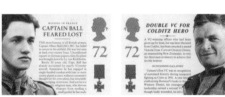

1922 Captain Albert Ball   **1923** Captain Charles Upham

2006 (21 Sept). 150th Anniversary of the Victoria Cross (1st issue). Multicoloured One side phosphor band. Perf 14½×14.

2659	**1918**	(1st) Corporal Agansing Rai	1·20	1·00
		a. Horiz pair. Nos. 2659/2660	2·40	2·00
2660	**1919**	(1st) Boy Seaman Jack Cornwell	1·20	1·00
2661	**1920**	64p. Midshipman Charles Lucas	90	90
		a. Horiz pair. Nos. 2661/2662	1·75	1·75
2662	**1921**	64p. Captain Noel Chavasse	90	90
2663	**1922**	72p. Captain Albert Ball	1·25	1·25
		a. Horiz pair. Nos. 2663/2664	2·40	2·40
2664	**1923**	72p. Captain Charles Upham	1·25	1·25
Set of 6			6·25	6·00
Set of 3 Gutter Strips of 4			12·20	
First Day Cover (Tallents House)				6·25
Presentation Pack (PO Pack No. 387)			6·50	
PHQ Cards (set of 7) (290)			2·00	13·50
MS2665 190×67 mm. Nos. 2659/2664 and 2666			6·50	6·50
First Day Cover (Tallents House)				6·50

Nos. 2659/2660, 2661/2662 and 2663/2664 were each printed together, *se-tenant*, as horizontal pairs in sheets of 60 (2 panes 6×5).

Nos. 2659/2660, 2661/2662 and 2663/2664 were issued in the £7·44 Victoria Cross booklet No. DX37.

The seven PHQ Cards depict the six individual stamps and the miniature sheet.

1914 *Charles Darwin* (John Collier)

2006 (18 July). 150th Anniversary of National Portrait Gallery, London. Multicoloured Two phosphor bands. Perf 14½.

2640	**1905**	(1st) Sir Winston Churchill	1·20	1·00
		a. Block of 10. Nos. 2640/2649	10·50	9·00
2641	**1906**	(1st) Sir Joshua Reynolds	1·20	1·00
2642	**1907**	(1st) T. S. Eliot	1·20	1·00
2643	**1908**	(1st) Emmeline Pankhurst	1·20	1·00

959 Victoria Cross

2006 (21 Sept). 150th Anniversary of the Victoria Cross (2nd issue). Booklet stamp. Design as No. 1517 (1990 Gallantry Awards). Multicoloured 'All-over' phosphor. Perf 14×14½.

2666	**959**	20p. Victoria Cross	1·50	1·50

No. 2666 was only issued in No. **MS**2665 and in the £7·44 Victoria Cross booklet, No. DX37. See also No. 1517.

1924 Sitar Player and Dancer

1925 1924 Reggae Bass Guitarist and African Drummer

1926 Fiddler and Harpist

1927 Sax Player and Blues Guitarist

1928 Maraca Player and Salsa Dancers

2006 (3 Oct). Europa. Integration. Sounds of Britain. Multicoloured 'All-over' phosphor. Perf 14½.

2667	**1924**	(1st) Sitar Player and Dancer	1·20	1·00
2668	**1925**	42p. Reggae Bass Guitarist and African Drummer	1·00	1·00
2669	**1926**	50p. Fiddler and Harpist	1·10	1·10
2670	**1927**	72p. Sax Player and Blues Guitarist	1·25	1·25
2671	**1928**	£1·19 Maraca Player and Salsa Dancers	1·75	1·75
Set of 5			5·50	5·50
Set of 5 Gutter Pairs			11·00	
Set of 5 Traffic Light Gutter Blocks of 4			26·00	
First Day Cover (Tallents House)				6·00
Presentation Pack (PO Pack No. 388)			6·00	
PHQ Cards (set of 5) (291)			1·50	6·25

The 1st class and 50p. values include the EUROPA emblem.

1929 'New Baby' (Alison Carmichael)

1930 'Best Wishes' (Alan Kitching)

1931 'THANK YOU' (Alan Kitching)

1932 Balloons (Ivan Chermayeff)

1933 Firework (Kam Tang)

1934 Champagne, Flowers and Butterflies (Olaf Hajek)

2006 (17 Oct). Smilers Booklet stamps (2nd series). Occasions. Self-adhesive. Multicoloured Two phosphor bands. Die-cut Perf 15×14.

2672	**1929**	(1st) 'New Baby'	1·20	1·00
2673	**1930**	(1st) 'Best Wishes'	1·20	1·00
2674	**1931**	(1st) 'THANK YOU'	1·20	1·00
2675	**1932**	(1st) Balloons	1·20	1·00
2676	**1933**	(1st) Firework	1·20	1·00
2677	**1934**	(1st) Champagne, Flowers and Butterflies	1·20	1·00
Set of 6			7·00	6·00
First Day Cover (Tallents House)				6·25
Presentation Pack (PO Pack No. M13)			10·00	
PHQ Cards (set of 6) (D29)			1·75	7·00

Nos. 2672/2677 were printed together, *se-tenant*, in booklet panes of six in which the surplus backing paper around each stamp was removed.

Nos. 2672/2677 were also issued in sheets of 20, containing four of Nos. 2672 and 2677 and three of each of the other designs, each stamp accompanied by a *se-tenant* greetings label.

These designs were available in separate sheets with personal photographs printed on the labels.

Stamps as No. 2672 but perforated with one elliptical hole on each vertical side were issued on 28 October 2008 in sheets of ten or 20 with circular *se-tenant* Peter Rabbit labels.

Stamps as Nos. 2674 but perforated with on elliptical hole in each vertical side were issued, together with Nos. 2569, 2572, 2821/2823 and four designs from No. **MS**3024, on 8 May 2010 in sheets of 20 stamps with *se-tenant* greetings labels.

These generic sheets were all printed in lithography instead of gravure.

1935 Snowman

1936 Father Christmas

1937 Snowman

1938 Father Christmas

1939 Reindeer

1940 Christmas Tree

2006 (7 Nov). Christmas. Multicoloured One centre phosphor band (No. 2678) or two phosphor bands (others). Perf 15×14.

(a) Self-adhesive.

2678	**1935**	(2nd) Snowman	90	90
2679	**1936**	(1st) Father Christmas	1·20	1·00
2680	**1937**	(2nd Large) Snowman	1·25	1·00
2681	**1938**	(1st Large) Father Christmas	1·70	1·25
2682	**1939**	72p. Reindeer	1·10	1·10
2683	**1940**	£1·19 Christmas Tree	1·50	1·50
Set of 6			6·75	6·00
First Day Cover (Tallents House)				7·00
Presentation Pack (PO Pack No. 389)			7·25	
PHQ Cards (set of 7) (292)			2·00	13·50

(b) Ordinary gum.

MS2684	115×102 mm. As Nos. 2678/2683	6·75	6·75
First Day Cover (Tallents House)			7·00

The 2nd and 1st class stamps were also issued together in sheets of 20 printed in lithography instead of gravure, containing ten 1st class and ten 2nd class stamps, each stamp accompanied by a *se-tenant* label.

Separate sheets of 20×1st or 20×2nd class were available with personalised photographs.

The seven PHQ Cards depict the six individual stamps and the miniature sheet.

1941 Lest We Forget

2006 (9 Nov). Lest We Forget (1st issue). 90th Anniversary of the Battle of the Somme. Sheet 124×71 mm containing new stamp as No. 2883 and designs as Nos. EN17, NI102, S120 and W109. Multicoloured Two phosphor bands. Perf 14½ (1st) or 15×14 (with one elliptical hole in each vertical side) (72p.).

MS2685 **1941** Lest We Forget (1st) Poppies on barbed
wire stems; 72p.×4	5·50	5·50
First Day Cover (Tallents House)		6·00
Presentation Pack (PO Pack No. 390)	7·25	

The 1st class stamp was also issued in sheets of 20 with *se-tenant* labels showing war memorials, and on 6 November 2008, in a *se-tenant* strip of three issues printed in lithography instead of gravure.

No. MS2685 (including the Northern Ireland stamp) is printed in gravure. See also Nos. MS2796 and MS2886.

Year Pack

2006 (9 Nov). Comprises Nos. 2589/2612, 2615/2649, 2659/2664, 2667/2671, 2678/2683 and MS2685.
CP2685a	Year Pack (Pack No. 391)	65·00

Post Office Yearbook

2006 (9 Nov). Comprises Nos. 2589/2612, 2615/2649, 2659/2664, 2667/2671, 2678/2683 and MS2685.
YB2685a	Yearbook	75·00

Miniature Sheet Collection

2006 (30 Nov). Comprises Nos. MS2613, MS2658, MS2665, MS2684/ MS2685, MSS153 and MSW143.
MS2685a Miniature Sheet Collection	38·00	

1942 *with the beatles*

1943 *Sgt Pepper's Lonely Hearts Club Band*

1944 *Help!*

1945 *Abbey Road*

1946 *Revolver*

1947 *Let It Be*

1948 Beatles Memorabilia

2007 (9 Jan). The Beatles. Album Covers. Multicoloured Two phosphor bands.

(a) Self-adhesive. Gravure Walsall. Die-cut irregular Perf 13½-14½.
2686	**1942**	(1st) *with the beatles*	1·20	1·00
		a. Horiz pair. Nos. 2686/2687	2·40	
2687	**1943**	(1st) *Sgt Pepper's Lonely Hearts Club Band*	1·20	1·00
2688	**1944**	64p. *Help!*	90	90
		a. Horiz pair. Nos. 2688/2689	1·80	
2689	**1945**	64p. *Abbey Road*	90	90
2690	**1946**	72p. *Revolver*	1·25	1·25
		a. Horiz pair. Nos. 2690/2691	2·50	
2691	**1947**	72p. *Let It Be*	1·25	1·25
Set of 6			6·25	6·00
First Day Cover (Tallents House)				6·25
Presentation Pack (PO Pack No. 392) (Nos. 2686/ MS2692)			10·00	
PHQ Cards (set of 11) (293)			3·25	15·50

(b) Ordinary gum. Litho Walsall. Perf 14.
MS2692 115×89 mm. **1948** Beatles Memorabilia (1st) Guitar; (1st) Yellow Submarine lunch box and keyrings; (1st) Record *Love Me Do*; (1st) Beatles tea tray and badges	3·75	3·75
First Day Cover (Tallents House)		6·25

Nos. 2686/2691 are all die-cut in the shape of a pile of records.

Nos. 2686/2687, 2688/2689 and 2690/2691 were each printed together in sheets of 60 (2 panes of 30), with the two designs alternating horizontally and the surplus backing paper around each stamp removed.

Nos. 2686/MS2692 commemorate the 50th anniversary of the first meeting of Paul McCartney and John Lennon.

The complete miniature sheet is on one of the 11 PHQ cards, with the others depicting individual stamps, including those from No. MS2692.

2007 (16 Jan)–**2008**. Smilers Booklet stamp (3rd series). 'LOVE' design as No. 2569. Self-adhesive. Multicoloured. Two phosphor bands. Die-cut Perf 15×14 (with one elliptical hole in each vertical side).
2693	(1st) multicoloured	5·50	5·50

No. 2693 was issued in stamp booklets in which the surplus backing paper around each stamp was removed.

Nos. 2694/2698 are left vacant.

1949 Moon Jellyfish

1950 Common Starfish

1951 Beadlet Anemone

1952 Bass

1953 Thornback Ray   **1954** Lesser Octopus

1955 Common Mussels   **1956** Grey Seal

1957 Shore Crab   **1958** Common Sun Star

2007 (1 Feb). Sea Life. Multicoloured Two phosphor bands. Perf 14½.

2699	**1949**	(1st) Moon Jellyfish	1·20	1·00
		a. Block of 10. Nos. 2699/2708	10·50	9·00
2700	**1950**	(1st) Common Starfish	1·20	1·00
2701	**1951**	(1st) Beadlet Anemone	1·20	1·00
2702	**1952**	(1st) Bass	1·20	1·00
2703	**1953**	(1st) Thornback Ray	1·20	1·00
2704	**1954**	(1st) Lesser Octopus	1·20	1·00
2705	**1955**	(1st) Common Mussels	1·20	1·00
2706	**1956**	(1st) Grey Seal	1·20	1·00
2707	**1957**	(1st) Shore Crab	1·20	1·00
2708	**1958**	(1st) Common Sun Star	1·20	1·00
Set of 10			10·50	9·00
Gutter Block of 20			21·00	
First Day Cover (Tallents House)				9·25
Presentation Pack (PO Pack No. 393)			11·00	
PHQ Cards (set of 10) (294)			3·00	10·50

Nos. 2699/2708 were printed together, *se-tenant*, as blocks of ten (5×2) in sheets of 60 (2 panes of 30).

1959 Saturn Nebula C55   **1960** Eskimo Nebula C39

1961 Cat's Eye Nebula C6   **1962** Helix Nebula C63

1963 Flaming Star Nebula C31   **1964** The Spindle C53

2007 (13 Feb). 50th Anniversary of *The Sky at Night* (TV programme). Nebulae. Self-adhesive. Multicoloured Two phosphor bands. Die-cut Perf 14½×14.

2709	**1959**	(1st) Saturn Nebula C55	1·20	1·00
		a. Horiz pair. Nos. 2709/2710	2·40	
2710	**1960**	(1st) Eskimo Nebula C39	1·20	1·00
2711	**1961**	50p. Cat's Eye Nebula C6	1·00	1·00
		a. Horiz pair. Nos. 2711/2712	2·00	
2712	**1962**	50p. Helix Nebula C63	1·00	1·00
2713	**1963**	72p. Flaming Star Nebula C31	1·25	1·25
		a. Horiz pair. Nos. 2713/2714	2·40	
2714	**1964**	72p. The Spindle C53	1·25	1·25
Set of 6			6·00	5·75
First Day Cover (Tallents House)				6·25
Presentation Pack (PO Pack No. 394)			7·00	
PHQ Cards (set of 6) (295)			1·75	7·00

Nos. 2709/2710, 2711/2712 and 2713/2714 were each printed together in sheets of 60 (2 panes of 30), with the two designs alternating horizontally and the surplus backing paper around each stamp removed.

1965 Iron Bridge (Thomas Telford)   **1966** Steam Locomotive and Railway Tracks

1967 Map of British Isles and Australia (telephone)   **1968** Camera and Television (John Logie Baird)

1969 Globe as Web (email and internet)   **1970** Couple with Suitcases on Moon (space travel)

2007 (1 Mar). World of Invention (1st issue). Self-adhesive. Multicoloured Two phosphor bands. Die-cut Perf 14½×14.

2715	**1965**	(1st) Iron Bridge	1·20	1·00
		a. Horiz pair. Nos. 2715/2716	2·40	
2716	**1966**	(1st) Steam Locomotive and Railway Tracks	1·20	1·00
2717	**1967**	64p. Map of British Isles and Australia	90	90
		a. Horiz pair. Nos. 2717/2718	1·75	
2718	**1968**	64p. Camera and Television	90	90
2719	**1969**	72p. Globe as Web	1·25	1·25
		a. Horiz pair. Nos. 2719/2720	2·50	
2720	**1970**	72p. Couple with Suitcases on Moon	1·25	1·25
Set of 6			6·25	6·00
First Day Cover (Tallents House)				6·25
Presentation Pack (PO Pack No. 395)			6·50	
PHQ Cards (set of 7) (296)			2·00	7·25

Nos. 2715/2716, 2717/2718 and 2719/2720 were each printed together in sheets of 60 (2 panes of 30), with the two designs alternating horizontally and the surplus backing paper around each stamp removed.

The seven PHQ Cards depict the six individual stamps and No. **MS**2727.

2007 (1 Mar). World of Invention (2nd issue). Ordinary gum. Multicoloured
Two phosphor bands. Perf 14½×14.

2721	**1965**	(1st) Iron Bridge	1·20	1·00
2722	**1966**	(1st) Steam Locomotive and Railway Tracks	1·20	1·00
2723	**1967**	64p. Map of British Isles and Australia	2·50	2·50
2724	**1968**	64p. Camera and Television	2·50	2·50
2725	**1969**	72p. Globe as Web	2·50	2·50
2726	**1970**	72p. Couple with Suitcases on Moon	2·50	2·50
Set of 6			11·00	11·00
MS2727 115×104 mm. Nos. 2721/2726			12·00	12·00
First Day Cover (Tallents House)				12·50

Nos. 2721/2726 were only issued in the £7·49 World of Invention booklet,
No. DX38 and in No. **MS**2727.

1971 William Wilberforce and Anti-slavery Poster

1972 Olaudah Equiano and Map of Slave Trade Routes

1973 Granville Sharp and Slave Ship

1974 Thomas Clarkson and Diagram of Slave Ship

1975 Hannah More and Title Page of *The Sorrows of Yamba*

1976 Ignatius Sancho and Trade/Business Card

2007 (22 Mar). Bicentenary of the Abolition of the Slave Trade.
Multicoloured Two phosphor bands. Perf 14½.

2728	**1971**	(1st) William Wilberforce	1·00	1·00
		a. Horiz pair. Nos. 2728/2729	2·00	
2729	**1972**	(1st) Olaudah Equiano	1·00	1·00
2730	**1973**	50p. Granville Sharp	80	80
		a. Horiz pair. Nos. 2730/2731	1·60	
2731	**1974**	50p. Thomas Clarkson	80	80
2732	**1975**	72p. Hannah More	90	90
		a. Horiz pair. Nos. 2732/2733	1·75	
2733	**1976**	72p. Ignatius Sancho	90	90
Set of 6			5·00	5·00
Set of 3 Gutter Strips of 4			11·00	
Set of 3 Traffic Light Gutter Strips of 4			42·00	
First Day Cover (Tallents House)				5·75
Presentation Pack (PO Pack No. 396)			6·00	
PHQ Cards (set of 6) (297)			1·75	6·00

Nos. 2728/2729, 2730/2731 and 2732/2733 were each printed together,
se-tenant, in horizontal pairs throughout the sheets.

For miniature sheet entitled Celebrating England, issued 23 April 2007,
see Regionals Section

1977 Ice Cream Cone

1978 Sandcastle

1979 Carousel Horse

1980 Beach Huts

1981 Deckchairs

1982 Beach Donkeys

2007 (15 May). Beside the Seaside. Multicoloured Two phosphor bands.
Perf 14½.

2734	**1977**	1st Ice Cream Cone	1·20	1·00
2735	**1978**	46p. Sandcastle	80	80
2736	**1979**	48p. Carousel Horse	90	90
2737	**1980**	54p. Beach Huts	1·00	1·00
2738	**1981**	69p. Deckchairs	1·10	1·10
2739	**1982**	78p. Beach Donkeys	1·25	1·25
Set of 6			5·50	5·50
Set of 6 Gutter Pairs			11·00	
First Day Cover (Tallents House)				5·75
Presentation Pack (PO Pack No. 397)			6·00	
PHQ Cards (set of 6) (298)			1·75	6·25

For T **1977**, but self-adhesive, see No. 2848

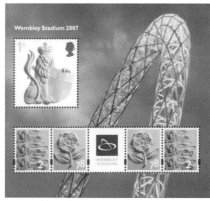

1983 Wembley Stadium

2007 (17 May). New Wembley Stadium, London. Sheet 113×103 mm
containing design as T **1593** but with 'WORLD CUP 2002' inscription
omitted, and Nos. EN6 and EN18, each×2. Multicoloured One centre
phosphor band (2nd) or two phosphor bands (others). Perf 14½×14
(1st) or 15×14 (with one elliptical hole in each vertical side) (2nd, 78p.).

MS2740	**1983**	Wembley Stadium (1st) As Type **1593**;		
		(2nd) No. EN6×2; 78p. No. EN18×2 and one central		
		stamp-size label	4·75	4·75
First Day Cover (Tallents House)				5·00

The design as T **1593** was also issued in sheets of 20 with *se-tenant*
labels showing scenes from Wembley Stadium.

1984 Arnold Machin

1985 1967 4d. Machin

1986 The Machin Definitives

2007 (5 June). 40th Anniversary of the First Machin Definitives. 'All-over' phosphor (1st) or two phosphor bands (others). Perf 14½ (1st) or 15×14 (with one elliptical hole in each vertical side) (£1).

2741	**1984**	(1st) Arnold Machin	1·75	1·75
2742	**1985**	(1st) 1967 4d. Machin	1·75	1·75

MS2743 127×73mm **1986** The Machin Definitives Nos.
2741/2742, Y1743 and Y1744 .... 4·75 4·75
First Day Cover (Tallents House) (No. **MS**2743) ...... 5·00
Presentation Pack (PO Pack No. 398) (No. **MS**2743) 5·50
PHQ Cards (set of 3) (299) (Nos. 2741/**MS**2743) 1·00 7·50

Nos. 2741/2742 were only issued in the £7·66 The Machin, The Making of a Masterpiece booklet, No. DX39 and in No. **MS**2743.

Stamps as T **1984** but with phosphor frames were issued in sheets of 20 with *se-tenant* labels showing the 1967–1969 Machin definitives.

1987 Stirling Moss in Vanwall 2.5L, 1957

1988 Graham Hill in BRM P57, 1962

1989 Jim Clark in Lotus 25 Climax, 1963

1990 Jackie Stewart in Tyrrell 006/2, 1973

1991 James Hunt in McLaren M23, 1976

1992 Nigel Mansell in Williams FW11, 1986

2007 (3 July). Grand Prix. Racing Cars. Multicoloured Two phosphor bands. Perf 14½.

2744	**1987**	(1st) Stirling Moss in Vanwall 2.5L	1·20	1·00
2745	**1988**	(1st) Graham Hill in BRM P57	1·20	1·00
2746	**1989**	54p. Jim Clark in Lotus 25 Climax	90	90
2747	**1990**	54p. Jackie Stewart in Tyrrell 006/2	90	90
2748	**1991**	78p. James Hunt in McLaren M23	1·25	1·25
2749	**1992**	78p. Nigel Mansell in Williams FW11	1·25	1·25
Set of 6			5·75	5·50
Set of 6 Gutter Pairs			11·00	
First Day Cover (Tallents House)				6·00
Presentation Pack (PO Pack No. 399)			6·00	
PHQ Cards (set of 6) (300)			1·75	6·25

1993 *Harry Potter and the Philosopher's Stone*

1994 *Harry Potter and the Chamber of Secrets*

1995 *Harry Potter and the Prisoner of Azkaban*

1996 *Harry Potter and the Goblet of Fire*

1997 *Harry Potter and the Order of the Phoenix*

1998 *Harry Potter and the Half-Blood Prince*

1999 *Harry Potter and the Deathly Hallows*

2000 Crests of Hogwarts School and its Four Houses

2007 (17 July). Publication of Final Book in the Harry Potter Series. Multicoloured

(a) Book Covers. 'All-over' phosphor. Perf 14½.

2750	**1993**	(1st) Harry Potter and the Philosopher's Stone	1·20	1·00
		a. Horiz strip of 7. Nos. 2750/2756	7·25	6·25
2751	**1994**	(1st) Harry Potter and the Chamber of Secrets	1·20	1·00
2752	**1995**	(1st) Harry Potter and the Prisoner of Azkaban	1·20	1·00
2753	**1996**	(1st) Harry Potter and the Goblet of Fire	1·20	1·00
2754	**1997**	(1st) Harry Potter and the Order of the Phoenix	1·20	1·00
2755	**1998**	(1st) Harry Potter and the Half-Blood Prince	1·20	1·00
2756	**1999**	(1st) Harry Potter and the Deathly Hallows	1·20	1·00
Set of 7			7·25	6·25
Gutter Block of 14			14·50	
Traffic Light Gutter Block of 14			32·00	
First Day Cover (Tallents House)				6·50
Presentation Pack (Nos. 2750/2757) (PO Pack No. M16)			12·00	
PHQ Cards (set of 13) (HP)			4·00	19·50

(b) Crests of Hogwarts School and its Four Houses. Multicoloured Two phosphor bands. Perf 15×14.

MS2757 123×70 mm. **2000** Crests of Hogwarts School and its Four Houses (1st) Gryffindor; (1st) Hufflepuff; (1st) Hogwarts; (1st) Ravenclaw; (1st) Slytherin	5·50	5·50
First Day Cover (Tallents House)		5·75

Nos. 2750/2756 were printed together, *se-tenant*, as horizontal strips of seven stamps in sheets of 56 (2 panes 7×4).

Stamps as those within No. **MS**2757 but self-adhesive were issued in sheets of 20 containing the five designs *se-tenant* with labels depicting either magic spells or personal photographs. The magic spells labels are printed in thermochromic ink which fades temporarily when exposed to heat, revealing the meaning of the spells.

The complete miniature sheet is shown on one of the 13 PHQ cards with the others depicting individual stamps including those from No. **MS**2757.

2001 Scout and Campfire

2002 Scouts Rock Climbing

2003 Scout Planting Tree

2004 Adult Volunteer Teaching Scout Archery

2005 Scouts Learning Gliding

2006 Scouts From Many Nations

2007 (26 July). Europa. Centenary of Scouting and 21st World Scout Jamboree, Chelmsford, Essex. Multicoloured Two phosphor bands. Perf 14½×14.

2758	**2001**	(1st) Scout and Campfire	1·20	1·00
2759	**2002**	46p. Scouts Rock climbing	80	80
2760	**2003**	48p. Scout planting Tree	85	85
2761	**2004**	54p. Adult Volunteer teaching Scout Archery	95	95
2762	**2005**	69p. Scouts learning gliding	1·10	1·10
2763	**2006**	78p. Scouts from Many Nations	1·25	1·25
Set of 6			5·50	5·50
Set of 6 Gutter Pairs			11·00	
First Day Cover (Tallents House)				6·00
Presentation Pack (PO Pack No. 400)			6·00	
PHQ Cards (*set of 6*) (301)			1·75	6·25

The 1st class and 48p. values include the EUROPA emblem.

2007 White-tailed Eagle   **2008** Bearded Tit

2009 Red Kite   **2010** Cirl Bunting

2011 Marsh Harrier   **2012** Avocet

2013 Bittern   **2014** Dartford Warbler

2015 Corncrake   **2016** Peregrine Falcon

2007 (4 Sept). Action for Species (1st series). Birds. Multicoloured Two phosphor bands. Perf 14½.

2764	**2007**	(1st) White-tailed Eagle	1·20	1·00
		a. Block of 10. Nos. 2764/2773	10·50	9·00
2765	**2008**	(1st) Bearded Tit	1·20	1·00
2766	**2009**	(1st) Red Kite	1·20	1·00
2767	**2010**	(1st) Cirl Bunting	1·20	1·00
2768	**2011**	(1st) Marsh Harrier	1·20	1·00
2769	**2012**	(1st) Avocet	1·20	1·00
2770	**2013**	(1st) Bittern	1·20	1·00
2771	**2014**	(1st) Dartford Warbler	1·20	1·00
2772	**2015**	(1st) Corncrake	1·20	1·00
2773	**2016**	(1st) Peregrine Falcon	1·20	1·00
Set of 10			10·50	9·00
Gutter Block of 20			21·00	
First Day Cover (Tallents House)				9·50
Presentation Pack (PO Pack No. 401)			11·00	
PHQ Cards (*set of 10*) (302)			3·00	9·75

Nos. 2764/2773 were printed together, *se-tenant*, as blocks of ten (5×2) in sheets of 60 (2 panes of 30).

2017 NCO, Royal Military Police, 1999   **2018** Tank Commander, 5th Royal Tank Regiment, 1944   **2019** Observer, Royal Field Artillery, 1917

2020 Rifleman, 95th Rifles, 1813

2021 Grenadier, Royal Regiment of Foot of Ireland, 1704

2022 Trooper, Earl of Oxford's Horse, 1661

2007 (20 Sept). Military Uniforms (1st series). British Army Uniforms. Multicoloured Two phosphor bands. Perf 14½.

2774	**2017**	(1st) NCO, Royal Military Police	1·20	1·00
		a. Horiz strip of 3. Nos. 2774/2776	3·60	3·00
2775	**2018**	(1st) Tank Commander, 5th Royal Tank Regiment	1·00	1·00
2776	**2019**	(1st) Observer, Royal Field Artillery	1·00	1·00
		a. Booklet pane. No. 2776×4 with margins all round (14.5.15)	1·00	1·00
2777	**2020**	78p. Rifleman, 95th Rifles	1·25	1·25
		a. Horiz strip of 3. Nos. 2777/2779	3·75	3·75
2778	**2021**	78p. Grenadier, Royal Regiment of Foot of Ireland	1·25	1·25
2779	**2022**	78p. Trooper, Earl of Oxford's Horse	1·25	1·25
Set of 6			7·00	6·50
Set of 2 Gutter blocks of 6			14·00	
Set of 2 Traffic Light Gutter blocks of 6			30·00	
First Day Cover (Tallents House)				7·00
Presentation Pack (PO Pack No. 402)			7·25	
PHQ Cards (set of 6) (303)			1·75	7·00

Nos. 2774/2776 and 2777/2779 were each printed together, se-tenant, in horizontal strips of three stamps in sheets of 60 (2 panes 6×5).

Nos. 2774/2776 and 2777/2779 were issued in the £7·66 British Army Uniforms booklet, No., DX40.

See also Nos. 2862/2867 and 2964/2969.

2029 Photographs of the Royal Family

2007 (16 Oct). Diamond Wedding of Queen Elizabeth II and Duke of Edinburgh. Blackish brown and black.

(a) Ordinary gum. Litho Cartor. 'All-over' phosphor. Perf 14½×14.

2780	**2023**	(1st) Leaving St Paul's Cathedral	1·20	1·00
		a. Horiz pair. Nos. 2780/2781	2·40	2·00
2781	**2024**	(1st) Inspecting King's Troop Royal Horse Artillery	1·20	1·00
2782	**2025**	54p. At Garter Ceremony	85	85
		a. Horiz pair. Nos. 2782/2783	1·75	1·75
2783	**2026**	54p. At Royal Ascot	85	85
2784	**2027**	78p. At Premiere of The Guns of Navarone	1·25	1·25
		a. Horiz pair. Nos. 2784/2785	2·50	2·50
2785	**2028**	78p. At Clydebank	1·25	1·25
Set of 6			5·75	5·50
Set of 3 Gutter blocks of 4			11·50	
First Day Cover (Tallents House)				7·25
Presentation Pack (PO Pack No. 403) (Nos. 2780/ MS2786)			11·50	
PHQ Cards (set of 11) (304)			3·25	15·50

(b) Self-adhesive. Gravure Walsall. Multicoloured Two phosphor bands. Perf 14½.

MS2786 115×89 mm. **2029** Photographs of the Royal Family (1st) Royal family, Balmoral, 1972; (1st) Queen and Prince Philip, Buckingham Palace, 2007; 69p. Royal family, Windsor Castle, 1965; 78p. Princess Elizabeth, Prince Philip, Prince Charles and Princess Anne, Clarence House, 1951 ... 4·25 4·25

First Day Cover (Tallents House) ... 5·75

Nos. 2780/2781, 2782/2783 and 2784/2785 were each printed together, se-tenant, in horizontal pairs throughout the sheets.

The complete miniature sheet is shown on one of the 11 PHQ cards with the others depicting individual stamps including those from No. **MS**2786.

2023 Leaving St Paul's Cathedral after Thanksgiving Service, 2006

2024 Inspecting King's Troop Royal Horse Artillery, Regents Park, 1997

2030 Madonna and Child (William Dyce), circa 1827

2031 The Madonna of Humility (Lippo di Dalmasio), circa 1390–1400)

2007 (6 Nov). Christmas (1st issue). Paintings of the Madonna and Child. Self-adhesive. Multicoloured One centre phosphor band (2nd) or two phosphor bands (1st). Die-cut Perf 15×14 (with one elliptical hole in each vertical side).

2787	**2030**	(2nd) Madonna and Child	90	90
2788	**2031**	(1st) The Madonna of Humility	1·20	1·10
First Day Cover (Tallents House)				2·75

2025 At Garter Ceremony, Windsor, 1980

2026 At Royal Ascot, 1969

2027 At Premiere of The Guns of Navarone, 1961

2028 At Clydebank, 1947

2032 Angel playing Trumpet ('PEACE')

2033 Angel playing Lute ('GOODWILL')

2034 Angel playing Trumpet ('PEACE')

2035 Angel playing Lute ('GOODWILL')

2036 Angel playing Flute ('JOY')

2037 Angel playing Tambourine ('GLORY')

2007 (6 Nov). Christmas (2nd issue). Angels. Multicoloured One centre phosphor band (No. 2789) or two phosphor bands (others). Perf 15×14.

		(a) Self-adhesive.		
2789	**2032**	(2nd) Angel playing Trumpet	90	90
2790	**2033**	(1st) Angel playing Lute	1·20	1·00
2791	**2034**	(2nd Large) Angel playing Trumpet	1·25	1·25
2792	**2035**	(1st Large) Angel playing Lute	1·70	1·50
2793	**2036**	78p. Angel playing Flute	1·50	1·50
2794	**2037**	£1·24 Angel playing Tambourine	2·25	2·25
Set of 6			7·75	7·50
First Day Cover (Tallents House)				7·75
Presentation Pack (Nos. 2787/2794) (PO Pack No. 404)			9·75	
PHQ Cards (set of 9) (305)			2·75	17·50

	(b) Ordinary gum.		
MS2795 115×102 mm. As Nos. 2789/2794		7·75	7·50
First Day Cover (Tallents House)			7·75

The phosphor bands on Nos. 2791/2792 are at the centre and right of each stamp.

The 2nd class, 1st class and 78p. stamps were also issued together in sheets of 20 printed in lithography instead of gravure containing 8×1st class, 8×2nd class and 4×78p. stamps, each stamp accompanied by a *se-tenant* label.

Separate sheets of 20×1st, 20×2nd or 10×78p. were available with personalised photographs.

The PHQ cards depict Nos. 2787/2794 and **MS**2795.

2038 Lest We Forget

2007 (8 Nov). Lest We Forget (2nd issue). 90th Anniversary of the Battle of Passchendaele. Sheet 124×70 mm containing new stamp as No. 2884 and designs as Nos. EN18, NI128, S121 and W110. Multicoloured Two phosphor bands. Perf 14½ (1st) or 15×14 (with one elliptical hole in each vertical side) (78p.).

MS2796	2038 Lest We Forget (1st) Soldiers in poppy flower; 78p.×4		6·00	6·00
First Day Cover (Tallents House)			6·25
Presentation Pack (PO Pack No. 405)		6·50	

The 1st class stamp was also issued in sheets of 20 with *se-tenant* labels showing soldiers and their letters home and, on 6 November 2008 in a *se-tenant* strip of three, see No. 2884.

Year Pack

2007 (8 Nov). Comprises Nos. 2686/2692, 2699/2720, 2728/2739, **MS**2743/2794 and **MS**2796.

CP2796a	Year Pack (Pack No. 406)	£120

Post Office Yearbook

2007 (8 Nov). Comprises Nos. 2686/2692, 2699/2720, 2728/2739, **MS**2743/2794 and **MS**2796.

YB2796a	Yearbook	80·00

Miniature Sheet Collection

2007 (8 Nov). Comprises Nos. **MS**2692, **MS**2727, **MS**2740, **MS**2743, **MS**2757, **MS**2786 and **MS**2795/**MS**2796.

MS2796a	Miniature Sheet Collection	48·00

2039 Casino Royale

2040 Dr No

2041 Goldfinger

2042 Diamonds are Forever

2043 For Your Eyes Only

2044 From Russia with Love

2008 (8 Jan). Birth Centenary of Ian Fleming (author of James Bond books). Book Covers. Multicoloured Two phosphor bands. Perf 14½×14.

2797	**2039**	(1st) Casino Royale	1·20	1·00
2798	**2040**	(1st) Dr No	1·20	1·00
2799	**2041**	54p. Goldfinger	90	90
2800	**2042**	54p. Diamonds are Forever	90	90
2801	**2043**	78p. For Your Eyes Only	1·25	1·25
2802	**2044**	78p. From Russia with Love	1·25	1·25
Set of 6			5·50	5·50
Set of 6 Gutter Pairs			11·00	
First Day Cover (Tallents House)				6·75
Presentation Pack (PO Pack No. 407)			6·50	
PHQ Cards (set of 7) (306)			2·00	15·00
MS2803 189×68 mm. Nos. 2797/2802			9·25	9·25
First Day Cover (Tallents House)				9·50

Nos. 2797/2802 were issued in the £7·40 Ian Fleming's James Bond booklet, No. DX41.

The seven PHQ cards depict the individual stamps and No. **MS**2803.

No. 2804 is vacant.

2008 (8 Jan). Ian Fleming's James Bond. Booklet stamp. Design as T **1517** (2001 Union Jack from Submarine Centenary). Multicoloured Two phosphor bands. Perf 14½.

2805	**1517**	(1st) multicoloured	2·00	2·00

No. 2805 was issued in the £7·40 Ian Fleming's James Bond booklet, No. DX41.

For White Ensign stamp from booklet No. DX41 see No. 2581.

2045 Assistance Dog carrying Letter (Retriever, Rowan)

2046 Mountain Rescue Dog (Cross-bred, Merrick)

2047 Police Dog (German Shepherd, Max)

2048 Customs Dog (Springer Spaniel, Max)

2049 Sheepdog (Border Collie, Bob)

2050 Guide Dog (Labrador, Warwick)

2008 (5 Feb). Working Dogs. Multicoloured Two phosphor bands. Perf 14½.

2806	**2045**	(1st) Assistance Dog carrying Letter	1·20	1·00
2807	**2046**	46p. Mountain Rescue Dog	80	80
2808	**2047**	48p. Police Dog	80	80
2809	**2048**	54p. Customs Dog	1·00	1·00
2810	**2049**	69p. Sheepdog	1·10	1·10
2811	**2050**	78p. Guide Dog	1·25	1·25
Set of 6			5·25	5·25
Set of 6 Gutter Pairs			10·50	
First Day Cover (Tallents House)				6·75
Presentation Pack (PO Pack No. 408)			6·50	
PHQ Cards (set of 6) (307)			1·75	6·25

The 1st class value includes the EUROPA emblem.

2051 Henry IV (1399–1413)

2052 Henry V (1413–1422)

2053 Henry VI (1422–1461 and 1470–1471)

2054 Edward IV (1461–1470 and 1471–1483)

2055 Edward V (1483)

2056 Richard III (1483–1485)

2057 The Age of Lancaster and York

2008 (28 Feb). Kings and Queens (1st issue). Houses of Lancaster and York. Multicoloured Two phosphor bands. Perf 14½.

2812	**2051**	(1st) Henry IV	1·20	1·00
2813	**2052**	(1st) Henry V	1·20	1·00
2814	**2053**	54p. Henry VI	90	1·00
2815	**2054**	54p. Edward IV	90	1·00
2816	**2055**	69p. Edward V	1·10	1·10
2817	**2056**	69p. Richard III	1·10	1·10
Set of 6			5·25	5·25
Set of 6 Gutter Pairs			10·50	
Set of 6 Traffic Light Gutter Blocks of 4			35·00	
First Day Cover (Tallents House)				6·75
Presentation Pack (PO Pack No. 409) (Nos. 2812/ **MS**2818)			11·00	
PHQ Cards (set of 11) (308)			3·25	15·00

MS2818 123×70 mm. **2057** The Age of Lancaster and York (1st) Owain Glyn Dwr (Parliament), 1404; (1st) Henry V's triumph at Battle of Agincourt, 1415; 78p. Yorkist victory at Battle of Tewkesbury, 1471; 78p. William Caxton, first English printer, 1477   4·00   4·25

First Day Cover (Tallents House)   5·00

The complete miniature sheet is shown on one of the 11 PHQ cards with the others depicting individual stamps including those from No. **MS**2818.

2008 (28 Feb). Smilers Booklet stamps (4th series). Self-adhesive. Multicoloured Two phosphor bands. Die-cut Perf 15×14 (with one elliptical hole in each vertical side).

2819	**1842a**	(1st) Aircraft Skywriting 'hello'	5·50	5·50
2820	**1842**	(1st) Gazania splendens	5·50	5·50
2821	**1842c**	(1st) Union Jack	5·50	5·50
2822	**1932**	(1st) Balloons	5·50	5·50
2823	**1933**	(1st) Firework	5·50	5·50
2824	**1934**	(1st) Champagne, Flowers and Butterflies	5·50	5·50
Set of 6			30·00	30·00

Nos. 2819/2824 were issued in £2·04 booklets in which the surplus backing paper around each stamp was removed.

No. 2819 was issued in sheets of 20 with se-tenant labels on 8 May 2010 for London 2010 Festival of Stamps, 28 July 2011 for Philanippon '11 World Stamp Exhibition, Yokohama, on 28 June 2012 for Indonesia 2012 International Stamp Exhibition, Jakarta, on 10 May 2013 for Australia 2013 World Stamp Exhibition, Melbourne, on 2 August 2013 for Bangkok 2013 World Stamp Exhibition, Thailand, on 1 December 2014 for Kuala Lumpur 2014 FIF Exhibition, on 13 May 2015 for Europhilex London 2015 Exhibition, on 28 May 2016 for New York World Stamp Show, on 28 May 2017 for Finlandia 2017 FIP Exhibition, Tampere, on 29 May 2019 for Stockholmia 2019 International Stamp Exhibition and on 19 February 2022 for London International Stamp Exhibition.

Nos. 2819, 2820 and 2822 were issued again on 30 April 2009 in separate sheets often or 20 with circular se-tenant labels showing Jeremy Fisher (No. 2819), Wild Cherry fairy (No. 2820), Little Miss Sunshine or Big Ears (No. 2822).

Nos. 2820 and 2822 were each issued on 28 October 2008 in separate sheets of ten or 20 with circular se-tenant labels showing the Almond Blossom fairy (No. 2820), Mr Men or Noddy (No. 2822).

No. 2821 (and Nos. 2822/2823) were issued, together with Nos. 2569, 2572, 2674 and four designs from No. **MS**3024, on 8 May 2010 in sheets of 20 with se-tenant greetings labels.

No. 2821 was issued on 12 February 2011 in sheets of 20 with se-tenant labels for Indipex International Stamp Exhibition.

No. 2821 was issued on 30 March 2011 in sheets of ten with se-tenant labels for the 50th Anniversary of the Jaguar E-type car.

No. 2823 was issued in sheets of 20 with se-tenant labels on 20 January 2012 for Lunar New Year, Year of the Dragon, on 7 February 2013 for Year of the Snake, 10 December 2013 for Year of the Horse, on 19 November 2014 for Year of the Sheep, on 9 November 2015 for Year of the Monkey, on 15 November 2016 for Year of the Rooster, on 16 November 2017 for Year of the Dog, on 15 November 2018 for Year of the Pig, on 18 November 2019 for Year of the Rat, on 8 December 2020 for Year of the Ox, on 8 December 2021 for Year of the Tiger and on 8 December 2022 for Year of the Rabbit. All the above sheets were printed in lithography instead of photogravure.

For the miniature sheet entitled Celebrating Northern Ireland, issued 11 March 2008, see Regionals Section.

2058 Lifeboat, Barra

2059 Lifeboat approaching Dinghy, Appledore

2060 Helicopter Winchman, Portland

2061 Inshore lifeboat, St Ives

2062 Rescue Helicopter, Lee-on-Solent

2063 Launch of Lifeboat, Dinbych-y-Pysgod, Tenby

2008 (13 Mar). Rescue at Sea. Multicoloured 'All-over' phosphor. Perf 14½×14*.

2825	**2058**	(1st) Lifeboat, Barra	1·20	1·00
2826	**2059**	46p. Lifeboat approaching Dinghy, Appledore	80	80
2827	**2060**	48p. Helicopter Winchman, Portland	90	90
2828	**2061**	54p. Inshore lifeboat, St Ives	1·00	1·00
2829	**2062**	69p. Rescue Helicopter, Lee-on- Solent	1·10	1·10
2830	**2063**	78p. Launch of Lifeboat, Dinbych-y-Pysgod, Tenby	1·25	1·25
		Set of 6	5·25	5·25
		Set of 6 Gutter Pairs	10·50	
		First Day Cover (Tallents House)		6·50
		Presentation Pack (PO Pack No. 411)	6·00	
		PHQ Cards (set of 6) (309)	1·50	6·25

*   Nos. 2825/2830 have interrupted perforations along the top and bottom edges of the stamps, the gaps in the perforations forming the three dots and three dashes that spell out 'SOS' in morse code.

2064 Lysandra bellargus (Adonis Blue)

2065 Coenagrion mercuriale (Southern Damselfly)

2066 Formica rufibarbis (Red-barbed Ant)

2067 Pareulype berberata (Barberry Carpet Moth)

2068 Lucanus cervus (Stag Beetle)

2069 Cryptocephalus coryli (Hazel Pot Beetle)

2070 Gryllus campestris (Field Cricket)

2071 Hesperia comma (Silver-spotted Skipper)

2072 Pseudepipona herrichii (Purbeck Mason Wasp)

2073 Gnorimus nobilis (Noble Chafer)

2008 (15 Apr). Action for Species (2nd series). Insects. Multicoloured Phosphor background. Perf 14½.

2831	**2064**	(1st) Lysandra bellargus (Adonis blue)	1·20	1·00
		a. Block of 10. Nos. 2831/2840	10·50	9·00
2832	**2065**	(1st) Coenagrion mercuriale (southern damselfly)	1·20	1·00
2833	**2066**	(1st) Formica rufibarbis (red-barbed ant)	1·20	1·00
2834	**2067**	(1st) Pareulype berberata (barberry carpet moth)	1·20	1·00
2835	**2068**	(1st) Lucanus cervus (stag beetle)	1·20	1·00
2836	**2069**	(1st) Cryptocephalus coryli (hazel pot beetle)	1·20	1·00
2837	**2070**	(1st) Gryllus campestris (field cricket)	1·20	1·00
2838	**2071**	(1st) Hesperia comma (silver-spotted skipper)	1·20	1·00
2839	**2072**	(1st) Pseudepipona herrichii (Purbeck mason wasp)	1·20	1·00
2840	**2073**	(1st) Gnorimus nobilis (noble chafer)	1·20	1·00
		Set of 10	10·50	9·00
		Gutter Block of 20	21·00	
		First Day Cover (Tallents House)		9·25
		Presentation Pack (PO Pack No. 412)	11·00	
		PHQ Cards (set of 10) (310)	3·00	9·75

Nos. 2831/2840 were printed together, se-tenant, as blocks of ten (5×2) in sheets of 60 (2 panes of 30).

2074 Lichfield Cathedral

2075 Belfast Cathedral

2076 Gloucester Cathedral

2077 St David's Cathedral

2078 Westminster Cathedral

2079 St Magnus Cathedral, Kirkwall, Orkney

2080 St Paul's Cathedral

2008 (13 May). Cathedrals. Multicoloured 'All-over' phosphor. Perf 14½.

2841	**2074**	(1st) Lichfield Cathedral	1·20	1·00
2842	**2075**	48p. Belfast Cathedral	85	85
2843	**2076**	50p. Gloucester Cathedral	1·00	1·00
2844	**2077**	56p. St David's Cathedral	1·10	1·10
2845	**2078**	72p. Westminster Cathedral	1·25	1·25
2846	**2079**	81p. St Magnus Cathedral, Kirkwall, Orkney	1·40	1·40
Set of 6			6·00	6·00
Set of 6 Gutter Pairs			12·00	
Set of 6 Traffic Light Gutter Pairs			32·00	
First Day Cover (Tallents House)			6·75	
Presentation Pack (PO Pack No. 413) (Nos. 2841/ **MS**2847)			11·00	
PHQ Cards (set of 11) (311)			3·25	16·00

MS2847 115×89 mm. **2080** St Paul's Cathedral (1st) multicoloured; (1st) multicoloured; 81p. multicoloured; 81p. multicoloured. Perf 14½×14   4·00   4·00

First Day Cover (Tallents House)   4·50

No. **MS**2847 commemorates the 300th anniversary of St Paul's Cathedral. The complete miniature sheet is shown on one of the 11 PHQ cards with the others depicting individual stamps including those from No. **MS**2847.

2008 (13 May). Beside the Seaside (2nd series). As T **1977** but self-adhesive. Multicoloured Two phosphor bands. Die-cut Perf 14½.

2848	**1977**	(1st) Ice Cream Cone. Multicoloured	3·00	3·00

No. 2848 was only issued in £2·16 booklets.

2081 *Carry on Sergeant*   **2082** *Dracula*

2083 *Carry on Cleo*   **2084** *The Curse of Frankenstein*

2085 *Carry on Screaming*   **2086** *The Mummy*

2008 (10 June). Posters for Carry On and Hammer Horror Films. Multicoloured Two phosphor bands. Perf 14.

2849	**2081**	(1st) *Carry on Sergeant*	1·20	1·00
2850	**2082**	48p. *Dracula*	80	80
2851	**2083**	50p. *Carry on Cleo*	90	90
2852	**2084**	56p. *The Curse of Frankenstein*	1·00	1·00
2853	**2085**	72p. *Carry on Screaming*	1·10	1·10
2854	**2086**	81p. *The Mummy*	1·25	1·25
Set of 6			5·50	5·50
Set of 6 Gutter Pairs			11·00	
First Day Cover (Tallents House)			6·25	
Presentation Pack (PO Pack No. 414)			6·25	
PHQ Cards (set of 6) (312)			1·50	7·00
PHQ Cards (brick wall background) and Stamps Set			7·00	

Nos. 2849/2854 commemorate the 50th anniversary of *Dracula* and the first Carry On film (*Carry on Sergeant*).

2087 Red Arrows, Dartmouth Regatta Airshow, 2006   **2088** RAF Falcons Parachute Team, Biggin Hill, 2006

2089 Spectator watching Red Arrows, Farnborough, 2006   **2090** Prototype Avro Vulcan Bombers and Avro 707s, Farnborough, 1953

2091 Parachutist Robert Wyndham on Wing of Avro 504, 1933   **2092** Air Race rounding the Beacon, Hendon, c 1912

2008 (17 July). Air Displays. Multicoloured Two phosphor bands. Perf 14½×14.

2855	**2087**	(1st) Red Arrows	1·20	1·00
2856	**2088**	48p. RAF Falcons Parachute Team	80	80
2857	**2089**	50p. Spectator watching Red Arrows	90	90
2858	**2090**	56p. Prototype Avro Vulcan Bombers and Avro 707s	1·00	1·00
2859	**2091**	72p. Parachutist Robert Wyndham on Wing of Avro 504	1·10	1·10
2860	**2092**	81p. Air Race rounding the Beacon	1·25	1·25
Set of 6			5·50	5·50
Set of 6 Gutter Pairs			11·00	
First Day Cover (Tallents House)			6·25	
Presentation Pack (PO Pack No. 415)			6·25	
PHQ Cards (set of 6) (313)			1·75	6·25

The 1st class stamp was also issued in sheets of 20 with *se-tenant* labels. See also No. 2869.

2093 Landmarks of Beijing and London

2008 (22 Aug). Handover of Olympic Flag from Beijing to London. Sheet 115×76 mm. Multicoloured Phosphorised paper. Perf 14½.

MS2861	**2093**	Landmarks of Beijing and London (1st) National Stadium, Beijing; (1st) London Eye; (1st) Tower of London; (1st) Corner Tower of the Forbidden City, Beijing	5·00	5·00
		First Day Cover (Talents House)		5·25
		Presentation Pack (PO Pack No. M17)	30·00	
		PHQ Cards (set of 5) (OGH)	60	5·00

The Olympic rings overprinted on No. **MS**2861 are in silk-screen varnish. The five PHQ cards show the four individual stamps and the complete miniature sheet.

2094 Drum Major, RAF Central Band, 2007

2095 Helicopter Rescue Winchman, 1984

2096 Hawker Hunter Pilot, 1951

2097 Lancaster Air Gunner, 1944

2098 WAAF Plotter, 1940

2099 Pilot, 1918

2008 (18 Sept). Military Uniforms (2nd series). RAF Uniforms. Multicoloured Two phosphor bands. Perf 14.

2862	**2094**	(1st) Drum Major, RAF Central Band	1·20	1·00
		a. Horiz strip of 3. Nos. 2862/2864	3·50	3·00
2863	**2095**	(1st) Helicopter Rescue Winchman	1·20	1·00
2864	**2096**	(1st) Hawker Hunter Pilot	1·20	1·00
2865	**2097**	81p. Lancaster Air Gunner	1·40	1·40
		a. Horiz strip of 3. Nos. 2865/2867	4·25	4·25
2866	**2098**	81p. WAAF Plotter	1·40	1·40
2867	**2099**	81p. Pilot	1·40	1·40
		Set of 6	7·00	6·75
		Set of 2 Gutter Strips of 6	14·00	
		Set of 2 Traffic Light Gutter Blocks of 12	28·00	
		First Day Cover (Talents House)		7·00
		Presentation Pack (PO Pack No. 416)	7·00	
		PHQ Cards (set of 6) (314)	1·75	7·75

Nos. 2862/2864 and 2865/2867 were each printed together, *se-tenant*, as horizontal strips of three stamps in sheets of 60 (2 panes 6×5).

Nos. 2862/2867 were issued in the £7·15 Pilot to Plane, RAF Uniforms booklet No. DX42.

See also Nos. 2774/2779 and 2964/2969.

2008 (18 Sept). Pilot to Plane. RAF Uniforms. Booklet stamps. Designs as T **1307** (Spitfire from 1997 British Aircraft Designers) and T **2087** (Red Arrows from 2008 Air Displays). Multicoloured Two phosphor bands. Perf 14.

2868	**1307**	20p. Reginald Mitchell and Supermarine Spitfire MkIIA	1·25	1·25
2869	**2087**	(1st) Red Arrows	1·25	1·25

Nos. 2868/2869 were only issued in the £7·15 Pilot to Plane, RAF Uniforms booklet, No. DX42.

2100 Millicent Garrett Fawcett (suffragist)

2101 Elizabeth Garrett Anderson (physician, women's health)

2102 Marie Stopes (family planning pioneer)

2103 Eleanor Rathbone (family allowance campaigner)

2104 Claudia Jones (civil rights activist)

2105 Barbara Castle (politician, Equal Pay Act)

2008 (14 Oct). Women of Distinction. Multicoloured 'All-over' phosphor. Perf 14×14½.

2870	**2100**	(1st) Millicent Garrett Fawcett	1·20	1·00
2871	**2101**	48p. Elizabeth Garrett Anderson	80	80
2872	**2102**	50p. Marie Stopes	90	90
2873	**2103**	56p. Eleanor Rathbone	1·00	1·00
2874	**2104**	72p. Claudia Jones	1·10	1·10
2875	**2105**	81p. Barbara Castle	1·25	1·25
		Set of 6	5·25	5·25
		Set of 6 Gutter Pairs	10·50	
		First Day Cover (Talents House)		6·25
		Presentation Pack (PO Pack No. 417)	6·00	
		PHQ Cards (set of 6) (315)	1·75	6·25

2106 Ugly Sisters from *Cinderella*

2107 Genie from *Aladdin*

2108 Ugly Sisters from *Cinderella*

2109 Captain Hook from *Peter Pan*

2110 Genie from *Aladdin*

2111 Wicked Queen from *Snow White*

2008 (4 Nov). Christmas. Multicoloured One centre band (No. 2876) or two phosphor bands (others). Perf 15×14.

(a) Self-adhesive.

2876	**2106**	(2nd) Ugly Sisters	90	90
2877	**2107**	(1st) Genie	1·20	1·00
2878	**2108**	(2nd Large) Ugly Sisters	1·25	1·25
2879	**2109**	50p. Captain Hook	1·00	1·00
2880	**2110**	(1st Large) Genie	1·70	1·50
2881	**2111**	81p. Wicked Queen	1·75	1·75
		Set of 6	6·25	6·25
		First Day Cover (Talents House)		6·50
		Presentation Pack (PO Pack No. 418)	7·00	
		PHQ Cards (set of 7) (316)	2·00	12·00

(b) Ordinary gum.

MS2882	114×102 mm. As Nos. 2876/2881	6·50	6·50
	First Day Cover (Talents House)		6·75

The phosphor bands on Nos. 2878 and 2880 are at the centre and right of each stamp.

The 2nd class, 1st class and 81p. stamps were also issued together in sheets of 20 containing 8×1st class, 8×2nd class and 4×81p. stamps, each stamp accompanied by a *se-tenant* label.

Separate sheets of 10×1st, 20×1st, 20×2nd or 10×81p. stamps were available with personalised photographs.

All these sheets were printed in lithography and had the backing paper around the stamps retained.

The seven PHQ cards depict the six stamps and No. **MS**2882.

2112 Seven Poppies on Barbed Wire Stems

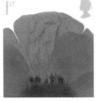

2113 Soldiers in Poppy Flower

2114 Soldier's Face in Poppy Flower

2115 Lest We Forget

2008 (6 Nov)–**2017**. Lest We Forget (3rd issue). 90th Anniversary of the Armistice. Multicoloured Two phosphor bands. Perf 14½ (1st) or 15×14 (with one elliptical hole in each vertical side) (81p.).

2883	**2112**	(1st) Seven Poppies on Barbed Wire Stems	1·20	1·00
		a. Horiz strip of 3. Nos. 2883/2885	3·50	4·50
2884	**2113**	(1st) Soldiers in Poppy Flower	1·20	1·00
2885	**2114**	(1st) Soldier's Face in Poppy Flower	1·20	1·00
Set of 3			3·50	4·50
Gutter Strip of 6			7·00	
Traffic Light Gutter Block of 12			25·00	
MS2886 124×70 mm. **2115** Lest We Forget No. 2885 and as Nos. EN19, NI129, S122 and W111			5·75	5·75
First Day Cover (Tallents House)				6·75
Presentation Pack (PO Pack No. 419)			7·25	
PHQ Cards (set of 6) (317)			1·80	9·50

Nos. 2883/2885 were printed together, *se-tenant*, in horizontal strips of three stamps in sheets of 30.

No. **MS**2886 (including the England, Northern Ireland, Scotland and Wales stamps) is printed in lithography.

The 1st class stamp, T **2114**, was also issued in sheets of 20 with *se-tenant* labels.

The six PHQ cards depict Nos. **MS**2685, **MS**2796 and 2883/**MS**2886.

Year Pack

2008 (6 Nov). Comprises Nos. 2797/2802, 2806/**MS**2818, 2825/**MS**2847, 2849/2867, 2870/2881, **MS**2886 and **MS**NI152

CP2886a	Year Pack (Pack No. 420)	85·00

Post Office Yearbook

2008 (6 Nov). Comprises Nos. 2797/2802, 2806/**MS**2818, 2825/**MS**2847, 2849/2867, 2870/2881, **MS**2886 and **MS**NI152/**MS**NI153

YB2886a	Yearbook	85·00

Miniature Sheet Collection

2008 (6 Nov). Comprises Nos. **MS**2803, **MS**2818, **MS**2847, **MS**2861, **MS**2882, **MS**2886 and **MS**NI152/**MS**NI153

MS2886a	Miniature Sheet Collection	45·00

2116 Supermarine Spitfire (R. J. Mitchell)

2117 Mini Skirt (Mary Quant)

2118 Mini (Sir Alec Issigonis)

2119 Anglepoise Lamp (George Carwardine)

2120 Concorde (Aérospatiale-BAC)

2121 K2 Telephone Kiosk (Sir Giles Gilbert Scott)

2122 Polypropylene Chair (Robin Day)

2123 Penguin Books (Edward Young)

2124 London Underground Map (based on original design by Harry Beck)

2125 Routemaster Bus (design team led by AAM Durrant)

2009 (13 Jan). British Design Classics (1st series). Multicoloured Phosphor background. Perf 14½.

2887	**2116**	(1st) Supermarine Spitfire	1·20	1·00
		a. Block of 10. Nos. 2887/2896	10·50	9·00
2888	**2117**	(1st) Mini Skirt	1·20	1·00
2889	**2118**	(1st) Mini	1·20	1·00
2890	**2119**	(1st) Anglepoise Lamp	1·20	1·00
2891	**2120**	(1st) Concorde	1·20	1·00
2892	**2121**	(1st) K2 Telephone Kiosk	1·20	1·00
2893	**2122**	(1st) Polypropylene Chair	1·20	1·00
2894	**2123**	(1st) Penguin Books	1·20	1·00
2895	**2124**	(1st) London Underground Map	1·20	1·00
2896	**2125**	(1st) Routemaster Bus	1·20	1·00
Set of 10			10·50	9·00
Gutter Block of 20			21·00	
First Day Cover (Tallents House)				9·00
Presentation Pack (PO Pack No. 421)			11·00	
PHQ Cards (set of 10) (318)			3·00	9·75

No. 2887 was also issued on 15 September 2010 in sheets of 20 with *se-tenant* labels.

Nos. 2887/2896 were printed together, *se-tenant*, in blocks of ten (2×5) throughout sheets of 30 stamps.

Nos. 2887/2896 were also issued in the £7·68 British Design Classics booklet, No. DX44.

No. 2889 was also issued in sheets of 20 with *se-tenant* labels, on 13 January 2009.

No. 2891 was also issued on 2 March 2009 in sheets of 20 with *se-tenant* labels.

The above sheets were all printed in lithography and perforated 14×14½. For self-adhesive versions of these stamps see Nos. 2911/2915b.

2009 (13 Jan). British Design Classics (2nd series). Booklet stamp. Design as No. 2285 (Concorde from 2002 Passenger Jet Aviation). Multicoloured Two phosphor bands. Perf 14½.

2897	**1589**	(1st) Concorde (1976). Multicoloured	4·50	4·50

No. 2897 was only issued in the £7·68 British Design Classics booklet, No. DX44.

> For the miniature sheet entitled Robert Burns 250th Anniversary, issued on 22 January, see the Regional Section.

2126 Charles Darwin

2127 Marine Iguana

2128 Finches

2129 Atoll

2130 Bee Orchid

2131 Orangutan

2132 Fauna and Map of the Galapagos Islands

2009 (12 Feb). Birth Bicentenary of Charles Darwin (naturalist and evolutionary theorist) (1st issue). Multicoloured

(a) Self-adhesive. Gravure De La Rue. 'All-over' phosphor. Perf 14.

2898	**2126**	(1st) Charles Darwin	1·20	1·00
2899	**2127**	48p. Marine Iguana	1·10	1·10
2900	**2128**	50p. Finches	1·25	1·25
2901	**2129**	56p. Atoll	1·40	1·40
2902	**2130**	72p. Bee Orchid	1·75	1·75

2903	**2131**	81p. Orangutan	2·00	2·00
Set of 6			7·50	7·50
First Day Cover (Tallents House)				8·25
Presentation Pack (PO Pack No. 423) (Nos. 2898/				
MS2904)			10·50	
PHQ Cards (set of 11) (320)			3·25	16·50

(b) Ordinary gum. Litho De La Rue. Two phosphor bands. Perf 14.

MS2904 115×89 mm. **2132** Fauna and Map of the
Galapagos Islands (1st) Flightless Cormorant;
(1st) Giant Tortoise and Cactus Finch; 81p. Marine
Iguana; 81p. Floreana Mockingbird ..... 5·00   5·00

First Day Cover (Tallents House) ..... 6·00

Nos. 2898/2903 have jigsaw perforations on the two vertical sides.

The complete miniature sheet is shown on one of the 11 PHQ cards with the others depicting individual stamps, including those from No. **MS**2904.

2009 (12 Feb). Birth Bicentenary of Charles Darwin (naturalist and evolutionary theorist) (2nd issue). Multicoloured Phosphorised paper. Perf 14.

2905	**2126**	(1st) Charles Darwin	6·00	6·00
2906	**2127**	48p. Marine Iguana	6·00	6·00
2907	**2128**	50p. Finches	6·00	6·00
2908	**2129**	56p. Atoll	6·00	6·00
2909	**2130**	72p. Bee Orchid	6·00	6·00
2910	**2131**	81p. Orangutan	6·00	6·00
Set of 6			32·00	32·00

Nos. 2905/2910 were only issued in the £7·75 Charles Darwin booklet, No. DX45.

Nos, 2905/2910 have Jigsaw perforations on both vertical sides.

> For Nos. U2911/U3109 and Types **2132a/2132d** see Decimal Machin Definitives section.

2009 (10 Mar)–**2010**. British Design Classics (3rd series). Booklet stamps. Designs as Nos. 2887/2889, 2891/2892 and 2896. Self-adhesive. Multicoloured. Phosphor background. Die-cut perf 14½.

2911	**2121**	(1st) K2 Telephone Kiosk	2·00	2·00
2912	**2125**	(1st) Routemaster Bus	2·00	2·00
2913	**2118**	(1st) Mini (21.4.09)	2·00	2·00
2914	**2120**	(1st) Concorde (18.8.09)	2·00	2·00
2915	**2117**	(1st) Mini Skirt (17.9.09)	2·00	2·00
2915*b*	**2116**	(1st) Supermarine Spitfire (15.9.10)	2·00	2·00
Set of 6			10·00	10·00

Nos. 2911/2915b were only issued in booklets.

2133 Matthew Boulton and Factory (manufacturing)

2134 James Watt and Boulton & Watt Condensing Engine (steam engineering)

2135 Richard Arkwright and Spinning Machine (textiles)

2136 Josiah Wedgwood and Black Basalt Teapot and Vase (ceramics)

2137 George Stephenson and Locomotion (railways)

2138 Henry Maudslay and Table Engine (machine making)

2139 James Brindley and Bridgewater Canal Aqueduct (canal engineering)

2140 John McAdam (road building)

2009 (10 Mar). Pioneers of the Industrial Revolution. Multicoloured 'All-over' phosphor. Perf 14×14½.

2916	**2133**	(1st) Matthew Boulton	1·20	1·00
		a. Horiz pair. Nos. 2916/2917	2·40	2·00
2917	**2134**	(1st) James Watt	1·20	1·00
2918	**2135**	50p. Richard Arkwright	70	70
		a. Horiz pair. Nos. 2918/2919	1·40	1·40
2919	**2136**	50p. Josiah Wedgwood	70	70
2920	**2137**	56p. George Stephenson	85	85
		a. Horiz pair. Nos. 2920/2921	1·75	1·75
2921	**2138**	56p. Henry Maudslay	85	85
2922	**2139**	72p. James Brindley	1·00	1·00
		a. Horiz pair. Nos. 2922/2923	2·00	2·00
2923	**2140**	72p. John McAdam	1·00	1·00
Set of 8			6·75	6·50
Set of 4 Gutter Strips of 4			13·50	
First Day Cover (Tallents House)				7·50
Presentation Pack (PO Pack No. 425)			7·25	
PHQ Cards (set of 8) (321)			2·40	8·00

Nos. 2916/2917, 2918/2919, 2920/2921 and 2922/2923 were each printed together, *se-tenant*, as horizontal pairs in sheets of 60 (2 panes 6×5).

2141 Henry VII (1485–1509)

2142 Henry VIII (1509–1547)

2143 Edward VI (1547–1553)

2144 Lady Jane Grey (1553)

2145 Mary I (1553–1558)

2146 Elizabeth I (1558–1603)

2147 The Age of the Tudors

2009 (21 Apr). Kings and Queens (2nd issue). House of Tudor. Multicoloured Two phosphor bands. Perf 14.

2924	**2141**	(1st) Henry VII	1·20	1·00
2925	**2142**	(1st) Henry VIII	1·20	1·00
2926	**2143**	62p. Edward VI	90	90
2927	**2144**	62p. Lady Jane Grey	90	90
2928	**2145**	81p. Mary I	1·25	1·25

2929	**2146**	81p. Elizabeth I	1·25	1·25
Set of 6			5·75	5·50
Set of 6 Gutter Pairs			11·50	
Set of 6 Traffic Light Gutter Blocks of 4			30·00	
First Day Cover (Tallents House)				7·50
Presentation Pack (PO Pack No. 426) (Nos. 2924/MS2930)			7·25	
PHQ Cards (set of 11) (322)			3·25	16·00
MS2930 123×70 mm. **2147** The Age of the Tudors (1st) *Mary Rose* (galleon), 1510; (1st) Field of Cloth of Gold Royal Conference, 1520; 90p. Royal Exchange (centre of commerce), 1565; 90p. Francis Drake (circumnavigation), 1580			4·25	4·25
First Day Cover (Tallents House)				5·00

The complete miniature sheet is shown on one of the 11 PHQ cards with the others depicting individual stamps including those from No. **MS**2930.

2148 *Allium sphaerocephalon* (Round-headed Leek)

2149 *Luronium natans* (Floating Water-plantain)

2150 *Cypripedium calceolus* (Lady's Slipper Orchid)

2151 *Polygala amarella* (Dwarf Milkwort)

2152 *Saxifraga hirculus* (Marsh Saxifrage)

2153 *Stachys germanica* (Downy Woundwort)

2154 *Euphorbia serrulata* (Upright Spurge)

2155 *Pyrus cordata* (Plymouth Pear)

2156 *Polygonum maritimum* (Sea Knotgrass)

2157 *Dianthus armeria* (Deptford Pink)

2158 Royal Botanic Gardens, Kew

2009 (19 May). Action for Species (3rd series). Plants. Multicoloured

(a) Phosphor background. Perf 14½.

2931	**2148**	(1st) *Allium sphaerocephalon* (Round-headed Leek)	1·20	1·00
		a. Block of 10. Nos. 2931/2940	10·50	9·00
2932	**2149**	(1st) *Luronium natans* (Floating Water-plantain)	1·20	1·00
2933	**2150**	(1st) *Cypripedium calceolus* (Lady's Slipper Orchid)	1·20	1·00
2934	**2151**	(1st) *Polygala amarella* (Dwarf Milkwort)	1·20	1·00
2935	**2152**	(1st) *Saxifraga hirculus* (Marsh Saxifrage)	1·20	1·00
2936	**2153**	(1st) *Stachys germanica* (Downy Woundwort)	1·20	1·00
2937	**2154**	(1st) *Euphorbia serrulata* (Upright Spurge)	1·20	1·00
2938	**2155**	(1st) *Pyrus cordata* (Plymouth Pear)	1·20	1·00
2939	**2156**	(1st) *Polygonum maritimum* (Sea Knotgrass)	1·20	1·00
2940	**2157**	(1st) *Dianthus armeria* (Deptford Pink)	1·20	1·00
Set of 10			10·50	9·00
Gutter Block of 10			21·00	
First Day Cover (Tallents House)				11·00
Presentation Pack (PO Pack No. 427) (Nos. 2931/**MS**2941)			15·00	
PHQ Cards (*set of* 15) (323)			4·50	13·50

(b) 250th Anniversary of Royal Botanic Gardens, Kew. Two phosphor bands. Perf 14×14½.

MS2941 **2158** 115×89 mm. (1st) Palm House, Kew Gardens; (1st) Millennium Seed Bank, Wakehurst Place; 90p. Pagoda, Kew Gardens; 90p. Sackler Crossing, Kew Gardens	4·25	4·25
First Day Cover (Tallents House)		5·00

Nos. 2931/2940 were printed together, *se-tenant*, as blocks of ten (5×2) in sheets of 60 (2 panes of 30).

The complete miniature sheet is shown on one of the 15 PHQ cards with the others depicting individual stamps including those from No. **MS**2941.

2009 (21 May). 50th Anniversary of NAFAS (National Association of Flower Arrangement Societies). Booklet stamps. Designs as Nos. 1958 and 1962 (1997 Greetings Stamps, 19th-century Flower Paintings). Self-adhesive. Multicoloured Two phosphor bands. Die-cut Perf 14 (with one elliptical hole in each vert side).

2942	**1287**	(1st) *Iris latifolia*	4·25	4·25
2943	**1283**	(1st) *Tulipa*		
			4·25	4·25

Nos. 2942/2943 were only issued in stamp booklets.

2159 Dragon

2160 Unicorn

2161 Giant

2162 Pixie

2163 Mermaid

2164 Fairy

2009 (16 June). Mythical Creatures. Multicoloured 'All-over' phosphor. Perf 14½.

2944	**2159**	(1st) Dragon	1·20	1·00
2945	**2160**	(1st) Unicorn	1·20	1·00
2946	**2161**	62p. Giant	1·00	1·00
2947	**2162**	62p. Pixie	1·00	1·00
2948	**2163**	90p. Mermaid	1·50	1·50
2949	**2164**	90p. Fairy	1·50	1·50
Set of 6			6·50	6·25
Set of 6 Gutter Pairs			13·00	
First Day Cover (Tallents House)				8·00
Presentation Pack (PO Pack No. 428)			7·00	
PHQ Cards (*set of* 6) (324)			1·75	8·00

2165 George V Type B Wall Letter Box, 1933–1936

2166 Edward VII Ludlow Letter Box, 1901–1910

2167 Victorian Lamp Letter Box, 1896

2168 Elizabeth II Type A Wall Letter Box, 1962–1963

2169 Post Boxes

2009 (18 Aug). Post Boxes. Multicoloured 'All-over' phosphor. Perf 14.

2950	**2165**	(1st) George V Type B Wall Letter Box	1·20	1·00
2951	**2166**	56p. Edward VII Ludlow Letter Box	1·10	1·10

2952	**2167**	81p. Victorian Lamp Letter Box	1·25	1·25
2953	**2168**	90p. Elizabeth II Type A Wall Letter Box	1·25	1·25
Set of 4			4·25	4·25

MS2954 145×74 mm **2169** Post Boxes Nos.
2950/2953   4·25   4·25
First Day Cover (Tallents House)   5·00
Presentation Pack (PO Pack No. 430)   4·75
PHQ Cards (set of 5) (326)   1·50   9·25

Nos. 2950/2953 were only issued in the £8·18 Treasures of the Archive booklet, No. DX46 and in No. **MS**2954.

T **2165** was also issued in sheets of 20 with *se-tenant* labels showing post boxes.

The five PHQ cards show the four individual stamps and the miniature sheet.

2009 (18 Aug). Treasures of the Archive (1st series). Booklet stamps. Designs as T **929** (1990 150th anniversary of the Penny Black) and T **1446** (with redrawn 1st face value). Printed in lithography. Two phosphor bands. Perf 14½×14 (with one elliptical hole in each vert side).

2955	**929**	20p. brownish-black and grey-brown	80	80
2956	**1446**	(1st) brownish-black and grey-brown	1·25	1·25

Nos. 2955/2956 were only issued in the £8·18 Treasures of the Archive booklet, No. DX46.

Also see Nos. 1478, 2133/2133a, **MS**1501 and **MS**3695.

2009 (18 Aug). Treasures of the Archive (2nd series). Booklet stamps. Design as T **919** (1989 Lord Mayor's Show). Multicoloured 'All-over' phosphor. Perf 14.

2957	**919**	20p. Royal Mail Coach. Multicoloured	1·50	1·50

No. 2957 was only issued in the £8·18 Treasures of the Archive booklet, No. DX46.

2170 Firefighting

2171 Chemical Fire

2172 Emergency Rescue

2173 Flood Rescue

2174 Search and Rescue

2175 Fire Safety

2009 (1 Sept). Fire and Rescue Service. Multicoloured 'All-over' phosphor. Perf 14×14½.

2958	**2170**	(1st) Firefighting	1·20	1·00
2959	**2171**	54p. Chemical Fire	90	90
2960	**2172**	56p. Emergency Rescue	1·10	1·10
2961	**2173**	62p. Flood Rescue	1·25	1·25
2962	**2174**	81p. Search and Rescue	1·25	1·40
2963	**2175**	90p. Fire Safety	1·40	1·40
Set of 6			6·25	6·25
Set of 6 Gutter Pairs			12·50	
First Day Cover (Tallents House)				7·50
Presentation Pack (PO Pack No. 429)			6·75	
PHQ Cards (set of 6) (325)			1·75	7·50

2176 Flight Deck Officer, 2009   2177 Captain, 1941   2178 Second Officer WRNS, 1918

2179 Able Seaman, 1880   2180 Royal Marine, 1805   2181 Admiral, 1795

2009 (17 Sept). Military Uniforms (3rd series). Royal Navy Uniforms. Multicoloured Phosphor background. Perf 14.

2964	**2176**	(1st) Flight Deck Officer	1·20	1·00
		a. Horiz strip of 3. Nos. 2964/2966	3·50	3·00
2965	**2177**	(1st) Captain	1·20	1·00
2966	**2178**	(1st) Second Officer WRNS	1·20	1·00
2967	**2179**	90p. Able Seaman	1·40	1·40
		a. Horiz strip of 3. Nos. 2967/2969	4·00	4·00
2968	**2180**	90p. Royal Marine	1·40	1·40
2969	**2181**	90p. Admiral	1·40	1·40
Set of 6			7·00	6·50
Set of 2 Gutter Strips of 6			14·00	
Set of 2 Traffic Light Gutter Blocks of 12			30·00	
First Day Cover (Tallents House)				7·75
Presentation Pack (PO Pack No. 431)			7·50	
PHQ Cards (set of 6) (327)			21·00	13·00

Nos. 2964/2966 and 2967/2969 were each printed together, *se-tenant*, as horizontal strips of three in sheets of 60 (2 panes 6×5).

Nos. 2964/2969 were also issued in the £7·93 Royal Navy Uniforms booklet, No. DX47.

2009 (17 Sept). Royal Navy Uniforms. Booklet stamp. Design as T **1518** (Jolly Roger flag from 2001 Submarine Centenary). Multicoloured Two phosphor bands. Perf 14½.

2970	**1518**	(1st) Jolly Roger flown by HMS *Proteus* (submarine)	4·75	6·00

No. 2970 was only issued in the £7·93 Royal Navy Uniforms booklet, No. DX47.

2182 Fred Perry 1909–1995 (lawn tennis champion)   2183 Henry Purcell 1659–1695 (composer and musician)

2184 Sir Matt Busby 1909–1994 (footballer and football manager)   2185 William Gladstone 1809–1898 (statesman and Prime Minister)

2186 Mary Wollstonecraft 1759–1797 (pioneering feminist)

2187 Sir Arthur Conan Doyle 1859–1930 (writer and creator of Sherlock Holmes)

2188 Donald Campbell 1921–1967 (water speed record broken 1959)

2189 Judy Fryd 1909–2000 (campaigner and founder of MENCAP)

2190 Samuel Johnson 1709–1784 (lexicographer, critic and poet)

2191 Sir Martin Ryle 1918–1984 (radio survey of the Universe 1959)

2009 (8 Oct). Eminent Britons. Multicoloured Phosphor background. Perf 14½.

2971	**2182**	(1st) Fred Perry	1·20	1·00
		a. Horiz strip of 5. Nos. 2971/2975	5·25	4·50
2972	**2183**	(1st) Henry Purcell	1·20	1·00
2973	**2184**	(1st) Sir Matt Busby	1·20	1·00
2974	**2185**	(1st) William Gladstone	1·20	1·00
2975	**2186**	(1st) Mary Wollstonecraft	1·20	1·00
2976	**2187**	(1st) Sir Arthur Conan Doyle	1·20	1·00
		a. Horiz strip of 5. Nos. 2976/2980	5·25	4·50
2977	**2188**	(1st) Donald Campbell	1·20	1·00
2978	**2189**	(1st) Judy Fryd	1·20	1·00
2979	**2190**	(1st) Samuel Johnson	1·20	1·00
2980	**2191**	(1st) Sir Martin Ryle	1·20	1·00
Set of 10			10·50	9·00
Set of 2 Gutter Strips of 10			21·00	
First Day Cover (Tallents House)				9·25
Presentation Pack (PO Pack No. 432)			11·00	
PHQ Cards (set of 10) (328)			3·00	9·75

Nos. 2971/2975 and 2976/2980 were each printed together, *se-tenant*, as horizontal strips of five stamps in sheets of 50 (2 panes 5×5).

No. 2980 includes the EUROPA emblem.

2192 Canoe Slalom

2193 Paralympic Games Archery

2194 Athletics, Track

2195 Diving

2196 Paralympic Games, Boccia

2197 Judo

2198 Paralympic Games, Dressage

2199 Badminton

2200 Weightlifting

2201 Basketball

2009 (22 Oct). Olympic and Paralympic Games, London (2012) (1st issue). Multicoloured 'All-over' phosphor. Perf 14½.

2981	**2192**	(1st) Canoe Slalom	1·20	1·00
		a. Horiz strip of 5. Nos. 2981/2985	5·25	4·50
2982	**2193**	(1st) Paralympic Games Archery	1·20	1·00
2983	**2194**	(1st) Athletics, Track	1·20	1·00
2984	**2195**	(1st) Diving	1·20	1·00
2985	**2196**	(1st) Paralympic Games Boccia	1·20	1·00
2986	**2197**	(1st) Judo	1·20	1·00
		a. Horiz strip of 5. Nos. 2986/2990	5·25	4·50
2987	**2198**	(1st) Paralympic Games Dressage	1·20	1·00
2988	**2199**	(1st) Badminton	1·20	1·00
2989	**2200**	(1st) Weightlifting	1·20	1·00
2990	**2201**	(1st) Basketball	1·20	1·00
Set of 10			10·50	9·00
Set of 2 Gutter Strips of 10			21·00	
First Day Cover (Tallents House)				9·25
Presentation Pack (PO Pack No. M18)			11·00	
PHQ Cards (set of 10) (OXPG1)			3·00	10·00

Nos. 2981/2985 and 2986/2990 were each printed together, *se-tenant*, as horizontal strips of five stamps throughout the sheets and were also issued on 27 July 2011, in a sheetlet containing all 30 stamps in the series. See No. **MS**3204*a*.

Booklet panes Nos. 2982*b*, 2983*b* and 2984*b* were from the £10.71 Olympic and Paralympic Games, London booklet, No. DY5.

See also Nos. 3020/3023.

2202 Angel playing Lute

2203 Madonna and Child

2204 Angel playing Lute

2205 Joseph

2206 Madonna and Child

2207 Wise Man

2208 Shepherd

2009 (3 Nov). Christmas. Stained-glass Windows. Multicoloured. One centre band (No. 2202) or two phosphor bands (others). Perf 14½×14 (with one elliptical hole in each vert side).

(a) Self-adhesive.

2991	**2202**	(2nd) Angel playing Lute	90	90
2992	**2203**	(1st) Madonna and Child	1·20	1·00
2993	**2204**	(2nd Large) Angel playing Lute	1·25	1·10
2994	**2205**	56p. Joseph	1·10	1·10
2995	**2206**	(1st Large) Madonna and Child	1·70	1·40
2996	**2207**	90p. Wise Man	1·75	1·75
2997	**2208**	£1·35 Shepherd	2·40	2·40
	Set of 7		9·25	8·75
	First Day Cover (Tallents House)			9·00
	Presentation Pack (PO Pack No. 433)		9·50	
	PHQ Cards (*set of 8*) (328)		2·40	17·50

(b) Ordinary gum.

MS2998	115×102 mm. As Nos. 2991/2997	9·25	8·75
	First Day Cover (Tallents House)		9·00

The 2nd class, 1st class, 56p. and 90p. stamps were also issued together in sheets of 20 containing 8×2nd class, 8×1st class, 2×56p. and 2×90p. stamps, each stamp accompanied by a *se-tenant* label.

Separate sheets of 20×2nd, 20×1st, 10×1st, 10×56p. and 10×90p. were available with personal photographs.

All these sheets were printed in lithography instead of gravure.

For the 2nd class stamp printed in lithography with ordinary gum see No. 3186a.

The eight PHQ cards show the seven stamps and No. **MS**2998.

For Nos. U3045/U3052 see Decimal Machin Definitives section.

Year Pack

2009 (3 Nov). Comprises Nos. 2887/2896, 2898/**MS**2904, 2916/**MS**2941, 2944/2949, **MS**2954, 2958/2969, 2971/2997, **MS**S157 and **MS**W147.

CP2998a	Year Pack (Pack No. 434) (*sold for £60*)	95·00

Post Office Yearbook

2009 (3 Nov). Comprises Nos. 2887/2896, 2898/**MS**2904, 2916/**MS**2941, 2944/2949, **MS**2954, 2958/2969, 2971/2997, **MS**S157 and **MS**W147.

YB2998a	Yearbook (*sold for £65*)	95·00

Miniature Sheet Collection

2009 (3 Nov). Comprises Nos. **MS**2904, **MS**2930, **MS**2941, **MS**2954, **MS**2998, **MS**S157 and **MS**W147.

MS2998a	Miniature Sheet Collection (*sold for £21·30*)	32·00

2209 *The Division Bell* (Pink Floyd)

2210 *A Rush of Blood to the Head* (Coldplay)

2211 *Parklife* (Blur)

2212 *Power Corruption and Lies* (New Order)

2213 *Let It Bleed* (Rolling Stones)

2214 *London Calling* (The Clash)

2215 *Tubular Bells* (Mike Oldfield)

2216 *Led Zeppelin IV* (Led Zeppelin)

2217 *Screamadelica* (Primal Scream)

2218 *The Rise and Fall of Ziggy Stardust and the Spiders from Mars* (David Bowie)

2010 (7 Jan). Classic Album Covers (1st issue). Multicoloured 'All-over' phosphor.

(a) Self-adhesive. Gravure De La Rue. Die-cut Perf 14½ (interrupted).

2999	**2209**	(1st) *The Division Bell* (Pink Floyd)	1·20	1·00
		a. Horiz strip of 5. Nos. 2999/3003	5·25	—
3000	**2210**	(1st) *A Rush of Blood to the Head* (Coldplay)	1·20	1·00
3001	**2211**	(1st) *Parklife* (Blur)	1·20	1·00
3002	**2212**	(1st) *Power Corruption and Lies* (New Order)	1·20	1·00
3003	**2213**	(1st) *Let It Bleed* (Rolling Stones)	1·20	1·00
3004	**2214**	(1st) *London Calling* (The Clash)	1·20	1·00
		a. Horiz strip of 5. Nos. 3004/3008	5·25	—
3005	**2215**	(1st) *Tubular Bells* (Mike Oldfield)	1·20	1·00
3006	**2216**	(1st) *IV* (Led Zeppelin)	1·20	1·00
3007	**2217**	(1st) *Screamadelica* (Primal Scream)	1·20	1·00
3008	**2218**	(1st) *The Rise and Fall of Ziggy Stardust and the Spiders from Mars* (David Bowie)	1·20	1·00
	Set of 10		10·50	9·00
	First Day Cover (Tallents House)			9·25
	Presentation Pack (PO Pack No. 435)		11·00	
	PHQ Cards (*set of 10*) (330)		4·00	12·00

Nos. 2999/3003 and 3004/3008 were each printed together, as horizontal strips of five stamps in sheets of 50 (2 panes of 25).

2218a Album Covers

2010 (7 Jan). Classic Album Covers (2nd issue). Multicoloured 'All-over' phosphor. Litho Cartor. Perf 14½ (interrupted).

3009	**2213**	(1st) *Let It Bleed* (Rolling Stones).	1·25	1·25
3010	**2216**	(1st) *Led Zeppelin IV* (Led Zeppelin)	1·25	1·25
3011	**2218**	(1st) *The Rise and Fall of Ziggy Stardust and the Spiders from Mars* (David Bowie)	1·25	1·25
3012	**2212**	(1st) *Power Corruption and Lies* (New Order)	1·25	1·25
3013	**2217**	(1st) *Screamadelica* (Primal Scream)	1·25	1·25
3014	**2209**	(1st) *The Division Bell* (Pink Floyd)	1·25	1·25
3015	**2215**	(1st) *Tubular Bells* (Mike Oldfield)	1·25	1·25
3016	**2214**	(1st) *London Calling* (The Clash)	1·25	1·25
3017	**2211**	(1st) *Parklife* (Blur)	1·25	1·25
3018	**2210**	(1st) *A Rush of Blood to the Head* (Coldplay)	1·25	1·25
Set of 10			13·00	13·00
MS3019 **2218a** 223×189 mm. Nos. 3009/3018			25·00	25·00
First Day Cover (Tallents House)				25·00

Nos. 3009/3018 were only issued in the £8·06 Classic Album Covers booklet, No. DX48 and in No. **MS**3019.

The right-hand edges of Nos. 3009/3018 and the miniature sheet No. **MS**3019 are all cut around in an imperforate section to show the vinyl disc protruding from the open edge of the album cover.

Stamps from the miniature sheet have a white background, while those from the booklet have a brown background containing descriptive texts.

A miniature sheet containing No. 3014×10 *The Division Bell* (Pink Floyd) was issued on 6 March 2010 and sold for £4·75 per sheet.

2010 (7 Jan–25 Feb). Olympic and Paralympic Games, London (2012) (2nd issue). Booklet stamps. Designs as Nos. 2982/2983, 2986 and 2990. Self-adhesive. Multicoloured 'All-over' phosphor. Die-cut Perf 14½.

3020	**2197**	(1st) Judo	2·00	2·00
3021	**2193**	(1st) Paralympic Games Archery	2·00	2·00
3022	**2194**	(1st) Athletics, Track (25.2.10)	2·00	2·00
3023	**2201**	(1st) Basketball (25.2.10)	2·00	2·00
Set of 4			5·50	5·50

Nos. 3020/3021 and 3022/3023 were only issued in separate booklets, each originally sold for £2·34.

2219 Smilers

2010 (26 Jan). Business and Consumer Smilers. Sheet 124×71 mm. Multicoloured Two phosphor bands. Perf 14½×14 (with one elliptical hole in each vertical side).

MS3024 **2219** Smilers (1st) Propellor driven aircraft (Andrew Davidson); (1st) Vintage sports roadster (Andrew Davidson); (1st) Recreation of crown seal (Neil Oliver); (1st) Birthday cake (Annabel Wright); (1st) Steam locomotive (Andrew Davidson); (1st) Ocean liner (Andrew Davidson); (1st) Six poppies on barbed wire stems; (1st) Birthday present (Annabel Wright); (Europe up to 20 grams) Bird carrying envelope (Lucy Davey); (Worldwide up to 20 grams) 'hello' in aeroplane vapour trail (Lucy Davey)

	12·50	10·00
First Day Cover (Tallents House)		10·50
PHQ Cards (*set of 11*) (D31)	4·25	20·00

No. **MS**3024 was sold for £4·58.

Stamps in designs as within No. **MS**3024 but self-adhesive were available printed together, *se-tenant*, in sheets of 20 containing two of each design with greetings labels.

The (1st) birthday present, Europe and Worldwide designs were also available in separate sheets with personal photographs.

A stamp as the crown seal design in No. **MS**3024 but self-adhesive was issued on 15 September 2011 in sheets of 20 with postmark labels for the 350th Anniversary of the Postmark.

The other 1st class designs were for the business customised service.

Stamps as the (1st) birthday cake (×4), (1st) birthday present (×4), Europe bird carrying envelope (×2) and Worldwide 'hello' in aeroplane vapour trail (×2) designs but self-adhesive were issued together with Nos. 2572, 2674, 2693 and 2821/2823 on 8 May 2010 in sheets of 20 stamps with *se-tenant* greetings labels printed in lithography.

For the self-adhesive (1st) six Poppies stamp, see No. 3414.

The 11 PHQ cards show the ten individual stamps and the complete miniature sheet.

2220 Girlguiding UK

2010 (2 Feb). Centenary of Girlguiding. Sheet 190×67 mm. Multicoloured Phosphor background. Perf 14×14½.

MS3025 **2220** Girlguiding UK (1st) Rainbows; 56p. Brownies; 81p. Guides; 90p. Senior Section members

	4·25	4·50
First Day Cover (Tallents House)		5·25
Presentation Pack (PO Pack No. 436)	5·50	
PHQ Cards (*set of 5*) (331)	2·00	9·00

The five PHQ cards show the four individual stamps and the complete miniature sheet.

2221 Sir Robert Boyle (chemistry)

2222 Sir Isaac Newton (optics)

2223 Benjamin Franklin (electricity)

2224 Edward Jenner (pioneer of smallpox vaccination)

2225 Charles Babbage (computing)

2226 Alfred Russel Wallace (theory of evolution)

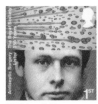

2227 Joseph Lister (antiseptic surgery)

2228 Ernest Rutherford (atomic structure)

2229 Dorothy Hodgkin (crystallography)

2230 Sir Nicholas Shackleton (earth sciences)

2010 (25 Feb). 350th Anniversary of the Royal Society. Multicoloured 'All-over' phosphor. Perf 14½.

3026	**2221**	(1st) Sir Robert Boyle	1·20	1·00
		a. Block of 10. Nos. 3026/3035	10·50	9·00
3027	**2222**	(1st) Sir Isaac Newton	1·20	1·00
3028	**2223**	(1st) Benjamin Franklin	1·20	1·00
3029	**2224**	(1st) Edward Jenner	1·20	1·00
3030	**2225**	(1st) Charles Babbage	1·20	1·00
3031	**2226**	(1st) Alfred Russell Wallace	1·20	1·00
3032	**2227**	(1st) Joseph Lister	1·20	1·00
3033	**2228**	(1st) Ernest Rutherford	1·20	1·00
3034	**2229**	(1st) Dorothy Hodgkin	1·20	1·00
3035	**2230**	(1st) Sir Nicholas Shackleton	1·20	1·00
Set of 10			10·50	9·00
Gutter Block of 20			21·00	
First Day Cover (Tallents House)				10·00
Presentation Pack (PO Pack No. 437)			11·00	
PHQ Cards (set of 10) (332)			4·00	11·50

Nos. 3026/3035 were printed together, *se-tenant*, as blocks of ten (5×2) in sheets of 60 (2 panes of 30).

Nos. 3026/3035 were issued in the £7·72 350th Anniversary of The Royal Society booklet, No. DX49.

2231 Pixie (mastiff cross)

2232 Button

2233 Herbie (mongrel)

2234 Mr Tumnus

2235 Tafka (border collie)

2236 Boris (bulldog cross)

2237 Casey (lurcher)

2238 Tigger

2239 Leonard (Jack Russell cross)

2240 Tia (terrier cross)

2010 (11 Mar). 150th Anniversary of Battersea Dogs and Cats Home. Multicoloured. Phosphor background. Perf 14½.

3036	**2231**	(1st) Pixie (mastiff cross)	1·20	1·00
		a. Block of 10. Nos. 3036/3045	10·50	9·00
3037	**2232**	(1st) Button	1·20	1·00
3038	**2233**	(1st) Herbie (mongrel)	1·20	1·00
3039	**2234**	(1st) Mr Tumnus	1·20	1·00
3040	**2235**	(1st) Tafka (border collie)	1·20	1·00
3041	**2236**	(1st) Boris (bulldog cross)	1·20	1·00
3042	**2237**	(1st) Casey (lurcher)	1·20	1·00
3043	**2238**	(1st) Tigger	1·20	1·00
3044	**2239**	(1st) Leonard (Jack Russell cross)	1·20	1·00
3045	**2240**	(1st) Tia (terrier cross)	1·20	1·00
Set of 10			10·50	9·00
Gutter Block of 20			21·00	
First Day Cover (Tallents House)				9·50
Presentation Pack (PO Pack No. 438)			11·00	
PHQ Cards (set of 10) (333)			4·00	11·50

Nos. 3036/3045 were printed together, *se-tenant*, as blocks of ten (5×2) in sheets of 60 (2 panes of 30).

2241 James I (1406–1437)

2242 James II (1437–1460)

2243 James III (1460–1488)

2244 James IV (1488–1513)

2245 James V (1513–1542)

2246 Mary (1542–1567)

2247 James VI
(1567–1625)

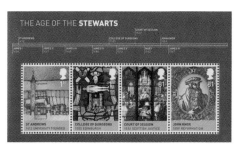

2248 The Age of the Stewarts

2010 (23 Mar). Kings and Queens (3rd issue). House of Stewart. Multicoloured Two phosphor bands. Perf 14.

3046	**2241**	(1st) James I	1·20	1·00
3047	**2242**	(1st) James II	1·20	1·00
3048	**2243**	(1st) James III	1·20	1·00
3049	**2244**	62p. James IV	1·00	1·00
3050	**2245**	62p. James V	1·00	1·00
3051	**2246**	81p. Mary	1·25	1·25
3052	**2247**	81p. James VI	1·25	1·25
Set of 7			7·25	6·75
Set of 7 Gutter Pairs			14·50	
Set of 7 Traffic Light Gutter Blocks of 4			32·00	
First Day Cover (Tallents House)				8·00
Presentation Pack (PO Pack No. 439) (Nos. 3046/				
MS3053)			12·00	
PHQ Cards (set of 12) (334)			4·75	11·50

MS3053 123×70 mm. **2248** The Age of the Stewarts (1st) Foundation of the University of St Andrews, 1413; (1st) Foundation of the College of Surgeons, Edinburgh, 1505; 81p. Foundation of Court of Session, 1532; 81p. John Knox (Reformation, 1559)   4·25   4·25

First Day Cover (Tallents House)   4·75

The complete miniature sheet is shown on one of the 12 PHQ cards with the others depicting individual stamps including those from No. **MS**3053.

2249 Humpback Whale (*Megaptera novaeangliae*)

2250 Wildcat (*Felis silvestris*)

2251 Brown Long-eared Bat (*Plecotus auritus*)

2252 Polecat (*Mustela putorius*)

2253 Sperm Whale (*Physeter macrocephalus*)

2254 Water Vole (*Arvicola terrestris*)

2255 Greater Horseshoe Bat (*Rhinolophus ferrumequinum*)

2256 Otter (*Lutra lutra*)

2257 Dormouse (*Muscardinus avellanarius*)

2258 Hedgehog (*Erinaceus europaeus*)

2010 (13 Apr). Action for Species (4th series). Mammals. Multicoloured 'All-over' phosphor. Perf 14½.

3054	**2249**	(1st) Humpback Whale	1·20	1·00
		a. Block of 10. Nos. 3054/3063	10·50	9·00
3055	**2250**	(1st) Wildcat	1·20	1·00
3056	**2251**	(1st) Brown Long-eared Bat	1·20	1·00
3057	**2252**	(1st) Polecat	1·20	1·00
3058	**2253**	(1st) Sperm Whale	1·20	1·00
3059	**2254**	(1st) Water Vole	1·20	1·00
3060	**2255**	(1st) Greater Horseshoe Bat	1·20	1·00
3061	**2256**	(1st) Otter	1·20	1·00
3062	**2257**	(1st) Dormouse	1·20	1·00
3063	**2258**	(1st) Hedgehog	1·20	1·00
Set of 10			10·50	9·00
Gutter Block of 20			21·00	
First Day Cover (Tallents House)				9·50
Presentation Pack (PO Pack No. 440)			11·00	
PHQ Cards (set of 10) (335)			4·00	11·00

Nos. 3054/3063 were printed together, *se-tenant*, as blocks of ten (5×2) in sheets of 60 (2 panes of 30).
See also Nos. 3095/3096.

No. 3064, T **2259** is vacant.

2260 King George V and Queen Elizabeth II (1st); Two portraits of King George V (£1)

2010 (6 May). London 2010 Festival of Stamps and Centenary of Accession of King George V (1st issue). 'All-over' phosphor. Perf 14½×14.
MS3065 141×74 mm **2260** (1st) rosine; £1 blackish brown, grey-brown and silver   3·75   4·00

First Day Cover (Tallents House)   12·00

A miniature sheet as No. **MS**3065 but inscr 'BUSINESS DESIGN CENTRE, LONDON 8–15 MAY 2010' along the top right margin was only available at London 2010 Festival of Stamps (*Price* £9·75).
For presentation pack and PHQ cards for No. **MS**3065 see below No. **MS**3072.

2261 King George V and
Queen Elizabeth II

2262 1924 British Empire
Exhibition 1½d. Brown Stamp

2263 1924 British Empire Exhibition
1d. Scarlet Stamp

2264 Two Portraits of
King George V

2265 1913 £1 Green Sea Horses Design Stamp

2266 1913 10s. Blue Sea Horses Design Stamp

LONDON 2010 FESTIVAL OF STAMPS

2267 London 2022 Festival of Stamps

2010 (6–8 May). London 2010 Festival of Stamps and Centenary of
Accession of King George V (2nd issue). (except Nos. 3066, 3069)
'All-over' phosphor. Perf 14½×14.

3066	**2261**	(1st) rosine (6.5.10)	1·25	1·25
3067	**2262**	(1st) 1924 British Empire Exhibition 1½d. Brown Stamp (8.5.10)	1·50	1·50
3068	**2263**	(1st) 1924 British Empire Exhibition 1d. Scarlet Stamp (8.5.10)	1·50	1·50
3069	**2264**	£1 blackish brown, grey-brown and silver (8.5.10)	2·50	2·50
3070	**2265**	£1 1913 £1 Green Sea Horses Design Stamp (8.5.10)	2·25	2·25
3071	**2266**	£1 1913 10s. Blue Sea Horses Design Stamp (8.5.10)	2·25	2·25
Set of 6			11·00	11·00
Gutter Pair (No. 3066)			2·50	

MS3072	**2267**	115×90 mm. Nos. 3067/3068 and 3070/3071 (8.5.10)	4·50	4·75
First Day Cover (Tallents House) (No. MS3072)				12·00
Presentation Pack (PO Pack No. 441) (Nos. MS3065 and MS3072)			8·50	
PHQ Cards (set of 8) (336)			3·25	13·00

No. 3066 was also issued as a sheet stamp on 6 May 2010.

Nos. 3066/3071 come from the £11·15 1910–1936, King George V
booklet, No. DX50.

Nos. 3066 and 3069 also come from No. MS3065, issued on 6 May 2010.

Nos. 3067/3068 and 3070/3071 also come from No. MS3072, issued
on 8 May 2010.

For presentation pack and PHQ cards for No. MS3072 see under MS3065.

The eight PHQ cards depict the individual stamps from Nos. MS3065
and MS3072 and the complete miniature sheets.

For No. MS3073, T **2268**, see Decimal Machin Definitives section.

2269 Winston Churchill

2270 Land Girl

2271 Home Guard

2272 Evacuees

2273 Air Raid Wardens

2274 Woman working in
Factory

2275 Royal Broadcast by
Princess Elizabeth and
Princess Margaret

2276 Fire Service

2010 (13 May). Britain Alone (1st issue). Pale stone, pale bistre and black.
'All-over' phosphor. Perf 14½.

3074	**2269**	(1st) Winston Churchill	1·20	1·00
3075	**2270**	(1st) Land Girl	1·20	1·00
3076	**2271**	60p. Home Guard	90	90
3077	**2272**	60p. Evacuees	90	90
3078	**2273**	67p. Air Raid Wardens	1·00	1·00
3079	**2274**	67p. Woman working in Factory	1·00	1·00
3080	**2275**	97p. Royal Broadcast by Princess Elizabeth and Princess Margaret	1·40	1·40
3081	**2276**	97p. Fire Service	1·40	1·40
Set of 8			7·75	7·50
Set of 8 Gutter Pairs			15·50	

First Day Cover (Tallents House) 8·50
Presentation Pack (PO Pack No. 442) (Nos. 3074/3081
and **MS**3086) 13·00
PHQ Cards (set of 13) (337) 5·25 11·00

Nos. 3074/3081 were also issued in the £9·76 Britain Alone booklet, No. DX51.

The 13 PHQ cards depict Nos. 3074/3085 and the complete miniature sheet No. **MS**3086.

2277 Evacuation of British Soldiers from Dunkirk

2278 Vessels from Upper Thames Patrol in Operation Little Ships

2279 Rescued Soldiers on Board Royal Navy Destroyer, Dover

2280 Steamship and Other Boat loaded with Troops

2281 Evacuation of British Troops from Dunkirk, 1940

2010 (13 May). Britain Alone (2nd issue). Pale stone, pale bistre and black. 'All-over' phosphor. Perf 14½.

3082	**2277**	(1st) Evacuation of British Soldiers	1·40	1·40
3083	**2278**	60p. Vessels from Upper Thames Patrol	1·40	1·40
3084	**2279**	88p. Rescued Soldiers	1·40	1·40
3085	**2280**	97p. Steamship and Other Boat loaded with Troops	1·40	1·40
Set of 4			5·00	5·00

MS3086 115×89 mm. **2281** Evacuation of British Troops from Dunkirk, 1940 Nos. 3082/3085 5·00 5·00
First Day Cover (Tallents House) (No. **MS**3086) 5·50

Nos. 3082/3085 were only issued in the £9·76 Britain Alone booklet, No. DX51, and in No. **MS**3086.

2282 James I (1603–1625)

2283 Charles I (1625–1649)

2284 Charles II (1660–1685)

2285 James II (1685–1688)

2286 William III (1689–1702)

2287 Mary II (1689–1694)

2288 Anne (1702–1714)

2289 The Age of the Stuarts

2010 (15 June). Kings and Queens (4th issue). House of Stuart. Multicoloured Two phosphor bands. Perf 14.

3087	**2282**	(1st) James I	1·20	1·00
3088	**2283**	(1st) Charles I	1·20	1·00
3089	**2284**	60p. Charles II	90	90
3090	**2285**	60p. James II	90	90
3091	**2286**	67p. William III	1·10	1·10
3092	**2287**	67p. Mary II	1·10	1·10
3093	**2288**	88p. Anne	1·40	1·40
Set of 7			6·75	6·50
Set of 7 Gutter Pairs			13·50	
Set of 7 Traffic Light Gutter Blocks of 4			30·00	
First Day Cover (Tallents House)				8·50
Presentation Pack (PO Pack No. 443) (Nos. 3087/3093 and **MS**3094)			12·00	
PHQ Cards (set of 12) (338)			4·75	16·00

MS3094 123×70 mm. **2289** The Age of the Stuarts (1st) William Harvey (discovery of blood circulation, 1628); 60p. Civil War Battle of Naseby, 1645; 88p. John Milton (*Paradise Lost*, 1667); 97p. Castle Howard (John Vanbrugh, 1712) 4·75 4·75
First Day Cover (Tallents House) 5·00

The complete miniature sheet is shown on one of the 12 PHQ cards with the others depicting individual stamps including those from No. **MS**3094.

2010 (15 June). Mammals. Booklet stamps. Designs as Nos. 3061 and 3063. Self-adhesive. Multicoloured Die-cut Perf 14½.

3095	**2256**	(1st) Otter	3·00	3·00
3096	**2258**	(1st) Hedgehog	3·00	3·00

Nos. 3095/3096 were only issued in booklets, originally sold for £2·46.

2290 Paralympic Games, Rowing

2291 Shooting

2292 Modern Pentathlon   **2293** Taekwondo

2294 Cycling   **2295** Paralympic Games, Table Tennis

2296 Hockey   **2297** Football

2298 Paralympic Games, Goalball   **2299** Boxing

2010 (27 July). Olympic and Paralympic Games, London (2012) (3rd issue). Multicoloured 'All-over' phosphor. Perf 14½.

3097	**2290**	(1st) Paralympic Games, Rowing	1·20	1·00
		a. Horiz strip of 5. Nos. 3097/3101	5·25	4·50
3098	**2291**	(1st) Shooting	1·20	1·00
3099	**2292**	(1st) Modern Pentathlon	1·20	1·00
3100	**2293**	(1st) Taekwondo	1·20	1·00
3101	**2294**	(1st) Cycling	1·20	1·00
3102	**2295**	(1st) Paralympic Games, Table Tennis	1·20	1·00
		a. Horiz strip of 5. Nos. 3102/3106	5·25	4·50
3103	**2296**	(1st) Hockey	1·20	1·00
3104	**2297**	(1st) Football	1·20	1·00
3105	**2298**	(1st) Paralympic Games, Goalball	1·20	1·00
3106	**2299**	(1st) Boxing	1·20	1·00
Set of 10			10·50	9·00
Set of 2 Gutter Strips of 10			21·00	
First Day Cover (Tallents House)				9·25
Presentation Pack (PO Pack No. 444)			11·00	
PHQ Cards (set of 10) (339)			4·00	11·00

Nos. 3097/3101 and 3102/3106 were each printed together, se-tenant, in horizontal strips of five stamps in sheets of 50 (2 panes 5×5).

Nos. 3097/3101 and 3102/3106 were also issued on 27 July 2011 in a miniature sheet containing all 30 stamps in the series.

See also No. **MS3204a.**

2010 (27 July–12 Oct). Olympic and Paralympic Games, London (2012) (4th issue). Booklet stamps. Designs as Nos. 3097, 3101/3102 and 3104. Self-adhesive. Multicoloured 'All-over' phosphor. Die-cut perf 14½.

3107	**2290**	(1st) Paralympic Games, Rowing	2·00	2·00
3108	**2295**	(1st) Paralympic Games, Table Tennis	2·00	2·00

3108a	**2297**	(1st) Football (12.10.10)	2·00	2·00
3108b	**2294**	(1st) Cycling (12.10.10)	2·00	2·00
Set of 4			7·50	7·50

Nos. 3107/3108 and 3108a/3108b were only issued in two separate stamp booklets each originally sold for £2·46.

2300 LMS Coronation Class Locomotive, Euston Station, 1938   **2301** BR Class 9F Locomotive *Evening Star*, Midsomer Norton, 1962

2302 GWR King Class Locomotive *King William IV*, near Teignmouth, 1935   **2303** LNER Class A1 Locomotive *Royal Lancer*, 1929

2304 SR King Arthur Class Locomotive *Sir Mador de la Porte*, Bournemouth Central Station, 1935–1939   **2305** LMS NCC Class WT No. 2, Larne Harbour, c 1947

2010 (19 Aug). Great British Railways. Gold, bluish grey and black. 'All-over' phosphor. Perf 14.

3109	**2300**	(1st) LMS Coronation Class Locomotive	1·20	1·00
3110	**2301**	(1st) BR Class 9F Locomotive *Evening Star*	1·20	1·00
3111	**2302**	67p. GWR King Class Locomotive *King William IV*	90	90
3112	**2303**	67p. LNER Class A1 Locomotive *Royal Lancer*	90	90
3113	**2304**	97p. SR King Arthur Class Locomotive *Sir Mador de la Porte*	1·25	1·25
3114	**2305**	97p. LMS NCC Class WT No. 2	1·25	1·25
Set of 6			6·00	5·75
Set of 6 Gutter Pairs			12·00	
First Day Cover (Tallents House)				7·00
Presentation Pack (PO Pack No. 445)			7·00	
PHQ Cards (set of 6) (340)			2·50	7·50

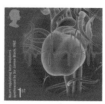 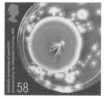

2306 Heart-regulating Beta Blockers (Sir James Black, 1962)   **2307** Antibiotic Properties of Penicillin (Sir Alexander Fleming, 1928)

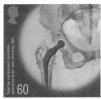

2308 Total Hip Replacement Operation (Sir John Charnley, 1962)

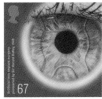

2309 Artificial Lens Implant Surgery (Sir Harold Ridley, 1949)

2310 Malaria Parasite transmitted by Mosquitoes (proved by Sir Ronald Ross, 1897)

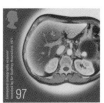

2311 Computed Tomography Scanner (Sir Godfrey Hounsfield, 1971)

2010 (16 Sept). Medical Breakthroughs. Multicoloured 'All-over' phosphor. Perf 14×14½.

3115	**2306**	(1st) Heart-regulating Beta Blockers	1·20	1·00
3116	**2307**	58p. Antibiotic Properties of Penicillin	90	90
3117	**2308**	60p. Total Hip Replacement Operation	1·00	1·00
3118	**2309**	67p. Artificial Lens Implant Surgery	1·10	1·10
3119	**2310**	88p. Malaria Parasite transmitted by Mosquitoes	1·25	1·25
3120	**2311**	97p. Computed Tomography Scanner	1·40	1·40
Set of 6			6·00	6·00
Set of 6 Gutter Pairs			12·00	
First Day Cover (Tallents House)				8·00
Presentation Pack (PO Pack No. 446)			7·25	
PHQ Cards (set of 6) (341)			2·50	7·50

See also No. 3153.

2312 Winnie-the-Pooh and Christopher Robin (*Now we are Six*)

2313 Winnie-the-Pooh and Piglet (*The House at Pooh Corner*)

2314 Winnie-the-Pooh and Rabbit (*Winnie-the-Pooh*)

2315 Winnie-the-Pooh and Eeyore (*Winnie-the-Pooh*)

2316 Winnie-the-Pooh and Friends (*Winnie-the-Pooh*)

2317 Winnie-the-Pooh and Tigger (The House at Pooh Corner)

2318 Winnie-the-Pooh

2010 (12 Oct). Europa. Children's Books. Winnie-the-Pooh by A. A. Milne. Book Illustrations by E. H. Shepard. Yellow-brown, pale stone and black. 'All-over' phosphor. Perf 14×14½.

3121	**2312**	(1st) Winnie-the-Pooh and Christopher Robin	1·20	1·00
3122	**2313**	58p. Winnie-the-Pooh and Piglet	90	90
3123	**2314**	60p. Winnie-the-Pooh and Rabbit	1·00	1·00
3124	**2315**	67p. Winnie-the-Pooh and Eeyore	1·10	1·10
3125	**2316**	88p. Winnie-the-Pooh and Friends	1·25	1·25
3126	**2317**	97p. Winnie-the-Pooh and Tigger	1·40	1·40
Set of 6			6·00	6·00
Set of 6 Gutter Pairs			12·00	
First Day Cover (Tallents House)				8·00
Presentation Pack (PO Pack No. 447) (Nos. 3121/3126 and **MS**3127)			11·50	
PHQ Cards (set of 11) (342)			4·25	15·00

MS3127 115×89 mm. **2318** Winnie-the-Pooh (1st) Winnie-the-Pooh and Christopher Robin (from *Now we are Six*); 60p. Christopher Robin reads to Winnie-the-Pooh (from *Winnie-the-Pooh*); 88p. Winnie-the-Pooh and Christopher Robin sailing in umbrella (from *Winnie-the-Pooh*); 97p. Christopher Robin (putting on wellingtons) and Pooh (from *Winnie-the-Pooh*). Perf 14½ .... 4·75 ... 4·75

First Day Cover (Tallents House) ... 6·25

The 1st class value includes the EUROPA emblem.

Stamps from No. **MS**3127 show lines from poem *We Too* by A. A. Milne. 'Wherever I am, there's always Pooh' (1st); 'There's always Pooh and Me. Whatever I do, he wants to do' (60p.); 'Where are you going to-day?' says Pooh: 'Well that's very odd 'cos I was too' (88p.); 'Let's go together,' says Pooh, says he. 'Let's go together,' says Pooh (97p.).

The 11 PHQ cards show the six stamps, the four individual stamps within No. **MS**3127 and the complete miniature sheet.

2319 Wallace and Gromit Carol singing

2320 Gromit posting Christmas Cards

2321 Wallace and Gromit Carol singing

2322 Wallace and Gromit decorating Christmas Tree

2323 Gromit posting Christmas Cards

2324 Gromit carrying Christmas Pudding

2325 Gromit wearing Oversized Sweater

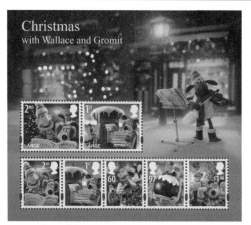

2325a Wallace and Gromit

2010 (2 Nov). Christmas with Wallace and Gromit. Multicoloured One centre band (No. 3128) or two bands (others). Perf 14½×14 (with one elliptical hole in each vert side).

(a) Self-adhesive.

3128	**2319**	(2nd) Wallace and Gromit Carol singing	90	90
3129	**2320**	(1st) Gromit posting Christmas Cards	1·20	1·00
3130	**2321**	(2nd Large) Wallace and Gromit Carol singing	1·25	1·00
3131	**2322**	60p. Wallace and Gromit decorating Christmas Tree	1·10	1·10
3132	**2323**	(1st Large) Gromit posting Christmas Cards	1·70	1·40
3133	**2324**	97p. Gromit carrying Christmas Pudding	1·40	1·40
3134	**2325**	£1·46 Gromit wearing Oversized Sweater	2·00	2·00
		Set of 7	8·25	8·00
		First Day Cover (Tallents House)		9·50
		Presentation Pack (PO Pack No. 448)	10·00	
		PHQ Cards (set of 8) (343)	3·25	16·50

(b) Ordinary gum.

MS3135 2325a	115×102 mm. Nos. 3128/3134	8·25	8·00
First Day Cover (Tallents House)			9·50

The 2nd class, 1st class, 60p. and 97p. stamps were also issued together in sheets of 20 containing 8×2nd class, 8×1st class, 2×60p. and 2×97p. stamps, each stamp accompanied by a se-tenant label.

Separate sheets of 20×2nd, 20×1st, ten 1st, 10×60p. and 10×97p. were available with personal photographs on the labels.

All these sheets were printed in lithography instead of gravure.

The eight PHQ cards show the seven individual stamps and the miniature sheet.

Year Pack

2010 (2 Nov). Comprises Nos. 2999/3008, MS3025/3063, MS3065, MS3072, 3074/3081, MS3086/MS3094, 3097/3106 and 3109/3134.

CP3135a	Year Pack (Pack No. 449) (sold for £80)	£125

Post Office Yearbook

2010 (2 Nov). Comprises Nos. 2999/3008, MS3025/3063, MS3065, MS3072, 3074/3081, MS3086/MS3094, 3097/3106 and 3109/3134.

YB3135a	Yearbook (sold for £85)	£110

Miniature Sheet Collection

2010 (2 Nov). Comprises Nos. MS3024, MS3025, MS3053, MS3065, MS3072, MS3086, MS3094, MS3127 and MS3135.

MS3135a	Miniature Sheet Collection (sold for £32)	50·00

2326 Joe 90

2327 Captain Scarlet

2328 Thunderbird 2 (Thunderbirds)

2329 Stingray

2330 Fireball XL5

2331 Supercar

2332 Thunderbird 4; Thunderbird 3; Thunderbird 2; Thunderbird 1

2011 (11 Jan). F.A.B. The Genius of Gerry Anderson (producer of TV programmes). Multicoloured 'All-over' phosphor.

(a) Ordinary gum. Litho Cartor. Perf 14.

3136	**2326**	(1st) Joe 90	1·20	1·00
		a. Horiz strip of 3. Nos. 3136/3138	3·50	3·00
3137	**2327**	(1st) Captain Scarlet	1·20	1·00
3138	**2328**	(1st) Thunderbird 2 (Thunderbirds)	1·20	1·00
3139	**2329**	97p. Stingray	1·50	1·50
		a. Horiz strip of 3. Nos. 3139/3141	4·50	4·50
3140	**2330**	97p. Fireball XL5	1·50	1·50
3141	**2331**	97p. Supercar	1·50	1·50
		Set of 6	7·25	6·75
		Set of 2 Gutter Strips of 6	14·50	
		First Day Cover (Tallents House)		7·75
		Presentation Pack (PO Pack No. 450) (Nos. 3136/3141 and MS3142)	12·50	
		PHQ Cards (set of 11) (344)	4·25	17·00

(b) Microlenticular Cartor and Outer Aspect Ltd, New Zealand. Perf 14.

MS3142	116×89 mm. **2332** 41p. Thunderbird 4; 60p. Thunderbird 3; 88p. Thunderbird 2; 97p. Thunderbird 1	5·25	5·50
First Day Cover (Tallents House)			6·00

(c) Self-adhesive. Gravure Walsall. Die-cut Perf 14.

3143	**2328**	(1st) Thunderbird 2 (Thunderbirds)	2·00	2·00

Nos. 3136/3138 and 3139/3141 were each printed together, se-tenant, as horizontal strips of three stamps in sheets of 60 (2 panes 6×5).

The stamps within No. MS3142 use microlenticular technology to show each vehicle's launch sequences when the miniature sheet is tilted. No. 3143 was only issued in booklets originally sold for £2·46.

The complete miniature sheet is shown on one of the 11 PHQ cards with the others depicting individual stamps including those from No. MS3142.

2333 Classic Locomotives of England

2011 (1 Feb). Classic Locomotives (1st series). England. Sheet 180×74 mm. Multicoloured 'All-over' phosphor. Perf 14.

MS3144 **2333** Classic Locomotives of England (1st) BR
Dean Goods No. 2532; 60p. Peckett R2 *Thor*; 88p.
Lancashire and Yorkshire Railway 1093 No. 1100;

97p. BR WD No. 90662		4·25	4·50
First Day Cover (Tallents House)			5·00
Presentation Pack (PO Pack No. 451)		5·25	
PHQ Cards (set of 5) (345)		2·00	9·00

The five PHQ cards show the four individual stamps and the complete miniature sheet.

See also No. 3215.

2334 *Oliver*   **2335** *Blood Brothers*   **2336** *We Will Rock You*

2337 *Spamalot*   **2338** *Rocky Horror Show*   **2339** *Me and My Girl*

2340 *Return to the Forbidden Planet*   **2341** *Billy Elliot*

2011 (24 Feb). Musicals. Multicoloured 'All-over' phosphor. Perf 14.

3145	**2334**	(1st) *Oliver*	1·20	1·00
3146	**2335**	(1st) *Blood Brothers*	1·20	1·00
3147	**2336**	(1st) *We Will Rock You*	1·20	1·00
3148	**2337**	(1st) *Spamalot*	1·20	1·00
3149	**2338**	97p. *Rocky Horror Show*	1·30	1·30
3150	**2339**	97p. *Me and My Girl*	1·30	1·30
3151	**2340**	97p. *Return to the Forbidden Planet*	1·30	1·30
3152	**2341**	97p. *Billy Elliot*	1·30	1·30
Set of 8			8·75	8·25
Set of 8 Gutter Pairs			17·50	
Set of 8 Traffic Light Gutter Pairs			25·00	
First Day Cover (Tallents House)				9·25
Presentation Pack (PO Pack No. 452)			9·75	
PHQ Cards (set of 8) (346)			3·25	11·00

2011 (24 Feb). 50th Anniversary of the British Heart Foundation. Booklet stamp. Design as No. 3115. Self-adhesive. Multicoloured 'All-over' phosphor. Die-cut Perf 14×14½.

3153	**2306**	(1st) Heart-regulating Beta Blockers	2·00	2·00

No. 3153 was only issued in booklets originally sold for £2·46.

2342 Rincewind (Terry Pratchett's *Discworld*)   **2343** Nanny Ogg (Terry Pratchett's *Discworld*)

2344 Michael Gambon as Dumbledore (J. K. Rowling's Harry Potter)   **2345** Ralph Fiennes as Lord Voldemort (J. K. Rowling's Harry Potter)

2346 Merlin (Arthurian Legend)   **2347** Morgan Le Fay (Arthurian Legend)

2348 Aslan (C. S. Lewis's *Narnia*)   **2349** Tilda Swinton as The White Witch (C. S. Lewis's *Narnia*)

2011 (8 Mar). Magical Realms. Multicoloured 'All-over' phosphor. Perf 14½.

3154	**2342**	(1st) Rincewind	1·20	1·00
		a. Vert pair. Nos. 3154/3155	2·40	2·00
3155	**2343**	(1st) Nanny Ogg	1·20	1·00
3156	**2344**	(1st) Michael Gambon as Dumbledore	1·20	1·00
		a. Vert pair. Nos. 3156/3157	2·40	2·00
3157	**2345**	(1st) Ralph Fiennes as Lord Voldemort	1·20	1·00
3158	**2346**	60p. Merlin	95	95
		a. Vert pair. Nos. 3158/3159	1·90	1·90
3159	**2347**	60p. Morgan Le Fay	95	95
3160	**2348**	97p. Aslan	1·25	1·25
		a. Vert pair. Nos. 3160/3161	2·50	2·50
3161	**2349**	97p. Tilda Swinton as The White Witch	1·25	1·25
Set of 8			8·00	7·50
Set of 4 Gutter Strips of 4			16·00	
First Day Cover (Tallents House)				7·75
Presentation Pack (PO Pack No. 453)			8·50	
Presentation Pack (Heroes and Villains containing Nos. 3156/3157, each×5) (2.12.11)			14·00	
PHQ Cards (set of 8) (347)			3·25	9·25

Nos. 3154/3155, 3156/3157, 3158/3159 and 3160/3161 were each printed together, *se-tenant*, as vertical pairs in sheets of 60 (2 panes 5×6).

For Nos. U3055/U3059 see Decimal Machin Definitives section

2350 African Elephant   **2351** Mountain Gorilla

2352 Siberian Tiger

2353 Polar Bear

2354 Amur Leopard

2355 Iberian Lynx

2356 Red Panda

2357 Black Rhinoceros

2358 African Wild Dog

2359 Golden Lion Tamarin

2360 Wildlife of the Amazon Rainforest

2011 (22 Mar). 50th Anniversary of the WWF. Multicoloured 'All-over' phosphor. Perf 14 (No. **MS**3172) or 14½ (others).

3162	**2350**	(1st) African Elephant	1·20	1·00
		a. Horiz strip of 5. Nos. 3162/3166	5·25	4·50
3163	**2351**	(1st) Mountain Gorilla	1·20	1·00
3164	**2352**	(1st) Siberian Tiger	1·20	1·00
3165	**2353**	(1st) Polar Bear	1·20	1·00
3166	**2354**	(1st) Amur Leopard	1·20	1·00
3167	**2355**	(1st) Iberian Lynx	1·20	1·00
		a. Horiz strip of 5. Nos. 3167/3171	5·25	4·50
3168	**2356**	(1st) Red Panda	1·20	1·00
3169	**2357**	(1st) Black Rhinoceros	1·20	1·00
3170	**2358**	(1st) African Wild Dog	1·20	1·00
3171	**2359**	(1st) Golden Lion Tamarin	1·20	1·00
Set of 10			10·50	9·00
Set of 2 Gutter Strips of 10			21·00	
First Day Cover (Tallents House)				9·50

Presentation Pack (PO Pack No. 454) (Nos. 3162/3171 and **MS**3172)	16·00	
PHQ Cards (set of 15) (348)	6·00	21·00

MS3172 115×89 mm. **2360** Wildlife of the Amazon Rainforest (1st) Spider monkey; 60p. Hyacinth macaw; 88p. Poison dart frog; 97p. Jaguar — 4·50 4·50

First Day Cover (Tallents House) — 5·25

Nos. 3162/3166 and 3167/3171 were each printed together, se-tenant, as horizontal strips of five stamps in sheets of 50 (2 panes 5×5).

Nos. 3162/3171 were issued in the £9·05 50th Anniversary of the WWF booklet, No. DX52.

The 1st class value from No. **MS**3172 includes the EUROPA emblem.

The complete miniature sheet is shown on one of the 15 PHQ cards with the others depicting individual stamps including those from No. **MS**3172.

2361 David Tennant as Hamlet, 2008

2362 Antony Sher as Prospero, The Tempest, 2009

2363 Chuk Iwuji as Henry VI, 2006

2364 Paul Schofield as King Lear, 1962

2365 Sara Kestelman as Titania, A Midsummer Night's Dream, 1970

2366 Ian McKellen and Francesca Annis as Romeo and Juliet, 1976

2367 The Four Theatres of the Royal Shakespeare Company, Stratford-upon-Avon

2011 (12 Apr). 50th Anniversary of the Royal Shakespeare Company. Black, brownish black and bright scarlet. 'All-over' phosphor. Perf 14½ (Nos. 3173/3178) or 14 (No. **MS**3179).

3173	**2361**	(1st) David Tennant as Hamlet	1·20	1·00
3174	**2362**	66p. Antony Sher as Prospero, The Tempest	1·00	1·00
3175	**2363**	68p. Chuk Iwuji as Henry VI	1·10	1·10
3176	**2364**	76p. Paul Schofield as King Lear	1·25	1·25
3177	**2365**	£1 Sara Kestelman as Titania, A Midsummer Night's Dream	1·50	1·50

3178 **2366** £1·10 Ian McKellen and Francesca Annis

as Romeo and Juliet	1·75	1·75
Set of 6	6·75	6·75
Set of 6 Gutter Pairs	13·50	
First Day Cover (Tallents House)		8·00
Presentation Pack (PO Pack No. 455) (Nos. 3173/3178 and **MS**3179)	13·00	
PHQ Cards (set of 11) (349)	4·50	18·00

MS3179 115×89 mm. 2367 The Four Theatres of the Royal Shakespeare Company, Stratford-upon-Avon (1st) Janet Suzman as Ophelia, *Hamlet*, 1965, Royal Shakespeare Theatre; 68p. Patrick Stewart in *Antony and Cleopatra*, 2006, Swan Theatre; 76p. Geoffrey Streatfield in *Henry V*, 2007, The Courtyard Theatre; £1 Judy Dench as Lady Macbeth, 1976, The Other Place 4·25 4·25

First Day Cover (Tallents House) 5·00

The 11 PHQ cards show the six stamps, the four individual stamps within No. **MS**3179 and the complete miniature sheet.

2368 Prince William and Miss Catherine Middleton

2011 (21 Apr). Royal Wedding. Official Engagement Portraits by Mario Testino. Sheet 115×89 mm. Multicoloured 'All-over' phosphor. Perf 14½×14.

MS3180 **2368** Prince William and Miss Catherine Middleton (1st)×2 Prince William and Miss Catherine Middleton embracing; £1·10×2 Formal portrait of Prince William and Miss Catherine Middleton in Council Chamber, St James's Palace 5·50 5·50

First Day Cover (Tallents House)		7·00
Presentation Pack (PO Pack No. M20)	13·00	
Commemorative Document	15·00	

2369 Cray (fabric print by William Morris), 1884

2370 Cherries (detail from panel by Philip Webb), 1867

2371 Seaweed (wallpaper pattern by John Henry Dearle), 1901

2372 Peony (ceramic tile design by Kate Faulkner), 1877

2373 Acanthus (tile by William Morris and William de Morgan), 1876

2374 The Merchant's Daughter (detail of stained-glass window by Edward Burne-Jones), 1864

2011 (5 May). 150th Anniversary of Morris and Company (designers and manufacturers of textiles, wallpaper and furniture) (1st issue). Multicoloured 'All-over' phosphor. Perf 14×14½.

3181	**2369**	(1st) Cray	1·20	1·00
3182	**2370**	(1st) Cherries	1·20	1·00
3183	**2371**	76p. Seaweed	1·25	1·25
3184	**2372**	76p. Peony	1·25	1·25
3185	**2373**	£1·10 Acanthus	1·75	1·75
3186	**2374**	£1·10 The Merchant's Daughter	1·75	1·75
Set of 6			7·25	7·00
Set of 6 Gutter Pairs			14·50	
First Day Cover (Tallents House)				8·00
Presentation Pack (PO Pack No. 456)			7·75	
PHQ Cards (set of 6) (350)			2·50	8·25

Booklet panes Nos. 3181a and 3182a come from the £9·99 150th Anniversary of Morris and Company booklet, No. DY1.

2011 (5 May). 150th Anniversary of Morris and Company (2nd issue). Design as T **2202** (2009 Christmas. Stained-glass Windows). Multicoloured One centre band. Perf 14½×14 (with one elliptical hole in each vert side).

3186a **2202** (2nd) Angel playing Lute (William Morris), Church of St James, Staveley, Kendal, Cumbria 1·50 1·50

No. 3186a was only issued in the £9·99 150th Anniversary of Morris and Company booklet, No. DY1.

2375 Thomas the Tank Engine

2376 James the Red Engine

2377 Percy the Small Engine

2378 Daisy (diesel railcar)

2379 Toby the Tram Engine

2380 Gordon the Big Engine

2381 Book Illustrations by John T. Kenny (76p.) or C. Reginald Dalby (others)

2382 "Goodbye, Bertie", called Thomas (from *Tank Engine Thomas Again*)

2011 (14 June). Thomas the Tank Engine. Multicoloured 'All-over' phosphor.

(a) Ordinary gum. Perf 14 (No. **MS**3193) or 14½×14 (others).

3187	**2375**	(1st) Thomas the Tank Engine	1·20	1·00
3188	**2376**	66p. James the Red Engine	1·00	1·00
3189	**2377**	68p. Percy the Small Engine	1·10	1·10
3190	**2378**	76p. Daisy (diesel railcar)	1·25	1·25
3191	**2379**	£1 Toby the Tram Engine	1·50	1·50
3192	**2380**	£1·10 Gordon the Big Engine	1·75	1·75
Set of 6			6·75	6·75
Set of 6 Gutter Pairs			13·50	
First Day Cover (Tallents House)				8·00
Presentation Pack (PO Pack No. 457) (Nos. 3187/3192 and **MS**3193)			13·00	
PHQ Cards (set of 11) (351)			4·50	18·00

MS3193 115×89 mm. **2381** (1st) "Goodbye, Bertie", called Thomas (from *Tank Engine Thomas Again*); 68p. James was more dirty than hurt (from *Toby the Tram Engine*); 76p. "Yes, Sir", Percy shivered miserably (from *The Eight Famous Engines*); £1. They told Henry, "We shall leave you there for always" (from *The Three Railway Engines*) ... 4·25 ... 4·25

First Day Cover (Tallents House) ... 5·00

(b) Self-adhesive. Die-cut perf 14 (Gravure Walsall).

3194	**2382**	(1st) "Goodbye, Bertie", called Thomas (from *Tank Engine Thomas Again*)	2·00	2·00

Nos. 3187/3192 show scenes from TV series *Thomas and Friends*, and Nos. **MS**3193/3194 book illustrations from The Railway Series.

No. 3194 was only issued in stamp booklets originally sold for £2·76.

The 11 PHQ cards show the six stamps, the four individual stamps within No. **MS**3193 and the complete miniature sheet.

2383 Paralympic Games, Sailing

2384 Athletics, Field

2385 Volleyball

2386 Wheelchair Rugby

2387 Wrestling

2388 Wheelchair Tennis

2389 Fencing

2390 Gymnastics

2391 Triathlon

2392 Handball

2011 (27 July). Olympic and Paralympic Games, London (2012) (5th issue). Multicoloured 'All-over' phosphor. Perf 14½.

3195	**2383**	(1st) Paralympic Games, Sailing	1·20	1·00
		a. Horiz strip of 5. Nos. 3195/3199	5·25	4·50
3196	**2384**	(1st) Athletics, Field	1·20	1·00
3197	**2385**	(1st) Volleyball	1·20	1·00
3198	**2386**	(1st) Wheelchair Rugby	1·20	1·00
3199	**2387**	(1st) Wrestling	1·20	1·00
3200	**2388**	(1st) Wheelchair Tennis	1·20	1·00
		a. Horiz strip of 5. Nos. 3200/3204	5·25	4·50
3201	**2389**	(1st) Fencing	1·20	1·00
3202	**2390**	(1st) Gymnastics	1·20	1·00
3203	**2391**	(1st) Triathlon	1·20	1·00
3204	**2392**	(1st) Handball	1·20	1·00
Set of 10			10·50	9·00
Set of 2 Gutter Strips of 10			21·00	
First Day Cover (Tallents House)				9·50
Presentation Pack (PO Pack No. 458)			11·00	
PHQ Cards (set of 10) (352)			4·00	12·00

MS3204a 210×300 mm. Nos. 2981/2990, 3097/3106 and 3195/3204 ... 35·00 ... 35·00

Nos. 3195/3199 and 3200/3204 were each printed together, *se-tenant*, in horizontal strips of five stamps in sheets of 50 (2 panes 5×5) and in No. **MS**3204a.

2011 (27 July–15 Sept). Olympic and Paralympic Games (2012) (6th issue). Booklet stamps. Designs as Nos. 3195, 3198 and 3201/32022 . Self-adhesive. Multicoloured 'All-over' phosphor. Die-cut Perf 14½×14.

3205	**2386**	(1st) Wheelchair Rugby	2·00	2·00
3206	**2383**	(1st) Paralympic Games, Sailing	2·00	2·00
3206a	**2390**	(1st) Gymnastics (15.9.11)	2·00	2·00
3206b	**2389**	(1st) Fencing (15.9.11)	2·00	2·00
Set of 4			7·50	7·50

Nos. 3205/3206 and 3206a/3206b were only issued in two separate stamp booklets each originally sold for £2·76.

2393 The Sovereign's Sceptre with Cross

2394 St Edward's Crown

2395 Rod and Sceptre with Doves

2396 Queen Mary's Crown

2397 The Sovereign's Orb

2398 Jewelled Sword of Offering

2399 Imperial State Crown

2400 Coronation Spoon

2011 (23 Aug). Crown Jewels. Multicoloured Phosphor background. Perf 14×14½.

3207	**2393**	(1st) The Sovereign's Sceptre with Cross	1·20	1·00
3208	**2394**	(1st) St Edward's Crown	1·20	1·00
3209	**2395**	68p. Rod and Sceptre with Doves	1·10	1·10
3210	**2396**	68p. Queen Mary's Crown	1·10	1·10
3211	**2397**	76p. The Sovereign's Orb	1·25	1·25
3212	**2398**	76p. Jewelled Sword of Offering	1·25	1·25
3213	**2399**	£1·10 Imperial State Crown	1·60	1·60
3214	**2400**	£1·10 Coronation Spoon	1·60	1·60
Set of 8			9·00	8·75
Set of 8 Gutter Pairs			18·00	
First Day Cover (Tallents House)				10·00
Presentation Pack (PO Pack No. 459)			10·00	
PHQ Cards (set of 8) (353)			3·25	11·00

2401 BR Dean Goods No. 2532

2011 (23 Aug). Classic Locomotives. Black and gold. Booklet stamp. Design as 1st class stamp within No. **MS**3144. Self-adhesive. Die-cut Perf 14.

3215	**2401**	(1st) BR Dean Goods No. 2532	2·00	2·00

No. 3215 was only issued in booklets originally sold for £2·76.
See also No. 3570.

2402 Pilot Gustav Hamel receiving Mailbag

2403 Gustav Hamel in Cockpit

2404 Pilot Clement Greswell and Blériot Monoplane

2405 Delivery of First Airmail to Postmaster General at Windsor

2406 First United Kingdom Aerial Post, 9 September 1911

2011 (9 Sept). Centenary of First United Kingdom Aerial Post (1st issue). Multicoloured 'All-over' phosphor. Perf 14.

3216	**2402**	(1st) Pilot Gustav Hamel receiving Mailbag	1·75	1·75
3217	**2403**	68p. Pilot Gustav Hamel receiving Mailbag	1·75	1·75
3218	**2404**	£1 Pilot Clement Greswell and Blériot Monoplane	5·00	5·00
3219	**2405**	£1·10 Delivery of First Airmail to Postmaster General at Windsor	5·00	5·00
Set of 4			13·50	13·50
MS3220 146×74 mm. **2406** First United Kingdom Aerial Post, 9 September 1911 Nos. 3216/3219			8·50	8·50
First Day Cover (Tallents House)				9·50
Presentation Pack (PO Pack No. 460)			9·50	
PHQ Cards (set of 5) (354)			2·00	21·00

Nos. 3216/3219 were only issued in £9·99 First United Kingdom Aerial Post stamp booklet, No. DY2, and in No. **MS**3220.
The five PHQ cards show the four individual stamps and the complete miniature sheet.

2407 Windsor Castle

2011 (9 Sept). Centenary of First United Kingdom Aerial Post (2nd issue). Black and cream. Perf 11×11½.

3221	**2407**	50p. Windsor Castle	2·00	2·00

No. 3221 was only issued in £9·97 First United Kingdom Aerial Post stamp booklet, No. DY2.

For No. **MS**3222, T **2408**, see Decimal Machin Definitives section

2409 George I (1714–1727)   **2410** George II (1727–1760)   **2411** George III (1760–1820)

2412 George IV (1820–1830)   **2413** William IV (1830–1837)   **2414** Victoria (1837–1901)

2415 The Age of the Hanoverians

2011 (15 Sept). Kings and Queens (5th issue). House of Hanover. Multicoloured Two phosphor bands. Perf 14.

3223	**2409**	(1st) George I	1·20	1·00
3224	**2410**	(1st) George II	1·20	1·00
3225	**2411**	76p. George III	1·25	1·25
3226	**2412**	76p. George IV	1·25	1·25
3227	**2413**	£1·10 William IV	1·75	1·75
3228	**2414**	£1·10 Victoria	1·75	1·75
Set of 6			7·25	7·00
Set of 6 Gutter Pairs			14·50	
Set of 6 Traffic Light Gutter Blocks of 4			50·00	
First Day Cover (Tallents House)			8·00	
Presentation Pack (PO Pack No. 461) (Nos. 3223/3228 and **MS**3229)			13·00	
PHQ Cards (set of 11) (355)			4·50	18·00

MS3229 123×70 mm. **2415** The Age of the Hanoverians (1st) Robert Walpole (first Prime Minister), 1721; 68p. Ceiling by Robert Adam, Kedleston Hall, 1763; 76p. Penny Black (uniform postage), 1840; £1 Queen Victoria (Diamond Jubilee), 1897 .... 4·25   4·25

First Day Cover (Tallents House) .... 5·00

The complete miniature sheet is shown on one of the 11 PHQ cards with the others depicting individual stamps including those from No. **MS**3229.

2416 *Angel of the North*   **2417** Blackpool Tower

2418 Carrick-a-Rede, Co. Antrim   **2419** Downing Street

2420 Edinburgh Castle   **2421** Forth Railway Bridge

2422 Glastonbury Tor   **2423** Harlech Castle

2424 Ironbridge   **2425** Jodrell Bank

2426 Kursaal, Southend, Essex   **2427** Lindisfarne Priory

2011 (13 Oct). UK A–Z (1st series). Multicoloured 'All-over' phosphor. Perf 14½.

3230	**2416**	(1st) *Angel of the North*	1·20	1·00
		a. Horiz strip of 6. Nos. 3230/3235	5·25	4·50
3231	**2417**	(1st) Blackpool Tower	1·20	1·00
3232	**2418**	(1st) Carrick-a-Rede, Co. Antrim	1·20	1·00
3233	**2419**	(1st) Downing Street	1·20	1·00
3234	**2420**	(1st) Edinburgh Castle	1·20	1·00
3235	**2421**	(1st) Forth Railway Bridge	1·20	1·00
3236	**2422**	(1st) Glastonbury Tor	1·20	1·00
		a. Horiz strip of 6. Nos. 3236/3241	5·25	4·50

3237	**2423**	(1st) Harlech Castle	1·20	1·00
3238	**2424**	(1st) Ironbridge	1·20	1·00
3239	**2425**	(1st) Jodrell Bank	1·20	1·00
3240	**2426**	(1st) Kursaal, Southend, Essex	1·20	1·00
3241	**2427**	(1st) Lindisfarne Priory	1·20	1·00
Set of 12			10·50	9·00
Set of 2 Gutter Strips of 12			21·00	
Set of 2 Traffic Light Gutter Strips of 24			48·00	
First Day Covers (Tallents House) (2)				11·00
Presentation Pack (PO Pack No. 462)			12·00	
PHQ Cards (set of 12) (356)			4·75	13·00

Nos. 3230/3235 and 3236/3241 were each printed together, *se-tenant*, as horizontal strips of six stamps in sheets of 60 (2 panes of 30) and were also issued on 10 April 2012 in a sheet containing all 26 UK A–Z stamps. See No. **MS**3308.

2428 Joseph visited by the Angel (Matthew 1:21)

2429 Madonna and Child (Matthew 1:23)

2430 Joseph visited by the Angel (Matthew 1:21)

2431 Madonna and Child (Matthew 1:23)

2432 Baby Jesus in the Manger (Luke 2:7)

2433 Shepherds visited by the Angel (Luke 2:10)

2434 Wise Men and Star (Matthew 2:10)

2434a *The King James Bible*

2011 (8 Nov). Christmas. 400th Anniversary of the *King James Bible*. Multicoloured One centre band (No. 3242) or two phosphor bands (others). Perf 14½×14 (with one elliptical hole in each vert side).
(a) Self-adhesive.

3242	**2428**	(2nd) Joseph visited by the Angel	90	90
3243	**2429**	(1st) Madonna and Child	1·20	1·00
3244	**2430**	(2nd Large) Joseph visited by the Angel	1·25	1·10

3245	**2431**	(1st Large) Madonna and Child	1·70	1·40
3246	**2432**	68p. Baby Jesus in the Manger	1·25	1·25
3247	**2433**	£1·10 Shepherds visited by the Angel	1·90	1·90
3248	**2434**	£1·65 Wise Men and Star	2·50	2·50
Set of 7			9·25	9·00
First Day Cover (Tallents House)				11·00
Presentation Pack (PO Pack No. 463)			10·00	
PHQ Cards (set of 8) (357)			3·25	19·50

(b) Ordinary gum.

MS3249 **2434a** 116×102 mm. As Nos. 3242/3248	9·25	9·00
First Day Cover (Tallents House)		10·00

The 2nd class, 1st class, 68p., and £1·10 stamps were also issued in sheets of 20 containing 8×2nd class, 8×1st class, 2×68p. and 2×£1·10 stamps, each stamp accompanied by a *se-tenant* label with a verse from the *King James Bible*.

Separate sheets of 20×2nd, 10×1st, 10×68p. and 10×£1·10 were available with personal photographs.

The eight PHQ cards show the seven individual stamps and the miniature sheet.

Year Pack

2011 (8 Nov). Comprises Nos. 3136/3142, **MS**3144/3152, 3154/3193, 3195/3204, 3207/3214, **MS**3220 and 3223/3248.

CP3244a	Year Pack (Pack No. 464) (*sold for £94*)	£130

Post Office Yearbook

2011 (8 Nov). Comprises Nos. 3136/3142, **MS**3144/3152, 3154/3193, 3195/3204, 3207/3214, **MS**3220 and 3223/3248.

YB3244a	Yearbook (*sold for £99*)	£130

Miniature Sheet Collection

2011 (8 Nov). Comprises Nos. **MS**3142, **MS**3144, **MS**3172, **MS**3179/ **MS**3180, **MS**3193, **MS**3220, **MS**3229 and **MS**3249.

MS3244a Miniature Sheet Collection	45·00	

2435 Paralympic Games Emblem

2436 Olympic Games Emblem

2012 (5 Jan). Olympic and Paralympic Games (7th issue). Self-adhesive. Two phosphor bands. Die-cut Perf 14½×14 (with one elliptical hole on each vert side).

3250	**2435**	(1st) Paralympic Games Emblem. Black and orange-red	1·25	1·25
3251	**2436**	(1st) Olympic Games Emblem. Black and orange-red	1·25	1·25
3252	**2435**	(Worldwide up to 20 g) Paralympic Games Emblem. Black, bright scarlet and greenish blue	2·25	2·25
3253	**2436**	(Worldwide up to 20 g) Olympic Games Emblem. Black, bright scarlet and greenish blue	2·25	2·25
Set of 4			7·00	7·00
First Day Cover (Tallents House)				8·00
Presentation Pack (PO Pack No. D92)			9·00	
PHQ Cards (set of 4) (D32)			1·50	8·00

Nos. 3250/3251 were printed together in sheets of 50 (2 panes 5×5), with the two designs alternating horizontally and vertically. The upper pane had No. 3250 at top left and contained 13 of No. 3250 and 12 of No. 3251. The lower pane had No. 3251 at top left and contained 13 of No. 3251 and 12 of No. 3250.

Nos. 3250/3251 were also issued in stamp booklets of six originally sold for £2·76.

the panes from this booklet exists in two versions which differ in the order of the stamps within the block of six.

Nos. 3252/3253 were printed together in sheets of 25 (5×5) with the two designs alternating horizontally and vertically. There were two versions of the sheets of 25, one having No. 3252 at top left and containing 13 of No. 3252 and 12 of No. 3253, and the other having No. 3253 at top left and containing 13 of No. 3253 and 12 of No. 3252.

Nos. 3250/3253 were also issued on 27 June 2012 in sheets of 20 containing Nos. 3250/3251, each×8, and Nos. 3252/3253, each×2, all with *se-tenant* labels showing Games venues. These sheets were printed in lithography instead of gravure.

See also Nos. 3337/3340.

2437 *Charlie and the Chocolate Factory*

2438 *Fantastic Mr Fox*

2439 *James and the Giant Peach*

2440 *Matilda*

2441 *The Twits*

2442 *The Witches*

2012 (10 Jan). Roald Dahl's Children's Stories (1st issue). Book Illustrations by Quentin Blake. Multicoloured 'All-over' phosphor. Perf 14.

3254	**2437**	(1st) *Charlie and the Chocolate Factory*	1·20	1·00
3255	**2438**	66p. *Fantastic Mr Fox*	1·00	1·00
3256	**2439**	68p. *James and the Giant Peach*	1·10	1·10
3257	**2440**	76p. *Matilda*	1·25	1·25
3258	**2441**	£1 *The Twits*	1·50	1·50
3259	**2442**	£1·10 *The Witches*	1·75	1·75
Set of 6			6·75	6·75
Set of 6 Gutter Pairs			13·50	
Set of 6 Traffic Light Gutter Blocks of 4			30·00	
First Day Cover (Tallents House)				9·00
Presentation Pack (PO Pack No. 465) (Nos. 3254/3259 and **MS**3264)			16·00	
PHQ Cards (set of 11) (358)			4·25	25·00

Booklet panes Nos. 3254a and 3255a come from the £11·47 Roald Dahl, Master Storyteller premium booklets, No. DY3.

2443 The BFG Carrying Sophie in his Hand

2444 The BFG Wakes up the Giants

2445 Sophie Sitting on Buckingham Palace Window Sill

2446 The BFG and Sophie at Writing Desk

2447 Roald Dahl's The BFG

2012 (10 Jan). Roald Dahl's Children's Stories (2nd issue). Book Illustrations by Quentin Blake. Multicoloured 'All-over' phosphor. Perf 14×14½.

3260	**2443**	(1st) The BFG carrying Sophie in his Hand	2·40	2·40
3261	**2444**	68p. The BFG wakes up the Giants	2·40	2·40
3262	**2445**	76p. Sophie sitting on Buckingham Palace Window sill	2·40	2·40
3263	**2446**	£1 The BFG and Sophie at Writing Desk	2·40	2·40
Set of 4			9·00	9·00
MS3264 115×89 mm. **2447** Roald Dahl's The BFG Nos. 3260/3263			9·00	9·00
First Day Cover (Tallents House)				9·50

Nos. 3260/3263 were only issued in £11·47 Roald Dahl, Master Storyteller premium booklet, No. DY3, and in No. **MS**3264.

No. **MS**3264 commemorates the 30th anniversary of the publication of *The BFG*.

The complete miniature sheet is shown on one of the 11 PHQ cards with the others showing individual stamps including those from No. **MS**3264.

2448 Edward VII (1901–1910)

2449 George V (1910–1936)

2450 Edward VIII (1936)

2451 George VI (1936–1952)

2452 Elizabeth II (1952–)

2453 The Age of the Windsors

2012 (2 Feb). Kings and Queens (6th issue). House of Windsor. Multicoloured Two phosphor bands. Perf 14.

3265	**2448**	(1st) Edward VII	1·20	1·00
3266	**2449**	68p. George V	1·00	1·00
3267	**2450**	76p. Edward VIII	1·40	1·40
3268	**2451**	£1 George VI	1·90	1·90
3269	**2452**	£1·10 Elizabeth II	2·25	2·25
Set of 5			6·75	6·75
Set of 5 Gutter Pairs			13·50	
Set of 5 Traffic Light Gutter Blocks of 4			25·00	
First Day Cover (Tallents House)				7·50
Presentation Pack (PO Pack No. 466) (Nos. 3265/3269 and **MS**3270)			11·50	
PHQ Cards (set of 10) (359)			4·00	16·50

MS3270 123×70 mm. **2453** The Age of the Windsors (1st) Scott Expedition to South Pole, 1912; 68p. Queen Elizabeth the Queen Mother and King George VI in bomb damaged street, *circa* 1940; 76p. England's winning World Cup football team, 1966; £1 Channel Tunnel, 1996 — 4·25 / 4·25

First Day Cover (Tallents House) — 5·50

The complete miniature sheet is shown on one of the ten PHQ cards with the others depicting individual stamps including those from No. **MS**3270.

No. 3271 is vacant.

For Nos. U3271/U3278 see Decimal Machin Definitives section

2454 Diamond Jubilee

2012 (6 Feb). Diamond Jubilee. (2nd issue). Multicoloured Two phosphor bands. Perf 14½×14 (with one elliptical hole in each vertical side).

MS3272 146×74 mm. **2454** Diamond Jubilee (1st)×6 Portrait from photograph by Dorothy Wilding; 1960 £1 Banknote portrait by Robert Austin; 1971 £5 Banknote portrait by Harry Eccleston; 1953 Coinage portrait by Mary Gillick; 1971 decimal coin portrait by Arnold Machin; As No. U3279 — 7·25 / 7·25

First Day Cover (Tallents House) — 7·75

Presentation Pack (PO Pack No. 93) — 7·25

PHQ Cards (set of 7) (D33) — 2·75 / 14·50

Commemorative Document — 12·00

The 1st class slate-blue Machin stamp from No. **MS**3272 has an iridescent overprint reading 'DIAMOND JUBILEE' and the source code 'MMND'.

The seven PHQ cards show the six individual stamps and the complete miniature sheet.

2455 Coventry Cathedral, 1962 (Sir Basil Spence, architect)

2456 Frederick Delius (1862–1934, composer)

2457 Orange Tree, Embroidery (Mary 'May' Morris 1862–1938, designer and textile artist)

2458 Odette Hallowes (1912–1995, SOE agent in occupied France)

2459 Steam Engine, 1712 (Thomas Newcomen, inventor of atmospheric steam engine)

2460 Kathleen Ferrier (1912–1953, contralto)

2461 Interior of Palace of Westminster (Augustus Pugin 1812–1852, Gothic revival architect and designer)

2462 Montagu Rhodes James (1862–1936 scholar and author)

2463 Bombe Code Breaking Machine (Alan Turing 1912–1954, mathematician and World War II code breaker)

2464 Joan Mary Fry (1862–1955 relief worker and social reformer)

2012 (23 Feb). Britons of Distinction. Multicoloured 'All-over' phosphor. Perf 14½.

3273	**2455**	(1st) Coventry Cathedral	1·20	1·00
		a. Horiz strip of 5. Nos. 3273/3277	5·25	4·50
3274	**2456**	(1st) Frederick Delius	1·20	1·00
3275	**2457**	(1st) Orange Tree, Embroidery	1·20	1·00
3276	**2458**	(1st) Odette Hallowes	1·20	1·00
3277	**2459**	(1st) Steam Engine, 1712	1·20	1·00
3278	**2460**	(1st) Kathleen Ferrier	1·20	1·00
		a. Horiz strip of 5. Nos. 3278/3282	5·25	4·50
3279	**2461**	(1st) Interior of Palace of Westminster	1·20	1·00
3280	**2462**	(1st) Montagu Rhodes James	1·20	1·00
3281	**2463**	(1st) Bombe Code Breaking Machine	1·20	1·00
3282	**2464**	(1st) Joan Mary Fry	1·20	1·00
Set of 10			10·50	9·00
Set of 2 Gutter Strips of 10			21·00	
First Day Cover (Tallents House)				9·25
Presentation Pack (PO Pack No. 467)			11·00	
PHQ Cards (set of 10) (360)			4·00	11·50

Nos. 3273/3277 and 3278/3282 were each printed together, *se-tenant*, as horizontal strips of five stamps in sheets of 50 (2 panes 5×5).

2465 Classic Locomotives of Scotland

2012 (8 Mar). Classic Locomotives (2nd series). Scotland. Sheet 180×74 mm. Multicoloured 'All-over' phosphor. Perf 14.

MS3283 **2465** Classic Locomotives of Scotland (1st) BR Class D34 Nos. 62471 *Glen Falloch* and 62496 *Glen Loy* at Ardlui, 9 May 1959; 68p. BR Class D40 No. 62276 *Andrew Bain* at Macduff, July 1950; £1 Andrew Barclay No. 807 *Bon Accord* propelling wagons along Miller Street, Aberdeen, June 1962; £1·10 BR Class 4P No. 54767 *Clan Mackinnon* pulling fish train, Kyle of Lochalsh, October 1948

	4·75	4·75
		6·00
First Day Cover (Tallents House)		
Presentation Pack (PO Pack No. 468)	5·50	
PHQ Cards (set of 5) (361)	2·00	9·00

The five PHQ cards show the four individual stamps and the complete miniature sheet.

2012 (20 Mar). Comics. Multicoloured 'All-over' phosphor. Perf 14½.

3284	2466	(1st) *The Dandy* and Desperate Dan	1·20	1·00
		a. Horiz strip of 5. Nos. 3284/3288	5·25	4·50
3285	2467	(1st) *The Beano* and Dennis the Menace	1·20	1·00
3286	2468	(1st) *Eagle* and Dan Dare	1·20	1·00
3287	2469	(1st) *The Topper* and Beryl the Peril	1·20	1·00
3288	2470	(1st) *Tiger* and Roy of the Rovers	1·20	1·00
3289	2471	(1st) *Bunty* and the Four Marys	1·20	1·00
		a. Horiz strip of 5. Nos. 3289/3293	5·25	4·50
3290	2472	(1st) *Buster* and Cartoon Character Buster	1·20	1·00
3291	2473	(1st) *Valiant* and the Steel Claw	1·20	1·00
3292	2474	(1st) *Twinkle* and Nurse Nancy	1·20	1·00
3293	2475	(1st) *2000 AD* and Judge Dredd	1·20	1·00
Set of 10			10·50	9·00
Set of 2 *Gutter Strips* of 5			21·00	
First Day Cover (Tallents House)				15·00
Presentation Pack (PO Pack No. 469)			11·00	
PHQ Cards (set of 10)			4·00	11·50

2466 *The Dandy* and Desperate Dan

2467 *The Beano* and Dennis the Menace

2468 *Eagle* and Dan Dare

2469 *The Topper* and Beryl the Peril

2470 *Tiger* and Roy of the Rovers

2471 *Bunty* and the Four Marys

2472 *Buster* and Cartoon Character Buster

2473 *Valiant* and the Steel Claw

2474 *Twinkle* and Nurse Nancy

2475 *2000 AD* and Judge Dredd

2476 Manchester Town Hall

2477 Narrow Water Castle, Co. Down

2478 Old Bailey, London

2479 Portmeirion, Wales

2480 The Queen's College, Oxford

2481 Roman Baths, Bath

2482 Stirling Castle, Scotland

2483 Tyne Bridge, Newcastle

2484 Urquhart Castle, Scotland

2485 Victoria and Albert Museum, London

2486 White Cliffs of Dover

2487 Station X, Bletchley Park, Buckinghamshire

2488 York Minster

2489 London Zoo

2489a Composite sheet

2012 (10 Apr). UK A–Z (2nd series). Multicoloured 'All-over' phosphor. Perf 14½.

3294	**2476**	(1st) Manchester Town Hall	1·20	1·00
		a. Horiz strip of 6. Nos. 3294/3299	6·50	5·50
3295	**2477**	(1st) Narrow Water Castle, Co. Down	1·20	1·00
3296	**2478**	(1st) Old Bailey, London	1·20	1·00
3297	**2479**	(1st) Portmeirion, Wales	1·20	1·00
3298	**2480**	(1st) The Queen's College, Oxford	1·20	1·00
3299	**2481**	(1st) Roman Baths, Bath	1·20	1·00
3300	**2482**	(1st) Stirling Castle, Scotland	1·20	1·00
		a. Horiz strip of 6. Nos. 3300/3305	6·50	5·50
3301	**2483**	(1st) Tyne Bridge, Newcastle	1·20	1·00
3302	**2484**	(1st) Urquhart Castle, Scotland	1·20	1·00
3303	**2485**	(1st) Victoria and Albert Museum, London	1·20	1·00
3304	**2486**	(1st) White Cliffs of Dover	1·20	1·00
3305	**2487**	(1st) Station X, Bletchley Park, Buckinghamshire	1·20	1·00
3306	**2488**	(1st) York Minster	1·20	1·00
		a. Horiz pair. Nos. 3306/3307	2·25	2·00
3307	**2489**	(1st) London Zoo	1·20	1·00
Set of 14			15·00	12·50

Set of 2 Gutter Strips of 12 and 1 Gutter Strip of 4	30·00	
Set of 2 Traffic Light Gutter Strips of 24 and 1 Gutter Block of 8	50·00	
First Day Covers (Tallents House) (2)		15·00
Presentation Pack (PO Pack No. 470)	16·00	
PHQ Cards (set of 14) (363)	5·50	15·00
MS3308 297×210 mm. Nos. 3230/3241 and 3294/3307	£100	£110

Nos. 3294/3299 and 3300/3305 were each printed together, *se-tenant*, as horizontal strips of six stamps in sheets of 60 (2 panes 6×5).

Nos. 3306/3307 were printed together, *se-tenant*, as horizontal pairs in sheets of 60 (2 panes 6×5).

No. 3303 includes the EUROPA emblem.

2490 Skirt Suit by Hardy Amies, late 1940s

2491 Outfit by Norman Hartnell, 1950s

2492 Jacket designed by John Pearce for Granny Takes a Trip Boutique, 1960s

2493 Print by Celia Birtwell for Outfit by Ossie Clark, late 1960s

2494 Suit designed for Ringo Starr by Tommy Nutter

2495 Outfit by Jean Muir, late 1970s/early 1980s

2496 'Royal' Dress by Zandra Rhodes, 1981

2497 Harlequin dress by Vivienne Westwood, 1993

2498 Suit by Paul Smith, 2003

2499 'Black Raven' by Alexander McQueen, 2009

2012 (15 May). Great British Fashion. Multicoloured Phosphor background. Perf 14½×14.

3309	**2490**	(1st) Skirt Suit by Hardy Amies	1·20	1·00
		a. Horiz strip of 5. Nos. 3309/3313	5·25	4·50
3310	**2491**	(1st) Outfit by Norman Hartnell	1·20	1·00
3311	**2492**	(1st) Jacket designed by John Pearce	1·20	1·00
3312	**2493**	(1st) Print by Celia Birtwell for Outfit by Ossie Clark	1·20	1·00
3313	**2494**	(1st) Suit designed	1·20	1·00
3314	**2495**	(1st) Outfit by Jean Muir	1·20	1·00
		a. Horiz strip of 5. Nos. 3314/3318	5·25	4·50
3315	**2496**	(1st) 'Royal' Dress by Zandra Rhodes	1·20	1·00
3316	**2497**	(1st) Harlequin dress by Vivienne Westwood	1·20	1·00
3317	**2498**	(1st) Suit by Paul Smith	1·20	1·00
3318	**2499**	(1st) 'Black Raven' by Alexander McQueen	1·20	1·00
Set of 10			10·50	9·00
Set of 2 Gutter Strips of 10			21·00	
Set of 2 Traffic Light Gutter Strips of 20			40·00	
First Day Cover (Tallents House)				11·00
Presentation Pack (PO Pack No. 471)			11·00	
PHQ Cards (set of 10) (364)			4·00	12·00

Nos. 3309/3313 and 3314/3318 were each printed together, *se-tenant*, as horizontal strips of five stamps in sheets of 50 (2 panes 5×5).

2500 Queen Elizabeth II at Golden Jubilee Thanksgiving Service, St Paul's Cathedral, London, 2002

2501 Queen Elizabeth II Trooping the Colour, 1967

2502 Queen Elizabeth II inspecting 2nd Battalion Royal Welsh, Tidworth, 1 March 2007

2503 First Christmas Television Broadcast, 1957

2504 Silver Jubilee Walkabout, 1977

2505 Queen Elizabeth II in Garter Ceremony Procession, 1997

2506 Queen Elizabeth II addressing the UN General Assembly, 1957

2507 Queen Elizabeth II at Commonwealth Games, Brisbane, Australia, 1982

2012 (31 May)–**22**. Diamond Jubilee. Multicoloured. 'All-over' phosphor.

(a) Sheet stamps. Gravure. Ordinary gum. Perf 14×14½.

3319A	**2500**	(1st) Queen Elizabeth II at Golden Jubilee Service, St Paul's Cathedral, London, 2002	1·20	1·00
		a. Horiz pair. Nos. 3319A/3320A	2·40	2·00
3320A	**2501**	(1st) Queen Elizabeth II Trooping the Colour, 1967	1·20	1·00
3321A	**2502**	77p. Queen Elizabeth II inspecting 2nd Battalion Royal Welsh, Tidworth, 1 March 2007	1·00	1·00
		a. Horiz pair. Nos. 3321A/3322A	2·00	2·00
3322A	**2503**	77p. First Christmas Television Broadcast, 1957	1·00	1·00
3323A	**2504**	87p. Silver Jubilee Walkabout, 1977	1·25	1·25
		a. Horiz pair. Nos. 3323A/3324A	2·50	2·50
3324A	**2505**	87p. Queen Elizabeth II in Garter Ceremony Procession, 1997	1·25	1·25
3325A	**2506**	£1·28 Queen Elizabeth II addressing the UN General Assembly, 1957	1·75	1·75
		a. Horiz pair. Nos. 3325A/3326A	2·50	3·50
3326A	**2507**	£1·28 Queen Elizabeth II at Commonwealth Games, Brisbane, Australia, 1982	1·75	1·75
Set of 8			9·25	9·00
Set of 4 Gutter Strips of 4			18·50	
First Day Cover (Tallents House)				11·00
Presentation Pack (PO Pack No. 72)			19·00	
PHQ Cards (Set of 8) (365)			3·25	12·00

(b) Booklet stamps. Litho. Ordinary gum. Perf 14×14½.

3319B	**2500**	(1st) Queen Elizabeth II at Golden Jubilee Service, St Paul's Cathedral, London, 2002	1·40	1·40
3320B	**2501**	(1st) Queen Elizabeth II Trooping the Colour, 1967	1·40	1·40
3321B	**2502**	77p. Queen Elizabeth II inspecting 2nd Battalion Royal Welsh, Tidworth, 1 March 2007	1·40	1·40
3322B	**2503**	77p. First Christmas Television Broadcast, 1957	1·40	1·40
3323B	**2504**	87p. Silver Jubilee Walkabout, 1977	1·40	1·40
3324B	**2505**	87p. Queen Elizabeth II in Garter Ceremony Procession, 1997	1·40	1·40
3325B	**2506**	£1·28 Queen Elizabeth II addressing the UN General Assembly, 1957	1·75	1·75
3326B	**2507**	£1·28 Queen Elizabeth II at Commonwealth Games, Brisbane, Australia, 1982	1·75	1·75
Set of 8			11·00	11·00

(c) Self-adhesive booklet stamp. Die-cut perf 14.

3327	**2500**	(1st) Queen Elizabeth II at Golden Jubilee Service, St Paul's Cathedral, London, 2002	2·00	2·00

Nos. 3319A/3320A, 3321A/3322A, 3323A/3324A and 3325A/3326A were printed together, *se-tenant*, as horizontal pairs in sheets of 60 (2 panes 6×5).

Booklet pane Nos. 3319Bb and 3326Bb come from the £12·77 Diamond Jubilee booklet, No. DY4.

Booklet pane No. 3319Bc comes from the £19·50 Platinum Jubilee booklet, No. DY42.

No. 3327 was only issued in stamp booklet, No. PM33, originally sold for £3·60.

No. 3328 is vacant.

2507a Queen Elizabeth II

2012 (31 May). Diamond Jubilee (4th issue). As T **2507a**. Two phosphor bands. Perf 14½×14 (with one elliptical hole in each vert side).

3329	**2507a**	(1st) light brown	1·25	1·25

No 3329 comes from the £12·27 Diamond Jubilee booklet, No. DY4. A similar stamp was issued in No. **MS**3272.

The stamp and pane, formerly listed as Nos. 3328/3328a have been renumbered as U3279/U3279I and will be found in the Machins section of this catalogue.

2508 Mr Bumble (*Oliver Twist*)

2509 Mr Pickwick (*The Pickwick Papers*)

2510 The Marchioness (*The Old Curiosity Shop*)

2511 Mrs Gamp (*Martin Chuzzlewit*)

2512 Captain Cuttle (*Dombey and Son*)

2513 Mr Micawber (*David Copperfield*)

2514 Scenes from *Nicholas Nickleby, Bleak House, Little Dorrit* and *A Tale of Two Cities*

2012 (19 June). Birth Bicentenary of Charles Dickens. Illustrations from Character Sketches from Charles Dickens, *circa* 1890 by Joseph Clayton Clarke ('Kyd') (Nos. 3330/3335) or Book Illustrations by Hablot Knight Browne ('Phiz') (No. **MS**3336). Multicoloured One centre band (2nd) or 'all-over' phosphor (others). Perf 14 (Nos. 3330/3335) or 14×14½ (No. **MS**3336).

3330	**2508**	(2nd) Mr Bumble (*Oliver Twist*)	90	90
3331	**2509**	(1st) Mr Pickwick (*The Pickwick Papers*)	1·20	1·00
3332	**2510**	77p. The Marchioness (*The Old Curiosity Shop*)	1·00	1·00
3333	**2511**	87p. Mrs Gamp (*Martin Chuzzlewit*)	1·40	1·40
3334	**2512**	£1·28 Captain Cuttle (*Dombey and Son*)	2·00	2·00
3335	**2513**	£1·90 Mr Micawber (*David Copperfield*)	3·00	3·00
Set of 6			8·50	8·50
Set of 6 Gutter Pairs			17·00	
Set of 6 Traffic Light Gutter Blocks of 4			38·00	
First Day Cover (Tallents House)				11·00
Presentation Pack (PO Pack No. 473) (Nos. 3330/3335 and **MS**3336)			14·00	
PHQ Cards (set of 11) (366)			4·50	17·00

MS3336 190×67 mm. **2514** Scenes from *Nicholas Nickleby, Bleak House, Little Dorrit* and *A Tale of Two Cities* (1st)×4 Nicholas Nickleby caning headmaster Wackford Squeers (*Nicholas Nickleby*); Mrs Bagnet is charmed with Mr Bucket (*Bleak House*); Amy Dorrit introduces Maggy to Arthur Clennam (*Little Dorrit*); Charles Darnay arrested by French revolutionaries (*A Tale of Two Cities*) — 3·75 / 3·75

First Day Cover (Tallents House) — 4·50

The complete miniature sheet is shown on one of the 11 PHQ cards with the others depicting individual stamps including those from No. **MS**3336.

2435 Paralympic Games Emblem

2436 Olympic Games Emblem

2012 (27 July). Olympic and Paralympic Games (8th issue). Designs as Nos. 3250/3253. Multicoloured Two phosphor bands. Perf 14½×14 (with one elliptical hole in each vert side).

3337	**2436**	(1st) Olympic Games Emblem. Black and orange-red	4·00	4·00
3338	**2435**	(1st) Paralympic Games Emblem. Black and orange-red	4·00	4·00
3339	**2436**	(Worldwide up to 20 g) Olympic Games Emblem. Black, bright scarlet and greenish blue	6·00	6·00
3340	**2435**	(Worldwide up to 20 g) Paralympic Games Emblem. Black, bright scarlet and greenish blue	6·00	6·00
Set of 4			18·00	18·00
First Day Cover (Tallents House) (No. 3337)				20·00

Nos. 3339/3340 were for use on Worldwide Mail up to 20 grams.
Nos. 3337/3340 were only issued in the £10·71 Olympic and Paralympic Games, London booklet, No. DY5.

2515 Sports and London Landmarks

2012 (27 July). Welcome to London, Olympic Games. Sheet 192×75 mm. Multicoloured 'All-over' phosphor. Perf 14½.

MS3341 **2515** Sports and London Landmarks (1st) Fencer and Tower Bridge; (1st) Athletes in race and Olympic Stadium; £1·28 Diver and Tate Modern; £1·28 Cyclist and London Eye		5·50	5·50
First Day Cover (Tallents House)			10·00
Presentation Pack (PO Pack No. 474)		20·00	
PHQ Cards (set of 5) (367)		2·00	9·00

The five PHQ Cards show the four individual stamps and the complete miniature sheet.

2516 Helen Glover and Heather Stanning (rowing, women's pairs)

2517 Bradley Wiggins (cycling, road, men's time trial)

2518 Tim Baillie and Etienne Stott (canoe slalom, men's canoe double (C2))

2519 Peter Wilson (shooting, shotgun men's double trap)

2520 Philip Hindes, Chris Hoy and Jason Kenny (cycling, track men's team sprint)

2521 Katherine Grainger and Anna Watkins (rowing, women's double sculls)

2522 Steven Burke, Ed Clancy, Peter Kennaugh and Geraint Thomas (cycling, track men's team pursuit)

2523 Victoria Pendleton (cycling, track women's keirin)

2524 Alex Gregory, Tom James, Pete Reed and Andrew Triggs Hodge (rowing, men's fours)

2525 Katherine Copeland and Sophie Hosking (rowing, lightweight women's double sculls)

2526 Dani King, Joanna Rowsell and Laura Trott (cycling, track women's team pursuit)

2527 Jessica Ennis (athletics, combined women's heptathlon)

2528 Greg Rutherford (athletics, field men's long jump)

2529 Mo Farah (athletics, track men's 10,000 m)

2530 Ben Ainslie (sailing, Finn men's heavyweight dinghy)

2531 Andy Murray (tennis, men's singles)

2532 Scott Brash, Peter Charles, Ben Maher and Nick Skelton (equestrian, jumping team)

2533 Jason Kenny (cycling, track men's sprint)

2534 Alistair Brownlee (men's triathlon)

2535 Carl Hester, Laura Bechtolsheimer and Charlotte Dujardin (equestrian, dressage team)

2536 Laura Trott (cycling, track women's omnium)

2537 Chris Hoy (cycling, track men's keirin)

2538 Charlotte Dujardin (equestrian, dressage individual)

2539 Nicola Adams (boxing, women's fly weight)

2540 Jade Jones (taekwondo, women's under 57 kg)

2541 Ed McKeever (canoe sprint, men's kayak single (K1) 200 m)

2542 Mo Farah (athletics, track men's 5000 m)

2543 Luke Campbell (boxing, men's bantam weight)

2544 Anthony Joshua (boxing, men's super heavy weight)

2012 (2 Aug–1 Sept). British Gold Medal Winners at London Olympic Games. Self-adhesive. Multicoloured Two phosphor panels. Die-cut perf 15×14½.

3342	**2516**	(1st) Helen Glover and Heather Stanning	1·25	1·25
		a. Sheetlet. No. 3342×6	6·75	6·75
3343	**2517**	(1st) Bradley Wiggins (1.9.12)	1·25	1·25
		a. Sheetlet. No. 3343×6	6·75	6·75
3344	**2518**	(1st) Tim Baillie and Etienne Stott (3.8.12)	1·25	1·25
		a. Sheetlet. No. 3344×6	6·75	6·75
3345	**2519**	(1st) Peter Wilson (3.8.12)	1·25	1·25
		a. Sheetlet. No. 3345×6	6·75	6·75
3346	**2520**	(1st) Philip Hindes, Chris Hoy and Jason Kenny (3.8.12)	1·25	1·25
		a. Sheetlet. No. 3346×6	6·75	6·75
3347	**2521**	(1st) Katherine Grainger and Anna Watkins (4.8.12)	1·25	1·25
		a. Sheetlet. No. 3347×6	6·75	6·75
3348	**2522**	(1st) Steven Burke, Ed Clancy, Peter Kennaugh and Geraint Thomas (4.8.12)	1·25	1·25
		a. Sheetlet. No. 3348×6	6·75	6·75
3349	**2523**	(1st) Victoria Pendleton (4.8.12)	1·25	1·25
		a. Sheetlet. No. 3349×6	6·75	6·75
3350	**2524**	(1st) Alex Gregory, Tom James, Pete Reed and Andrew Triggs Hodge (5.8.12)	1·25	1·25
		a. Sheetlet. No. 3350×6	6·75	6·75

3351	**2525**	(1st) Katherine Copeland and Sophie Hosking (5.8.12)	1·25	1·25
		a. Sheetlet. No. 3351×6	6·75	6·75
3352	**2526**	(1st) Dani King, Joanna Rowsell and Laura Trott (5.8.12)	1·25	1·25
		a. Sheetlet. No. 3352×6	6·75	6·75
3353	**2527**	(1st) Jessica Ennis (5.8.12)	1·25	1·25
		a. Sheetlet. No. 3353×6	6·75	6·75
3354	**2528**	(1st) Greg Rutherford (5.8.12)	1·25	1·25
		a. Sheetlet. No. 3354×6	6·75	6·75
3355	**2529**	(1st) Mo Farah (5.8.12)	1·25	1·25
		a. Sheetlet. No. 3355×6	6·75	6·75
3356	**2530**	(1st) Ben Ainslie (6.8.12)	1·25	1·25
		a. Sheetlet. No. 3356×6	6·75	6·75
3357	**2531**	(1st) Andy Murray (6.8.12)	1·25	1·25
		a. Sheetlet. No. 3357×6	6·75	6·75
3358	**2532**	(1st) Scott Brash, Peter Charles, Ben Maher and Nick Skelton (7.8.12)	1·25	1·25
		a. Sheetlet. No. 3358×6	6·75	6·75
3359	**2533**	(1st) Jason Kenny (7.8.12)	1·25	1·25
		a. Sheetlet. No. 3359×6	6·75	6·75
3360	**2534**	(1st) Alistair Brownlee (8.8.12)	1·25	1·25
		a. Sheetlet. No. 3360×6	6·75	6·75
3361	**2535**	(1st) Carl Hester, Laura Bechtolsheimer and Charlotte Dujardin (8.8.12)	1·25	1·25
		a. Sheetlet. No. 3361×6	6·75	6·75
3362	**2536**	(1st) Laura Trott (8.8.12)	1·25	1·25
		a. Sheetlet. No. 3362×6	6·75	6·75
3363	**2537**	(1st) Chris Hoy (8.8.12)	1·25	1·25
		a. Sheetlet. No. 3363×6	6·75	6·75
3364	**2538**	(1st) Charlotte Dujardin (10.8.12)	1·25	1·25
		a. Sheetlet. No. 3364×6	6·75	6·75
3365	**2539**	(1st) Nicola Adams (10.8.12)	1·25	1·25
		a. Sheetlet. No. 3365×6	6·75	6·75
3366	**2540**	(1st) Jade Jones (10.8.12)	1·25	1·25
		a. Sheetlet. No. 3366×6	6·75	6·75
3367	**2541**	(1st) Ed McKeever (12.8.12)	1·25	1·25
		a. Sheetlet. No. 3367×6	6·75	6·75
3368	**2542**	(1st) Mo Farah (12.8.12)	1·25	1·25
		a. Sheetlet. No. 3368×6	6·75	6·75
3369	**2543**	(1st) Luke Campbell (12.8.12)	1·25	1·25
		a. Sheetlet. No. 3369×6	6·75	6·75
3370	**2544**	(1st) Anthony Joshua (13.8.12)	1·25	1·25
		a. Sheetlet. No. 3370×6	6·75	6·75
		Set of 29 Single Stamps	35·00	35·00
		First Day Covers (Tallents House) (Sheetlets, Nos. 3342a/3370a) (29)		£250
		First Day Cover (Tallents House) (any single gold medal stamp)		4·25

The self-adhesive base sheetlets for Nos. 3342/3370 were produced by Walsall with the image, name and event of the winning athletes digitally printed by regional printers in six different locations: Attleborough, Edinburgh, London, Preston, Solihull and Swindon.

Nos. 3368/3370 were not produced by the Preston printer due to machinery breakdown.

Post office sheets comprised four sheetlets of six stamps (3×2), the sheetlets being separated by roulettes. The four sheetlets had one of the following inscriptions on the left margin: emblem 'TEAM GB' and Olympic rings; 'The XXX Olympiad'; barcode; Sheet number, Issue date and Printer location.

2545 Paralympic Sports and London Landmarks (*Illustration reduced. Actual size 193×75 mm*)

2012 (29 Aug). Welcome to London, Paralympic Games. Sheet 193×75 mm. Multicoloured 'All-over' phosphor. Perf 14½.

MS3371	**2545**	Paralympic Sports and London Landmarks (1st) Athlete wearing running blades and Olympic Stadium; (1st) Wheelchair basketball player and Palace of Westminster; £1·28 Powerlifter, Millennium Bridge and St Paul's Cathedral; £1·28 Cyclist and London Eye	5·50	5·50
		First Day Cover (Tallents House)		10·00
		Presentation Pack (PO Pack No. 475)	9·00	
		PHQ Cards (set of 5) (368)	2·00	9·00

The five PHQ Cards show the four individual stamps and the complete miniature sheet.

2546 Sarah Storey (cycling, track women's C5 pursuit)

2547 Jonathan Fox (swimming, men's 100 m backstroke, S7)

2548 Mark Colbourne (cycling, track men's C1 pursuit)

2549 Hannah Cockroft (athletics, track women's 100 m, T34)

2550 Neil Fachie and Barney Storey (cycling, men's B 1 km time trial)

2551 Richard Whitehead (athletics, track men's 200 m, T42)

2552 Natasha Baker (equestrian, individual championship test, grade II)

2553 Sarah Storey (cycling : track women's C4-5 500 m time trial)

2554 Ellie Simmonds (swimming, women's 400 m freestyle, S6)

2555 Pamela Relph, Naomi Riches, James Roe, David Smith and Lily van den Broecke (rowing, mixed coxed four, LTAmix4+)

2556 Aled Davies (athletics, field men's discus, F42)

2557 Anthony Kappes and Craig MacLean (cycling, track men's B sprint)

2558 Jessica-Jane Applegate (swimming, women's 200 m freestyle, S14)

2559 Sophie Christiansen (equestrian, individual championship test, grade 1a)

2560 David Weir (athletics, track men's 5000 m, T54)

2561 *Natasha Baker* (equestrian, individual freestyle test, grade II)

2562 *Ellie Simmonds* (swimming, women's 200 m individual medley, SM6)

2563 *Mickey Bushell* (athletics, track men's 100 m, T53)

2564 Danielle Brown (archery, women's individual compound, open)

2565 Heather Frederiksen (swimming, women's 100 m backstroke, S8)

2566 Sophie Christiansen (equestrian, individual freestyle test, grade 1a)

2567 David Weir (athletics, track men's 1500 m, T54)

2568 Sarah Storey (cycling, road women's C5 time trial)

2569 Ollie Hynd (swimming, men's 200 m individual medley, SM8)

2570 Sophie Christiansen, Deb Criddle, Lee Pearson and Sophie Wells (equestrian team, open)

2571 Helena Lucas (sailing, single-person keelboat, 2·4mR)

2572 Sarah Storey (cycling, road women's C4-5 road race)

2573 Josef Craig (swimming, men's 400 m freestyle, S7)

2574 Hannah Cockroft (athletics, track women's 200 m, T34)

2575 David Weir (athletics, track men's 800 m, T54)

2576 Jonnie Peacock (athletics, track men's 100 m, T44)

2577 Josie Pearson (athletics, field women's discus, F51/52/53)

2578 David Stone (cycling, road mixed T1-2 road race)

2579 David Weir (athletics, road men's marathon, T54)

2012 (31 Aug–10 Sept). British Gold Medal Winners at London Paralympic Games. Self-adhesive. Multicoloured Two phosphor panels. Die-cut Perf 15×14½.

3372	**2546**	(1st) Sarah Storey	1·25	1·25
		a. Sheetlet. No. 3372×2	2·50	2·50

3373	**2547**	(1st) Jonathan Fox (1.9.12)	1·25	1·25
		a. Sheetlet. No. 3373×2	2·50	2·50
3374	**2548**	(1st) Mark Colbourne (3.9.12)	1·25	1·25
		a. Sheetlet. No. 3374×2	2·50	2·50
3375	**2549**	(1st) Hannah Cockroft (3.9.12)	1·25	1·25
		a. Sheetlet. No. 3375×2	2·50	2·50
3376	**2550**	(1st) Neil Fachie and Barney Storey		
		(3.9.12)	1·25	1·25
		a. Sheetlet. No. 3376×2	2·50	2·50
3377	**2551**	(1st) Richard Whitehead (3.9.12)	1·25	1·25
		a. Sheetlet. No. 3377×2	2·50	2·50
3378	**2552**	(1st) Natasha Baker (3.9.12)	1·25	1·25
		a. Sheetlet. No. 3378×2	2·50	2·50
3379	**2553**	(1st) Sarah Storey (3.9.12)	1·25	1·25
		a. Sheetlet. No. 3379×2	2·50	2·50
3380	**2554**	(1st) Ellie Simmonds (3.9.12)	1·25	1·25
		a. Sheetlet. No. 3380×2	2·50	2·50
3381	**2555**	(1st) Pamela Relph, Naomi Riches,		
		James Roe, David Smith and Lily		
		van den Broecke (4.9.12)	1·25	1·25
		a. Sheetlet. No. 3381×2	2·50	2·50
3382	**2556**	(1st) Aled Davies (4.9.12)	1·25	1·25
		a. Sheetlet. No. 3382×2	2·50	2·50
3383	**2557**	(1st) Anthony Kappes and Craig		
		MacLean (4.9.12)	1·25	1·25
		a. Sheetlet. No. 3383×2	2·50	2·50
3384	**2558**	(1st) Jessica-Jane Applegate (4.9.12)	1·25	1·25
		a. Sheetlet. No. 3384×2	2·50	2·50
3385	**2559**	(1st) Sophie Christiansen (4.9.12)	1·25	1·25
		a. Sheetlet. No. 3385×2	2·50	2·50
3386	**2560**	(1st) David Weir (4.9.12)	1·25	1·25
		a. Sheetlet. No. 3386×2	2·50	2·50
3387	**2561**	(1st) Natasha Baker (4.9.12)	1·25	1·25
		a. Sheetlet. No. 3387×2	2·50	2·50
3388	**2562**	(1st) Ellie Simmonds (4.9.12)	1·25	1·25
		a. Sheetlet. No. 3388×2	2·50	2·50
3389	**2563**	(1st) Mickey Bushell (5.9.12)	1·25	1·25
		a. Sheetlet. No. 3389×2	2·50	2·50
3390	**2564**	(1st) Danielle Brown (5.9.12)	1·25	1·25
		a. Sheetlet. No. 3390×2	2·50	2·50
3391	**2565**	(1st) Heather Frederiksen (5.9.12)	1·25	1·25
		a. Sheetlet. No. 3391×2	2·50	2·50
3392	**2566**	(1st) Sophie Christiansen (5.9.12)	1·25	1·25
		a. Sheetlet. No. 3392×2	2·50	2·50
3393	**2567**	(1st) David Weir (7.9.12)	1·25	1·25
		a. Sheetlet. No. 3393×2	2·50	2·50
3394	**2568**	(1st) Sarah Storey (7.9.12)	1·25	1·25
		a. Sheetlet. No. 3394×2	2·50	2·50
3395	**2569**	(1st) Ollie Hynd (7.9.12)	1·25	1·25
		a. Sheetlet. No. 3395×2	2·50	2·50
3396	**2570**	(1st) Sophie Christiansen, Deb Criddle,		
		Lee Pearson and Sophie Wells		
		(7.9.12)	1·25	1·25
		a. Sheetlet. No. 3396×2	2·50	2·50
3397	**2571**	(1st) Helena Lucas (8.9.12)	1·25	1·25
		a. Sheetlet No. 3397×2	2·50	2·50
3398	**2572**	(1st) Sarah Storey (8.9.12)	1·25	1·25
		a. Sheetlet. No. 3398×2	2·50	2·50
3399	**2573**	(1st) Josef Craig (8.9.12)	1·25	1·25
		a. Sheetlet. No. 3399×2	2·50	2·50
3400	**2574**	(1st) Hannah Cockroft (8.9.12)	1·25	1·25
		a. Sheetlet. No. 3400×2	2·50	2·50
3401	**2575**	(1st) David Weir (10.9.12)	1·25	1·25
		a. Sheetlet. No. 3401×2	2·50	2·50
3402	**2576**	(1st) Jonnie Peacock (10.9.12)	1·25	1·25
		a. Sheetlet. No. 3402×2	2·50	2·50
3403	**2577**	(1st) Josie Pearson (10.9.12)	1·25	1·25
		a. Sheetlet. No. 3403×2	2·50	2·50
3404	**2578**	(1st) David Stone (10.9.12)	1·25	1·25
		a. Sheetlet. No. 3404×2	2·50	2·50
3405	**2579**	(1st) David Weir (10.9.12)	1·25	1·25
		a. Sheetlet. No. 3405×2	2·50	2·50
Set of 34			40·00	40·00

First Day Covers (Tallents House) (Sheetlets Nos.
3372a/3405a) (34) £125
First Day Covers (Tallents House) (any single gold
medal stamp) 4·25

The self-adhesive base sheetlets for Nos. 3372/3405 were produced by Walsall with the image, name and event of the winning athletes digitally printed by regional printers in six different locations: Attleborough, Edinburgh, London, Preston, Solihull and Swindon.

These sheetlets of 16 stamps were divided by roulettes into eight panes of two stamps (1×2). The left margins were inscribed as follows (reading downwards): emblem and 'ParalympicsGB'; 'London 2012 Paralympic Games'; barcode; Sheet number, Issue date and Printer location.

Nos. 3372, 3373 and 3405 were each printed in separate sheetlets of 16 stamps.

Nos. 3374/3377, 3381/3384, 3385/3388, 3389/3392, 3393/3396, 3397/3400 and 3401/3404 were printed in sheetlets of 16 containing four stamps of each design.

The sheetlets of 16 containing Nos. 3378/3380 contained four each of Nos. 3378/3379 and eight of No. 3380.

2580 Scenes from Olympic and Paralympic Games

2012 (27 Sept). Memories of London 2012 Olympic and Paralympic Games. Sheet 192×75 mm. Multicoloured 'All-over' phosphor. Perf 14½.

MS3406 **2580** Scenes from Olympic and Paralympic
Games (1st) Procession of athletes, Paralympic
Games; (1st) Games makers and Olympic Stadium;
£1·28 Opening ceremony of Paralympic Games;
£1·28 Olympic Games closing ceremony and
handover to Rio 9·00 9·00
First Day Cover (Tallents House) 13·00
Presentation Pack (PO Pack No. 476) 17·50
PHQ Cards (set of 5) (369) 2·00 16·50
The five PHQ Cards show the four individual stamps and the complete miniature sheet.

2581 BR Class D34 Nos. 62471
Glen Falloch and 62496 *Glen Loy*
at Ardlui, 9 May 1959

2012 (27 Sept). Classic Locomotives of Scotland. Booklet stamp. Design as 1st class stamp within No. **MS**3283. Self-adhesive. Multicoloured 'All-over' phosphor. Die-cut perf 14.
3407 **2581** (1st) BR Class D34 Nos. 62471 *Glen
Falloch* and 62496 *Glen Loy* 2·00 2·00
No. 3407 was only issued in booklets containing No. 3407×2 and U3274×4, originally sold for £3·60.

2582 Sun and Particles ejected
from Solar Surface seen from
SOHO Observatory

2583 Venus with Clouds in
Southern Hemisphere seen
from *Venus Express*

2584 Ice in Martian Impact
Crater seen from *Mars Express*

2585 Surface of Asteroid
Lutetia seen from *Rosetta* Probe

2586 Saturn and its Rings seen
from *Cassini* Satellite

2587 Titan (Saturn's largest
moon) seen from *Huygens*
Probe

2012 (16 Oct). Space Science. Multicoloured 'All-over' phosphor. Perf 14.
| 3408 | **2582** | (1st) Sun | 1·20 | 1·00 |
| 3409 | **2583** | (1st) Venus | 1·20 | 1·00 |

3410	2584	77p. Ice in Martian Impact Crater	1·25	1·25
3411	2585	77p. Surface of Asteroid Lutetia	1·25	1·25
3412	2586	£1·28 Saturn and its Rings	2·00	2·00
3413	2587	£1·28 Titan (Saturn's largest moon)	2·00	2·00
Set of 6			8·00	7·50
Set of 6 Gutter Pairs			16·00	
First Day Cover (Tallents House)				9·75
Presentation Pack (PO Pack No. 477)			8·75	
PHQ Cards (set of 6) (370)			2·40	9·00

2588 Six
Poppies on
Barbed Wire
Stems

2012 (23 Oct). Lest We Forget (4th issue). Self-adhesive. Multicoloured
Two phosphor bands. Die-cut perf 14½×14 (with one elliptical hole
in each vert side).

3414	2588	(1st) Six Poppies on Barbed Wire Stems	1·25	1·25

For T **2588** with ordinary gum, see No. 3717.

2589
Reindeer with
Decorated
Antlers

2590 Santa
with Robin

2591 Reindeer with
Decorated Antlers

2592
Snowman and
Penguin

2593 Santa with
Robin

2594 Robin
with Star
Decoration in
Beak

2595 Cat
and Mouse
decorating
Christmas
Tree

2012 (6 Nov). Christmas. Illustrations by Axel Scheffler. Multicoloured One
centre band (No. 3415) or two phosphor bands (others).

(a) Self-adhesive. Die-cut perf 14½×14 (with elliptcal hole on each vert
side).

3415	2589	(2nd) Reindeer with Decorated Antlers	90	90
3416	2590	(1st) Santa with Robin	1·20	1·00
3417	2591	(2nd Large) Reindeer with Decorated Antlers	1·25	1·10
3418	2592	87p. Snowman and Penguin	1·40	1·40
3419	2593	(1st Large) Santa with Robin	1·70	1·40
3420	2594	£1·28 Robin with Star Decoration in Beak	2·00	2·00
3421	2595	£1·90 Cat and Mouse decorating Christmas Tree	3·00	3·00
Set of 7			10·00	9·75
First Day Cover (Tallents House)				12·50
Presentation Pack (PO Pack No. 478)			11·00	
PHQ Cards (set of 8) (371)			3·25	21·00

(b) Ordinary gum. Perf 14½×14.

MS3422 115×102 mm. As Nos. 3415/3421	10·00	9·75
First Day Cover (Tallents House)		10·00

The 2nd class, 1st class, 87p. and £1·28 stamps were also issued in sheets
of 20 containing 8×2nd class, 8×1st class, 2×87p. and 2×£1·28 stamps,
each with a *se-tenant* label. These sheets were printed in lithography
instead of gravure.

Separate sheets of 20×2nd, 20×1st, 10×1st, 10×87p. and 10×£1·28 were
available with personal photographs.

The eight PHQ cards depict the seven individual stamps and the
miniature sheet.

Year Pack

2012 (6 Nov). Comprises Nos. 3254/3259, **MS**3264/**MS**3270, **MS**3272/3307,
3309/3318, 3319A/3326A, 3330/3336, **MS**3341, **MS**3371, **MS**3406,
3408/3413 and 3415/3421

CP3422a	Year Pack (Pack No. 479) (sold for £80)	£125

Post Office Yearbook

2012 (6 Nov). Comprises Nos. 3254/3259, **MS**3264/**MS**3270, **MS**3272/3307,
3309/3318, 3319A/3326A, 3330/3336, **MS**3341, **MS**3371, **MS**3406,
3408/3413 and 3415/3421

YB3422a	Yearbook (sold for £90)	£140

Miniature Sheet Collection

2012 (6 Nov). Comprises Nos. **MS**3264, **MS**3270, **MS**3272, **MS**3283,
MS3336, **MS**3341, **MS**3371, **MS**3406 and **MS**3422

MS3422a Miniature Sheet Collection (sold for £35)	55·00	

2596 Steam Locomotive on
Metropolitan Railway, 1863

2597 Navvies excavating
'Deep Cut' Tube Tunnel,
1898

2598 Commuters in
Carriage, 1911

2599 Boston Manor Art
Deco Station, 1934

2600 Train on 'Deep Cut'
Line, 1938

2601 Canary Wharf Station,
1999

2602 Classic London Underground Posters

2013 (9 Jan). 150th Anniversary of the London Underground.
Multicoloured One centre band (2nd) or 'all-over' phosphor (others).

(a) Ordinary gum. Perf 14½.

3423	2596	(2nd) Steam Locomotive on Metropolitan Railway	90	90
3424	2597	(2nd) Navvies excavating Deep Cut Tube Tunnel	90	90
3425	2598	(1st) Commuters in Carriage	1·20	1·00
3426	2599	(1st) Boston Manor Art Deco Station	1·20	1·00

3427	**2600**	£1·28 Train on Deep Cut Line	2·00	2·00
3428	**2601**	£1·28 Canary Wharf Station	2·00	2·00

Set of 6   7·25   7·00
Set of 6 Gutter Pairs   14·50
First Day Cover (Tallents House)   8·75
Presentation Pack (PO Pack No. 480) (Nos. 3423/3428 and **MS**3429)   15·00
PHQ Cards (set of 11) (372)   4·50   18·00

MS3429 184×74 mm. **2602** Classic London Underground Posters (1st) Golders Green, 1908, By Underground to fresh air (Maxwell Armfield), 1915 and Summer Sales (Mary Koop), 1925; 77p. For the Zoo (Charles Paine), 1921, Power (Edward McKnight-Kauffer), 1931 and The Seen (James Fitton), 1948; 87p. A train every 90 seconds (Abram Games), 1937, Thanks to the Underground (Zero (Hans Schleger)), 1935 and Cut travelling time, Victoria Line (Tom Eckersley), 1969; £1·28 The London Transport Collection (Tom Eckersley), 1975, London Zoo (Abram Games), 1976 and The Tate Gallery by Tube (David Booth), 1987   5·00   5·25
First Day Cover (Tallents House)   6·50

(b) Self-adhesive. Die-cut perf 14½. Die-cut perf 14½.

3430	**2599**	(1st) Boston Manor Art Deco Station, 1934	2·00	2·00

No. 3430 was issued in stamp booklets containing No. 3430×2 and 1st vermilion stamps×4, each booklet originally sold for £3·60.
The complete miniature sheet is shown on one of the 11 PHQ cards with the others depicting individual stamps, including those from No. **MS**3429.

2603 Elinor and Marianne Dashwood (Sense and Sensibility)

2604 Elizabeth Bennet and Portrait of Mr Darcy (Pride and Prejudice)

2605 Fanny Price (Mansfield Park)

2606 Emma Woodhouse and Mr Knightley (Emma)

2607 Catherine Morland (Northanger Abbey)

2608 Anne Elliot and Captain Wentworth (Persuasion)

2013 (21 Feb). Bicentenary of the Publication of Jane Austen's Pride and Prejudice. Multicoloured 'All-over' phosphor. Perf 14.

3431	**2603**	(1st) Elinor and Marianne Dashwood	1·20	1·00
3432	**2604**	(1st) Elizabeth Bennet and Portrait of Mr Darcy	1·20	1·00
3433	**2605**	77p. Fanny Price	1·25	1·25
3434	**2606**	77p. Emma Woodhouse and Mr Knightley	1·25	1·25
3435	**2607**	£1·28 Catherine Morland	2·00	2·00
3436	**2608**	£1·28 Anne Elliot and Captain Wentworth	2·00	2·00

Set of 6   7·75   7·50
Set of 6 Gutter Pairs   15·50
Set of 6 Traffic Light Gutter Pairs   32·00
First Day Cover (Tallents House)   10·00
Presentation Pack (PO Pack No. 481)   9·00
PHQ Cards (set of 6) (373)   2·50   9·25

2609 The 11th Doctor (Matt Smith, 2010–2014)

2610 The Tenth Doctor (David Tennant, 2005–2010)

2611 The Ninth Doctor (Christopher Eccleston, 2005)

2612 The Eighth Doctor (Paul McGann, 1996)

2613 The Seventh Doctor (Sylvester McCoy, 1987–1989)

2614 The Sixth Doctor (Colin Baker, 1984–1986)

2615 The Fifth Doctor (Peter Davison, 1982–1984)

2616 The Fourth Doctor (Tom Baker, 1974–1981)

2617 The Third Doctor (Jon Pertwee, 1970–1974)

2618 The Second Doctor (Patrick Troughton, 1966–1969)

2619 The First Doctor (William Hartnell, 1963–1966)

2620 Tardis

2621 Dr Who 1963–2013

2013 (26 Mar). 50th Anniversary of *Doctor Who* (TV programme) (1st issue). Multicoloured 'All-over' phosphor.

(a) Ordinary gum. 'All-over' phosphor. Perf 14.

3437	**2609**	(1st) Matt Smith	1·20	1·00
		a. Horiz strip of 3. Nos. 3437/3439	3·50	3·00
3438	**2610**	(1st) David Tennant	1·20	1·00
3439	**2611**	(1st) Christopher Eccleston	1·20	1·00
3440	**2612**	(1st) Paul McGann	1·20	1·00
		a. Horiz strip of 4. Nos. 3440/3443	4·25	4·00
3441	**2613**	(1st) Sylvester McCoy	1·20	1·00
3442	**2614**	(1st) Colin Baker	1·20	1·00
3443	**2615**	(1st) Peter Davison	1·20	1·00
3444	**2616**	(1st) Tom Baker	1·20	1·00
		a. Horiz strip of 4. Nos. 3444/3447	4·25	4·00
3445	**2617**	(1st) Jon Pertwee	1·20	1·00
3446	**2618**	(1st) Patrick Troughton	1·20	1·00
3447	**2619**	(1st) William Hartnell	1·20	1·00
Set of 11			12·00	10·00
Set of 1 Gutter Strip of 3 and 2 Gutter Strips of 8			24·00	
First Day Covers (Tallents House) (2)				12·00
Presentation Pack (PO Pack No. 482) (Nos. 3437/3447 and **MS**3451)			18·00	
PHQ Cards (set of 17)			6·75	18·50

(b) Self-adhesive. One centre band (2nd) or two bands. Die-cut perf 14½ (2nd) or 14½×14 (with one elliptical hole in each vert side) (1st).

3448	**2609**	(1st) Matt Smith	4·50	4·50
3449	**2620**	(1st) Tardis	1·25	1·25
3450	**2619**	(1st) William Hartnell	4·50	4·50

MS3451 115×89 mm. **2621** *Dr Who* 1963–2013 (2nd) Dalek; (2nd) The Ood; (2nd) Weeping Angel; (2nd) Cyberman; (1st) TARDIS — 5·00 / 4·75

First Day Cover (Tallents House) — 5·00

Nos. 3437/3439 were printed together, *se-tenant*, as horizontal strips of three stamps in sheets of 48 (2 panes 6×4).

Nos. 3440/3443 and 3444/3447 were each printed together, *se-tenant*, as horizontal strips of four stamps in sheets of 48 (2 panes 4×6).

Nos. 3448/3450 were issued in stamp booklets, each booklet containing No. 3448, 3449×4 and 3450 and originally sold for £3·60.

The 1st class TARDIS stamp perforated 15 all round comes from the £13·37 *Dr Who* premium booklet, No. DY6

The design area of No. 3449 measures 17½×21½ mm, slightly larger than the same TARDIS design (T **2620**) from the miniature sheet and premium booklet pane which measures 17×21mm. (All are 20×24 mm measured perf to perf edge).

The 1st class TARDIS stamp was also issued in sheets of 20, each stamp accompanied by a *se-tenant* label. These sheets were printed in lithography.

No. 3449 was also issued in sheets of 20 with *se-tenant* labels, printed in lithography instead of gravure.

The complete miniature sheet is shown on one of the 17 PHQ cards with the others depicting individual stamps including those from the miniature sheet.

2013 (26 Mar). 50th Anniversary of *Doctor Who* (TV programme) (2nd issue). As No. 3449 but ordinary gum. Multicoloured Two phosphor bands. Perf 14½×14 with one elliptical hole in each vertical side

3452	**2620**	(1st) Tardis	1·25	1·25

No. 3452 only comes from the £13·37 *Dr Who* premium booklet, No. DY6.

2622 Norman Parkinson (1913–1990, portrait and fashion photographer)

2623 Vivien Leigh (1913–1967, actress)

2624 Peter Cushing (1913–1994, actor)

2625 David Lloyd George (1863–1945, Prime Minister 1916–1922)

2626 Elizabeth David (1913–1992, cookery writer)

2627 John Archer (1863–1932, politician and civil rights campaigner)

2628 Benjamin Britten (1913–1976, composer and pianist)

2629 Mary Leakey (1913–1996, archaeologist and anthropologist)

2630 Bill Shankly (1913–1981, football player and manager)

2631 Richard Dimbleby (1913–1965, journalist and broadcaster)

2013 (16 Apr). Great Britons. Multicoloured 'All-over' phosphor. Perf 14½.

3453	**2622**	(1st) Norman Parkinson	1·20	1·00
		a. Horiz strip of 5. Nos. 3453/3457	5·25	4·50
3454	**2623**	(1st) Vivien Leigh	1·20	1·00
3455	**2624**	(1st) Peter Cushing	1·20	1·00
3456	**2625**	(1st) David Lloyd George	1·20	1·00
3457	**2626**	(1st) Elizabeth David	1·20	1·00
3458	**2627**	(1st) John Archer	1·20	1·00
		a. Horiz strip of 5. Nos. 3458/3462	5·25	4·50
3459	**2628**	(1st) Benjamin Britten	1·20	1·00
3460	**2629**	(1st) Mary Leakey	1·20	1·00
3461	**2630**	(1st) Bill Shankly	1·20	1·00
3462	**2631**	(1st) Richard Dimbleby	1·20	1·00
Set of 10			10·50	9·00
Set of 2 Gutter Strips of 10			21·00	
First Day Cover (Tallents House)				11·00
Presentation Pack (PO Pack No. 483)			11·00	
PHQ Cards (set of 10) (375)			4·00	12·00

Nos. 3453/3457 and 3458/3462 were each printed together, *se-tenant*, as horizontal strips of five stamps in sheets of 50 (2 panes 5×5).

2632 Jimmy Greaves (England)

2633 John Charles (Wales)

2634 Gordon Banks (England)

2635 George Best (Northern Ireland)

2636 John Barnes (England)

2637 Kevin Keegan (England)

2638 Denis Law (Scotland)

2639 Bobby Moore (England)

2640 Bryan Robson (England)

2641 Dave Mackay (Scotland)

2642 Bobby Charlton (England)

2013 (9 May)–**2014**. Football Heroes (1st issue). Multicoloured 'All-over' phosphor.

(a) Ordinary gum. Perf 14½.

3463	2632	(1st) Jimmy Greaves	1·20	1·00
		a. Horiz strip of 5. Nos. 3463/3467	5·50	4·50
3464	2633	(1st) John Charles	1·20	1·00
3465	2634	(1st) Gordon Banks	1·20	1·00
3466	2635	(1st) George Best	1·20	1·00
3467	2636	(1st) John Barnes	1·20	1·00
3468	2637	(1st) Kevin Keegan	1·20	1·00
		a. Horiz strip of 6. Nos. 3468/3473	6·50	5·50
3469	2638	(1st) Denis Law	1·20	1·00
3470	2639	(1st) Bobby Moore	1·20	1·00
3471	2640	(1st) Bryan Robson	1·20	1·00
3472	2641	(1st) Dave Mackay	1·20	1·00
3473	2642	(1st) Bobby Charlton	1·20	1·00
Set of 11			12·00	10·00

Set of 1 Gutter Strip of 12 and 1 Gutter Strip of 10	24·00	
First Day Cover (Tallents House)		11·00
Presentation Pack (PO Pack 484)	13·00	
PHQ Cards (set of 12) (376)	4·75	11·00
MS3474 192×74 mm. Nos. 3463/3473	12·00	10·00
First Day Cover		12·00

(b) Self-adhesive. Die-cut perf 14½.

3475	2635	(1st) George Best	4·50	4·50
3476	2639	(1st) Bobby Moore	4·50	4·50
3477	2633	(1st) John Charles (20.2.14)	4·50	4·50
3478	2641	(1st) Dave Mackay (20.2.14)	4·50	4·50
Set of 4			16·00	16·00

Nos. 3463/3489 commemorate the 150th anniversary of the Football Association and the 140th Anniversary of the Scottish Football Association.

Nos. 3463/3467 were printed together, se-tenant, as horizontal strips of five stamps in sheets of 30 (5×6).

Nos. 3468/3473 were printed together, se-tenant, as horizontal strips of six stamps in sheets of 30 (6×5).

Nos. 3475/3476 were issued in booklets, containing Nos. 3475/3476 and 1st vermilion stamp×4, originally sold for £3·60.

The 12 PHQ cards depict the 11 individual stamps and the complete miniature sheet.

2013 (9 May). Football Heroes (2nd issue). Self-adhesive. Multicoloured 'All-over'. phosphor. Die-cut perf 14½×14.

3479	2632	(1st) Jimmy Greaves	1·60	1·60
3480	2633	(1st) John Charles	1·60	1·60
3481	2637	(1st) Kevin Keegan	1·60	1·60
3482	2638	(1st) Denis Law	1·60	1·60
3483	2639	(1st) Bobby Moore	1·60	1·60
3484	2634	(1st) Gordon Banks	1·60	1·60
3485	2635	(1st) George Best	1·60	1·60
3486	2636	(1st) John Barnes	1·60	1·60
3487	2640	(1st) Bryan Robson	1·60	1·60
3488	2641	(1st) Dave Mackay	1·60	1·60
3489	2642	(1st) Bobby Charlton	1·60	1·60
Set of 11			16·00	16·00

Nos. 3479/3489 were issued in £11·11 Football Heroes premium booklet, No. DY7.

No. 3490 is vacant.

2646 Preliminary Oil Sketch for The Coronation of Queen Elizabeth II (Terence Cuneo), 1953

2647 Queen Elizabeth II in Garter Robes (Nicky Philipps), 2012

2648 Portrait by Andrew Festing, 1999

2649 Portrait by Pietro Annigoni, 1955

2650 Portrait by Sergei Pavlenko, 2000

2651 Her Majesty Queen Elizabeth II (Richard Stone), 1992

2013 (30 May). 60th Anniversary of the Coronation. Six Decades of Royal Portraits. Multicoloured. Phosphor band at left (2nd) or 'all-over' phosphor (others). Perf 14.

3491	2646	(2nd) Preliminary Oil Sketch for The Coronation of Queen Elizabeth II (Terence Cuneo), 1953	90	90
3492	2647	(1st) Queen Elizabeth II in Garter Robes (Nicky Philipps), 2012	1·20	1·00
3493	2648	78p. Portrait by Andrew Festing, 1999	1·10	1·10
3494	2649	88p. Portrait by Pietro Annigoni, 1955	1·50	1·50

3495	**2650**	£1·28 Portrait by Sergei Pavlenko, 2000	2·10	2·10
3496	**2651**	£1·88 Her Majesty Queen Elizabeth II		
		(Richard Stone), 1992	3·00	3·00
Set of 6			8·50	8·50
Set of 6 Gutter Pairs			17·00	
Set of 6 Traffic Light Gutter Blocks of 4			36·00	
First Day Cover (Tallents House)				11·00
Presentation Pack (PO Pack No. 485)			10·00	
PHQ Cards (set of 6) (377)			12·50	10·50

2652 UTA Class W No. 103
Thomas Somerset with Belfast
Express, Downhill, near
Castlerock, *c* 1950

2653 Classic Locomotives of Northern Ireland

2013 (18 June). Classic Locomotives (3rd series). Northern Ireland. Black, grey and gold. 'All-over' phosphor.
(a) Self-adhesive. Die-cut perf 14.

| 3497 | **2652** | (1st) UTA Class W No. 103 *Thomas* | | |
| | | *Somerset* with Belfast Express | 2·00 | 2·00 |

(b) Ordinary gum. Sheet 180×74 mm. Perf 14.
MS3498 Classic Locomotives of Northern Ireland. As
T **2652**; 78p. UTA SG3 No. 35; 88p. Peckett No. 2;

£1·28 CDRJC Class 5 No. 4	5·00	5·25
First Day Cover (Tallents House)		6·50
Presentation Pack (PO Pack No. 486)	6·25	
PHQ Cards (set of 5) (378)	2·00	6·50

No. 3497 was issued in booklets containing No. 3497×2 and 1st vermilion stamps×4 and sold for £3·60.
The five PHQ cards show the four individual stamps and the complete miniature sheet.

2654 Comma *(Polygonia c-album)*

2655 Orange-tip *(Anthocharis cardamines)*

2656 Small Copper *(Lycaena phlaeas)*

2657 Chalkhill Blue *(Polyommatus coridon)*

2658 Swallowtail *(Papilio machaon)*

2659 Purple Emperor *(Apatura iris)*

2660 Marsh Fritillary *(Euphydryas aurinia)*

2661 Brimstone *(Gonepteryx rhamni)*

2662 Red Admiral *(Vanessa atalanta)*

2663 Marbled White *(Melanargia galathea)*

2013 (11 July). Butterflies. Multicoloured 'All-over' phosphor.
(a) Ordinary paper. Perf 14×14½.

3499	**2654**	(1st) Comma	1·20	1·00
		a. Horiz strip of 5. Nos. 3499/3503	5·25	4·50
3500	**2655**	(1st) Orange-tip	1·20	1·00
3501	**2656**	(1st) Small Copper	1·20	1·00
3502	**2657**	(1st) Chalkhill Blue	1·20	1·00
3503	**2658**	(1st) Swallowtail	1·20	1·00
3504	**2659**	(1st) Purple Emperor	1·20	1·00
		a. Horiz strip of 5. Nos. 3504/3508	5·25	4·50
3505	**2660**	(1st) Marsh Fritillary	1·20	1·00
3506	**2661**	(1st) Brimstone	1·20	1·00
3507	**2662**	(1st) Red Admiral	1·20	1·00
3508	**2663**	(1st) Marbled White	1·20	1·00
Set of 10			10·50	9·00
Set of 2 Gutter Strips of 10			21·00	
First Day Cover (Tallents House)				12·00
Presentation Pack (PO Pack No. 487)			11·00	
PHQ Cards (set of 10) (379)			4·00	11·00

(b) Self-adhesive. Die-cut perf 14×14½.

| 3509 | **2657** | (1st) Chalkhill Blue. | 2·00 | 2·00 |
| 3510 | **2654** | (1st) Comma. | 2·00 | 2·00 |

Nos. 3499/3503 and 3504/3508 were each printed together, *se-tenant*, as horizontal strips of five stamps in sheets of 50 (2 panes 5×5).
Nos. 3509/3510 were issued in stamp booklets containing Nos. 3509/3510 and 1st vermilion stamp×4 and sold for £3·60.

2664 Andy Murray's Wimbledon Victory

2013 (8 Aug). Andy Murray, Men's Singles Champion, Wimbledon. Sheet 192×75 mm. Multicoloured 'All-over' phosphor. Perf 14½.

MS3511	2664	Andy Murray's Wimbledon Victory		
		(1st) Andy Murray kissing Wimbledon Trophy;		
		(1st) Andy Murray serving; £1·28 In action; £1·28		
		Holding Trophy	5·25	5·50

First Day Cover (Tallents House) 7·00
Presentation Pack (PO Pack No. M21) 6·50

2665 Jaguar E-Type, 1961

2666 Rolls-Royce Silver Shadow, 1965

2667 Aston Martin DB5, 1963

2668 MG MGB, 1962

2669 Morgan Plus 8, 1968

2670 Lotus Esprit, 1976

2671 The Workhorses

2013 (13 Aug). British Auto Legends. Multicoloured 'All-over' phosphor. Perf 13½ (Nos. 3512/3517) or 14 (No. **MS**3518).

3512	2665	(1st) Jaguar E-Type, 1961	1·20	1·00
		a. Horiz strip of 3. Nos. 3512/3514	3·25	2·75
3513	2666	(1st) Rolls-Royce Silver Shadow, 1965	1·20	1·00
3514	2667	(1st) Aston Martin DB5, 1963	1·20	1·00
3515	2668	£1·28 MG MGB, 1962	1·60	1·60
		a. Horiz strip of 3. Nos. 3515/3517	4·25	4·25
3516	2669	£1·28 Morgan Plus 8, 1968	1·60	1·60
3517	2670	£1·28 Lotus Esprit, 1976	1·60	1·60
		Set of 6	7·50	7·00

Set of 2 Gutter Strips of 6 15·00
First Day Cover (Tallents House) 9·00
Presentation Pack (PO Pack No. 488) (Nos. 3512/3517 and **MS**3518) 13·50
PHQ Cards (set of 11) (380) 4·50 17·00

MS3518	180×74 mm. **2671** The Workhorses (1st)×4	
	Morris Minor Royal Mail van (1953–1971); Austin	
	FX4 (1958–1997) London taxi; Ford Anglia 105E	
	(1959–1967) police car; Coastguard Land Rover	
	Defender 110 (from 1990) (all 40×30 mm)	4·50 4·00

First Day Cover (Tallents House) 4·50

Nos. 3512/3514 and 3515/3517 were each printed together, *se-tenant*, as horizontal strips of three stamps in sheets of 60 (2 panes 6×5).

The 1st value from No. **MS**3518 is inscr EUROPA.

The complete miniature sheet is shown on one of the 11 PHQ cards with the others depicting individual stamps including those from the miniature sheet.

2672 East Indiaman *Atlas*, 1813

2673 Royal Mail Ship *Britannia*, 1840

2674 Tea Clipper *Cutty Sark*, 1870

2675 Cargo Liner *Clan Matheson*, 1919

2676 Royal Mail Ship *Queen Elizabeth*, 1940

2677 Bulk Carrier *Lord Hinton*, 1986

2013 (19 Sept). Merchant Navy (1st issue). Multicoloured 'All-over' phosphor. Perf 14.

3519	2672	(1st) East Indiaman *Atlas*, 1813	1·20	1·00
3520	2673	(1st) Royal Mail Ship *Britannia*, 1840	1·20	1·00
3521	2674	(1st) Tea Clipper *Cutty Sark*, 1870	1·20	1·00
3522	2675	£1·28 Cargo Liner *Clan Matheson*, 1919	1·60	1·60
3523	2676	£1·28 Royal Mail Ship *Queen Elizabeth*, 1940	1·60	1·60
3524	2677	£1·28 Bulk Carrier *Lord Hinton*, 1986	1·60	1·60
		Set of 6	7·50	7·00

Set of 6 Gutter Pairs 15·00
First Day Cover (Tallents House) 9·00
Presentation Pack (PO Pack No. 489) (Nos. 3519/3524 and **MS**3529) 14·50
PHQ Cards (set of 11) (381) 4·50 17·00

The complete miniature sheet is shown on one of the 11 PHQ cards with the others depicting individual stamps including those from No. **MS**3529.

2678 Destroyer HMS *Vanoc* escorting Atlantic Convoy

2679 Merchant Ship passing the Naval Control Base in the Thames Estuary

2680 Sailors clearing Ice from the Decks of HMS *King George V* in Arctic Waters

2681 Naval Convoy of 24 Merchant Ships in the North Sea

2682 Second World War Atlantic and Arctic Convoys

2013 (19 Sept). Merchant Navy. Multicoloured 'All-over' phosphor.Perf 14.

3525	2678	(1st) Destroyer HMS *Vanoc* escorting Atlantic Convoy	2·25	2·25
3526	2679	(1st) Merchant Ship passing the Naval Control Base in the Thames Estuary	2·25	2·25
3527	2680	(1st) Sailors clearing Ice from the Decks of HMS *King George V* in Arctic Waters	2·25	2·25
3528	2681	(1st) Naval Convoy of 24 Merchant Ships in the North Sea	2·25	2·25
Set of 4			8·00	8·00
MS3529 115×89 mm. **2682** Second World War Atlantic and Arctic Convoys. Nos. 3525/3528			6·00	6·00
First Day Cover (Tallents House)				6·75

Nos. 3525/3528 were only issued in the £11·19 Merchant Navy premium booklet, No. DY8, and in No. **MS**3529.

2683 Royal Mail Van

2673 Royal Mail Ship *Britannia*, 1840

2013 (19 Sept). Royal Mail Transport By Land and Sea. Multicoloured Die-cut perf 14.

3530	2683	(1st) Royal Mail Van	5·50	5·50
3531	2673	(1st) Royal Mail Ship *Britannia*, 1840.	5·50	5·50

The design of No. 3530 is as the Royal Mail van stamp within No. **MS**3518.

Nos. 3530/3531 were only issued in booklets containing Nos. 3530/3531 and 1st vermilion stamp×4 and originally sold for £3·60.

No. 3530 includes the EUROPA emblem.

2684 Polacanthus

2685 Ichthyosaurus

2686 Iguanodon

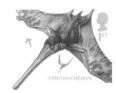

2687 Ornithocheirus

2688 Baryonyx

2689 Dimorphodon

2690 Hypsilophodon

2691 Cetiosaurus

2692 Megalosaurus

2693 Plesiosaurus

2013 (10 Oct). Dinosaurs. Multicoloured 'All-over' phosphor. Die-cut perf 13½×14 (with no teeth around protruding parts at top or foot of the designs).

3532	2684	(1st) Polacanthus	1·20	1·00
		a. Horiz strip of 5. Nos. 3532/3536	5·25	
3533	2685	(1st) Ichthyosaurus	1·20	1·00
3534	2686	(1st) Iguanodon	1·20	1·00
3535	2687	(1st) Ornithocheirus	1·20	1·00
3536	2688	(1st) Baryonyx	1·20	1·00
3537	2689	(1st) Dimorphodon	1·20	1·00
		a. Horiz strip of 5. Nos. 3537/3541	5·25	
3538	2690	(1st) Hypsilophodon	1·20	1·00
3539	2691	(1st) Cetiosaurus	1·20	1·00
3540	2692	(1st) Megalosaurus	1·20	1·00
3541	2693	(1st) Plesiosaurus	1·20	1·00
Set of 10			10·50	9·00
First Day Cover (Tallents House)				11·00
Presentation Pack (PO Pack 490)			11·00	
PHQ Cards (set of 10) (382)			4·00	11·00

Nos. 3532/3536 and 3537/3541 were each printed together as horizontal strips of five stamps in sheets of 50 (2 panes 5×5).

2694 *Madonna and Child*

2695 *Virgin and Child with the Young St John the Baptist*

2696 *Madonna and Child*

2697 *St Roch Praying to the Virgin for an End to the Plague*

2698 *Virgin and Child with the Young St John the Baptist*

2699 *La Vierge au Lys*

2700 *Theotokos, Mother of God*

2700a Madonna and Child

2013 (5 Nov). Christmas. Madonna and Child Paintings. Multicoloured One centre band (No. 3542) or two bands (others).

(a) Self-adhesive. Die-cut perf 14½×15.

3542	**2694**	(2nd) *Madonna and Child*	90	90
3543	**2695**	(1st) *Virgin and Child with the Young St John the Baptist* (detail)	1·20	1·00
3544	**2696**	(2nd Large) *Madonna and Child*	1·25	1·10
3545	**2697**	88p. *St Roch Praying to the Virgin for an End to the Plague* (detail)	1·40	1·40
3546	**2698**	(1st Large) *Virgin and Child with the Young St John the Baptist* (detail)	1·70	1·40
3547	**2699**	£1·28 *La Vierge au Lys*	2·00	2·00
3548	**2700**	£1·88 *Theotokos*, Mother of God	3·00	3·00
Set of 7			9·75	9·50
First Day Cover (Tallents House)				12·50
Presentation Pack (PO Pack No. 491) (383)			11·50	
PHQ Cards (set of 8) (383)			3·25	19·00

(b) Ordinary gum. Perf 14½×15.

MS3549 146×74 mm. **2700a** As Nos. 3542/3548		9·75	9·50
First Day Cover			12·50

The 2nd class, 1st class, 88p., £1·28 and £1·88 stamps were also issued in sheets of 20 containing 8×2nd class, 8×1st class, 2×88p., 1×£1·28 and 1×£1·88 stamps, each stamp accompanied by a *se-tenant* label.

Separate sheets of 20×2nd, 10×1st, 10×88p. and 10×£1·28 were available with personal photographs.

The eight PHQ cards show the seven individual stamps and the complete miniature sheet.

2701 Angels (Rosie Hargreaves)

2702 Santa (Molly Robson)

2013 (5 Nov). Children's Christmas. Self-adhesive. Multicoloured One phosphor band at right (2nd) or two phosphor bands (1st). Die-cut perf 14½.

3550	**2701**	(2nd) Angels	1·00	1·00
3551	**2702**	(1st) Santa	1·25	1·25
First Day Cover (Tallents House)				4·25
Presentation Pack (PO Pack No. M22)			4·25	

Year Pack

2013 (5 Nov). Comprises Nos. 3423/3429, 3431/3447, **MS**3451, 3453/3473, 3491/3496, **MS**3498/3508, **MS**3511/3524, **MS**3529 and 3532/3548

CP3551a	Year Pack (Pack No. 492) (sold for £85)	£130

Post Office Yearbook

2013 (5 Nov). Comprises Nos. 3423/3429, 3431/3447, **MS**3451, 3453/3473, 3491/3496, **MS**3498/3508, **MS**3511/3524, **MS**3529, 3532/3548 and 3550/3551

YB3551a	Yearbook (sold for £90)	£135

Miniature Sheet Collection

2013 (5 Nov). Comprises Nos. **MS**3429, **MS**3451, **MS**3474, **MS**3498, **MS**3511, **MS**3518, **MS**3529 and **MS**3549

MS3551a Miniature Sheet Collection (sold for £33)   45·00

2703 *Andy Pandy*

2704 *Ivor the Engine*

2705 *Dougal (The Magic Roundabout)*

2706 Windy Miller *(Camberwick Green)*

2707 *Mr Benn*

2708 Great Uncle Bulgaria *(The Wombles)*

2709 *Bagpuss*

2710 *Paddington Bear* **2711** *Postman Pat*

2712 *Bob the Builder* **2713** *Peppa Pig* **2714** *Shaun the Sheep*

2014 (7 Jan). Classic Children's TV. Self-adhesive. Multicoloured 'All-over' phosphor. Die-cut perf 15.

3552	**2703**	(1st) *Andy Pandy*	1·20	1·00
		a. Horiz strip of 6. Nos. 3552/3557	6·50	
3553	**2704**	(1st) *Ivor the Engine*	1·20	1·00
3554	**2705**	(1st) *Dougal (The Magic Roundabout)*	1·20	1·00
3555	**2706**	(1st) *Windy Miller (Camberwick Green)*	1·20	1·00
3556	**2707**	(1st) *Mr Benn*	1·20	1·00
3557	**2708**	(1st) *Great Uncle Bulgaria (The Wombles)*	1·00	1·00
3558	**2709**	(1st) *Bagpuss*	1·20	1·00
		a. Horiz strip of 6. Nos. 3558/3563	6·50	
3559	**2710**	(1st) *Paddington Bear*	1·20	1·00
3560	**2711**	(1st) *Postman Pat*	1·20	1·00
3561	**2712**	(1st) *Bob the Builder*	1·20	1·00
3562	**2713**	(1st) *Peppa Pig*	1·20	1·00
3563	**2714**	(1st) *Shaun the Sheep*	1·20	1·00
Set of 12			13·00	11·00
Set of 2 Gutter Strips of 12			26·00	
First Day Cover (Tallents House)				13·50
Presentation Pack (PO Pack No. 493)			14·00	
PHQ Cards (set of 12) (384)			4·75	12·50

Nos. 3552/3557 and 3558/3563 were each printed together, *se-tenant*, in horizontal strips of six stamps in sheets of 60 (6×10).

2715 Riding for the Disabled Association

2716 The King's Troop Ceremonial Horses

2717 Dray Horses

2718 Royal Mews Carriage Horses

2719 Police Horses

2720 Forestry Horse

2014 (4 Feb). Working Horses. Multicoloured 'All-over' phosphor. Perf 14.

3564	**2715**	(1st) Riding for the Disabled Association	1·20	1·00
3565	**2716**	(1st) The King's Troop Ceremonial Horses	1·20	1·00
3566	**2717**	88p. Dray Horses	1·40	1·40
3567	**2718**	88p. Royal Mews Carriage Horses	1·40	1·40
3568	**2719**	£1·28 Police Horses	2·10	2·10

3569	**2720**	£1·28 Forestry Horse	2·10	2·10
Set of 6			8·25	8·00
Set of 6 Gutter Pairs			16·50	
First Day Cover (Tallents House)				10·00
Presentation Pack (PO Pack No. 494)			9·50	
PHQ Cards (set of 6) (385)			2·50	9·50

2721 BR Dean Goods No. 2532 **2722** BR D34 Nos. 62471 and 62496

2723 UTA Class W No. 103 *Thomas Somerset*

2724 LMS No. 7720

2725 Peckett R2 *Thor* **2726** BR D40 No. 62276

2727 UTA SG3 No. 35 **2728** Hunslet No. 589 *Blanche*

2729 Classic Locomotives of Wales

2014 (20 Feb). Classic Locomotives (4th and 5th series). Wales (No. **MS**3578) and United Kingdom. Multicoloured 'All-over' phosphor. Perf 14.

3570	**2721**	(1st) BR Dean Goods No. 2532	2·75	2·75
3571	**2722**	(1st) BR D34 Nos. 62471 and 62496	2·75	2·75
3572	**2723**	(1st) UTA Class W No. 103	2·75	2·75
3573	**2724**	(1st) LMS No. 7720	2·75	2·75
3574	**2725**	60p. Peckett R2 *Thor*	2·75	2·75
3575	**2726**	68p. BR D40 No. 62276	2·75	2·75
3576	**2727**	78p. UTA SG3 No. 35	2·75	2·75
3577	**2728**	78p. Hunslet No. 589 *Blanche*	2·75	2·75
Set of 8			15·00	15·00

MS3578 180×74 mm. **2729** Classic Locomotives of Wales No. 3573; No. 3577; 88p. W&LLR No. 822 *The Earl*; £1·28 BR 5600 No. 5652 — 5·00 / 5·25

First Day Cover (Tallents House)		6·50
Presentation Pack (PO Pack No. 495)	6·00	
PHQ Cards (set of 5) (386)	2·00	10·00

Nos. 3570/3577 were issued in the £13·97 Classic Locomotives booklet, No. DY9, or in No. **MS**3578 (Nos. 3573 and 3577).

For the self-adhesive version of No. 3573, see No. 3634

The five PHQ cards show the four individual stamps and the complete miniature sheet.

2730 Roy Plomley (1914–1985, broadcaster and writer)

2731 Barbara Ward (1914–1981, economist and broadcaster)

2732 Joe Mercer (1914–1990, football player and manager)

2733 Kenneth More (1914–1982, stage and screen actor)

2734 Dylan Thomas (1914–1953, poet and writer)

2735 Sir Alec Guinness (1914–2000, stage and screen actor)

2736 Noorunissa Inayat Khan (1914–1944, SOE agent in occupied France)

2737 Max Perutz (1914–2002, molecular biologist and Nobel laureate)

2738 Joan Littlewood (1914–2002, theatre director and writer)

2739 Abram Games (1914–1996, graphic designer)

2014 (25 Mar). Remarkable Lives. Multicoloured 'All-over' phosphor. Perf 14½.

3579	**2730**	(1st) Roy Plomley	1·20	1·00
		a. Horiz strip of 5. Nos. 3579/3583	5·25	4·50
3580	**2731**	(1st) Barbara Ward	1·20	1·00
3581	**2732**	(1st) Joe Mercer	1·20	1·00
3582	**2733**	(1st) Kenneth More	1·20	1·00
3583	**2734**	(1st) Dylan Thomas	1·20	1·00
3584	**2735**	(1st) Sir Alec Guinness	1·20	1·00
		a. Horiz strip of 5. Nos. 3584/3588	5·25	4·50
3585	**2736**	(1st) Noorunissa Inayat Khan	1·20	1·00
3586	**2737**	(1st) Max Perutz	1·20	1·00
3587	**2738**	(1st) Joan Littlewood	1·20	1·00
3588	**2739**	(1st) Abram Games	1·20	1·00
Set of 10			10·50	9·00

Set of 2 Gutter Strips of 10	21·00	
First Day Cover (Tallents House)		11·00
Presentation Pack (PO Pack No. 496)	11·00	
PHQ Cards (set of 10) (387)	4·00	11·00

Nos. 3579/3583 and 3584/3588 were each printed together, *se-tenant*, as horizontal strips of five stamps in sheets of 50 (2 panes 5×5).

2740 Buckingham Palace, 2014

2741 Buckingham Palace, *circa* 1862

2742 Buckingham Palace, 1846

2743 Buckingham House, 1819

2744 Buckingham House, 1714

2745 Buckingham House, *circa* 1700

2746 The Grand Staircase

2747 The Throne Room

2014 (15 Apr). Buckingham Palace, London (1st issue). Multicoloured 'All-over phosphor'.

(a) Ordinary gum. Perf 14½.

3589	**2740**	(1st) Buckingham Palace, 2014	1·20	1·00
		a. Horiz strip of 3. Nos. 3589/3591	3·25	2·75
		b. Perf 14×13½	1·25	1·25
3590	**2741**	(1st) Buckingham Palace, *circa* 1862	1·20	1·00
		b. Perf 14×13½	1·25	1·25
3591	**2742**	(1st) Buckingham Palace, 1846	1·20	1·00
		b. Perf 14×13½	1·25	1·25
3592	**2743**	(1st) Buckingham House, 1819	1·20	1·00
		a. Horiz strip of 3. Nos. 3592/3594	3·25	2·75
		b. Perf 14×13½	1·25	1·25
3593	**2744**	(1st) Buckingham House, 1714	1·20	1·00
		b. Perf 14×13½	1·25	1·25
3594	**2745**	(1st) Buckingham House, *circa* 1700	1·20	1·00
		b. Perf 14×13½	1·25	1·25
Set of 6 (Nos. 3589/3594)			6·50	5·50
Set of 6 (Nos. 3589b/3594b)			7·50	7·50
Set of 2 Gutter Strips of 6			13·00	
First Day Cover (Tallents House)				6·75
Presentation Pack (PO Pack No. 497) (Nos. 3589/3594 and **MS**3601)			11·50	
PHQ Cards (set of 11) (388)			4·50	13·00

(b) Self-adhesive. Die-cut perf 14.

3595	**2746**	(1st) The Grand Staircase	2·25	2·25
3596	**2747**	(1st) The Throne Room	2·25	2·25

Nos. 3589/3591 and 3592/3594 were each printed together, *se-tenant*, as horizontal strips of three in sheets of 36 (2 panes 3×6).

Nos. 3589b and 3591b come from £11·39 premium booklet, No. DY10.

Nos. 3595/3596 were issued in stamp booklets containing Nos. 3595/3596 and 1st vermilion stamps×4 and originally sold for £3·72.

The complete miniature sheet is shown on one of the 11 PHQ cards with the others depicting individual stamps including those from No. **MS**3601.

2748 The Blue Drawing Room

2749 The Green Drawing Room

2750 Buckingham Palace

2014 (15 Apr). Buckingham Palace, London (2nd issue). Multicoloured 'All-over' phosphor. Perf 14.

3597	**2747**	(1st) The Throne Room	1·20	1·00
3598	**2746**	(1st) The Grand Staircase	1·20	1·00
3599	**2748**	(1st) The Blue Drawing Room	1·20	1·00
3600	**2749**	(1st) The Green Drawing Room	1·20	1·00
Set of 4			4·25	3·50
MS3601 146×74 mm. **2750** Buckingham Palace Nos. 3597/3600			4·25	3·50
First Day Cover (Tallents House)				4·50

Nos. 3597/3600 were only issued in the £11·39 premium booklet, No. DY10 and No. **MS**3601.

2751 *A Matter of Life and Death* (1946)

2752 *Lawrence of Arabia* (1962)

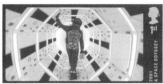

2753 *2001 A Space Odyssey* (1968)

2754 *Chariots of Fire* (1981)

2755 *Secrets and Lies* (1996)

2756 *Bend It Like Beckham* (2002)

2757 Films by GPO Film Unit

2014 (13 May). Great British Films. Multicoloured 'All-over' phosphor. Perf 14½ (Nos. 3602/3607) or 14 (No. **MS**3608).

3602	**2751**	(1st) *A Matter of Life and Death*	1·20	1·00
		a. Horiz strip of 3. Nos. 3602/3604	3·25	2·75
3603	**2752**	(1st) *Lawrence of Arabia*	1·20	1·00
3604	**2753**	(1st) *2001 A Space Odyssey*	1·20	1·00
3605	**2754**	£1·28 *Chariots of Fire*	1·60	1·60
		a. Horiz strip of 3. Nos. 3605/3607	4·25	4·25
3606	**2755**	£1·28 *Secrets and Lies*	1·60	1·60
3607	**2756**	£1·28 *Bend It Like Beckham*	1·60	1·60
Set of 6			7·50	7·00

Set of 2 Gutter Strips of 6			15·00	
First Day Cover (Tallents House)				10·00
Presentation Pack (PO Pack No. 498) (Nos. 3602/3607 and **MS**3608)			15·00	
PHQ Cards (set of 11) (389)			4·50	18·00

MS3608 115×89 mm. **2757** Films by GPO Film Unit (1st)×4 *Night Mail* (1936) directed by Harry Watt and Basil Wright; *Love on the Wing* (1938) directed by Norman McLaren; *A Colour Box* (1935) directed by Len Lye; *Spare Time* (1939) directed by Humphrey Jennings 5·00 4·75

First Day Cover (Tallents House) 5·00

Nos. 3602/3604 and 3605/3607 were each printed together, *se-tenant*, as horizontal strips of three stamps in sheets of 36 (2 panes 3×6).

The complete miniature sheet is shown on one of the 11 PHQ cards with the others depicting individual stamps including those from No. **MS**3608.

 **2758** Herring
 **2759** Red Gurnard
 2760 Dab
 **2761** Pouting
 **2762** Cornish Sardine
 **2763** Common Skate
 **2764** Spiny Dogfish
 2765 Wolffish
 2766 Sturgeon
 **2767** Conger Eel

2014 (5 June). Sustainable Fish (Nos. 3609/3613) and Threatened Fish (Nos. 3614/3618). Multicoloured 'All-over' phosphor. Perf 14×14½.

3609	**2758**	(1st) Herring	1·20	1·00
		a. Horiz strip of 5. Nos. 3609/3613	5·25	4·50
3610	**2759**	(1st) Red Gurnard	1·20	1·00
3611	**2760**	(1st) Dab	1·00	1·00
3612	**2761**	(1st) Pouting	1·20	1·00
3613	**2762**	(1st) Cornish Sardine	1·20	1·00
3614	**2763**	(1st) Common Skate	1·20	1·00
		a. Horiz strip of 5. Nos. 3614/3618	5·25	4·50
3615	**2764**	(1st) Spiny Dogfish	1·20	1·00
3616	**2765**	(1st) Wolffish	1·20	1·00
3617	**2766**	(1st) Sturgeon	1·20	1·00
3618	**2767**	(1st) Conger Eel	1·20	1·00
Set of 10			10·50	9·00
Set of 2 Gutter Strips of 10			21·00	
First Day Cover (Tallents House)				11·50
Presentation Pack (PO Pack No. 499)			11·00	
PHQ Cards (set of 10) (390)			4·00	11·00

Nos. 3609/3613 and 3614/3618 were each printed together, *se-tenant*, as horizontal strips of five in sheets of 50 (2 panes 5×5).

 **2768** Judo
 **2769** Swimming
 **2770** Marathon
 **2771** Squash
 **2772** Netball
 **2773** Para-athlete Cycling

2014 (17 July). Commonwealth Games, Glasgow. Multicoloured One phosphor band (No. 3619) or two bands (others).

(a) Ordinary gum. Perf 14×14½.

3619	**2768**	(2nd) Judo	90	90
3620	**2769**	(1st) Swimming	1·00	1·00
3621	**2770**	97p. Marathon	1·40	1·40
3622	**2771**	£1·28 Squash	1·75	1·75
3623	**2772**	£1·47 Netball	2·50	2·50
3624	**2773**	£2·15 Para-athlete Cycling	3·50	3·50
Set of 6			10·00	10·00
Set of 6 Gutter Pairs			20·00	
First Day Cover (Tallents House)				11·50
Presentation Pack (PO Pack No. 500)			10·50	
PHQ Cards (set of 6) (391)			2·50	11·50

(b) Self-adhesive. Die-cut perf 14×14½.

3625	**2769**	(1st) Swimming	2·00	2·00

The phosphor band on No. 3619 is at centre right of the stamps.

No. 3625 was issued in stamp booklets containing No. 3625×2 and 1st vermilion stamps×4 and originally sold for £3·72.

 **2774** *Poppy* (Fiona Strickland)
 **2775** Lines from *For the Fallen* (Laurence Binyon)

2776 Private William Cecil Tickle

2777 *A Star Shell* (C. R. W. Nevinson)

2778 *The Response* (sculpture by William Goscombe John)

2779 Princess Mary's Gift Box Fund

2014 (28 July). Centenary of the First World War (1st issue). Multicoloured 'All-over' phosphor (Nos. 3627, 3629) or two bands (others). Perf 14½.

3626	**2774**	(1st) *Poppy*	1·20	1·00
		a. 'All-over' phosphor	1·25	1·50
3627	**2775**	(1st) Lines from *For the Fallen*	1·20	1·00
3628	**2776**	(1st) Private William Cecil Tickle	1·20	1·00
		a. 'All-over' phosphor	1·25	1·50
3629	**2777**	£1·47 *A Star Shell*	2·50	2·50
3630	**2778**	£1·47 *The Response*	2·50	2·50
		a. 'All-over' phosphor	3·25	3·50
3631	**2779**	£1·47 Princess Mary's Gift Box Fund	2·50	2·50
		a. 'All-over' phosphor	3·25	3·50
Set of 6			10·00	9·25
Set of 6 Gutter Pairs			20·00	
First Day Cover (Tallents House)				11·50
Presentation Pack (PO Pack No. 501)			11·50	
PHQ Cards (set of 6) (392)			2·50	10·50

Nos. 3626a, 3628a, 3630a and 3631a only come from £11·30 Centenary of the First World War premium booklet, No. DY11.

No. 3627 also comes from £15·65 premium booklet, No. DY26.

2014 (18 Aug). Sustainable Fish and Threatened Fish (2nd issue). Designs as Nos. 3613/3614. Self-adhesive. Multicoloured Die-cut perf 14×14½.

3632	**2763**	(1st) Common Skate.	2·00	2·00
3633	**2762**	(1st) Cornish Sardine.	2·00	2·00

Nos. 3632/3633 were only issued in stamp booklets containing Nos. 3632/3633 and 1st vermilion stamps×4 and originally sold for £3·72.

2724 LMS No. 7720

2014 (18 Sept). Classic Locomotives of Wales. Booklet stamp as T **2724**. 'All-over' phosphor. Self-adhesive. Multicoloured Die-cut perf 14.

3634	**2724**	(1st) LMS No. 7720	2·00	2·00

No. 3634 was only issued in booklets originally sold for £3·72.

2780 Eastbourne Bandstand

2781 Tinside Lido, Plymouth

2782 Bangor Pier

2783 Southwold Lighthouse

2784 Blackpool Pleasure Beach

2785 Bexhill-on-Sea Shelter

2786 British Piers

2014 (18 Sept). Seaside Architecture. Multicoloured Two bands (Nos. 3635/3640) or 'All-over' phosphor (No. **MS**3641). Perf 14.

3635	**2780**	(1st) Eastbourne Bandstand	1·20	1·00
3636	**2781**	(1st) Tinside Lido, Plymouth	1·20	1·00
3637	**2782**	97p. Bangor Pier	1·40	1·40
3638	**2783**	97p. Southwold Lighthouse	1·40	1·40
3639	**2784**	£1·28 Blackpool Pleasure Beach	2·10	2·10
3640	**2785**	£1·28 Bexhill-on-Sea Shelter	2·10	2·10
Set of 6			8·50	8·00
Set of 6 Gutter Pairs			17·00	
First Day Cover (Tallents House)				10·00
Presentation Pack (PO Pack No. 502) (Nos. 3635/3640 and **MS**3641)			16·00	
PHQ Cards (set of 11) (393)			4·50	19·00
MS3641 125×89 mm. **2786** British Piers (1st) Llandudno Pier; (1st) Worthing Pier; £1·28 Dunoon Pier; £1·28 Brighton Pier			5·50	5·50
First Day Cover (Tallents House)				7·00

No. 3635 includes the EUROPA emblem.

The complete miniature sheet is shown on one of the 11 PHQ cards with the others depicting individual stamps including those from the miniature sheet.

2787 Margaret Thatcher

2788 Harold Wilson

2789 Clement Attlee

2790 Winston Churchill

2791 William Gladstone

2792 Robert Peel

2793 Charles Grey

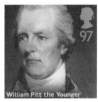
2794 William Pitt the Younger

2014 (14 Oct). Prime Ministers. Multicoloured. 'All-over' phosphor. Perf 14½.

3642	**2787**	(1st) Margaret Thatcher	1·20	1·00
		a. Horiz strip of 4. Nos. 3642/3645	4·25	3·75
3643	**2788**	(1st) Harold Wilson	1·20	1·00
3644	**2789**	(1st) Clement Attlee	1·20	1·00
3645	**2790**	(1st) Winston Churchill	1·20	1·00
3646	**2791**	97p. William Gladstone	1·60	1·60
		a. Horiz strip of 4. Nos. 3646/3649	5·75	5·75
3647	**2792**	97p. Robert Peel	1·60	1·60
3648	**2793**	97p. Charles Grey	1·60	1·60
3649	**2794**	97p. William Pitt the Younger	1·60	1·60
Set of 8			10·00	9·50
Set of 2 Gutter strips of 4			20·00	
First Day Cover (Tallents House)				11·00
Presentation Pack (PO Pack No. 503)			11·00	
PHQ Cards (set of 8) (394)			3·25	11·50

Nos. 3642/3645 and 3646/3649 were each printed together, *se-tenant*, as horizontal strips of four stamps in sheets of 48 (2 panes 4×6).

2795 Collecting the Christmas Tree

2796 Posting Christmas Cards

2797 Collecting the Christmas Tree

2798 Posting Christmas Cards

2799 Building a Snowman

2800 Carol Singing

2801 Ice Skating

2014 (4 Nov). Christmas. Illustrations by Andrew Bannecker. Multicoloured One centre band (No. 3650) or two bands (others)
(a) Self-adhesive. Die-cut perf 14½×15.

3650	**2795**	(2nd) Collecting the Christmas Tree	90	90
3651	**2796**	(1st) Posting Christmas Cards	1·20	1·00
3652	**2797**	(2nd Large) Collecting the Christmas Tree	1·25	1·10
3653	**2798**	(1st Large) Posting Christmas Cards	1·70	1·40
3654	**2799**	£1·28 Building a Snowman	2·00	2·00
3655	**2800**	£1·47 Carol Singing	2·50	2·50
3656	**2801**	£2·15 Ice Skating	3·25	3·25
Set of 7			11·50	11·00
First Day Cover (Tallents House)				14·00
Presentation Pack (PO Pack No. 504)			13·00	
PHQ Cards (set of 8) (395)			3·25	20·00

(b) Ordinary gum. Perf 14½×15.

MS3657 156×74 mm. Nos. 3650/3656	11·50	11·00
First Day Cover (Tallents House)		14·00

The 2nd class, 1st class, £1·28 and £1·47 stamps were also issued in sheets of 20 containing 8×2nd class, 8×1st class, 2×£1·28 and 2×£1·47 stamps, each stamp accompanied by a *se-tenant* label.

Separate sheets of 20×2nd, 20×1st, 10×1st, 10×£1·28 and 10×£1·47 were available with personal photographs.

The eight PHQ cards show the seven individual stamps and the complete miniature sheet.

Year Pack

2014 (4 Nov). Comprises Nos. 3552/3569, **MS**3578/3594, **MS**3601/3624, 3626/3631, 3635/3656.

CP3657a	Year Pack (Pack No. 505) (sold for £86)		£130

Post Office Yearbook

2014 (4 Nov). Comprises Nos. 3552/3569, **MS**3578/3594, **MS**3601/3624, 3626/3631, 3635/3656.

YB3657a	Yearbook (sold for £106)		£160

Miniature Sheet Collection

2014 (4 Nov). Comprises Nos. **MS**3578, **MS**3601, **MS**3608, **MS**3641 and **MS**3657.

MS3657a Miniature Sheet Collection (sold for £23)	30·00	

2802 The White Rabbit

2803 Down the Rabbit Hole

2804 Drink Me

2805 The White Rabbit's House

2806 The Cheshire Cat   **2807** A Mad Tea Party

2808 The Queen of Hearts   **2809** The Game of Croquet

2810 Alice's Evidence   **2811** A Pack of Cards

2015 (6 Jan). Alice in Wonderland. Multicoloured One phosphor band at right (2nd) or two phosphor bands (others).

(a) Ordinary gum. Perf 14½.

3658	2802	(2nd) The White Rabbit	90	90
		a. Vert pair. Nos. 3658/3659	1·75	1·75
3659	2803	(2nd) Down the Rabbit Hole	90	90
3660	2804	(1st) Drink Me	1·20	1·00
		a. Vert pair. Nos. 3660/3661	2·40	2·00
3661	2805	(1st) The White Rabbit's House	1·20	1·00
3662	2806	81p. The Cheshire Cat	1·50	1·50
		a. Vert pair. Nos. 3662/3663	3·00	3·00
3663	2807	81p. A Mad Tea Party	1·50	1·50
3664	2808	£1·28 The Queen of Hearts	2·50	2·50
		a. Vert pair. Nos. 3664/3665	5·00	5·00
3665	2809	£1·28 The Game of Croquet	2·50	2·50
3666	2810	£1·47 Alice's Evidence	3·25	3·25
		a. Vert pair. Nos. 3666/3667	6·50	6·50
3667	2811	£1·47 A Pack of Cards	3·25	3·25
Set of 10			16·75	16·50
Set of 5 Gutter Strips of 4			35·00	
First Day Cover (Tallents House)				17·50
Presentation Pack (PO Pack No. 506)			25·00	
PHQ Cards (Set of 10) (396)			5·00	18·00

(b) Self-adhesive. Die-cut perf 14½.

3668	2804	(1st) Drink Me	5·00	5·00
3669	2805	(1st) The White Rabbit's House	5·00	5·00

Nos. 3658/3659, 3660/3661, 3662/3663, 3664/3665 and 3666/3667 were each printed together, *se-tenant*, as vertical pairs in sheets of 60 (2 panes 5×6).

Nos. 3658/3667 commemorate the 150th anniversary of the Publication of *Alice's Adventures in Wonderland* by Lewis Carroll.

Nos. 3668/3669 were only issued in stamp booklets containing Nos. 3668/3669 and 1st vermilion stamps×4 and originally sold for £3·72

2812 Happy Birthday (NB Studio)

2813 Well Done (Webb & Webb Design Ltd)

2814 Wedding (Caroline Gardner Ltd)

2815 Love (Rebecca Sutherland)

2816 Mum (The Chase)

2817 New Baby (NB Studio)

2818 Grandparent (NB Studio)

2819 Dad (Webb & Webb Design Ltd)

2015 (20 Jan). Smilers (5th series). Multicoloured Two phosphor bands.

(a) Self-adhesive booklet stamps. Die-cut perf 14½×14 (with one elliptical hole in each vert side).

3670	2812	(1st) Happy Birthday	1·90	1·90
3671	2813	(1st) Well Done	2·75	2·75
3672	2814	(1st) Wedding	1·90	1·90
3673	2815	(1st) Love	1·90	1·90
3674	2816	(1st) Mum	2·75	2·75
3675	2817	(1st) New Baby	1·90	1·90
3676	2818	(1st) Grandparent	2·75	2·75
3677	2819	(1st) Dad	2·75	2·75
Set of 8			15·00	15·00

(b) Ordinary gum. Perf 14½×14 (with one elliptical hole in each vert side).

MS3678 134×70 mm. As Nos. 3670/3677	10·00	10·00
First Day Cover (Tallents House)		10·00
Presentation Pack (PO Pack No. M23)	12·00	
PHQ Cards (set of 9) (D34)	6·75	25·00

Nos. 3670/3677 were issued in booklets of 12 originally sold for £7·44.

Nos. 3670/3677 were also issued in sheets of 20 with *se-tenant* greetings labels printed in lithography.

Sheets of 20 stamps of the same design were available with personal photographs.

The complete miniature sheet is shown on one of the nine PHQ cards with the others depicting individual stamps.

2820 Colossus, World's First Electronic Digital Computer

2821 World Wide Web, Revolutionary Global Communications System

2822 Cats Eyes, Light-reflecting Road Safety Innovation

2823 Fibre Optics, Pioneering Rapid-data-transfer Technology

2824 Stainless Steel, Non-corrosive, Versatile, 100% Recyclable Alloy

2825 Carbon Fibre, High-strength, Lightweight, Composite Material

2826 DNA Sequencing, Revolution in Understanding the Genome

2827 i-LIMB, Bionic Hand with Individually Powered Digits

2015 (19 Feb). Inventive Britain. Multicoloured Two phosphor bands. Perf 14½.

3679	**2820**	(1st) Colossus	1·20	1·00
		a. Horiz pair. Nos. 3679/3680	2·40	2·00
3680	**2821**	(1st) World Wide Web	1·20	1·00
3681	**2822**	81p. Cats eyes	1·10	1·10
		a. Horiz pair. Nos. 3681/3682	2·25	2·25
3682	**2823**	81p. Fibre Optics	1·10	1·10
3683	**2824**	£1·28 Stainless Steel	1·75	1·75
		a. Horiz pair. Nos. 3683/3684	3·75	3·75
3684	**2825**	£1·28 Carbon Fibre	1·75	1·75
3685	**2826**	£1·47 DNA Sequencing	2·25	2·25
		a. Horiz pair. Nos. 3685/3686	4·50	4·50
3686	**2827**	£1·47 i-LIMB	2·25	2·25
Set of 8			11·50	11·25
Set of 4 Gutter Blocks of 4			23·00	
First Day Cover (Tallents House)				15·50
Presentation Pack (PO Pack No. 507)			13·50	
PHQ Cards (set of 8) (397)			4·00	17·00

Nos. 3679/3680, 3681/3682, 3683/3684 and 3685/3686 were each printed together, *se-tenant*, as horizontal pairs in sheets of 60 (2 panes 6×5).

2828 Tarr Steps, River Barle

2829 Row Bridge, Mosedale Beck

2830 Pulteney Bridge, River Avon

2831 Craigellachie Bridge, River Spey

2832 Menai Suspension Bridge, Menai Strait

2833 High Level Bridge, River Tyne

2834 Royal Border Bridge, River Tweed

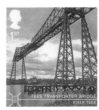

2835 Tees Transporter Bridge, River Tees

2836 Humber Bridge, River Humber

2837 Peace Bridge, River Foyle

2015 (5 Mar). Bridges. Multicoloured Two phosphor bands. Perf 14½×14.

3687	**2828**	(1st) Tarr Steps, River Barle	1·20	1·00
		a. Horiz strip of 5. Nos. 3687/3691	5·25	4·50
3688	**2829**	(1st) Row Bridge, Mosedale Beck	1·20	1·00
3689	**2830**	(1st) Pulteney Bridge, River Avon	1·20	1·00
3690	**2831**	(1st) Craigellachie Bridge, River Spey	1·20	1·00
3691	**2832**	(1st) Menai Suspension Bridge, Menai Strait	1·20	1·00
3692	**2833**	(1st) High Level Bridge, River Tyne	1·20	1·00
		a. Horiz strip of 5. Nos. 3692/3696	5·25	4·50
3693	**2834**	(1st) Royal Border Bridge, River Tweed	1·20	1·00
3694	**2835**	(1st) Tees Transporter Bridge, River Tees	1·20	1·00
3695	**2836**	(1st) Humber Bridge, River Humber	1·20	1·00
3696	**2837**	(1st) Peace Bridge, River Foyle	1·20	1·00
Set of 10			10·50	9·00
Set of 2 Gutter Strips of 10			21·00	
Set of 2 Traffic Light Gutter Strips of 10			26·00	
First Day Cover (Tallents House)				11·50
Presentation Pack (PO Pack No. 508)			11·50	
PHQ Cards (set of 10) (398)			5·00	12·50

Nos. 3687/3691 and 3692/3696 were each printed together, *se-tenant*, as horizontal strips of five stamps in sheets of 50 (2 panes 5×5).

2838 Spike Milligan

2839 The Two Ronnies

2840 Billy Connolly

2841 Morecambe and Wise

2842 Norman Wisdom

2843 Lenny Henry

2844 Peter Cook and Dudley Moore

2845 Monty Python

2846 French and Saunders

2847 Victoria Wood

2015 (1 Apr). Comedy Greats. Multicoloured Two phosphor bands.

(a) Ordinary gum. Perf 14.

3697	**2838**	(1st) Spike Milligan	1·20	1·00
		a. Horiz strip of 5. Nos. 3697/3701	5·25	4·50
3698	**2839**	(1st) The Two Ronnies	1·20	1·00
3699	**2840**	(1st) Billy Connolly	1·20	1·00
3700	**2841**	(1st) Morecambe and Wise	1·20	1·00
3701	**2842**	(1st) Norman Wisdom	1·20	1·00
3702	**2843**	(1st) Lenny Henry	1·20	1·00
		a. Horiz strip of 5. Nos. 3702/3706	5·25	4·50
3703	**2844**	(1st) Peter Cook and Dudley Moore	1·20	1·00
3704	**2845**	(1st) Monty Python	1·20	1·00
3705	**2846**	(1st) French and Saunders	1·20	1·00
3706	**2847**	(1st) Victoria Wood	1·20	1·00
Set of 10			10·50	9·00
Set of 2 Gutter Strips of 10			21·00	
First Day Cover (Tallents House)				11·50
Presentation Pack (PO Pack No. 509)			11·50	
PHQ Cards (set of 10) (399)			5·00	12·50

(b) Self-adhesive. Die-cut perf 14.

3707	**2842**	(1st) Norman Wisdom	5·50	5·50
3708	**2841**	(1st) Morecambe and Wise	5·50	5·50

Nos. 3697/3701 and 3702/3706 were each printed together, se-tenant, as horizontal strips of five stamps in sheets of 50 (2 panes 5×5).

Nos. 3707/3708 were issued in stamp booklets containing No. 3707/3708 and 1st vermilion stamps×4 and originally sold for £3·72.

2848 Penny Black

2849 Penny Black and 1840 2d. blue

2015 (6 May). 175th Anniversary of the Penny Black. Multicoloured Two phosphor bands.

(a) Self-adhesive booklet stamps. Die-cut perf 14½×14 (with one elliptical hole in each vert side).

3709	**2848**	(1st) Penny Black	2·00	2·00

(b) Ordinary gum. Perf 14½×14 (with one elliptical hole in each vert side).

MS3710 156×74 mm. **2849** (1st) Penny Black×2; (1st) 1840 2d. blue×2			3·50	3·75
First Day Cover (Tallents House)				4·75
Presentation Pack (PO Pack No. 510)			4·25	
PHQ Cards (set of 3) (400)			1·50	4·00

No. 3709 was issued in booklets of six.

Designs as No. 3709 and (1st) Twopenny Blue as within No. **MS**3710 but self-adhesive were also issued in sheets of 20, containing ten 1st class Penny Black and ten 1st class Twopenny Blue, each stamp accompanied by a se-tenant label. These sheets were printed in lithography.

Sheets of ten or 20 1st Penny Black were available with personal photographs.

The three PHQ cards show the two individual stamps and the complete miniature sheet.

See also Nos. 3806/3809, 4331 and **MS**4355.

2850 Poppies (Howard Hodgkin)

2851 All the Hills and Vales Along (Charles Hamilton Sorley)

2852 Rifleman Kulbir Thapa

2853 The Kensingtons at Laventie (Eric Kennington)

2854 A British Soldier visits his Comrade's Grave

2855 London Irish Rifles' Football from Loos

2015 (14 May). Centenary of the First World War (2nd issue). Multicoloured. Two phosphor bands. Perf 14½.

3711	**2850**	(1st) Poppies	1·20	1·00
3712	**2851**	(1st) All the Hills and Vales Along	1·20	1·00
3713	**2852**	(1st) Rifleman Kulbir Thapa	1·20	1·00
3714	**2853**	£1·52 The Kensingtons at Laventie	2·40	2·40
3715	**2854**	£1·52 A British Soldier visits his Comrade's Grave on the Cliffs	2·40	2·40
3716	**2855**	£1·52 London Irish Rifles' Football from Loos	2·40	2·40
Set of 6			9·50	9·00
Set of 6 Gutter Pairs			19·00	
First Day Cover (Tallents House)				12·00
Presentation Pack (PO Pack No. 511)			11·00	
PHQ Cards (set of 6) (401)			3·00	11·50

2588 Six
Poppies on
Barbed Wire
Fence

2015 (14 May). Centenary of the First World War. Premium Booklet stamp.
As No. 3414 but ordinary gum. Multicoloured Two phosphor bands.
Perf 14½×14 (with one elliptical hole in each vertical side).

| 3717 | **2588** | (1st) Six Poppies on Barbed Wire Stems | 1·50 | 1·50 |

No. 3717 comes from the Centenary of the First World War premium
booklets, (2nd, 3rd, 4th and 5th issues), Nos. DY13, DY18, DY22 and DY26.

2856 Magna Carta 1215

2857 Simon de Montfort's Parliament, 1265

2858 Bill of Rights, 1689

2859 American Bill of Rights, 1791

2860 Universal Declaration of Human Rights,
1948

2861 Charter of the Commonwealth, 2013

2015 (2 June). 800th Anniversary of the *Magna Carta*. Multicoloured Two
phosphor bands. Perf 14½.

3718	**2856**	(1st) Magna Carta	1·20	1·00
3719	**2857**	(1st) Simon de Montfort's Parliament	1·20	1·00
3720	**2858**	£1·33 Bill of Rights	1·60	1·60
3721	**2859**	£1·33 American Bill of Rights	1·60	1·60
3722	**2860**	£1·52 Universal Declaration of Human Rights	3·00	3·00
3723	**2861**	£1·52 Charter of the Commonwealth	3·00	3·00
Set of 6			10·00	10·00
Set of 6 Gutter pairs			20·00	
First Day Cover (Tallents House)				12·00
Presentation Pack (PO Pack No. 512)			13·00	
PHQ Cards (set of 6) (402)			3·00	12·50

2862 The Defence of Hougoumont

2863 The Scots Greys during the Charge of the
Union Brigade

2864 The French Cavalry's Assault on Allied
Defensive Squares

2865 The Defence of La Haye Sainte by the
King's German Legion

2866 The Capture of Plancenoit by the Prussians

2867 The French Imperial Guard's Final Assault

2015 (18 June). Bicentenary of the Battle of Waterloo (1st issue). Multicoloured Two phosphor bands. Perf 14½.

3724	**2862**	(1st) The Defence of Hougoumont	1·20	1·00
3725	**2863**	(1st) The Scots Greys during the charge of the Union Brigade	1·20	1·00
3726	**2864**	£1 The French Cavalry's assault on Allied defensive Squares	1·40	1·40
3727	**2865**	£1 The Defence of La Haye Sainte by the King's German Legion	1·40	1·40
3728	**2866**	£1·52 The Capture of Plancenoit by the Prussians	2·50	2·50
3729	**2867**	£1·52 The French Imperial Guard's Final Assault	2·50	2·50
Set of 6			9·00	8·75
Set of 6 Gutter Pairs			18·00	
First Day Cover (Tallents House)				11·50
Presentation Pack (PO Pack No. 513) (Nos. 3724/3729 and **MS**3734)			17·00	
PHQ Cards (set of 11) (403)			5·50	22·00

The 11 PHQ cards depict the individual stamps, including those from No. **MS**3734, and the complete miniature sheet.

2868 15th Infantry Regiment, IV Corps, Prussian Army

2869 Light Infantry, King's German Legion, Anglo-Allied Army

2870 92nd Gordon Highlanders, Anglo-Allied Army

2871 Grenadiers, Imperial Guard, French Army

2872 Soldiers and Battle of Waterloo Map

2015 (18 June). Bicentenary of the Battle of Waterloo (2nd issue). Multicoloured Two phosphor bands. Perf 14.

3730	**2868**	(1st) 15th Infantry Regiment, IV Corps	1·50	1·50
3731	**2869**	(1st) Light Infantry, King's German Legion	1·50	1·50
3732	**2870**	£1·33 92nd Gordon Highlanders	1·75	1·75
3733	**2871**	£1·33 Grenadiers, Imperial Guard	1·75	1·75
Set of 4			6·00	6·00
MS3734 156×74 mm. **2872** Soldiers and Battle of Waterloo Map Nos. 3730/3733			6·00	6·00
First Day Cover (Tallents House)				7·50

Nos. 3730/3733 come from £14·47 Bicentenary of the Battle of Waterloo booklet, No. DY14, and No. **MS**3734.

2873 Battle of Britain

2015 (16 July). 75th Anniversary of the Battle of Britain. Multicoloured 'All-over' phosphor. Perf 14½×14.

MS3735 190×74 mm. **2873** (1st) Pilots scramble to their Hurricanes; (1st) Supermarine Spitfires of 610 Squadron, Biggin Hill, on patrol; (1st) Armourer Fred Roberts replaces ammunition boxes on Supermarine Spitfire; £1·33 Spotters of the Auxiliary Territorial Service looking for enemy aircraft; £1·33 Operations Room at Bentley Priory; £1·33 Pilots of 32 Squadron await orders, RAF Hawkinge, Kent ...... 8·25 ...... 8·25

First Day Cover (Tallents House) ...... 11·00
Presentation Pack (PO Pack No. 514) ...... 10·00
PHQ Cards (set of 7) (404) ...... 3·50 ...... 13·50

The seven PHQ cards show the six individual stamps and the complete miniature sheet.

See also Nos. 4071/4073.

2874 Scabious Bee (*Andrena hattorfiana*) on Field Scabious (*Knautia arvensis*)

2875 Great Yellow Bumblebee (*Bombus distinguendus*) on Bird's-foot Trefoil (*Lotus corniculatus*)

2876 Northern Colletes Bee (*Colletes floralis*) on Wild Carrot (*Daucus carota*)

2877 Bilberry Bumblebee (*Bombus monticola*) on Bilberry (*Vaccinium myrtillus*)

2878 Large Mason Bee (*Osmia xanthomelana*) on Horseshoe Vetch (*Hippocrepis comosa*)

2879 Potter Flower Bee (*Anthophora retusa*) on Ground Ivy (*Glechoma hederacea*)

2880 The Honey Bee

2015 (18 Aug). Bees. Multicoloured

(a) Ordinary gum. One centre band (No. 3736), two phosphor bands (Nos. 3737/3741) or phosphor background (No. **MS**3742). Perf 14×14½.

3736	**2874**	(2nd) Scabious Bee on Field Scabious	90	90
3737	**2875**	(1st) Great Yellow Bumblebee on Bird's-foot Trefoil	1·20	1·20
3738	**2876**	£1 Northern Colletes Bee on Wild Carrot	1·50	1·50
3739	**2877**	£1·33 Bilberry Bumblebee on Bilberry	1·75	1·75
3740	**2878**	£1·52 Large Mason Bee on Horseshoe Vetch	2·25	2·25
3741	**2879**	£2·25 Potter Flower Bee on Ground Ivy	3·75	3·75
Set of 6			10·00	10·00
Set of 6 Gutter Pairs			20·00	
First Day Cover (Tallents House)				13·50
Presentation Pack (PO Pack No. 515) (Nos. 3736/3741 and **MS**3743)			19·00	
PHQ Cards (set of 7) (405)			3·50	18·00

MS3742 191×74 mm. **2880** (1st) Waggle dance; (1st) Pollination; £1·33 Making honey; £1·33 Tending young .... 5·50 5·75

First Day Cover (Tallents House) .... 6·00

(b) Self-adhesive. Two phosphor bands. Die-cut perf 14×14½.

3743	**2875**	(1st) Great Yellow Bumblebee (*Bombus distinguendus*) on Bird's-foot Trefoil (*Lotus corniculatus*)	2·00	2·00

No. 3743 was issued in stamp booklets containing No. 3743×2 and 1st vermilion stamps×4 and originally sold for £3·78.

The seven PHQ cards depict the six individual stamps and the complete miniature sheet.

Nos. 3744/3746 are vacant.

2881 'Long to Reign Over Us'

2015 (9 Sept) Long to Reign Over Us (2nd issue). Multicoloured Two phosphor bands. Perf 14½×14 (with one elliptical hole in each vertical side) (Machin) or 14 (others).

MS3747 194×75 mm. **2881** Long to Reign Over Us (1st) William Wyon's City Medal depicting Queen Victoria; (1st) Portrait of Queen Elizabeth II from photograph by Dorothy Wilding; As No. U3747 (but printed gravure); £1·52 Badge of the House of Windsor depicting Round Tower of Windsor Castle; £1·52 Device from The Queen's Personal Flag ...... 8·00 8·00

First Day Cover (Tallents House) .... 10·00
Presentation Pack (PO Pack No. 516) ...... 3·00
PHQ Cards (set of 6) (406) ...... 3·00 12·00

Stamps from No. **MS**3747 all have an iridescent overprint reading LONG TO REIGN OVER US.

The PHQ cards depict the five individual stamps and the complete miniature sheet.

2882 Tackle

2883 Scrum

2884 Try

2885 Conversion

2886 Pass

2887 Drop Goal

2888 Ruck   **2889** Line-Out

2015 (18 Sept). Rugby World Cup. Multicoloured One centre band (Nos. 3748/3749) or two bands (others).

(a) Ordinary gum. Perf 14.

3748	**2882**	(2nd) Tackle	90	90
		a. Horiz pair. Nos. 3748/3749	1·75	1·75
3749	**2883**	(2nd) Scrum	90	90
3750	**2884**	(1st) Try	1·20	1·00
		a. Horiz pair. Nos. 3750/3751	2·40	2·00
3751	**2885**	(1st) Conversion	1·20	1·00
3752	**2886**	£1 Pass	1·50	1·50
		a. Horiz pair. Nos. 3752/3753	3·00	3·00
3753	**2887**	£1 Drop Goal	1·50	1·50
3754	**2888**	£1·52 Ruck	2·00	2·00
		a. Horiz pair. Nos. 3754/3755	4·00	4·00
3755	**2889**	£1·52 Line-Out	2·00	2·00
Set of 8			10·00	9·75
Set of 4 Gutter Blocks of 4			20·00	
First Day Cover (Tallents House)				12·50
Presentation Pack (PO Pack No. 517)			12·50	
PHQ Cards (set of 8) (407)			4·00	13·00

(b) Self-adhesive. Die-cut perf 14.

3756	**2884**	(1st) Try	4·00	4·00
3757	**2885**	(1st) Conversion	4·00	4·00

Nos. 3748/3749, 3750/3751, 3752/3753 and 3754/3755 were each printed together, *se-tenant*, as horizontal pairs in sheets of 60 (2 panes 6×5).

Nos. 3756/3757 were issued in stamp booklets containing Nos. 3756/3757 and 1st vermilion stamps×4 and originally sold for £3·78.

2890 Darth Vader   **2891** Yoda

2892 Obi-Wan Kenobi   **2893** Stormtrooper

2894 Han Solo   **2895** Rey

2896 Princess Leia

2897 The Emperor

2898 Luke Skywalker

2899 Boba Fett

2900 Finn

2901 Kylo Ren

2902 Star Wars

2015 (20 Oct). *Star Wars* (1st issue). Multicoloured Two phosphor bands and fluorescent emblems (Nos. 3758/3769) or 'All-over' phosphor (No. **MS**3770).

(a) Ordinary gum. Perf 14½.

3758	**2890**	(1st) Darth Vader	1·20	1·00
		a. Horiz strip of 6. Nos. 3758/3763	6·50	5·50
3759	**2891**	(1st) Yoda	1·20	1·00
3760	**2892**	(1st) Obi-Wan Kenobi	1·20	1·00
3761	**2893**	(1st) Stormtrooper	1·20	1·00
3762	**2894**	(1st) Han Solo	1·20	1·00
3763	**2895**	(1st) Rey	1·20	1·00
3764	**2896**	(1st) Princess Leia	1·20	1·00
		a. Horiz strip of 6. Nos. 3764/3769	6·50	5·50
3765	**2897**	(1st) The Emperor	1·20	1·00
3766	**2898**	(1st) Luke Skywalker	1·20	1·00
3767	**2899**	(1st) Boba Fett	1·20	1·00
3768	**2900**	(1st) Finn	1·20	1·00
3769	**2901**	(1st) Kylo Ren	1·20	1·00
Set of 12			13·00	11·00
Set of 2 Gutter Strips of 12			26·00	
First Day Cover (Tallents House)				14·00
Presentation Pack (PO Pack No. 518) (Nos. 3758/3769 and **MS**3770)			21·00	
PHQ Cards (set of 19) (408)			9·50	28·00

(b) Self-adhesive.

MS3770 204×75 mm. **2902** (1st) X-wing Starfighter (60×21 mm, perf 14½×14); (1st) TIE fighters (35×36 mm, perf 14); (1st) X-wing Starfighters (60×21 mm, perf 14½×14); (1st) AT-AT Walkers (41×30 mm, Perf 14); (1st) TIE fighters (27×37 mm, perf 14); (1st) *Millennium Falcon* (60×30 mm, perf 14½)   7·00   6·50

First Day Cover (Tallents House)   7·00

Nos. 3758/3763 and 3764/3769 were each printed together, *se-tenant*, as horizontal strips of six stamps in sheets of 60 (2 panes 6×5).

Nos. 3758/3769 were re-issued on 12 October 2017 with Nos. 4007/4014 in a sheet entitled *Star Wars. The Ultimate Collectors' Sheet* (No. **MS**4014a).

Designs as Nos. 3758/3759 and 3761/3762 but self-adhesive were issued in sheets of ten with *se-tenant* labels, each sheet containing Nos. 3758/3759, each×3, and Nos. 3761/3762, each×2.

The 19 PHQ cards depict the individual stamps including those from No. **MS**3770 and the complete miniature sheet.

2903 The Journey to Bethlehem   **2904** The Nativity   **2905** The Journey to Bethlehem

2906 The Nativity   **2907** The Animals of the Nativity   **2908** The Shepherds

2909 The Three Wise Men   **2910** The Annunciation

2015 (3 Nov). Christmas. Multicoloured One centre band (No. 3771) or two bands (others).

(a) Self-adhesive. Die-cut perf 14½×15..

3771	**2903**	(2nd) The Journey to Bethlehem	90	90
3772	**2904**	(1st) The Nativity.	1·20	1·00
3773	**2905**	(2nd Large) The Journey to Bethlehem	1·25	1·10
3774	**2906**	(1st Large) The Nativity	1·70	1·40
3775	**2907**	£1·00 The Animals of the Nativity	1·75	1·75
3776	**2908**	£1·33 The Shepherds	2·10	2·10
3777	**2909**	£1·52 The Three Wise Men	2·50	2·50
3778	**2910**	£2·25 The Annunciation	3·50	3·50
Set of 8			13·25	12·75
First Day Cover (Tallents House)				16·75
Presentation Pack (PO Pack No. 519)			15·00	
PHQ Cards (set of 9) (409)			4·50	26·00

(b) Ordinary gum. Perf 14½×15..

MS3779 190×74 mm. As Nos. 3771/3778   13·25   12·75

First Day Cover (Tallents House)   16·75

The 2nd class, 1st class, £1, £1·33, £1·52 and £2·25 stamps were also issued in sheets of 20, containing 8×2nd class, 8×1st class, 1×£1, 1×£1·33, 1×£1·52 and 1×£2·25 stamps, each stamp accompanied by a *se-tenant* label with a verse from the *King James Bible*. These sheets were printed in lithography.

The nine PHQ cards show the eight individual stamps and the complete miniature sheet.

Year Pack

2015 (3 Nov). Comprises Nos. 3658/3667, **MS**3678/3706, **MS**3710/3716, 3718/3729. **MS**3734, **MS**3735/**MS**3742, **MS**3747/3755 and 3758/3778
CP3779a   Year Pack (Pack No. 520) (*sold for £117*)   £170

Post Office Yearbook

2015 (3 Nov). Comprises Nos. 3658/3667, **MS**3678/3706, **MS**3710/3729, **MS**3734, **MS**3735/**MS**3742, **MS**3747/3755 and 3758/3778
YB3779a   Yearbook (*sold for £137*)   £190

Miniature Sheet Collection

2015 (3 Nov). Comprises Nos. **MS**3678, **MS**3710, **MS**3734, **MS**3735, **MS**3742, **MS**3747, **MS**3770 and **MS**3779
MS3779a Minature Sheet Collection (*sold for £41*)   55·00

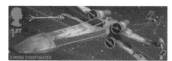

2911 X-wing Starfighter

2912 AT-AT Walkers

2913 TIE Fighters

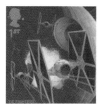

2914 TIE Fighters

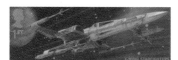

2915 X-wing Starfighters

2916 *Millennium Falcon*

2015 (17 Dec). *Star Wars* (2nd issue). Self-adhesive. Multicoloured 'All-over' phosphor. Die-cut perf 14½×14 (Nos. 3780, 3784), 14 (Nos. 3781/3783) or 14½ (No. 3785).

3780	**2911**	(1st) X-wing Starfighter	1·25	1·25
3781	**2912**	(1st) AT-AT Walkers	1·25	1·25
3782	**2913**	(1st) TIE fighters	1·25	1·25
3783	**2914**	(1st) TIE fighters	1·25	1·25
3784	**2915**	(1st) X-wing Starfighters	1·25	1·25
3785	**2916**	(1st) *Millennium Falcon*	1·25	1·25
Set of 6			6·75	6·75

Nos. 3780/3785 were only issued in £16·99 *Star Wars* premium booklet, No. DY15, or No. **MS**3770.

2917 Union
Flag

2015 (17 Dec). *Star Wars* (3rd issue). As No. 2570 but ordinary gum. Multicoloured Two phosphor bands. Perf 14½×14 (with one elliptical hole in each vert side).

3786	**2917**	(1st) Union Flag	1·50	1·50

No. 3786 comes from booklet pane No. U3150l from £16·99 *Star Wars* premium booklet, No. DY15.

2918 Entering the Antarctic Ice, December 1914

2919 *Endurance* Frozen in Pack Ice, January 1915

2920 Striving to Free *Endurance*, February 1915

2921 Trapped in a Pressure Crack, October 1915

2922 Patience Camp, December 1915–April 1916

2923 Safe Arrival at Elephant Island, April 1916

2924 Setting out for South Georgia, April 1916

2925 Rescue of *Endurance* Crew, August 1916

2016 (7 Jan). Shackleton and the *Endurance* Expedition. Multicoloured. Two phosphor bands. Perf 14×14½.

3787	**2918**	(1st) Entering the Antarctic Ice	1·20	1·00
		a. Horiz pair. Nos. 3787/3788	2·40	2·00
3788	**2919**	(1st) *Endurance* Frozen in Pack Ice	1·20	1·00
3789	**2920**	£1 Striving to Free *Endurance*	1·50	1·50
		a. Horiz pair. Nos. 3789/3790	3·00	3·00
3790	**2921**	£1 Trapped in a Pressure Crack	1·50	1·50
3791	**2922**	£1·33 Patience Camp	1·75	1·75
		a. Horiz pair. Nos. 3791/3792	3·75	3·75
3792	**2923**	£1·33 Safe Arrival at Elephant Island	1·75	1·75
3793	**2924**	£1·52 Setting out for South Georgia	2·25	2·25
		a. Horiz pair. Nos. 3793/3794	4·50	4·50
3794	**2925**	£1·52 Rescue of *Endurance* Crew	2·25	2·25
Set of 8			12·25	12·00
Set of 4 Gutter blocks of 4			24·50	
First Day Cover (Tallents House)				16·00
Presentation Pack (PO Pack No. 521)			15·00	
PHQ Cards (set of 8) (410)			4·00	15·00

Nos. 3787/3788, 3789/3790, 3791/3792 and 3793/3794 were each printed together, *se-tenant*, as horizontal pairs in sheets of 60 (2 panes 6×5).

2926 Sir Brian Tuke, Master of the Posts

2927 *Mail Packet off Eastbourne* (Captain Victor Howes)

2928 Penfold Pillar Box

2929 River Post

2930 Mail Coach

2931 Medway Mail Centre

2016 (17 Feb). Royal Mail 500 (1st issue). Multicoloured. Two phosphor bands. Perf 14½×14 (Nos.3795/3800) or 14 (No. **MS**3801)

3795	**2926**	(1st) Sir Brian Tuke	1·20	1·00
3796	**2927**	(1st) *Mail Packet off Eastbourne*	1·20	1·00
3797	**2928**	(1st) Penfold Pillar Box	1·20	1·00
3798	**2929**	£1·52 River Post	2·50	2·50
3799	**2930**	£1·52 Mail Coach	2·50	2·50
3800	**2931**	£1·52 Medway Mail Centre	2·50	2·50
Set of 6			10·00	9·50
Set of 6 Gutter Pairs			20·00	
Set of 6 Traffic light Gutter pairs (two stamps only in each pair)			21·00	
First Day Cover (Tallents House)				12·00
Presentation Pack (PO Pack No. 522) (Nos. 3795/3800 and **MS**3801)			18·00	
PHQ Cards (set of 11) (411)			5·50	24·00

2932 Classic GPO Posters
MS3801 125×89 mm. **2932** Classic GPO Posters (1st) 'QUICKEST WAY BY AIR MAIL' (Edward McKnight Kauffer, 1935); (1st) 'ADDRESS your letters PLAINLY' (Hans Schleger, 1942); £1·33 'pack your parcels carefully' (Hans Unger, 1950); £1·33 'STAMPS IN BOOKS SAVE TIME' (Harry Stevens, 1960)

		7·00	7·25

First Day Cover (Tallents House) 7·50

Nos. 3795/**MS**3801 commemorate 500 years of a regular, organised postal service.

The complete miniature sheet is shown on one of the 11 PHQ cards with the others depicting individual stamps including those from the miniature sheet.

2933 'QUICKEST WAY BY AIR MAIL' (Edward McKnight Kauffer, 1935)

2934 'ADDRESS your letters PLAINLY' (Hans Schleger, 1942)

2935 'STAMPS IN BOOKS SAVE TIME' (Harry Stevens, 1960)

2936 'pack your parcels carefully' (Hans Unger, 1950)

2016 (17 Feb). Royal Mail 500 (2nd issue). Multicoloured Perf 14.

3802	**2933**	(1st) 'QUICKEST WAY BY AIR MAIL'	1·75	1·75
3803	**2934**	(1st) 'ADDRESS your letters PLAINLY'	1·75	1·75
3804	**2935**	£1·33 'STAMPS IN BOOKS SAVE TIME'	1·75	1·75
3805	**2936**	£1·33 'pack your parcels carefully'	1·75	1·75
Set of 4			6·25	6·25

Nos. 3802/3805 come from No. **MS**3801 and £16·36 500 years of Royal Mail premium booklets, No. DY16, which was issued on 18 February 2016.

2937 Penny Red

2016 (18 Feb). 175th Anniversary of the Penny Red. Self-adhesive. Multicoloured Two phosphor bands. Die-cut perf 14½×14 (with one elliptical hole in each vert side).

3806	**2937**	(1st) Penny Red	1·50	1·50

No. 3806 comes from booklets of six stamps.

No. 3806 was also issued in sheets of 20 with attached labels showing the Rainbow Trials from which the Penny Red evolved. These sheets were printed in lithography.

Sheets of ten or 20 of these Penny Red stamps were available from Royal Mail with personal photographs on the labels.

2848 Penny Black

2938 Two Pence Blue

2016 (18 Feb). Royal Mail 500 (3rd issue). Multicoloured Two phosphor bands. 14½×14 (with one elliptical hole in each vert side).

3807	**2848**	(1st) Penny Black	1·75	1·75
3808	**2937**	(1st) Penny Red	1·50	1·50
3809	**2938**	(1st) 2d. Blue	1·50	1·50

Nos. 3807/3809 come from £16·36 500 Years of Royal Mail premium booklet, No. DY16.

2939 Nicholas Winton (1909–2015)

2940 Sue Ryder (1924–2000)

2941 John Boyd Orr (1880–1971)

2942 Eglantyne Jebb (1876–1928)

2943 Joseph Rowntree (1836–1925)

2944 Josephine Butler (1828–1906)

2016 (15 Mar). British Humanitarians. Multicoloured Two phosphor bands. Perf 14½.

3810	**2939**	(1st) Nicholas Winton	1·20	1·00
		a. Horiz strip of 3. Nos. 3810/3812	3·50	3·00
3811	**2940**	(1st) Sue Ryder	1·20	1·00
3812	**2941**	(1st) John Boyd Orr	1·20	1·00
3813	**2942**	£1·33 Eglantyne Jebb	2·00	2·00
		a. Horiz strip of 3. Nos. 3813/3815	6·00	6·00
3814	**2943**	£1·33 Joseph Rowntree	2·00	2·00
3815	**2944**	£1·33 Josephine Butler	2·00	2·00
Set of 6			8·75	8·25
Set of 2 Gutter Strips of 6			17·50	
First Day Cover (Tallents House)				11·00
Presentation Pack (PO Pack No. 523)			10·00	
PHQ Cards (set of 6) (412)			3·00	11·00

Nos. 3810/3812 and 3813/3815 were each printed together, *se-tenant*, as horizontal strips of three stamps in sheets of 60 (2 panes 6×5).

2945 'to thine own self be true' (*Hamlet*)

2946 'cowards die many times before their deaths. The valiant never taste of death but once.' (*Julius Caesar*)

2947 'Love is a smoke made with the fume of sighs' (*Romeo and Juliet*)

2948 'The fool doth think he is wise, but the wise man knows himself to be a fool.' (*As You Like It*)

2949 'There was a star danced, and under that was I born. (*Much Ado About Nothing*)

2950 'But if the while I think on thee, dear friend, all losses are restored and sorrows end.' (*Sonnet 30*)

2951 'LOVE comforteth like sunshine after rain' (*Venus and Adonis*)

2952 'We are such stuff as dreams are made on; and our little life is rounded with a sleep.' (*The Tempest*)

2953 'Life's but a walking shadow, a poor player That struts and frets his hour upon the stage' (*Macbeth*)

2954 'I wasted time, and now doth time waste me' (*Richard II*)

2016 (5 Apr). 400th Death Anniversary of William Shakespeare. Multicoloured Two phosphor bands. Perf 14½.

3816	**2945**	(1st) 'to thine own self be true'	1·20	1·00
		a. Horiz strip of 5. Nos. 3816/3820	5·25	4·50
3817	**2946**	(1st) 'cowards die many times before their deaths. The valiant never taste of death but once.'	1·20	1·00
3818	**2947**	(1st) 'Love is a smoke made with the fume of sighs'	1·20	1·00
3819	**2948**	(1st) 'The fool doth think he is wise, but the wise man knows himself to be a fool.'	1·20	1·00
3820	**2949**	(1st) 'There was a star danced, and under that was I born'	1·20	1·00
3821	**2950**	(1st) 'But if the while I think on thee, dear friend, all losses are restored and sorrows end.'	1·20	1·00
		a. Horiz strip of 5. Nos. 3821/3825	5·25	4·50
3822	**2951**	(1st) 'LOVE comforteth like sunshine after rain'	1·20	1·00
3823	**2952**	(1st) 'We are such stuff as dreams are made on; and our little life is rounded with a sleep.'	1·20	1·00
3824	**2953**	(1st) 'Life's but a walking shadow, a poor player That struts and frets his hour upon the stage'	1·20	1·00

3825	**2954**	(1st) 'I wasted time, and now doth time waste me' (Richard II)	1·20	1·00
		Set of 10	10·50	9·00
		Set of 2 Gutter Strips of 10	21·00	
		First Day Cover (Tallents House)		12·00
		Presentation Pack (PO Pack No. 524)	11·50	
		PHQ Cards (set of 10) (413)	5·00	12·00

Nos. 3816/3820 and 3821/3825 were each printed together, *se-tenant*, as horizontal strips of five stamps in sheets of 50 (2 panes 5×5).

2955 Princess Elizabeth and her Father the Duke of York (later King George VI), *circa* 1930

2956 Queen Elizabeth II at State Opening of Parliament, 2012

2957 Queen Elizabeth II with Prince Charles and Princess Anne, 1952

2958 Queen Elizabeth II on Visit to New Zealand, 1977

2959 Queen Elizabeth II and Duke of Edinburgh, 1957

2960 Queen Elizabeth II with Nelson Mandela, 1996

2961 Prince Charles, Queen Elizabeth II, Prince George and Prince William

2962 Prince Charles

2963 Queen Elizabeth II

2964 Prince George

2965 Prince William

2016 (21 Apr–9 June). 90th Birthday of Queen Elizabeth II. Multicoloured Two phosphor bands (Nos. 3826/3831) or 'all-over' phosphor (Nos. **MS**3832, 3833/38336).

(a) Ordinary gum. Perf 14×14½ (Nos. 3826/3831) or 14 (No. **MS**3832).

3826	**2955**	(1st) Princess Elizabeth and her Father the Duke of York	1·20	1·00
		a. Horiz strip of 3. Nos. 3826/3828	3·50	3·00
3827	**2956**	(1st) Queen Elizabeth II at State Opening of Parliament	1·20	1·00
3828	**2957**	(1st) Queen Elizabeth II with Prince Charles and Princess Anne	1·20	1·00
3829	**2958**	£1·52 Queen Elizabeth II on Visit to New Zealand	2·25	2·25
		a. Horiz strip of 3. Nos. 3829/38231	6·75	6·75
3830	**2959**	£1·52 Queen Elizabeth II and Duke of Edinburgh	2·25	2·25
3831	**2960**	£1·52 Queen Elizabeth II with Nelson Mandela	2·25	2·25
		Set of 6	9·25	8·75
		Set of 2 Gutter Strips of 6	18·50	
		First Day Cover (Tallents House)		11·50
		Presentation Pack (PO Pack No. 525) (Nos. 3826/3831 and **MS**3832)	14·50	
		PHQ Cards (set of 11) (414)	5·50	19·00

MS3832 189×75 mm. **2961** (1st×4) Prince Charles, Queen Elizabeth II, Prince George and Prince William ... 4·50 ... 4·25

First Day Cover (Tallents House) ... 4·75

(b) Self-adhesive. Die-cut perf 14.

3833	**2962**	(1st) Prince Charles	5·75	5·75
3834	**2963**	(1st) Queen Elizabeth II	5·75	5·75
3835	**2964**	(1st) Prince George (9.6.16)	5·75	5·75
3836	**2965**	(1st) Prince William (9.6.16)	2·00	2·00
		Set of 4	14·00	14·00

Nos. 3826/3828 and 3829/3831 were each printed together, *se-tenant*, as horizontal strips of three stamps in sheets of 60 (2 panes 6×5)

Nos. 3833/3836 were issued in stamp booklets either Nos. 3833/3834 or Nos. 3835/3836 and 1st bright lilac stamp×4 each booklet originally sold for £3·84 each.

2966 Animail

2016 (17 May). Animail. Sheet 203×74 mm. Multicoloured 'All-over' phosphor. Die-cut and die-cut perf 14.

MS3837 **2966** Animail (1st) Woodpecker; (1st) Snake; £1·05 Chimpanzee; £1·05 Bat; £1·33 Orangutan; £1·33 Koala ... 8·50 ... 8·75

First Day Cover (Tallents House) ... 11·00

Presentation Pack (PO Pack No. 526) ... 10·00

PHQ Cards (set of 7) (415) ... 3·50 ... 15·00

The seven PHQ cards show the six individual stamps and the complete miniature sheet.

2967 *Battlefield Poppy* (Giles Revell)

2968 'Your battle wounds are scars upon my heart' (poem *To My Brother,* Vera Brittain)

2969 Munitions Worker Lottie Meade

2970 *Travoys Arriving with Wounded at a Dressing-Station at Smol, Macedonia, September 1916* (Stanley Spencer)

2971 Thiepval Memorial, Somme, France

2972 Captain A. C. Green's Battle of Jutland Commemorative Medal

2016 (21 June). Centenary of the First World War (3rd issue). Multicoloured Two phosphor bands. Perf 14½.

3838	**2967**	(1st) *Battlefield Poppy*	1·20	1·00
3839	**2968**	(1st) 'Your battle wounds are scars upon my heart'	1·20	1·00
3840	**2969**	(1st) Munitions Worker Lottie Meade	1·20	1·00
3841	**2970**	£1·52 *Travoys Arriving with Wounded at a Dressing-Station at Smol, Macedonia, September 1916*	2·50	2·50
3842	**2971**	£1·52 Thiepval Memorial, Somme, France	2·50	2·50
3843	**2972**	£1·52 Captain A. C. Green's Battle of Jutland Commemorative Medal	2·50	2·50
Set of 6			10·00	9·50
Set of 6 Gutter Pairs			20·00	
First Day Cover (Tallents House)				12·00
Presentation Pack (PO Pack No. 527) (Nos. 3838/3843 and **MS**3848)			18·00	
PHQ Cards (set of 11) (416)			5·50	26·00

2973 The Post Office Rifles

2974 Writing a Letter from the Western Front

2975 Delivering the Mail on the Home Front

2976 Home Depot at Regent's Park, London

2977 The Post Office at War, 1914–1918

2016 (21 June). Centenary of the First World War (3rd issue). Multicoloured Two phosphor bands Perf 14.

3844	**2973**	(1st) The Post Office Rifles	1·60	1·60
3845	**2974**	(1st) Writing a Letter from the Western Front	1·60	1·60
3846	**2975**	£1·33 Delivering the Mail on the Home Front	2·50	2·50
3847	**2976**	£1·33 Home Depot at Regent's Park, London	2·50	2·50
Set of 4			7·25	7·25
MS3848 156×74 mm. **2977** The Post Office at War, 1914–1918 Nos. 3844/3847			7·25	7·25
First Day Cover (Tallents House)				8·25

Nos. 3844/3847 were issued in the £16·49 Centenary of the First Wold War (3rd issue) booklet, No. DY18, and in No. **MS**3848.

2978 *The Piper at the Gates of Dawn* (1967)

2979 *Atom Heart Mother* (1970)

2980 *The Dark Side of the Moon* (1973)

2981 *Animals* (1977)

2982 *Wish You Were Here* (1975)

2983 *The Endless River* (2014)

2984 Pink Floyd on Stage

2016 (7 July). Pink Floyd. Multicoloured
(a) Album Covers. Self-adhesive. Two phosphor bands. Die-cut perf 14½.

3849	**2978**	(1st) *The Piper at the Gates of Dawn*		
		(1967)	1·20	1·00
3850	**2979**	(1st) *Atom Heart Mother* (1970)	1·20	1·00
3851	**2980**	(1st) *The Dark Side of the Moon* (1973)	1·20	1·00
3852	**2981**	£1·52 *Animals* (1977)	2·50	2·50
3853	**2982**	£1·52 *Wish You Were Here* (1975)	2·50	2·50
3854	**2983**	£1·52 *The Endless River* (2014)	2·50	2·50
Set of 6			10·00	9·50
First Day Cover (Tallents House)				12·00
Presentation Pack (PO Pack No. 528) (Nos. 3849/3854				
and **MS**3855)			18·00	
PHQ Cards (set of 11) (417)			5·50	24·00

(b) Pink Floyd on Stage. Ordinary gum. Phosphor frame. Perf 14½.
MS3855 202×74 mm. **2984** Pink Floyd on Stage (1st)
  UFO Club, 1966; (1st) The Dark Side of the Moon
  Tour, 1973; £1·52 The Wall Tour, 1981; £1·52 The
  Division Bell Tour, 1994   6·25   6·25
First Day Cover (Tallents House)   8·00

The right-hand edges of Nos. 3849/3854 are all cut around to show the vinyl disc protruding from the open edge of the album cover.

A *Dark Side of the Moon* maxi sheet containing No. 3851×10 was sold at £12·95, a premium of £6·55 over face value.

The 11 PHQ cards depicts the individual stamps including those from No. **MS**3855 and the complete miniature sheet.

2985 Peter Rabbit   **2986** Mrs Tiggy-Winkle

2987 Squirrel Nutkin   **2988** Jemima Puddle-Duck

2989 Tom Kitten   **2990** Benjamin Bunny

2016 (28 July). 150th Birth Anniversary of Beatrix Potter (writer, illustrator and conservationist) (1st issue). Multicoloured Two phosphor bands.
(a) Ordinary gum. Perf 14½×14.

3856	**2985**	(1st) Peter Rabbit.	1·20	1·00
		a. Horiz pair. Nos. 3856/3857	2·40	2·00
3857	**2986**	(1st) Mrs Tiggy-Winkle.	1·20	1·00
3858	**2987**	£1·33 Squirrel Nutkin	2·00	2·00
		a. Horiz pair. Nos. 3858/3859	4·00	4·00
3859	**2988**	£1·33 Jemima Puddle-Duck	2·00	2·00
3860	**2989**	£1·52 Tom Kitten	2·25	2·25
		a. Horiz pair. Nos. 3860/3861	4·50	4·50

3861	**2990**	£1·52 Benjamin Bunny	2·25	2·25
Set of 6			9·75	9·50
Set of 3 Gutter Pairs (two stamps only in each pair)			19·50	
Set of 3 Traffic Light Gutter Pairs (two stamps only in				
each pair)			21·00	
First Day Cover (Tallents House)				12·00
Presentation Pack (PO Pack No. 529) (Nos. 3856/3856				
and **MS**3868)			18·50	
PHQ Cards (set of 11) (418)			5·50	24·00

(b) Self-adhesive. Die-cut perf 14½×14.

3862	**2985**	(1st) Peter Rabbit	4·00	4·00
3863	**2986**	(1st) Mrs Tiggy-Winkle	4·00	4·00

Nos. 3856/3857, 3858/3859 and 3860/3861 were printed together, se-tenant, as horizontal pairs in sheets of 60 (2 panes 6×5).

Nos. 3862/3863 were issued in stamp booklets containing Nos. 3862/3862 and 1st bright lilac stamp×4 and originally sold for £3·84.

The 11 PHQ cards depict the ten individual stamps including those from No. **MS**3868 and the complete miniature sheet.

2991 Now run along, and   **2992** And then, feeling
don't get into mischief.   rather sick, he went to
                                 look for some parsley.

2993 But Peter, who was   **2994** He slipped
very naughty, ran straight   underneath the gate, and
away to Mr McGregor's   was safe at last.
garden, and squeezed
under the gate!

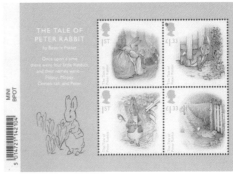

2995 Illustrations from *The Tale of Peter Rabbit*

2016 (28 July). 150th Birth Anniversary of Beatrix Potter (writer, illustrator and conservationist) (2nd issue). Multicoloured Two phosphor bands. Perf 14½.

3864	**2991**	(1st) Now run along, and don't get into		
		mischief.	2·25	2·25
3865	**2992**	(1st) And then, feeling rather sick, he		
		went to look for some parsley.	2·25	2·25
3866	**2993**	£1·33 But Peter, who was very		
		naughty, ran straight away to		
		Mr McGregor's garden, and		
		squeezed under the gate!	2·25	2·25
3867	**2994**	£1·33 He slipped underneath the gate,		
		and was safe at last.	2·25	2·25
Set of 4			8·25	8·25
MS3868 125×89 mm. **2995** Nos. 3864/3867 (The Tale				
of Peter Rabbit)			5·50	5·75
First Day Cover (Tallents House)				7·50

Nos. 3864/3867 were issued in £15·37 The Tale of Beatrix Potter booklet, DY19, and in No. **MS**3868.

2996 Blenheim Palace

2997 Longleat

2998 Compton Verney

2999 Highclere Castle

3000 Alnwick Castle

3001 Berrington Hall

3002 Stowe

3003 Croome Park

2016 (16 Aug). Landscape Gardens (300th Birth Anniversary of Capability Brown). Multicoloured One centre band (2nd) or two phosphor bands (others).

(a) Ordinary gum. Perf 14.

3869	**2996**	(2nd) Blenheim Palace	90	90
		a. Horiz pair. Nos. 3869/3870	1·80	1·80
3870	**2997**	(2nd) Longleat	90	90
3871	**2998**	(1st) Compton Verney	1·20	1·00
		a. Horiz pair. Nos. 3871/3872	2·40	2·00
3872	**2999**	(1st) Highclere Castle	1·20	1·00
3873	**3000**	£1·05 Alnwick Castle	1·50	1·50
		a. Horiz pair. Nos. 3873/3874	3·00	3·00
3874	**3001**	£1·05 Berrington Hall	1·50	1·50
3875	**3002**	£1·33 Stowe	2·00	2·00
		a. Horiz pair. Nos. 3875/3876	4·00	4·00
3876	**3003**	£1·33 Croome Park	2·00	2·00
Set of 8			10·00	10·00
Set of 4 Gutter Blocks of 4			20·00	
First Day Cover (Tallents House)				13·00
Presentation Pack (PO Pack No. 530)			13·00	
PHQ Cards (set of 8) (419)			4·00	12·00

(b) Self-adhesive. Die-cut perf 14.

3877	**2998**	(1st) Compton Verney	3·50	3·50
3878	**2999**	(1st) Highclere Castle	3·50	3·50

Nos. 3869/3870, 3871/3872, 3873/3874 and 3875/3876 were each printed together, se-tenant, as horizontal pairs in sheets of 60 (2 panes 6×5).

Nos. 3877/3878 were issued in stamp booklet, No. PM53, originally sold for £3·84.

Nos. 3877/3878 were issued in stamp booklets containing Nos. 3877/3878 and 1st bright lilac×4 and originally sold for £3·84.

3004 Fire Breaks Out in Bakery on Pudding Lane, Sunday 2nd September 1666

3005 The Fire Spreads Rapidly, Sunday 2nd September 1666

3006 Houses are Pulled, Monday 3rd September 1666

3007 As the Fire reaches St Paul's Citizens witness the Cathedral's Destruction, Tuesday 4th September 1666

3008 The Fire Dies Out, Wednesday 5th September 1666

3009 Christopher Wren develops Plans for the Regeneration of the City, Tuesday 11th September 1666

2016 (2 Sept). 350th Anniversary of the Great Fire of London. Multicoloured Two phosphor bands. Perf 14½.

3879	**3004**	(1st) Fire Breaks Out in Bakery on Pudding Lane	1·20	1·00
		a. Horiz pair. Nos. 3879/3880	2·40	2·00
3880	**3005**	(1st) The Fire Spreads Rapidly	1·20	1·00
3881	**3006**	£1·05 Houses are Pulled Down to Create Breaks	1·60	1·60
		a. Horiz pair. Nos. 3881/3882	3·25	3·25
3882	**3007**	£1·05 As the Fire reaches St Paul's Citizens witness the Cathedral's Destruction	1·60	1·60
3883	**3008**	£1·52 The Fire Dies Out	2·25	2·35
		a. Horiz pair. Nos. 3883/3884	4·50	4·50
3884	**3009**	£1·52 Christopher Wren develops Plans for the Regeneration of the City	2·25	2·35
Set of 6			9·25	9·25
Set of 3 Gutter Blocks of 4			18·50	
First Day Cover (Tallents House)				12·00
Presentation Pack (PO Pack No. 531)			11·00	
PHQ Cards (set of 6) (420)			3·00	11·00

Nos. 3879/3880, 3881/3882 and 3883/3884 were each printed together, se-tenant, as horizontal pairs in sheets of 60 (2 panes 6×5).

3010 Murder on the Orient Express

3011 *And Then There Were None*

3012 *The Mysterious Affair at Styles*

3013 *The Murder of Roger Ackroyd*

3014 *The Body in the Library*

3015 *A Murder is Announced*

2016 (15 Sept). 40th Death Anniversary of Agatha Christie (writer). Multicoloured Two phosphor bands. Perf 14½.

3885	**3010**	(1st) *Murder on the Orient Express*	1·20	1·00
		a. Vert pair. Nos. 3885/3886	2·40	2·00
3886	**3011**	(1st) *And There Were None*	1·20	1·00
3887	**3012**	£1·33 *The Mysterious Affair at Styles*	2·00	2·00
		a. Vert pair. Nos. 3887/3888	4·00	4·00
3888	**3013**	£1·33 *The Murder of Roger Ackroyd*	2·00	2·00
3889	**3014**	£1·52 *The Body in the Library*	2·25	2·25
		a. Vert pair. Nos. 3889/3890	4·50	4·50
3890	**3015**	£1·52 *A Murder is Announced*	2·25	2·25
Set of 6			9·75	9·50
Set of 3 Gutter Pairs (two stamps in each gutter pair)			10·25	
First Day Cover (Tallents House)				13·00
Presentation Pack (PO Pack No. 532)			12·00	
PHQ Cards (set of 6) (421)			3·00	11·00

Nos. 3885/3886, 3887/3888 and 3889/3890 were each printed together, *se-tenant*, as vertical pairs in sheets of 48 (2 panes 4×6).

3016 *Mr Happy*   **3017** *Little Miss Naughty*

3018 *Mr Bump*   **3019** *Little Miss Sunshine*

3020 *Mr Tickle*   **3021** *Mr Grumpy*

3022 *Little Miss Princess*   **3023** *Mr Strong*

3024 *Little Miss Christmas*   **3025** *Mr Messy*

2016 (20 Oct). Mr Men and Little Miss (children's books by Roger Hargreaves). Multicoloured Two phosphor bands.

(a) Ordinary gum. Perf 14½.

3891	**3016**	(1st) *Mr Happy*	1·20	1·00
		a. Horiz strip of 5. Nos. 3891/3895	5·25	4·50
3892	**3017**	(1st) *Little Miss Naughty*	1·20	1·00
3893	**3018**	(1st) *Mr Bump*	1·20	1·00
3894	**3019**	(1st) *Little Miss Sunshine*	1·20	1·00
3895	**3020**	(1st) *Mr Tickle*	1·20	1·00
3896	**3021**	(1st) *Mr Grumpy*	1·20	1·00
		a. Horiz strip of 5. Nos. 3896/3900	5·25	4·50
3897	**3022**	(1st) *Little Miss Princess*	1·20	1·00
3898	**3023**	(1st) *Mr Strong*	1·20	1·00
3899	**3024**	(1st) *Little Miss Christmas*	1·20	1·00
3900	**3025**	(1st) *Mr Messy*	1·20	1·00
Set of 10			10·50	9·00
Set of 2 Gutter Strips of 5			21·00	
First Day Cover (Tallents House)				11·50
Presentation Pack (PO Pack No. 533)			12·00	
PHQ Cards (set of 10) (422)			5·00	12·50

(b) Self-adhesive. Die-cut perf 14½.

3901	**3016**	(1st) *Mr Happy*	1·50	1·50
3902	**3020**	(1st) *Mr Tickle*	1·50	1·50

Nos. 3891/3895 and 3896/3900 were each printed together, *se-tenant*, as horizontal strips of five stamps in sheets of 50 stamps (2 panes 5×5).

Nos. 3901/3902 were issued in stamp booklets containing Nos. 3901/3902 and 1st vermilion stamp×4 and originally sold for £3·84.

Designs as Nos. 3891/3900 but self-adhesive were issued in sheets of ten with *se-tenant* labels.

Designs as Nos. 3891, 3893/3894, 3896/3897 and 3900 were also available in sheets of ten with personal photographs on the labels.

3026 Snowman **3027** Robin **3028** Snowman

3029 Robin **3030** Christmas Tree

3031 Lantern **3032** Stocking **3033** Christmas Pudding

3033a Christmas

2016 (8 Nov). Christmas. Multicoloured One centre band (No. 3903) or two bands (others).

(a) Self-adhesive. Die-cut perf 14½×15..

3903	**3026**	(2nd) Snowman	90	90
3904	**3027**	(1st) Robin	1·00	1·00
3905	**3028**	(2nd Large) Snowman	1·25	1·10
3906	**3029**	(1st Large) Robin	1·70	1·40
3907	**3030**	£1·05 Christmas Tree	1·75	1·75
3908	**3031**	£1·33 Lantern	2·00	2·00
3909	**3032**	£1·52 Stocking	2·50	2·50
3910	**3033**	£2·25 Christmas Pudding	3·50	3·50
Set of 8			13·25	13·00
First Day Cover (Tallents House)				16·50
Presentation Pack (PO Pack No. 534)			16·50	
PHQ Cards (set of 9) (423)			4·50	28·00

(b) Ordinary gum. Perf 14½×15.

MS3911 189×74 mm. **3033a** As Nos. 3903/3910			13·25	13·00
First Day Cover (Tallents House)				16·50

The 2nd class, 1st class, £1·05, £1·33, £1·52 and £2·25 values were also issued in sheets of 20, containing 8×2nd class, 8×1st class, 1×£1·05, 1×£1·33, 1×£1·52 and 1×£2·25 stamps, each stamp accompanied by a se-tenant label.

Separate sheets of 20×2nd, 20×1st, 10×1st, 10×£1·05, 10×£1·33 and 10×£1·52 were available with personal photographs on the labels.

The nine PHQ cards show the eight individual stamps and the complete miniature sheet.

Year Pack

2016 (8 Nov). Comprises Nos. 3787/**MS**3801, 3810/**MS**3832, **MS**3837/3843, **MS**3848/3861, **MS**3868/3876, 3879/3900 and 3903/3910

CP3911a	Year Pack (Pack No. 535) (sold for £120)	£175

Post Office Yearbook

2016 (8 Nov). Comprises Nos. 3787/**MS**3801, 3810/**MS**3832, **MS**3837/3843, **MS**3848/3861, **MS**3868/3876, 3879/3900 and 3903/3910

YB3911a	Yearbook (sold for £140)	£200

Miniature Sheet Collection

2016 (8 Nov). Comprises Nos. **MS**3801, **MS**3832, **MS**3837, **MS**3848, **MS**3855, **MS**3868 and **MS**3911

MS3911a	Miniature Sheet Collection (sold for £36)	50·00

3034 Battersea Shield, London, 350–50 BC

3035 Skara Brae Village, Orkney Islands, 3100–2500 BC

3036 Star Carr Headdress, Yorkshire, 9000 BC

3037 Maiden Castle Hill Fort, Dorset, 400 BC

3038 Avebury Stone Circles, Wiltshire, 2500 BC

3039 Drumbest Horns, County Antrim, 800 BC

3040 Grime's Graves Flint Mines, Norfolk, 2500 BC

3041 Mold Cape, Flintshire, 1900–1600 BC

2017 (17 Jan). Ancient Britain. Multicoloured Two phosphor bands. Perf 14.

3912	**3034**	(1st) Battersea Shield	1·20	1·00
		a. Horiz pair. Nos. 3912/3913	2·40	2·00
3913	**3035**	(1st) Skara Brae Village	1·20	1·00
3914	**3036**	£1·05 Star Carr Headdress	1·75	1·75
		a. Horiz pair. Nos. 3914/3915	3·50	3·50
3915	**3037**	£1·05 Maiden Castle Hill Fort	1·75	1·75
3916	**3038**	£1·33 Avebury Stone Circles	2·00	2·00
		a. Horiz pair. Nos. 3916/3917	4·00	4·00
3917	**3039**	£1·33 Drumbest Horns	2·00	2·00
3918	**3040**	£1·52 Grime's Graves Flint Mines	2·25	2·25
		a. Horiz pair. Nos. 3918/3919	4·50	4·50
3919	**3041**	£1·52 Mold Cape	2·25	2·25
Set of 8			13·00	13·00
Set of 4 Gutter Blocks of 4			26·00	
First Day Cover (Tallents House)				17·00
Presentation Pack (PO Pack No. 536)			15·50	
PHQ Cards (set of 8) (424)			4·00	15·00

Nos. 3912/3913, 3914/3915, 3916/3917 and 3918/3919 were each printed together, se-tenant, as horizontal pairs in sheets of 60 (2 panes 6×5).

For No. U3920, T **3041a**, See Decimal Machin section.

3042 The Long Walk

3043 The Round Tower

3044 The Norman Gate

3045 St George's Hall

3046 The Queen's Ballroom

3047 The Waterloo Chamber

2017 (15 Feb). Windsor Castle (1st issue). Multicoloured Two phosphor bands.

(a) Ordinary gum. Perf 14½.

3920	**3042**	(1st) The Long Walk	1·20	1·00
		a. Horiz strip of 3. Nos. 3920/3922	3·50	3·00
3921	**3043**	(1st) The Round Tower	1·20	1·00
3922	**3044**	(1st) The Norman Gate	1·00	1·00
3923	**3045**	£1·52 St George's Hall	2·00	2·00
		a. Horiz strip of 3. Nos. 3923/3925	6·00	6·00
3924	**3046**	£1·52 The Queen's Ballroom	2·00	2·00
3925	**3047**	£1·52 The Waterloo Chamber	2·00	2·00
Set of 6			8·75	8·25
Set of 2 Gutter Strips of 3			17·00	
First Day Cover (Tallents House)				11·00
Presentation Pack (PO Pack No. 537) (Nos. 3920/3925 and **MS**3932)			18·00	
PHQ Cards (set of 11) (425)			5·50	23·00

(b) Self-adhesive. Die-cut perf 14½.

3926	**3048**	(1st) Sir Reginald Bray Roof Boss	2·00	2·00
3927	**3049**	(1st) Fan-vaulted Roof	2·00	2·00

Nos. 3920/3922 and 3923/3925 were each printed together, *se-tenant*, as horizontal strips of three stamps in sheets of 60 (2 panes 6×5).

Booklet pane No. 3920b and No. 3921b come from the £14.58 Windsor Castle booklet, No. DY20.

Nos. 3926/3927 were issued in stamp booklets containing Nos. 3926/3926 and 1st bright scarlet stamp×4 and originally sold for £3·84.

The 11 PHQ cards show the individual stamps including those from No. **MS**3932 and the complete miniature sheet.

3048 St George's Chapel Nave: Sir Reginald Bray Roof Bass

3049 St George's Chapel Nave: Fan-vaulted Roof

3050 St George's Chapel Quire, Garter Banners

3051 St George's Chapel Quire, St George's Cross Roof Boss

3052 St George's Chapel

2017 (15 Feb). Windsor Castle (2nd issue). Multicoloured Two phosphor bands. Perf 14½.

3928	**3048**	(1st) Sir Reginald Bray Roof Boss	1·60	1·60
3929	**3049**	(1st) Fan-vaulted Roof	1·60	1·60
3930	**3050**	£1·33 Garter Banners	2·50	2·50
3931	**3051**	£1·33 St George's Cross Roof Boss	2·50	2·50
Set of 4			7·25	7·25
MS3932 125×89 mm. **3052** Nos. 3928/3931			7·25	7·25
First Day Cover (Tallents House)				8·00

Nos. 3928/3931 come from No. **MS**3932 and £14·58 Windsor Castle booklet, No. DY20.

3053 *Hunky Dory*

3054 *Aladdin Sane*

3055 *Heroes*

3056 *Let's Dance*

3057 *Earthling*   **3058** *Blackstar*

3064 Desert Orchid   **3065** Brigadier Gerard

3059 David Bowie Live

2017 (14 Mar). David Bowie (1947–2016, singer, songwriter and actor) Commemoration. Multicoloured Two phosphor bands.

(a) Self-adhesive. Die-cut perf 14½.

3933	**3053**	(1st) *Hunky Dory*	1·20	1·00
3934	**3054**	(1st) *Aladdin Sane*	1·20	1·00
3935	**3055**	(1st) *Heroes*	1·20	1·00
3936	**3056**	£1·52 *Let's Dance*	2·25	2·25
3937	**3057**	£1·52 *Earthling*	2·25	2·25
3938	**3058**	£1·52 *Blackstar*	2·25	2·25
	Set of 6		9·25	8·75
	First Day Cover (Tallents House)			11·50
	Presentation Pack (PO Pack No. 538) (Nos. 3933/3938 and **MS**3939)		17·00	
	PHQ Cards (set of 11) (426)		5·50	24·00

(b) Ordinary gum. Perf 14½.

MS3939 126×89 mm. **3059** David Bowie Live (1st) The Ziggy Stardust Tour, 1973; (1st) The Serious Moonlight Tour, 1983; £1·52 The Isolar II Tour, 1978; £1·52 A Reality Tour, 2004 ... 6·25 ... 6·25

First Day Cover (Tallents House) ... 8·25

Nos. 3933/3938 were printed in separate sheets of 50 (2 panes 5×5).

Nos. 3934/3935 were also issued in booklets containing Nos. 3934/3935 and 1st bright scarlet stamp×4 and originally sold for £3·84.

The right-hand edges of Nos. 3933/3938 are all cut around to show the vinyl disc protruding from the open edge of the album cover.

Four 'Fan sheets', printed on ordinary gummed paper, were available from Royal Mail at premium prices. The Album Fan Sheet contains the complete set, Types 3053/3058, T 3053×5, T 3054×5 and T **3055**×5

The 11 PHQ cards show the individual stamps including those from No. **MS**3939 and the complete miniature sheet all printed on ordinary gummed paper, were available from Royal Mail at premium prices.

3066 Arkle   **3067** Estimate

2017 (6 Apr). Racehorse Legends. Multicoloured Two phosphor bands. Perf 14.

3940	**3060**	(1st) Frankel	1·20	1·00
3941	**3061**	(1st) Red Rum	1·20	1·00
3942	**3062**	£1·17 Shergar	1·75	1·75
3943	**3063**	£1·17 Kauto Star	1·75	1·75
3944	**3064**	£1·40 Desert Orchid	2·25	2·25
3945	**3065**	£1·40 Brigadier Gerard	2·25	2·25
3946	**3066**	£1·57 Arkle	2·50	2·50
3947	**3067**	£1·57 Estimate	2·50	2·50
	Set of 8		13·75	13·50
	Set of 8 Gutter Pairs		27·50	
	First Day Cover (Tallents House)			17·00
	Presentation Pack (PO Pack No. 539)		16·00	
	PHQ Cards (set of 8) (427)		4·00	17·00

3068 Great Tit (*Parus major*)   **3069** Wren (*Troglodytes troglodytes*)

3060 Frankel   **3061** Red Rum

3070 Willow Warbler (*Phylloscopus trochilus*)   **3071** Goldcrest (*Regulus regulus*)

3062 Shergar   **3063** Kauto Star

3072 Skylark (*Alauda arvensis*)   **3073** Blackcap (*Sylvia atricapilla*)

3074 Song Thrush (*Turdus philomelos*)

3075 Nightingale (*Luscinia megarhynchos*)

3084 The Machin definitive 50 Years of a design icon

3076 Cuckoo (*Cuculus canorus*)

3077 Yellowhammer (*Emberiza citrinella*)

3085 The Machin definitive Golden Anniversary celebration

2017 (4 May). Songbirds. Multicoloured Two phosphor bands. Perf 14½.

3948	**3068**	(1st) Great Tit	1·20	1·00
		a. Horiz strip of 5. Nos. 3948/3952	5·25	4·50
3949	**3069**	(1st) Wren	1·20	1·00
3950	**3070**	(1st) Willow Warbler	1·20	1·00
3951	**3071**	(1st) Goldcrest	1·20	1·00
3952	**3072**	(1st) Skylark	1·20	1·00
3953	**3073**	(1st) Blackcap	1·20	1·00
		a. Horiz strip of 5. Nos. 3953/3957	5·25	4·50
3954	**3074**	(1st) Song Thrush	1·20	1·00
3955	**3075**	(1st) Nightingale	1·20	1·00
3956	**3076**	(1st) Cuckoo	1·20	1·00
3957	**3077**	(1st) Yellowhammer	1·20	1·00
Set of 10			10·50	9·00
Set of 2 Gutter Strips of 10			21·00	
First Day Cover (Tallents House)				12·00
Presentation Pack (PO Pack No. 540)			12·00	
PHQ Cards (set of 10) (428)			5·00	12·50

Nos. 3948/3952 and 3953/3957 were each printed together, *se-tenant*, as horizontal strips of five in sheets of 50 (2 panes 5×5).

3086 £1 gold foil Machin

3078 Preliminary sketch by Arnold Machin based on the Penny Black, January 1966

3079 Preparatory work by Arnold Machin using photograph of his coin mould, February 1966

2017 (5 June). 50th Anniversary of the Machin Definitive. Multicoloured Two phosphor bands. Perf 14×15

3958	**3078**	(1st) Preliminary sketch based on the Penny Black	1·25	1·25
3959	**3079**	(1st) Preparatory work using photograph of his coin mould	1·25	1·25
3960	**3080**	(1st) Essay with coinage head surrounded by Country symbols, April/May 1966	1·25	1·25
3961	**3081**	(1st) Essay of coinage head, with only the denomination	1·25	1·25
3962	**3082**	(1st) Photograph by John Hedgecoe	1·25	1·25
3963	**3083**	(1st) Essay of the first plaster cast of the Diadem Head	1·25	1·25
Set of 6			6·75	6·75
MS3964 202×74 mm. **3084** 6×(1st) Types **3078/3083**			11·00	11·00
First Day Cover (Tallents House) (No. **MS**3964)				12·00
PHQ Cards (Set of 11) (429)			5·50	21·00

Nos. 3958/3963 were issued in the £15·14 50th Anniversary of the Machin Definitive booklet, DY21, and in No. **MS**3964.

The 5p, 20p and £1 stamps in No. **MS**3965 do not have an elliptical hole in each vertical side.

On No. **MS**3965 only the £1 gold foil stamp is embossed.

3080 Essay with coinage head surrounded by Country symbols, April/May 1966

3081 Essay of Coinage head cropped and simplified, with only the denomination, October 1966

For No. U3966, T **3086**, see Decimal Machin section.

3082 Photo by John Hedgecoe with Queen Elizabeth II wearing the diadem, August 1966

3083 Essay of the first plaster cast of the Diadem Head, without corsage, October 1966

3087 Nutley Windmill, East Sussex

3088 New Abbey Corn Mill, Dumfries and Galloway

3089 Ballycopeland Windmill, County Down

3090 Cheddleton Flint Mill, Staffordshire

3091 Woodchurch Windmill, Kent

3092 Felin Cochwillan Mill, Gwynedd

2017 (20 June). Windmills and Watermills. Multicoloured Two phosphor bands. Perf 14½×14

3967	**3087**	(1st) Nutley Windmill, East Sussex	1·20	1·00
		a. Vert pair. Nos. 3967/3968	2·40	2·00
3968	**3088**	(1st) New Abbey Corn Mill, Dumfries and Galloway	1·20	1·00
3969	**3089**	£1·40 Ballycopeland Windmill, County Down	2·25	2·25
		a. Vert pair. Nos. 3969/3970	4·50	4·50
3970	**3090**	£1·40 Cheddleton Flint Mill, Staffordshire	2·25	2·25
3971	**3091**	£1·57 Woodchurch Windmill, Kent	2·50	2·50
		a. Vert pair. Nos. 3971/72	5·00	5·00
3972	**3092**	£1·57 Felin Cochwillan Mill, Gwynedd	2·50	2·50
Set of 6			10·75	10·50
Set of 3 Gutter Blocks of 4			21·50	
First Day Cover (Tallents House)				12·00
Presentation Pack (PO Pack No. 542)			12·00	
PHQ Cards (set of 6) (430)			3·00	12·00

Nos. 3967/3968, 3969/3970 and 3971/3972 were each printed together, *se-tenant*, as vertical pairs in sheets of 60 (2 panes 5×6).

3093 Aquatics Centre, Queen Elizabeth Olympic Park, London

3094 Library of Birmingham

3095 SEC Armadillo (formerly Clyde Auditorium), Glasgow

3096 Scottish Parliament, Edinburgh

3097 Giant's Causeway Visitor Centre, Co. Antrim

3098 National Assembly for Wales, Cardiff

3099 Eden Project, St Austell

3100 Everyman Theatre, Liverpool

3101 IWM (Imperial War Museum) North, Manchester

3102 Switch House, Tate Modern, London

2017 (13 July). Landmark Buildings. Multicoloured Two phosphor bands. Perf 14½

3973	**3093**	(1st) Aquatics Centre, Queen Elizabeth Olympic Park, London	1·20	1·00
		a. Horiz strip of 5. Nos. 3973/3977	5·25	5·00
3974	**3094**	(1st) Library of Birmingham	1·20	1·00
3975	**3095**	(1st) SEC Armadillo (formerly Clyde Auditorium), Glasgow	1·20	1·00
3976	**3096**	(1st) Scottish Parliament, Edinburgh	1·20	1·00
3977	**3097**	(1st) Giant's Causeway Visitor Centre, Co. Antrim	1·20	1·00
3978	**3098**	(1st) National Assembly for Wales, Cardiff	1·20	1·00
		a. Horiz strip of 5. Nos. 3978/3982	5·25	5·00
3979	**3099**	(1st) Eden Project, St Austell	1·20	1·00
3980	**3100**	(1st) Everyman Theatre, Liverpool	1·20	1·00
3981	**3101**	(1st) IWM (Imperial War Museum) North, Manchester	1·20	1·00
3982	**3102**	(1st) Switch House, Tate Modern, London	1·20	1·00
Set of 10			10·50	9·00
Set of 2 Gutter Strips of 5			21·00	
First Day Cover (Tallents House)				10·50
Presentation Pack (PO Pack No. 543)			12·00	
PHQ Cards (set of 10) (431)			5·00	10·00

Nos. 3973/3977 and 3978/3982 were each printed together, *se-tenant*, as horizontal strips of five stamps in sheets of 50 (2 panes 5×5).

3103 *Shattered Poppy* (John Ross)

3104 *Dead Man's Dump* (Isaac Rosenberg)

3105 Nurses Elsie Knocker and Mairi Chisholm

3106 *Dry Docked for Sealing and Painting* (Edward Wadsworth)

3115 Fuzzy-Felt Farm Set

3116 Meccano Ferris Wheel

3107 Tyne Cot Cemetery, Zonnebeke, Ypres Salient Battlefields, Belgium

3108 *Private Lemuel Thomas Rees's Life-saving Bible*

3117 Action Man Red Devil Parachutist

3118 Hornby Dublo Electric Train and TPO Mail Van

2017 (31 July). Centenary of the First World War (4th issue). Multicoloured Two phosphor bands. Perf 14½

3983	3103	(1st) *Shattered Poppy* (John Ross)	1·20	1·00
3984	3104	(1st) *Dead Man's Dump*	1·20	1·00
3985	3105	(1st) Nurses Elsie Knocker and Mairi Chisholm	1·20	1·00
3986	3106	£1·57 *Dry Docked for Sealing and Painting*	2·50	2·50
3987	3107	£1·57 Tyne Cot Cemetery, Belgium	2·50	2·50
3988	3108	£1·57 Private Lemuel Thomas Rees's Life-saving Bible	2·50	2·50
Set of 6			10·00	9·50
Set of 6 Gutter Pairs			20·00	
First Day Cover (Tallents House)				11·00
Presentation Pack (PO Pack No. 544)			11·50	
PHQ Cards (set of 6) (432)			3·00	11·00

2017 (22 Aug). Classic Toys. Multicoloured Two phosphor bands. Perf 14½

3989	3109	(1st) The Merrythought Bear	1·20	1·00
		a. Horiz strip of 5. Nos. 3989/3993	5·25	5·00
3990	3110	(1st) Sindy Weekender Doll	1·20	1·00
3991	3111	(1st) Spirograph	1·20	1·00
3992	3112	(1st) Stickle Bricks Super Set House	1·20	1·00
3993	3113	(1st) Herald Trojan Warriors	1·20	1·00
3994	3114	(1st) Spacehopper	1·20	1·00
		a. Horiz strip of 5. Nos. 3994/3998	5·25	5·00
3995	3115	(1st) Fuzzy-Felt Farm Set	1·20	1·00
3996	3116	(1st) Meccano Ferris Wheel	1·20	1·00
3997	3117	(1st) Action Man Red Devil Parachutist	1·20	1·00
3998	3118	(1st) Hornby Dublo Electric Train and TPO Mail Van	1·20	1·00
Set of 10			10·50	9·00
Set of 2 Gutter Strips of 5			21·00	
First Day Cover (Tallents House)				10·50
Presentation Pack (PO Pack No. 545)			12·00	
PHQ Cards (set of 10) (433)			5·00	10·00

Nos. 3989/3993 and 3994/3998 were each printed together, *se-tenant*, as horizontal strips of five stamps in sheets of 50 (2 panes 5×5).

3109 The Merrythought Bear

3110 Sindy Weekender Doll

3111 Spirograph

3112 Stickle Bricks Super Set House

3119 *The Story of Nelson, The Story of the First Queen Elizabeth* and *Florence Nightingale* (Adventures from History)

3120 *The Gingerbread Boy, Cinderella* and *The Elves and the Shoemaker* (Well-loved Tales)

3113 Herald Trojan Warriors

3114 Spacehopper

3121 *We have fun, Look at this* and *Things we do* (Key Words Reading Scheme)

3122 *Piggly Plays Truant, Tootles the Taxi and Other Rhymes* and *Smoke and Fluff* (Early Tales and Rhymes)

3123 *Things to Make, How it works: The Telephone* and *Tricks and Magic* (Hobbies and How it Works)

3124 *The Nurse, The Postman* and *The Fireman* (People at Work)

3125 *British Wild Flowers, Wild Life in Britain* and *Garden Flowers* (Nature and Conservation)

3126 *The Story of Ships, The Story of the Motor Car* and *The Story of Metals* (Achievements)

2017 (14 Sept). Ladybird Books. Multicoloured One centre band (Nos. 3999/4000) or two bands (others). Perf 14

3999	**3119**	(2nd) Adventures from History	90	90
		a. Horiz pair. Nos. 3999/4000	1·75	1·75
4000	**3120**	(2nd) Well-loved Tales	90	90
4001	**3121**	(1st) Key Words Reading Scheme	1·20	1·00
		a. Horiz pair. Nos. 4001/4002	2·40	2·00
4002	**3122**	(1st) Early Tales and Rhymes	1·20	1·00
4003	**3123**	£1·40 Hobbies and How it Works	2·25	2·25
		a. Horiz pair. Nos. 4003/4004	4·50	4·50
4004	**3124**	£1·40 People at Work	2·25	2·25
4005	**3125**	£1·57 Nature and Conservation	2·50	2·50
		a. Horiz pair. Nos. 4005/4006	5·00	5·00
4006	**3126**	£1·57 Achievements	2·50	2·50
Set of 8			12·25	12·00
Set of 4 Gutter Blocks of 4			24·50	
First Day Cover (Tallents House)				13·50
Presentation Pack (PO Pack No. 546)			14·00	
PHQ Cards (Set of 8) (434)			4·00	12·50

Nos. 3999/4000, 4001/4002, 4003/4004 and 4005/4006 were each printed together, *se-tenant*, as horizontal pairs in sheets of 60 (2 panes 6×5).

3127 Maz Kanata

3128 Chewbacca

3129 Supreme Leader Snoke

3130 Porg

3131 BB-8

3132 R2-D2

3133 C-3PO

3134 K-2SO

3134a Star Wars composite sheet

2017 (12 Oct). *Star Wars* (4th issue). Aliens and Droids. Multicoloured Two phosphor bands

(a) Ordinary gum. Perf 14½.

4007	**3127**	(1st) Maz Kanata	1·20	1·00
		a. Horiz strip of 4. Nos. 4007/4010	4·25	4·00
4008	**3128**	(1st) Chewbacca	1·20	1·00
4009	**3129**	(1st) Supreme Leader Snoke	1·20	1·00
4010	**3130**	(1st) Porg	1·20	1·00
4011	**3131**	(1st) BB-8	1·20	1·00
		a. Horiz strip of 4. Nos. 4011/4014	4·25	4·00
4012	**3132**	(1st) R2-D2	1·20	1·00
4013	**3133**	(1st) C-3PO	1·20	1·00
4014	**3134**	(1st) K-2SO	1·20	1·00
Set of 8			8·50	7·25
Set of 2 Gutter Strips of 4			17·00	
First Day Cover (Tallents House)				9·00
Presentation Pack (PO Pack No. 547)			10·00	
PHQ Cards (Set of 8) (435)			4·00	9·00
MS4014a 297×212 mm. **3134a** Nos. 3758/3769 and				
4007/4014			30·00	45·00

(b) Self-adhesive. Die-cut perf 14½.

4015	**3127**	(1st) Maz Kanata	1·75	1·75
4016	**3128**	(1st) Chewbacca	1·75	1·75
4017	**3131**	(1st) BB-8	1·75	1·75
4018	**3132**	(1st) R2-D2	1·75	1·75

Nos. 4007/4010 and 4011/4014 were each printed together, *se-tenant*, as horizontal strips of four stamps in sheets of 48 (2 panes 4×6).

No. **MS**4014a was inscribed 'THE ULTIMATE COLLECTOR'S SHEET' but was sold at face value (£13)

A 'DROID ALIENS AND CREATURES COLLECTOR'S SHEET' containing Nos. 4007/4010, 4011×2, 4012/4013 and 4014×2 and ten labels was sold at £7·20 a 70p. premium over face value.

Nos. 4015/4016 and 4017/4018 were each issued in stamp booklets with 1st bright scarlet stamp×4 stamps, and originally sold for £3·90 each.

Designs as Nos. 4007/4014 but self-adhesive were issued in sheets of ten with *se-tenant* labels. These sheets originally sold for £7·20.

3135 *Virgin and Child* (attributed to Gerard David)

3136 *The Madonna and Child* (William Dyce)

3137 *Virgin and Child* (attributed to Gerard David)

3138 *The Madonna and Child* (William Dyce)

3139 *Virgin Mary with Child* (attributed to Quinten Massys)

3140 *The Small Cowper Madonna* (Raphael)

3141 *The Sleep of the Infant Jesus* (Giovanni Battista Sassoferrato)

3142 *St Luke painting the Virgin* (detail) (Eduard Jakob von Steinle)

3142a Madonna and Child

2017 (7 Nov). Christmas. Madonna and Child. Multicoloured One centre phosphor band (No. 4019) or two bands.

(a) Self-adhesive. Die-cut perf 14½×15.

4019	**3135**	(2nd) *Virgin and Child* (attributed to Gerard David)	90	90
4020	**3136**	(1st) *The Madonna and Child* (William Dyce)	1·20	1·00
4021	**3137**	(2nd Large) *Virgin and Child* (attributed to Gerard David)	1·25	1·10
4022	**3138**	(1st Large) *The Madonna and Child* (William Dyce)	1·70	1·40
4023	**3139**	£1·17 *Virgin Mary with Child* (attributed to Quinten Massys)	1·80	1·80
4024	**3140**	£1·40 *The Small Cowper Madonna* (Raphael)	2·25	2·25
4025	**3141**	£1·57 *The Sleep of the Infant Jesus* (Giovanni Battista Sassoferrato)	2·50	2·50
4026	**3142**	£2·27 *St Luke painting the Virgin* (detail) (Eduard Jakob von Steinle)	3·50	3·50
Set of 8			13·50	13·00

First Day Cover (Tallents House) (Nos. 4019/4026 and 4028/4031) ... 18·00

Presentation Pack (PO Pack No. 548) (Nos. 4019/4026 and 4028/4031) ... 19·00

PHQ Cards (set of 13) (436) ... 6·50 ... 30·00

(b) Ordinary gum. Perf 14½×15.

MS4027 **3124a** 189×74 mm. As Nos. 4019/4026 ... 13·50 ... 13·00

First Day Cover (Tallents House) ... 17·00

The 2nd class (No. 4019), 1st class (No. 4020), £1·17, £1·40, £1·57 and £2·27 values were also issued in sheets of 20 containing 8×2nd class, 8×1st class, 1×£1·17, 1×£1·40, 1×£1·57 and 1×£2·27 values, each stamp accompanied by a *se-tenant* label.

The 13 PHQ cards show the 12 individual stamps and No. **MS**4027.

Arwen Wilson, age 9   Ted Lewis-Clark, age 10

3143 Snow Family (Arwen Wilson)

3144 Santa Claus on his sleigh on a starry night (Ted Lewis-Clark)

Arwen Wilson, age 9   Ted Lewis-Clark, age 10

3145 Snow Family (Arwen Wilson)

3146 Santa Claus on his sleigh on a starry night (Ted Lewis-Clark)

2017 (7 Nov). Children's Christmas. Multicoloured One centre phosphor band (No. 4028) or two bands. Self-adhesive. Die-cut perf 14½×15

4028	**3143**	(2nd) Snow Family (Arwen Wilson)	90	90
4029	**3144**	(1st) Santa Claus on his sleigh on a starry night (Ted Lewis-Clark)	1·20	1·00
4030	**3145**	(2nd Large) Snow Family (Arwen Wilson)	1·25	1·10
4031	**3146**	(1st Large) Santa Claus on his sleigh on a starry night (Ted Lewis-Clark)	1·70	1·40
Set of 4			4·00	4·00

The 2nd class (No. 4028) and 1st class (No. 4029) values were also issued in sheets of 20 containing 10×2nd class and 10×1st class, each stamp accompanied by a *se-tenant* label.

3147 Platinum Anniversary

2017 (20 Nov). Royal Platinum Wedding Anniversary of Queen Elizabeth II and Duke of Edinburgh. Multicoloured Two phosphor bands. Perf 14

MS4032 200×67 mm. **3147** (1st) Engagement of Princess Elizabeth and Lieutenant Philip Mountbatten; (1st) Princess Elizabeth and Duke of Edinburgh after their wedding at Westminster Abbey; (1st) Princess Elizabeth and Duke of Edinburgh looking at wedding photographs during their honeymoon; £1·57 Engagement photograph; £1·57 Princess Elizabeth and Duke of Edinburgh on their wedding day; £1·57 Princess Elizabeth and Duke of Edinburgh on honeymoon at Broadlands ... 10·00 ... 10·00

First Day Cover (Tallents House) ... 12·00

Presentation Pack (PO Pack No. 549) ... 12·00

PHQ Cards (set of 7) (437) ... 3·50 ... 18·00

Souvenir Pack ... 15·00

Collectors Pack

2017 (20 Nov). Comprises Nos. 3912/3925, **MS**3932/3957, **MS**3964/**MS**3965, 3967/4014, 4019/4029 and **MS**4032

CP4032*a*   Collectors Pack (Pack No. 550) (*sold for* £119) ... £180

Post Office Yearbook

2017 (20 Nov). Comprises Nos. 3912/3925, **MS**3932/3957, **MS**3964/**MS**3965, 3967/4014, 4019/4031 and **MS**4032

YB4032*a*   Yearbook (*sold for* £139) ... £210

Miniature Sheet Collection

2017 (20 Nov). Comprises Nos. **MS**3932, **MS**3939, **MS**3964/**MS**3965, **MS**4027 and **MS**4032

MS4032*a* Miniature Sheet Collection (*sold for* £35) ... 55·00

3148 Sansa Stark (Sophie Tucker)

3149 Jon Snow (Kit Harington)

3150 Eddard Stark (Sean Bean)

3151 Olenna Tyrell (Dianna Rigg)

3152 Tywin Lannister (Charles Dance)

3153 Tyrion Lannister (Peter Dinklage)

3154 Cersei Lannister (Lena Headey)

3155 Arya Stark (Maisie Williams)

3156 Jaime Lannister (Nicolaj Coster-Waldau)

3157 Daenerys Targaryen (Emilia Clarke)

3158 *Game of Thrones* non-human characters

3159 The Iron Throne

2018 (23 Jan) *Game of Thrones* (1st issue). Multicoloured Two phosphor bands.

(a) Ordinary gum. Perf 14.

4033	**3148**	(1st) Sansa Stark (Sophie Tucker)	1·20	1·00
		a. Horiz strip of 5. Nos. 4033/4037	5·25	4·50
4034	**3149**	(1st) Jon Snow (Kit Harington)	1·20	1·00
4035	**3150**	(1st) Eddard Stark (Sean Bean)	1·20	1·00
4036	**3151**	(1st) Olenna Tyrell (Dianna Rigg).	1·20	1·00
4037	**3152**	(1st) Tywin Lannister (Charles Dance)	1·20	1·00
4038	**3153**	(1st) Tyrion Lannister (Peter Dinklage)	1·20	1·00
		a. Horiz strip of 5. Nos. 4038/4042	5·25	4·50
4039	**3154**	(1st) Cersei Lannister (Lena Headey)	1·20	1·00
4040	**3155**	(1st) Arya Stark (Maisie Williams)	1·20	1·00
4041	**3156**	(1st) Jaime Lannister (Nicolaj Coster-Waldau)	1·20	1·00
4042	**3157**	(1st) Daenerys Targaryen (Emilia Clarke)	1·20	1·00
Set of 10			10·50	9·00
Set of 2 Gutter Strips of 10			21·00	
First Day Cover (Tallents House)				10·50
Presentation Pack (PO Pack No. 551)			12·00	
PHQ Cards (set of 16) (438)			8·00	23·00

(b) Self-adhesive. Die-cut perf 14½×14 (with one elliptical hole on each vert side) (Iron throne) or 14½ (others).

MS4043 202×75 mm. **3158** (1st) The Night King and White Walkers; (1st) Giants, (1st) The Iron Throne (18×22 mm); 1st Direwolves; 1st Dragons 7·50 7·50

First Day Cover (Tallents House) 8·50

(c) Self-adhesive booklet stamp. Die-cut perf 14½×14 with one elliptical hole in each vert side.

4044	**3159**	(1st) The Iron Throne	1·50	1·50

Nos. 4033/4037 and 4038/4042 were each printed together, *se-tenant*, as horizontal strips of five stamps in sheets of 60 (2 panes 5×6).

No. 4044 was issued in stamp booklets of six originally sold for £3.90

Designs as Nos. 4033/4042 but self-adhesive were issued in sheets of ten with *se-tenant* labels, originally sold for £7·50.

The 16 PHQ cards show the 15 individual stamps and No. **MS**4043.

3160 The Night King and White Walkers

3161 Giants

3162 Direwolves

3163 Dragons

2018 (23 Jan) *Game of Thrones* (2nd issue). Multicoloured Two phosphor bands. P.14

4045	**3160**	(1st) The Night King and White Walkers	1·50	1·50
4046	**3161**	(1st) Giants	1·50	1·50
4047	**3162**	(1st) Direwolves	1·50	1·50

4048	3163	(1st) Dragons	1·50	1·50
Set of 4			5·50	5·50

Nos. 4045/4048 were issued in £13·95 *Game of Thrones* booklet, No. DY24.

2018 (23 Jan) *Game of Thrones* (3rd issue). Multicoloured Two phosphor bands. Perf 14½×14 (with one elliptical hole in each vert side)

4049	3159	(1st) The Iron Throne	1·50	1·50

No. 4049 was issued in the Machin booklet pane from the £13·95 *Game of Thrones* booklet, No DY24.

3164 The Lone Suffragette in Whitehall, *circa* 1908

3165 The Great Pilgrimage of Suffragists, 1913

3166 Suffragette Leaders at Earl's Court, 1908

3167 Women's Freedom League poster parade, *circa* 1907

3168 Welsh Suffragettes, Coronation Procession, 1911

3169 Leigh and New Released from Prison, 1908

3170 Sophia Duleep Singh sells *The Suffragette*, 1913

3171 Suffragette Prisoners' Pageant, 1911

2018 (15 Feb) Votes for Women. Multicoloured One phosphor band (Nos. 4050/4051) or two bands. Perf 14½×14.

4050	3164	(2nd) The Lone Suffragette in Whitehall	90	90
		a. Horiz pair. Nos. 4050/4051	1·75	1·75
4051	3165	(2nd) The Great Pilgrimage of Suffragists	90	90
4052	3166	(1st) Suffragette Leaders at Earl's Court	1·20	1·00
		a. Horiz pair. Nos. 4052/4053	2·40	2·00
4053	3167	(1st) Women's Freedom League poster parade	1·20	1·00
4054	3168	£1·40 Welsh Suffragettes, Coronation Procession	2·25	2·25
		a. Horiz pair. Nos. 4054/4055	4·50	4·50
4055	3169	£1·40 Leigh and New Released from Prison	2·25	2·25
4056	3170	£1·57 Sophia Duleep Singh sells *The Suffragette*	2·50	2·50
		a. Horiz pair. Nos. 4056/4057	5·00	5·00
4057	3171	£1·57 Suffragette Prisoners' Pageant	2·50	2·50
Set of 8			12·25	12·00
Set of 4 Gutter Blocks of 4			24·50	
First Day Cover (Tallents House)				14·00
Presentation Pack (PO Pack No. 552)			15·00	
PHQ Cards (set of 8) (439)			4·00	13·00

Nos. 4050/4051, 4052/4053, 4054/4055 and 4056/4057 were each printed together, *se-tenant*, as horizontal pairs in sheets of 60 (2 panes 6×5).

3172 Lightning F6   **3173** Hawker Hurricane Mk.I

3174 Vulcan B2   **3175** Typhoon FGR4

3176 Sopwith Camel F.1   **3177** Nimrod MR2

3178 Royal Air Force Red Arrows

2018 (20 Mar) RAF Centenary (1st issue). Multicoloured Two phosphor bands.

(a) Ordinary gum. Perf 14½×14.

4058	3172	(1st) Lightning F6	1·50	1·40
		a. Horiz pair. Nos. 4058/4059	3·00	3·00
4059	3173	(1st) Hurricane Mk.I	1·50	1·40
4060	3174	£1·40 Vulcan B2	3·25	3·25
		a. Horiz pair. Nos. 4060/4061	6·50	6·50
4061	3175	£1·40 Typhoon FGR4	3·25	3·25
4062	3176	£1·57 Sopwith Camel F.1	3·75	3·75
		a. Horiz pair. Nos. 4062/4063	7·50	7·50
4063	3177	£1·57 Nimrod MR2	3·75	3·75
Set of 6			15·00	15·00
Set of 3 Gutter Blocks of 4			30·00	
First Day Cover (Tallents House)				16·00
Presentation Pack (PO Pack No. 553) (Nos. 4058/4063 and **MS**4064)			25·00	
PHQ Cards (set of 11) (440)			10·00	32·00
MS4064 192×74 mm. **3178** Nos. 4067/4070			9·50	9·50
First Day Cover (Tallents House)				10·50

(b) Self-adhesive. Die-cut perf 14½.

4065	3172	(1st) Lightning F6	1·75	1·75
4066	3173	(1st) Hurricane Mk.I	1·75	1·75

Nos. 4058/4059, 4060/4061 and 4062/4063 were each printed together, *se-tenant*, as horizontal pairs in sheets of 60 (2 panes 6×5).

Nos. 4065/4066 were issued in stamp booklets with 1st bright scarlet stamp×4 stamps originally sold for £3·90.

The 11 PHQ cards show the individual stamps including those from No. **MS**4064 and the complete miniature sheet.

3179 Red Arrows, Flypast   **3180** Red Arrows, Swan

3181 Red Arrows, Syncro pair   **3182** Red Arrows, Python

2018 (20 Mar) RAF Centenary (2nd issue). Red Arrows. Multicoloured Two phosphor bands. Perf 14½×14.

4067	**3179**	(1st) Red Arrows, Flypast	1·50	1·50
4068	**3180**	(1st) Red Arrows, Swan	1·50	1·50
4069	**3181**	£1·40 Red Arrows, Syncro pair	3·25	3·25
4070	**3182**	£1·40 Red Arrows, Python	3·25	3·25
Set of 4			7·00	7·00

Nos. 4067/4070 come from No. **MS**4064 and the £18·69 RAF Centenary booklet, No. DY25.

3183 Pilots scramble to their Hurricanes

3184 Supermarine Spitfires of 610 Squadron, Biggin Hill, on patrol

3185 Armourer Fred Roberts replaces ammunition boxes on Supermarine Spitfire

2018 (20 Mar) RAF Centenary (3rd issue). Battle of Britain. Multicoloured Two phosphor bands. Perf 14½×14.

4071	**3183**	(1st) Pilots scramble	1·50	1·50
4072	**3184**	(1st) Spitfires	1·50	1·50
4073	**3185**	(1st) Armourer replaces ammunition boxes	1·50	1·50
Set of 3			4·00	4·00

Nos. 4071/4073 come from the £18·69 RAF Centenary booklet, No. DY25. The images on these three stamps were previously used in No. **MS**3735 issued on 16 July 2015 to commemorate the 75th Anniversary of the Battle of Britain; those stamps were 'all-over' phosphor.

3186 Osprey (*Pandion haliaetus*)

3187 Large Blue Butterfly (*Maculinea arion*)

3188 Eurasian Beaver (*Castor fiber*)

3189 Pool Frog (*Pelophylax lessonae*)

3190 Stinking Hawk's-beard (*Crepis foetida*)

3191 Sand Lizard (*Lacerta agilis*)

2018 (17 Apr). Reintroduced Species. Multicoloured Two phosphor bands. Perf 14½.

4074	**3186**	(1st) Osprey (*Pandion haliaetus*)	1·20	1·00
		a. Horiz pair. Nos. 4074/4075	2·40	2·00
4075	**3187**	(1st) Large Blue Butterfly (*Maculinea arion*)	1·20	1·00
4076	**3188**	£1·45 Eurasian Beaver (*Castor fiber*)	2·25	2·25
		a. Horiz pair. Nos. 4076/4077	4·50	4·50
4077	**3189**	£1·45 Pool Frog (*Pelophylax lessonae*)	2·25	2·25
4078	**3190**	£1·55 Stinking Hawk's-beard (*Crepis foetida*)	2·50	2·50
		a. Horiz pair. Nos. 4078/4079	5·00	5·00
4079	**3191**	£1·55 Sand Lizard (*Lacerta agilis*)	2·50	2·50
Set of 6			10·75	10·50
Set of 3 Gutter Blocks of 4			21·50	
First Day Cover (Tallents House)				13·50
Presentation Pack (PO Pack No. 554)			13·50	
PHQ Cards (set of 6) (441)			4·00	12·00

Nos. 4074/4075, 4076/4077 and 4078/4079 were each printed together, *se-tenant*, as horizontal pairs in sheets of 60 (2 panes 6×5).

2018 (11 May). Centenary of the RAF (Royal Air Force) (4th issue). Multicoloured. Self-adhesive. Two phosphor bands. Die-cut perf 14

4080	**3179**	(1st) Red Arrows, Flypast	3·25	3·25
4081	**3180**	(1st) Red Arrows, Swan	3·25	3·25

Nos. 4080/4081 were issued in stamp booklets with 1st bright scarlet stamp×4 stamps and originally sold for £4·02.

3192 Barn Owl (*Tyto alba*)

3193 Little Owl (*Athene noctua*)

3194 Tawny Owl (*Strix aluco*)

3195 Short-eared Owl (*Asio flammeus*)

3196 Long-eared Owl (*Asio otus*)

3197 Two Young Barn Owls (*Tyto alba*)

3198 Little Owl Chicks
(*Athene noctua*)

3199 Tawny Owl Chick
(*Strix aluco*)

3203 *Summer Exhibition*
(Grayson Perry)

3204 *Queen of the Sky* (Fiona
Rae)

3200 Short-eared Owl
Chick (*Asio flammeus*)

3201 Long-eared Owl
Chick (*Asio otus*)

3205 *St. Kilda. The Great Sea
Stacs* (Norman Ackroyd)

3206 *Inverleith Allotments
and Edinburgh Castle*
(Barbara Rae)

2018 (11 May). Owls. Multicoloured Two phosphor bands. Perf 14½×14.

4082	**3192**	(1st) Barn Owl (*Tyto alba*)	1·20	1·00
		a. Horiz strip of 5. Nos. 4082/4086	5·25	4·50
4083	**3193**	(1st) Little Owl (*Athene noctua*)	1·20	1·00
4084	**3194**	(1st) Tawny Owl (*Strix aluco*)	1·20	1·00
4085	**3195**	(1st) Short-eared Owl (*Asio flammeus*)	1·20	1·00
4086	**3196**	(1st) Long-eared Owl (*Asio otus*)	1·20	1·00
4087	**3197**	(1st) Two Young Barn Owls (*Tyto alba*)	1·20	1·00
		a. Horiz strip of 5. Nos. 4087/4091	5·25	4·50
4088	**3198**	(1st) Little Owl Chicks (*Athene noctua*)	1·20	1·00
4089	**3199**	(1st) Tawny Owl Chick (*Strix aluco*)	1·20	1·00
4090	**3200**	(1st) Short-eared Owl Chick (*Asio flammeus*)	1·20	1·00
4091	**3201**	(1st) Long-eared Owl Chick (*Asio otus*)	1·20	1·00
Set of 10			10·50	9·00
Set of 2 Gutter Strips of 10			21·00	
Set of 2 Traffic Light Gutter Strips of 20			40·00	
First Day Cover (Tallents House)				12·50
Presentation Pack (PO Pack No. 555)			12·50	
PHQ Cards (set of 10) (442)			6·75	11·00

Nos. 4082/406 and 4087/4091 were each printed together, *se-tenant*, as horizontal strips of five stamps in sheets of 50 (2 panes 5×5).

3205 *St. Kilda. The Great Sea
Stacs* (Norman Ackroyd)

3206 *Inverleith Allotments
and Edinburgh Castle*
(Barbara Rae)

MINI
RW18

3202 Royal Wedding

2018 (19 May). Royal Wedding. Multicoloured. 'All-over' phosphor. Perf 14½×14.

MS4092 116×89 mm. **3202** (1st) Prince Harry and Ms
Meghan Markle×2; £1·55 Prince Harry and Ms
Meghan Markle (black and white photograph)×2   7·00   7·00
First Day Cover (Tallents House)   8·50
Presentation Pack (PO Pack No. M24)   7·50

A souvenir pack containing Nos. **MS**3932 and **MS**4092 with silver foil cachet postmarks and imagery from the Royal Wedding was available from Royal Mail from 29 June 2018 for £24·99.

3209 Sergeant Wilson (John Le
Mesurier) 'Do you think that's
wise, sir?'

3210 Private Pike (Ian Lavender)
'I'll tell Mum!'

2018 (5 June). 250th Anniversary of the Royal Academy of Arts, London. Multicoloured. Two phosphor bands. Perf 14×14½.

4093	**3203**	(1st) *Summer Exhibition* (Grayson Perry)	1·20	1·00
		a. Vert pair. Nos. 4093/4094	2·40	2·00
4094	**3204**	(1st) *Queen of the Sky* (Fiona Rae)	1·20	1·00
4095	**3205**	£1·25 *St Kilda. The Great Sea Stacs* (Norman Ackroyd)	1·90	1·90
		a. Vert pair. Nos. 4095/4096	3·75	3·75
4096	**3206**	£1·25 *Inverleith Allotments and Edinburgh Castle* (Barbara Rae)	1·90	1·90
4097	**3207**	£1·55 *Queuing at the RA* (Yinka Shonibare)	2·40	2·40
		a. Vert pair. Nos. 4097/4098	4·75	4·75
4098	**3208**	£1·55 *Saying Goodbye* (Tracey Emin)	2·40	2·40
Set of 6			9·75	9·50
Set of 3 Gutter Pairs (only 2 stamps in each gutter pair)			11·50	
First Day Cover (Tallents House)				13·00
Presentation Pack (PO Pack No. 556)			11·50	
PHQ Cards (set of 6) (443)			4·00	11·50

Nos. 4093/4094, 4095/4096 and 4097/4098 were each printed together, *se-tenant*, as vertical pairs in sheets of 60 (2 panes 5×6).

3211 Captain Mainwaring (Arthur Lowe) 'You stupid boy!'

3212 Lance Corporal Jones (Clive Dunn) 'Don't panic! Don't panic!'

3213 Private Walker (James Beck) 'It won't cost you much...'

3214 Private Frazer (John Laurie) 'We're doomed. Doomed!'

3215 Private Godfrey (Arnold Ridley) 'Do you think I might be excused?'

3216 Chief Warden Hodges (Bill Pertwee) 'Put that light out!'

2018 (26 June). 50th Anniversary of *Dad's Army* (BBC television sitcom 1968–1977). Multicoloured. One centre band (2nd) or two phosphor bands (others).

(a) Ordinary gum. Perf 14½×14.

4099	3209	(2nd) Sergeant Wilson (John Le Mesurier) 'Do you think that's wise, sir?'	90	90
		a. Horiz pair. Nos. 4099/4100	1·75	1·75
4100	3210	(2nd) Private Pike (Ian Lavender) 'I'll tell Mum!'	90	90
4101	3211	(1st) Captain Mainwaring (Arthur Lowe) 'You stupid boy!'	1·20	1·00
		a. Horiz pair. Nos. 4101/4102	2·40	2·00
4102	3212	(1st) Lance Corporal Jones (Clive Dunn) 'Don't panic! Don't panic!'	1·20	1·00
4103	3213	£1·45 Private Walker (James Beck) 'It won't cost you much...'	2·25	2·25
		a. Horiz pair. Nos. 4103/4104	4·50	4·50
4104	3214	£1·45 Private Frazer (John Laurie) 'We're doomed. Doomed!'	2·25	2·25
4105	3215	£1·55 Private Godfrey (Arnold Ridley) 'Do you think I might be excused?'	2·40	2·40
		a. Horiz pair. Nos. 4105/4106	4·75	4·75
4106	3216	£1·55 Chief Warden Hodges (Bill Pertwee) 'Put that light out!'	2·40	2·40
Set of 8			12·25	12·00
Set of 4 Gutter Blocks of 4			24·50	
First Day Cover (Tallents House)				16·00
Presentation Pack (PO Pack No. 557)			14·00	
PHQ Cards (set of 8) (444)			5·50	14·00

(b) Self-adhesive. Die-cut perf 14½×14.

4107	3211	(1st) Captain Mainwaring (Arthur Lowe) 'You stupid boy!'	1·75	1·75
4108	3212	(1st) Lance Corporal Jones (Clive Dunn) 'Don't panic! Don't panic!'	1·75	1·75

Nos. 4099/4100, 4101/4102, 4103/4104 and 4105/4106 were each printed, *se-tenant*, as horizontal pairs in sheets of 60 (2 pairs 6×5)

Nos. 4107/4108 were issued in stamp booklets with 1st bright scarlet stamp×4 stamps and originally sold for £4·02.

Stamps as Nos. 4101/4102 but self-adhesive and perforated 14×14½ were issued in sheets of ten containing five stamps of each design with labels showing stills from the television series. These sheets were printed in lithography.

3217 South Front

3218 West Front

3219 East Front

3220 Pond Gardens

3221 Maze

3222 Great Fountain Garden

3223 Hampton Court Palace

3224 Great Hall   **3225** King's Great
Bedchamber

2018 (31 July). Hampton Court Palace. Multicoloured Two phosphor
bands.

(a) Ordinary gum. Perf 14½.

4109	**3217**	(1st) South Front	1·20	1·00
		a. Horiz strip of 3. Nos. 4109/4111	3·50	3·00
4110	**3218**	(1st) West Front	1·20	1·00
4111	**3219**	(1st) East Front	1·20	1·00
4112	**3220**	£1·55 Pond Gardens	2·40	2·40
		a. Horiz strip of 3. Nos. 4112/4114	7·25	7·25
4113	**3221**	£1·55 Maze	2·40	2·40
4114	**3222**	£1·55 Great Fountain Garden	2·40	2·40
Set of 6			9·50	9·00
Set of 2 Gutter Strips of 6			19·00	
First Day Cover (Tallents House)				12·50
Presentation Pack (PO Pack No. 558) (Nos. 4104/4114 and **MS**4115)			17·50	
PHQ Cards (set of 11) (445)			7·50	22·00
MS4115 156×74 mm. **3223** (1st) Great Hall; (1st) King's Great Bedchamber; £1·45 Chapel Royal; £1·45 King's Staircase			6·50	6·50
First Day Cover (Tallents House)				8·25

(b) Self-adhesive. Die-cut perf 14.

4116	**3224**	(1st) Great Hall	1·75	1·75
4117	**3225**	(1st) King's Great Bedchamber	1·75	1·75

Nos. 4109/4111 and 4112/4114 were each printed together, *se-tenant*, as
horizontal strips of three stamps in sheets of 60 (2 panes 6×5).

Nos. 4116/4117 were issued in stamp booklets with 1st bright scarlet
stamp×4 stamps and originally sold for £4·02.

The 11 PHQ cards show the individual stamps including those from No.
MS4115 and the complete miniature sheet.

Joseph Banks · naturalist   The *Endeavour* voyage

3226 Joseph Banks, Red-
tailed Tropicbird and Red
Passion Flower   **3227** Chief Mourner of Tahiti
and a Scene with a Canoe

Captain James Cook   The *Endeavour* voyage

3228 Captain James Cook
and *Triumph of the Navigators*   **3229** Drawings of the
Observations of a Transit
of Venus

The *Endeavour* voyage   Sydney Parkinson · natural history artist

3230 Scarlet Clianthus and
Portrait of a Maori Chief   **3231** Blue-Black Grassquit
and Self-portrait of Sydney
Parkinson

3232 The *Endeavour* Voyage

2018 (16 Aug). Captain Cook and the *Endeavour* Voyage (1768–1771).
Multicoloured One centre band (2nd) or two phosphor bands
(others). Perf 14×14½ (Nos. 4118/4123) or 14 (No. **MS**4124).

4118	**3226**	(2nd) Joseph Banks, Red-tailed Tropicbird and Red Passion Flower	90	90
		a. Horiz pair. Nos. 4118/4119	1·75	1·75
4119	**3227**	(2nd) Chief Mourner of Tahiti and a Scene with a Canoe	90	90
4120	**3228**	(1st) Captain James Cook and *Triumph of the Navigators*	1·20	1·00
		a. Horiz pair. Nos. 4120/4121	2·40	2·00
4121	**3229**	(1st) Drawings of the Observations of a Transit of Venus	1·20	1·00
4122	**3230**	£1·45 Scarlet Clianthus and Portrait of a Maori Chief	2·25	2·25
		a. Horiz pair. Nos. 4122/4123	4·50	4·50
4123	**3231**	£1·45 Blue-Black Grassquit and Self-portrait of Sydney Parkinson	2·25	2·25
Set of 6			7·75	7·50
Set of 3 Gutter Blocks of 4			15·50	
First Day Cover (Tallents House)				10·50
Presentation Pack (PO Pack No.559). (Nos. 4118/4123 and **MS**4124)			15·00	
PHQ Cards (set of 11) (446)			7·50	20·00
MS4124 125×89 mm. **3232** (1st) Chart of the discoveries made by Captain James Cook (Lieutenant Roberts) ('Charting a new course: New Zealand and Australia'); (1st) Boathouse and canoes on Raiatea, Society Islands (after Sydney Parkinson); £1·45 Arched rock with Maori clifftop fort, New Zealand ('Mapping New Zealand: a Maori clifftop fort'); £1·45 Repairing the *Endeavour* on the Endeavour River, Australia (after Sydney Parkinson)			6·50	6·50
First Day Cover (Tallents House)				8·25

Nos. 4118/4119, 4120/4121 and 4122/4123 were each printed together,
se-tenant, as horizontal pairs in sheets of 60 (2 panes 6×5).

Nos. 4118/**MS**4124 commemorate the 250th Anniversary of the
Departure of the *Endeavour*.

The 11 PHQ cards show the ten individual stamps including those from
No. **MS**4124 and the complete miniature sheet.

3233 Laurence Olivier in
The Dance of Death   **3234** Glenda Jackson in
King Lear

3235 Albert Finney in
Hamlet   **3236** Maggie Smith in
Hedda Gabler

3237 John Gielgud and Ralph Richardson in *No Man's Land*

3238 Sharon Benson in *Carmen Jones*

3239 Judi Dench and John Stride in *Romeo and Juliet*

3240 Richard Burton in *Henry V*

2018 (30 Aug). Bicentenary of The Old Vic, London. Multicoloured. Two phosphor bands. Perf 14½×14

4125	**3233**	(1st) Laurence Olivier in *The Dance of Death*	1·20	1·00
		a. Horiz pair. Nos. 4125/4126	2·40	2·00
4126	**3234**	(1st) Glenda Jackson in *King Lear*	1·20	1·00
4127	**3235**	£1·25 Albert Finney in *Hamlet*	1·90	1·90
		a. Horiz pair. Nos. 4127/4128	3·75	3·75
4128	**3236**	£1·25 Maggie Smith in *Hedda Gabler*	1·90	1·90
4129	**3237**	£1·45 John Gielgud and Ralph Richardson in *No Man's Land*	2·25	2·25
		a. Horiz pair. Nos. 4129/4130	4·50	4·50
4130	**3238**	£1·45 Sharon Benson in *Carmen Jones*	2·25	2·25
4131	**3239**	£1·55 Judi Dench and John Stride in *Romeo and Juliet*	2·40	2·40
		a. Horiz pair. Nos. 4131/4132	4·75	4·75
4132	**3240**	£1·55 Richard Burton in *Henry V*	2·40	2·40
Set of 8			13·75	13·50
Set of 4 Gutter Pairs (only 2 stamps in each gutter pair)			14·50	
Set of 4 Traffic Light Gutter Blocks (4 stamps per block)			29·00	
First Day Cover (Tallents House)				18·50
Presentation Pack (PO Pack No. 560)			16·00	
PHQ Cards (set of 8) (447)			5·50	15·00

Nos. 4125/416, 4127/4128, 4129/4130 and 4131/4132 were each printed together, *se-tenant*, as horizontal pairs in sheets of 60 (2 panes 6×5).

3241 *100 Poppies* (Zafer and Barbara Baran)

3242 *Anthem for Doomed Youth* (poem by Wilfred Owen) (woodblock print by Andrew Davidson)

3243 Second Lieutenant Walter Tull (1888–1918)

3244 *We Are Making a New World* (Paul Nash)

3245 The Grave of the Unknown Warrior, Westminster Abbey, London

3246 Lieutenant Francis Hopgood's Goggles

2018 (13 Sept). Centenary of the First World War (5th issue). Multicoloured.
(a) Ordinary gum. Two phosphor bands. Perf 14½.

4133	**3241**	(1st) *100 Poppies* (Zafer and Barbara Baran)	1·20	1·00
4134	**3242**	(1st) *Anthem for Doomed Youth* (poem by Wilfred Owen) (woodblock print by Andrew Davidson)	1·20	1·00
4135	**3243**	(1st) Second Lieutenant Walter Tull (1888–1918)	1·20	1·00
4136	**3244**	£1·55 *We Are Making a New World* (Paul Nash)	2·40	2·40
4137	**3245**	£1·55 The Grave of the Unknown Warrior, Westminster Abbey, London	2·40	2·40
4138	**3246**	£1·55 Lieutenant Francis Hopgood's Goggles	2·40	2·40
Set of 6			9·50	9·00
Set of 6 Gutter Pairs			19·00	
First Day Cover (Tallents House)				12·50
Presentation Pack (PO Pack No. 561)			12·00	
PHQ Cards (set of 6) (448)			4·00	11·00
MS4138a 296×210 mm. Nos. 3626/3631, 3711/3716, 3838/3843, 3983/398 and 4133/4138			50·00	65·00

(b) Self-adhesive. Die-cut perf 14½.

4139	**2774**	(1st) *Poppy* (Fiona Strickland)	1·75	1·75
4140	**3241**	(1st) *100 Poppies* (Zafer and Barbara Baran)	1·75	1·75

Nos. 4139/4140 were issued in stamp booklets with 1st bright scarlet stamp×4 stamps and originally sold for £4·02.

No. **MS**4138a was a special composite sheet sold for £32·94.

No. 4139 was as T **2774**, the poppy stamp issued in 2014 for the first Centenary of the First World War series, but self-adhesive and printed in gravure.

A souvenir pack containing the poppy stamps Nos. 3626, 3711, 3838, 3983 and 4133 each affixed to a poem print was sold by Royal Mail for £24·99.

3247 Hermione Granger (Emma Watson)

3248 *Hogwarts Express*

3249 Harry Potter (Daniel Radcliffe)

3250 *Flying Ford Anglia*

3251 Ron Weasley (Rupert Grint)

3252 *Hagrid's Motorbike*

3253 Ginny Weasley (Bonnie Wright)

3254 Triwizard Cup

3255 Neville Longbottom (Matthew Lewis)

3256 Knight Bus

3257 Hogwarts Professors and The Marauders Map

2018 (16 Oct). Harry Potter (1st issue) Multicolour. 'All-over' phosphor (No. MS4151 stamps only) or two phosphor bands (others).

(a) Ordinary gum. Perf 14×14½.

4141	3247	(1st) Hermione Granger (Emma Watson)	1·20	1·00
		a. Horiz strip of 5. Nos. 4141/4145	5·25	5·00
4142	3248	(1st) Hogwarts Express	1·20	1·00
4143	3249	(1st) Harry Potter (Daniel Radcliffe)	1·20	1·00
4144	3250	(1st) Flying Ford Anglia	1·20	1·00
4145	3251	(1st) Ron Weasley (Rupert Grint)	1·20	1·00
4146	3252	(1st) Hagrid's Motorbike	1·20	1·00
		a. Horiz strip of 5. Nos. 4146/4150	5·25	5·00
4147	3253	(1st) Ginny Weasley (Bonnie Wright)	1·20	1·00
4148	3254	(1st) Triwizard Cup	1·20	1·00
4149	3255	(1st) Neville Longbottom (Matthew Lewis)	1·20	1·00
4150	3256	(1st) Knight Bus	1·20	1·00
Set of 10			10·50	9·00
Set of 2 Gutter Strips of 10			21·00	
First Day Cover (Tallents House)				13·00
Presentation Pack (PO Pack No. 562) (Nos. 4141/4150 and MS4151)			19·00	
PHQ Cards (set of 16) (449)			11·00	23·00

(b) Self-adhesive. Die-cut perf 14.

MS4151 202×74 mm. **3257** (1st) Pomona Sprout (Miriam Margolyes); (1st) Horace Slughorn (Jim Broadbent); (1st) Sybill Trelawney (Emma Thompson); (1st) Remus Lupin (David Thewlis); (1st) Severus Snape (Alan Rickman)

Severus Snape (Alan Rickman)	6·25 6·25
First Day Cover (Tallents House)	8·50

(c) Self-adhesive. Die-cut perf 14×14½.

4152	3247	(1st) Hermione Granger (Emma Watson)	1·75	1·75
4153	3249	(1st) Harry Potter (Daniel Radcliffe)	1·75	1·75

Nos. 4141/4145 and 4146/4150 were each printed together, se-tenant, as horizontal strips of five stamps in sheets of 50 (2 panes 5×5).

Nos. 4152/4153 were issued in stamp booklets with 1st bright scarlet stamp×4 stamps and originally sold for £4·02.

When placed under a UV light parts of the designs of Nos. 4141/4150 and 4152/4153 light up green, and No. **MS4151** reveals additional inscriptions.

A collectors sheet containing stamps as Nos. 4141/4150 but self-adhesive with labels showing Harry Potter film stills was sold for £7·70, a £1 premium over face value.

A Souvenir Stamp Art Folder containing pages of enlarged images of Nos. 4141/4150 with the stamps attached, cancelled with a special cachet postmark, and also a poster of the miniature sheet, were sold by Royal Mail for £24·99.

The 16 PHQ cards show the individual stamps including those from No. **MS4151** and the complete miniature sheet.

3258 Man and Girl posting Letters in Wall-mounted Post Box

3259 Postal Worker emptying Post Box

3260 Man and Girl posting Letters in Wall-mounted Post Box

3261 Postal Worker emptying Post Box

3262 Man and Boy approaching Rural Pillar Box

3263 Man approaching Post Box

3264 Woman with Dog posting Letter

3265 Pillar Box near Church

2018 (1 Nov). Christmas. Post Boxes. Multicoloured One centre band (No. 4154) or two bands (others).

(a) Self-adhesive. Die-cut perf 14½×15.

4154	3258	(2nd) Man and Girl posting Letters in Wall mounted Post box	90	90
4155	3259	(1st) Postal Worker emptying Post box	1·20	1·00
4156	3260	(2nd Large) Man and Girl posting Letters in Wall-mounted Post box	1·25	1·10
4157	3261	(1st Large) Postal Worker emptying Post box	1·70	1·40
4158	3262	£1·25 Man and Boy approaching Rural Pillar Box	1·90	1·90
4159	3263	£1·45 Man approaching Post Box	2·25	2·25
4160	3264	£1·55 Woman with Dog posting Letter	2·40	2·40
4161	3265	£2·25 Pillar Box near Church	3·50	3·50
Set of 8			13·50	13·00
First Day Cover (Tallents House)				18·00
Presentation Pack (PO Pack No. 563)			15·00	
PHQ Cards (set of 9) (450)			6·00	25·00

(b) Ordinary gum. Perf 14½×15.

MS4162 190×74 mm. As Nos. 4154/4161	13·50	13·00
First Day Cover (Tallents House)		18·00

The 2nd class, 1st class, £1·25, £1·45, £1·55 and £2·25 values were also issued in sheets of 20 containing 8×2nd class, 8×1st class, 1×£1·25, 1×£1·45, 1×£1·55 and 1×£2·25 values, each stamp accompanied by a se-tenant label.

The nine PHQ cards show the individual stamps and the complete miniature sheet.

3266 70th Birthday of Prince of Wales

2018 (14 Nov). 70th Birthday of the Prince of Wales. Multicolour. 'All-over' phosphor. Self-adhesive. Die-cut perf 14½×15

MS4163 203×74 mm. **3266** (1st) Prince Charles; (1st) Prince Charles with Camilla, Duchess of Cornwall; (1st) Prince Charles with Prince William and Prince Harry; £1·55 Prince Charles, Prince William and Prince Harry at Cirencester Park Polo Club; £1·55 Prince Charles at Castle of Mey; £1·55 Prince Charles with schoolchildren at Llancaiach Fawr Manor   10·50   10·50

First Day Cover (Tallents House)		13·00
Presentation Pack (PO Pack No. 564)	12·00	
PHQ Cards (set of 7) (451)	4·75	12·00

Collectors Pack

2018 (14 Nov). Comprises Nos. 4033/**MS**4043, 4050/**MS**4064, 4074/4079, 4082/4106, 4109/**MS**4115, 4118/4138, 4141/**MS**4151, 4154/4161 and **MS**4163

CP4163a	Collectors Pack (Pack No. 565) (sold for £133)	£200

Post Office Yearbook

2018 (14 Nov). Comprises Nos. 4033/**MS**4043, 4050/**MS**4064, 4074/4079, 4082/4106, 4109/**MS**4115, 4118/38, 4141/**MS**4151, 4154/4061 and **MS**4163

YB4163a	Yearbook (sold for £153)	£225

Miniature Sheet Collection

2018 (14 Nov). Comprises Nos. **MS**4043, **MS**4064, **MS**4092, **MS**4115, **MS**4124, **MS**4151, **MS**4162 and **MS**4163

MS4163a Miniature Sheet Collection (sold for £42)	65·00

3267 Pomona Sprout (Miriam Margolyes)

3268 Horace Slughorn (Jim Broadbent)

3269 Sybill Trelawney (Emma Thompson)

3270 Remus Lupin (David Thewlis)

3271 Severus Snape (Alan Rickman)

2018 (4 Dec). Harry Potter (2nd issue). Multicoloured. Self-adhesive. 'All-over' phosphor (stamps only). Die-cut perf 14.

4164	**3267**	(1st) Pomona Sprout (Miriam Margolyes)	1·40	1·40
4165	**3268**	(1st) Horace Slughorn (Jim Broadbent)	1·40	1·40
4166	**3269**	(1st) Sybill Trelawney (Emma Thompson)	1·40	1·40
4167	**3270**	(1st) Remus Lupin (David Thewlis)	1·40	1·40
4168	**3271**	(1st) Severus Snape (Alan Rickman)	1·40	1·40
Set of 5			6·25	6·25

Nos. 4164/4168 were issued in No. **MS**4151 and in two booklet panes from the £15·50 Harry Potter booklet No. DY27.

3273 The Skull Sectioned

3274 A Sprig of Guelder-rose

3275 Studies of Cats

3276 Star-of-Bethlehem and Other Plants

3277 The Anatomy of the Shoulder and Foot

3278 The Head of Leda

 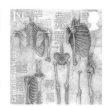

3279 The Head of a Bearded Man

3280 The Skeleton

3281 The Head of St Philip

3282 A Woman in a Landscape

2019 (15 Jan). Stamp Classics Multicoloured. Phosphor frame. Perf 14×13½.

MS4169 203×74 mm. **3272** (1st) Queen Victoria 1891 £1 green; (1st) King Edward VII 1910 2d. Tyrian plum; (1st) King George V 1913 Sea horse 2s.6d. brown; £1·55 King Edward VIII 1936 1½d. red-brown; £1·55 King George VI (and Queen Victoria) 1940 Penny Black Centenary ½d. green; £1·55 Queen Elizabeth II 1953 Coronation 2½d. carmine-red   13·50   13·50

First Day Cover (Tallents House)		16·00
Presentation Pack (PO Pack No. 566)	14·50	
PHQ Cards (set of 7) (452)	4·75	22·00

No. **MS**4169 commemorates the 150th Anniversary of the Royal Philatelic Society and the 50th Anniversary of Queen Elizabeth II opening the National Postal Museum, London.

3272 Stamp Classics

3283 A Design for an Equestrian Monument

3284 The Fall of Light on a Face

2019 (13 Feb). 500th Death Anniversary of Leonardo da Vinci (1452–1519, artist) Multicoloured. Two phosphor bands. Perf 14½.

4170	**3273**	(1st) The Skull Sectioned	1·20	1·00
		a. Horiz strip of 6. Nos. 4170/4175	6·50	5·50
4171	**3274**	(1st) A Sprig of Guelder-rose	1·20	1·00
4172	**3275**	(1st) Studies of Cats	1·20	1·00
4173	**3276**	(1st) A Star-of-Bethlehem and Other Plants	1·20	1·00
4174	**3277**	(1st) The Anatomy of the Shoulder and Foot	1·20	1·00
4175	**3278**	(1st) The Head of Leda	1·20	1·00
4176	**3279**	(1st) The Head of a Bearded Man	1·20	1·00
		a. Horiz strip of 6. Nos. 4176/4181	6·50	5·50
4177	**3280**	(1st) The Skeleton	1·20	1·00
4178	**3281**	(1st) The Head of St Philip	1·20	1·00
4179	**3282**	(1st) A Woman in a Landscape	1·20	1·00
4180	**3283**	(1st) A Design for an Equestrian Monument	1·20	1·00
4181	**3284**	(1st) The Fall of Light on a Face	1·20	1·00
Set of 12			13·00	11·00
Set of 2 Gutter Strips of 12			26·00	
First Day Cover (Tallents House)				14·00
Presentation Pack (PO Pack No. 567)			17·00	
PHQ Cards (set of 12) (453)			7·00	12·00

Nos. 4170/4175 and 4176/4181 were each printed together, *se-tenant*, as horizontal strips of six stamps in sheets of 60 (2 panes 6×5).

3291 Iron Man

3292 Union Jack

3293 Black Panther

3294 Thor

3295 Marvel Heroes UK

2019 (14 Mar). Marvel (1st issue) Multicoloured. Two phosphor bands.

(a) Ordinary gum. Perf 14½.

4182	**3285**	(1st) Spider-Man	1·20	1·00
		a. Horiz strip of 5. Nos. 4182/4186	5·25	4·50
4183	**3286**	(1st) Captain Marvel	1·20	1·00
4184	**3287**	(1st) Hulk	1·20	1·00
4185	**3288**	(1st) Doctor Strange	1·20	1·00
4186	**3289**	(1st) Captain Britain	1·20	1·00
4187	**3290**	(1st) Peggy Carter	1·20	1·00
		a. Horiz strip of 5. Nos. 4187/4191	5·25	4·50
4188	**3291**	(1st) Iron Man	1·20	1·00
4189	**3292**	(1st) Union Jack	1·20	1·00
4190	**3293**	(1st) Black Panther	1·20	1·00
4191	**3294**	(1st) Thor	1·20	1·00
Set of 10			10·50	9·00
Set of 2 Gutter Strips of 10			21·00	
First Day Cover (Tallents House)				17·00
Presentation Pack (PO Pack No. 568) (Nos. 4182/4191 and **MS**4192)			20·00	
PHQ Cards (set of 16) (454)			9·00	24·00

(b) Self-adhesive.

MS4192 203×74 mm. **3295** (1st) Thanos (Perf 14); (1st) Thor, Doctor Strange and Iron Man ('He's strong.') (Perf 14½×14); (1st) Hulk, Iron Man, Black Panther and Spider-Man ('but we're stronger...') (Perf 14); £1·25 Captain Britain, Spider-Man, Iron Man, Hulk, Thor and Black Panther ('...together!') (Perf 14); £1·45 Captain Britain ('Fury, a portal is opening.') (Perf 14½×14) ... 7·25 ... 7·25

First Day Cover (Tallents House) ... 10·00

(c) Self-adhesive booklet stamps. Die-cut perf 14½.

4193	**3285**	(1st) Spider-Man	3·50	3·50
4194	**3287**	(1st) Hulk	3·50	3·50

Nos. 4182/4186 and 4187/4191 were each printed together, *se-tenant*, as horizontal strips of five stamps in sheets of 50 (2 panes 5×5).

Nos. 4193/4194 were issued in stamp booklets with 1st bright scarlet stamp×4 stamps, originally sold for £4·02.

Nos. 4182/4194 commemorate the 80th Anniversary of Marvel Comics.

A collector's sheet containing stamps as Nos. 4182/4191 but self-adhesive was sold for £7·70, a £1 premium above face value.

The 16 PHQ cards show the 15 individual stamps, including those from No. **MS**4192, and the complete sheet.

3285 Spider-Man

3286 Captain Marvel

3287 Hulk

3288 Doctor Strange

3289 Captain Britain

3290 Peggy Carter

3296 'Thanos'

3297 Thor, Doctor Strange and Iron Man ('He's strong.')

3298 Hulk, Iron Man, Black Panther and Spider-Man ('but we're stronger...')

3299 Captain Britain, Spider-Man, Iron Man, Hulk, Thor and Black Panther ('...together!')

3300 Captain Britain ('Fury, a portal is opening.')

2019 (14 Mar). Marvel (2nd issue) Multicoloured. Self-adhesive. Two phosphor bands. Die-cut perf 14½×14 (Nos. 4196, 4199) or 14 (others).

4195	**3296**	(1st) Thanos	1·25	1·25
4196	**3297**	(1st) Thor, Doctor Strange and Iron Man ('He's strong.')	1·25	1·25
4197	**3298**	(1st) Hulk, Iron Man, Black Panther and Spider-Man ('but we're stronger...')	1·25	1·25
4198	**3299**	£1·25 Captain Britain, Spider-Man, Iron Man, Hulk, Thor and Black Panther ('...together!')	2·50	2·50
4199	**3300**	£1·45 Captain Britain ('Fury, a portal is opening.')	2·75	2·75
Set of 5			8·00	8·00

Nos. 4195/4199 were issued in No. **MS**4192 and in two booklet panes from the £17·45 Marvel booklet, No. DY29.

Booklet panes are as No. **MS**4192 but in two panes with enlarged margins.

3301 White-tailed Eagle

3302 Merlin

3303 Hobby

3304 Buzzard

3305 Golden Eagle

3306 Kestrel

3307 Goshawk

3308 Sparrowhawk

3309 Red Kite

3310 Peregrine Falcon

2019 (4 Apr). Birds of Prey. Multicoloured. Phosphor background.

(a) Ordinary gum. Perf 14×14½.

4200	**3301**	(1st) White-tailed Eagle (*Haliaeetus albicilla*)	1·20	1·00
		a. Horiz strip of 5. Nos. 4200/4204	5·25	4·50
4201	**3302**	(1st) Merlin (*Falco columbarius*)	1·20	1·00
4202	**3303**	(1st) Hobby (*Falco subbuteo*)	1·20	1·00
4203	**3304**	(1st) Buzzard (*Buteo buteo*)	1·20	1·00
4204	**3305**	(1st) Golden Eagle (*Aquila chrysaetos*)	1·20	1·00
4205	**3306**	(1st) Kestrel (*Falco tinnunculus*)	1·20	1·00
		a. Horiz strip of 5. Nos. 4205/4209	5·25	4·50
4206	**3307**	(1st) Goshawk (*Accipiter gentilis*)	1·20	1·00
4207	**3308**	(1st) Sparrowhawk (*Accipiter nisus*)	1·20	1·00
4208	**3309**	(1st) Red Kite (*Milvus milvus*)	1·20	1·00
4209	**3310**	(1st) Peregrine Falcon (*Falco peregrinus*)	1·20	1·00
Set of 10			10·50	9·00
Set of 2 Gutter Strips of 10			21·00	
First Day Cover (Tallents House)				13·00
Presentation Pack (PO Pack No. 569)			13·00	
PHQ Cards (set of 10) (455)			6·00	12·00

(b) Self-adhesive. Die-cut perf 14×14½.

4210	**3304**	(1st) Buzzard (*Buteo buteo*)	15·00	15·00
4211	**3303**	(1st) Hobby (*Falco subbuteo*)	15·00	15·00

Nos. 4200/4204 and 4205/4209 were each printed together, *se-tenant*, as horizontal strips of five stamps in sheets of 50 (2 panes 5×5).

Nos. 4210/4211 were issued in stamp booklets with 1st bright scarlet stamp×4 stamps, originally sold for £4·02.

Raspberry Pi microcomputer helps to teach programming

3311 Raspberry Pi Microcomputer

The Falkirk Wheel rotating boat lift connects Scottish waterways

3312 The Falkirk Wheel Rotating Boat Lift

Three-way catalytic converter
reduces pollutants in car exhaust

Crossrail created 26 miles (42km)
of new rail tunnels under London

3313 Three-way Catalytic
Converter

3314 Crossrail

Superconducting magnet allows
high-quality imaging in MRI

Synthetic bone-graft material
encourages new bone growth

3315 Superconducting
Magnet in MRI Scanner

3316 Synthetic Bone-graft

HARRIER JUMP JET
50TH ANNIVERSARY

3317 Harrier GR3

2019 (2 May). British Engineering. Multicoloured. Two phosphor bands.
Perf 14½×14 (Nos. 4212/4217) or 14 (No. **MS**4218)

4212	**3311**	(1st) Raspberry Pi Microcomputer	1·20	1·00
		a. Horiz pair. Nos. 4212/4213	2·40	2·00
4213	**3312**	(1st) The Falkirk Wheel	1·20	1·00
4214	**3313**	£1·55 Three-way catalytic converter	2·40	2·40
		a. Horiz pair. Nos. 4214/4215	4·75	4·75
4215	**3314**	£1·55 Crossrail	2·40	2·40
4216	**3315**	£1·60 Superconducting Magnet	2·50	2·50
		a. Horiz pair. Nos. 4216/4217	5·00	5·00
4217	**3316**	£1·60 Synthetic Bone-graft material	2·50	2·50
	Set of 6		10·75	10·50
	Set of 3 Gutter Pairs (only 2 stamps in each Gutter Pair)		11·50	
	Set of 3 Traffic Light Gutter Blocks of 4		23·00	
	First Day Cover (Tallents House)			14·50
	Presentation Pack (PO Pack No. 570) (Nos. 4212/4217 and **MS**4218)		20·00	
	PHQ Cards (set of 11) (456)		6·50	20·00

MS4218 203×75 mm. **3317** (1st) Harrier GR3 Short
Take-off; (1st) Harrier GR3 Conventional Flight;
£1·55 Harrier GR3 Transition to Landing; £1·55
Harrier GR3 Vertical Landing 6·75 6·75
First Day Cover (Tallents House) 8·50

Nos. 4212/4213, 4214/4215 and 4216/4217 were each printed together,
se-tenant, as horizontal pairs in sheets of 60 (2 panes 6×5).

The 11 PHQ cards show the ten individual stamps, including those from
No. **MS**4218, and the complete sheet.

3318 Queen Victoria
(Heinrich von Angeli), 1890

3319 Queen Victoria and
Benjamin Disraeli, 1878

3320 Queen Victoria with
servant John Brown, 1876

3321 Queen Victoria wearing
her Robes of State, 1859

3322 Marriage of Queen
Victoria and Prince Albert,
1840

3323 Princess Victoria aged
11, 1830

THE LEGACY OF
PRINCE ALBERT

3324 The Legacy of Prince Albert

2019 (24 May). Birth Bicentenary of Queen Victoria (1st issue).
Multicoloured. Two phosphor bands. Perf 14×14½ (Nos. 4219/4224)
or 14 (No. **MS**4225).

4219	**3318**	(1st) Queen Victoria (Heinrich von Angeli), 1890	1·20	1·00
		a. Horiz pair. Nos. 4219/4220	2·40	2·00
4220	**3319**	(1st) Queen Victoria and Benjamin Disraeli, 1878	1·20	1·00
4221	**3320**	£1·35 Queen Victoria with Servant John Brown, 1876	2·00	2·00
		a. Horiz pair. Nos. 4221/4222	4·00	4·00
4222	**3321**	£1·35 Queen Victoria wearing her Robes of State, 1859	2·00	2·00
4223	**3322**	£1·60 Marriage of Queen Victoria and Prince Albert, 1840	2·50	2·50
		a. Horiz pair. Nos. 4223/4224	5·00	5·00
4224	**3323**	£1·60 Princess Victoria aged 11, 1830	2·50	2·50
	Set of 6		10·50	10·00
	Set of 3 Gutter Pairs		21·00	
	First Day Cover (Tallents House)			13·50
	Presentation Pack (PO Pack No. 571)		20·00	
	PHQ Cards (set of 11) (457)		6·50	22·00

MS4225 156×74 mm. **3324** (1st) Model Lodge,
Kennington; (1st) Balmoral Castle, Scotland; £1·55
The New Crystal Palace, Sydenham; £1·55 Royal
Albert Hall, London 18·00 18·00
First Day Cover (Tallents House) 20·00

Nos. 4219/4220, 4221/4222 and 4223/4224 were each printed together,
se-tenant, as horizontal pairs in sheets of 60 (2 panes 6×5).

Booklet panes No. 4219b and 4222b come from the £17.20 Queen
Victoria booklet, No. DY30.

The 11 PHQ cards show the individual stamps including those from No.
MS4225 and the complete miniature sheet.

3325 Model Lodge, Kennington

3326 Balmoral Castle, Scotland

3327 The New Crystal Palace, Sydenham

3328 Royal Albert Hall, London

2019 (24 May). Birth Bicentenary of Queen Victoria (2nd issue). Multicoloured. Two phosphor bands. Perf 14

4226	**3325**	(1st) Model Lodge, Kennington	3·00	3·00
4227	**3326**	(1st) Balmoral Castle, Scotland	3·00	3·00
4228	**3327**	£1·55 The New Crystal Palace, Sydenham	6·00	6·00
4229	**3328**	£1·55 Royal Albert Hall, London	6·00	6·00
Set of 4			18·00	18·00

Nos. 4226/4229 come from No. **MS**4225 and the £17·20 Queen Victoria booklet, No. DY30.

3329 British soldiers are briefed before embarkation

3330 HMS *Warspite* shelling in support of beach landings

3331 Paratroopers synchronising watches

3332 Soldiers wade ashore on Juno Beach

3333 An American light bomber provides air support

3334 British troops take cover as they advance inland

3335 The Normandy Landings

⊛GOLD   ⊛SWORD

3336 Gold Beach   **3337** Sword Beach

2019 (6 June). 75th Anniversary of D-Day. Multicoloured. Two phosphor bands.

(a) Ordinary gum. Perf 14½.

4230	**3329**	(1st) No. 4 Commando, 1st Special Service Brigade briefed by Commanding Officer Lieutenant-Colonel R. Dawson before Embarkation	1·20	1·00
		a. Vert pair. Nos. 4230/4231	2·40	2·00
4231	**3330**	(1st) HMS *Warspite* shelling German Gun Batteries	1·20	1·00
4232	**3331**	£1·35 Paratroopers	2·00	2·00
		a. Vert pair. Nos. 4232/4233	4·00	4·00
4233	**3332**	£1·35 Commandos wade ashore on Juno Beach	2·00	2·00
4234	**3333**	£1·60 American A-20 Havoc Light Bomber	2·50	2·50
		a. Vert pair. Nos. 4234/4235	5·00	5·00
4235	**3334**	£1·60 Troops take cover from enemy shell	2·50	2·50
Set of 6			10·25	10·00
Set of 3 Gutter Pairs (only 2 stamps in each gutter pair)			11·50	
First Day Cover (Tallents House)				13·00
Presentation Pack (PO Pack No. 572) (Nos. 4230/4235 and **MS**4236)			18·00	
PHQ Cards (set of 12) (458)			7·00	22·00

MS4236 203×75 mm. **3335** (1st)×5 US 4th Infantry Division, Utah Beach; US troops going ashore at Omaha Beach; British 50th Division landing on Gold Beach; Canadian 3rd Division landing at Juno Beach; British 3rd Division landing at Sword Beach ... 6·25 / 6·25

First Day Cover (Tallents House) ... 7·50

(b) Self-adhesive. Die-cut perf 14½.

4237	**3336**	(1st) British 50th Division landing on Gold Beach	3·25	3·25
4238	**3337**	(1st) British 3rd Division landing at Sword Beach	3·25	3·25

Nos. 4230/4231, 4232/4233 and 4234/4235 were each printed together, *se-tenant*, as vertical pairs in sheets of 60 (5×6).

Nos. 4237/4238 were issued in stamp booklets 1st bright scarlet stamp×4 stamps originally sold for £4·20.

The 12 PHQ cards show each of the individual stamps including those from No. **MS**4236 and the complete miniature sheet.

No. **MS**4236 additionally inscribed 'Stampex International The British National Stamp Exhibition' 11-14 September 2019 was only available at that exhibition (*Price £7*)

3338 Burning the Clocks, Brighton

3339 'Obby 'Oss, Padstow

3340 World Gurning Championships, Egremont

3341 Up Helly Aa, Lerwick

3342 Halloween, Londonderry

3343 Cheese Rolling, Cooper's Hill

3344 Horn Dance, Abbots Bromley

3345 Bog Snorkelling, Llanwrtyd Wells

2019 (19 July). Curious Customs. Multicoloured. One centre bank (2nd) or two bands (others). Perf 14×14½.

4239	**3338**	(2nd) Burning the Clocks, Brighton	90	90
		a. Horiz pair. Nos. 4239/4240	1·75	1·75
4240	**3339**	(2nd) 'Obby 'Oss, Padstow, Cornwall	90	90
4241	**3340**	(1st) World Gurning Championships, Egremont, Cumbria	1·20	1·00
		a. Horiz pair. Nos. 4241/4242	2·40	2·00
4242	**3341**	(1st) Up Helly Aa, Lerwick, Shetland	1·20	1·00
4243	**3342**	£1·55 Halloween, Londonderry	2·40	2·40
		a. Horiz pair. Nos. 4243/4244	4·75	4·75
4244	**3343**	£1·55 Cheese Rolling, Cooper's Hill, Brockworth, Gloucestershire	2·40	2·40
4245	**3344**	£1·60 Horn Dance, Abbots Bromley, Staffordshire	2·50	2·50
		a. Horiz pair. Nos. 4245/4246	5·00	5·00
4246	**3345**	£1·60 Bog Snorkelling, Llanwrtyd Wells, Wales	2·50	2·50
Set of 8			12·75	12·50
Set of 4 Gutter Pairs			25·50	
First Day Cover (Tallents House)				14·00
Presentation Pack (PO Pack No. 573)			15·00	
PHQ Cards (set of 8) (459)			5·00	13·00

Nos. 4239/4240, 4241/4242, 4243/4244 and 4245/4246 were each printed together, *se-tenant*, as horizontal pairs in sheets of 60 (2 panes 6×5).

3346 Glen Affric

3347 The National Arboretum, Westonbirt

3348 Sherwood Forest

3349 Coed y Brenin

3350 Glenariff Forest

3351 Kielder Forest

2019 (13 Aug). Forests. Multicoloured. Two phosphor bands. Perf 14½.

4247	**3346**	(1st) Glen Affric	1·20	1·00
		a. Vert pair. Nos. 4247/4248	2·40	2·00
4248	**3347**	(1st) The National Arboretum, Westonbirt, Gloucestershire	1·20	1·00
4249	**3348**	£1·55 Sherwood Forest, Nottinghamshire	2·40	2·40
		a. Vert pair. Nos. 4249/4250	4·75	4·75
4250	**3349**	£1·55 Coed y Brenin, Gwynedd, Wales	2·40	2·40
4251	**3350**	£1·60 Glenariff Forest, County Antrim,	2·50	2·50
		a. Vert pair. Nos. 4251/4252	5·00	5·00
4252	**3351**	£1·60 Kielder Forest	2·50	2·50
Set of 6			10·75	10·50
Set of 3 Gutter Pairs (only 2 stamps in each gutter pair)			12·00	
First Day Cover (Tallents House)				13·50
Presentation Pack (PO Pack No. 574)			13·00	
PHQ Cards (set of 6) (460)			4·00	12·50

Nos. 4247/4248, 4249/4250 and 4251/4252 were each printed together, *se-tenant*, as vertical pairs in sheets of 60 (2 panes 5×6).

Nos. 4247/4252 commemorate the Centenary of the Forestry Commission.

3352 *Honky Château*   **3353** *Goodbye Yellow Brick Road*

3354 *Caribou*   **3355** *Captain Fantastic and The Brown Dirt Cowboy*

3356 *Sleeping with The Past*   **3357** *The One*

3358 *Made in England*   **3359** *Songs from The West Coast*

3360 Elton John Live

2019 (3 Sept). Elton John. Multicoloured. Two phosphor bands.

(a) Ordinary gum. Perf 14.

4253	**3352**	(1st) *Honky Château*	1·20	1·00
		a. Horiz strip of 4. Nos. 4253/4256	4·25	3·75
4254	**3353**	(1st) *Goodbye Yellow Brick Road*	1·20	1·00
4255	**3354**	(1st) *Caribou*	1·20	1·00
4256	**3355**	(1st) *Captain Fantastic and The Brown Dirt Cowboy*	1·20	1·00
4257	**3356**	£1·55 *Sleeping with The Past*	2·40	2·40
		a. Horiz strip of 4. Nos. 4257/4260	9·25	9·25
4258	**3357**	£1·55 *The One*	2·40	2·40
4259	**3358**	£1·55 *Made in England*	2·40	2·40
4260	**3359**	£1·55 *Songs from The West Coast*	2·40	2·40
Set of 8			13·00	12·50
Set of 2 Gutter Strips of 8			26·00	
First Day Cover (Tallents House)				15·50
Presentation Pack (PO Pack No. 575) (Nos. 4253/4260 and **MS**4261)			24·00	
Goodbye Yellow Brick Road Character Pack (containing No. 4254×10)			13·00	
Captain Fantastic and The Brown Dirt Cowboy Character Pack (containing No. 4256×10)			13·00	
PHQ Cards (set of 13) (461)			7·50	25·00

MS4261 156×74 mm. **3360** Elton John Live (1st) Madison Square Garden, 2018; (1st) Dodger Stadium, 1975; £1·55 Hammersmith Odeon, 1973; £1·55 Buckingham Palace, 2012   6·75   6·75
First day cover   8·50

(b) Self-adhesive. Die-cut perf 14.

4262	**3353**	(1st) *Goodbye Yellow Brick Road*	5·00	5·00
4263	**3355**	(1st) *Captain Fantastic and The Brown Dirt Cowboy*	5·00	5·00

Nos. 4253/4256 and 4257/4260 were each printed together, *se-tenant*, as horizontal strips of four stamps in sheets of 48 (2 panes 4×6).

Nos. 4262/4263 were issued in stamp booklets with 1st bright scarlet stamp×4, originally sold for £4·20.

A *Goodbye Yellow Brick Road* fan sheet containing No. 4254×4 was sold for £7·50.

A *Captain Fantastic and The Brown Dirt Cowboy* fan sheet containing No. 4256×4 was sold for £7·50.

A Album Collection fan sheet containing Nos. 4253/4260 was sold for £10·20.

The 13 PHQ cards show the individual stamps, including those from No. **MS**4261, and the complete miniature sheet.

3361 *Mary Rose*, 1511   **3362** HMS *Queen Elizabeth*, 2014

3363 HMS *Victory*, 1765   **3364** HMS *Dreadnought*, 1906

3365 HMS *Warrior*, 1860   **3366** *Sovereign of the Seas*, 1637

3367 HMS *King George V*, 1939   **3368** HMS *Beagle*, 1820

2019 (19 Sept). Royal Navy Ships. Multicoloured. Two phosphor bands.

(a) Ordinary gum. Perf 14.

4264	**3361**	(1st) *Mary Rose*, 1511 (Geoff Hunt)	1·20	1·00
		a. Horiz pair. Nos. 4264/4265	2·40	2·00
4265	**3362**	(1st) HMS *Queen Elizabeth*, 2014 (Robert G. Lloyd)	1·20	1·00
4266	**3363**	£1·35 HMS *Victory*, 1765 (Monamy Swaine)	2·00	2·00
		a. Horiz pair. Nos. 4266/4267	4·00	4·00
4267	**3364**	£1·35 HMS *Dreadnought*, 1906 (H. J. Morgan)	2·00	2·00
4268	**3365**	£1·55 HMS *Warrior*, 1860 (Thomas Goldsworth Dutton)	2·40	2·40
		a. Horiz pair. Nos. 4268/4269	4·75	4·75
4269	**3366**	£1·55 *Sovereign of the Seas*, 1637 (Paul Garnett)	2·40	2·40
4270	**3367**	£1·60 HMS *King George V*, 1939 (Robert G. Lloyd)	2·50	2·50
		a. Horiz pair. Nos. 4270/4271	5·00	5·00
4271	**3368**	£1·60 HMS *Beagle*, 1820 (John Chancellor)	2·50	2·50
Set of 8			14·25	14·00
Set of 4 Gutter Blocks of 4			28·50	

First Day Cover (Tallents House)		17·00
Presentation Pack (PO Pack No. 576)	17·00	
PHQ Cards (set of 8) (462)	5·00	16·00

(b) Self-adhesive. Die-cut perf 14.

4272	**3361**	(1st) *Mary Rose*, 1511 (Geoff Hunt)	15·00	15·00
4273	**3362**	(1st) HMS *Queen Elizabeth*, 2014 (Robert G. Lloyd)	15·00	15·00

Nos. 4264/4265, 4266/4267, 4268/4269 and 4270/4271 were each printed together, *se-tenant*, as horizontal pairs in sheets of 60 (2 panes 6×5).

Nos. 4272/4273 were issued in stamp booklets with 1st bright scarlet stamp×4 originally sold for £4·20.

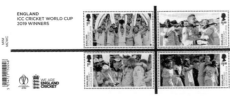

3369 Men's Cricket World Cup Winners

3370 Women's Cricket World Cup Winners

2019 (26 Sept). ICC Cricket World Cup Winners. Multicoloured. All over phosphor. Perf 14½.

MS4274 203×74 mm. **3369** (1st) England Captain Eoin Morgan lifting Cricket World Cup Trophy; (1st) Eoin Morgan (with trophy) and England team; £1·60 England players celebrating; £1·60 England players congratulating Ben Stokes	6·75	6·75
MS4275 203×74 mm. **3370** (1st) England team after their victory ('CHAMPIONS'); (1st) England players congratulating Anya Shrubsole; £1·60 England Captain Heather Knight and teammates celebrating; £1·60 England team celebrating on balcony at Lord's Cricket Ground (2017)	6·75	6·75
First Day Cover (Tallents House) (2)		16·00
Presentation Pack (PO Pack No. M25)	16·00	

3371 'Scrambled snake!'

3372 'Gruffalo crumble!'

3373 'All was quiet in the deep dark wood.'

3374 'A mouse took a stroll'

3375 'Roasted fox!'

3376 'Owl ice cream?'

3377 The Gruffalo

2019 (10 Oct). *The Gruffalo* (by Julia Donaldson, illustrated by Axel Scheffler). Multicoloured. Two phosphor bands. Perf 14 (No. 4276/4281) or 14½ (No. **MS**4282)

4276	**3371**	(1st) 'Scrambled snake!'	1·20	1·00
		a. Horiz strip of 3. Nos. 4276/4278	3·50	3·00
4277	**3372**	(1st) 'Gruffalo crumble!'	1·20	1·00
4278	**3373**	(1st) 'All was quiet in the deep dark wood.'	1·20	1·00
4279	**3374**	£1·60 'A mouse took a stroll'	2·50	2·50
		a. Horiz strip of 3. Nos. 4279/4281	7·50	7·50
4280	**3375**	£1·60 'Roasted fox!'	2·50	2·50
4281	**3376**	£1·60 'Owl ice cream?'	2·50	2·50
Set of 6			10·00	9·50
Set of 2 Gutter Strips of 6			11·50	
First Day Cover (Tallents House)				12·50
Presentation Pack (PO Pack No. 577) (Nos. 4276/4278 and **MS**4282)			19·00	
PHQ Cards (set of 11) (463)			7·50	22·00
MS4282 126×89 mm. **3377** (1st) Owl; (1st) Mouse; £1·55 Snake; £1·55 Fox			6·75	6·75
First Day Cover (Tallents House)				8·50

Nos. 4276/4278 and 4279/4281 were each printed together, *se-tenant*, as horizontal strips of three stamps in sheets of 60 (2 panes 6×5).

Stamps as within No. **MS**4282 but self-adhesive were issued in sheets of ten, containing three of each of the two 1st class designs and two of each of the two £1·55 designs, with attached labels.

The 11 PHQ cards show the individual stamps, including those from No. **MS**4282, and the complete miniature sheet.

3378 Angel and
Shepherd

3379 Mary and
Baby Jesus

3380 Angel and Shepherd

3381 Mary and Baby Jesus

3382 Joseph

3383 Baby Jesus
in Manger

3384 Shepherds
and Star

3385 Three Wise
Men

2019 (5 Nov). Christmas. Nativity. Multicoloured. One central band (No. 4283) or two (others).

(a) Self-adhesive. Gravure. Die-cut perf 14½×15..

4283	**3378**	(2nd) Angel and Shepherd	90	90
4284	**3379**	(1st) Mary and Baby Jesus	1·20	1·00
4285	**3380**	(2nd Large) Angel and Shepherd	1·25	1·25
4286	**3381**	(1st Large) Mary and Baby Jesus	1·70	1·60
4287	**3382**	£1·35 Joseph	2·00	2·00
4288	**3383**	£1·55 Baby Jesus in Manger	2·40	2·40
4289	**3384**	£1·60 Shepherds and Star	2·50	2·50
4290	**3385**	£2·30 Three Wise Men	3·50	3·50
Set of 8			13·75	13·50
First Day Cover (Tallents House)				17·00
Presentation Pack (PO Pack No. 578)			17·00	
PHQ Cards (set of 9) (464)			6·00	28·00

(b) Ordinary gum. Litho. Perf 14½×15..
MS4291 179×74 mm. Nos. 4283/4290 .... 13·75   13·50
First Day Cover (Tallents House) ....   17·00

The 2nd class, 1st class, £1·35, £1·55, £1·60 and £2·30 values were also issued in sheets of 20 containing 8×2nd class, 8×1st class, 1×£1·35, 1×£1·55, 1×£1·60 and 1×£2·30 values, each stamp accompanied by a *se-tenant* label.

The nine PHQ cards show the individual stamps and the complete miniature sheet.

3386 Count Dooku

3387 Lando Calrissian

3388 Sith Trooper

3389 Jannah

3390 Grand Moff Tarkin

3391 Darth Maul

3392 Zorii

3393 Wicket W. Warrick

3394 Poe Dameron

3395 Queen Amidala

3395a *Star Wars* Composite Sheet

3396 *Star Wars* Vehicles

2019 (26 Nov). *Star Wars*. (5th issue). Multicoloured. 'All-over' phosphor (No. **MS**4303 stamp only) or two phosphor bands (others).

(a) Ordinary gum. Perf 14½.

4292	**3386**	(1st) Count Dooku (Christopher Lee)	1·20	1·00
		a. Horiz strip of 5. Nos. 4292/4296	5·25	5·00
4293	**3387**	(1st) Lando Calrissian (Billy Dee Williams)	1·20	1·00
4294	**3388**	(1st) Sith Trooper	1·20	1·00
4295	**3389**	(1st) Jannah (Naomi Ackie)	1·20	1·00
4296	**3390**	(1st) Grand Moff Tarkin (Peter Cushing)	1·20	1·00
4297	**3391**	(1st) Darth Maul (Ray Park)	1·20	1·00
		a. Horiz strip of 5. Nos. 4297/4301	5·25	5·00
4298	**3392**	(1st) Zorii (Kerri Russell)	1·20	1·00
4299	**3393**	(1st) Wicket W. Warrick (Warwick Davis)	1·20	1·00
4300	**3394**	(1st) Poe Dameron (Oscar Isaac)	1·20	1·00
4301	**3395**	(1st) Queen Amidala (Natalie Portman)	1·20	1·00
Set of 10			9·00	9·00
Set of 2 Gutter Strips of 10			21·00	
First Day Cover (Tallents House)				12·00
Presentation Pack (PO Pack No. 579) (Nos. 4292/4301 and **MS**4303)			20·00	
PHQ Cards (set of 16)			11·50	20·00
MS4302 210×297 mm. **3395a** Nos. 3758/3769, 4007/4014 and 4292/4301			35·00	50·00

(b) Self-adhesive.

MS4303 192×74 mm. **3396** (1st) Poe's X-wing fighter (41×30 mm) (Perf 14); (1st) Jedi starfighter (27×37 mm) (Perf 14); (1st) Slave 1 (27×37 mm) (Perf 14); (1st) TIE silencer (41×30 mm) (Perf 14); (1st) Podracers (60×21 mm) (Perf 14½×14); (1st) Speeder bikes (60×21 mm) (Perf 14½×14)			7·00	7·00
First Day Cover (Tallents House)				8·75

(c) Self-adhesive. Die-cut perf 14½.

4304	**3394**	(1st) Poe Dameron (Oscar Isaac)	1·75	1·75
4305	**3388**	(1st) Sith Trooper	1·75	1·75

Nos. 4292/4296 and 4297/4301 were each printed together, *se-tenant*, as horizontal strips of five stamps in sheets of 50 (2 panes 5×5).

Booklet panes Nos. 4292b and 4393b come from the £17·65 *Star Wars: The Making of the Vehicles* booklet, No. DY31.

Nos. 4304/4305 were issued in stamp booklets with 1st bright scarlet stamp×4, originally sold for £4·20.

A collectors sheet containing stamps as Nos. 4292/4301 but self-adhesive with labels showing film scenes was sold for £8·10, a £1·10 premium over face value.

3397 Poe's X-wing Fighter   **3398** Jedi Starfighter

3399 Podracers

3400 Slave 1   **3401** TIE Silencer

3402 Speeder Bikes

2019 (26 Nov). *Star Wars* (6th issue). Multicoloured. 'All-over' phosphor (stamps only). Self-adhesive. Die-cut perf 14 (Nos. 4306/4307, 4309/4310) or 14½×14 (Nos. 4308, 4311).

4306	**3397**	(1st) Poe's X-wing Fighter	1·30	1·30
4307	**3398**	(1st) Jedi Starfighter	1·30	1·30
4308	**3399**	(1st) Podracers	1·30	1·30
4309	**3400**	(1st) Slave 1	1·30	1·30
4310	**3401**	(1st) TIE Silencer	1·30	1·30
4311	**3402**	(1st) Speeder Bikes	1·30	1·30
Set of 6			7·00	7·00

The booklet panes are as No. **MS**4303 but in two panes with margins giving information about *Star Wars* vehicles.

Nos. 4306/4311 were issued in No. **MS**4303 and in two booklet from the £17·65 *Star Wars The Making of the Vehicles* booklet, No. DY31.

Collectors Pack

2019 (26 Nov). Comprises Nos. **MS**4169/**MS**4192, 4200/4209, 4212/ **MS**4225, 4230/**MS**4236, 4239/**MS**4261, **MS**4274/4290, 4292/**MS**4301 and **MS**4303

CP4311a	Collectors Pack (Pack No. 580) (*sold for £156*)	£250

Post Office Yearbook

2019 (26 Nov). Comprises Nos. **MS**4169/**MS**4192, 4200/4209, 4212/ **MS**4225, 4230/**MS**4236, 4239/**MS**4261, 4264/4271, **MS**4274/4290, 4294/4301 and **MS**4303

YB4311a	Yearbook (*sold for £176*)	£275

Miniature Sheet Collection

2019 (26 Nov). Comprises Nos. **MS**4169, **MS**4192, **MS**4218, **MS**4225/ **MS**4236, **MS**4261, **MS**4274/**MS**4275, **MS**4282, **MS**4291 and **MS**4303.

MS4311a	Miniature Sheet Collection (*sold for £58*)	70·00

3403 *Elite*, 1984

3404 *Worms*, 1995

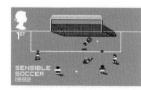

3405 *Sensible Soccer*, 1992

3406 *Lemmings*, 1991

3407 *Wipeout*, 1995

3408 *Micro Machines,* 1991

3409 *Dizzy,* 1987

3410 *Populous,* 1989

3411 *Tomb Raider*

3412 *Tomb Raider,* 1996

3413 *Tomb Raider,* 2013

2020 (21 Jan). Video Games. Multicoloured.
(a) Ordinary gum. Band at right (No. 4312), centre band (No. 4313) or two bands (others). Perf 14.

4312	**3403**	(2nd) *Elite,* 1984	1·25	1·25
		a. Vert pair. Nos. 4312/4313	2·50	2·50
4313	**3404**	(2nd) *Worms,* 1995	1·25	1·25
4314	**3405**	(1st) *Sensible Soccer,* 1992	1·90	1·90
		a. Vert pair. Nos. 4314/4315	3·75	3·75
4315	**3406**	(1st) *Lemmings,* 1991	1·90	1·90
4316	**3407**	£1·55 *Wipeout,* 1995	2·40	2·40
		a. Vert pair. Nos. 4316/4317	4·75	4·75
4317	**3408**	£1·55 *Micro Machines,* 1991	2·40	2·40
4318	**3409**	£1·60 *Dizzy,* 1987	2·50	2·50
		a. Vert pair. Nos. 4318/4319	5·00	5·00
4319	**3410**	£1·60 *Populous,* 1989	2·50	2·50
Set of 8			15·00	15·00
Set of 4 Gutter Blocks of 4			30·00	
First Day Cover (Tallents House)				17·50
Presentation Pack (PO Pack No. 581) (Nos. 4312/4319				
and **MS**4320)			26·00	
PHQ Cards (*set of 13*)			8·75	27·00

MS4320 126×90 mm. **3411** (1st) *Tomb Raider,* 1996; (1st) *Tomb Raider,* 2013; £1·55 *Adventures of Lara Croft,* 1998; £1·55 *Tomb Raider Chronicles,* 2000   8·75   8·75
First Day Cover (Tallents House)   11·00

(b) Self-adhesive. Two phosphor bands. Die-cut perf 14.

4321	**3412**	(1st) *Tomb Raider,* 1996	5·25	5·25
4322	**3413**	(1st) *Tomb Raider,* 2013	5·25	5·25

Nos. 4312/4313, 4314/4315, 4316/4317 and 4318/4319 were printed together, *se-tenant,* as vertical pairs in sheets of 60 (2 panes 5×6).

Nos. 4321/4322 were issued in stamp booklets with 1st bright scarlet stamp×4, originally sold for £4·20.

Stamps as within No. **MS**4320 but self-adhesive were issued in sheets of ten containing three of each of the 1st class designs and two of each of the £1·55 designs, with *se-tenant* labels. These sheets were printed in lithography.

The 13 PHQ cards show the 12 individual stamps, including those from No. **MS**4320, and the complete miniature sheet.

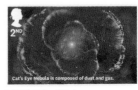

3414 Cat's Eye Nebula

3415 Enceladus

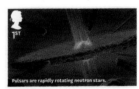

3416 Pulsars

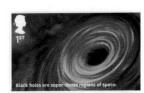

3417 Black Holes

3418 Jupiter's Auroras

3419 Gravitational Lensing

3420 Comet 67P

3421 Cygnus A Galaxy

2020 (11 Feb). Visions of the Universe. Multicoloured. One centre band (2nd) or two bands (others). Perf 14.

4323	**3414**	(2nd) Cat's Eye Nebula	1·25	1·25
		a. Horiz pair. Nos. 4323/4324	2·50	2·50
4324	**3415**	(2nd) Enceladus (Saturn's moon)	1·25	1·25
4325	**3416**	(1st) Pulsars	1·90	1·90
		a. Horiz pair. Nos. 4325/4326	3·75	3·75
4326	**3417**	(1st) Black holes	1·90	1·90
4327	**3418**	£1·55 Jupiter's auroras	2·40	2·40
		a. Horiz pair. Nos. 4327/4328	4·75	4·75
4328	**3419**	£1·55 Gravitational lensing	2·40	2·40
4329	**3420**	£1·60 Comet 67P	2·50	2·50
		a. Horiz pair. Nos. 4329/4330	5·00	5·00
4330	**3421**	£1·60 Cygnus A	2·50	2·50
Set of 8			15·00	15·00
Set of 4 Gutter Pairs			30·00	
First Day Cover (Tallents House)				17·00
Presentation Pack (PO Pack No. 582)			17·00	
PHQ Cards (set of 8)			5·50	16·00

Nos. 4323/4324, 4325/4326, 4327/4328 and 4329/4330 were each printed together, se-tenant, as horizontal pairs in sheets of 60 (2 panes 6×5).

2020 (10 Mar). London 2020 International Stamp Exhibition. Multicoloured. Self-adhesive. Two phosphor bands. Die-cut perf 14½×14 (with one elliptical hole in each vert side).

4331	**2938**	(1st) Two Pence Blue	1·90	1·90

No. 4331 comes from booklet containing Nos. 3709, 3806 and 4331, each×2 which was originally sold for £4·20.

3422 James Bond in *Casino Royale*

3423 James Bond in *Goldeneye*

3424 James Bond in *The Living Daylights*

3425 James Bond in *Live and Let Die*

3426 James Bond in *On Her Majesty's Secret Service*

3427 James Bond in *Goldfinger*

3428 Q Branch

3429 Bell-Textron Jet Pack, *Thunderball*

3430 Aston Martin DB5, *Skyfall*

2020 (17 Mar). James Bond. Multicoloured. (a) Ordinary gum. Two phosphor bands or 'all-over' phosphor (No. **MS**4338). Perf 14½ (No. 4332/4337) or 14×14½ (£1·55) or 14 (1st) (No. **MS**4338)

4332	**3422**	(1st) James Bond (Daniel Craig) in *Casino Royale*	1·90	1·90
		a. Horiz strip of 3. Nos. 4332/4334	5·75	5·75
4333	**3423**	(1st) James Bond (Pierce Brosnan) in *Goldeneye*	1·90	1·90
4334	**3424**	(1st) James Bond (Timothy Dalton) in *The Living Daylights*	1·90	1·90
4335	**3425**	£1·60 James Bond (Roger Moore) in *Live and Let Die*	2·50	2·50
		a. Horiz strip of 3. Nos. 4335/4337	7·50	
4336	**3426**	£1·60 James Bond (George Lazenby) in *On Her Majesty's Secret Service*	2·50	2·50
4337	**3427**	£1·60 James Bond (Sean Connery) in *Goldfinger*	2·50	2·50
Set of 6			13·00	13·00
Set of 2 Gutter Strips of 6			26·00	
First Day Cover (Tallents House)				15·00
Presentation Pack (Nos. 4332/4337 and **MS**4338) (PO Pack No. 583)			24·00	
PHQ Cards (set of 11)			7·50	24·00

MS4338 202×74 mm. **3428** (1st) Bell-Textron Jet Pack, *Thunderball*; (1st) Aston Martin DB5, *Skyfall*; £1·55 Lotus Esprit Submarine, *The Spy Who Loved Me*; £1·55 Little Nellie, *You Only Live Twice*

		8·75	8·75
First Day Cover (Tallents House)			11·00

(b) Self-adhesive. 'All-over' phosphor. Die-cut perf 14.

4339	**3429**	(1st) Bell-Textron Jet Pack, *Thunderball*	5·25	5·25
4340	**3430**	(1st) Aston Martin DB5, *Skyfall*	5·25	5·25

Nos. 4332/4334 and 4335/4337 were each printed together, *se-tenant*, as horizontal strips of three in sheets of 36 (2 panes 3×6).

Stamps from No. **MS**4338 have '007' perforations at top right, top left, bottom right or bottom left.

Nos. 4304/4305 were issued in stamp booklets with 1st bright scarlet stamp×4, originally sold for £4·20.

A collector's sheet with stamps as Nos 4332/4337 with attached labels was originally sold for £12·60. It contained Nos. 4332×2, 4333/4336 and 4337×3

A *No Time to Die* collector's sheet containing ten self-adhesive stamps as T **3430** perforated 14×14½ with attached labels was issued on 3 November 2020 and sold for £8·80.

The 11 PHQ cards show the ten individual stamps, including those from No. **MS**4338, and the complete miniature sheet.

3431 Little Nellie, *You Only Live Twice*

3432 Lotus Esprit Submarine, *The Spy Who Loved Me*

2020 (17 Mar). James Bond (2nd issue). Multicoloured. 'All-over' phosphor. Perf 14 (1st) or 14×14½ (£1·55), all with '007' perforations at top right, top left, bottom right or bottom left.

4341	**3429**	(1st) Bell-Textron Jet Pack, *Thunderball*	1·90	1·90
4342	**3430**	(1st) Aston Martin DB5, *Skyfall*	1·90	1·90
4343	**3431**	£1·55 Little Nellie, *You Only Live Twice*	2·40	2·40
4344	**3432**	£1·55 Lotus Esprit Submarine, *The Spy Who Loved Me*	2·40	2·40
Set of 4			8·75	8·75

Nos. 4341/4344 were issued in No. **MS**4338 and in a booklet pane from £16·99 James Bond booklet, No. DY33.

3433 The Progress of Rhyme (John Clare)

3434 Frost at Midnight (Samuel Taylor Coleridge)

3435 Auguries of Innocence (William Blake)

3436 The Lady of the Lake (Walter Scott)

3437 To a Skylark (Percy Bysshe Shelley)

3438 The Rainbow (William Wordsworth)

3439 Ode to the Snowdrop (Mary Robinson)

3440 The Fate of Adelaide (Letitia Elizabeth Landon)

3441 Ode to a Grecian Urn (John Keats)

3442 She Walks in Beauty (Lord Byron)

2020 (7 Apr). Romantic Poets. Black and orange-brown. Two phosphor bands. Perf 14.

4345	**3433**	(1st) *The Progress of Rhyme* (John Clare)	1·90	1·90
		a. Horiz strip of 5. Nos. 4345/4349	9·25	9·25
4346	**3434**	(1st) *Frost at Midnight* (Samuel Taylor Coleridge)	1·90	1·90
4347	**3435**	(1st) *Auguries of Innocence* (William Blake)	1·90	1·90
4348	**3436**	(1st) *The Lady of the Lake* (Walter Scott)	1·90	1·90
4349	**3437**	(1st) *To a Skylark* (Percy Bysshe Shelley)	1·90	1·90
4350	**3438**	(1st) *The Rainbow* (William Wordsworth)	1·90	1·90
		a. Horiz strip of 5. Nos. 4350/4354	9·25	9·25
4351	**3439**	(1st) *Ode to the Snowdrop* (Mary Robinson)	1·90	1·90
4352	**3440**	(1st) *The Fate of Adelaide* (Letitia Elizabeth Landon)	1·90	1·90
4353	**3441**	(1st) *Ode on a Grecian Urn* (John Keats)	1·90	1·90
4354	**3442**	(1st) *She Walks in Beauty* (Lord Byron)	1·90	1·90
Set of 10			18·00	18·00
Set of 2 Gutter Strips of 10			36·00	
First Day Cover (Tallents House)				20·00
Presentation Packs (PO Pack No. 584)			20·00	
PHQ Cards (set of 10) (469)			5·75	19·00

Nos. 4345/4349 and 4350/4354 were printed together, *se-tenant*, as horizontal strips of five in sheets of 50 (2 panes 5×5).

3442a

2020 (6 May). 180th Anniversary of the Penny Black. As T **2848** but ordinary gum. Litho. Perf 14½×14 (with one elliptical hole in each vert side).

MS4355 122×141 mm. **3442a** (1st) Penny Black×25   45·00   45·00

No. **MS**4355 was issued in sheets of 25 stamps and originally sold for £19.

3443 Servicemen returning home

3444 Nurses Celebrating

3445 Crowd Celebrating

3446 Evacuees Returning

3447 Marching Troops

3448 Demobilised Servicemen

3449 Liberated Prisoners

3450 Navy Personnel Celebrating

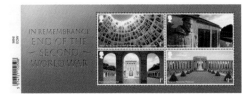

3451 Memorials

2020 (8 May). 75th Anniversary of the End of the Second World War (1st issue). Multicoloured. One centre band (2nd) or two phosphor bands (others). Perf 14 (Nos. 4356/4363) or 14½ (No. **MS**4364).

4356	**3443**	(2nd) Serviceman Returning Home	1·25	1·25
		a. Vert pair. Nos. 4356/4357	2·50	2·50
4357	**3444**	(2nd) Nurses celebrating VE Day, Liverpool, 1945	1·25	1·25
4358	**3445**	(1st) Crowds celebrating VE Day, Piccadilly, London, 1945	1·90	1·90
		a. Vert pair. Nos. 4358/4359	3·75	3·75
4359	**3446**	(1st) Evacuee children returning home, London, 1945	1·90	1·90
4360	**3447**	£1·42 Troops march along Oxford Street, London, 1945	2·00	2·00
		a. Vert pair. Nos. 4360/4361	4·00	4·00
4361	**3448**	£1·42 Soldiers and sailors leaving demobilisation centre with boxes of civilian clothes	2·00	2·00
4362	**3449**	£1·63 Liberated Allied prisoners of war, Aomori Camp, near Yokohama, Japan	2·25	2·25
		a. Vert pair. Nos. 4362/4363	4·50	4·50
4363	**3450**	£1·63 Navy personnel in VE Day celebrations, Glasgow, 1945	2·25	2·25
Set of 8			14·00	14·00
Set of 4 Gutter Strips of 4			28·00	
First Day Cover (Tallents House)				16·00
Presentation Pack (PO Pack No. 585) (Nos. 4356/4363 and **MS**4364)			20·00	
PHQ Cards (set of 13) (470)			7·75	25·00

MS4364 202×74 mm. **3451** (1st) Hall of Names, Holocaust History Museum, Yad Vashem, Jerusalem; (1st) Runnymede Memorial; £1·63 Plymouth Naval Memorial; £1·63 Rangoon Memorial, Myanmar (all 60×30 mm) 8·00 8·00
First Day Cover (Tallents House) 10·00

Nos. 4356/4357, 4358/4359, 4360/4361 and 4362/4363 were printed together, *se-tenant*, as vertical pairs in sheets of 60 (2 panes 5×6).

Nos. 4356/4363 also come from the £19·80 75th Anniversary of the End of the Second World War booklet, No. DY34.

The 13 PHQ cards show the ten individual stamps, including those from No. **MS**4364 and the complete miniature sheet.

3452 Hall of Names, Holocaust History Museum, Yad Vashem, Jerusalem

3453 Runnymede Memorial

3454 Plymouth Naval Memorial

3455 Rangoon Memorial, Myanmar

2020 (8 May). 75th Anniversary of the End of the Second World War (2nd issue). Multicoloured. Two phosphor bands. Perf 14½.

4365	**3452**	(1st) Hall of Names, Holocaust History Museum, Yad Vashem, Jerusalem	2·00	2·00
4366	**3453**	(1st) Runnymede Memorial	2·00	2·00
4367	**3454**	£1·63 Plymouth Naval Memorial	3·00	3·00
4368	**3455**	£1·63 Rangoon Memorial, Myanmar	3·00	3·00
Set of 4			10·50	10·50

Nos. 4365/4368 were issued in No. **MS**4364 and in booklet pane from the £19·80 75th Anniversary of the Second World War booklet, No. DY34.

3456 'That woman's tongue...' (Edna Sharples and Elsie Tanner)

3457 'Woman, Stanley, Woman' (Stan and Hilda Ogden)

3458 'Vera my little swamp duck' (Jack and Vera Duckworth)

3459 'Ken! do something!' (Deirdre and Ken Barlow)

3460 'I can't abide to see...' (Rita Sullivan and Norris Cole)

3461 'Be nice if everyday...' (Hayley and Roy Cropper)

3462 'I love you...' (Dev and Sunita Alahan)

3463 'I always thought...' (Tracy Barlow and Steve McDonald)

3464 *Rovers Return* Barmaids

2020 (28 May). *Coronation Street*. Multicoloured. One centre band (2nd) or two phosphor bands (others)

(a) Ordinary gum. Perf 14.

4369	**3456**	(2nd) 'That woman's tongue... (Ena Sharples and Elsie Tanner)	1·25	1·25
		a. Horiz pair. Nos. 4369/4370	2·50	2·50
4370	**3457**	(2nd) 'Woman, Stanley, woman.' Stan and Hilda Ogden	1·25	1·25
4371	**3458**	(1st) 'Vera, my little swamp duck.' (Jack and Vera Duckworth)	1·90	1·90
		a. Horiz pair. Nos. 4371/4372	3·75	3·75
4372	**3459**	(1st) 'Ken! Do something!' (Deirdre and Ken Barlow)	1·90	1·90
4373	**3460**	£1·42 'I can't abide to see people gossiping.' (Rita Sullivan and Norris Cole)	2·00	2·00
		a. Horiz pair. Nos. 4373/4374	4·00	4·00
4374	**3461**	£1·42 'Be nice if every day...'(Hayley and Roy Cropper)	2·00	2·00
4375	**3462**	£1·63 'I love you...' (Dev and Sunita Alahan)	2·25	2·25
		a. Horiz pair. Nos. 4375/4376	4·50	4·50
4376	**3463**	£1·63 'I always thought...' (Tracy Barlow and Steve McDonald)	2·25	2·25
Set of 8			14·00	14·00
Set of 8 Gutter Pairs			28·00	
First Day Cover (Tallents House)			16·00	
Presentation Pack (PO Pack No. 586) (Nos. 4369/4376 and **MS**4377)			24·00	
PHQ Card (set of 13) (471)			7·50	25·00

MS4377 156×74 mm. **3464** (1st) Bet Lynch; (1st) Raquel Watts; £1·42 Liz McDonald; £1·42 Gemma Winter (all 27×36 mm)

		8·00	8·00
First Day Cover (Tallents House)			10·00

(b) Self-adhesive. Die-cut perf 14.

4378	**3458**	(1st) 'Vera, my little swamp duck.' (Vera and Jack Duckworth)	2·00	2·00
4379	**3457**	(1st) 'Ken! Do something!' (Deirdre and Ken Barlow)	2·00	2·00

Nos. 4369/4370, 4371/4372, 4373/4374 and 4375/4376 were printed together, *se-tenant*, as horizontal pairs in sheets of 60 (2 panes 6×5).

Nos. 4378/4379 were issued in stamp booklets with 1st bright scarlet stamps×4, originally sold for £4·56.

Stamps as Nos. 4371/4372 but self-adhesive and perf 14×14½ were issued in collector's sheets containing five of each design, sold for £8·80.

The 13 PHQ cards show the 12 individual stamps, including those from No. **MS**4377, and the complete miniature sheet.

3465 Dover Lighthouse

3466 Bignor Mosaic

3467 Amphitheatre at Isca Fortress, Caerleon

3468 Ribchester Helmet

3469 Bridgeness Distance Slab at Eastern end of Antonine Wall

3470 Copper-alloy Figurine of Warrior God, Cambridgeshire

3471 Gorgon's Head from Temple to Sulis Minerva, Bath

3472 Hadrian's Wall

2020 (18 June). *Roman Britain*. Multicoloured. One centre band (2nd) or two bands (others). Perf 14½×14.

4380	**3465**	(2nd) Dover Lighthouse	1·25	1·25
		a. Horiz pair. Nos. 4380/4381	2·50	2·50
4381	**3466**	(2nd) Bignor Mosaic	1·25	1·25
4382	**3467**	(1st) Amphitheatre, Caerleon	1·90	1·90
		a. Horiz pair. Nos. 4382/4383	3·75	3·75
4383	**3468**	(1st) Ribchester Helmet	1·90	1·90
4384	**3469**	£1·63 Bridgeness distance slab, Antonine Wall	2·25	2·25
		a. Horiz pair. Nos. 4384/4385	4·50	4·50
4385	**3470**	£1·63 Copper-alloy figurine of Warrior God, Cambridgeshire	2·25	2·25
4386	**3471**	£1·68 Gorgon's head, Bath	2·40	2·40
		a. Horiz pair. Nos. 4386/4387	4·75	4·75
4387	**3472**	£1·68 Hadrian's Wall	2·40	2·40
Set of 8			15·00	15·00

Set of 4 *Gutter Pairs* (only 2 stamps in each gutter pair)   17·00
Set of 4 *Traffic Light Gutter Blocks* (4 stamps in each
gutter block)   30·00
First Day Cover (Tallents House)   17·00
Presentation Pack (PO Pack No. 587)   17·00
PHQ Cards (set of 8) (472)   4·75   16·00

Nos. 4380/4381, 4382/4383, 4384/4385 and 4386/4387 were each printed together, *se-tenant*, as horizontal pairs in sheets of 60 (2 panes 6×5).

3473 *Queen II*, 1974   **3474** *Sheer Heart Attack*, 1974

3475 *A Night At The Opera*,   **3476** *News of the World*, 1977
1975

3477 *The Game*, 1980   **3478** *Greatest Hits*, 1981

3479 *The Works*, 1984   **3480** *Innuendo*, 1991

3481 Queen Live

2020 (9 July). Queen (rock band) (1st issue). Multicoloured. Two phosphor bands.
(a) Ordinary gum. Perf 14 (Nos. 4388/4395), 14½×14 (Queen machin size stamp from No. **MS**4396) or 14½ (other stamps from No. **MS**4396).

4388	**3473**	(1st) *Queen II*, 1974	1·90	1·90
		a. Horiz strip of 4. Nos. 4388/4391	7·50	7·50
4389	**3474**	(1st) *Sheer Heart Attack*, 1974	1·90	1·90
4390	**3475**	(1st) *A Night At The Opera*, 1975	1·90	1·90
4391	**3476**	(1st) *News of the World*, 1977	1·90	1·90
4392	**3477**	£1·63 *The Game*, 1980	2·25	2·25
		a. Horiz strip of 4. Nos. 4392/4395	9·00	9·00
4393	**3478**	£1·63 *Greatest Hits*, 1981	2·25	2·25
4394	**3479**	£1·63 *The Works*, 1984	2·25	2·25
4395	**3480**	£1·63 *Innuendo*, 1991	2·25	2·25
Set of 8			16·50	16·50
Set of 2 Gutter Strips of 8			33·00	
First Day Cover (Tallents House)				19·00

Presentation Pack (PO Pack No. 588) (Nos. 4388/4395
and **MS**4396)   28·00
PHQ Cards (set of 15) (473)   8·25   27·00
MS4396 202×74 mm. **3481** (1st) Freddie Mercury,
Magic Tour, Wembley Stadium, 1986; (1st) Roger
Taylor, Hyde Park Concert, 1976; (1st) Queen,
Primrose Hill, London, 1974; £1·63 John Deacon,
A Night at the Opera Tour, Hammersmith Odeon,
1975; £1·63 Brian May, Magic Tour, Nepstadion,
Budapest, 1986   10·00   10·00
First Day Cover (Tallents House)   12·50

(b) Self-adhesive. Die-cut perf 14.

4397	**3473**	(1st) *Queen II*, 1974	2·00	2·00
4398	**3475**	(1st) *A Night At The Opera*, 1975	2·00	2·00

Nos. 4388/4395 were printed together, *se-tenant*, as horizontal strips of four stamps in sheets of 24 (2 panes 4×6).
Nos. 4388/4395 also come from the £19·10 Queen booklet, No. DY35.
Nos. 4397/4398 were issued in stamp booklets with 1st bright scarlet stamp×4, originally sold for £4·56.
Stamps as Nos. 4388×2, 4389, 4390×2 and 4391/4395 but self-adhesive were issued with labels in a Queen Album Cover collector's sheet, originally sold for £13·15.
An Album Cover Collection fan sheet containing Nos. 4388/4395 was originally sold for £10·20.
A *Night at the Opera* fan sheet containing No. 4390×4 was originally sold for £7·50.
The 15 PHQ cards show the 14 individual stamps including those from No. **MS**4396 and the complete miniature sheet.

3482 Freddie Mercury,   **3483** Roger Taylor, Hyde
Magic Tour, Wembley   Park Concert, 1976
Stadium, 1986

3484 John Deacon, A   **3485** Brian May, Magic
Night at the Opera Tour,   Tour, Nepstadion, Budapest,
Hammersmith Odeon, 1975   1986

2020 (9 July). Queen (rock band) (2nd issue). Multicoloured. Two phosphor bands. Perf 14½.

4399	**3482**	(1st) Freddie Mercury	2·00	2·00
4400	**3483**	(1st) Roger Taylor	2·00	2·00
4401	**3484**	£1·63 John Deacon	3·00	3·00
4402	**3485**	£1·63 Brian May	3·00	3·00
Set of 4			10·00	10·00

Nos. 4399/4402 were issued in No. **MS**4396 and booklet pane from the £19·10 Queen premium booklet, No. DY35.

3486 Queen,
Primrose Hill,
London, 1974

2020 (9 July). Queen (rock band) (3rd issue). Multicoloured. Two phosphor bands. Perf 14½×14 (with one elliptical hole in each vert side).

4403	**3486**	(1st) Queen, 1974	2·00	2·00

No. 4403 was issued in No. **MS**4396 and the machin booklet pane from the £19·10 Queen premium booklet, No. DY35.
A stamp as No. 4403 but self-adhesive was issued in a Queen Live Collector's Sheet containing ten stamps with labels, originally sold for £8·80.
See also No. 4502.

3487 Palace of Westminster from Old Palace Yard

3488 Palace of Westminster from River Thames

3489 Elizabeth Tower

3490 Commons Chamber

3491 Central Lobby

3492 Lords Chamber

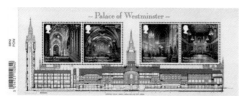

3493 Palace of Westminster

2020 (30 July). Palace of Westminster. Multicoloured. Two phosphor bands. Perf 14½.

4404	**3487**	(1st) Palace of Westminster from Old Palace Yard	1·90	1·90
		a. Horiz strip of 3. Nos. 4404/4406	5·75	5·75
4405	**3488**	(1st) Palace of Westminster from River Thames	1·90	1·90
4406	**3489**	(1st) Elizabeth Tower	1·90	1·90
4407	**3490**	£1·68 Commons Chamber	2·40	2·40
		a. Horiz strip of 3. Nos. 4407/4409	7·00	7·00
4408	**3491**	£1·68 Central Lobby	2·40	2·40
4409	**3492**	£1·68 Lords Chamber	2·40	2·40
Set of 6			12·00	12·00
Set of 2 Gutter Strips of 6			24·00	
First Day Cover (Tallents House)				14·00
Presentation Pack (PO Pack No. 589) (Nos. 4404/4409, **MS**4410)			22·00	
PHQ Cards (set of 11) (474)			6·50	22·00
MS4410 203×74 mm. **3493** (1st) Norman Porch; (1st) Chapel of St Mary Undercroft; £1·63 St Stephen's Hall; £1·63 Royal Gallery			8·00	8·00
First Day Cover (Tallents House)				10·00

Nos. 4404/4406 and 4407/4409 were each printed together, *se-tenant*, as horizontal strips of three in sheets of 36 (2 panes 3×6).

The 11 PHQ cards show the ten individual stamps, including those from No. **MS**4410, and the complete miniature sheet.

3494 *The Reichenbach Fall*

3495 *A Study in Pink*

3496 *The Great Game*

3497 *The Empty Hearse*

3498 *A Scandal in Belgravia*

3499 *The Final Problem*

3500 Sherlock Holmes Mysteries by Sir Arthur Conan Doyle

3501 *The Red-Headed League* **3502** *The Adventure of the Speckled band*

2020 (18 Aug). Sherlock. Multicoloured. Two phosphor bands.

(a) Ordinary gum. Perf 14½ (Nos. 4411/4416) or 14 (No. **MS**4417).

4411	**3494**	(1st) *The Reichenbach Fall*	1·90	1·90
		a. Vert pair. Nos. 4411/4412	3·75	3·75
4412	**3495**	(1st) *A Study in Pink*	1·90	1·90
4413	**3496**	£1·42 *The Great Game*	2·00	2·00
		a. Vert pair. Nos. 4413/4414	4·00	4·00
4414	**3497**	£1·42 *The Empty Hearse*	2·00	2·00
4415	**3498**	£1·68 *A Scandal in Belgravia*	2·40	2·40
		a. Vert pair. Nos. 4415/4416	4·75	4·75
4416	**3499**	£1·68 *The Final Problem*	2·40	2·40
Set of 6			12·00	12·00
Set of 3 Gutter Pairs (only 2 stamps in each gutter pair)			14·00	
First Day Cover (Tallents House)				14·00
Presentation Pack (PO Pack No. 590) (Nos. 4411/4416 and **MS**4417)			22·00	
PHQ Cards (set of 11) (475)			6·50	22·00

MS4417 126×89 mm. **3500** (1st) *The Adventure of the Speckled Band*; (1st) *The Red-Headed League*; £1·68 *The Adventure of the Second Stain*; £1·68 *The Adventure of the Dancing Men* ... 8·00 ... 8·00

First Day Cover (Tallents House) ... 10·00

(b) Self-adhesive. Die-cut perf 14.

4418	**3501**	(1st) *The Red-Headed League*	2·50	2·50
4419	**3502**	(1st) *The Adventure of the Speckled Band*	2·50	2·50

Nos. 4411/4412, 4413/4414 and 4415/4416 were each printed together, *se-tenant*, as vertical pairs in sheets of 36 (2 panes 3×6).

Nos. 4411/4416 show scenes from the *Sherlock* television series, and show additional inscriptions when UV light is shone over the stamps.
Nos. 4411 and 4413 have the two phosphor bands at left and right of the stamps as usual.
Nos. 4412 and 4414 have the two phosphor bands at left and centre of the stamp.
No. 4415 has the two phosphor bands at left and just right of centre.
No. 4416 has the two phosphor bands at left and centre right.
Nos. 4418/4419 were issued in stamp booklets with 1st bright scarlet stamp×4, originally sold for £4·56.
Stamps as Nos. 4411/4416 but self-adhesive were issued in collector's sheets, with labels containing Nos. 4411×4, 4412×2 and one each of Nos. 4413/4416, originally sold for £11·95.
The 11 PHQ cards show the ten individual stamps, including those from No. **MS**4417, and the complete miniature sheet.

3503 Then with a terrifying roar (*Rupert's Rainy Adventure*) **3504** The bath is rocked from side to side (*Rupert's Rainy Adventure*)

3505 Then Algy looks a trifle glum (*Rupert and the Mare's Nest*) **3506** The large bird says (*Rupert and the Mare's Nest*)

3507 'There's something puzzling all of you,' Says Rupert (*Rupert and the Lost Cuckoo*) **3508** 'My cuckoo's back again' (*Rupert and the Lost Cuckoo*)

3509 Though Rupert searches all around (*Rupert's Christmas Tree*) **3510** The tree is such a lovely sight (*Rupert's Christmas Tree*)

2020 (3 Sept). Rupert Bear. Multicoloured. Centre band (2nd) or two bands (others). Perf 14½×14

4420	**3503**	(2nd) Then with a terrifying roar... (*Rupert's Rainy Adventure*)	1·25	1·25
		a. Horiz pair. Nos. 4420/4421	2·50	2·50
4421	**3504**	(2nd) The bath is rocked... (*Rupert's Rainy Adventure*)	1·25	1·25
4422	**3505**	(1st) Then Algy looks a trifle glum... (*Rupert and the Mare's Nest*)	1·90	1·90
		a. Horiz pair. Nos. 4422/4423	3·75	3·75
4423	**3506**	(1st) The large bird says... (*Rupert and the Mare's Nest*)	1·90	1·90
4424	**3507**	£1·45 'There's something puzzling...' (*Rupert and the Lost Cuckoo*)	2·00	2·00
		a. Horiz pair. Nos. 4424/4425	4·00	4·00
4425	**3508**	£1·45 'My cuckoo's back again...' (*Rupert and the Lost Cuckoo*)	2·00	2·00
4426	**3509**	£1·70 Though Rupert searches... (*Rupert's Christmas Tree*)	2·40	2·40
		a. Horiz pair. Nos. 4426/4427	4·75	4·75
4427	**3510**	£1·70 The tree is such a lovely sight... (*Rupert's Christmas Tree*)	2·40	2·40
Set of 8			14·00	14·00
Set of 4 Gutter Pairs (only 2 stamps in each gutter pair)			16·00	
Set of 4 Traffic Light Blocks of 4			28·00	

First Day Cover (Tallents House)   16·00
Presentation Pack (PO Pack No. 591)   16·00
PHQ Cards (set of 8) (476)   7·50   15·00

Nos. 4420/4421, 4422/4423, 4424/4425 and 4426/4427 were each printed together, *se-tenant*, as horizontal pairs in sheets of 60 (2 panes 6×5).

3511 Common Carder Bee (*Bombus pascuorum*)

3512 Painted Lady Butterfly (*Vanessa cardui*)

3513 Longhorn Beetle (*Rutpela maculata*)

3514 Elephant Hawk-moth (*Deilephila elpenor*)

3515 Marmalade Hoverfly (*Episyrphus balteatus*)

3516 Ruby-tailed Wasp (*Chrysis ignita* agg)

2020 (1 Oct). Brilliant Bugs. Multicoloured. Two phosphor bands. Perf 14×14½.

4428	**3511**	(1st) Common Carder Bee (*Bombus pascuorum*)	1·90	1·90
		a. Vert pair. Nos. 4428/4429	3·75	3·75
4429	**3512**	(1st) Painted Lady Butterfly (*Vanessa cardui*)	1·90	1·90
4430	**3513**	£1·45 Longhorn Beetle (*Rutpela maculata*)	2·00	2·00
		a. Vert pair. Nos. 4430/4431	4·00	4·00
4431	**3514**	£1·45 Elephant Hawk-moth (*Deilephila elpenor*)	2·00	2·00
4432	**3515**	£1·70 Marmalade Hoverfly (*Episyrphus balteatus*)	2·40	2·40
		a. Vert pair. Nos. 4432/4433	4·75	4·75
4433	**3516**	£1·70 Ruby-tailed Wasp (*Chrysis ignita* agg)	2·40	2·40
Set of 6			12·00	12·00

Set of 3 Gutter Pairs (only 2 stamps in each gutter pair)   14·00
First Day Cover (Tallents House)   14·50
Presentation Pack (PO Pack No. 592)   14·00
PHQ Cards (set of 8) (477)   3·50   13·50

Nos. 4428/4429, 4430/4431 and 4432/4433 were each printed together, *se-tenant*, as vertical pairs in sheets of 60 (2 panes 5×6).

3517 Adoration of the Magi (detail), St Andrew's Church, East Lexham

3518 Virgin and Child, St Andrew's Church, Coln Rogers

3519 Adoration of the Magi, St Andrew's Church, Lexham

3520 Virgin and Child, St Andrew's Church, Coln Rogers

3521 Virgin and Child, Church of St James, Hollowell

3522 Virgin and Child, All Saints' Church, Otley

3523 The Holy Family (detail), St Columba's Church, Topcliffe

3524 Virgin and Child, Christ Church, Coalville

2020 (3 Nov). Christmas. Stained-glass Windows. Multicoloured. One centre band (No. 4434) or two bands (others).

(a) Self-adhesive. Die-cut perf 14½×15..

4434	**3517**	(2nd) Adoration of the Magi (detail), St Andrew's Church, East Lexham	1·25	1·25
4435	**3518**	(1st) Virgin and Child, St Andrew's Church, Coln Rogers	1·90	1·90
4436	**3519**	(2nd Large) Adoration of the Magi, St Andrew's Church, Lexham	2·50	2·50
4437	**3520**	(1st Large) Virgin and Child, St Andrew's Church, Coln Rogers	3·25	3·25
4438	**3521**	£1·45 Virgin and Child, Church of St James, Hollowell	2·00	2·00
4439	**3522**	£1·70 Virgin and Child, All Saints' Church, Otley	2·40	2·40
4440	**3523**	£2·50 The Holy Family (detail), St Columba's Church, Topcliffe	3·50	3·50
4441	**3524**	£2·55 Virgin and Child, Christ Church, Coalville	3·50	3·50
Set of 8			19·50	19·50

First Day Cover (Tallents House)   22·00
Presentation Pack (PO Pack No. 593)   22·00
PHQ Cards (set of 9) (478)   5·25   35·00

(b) Ordinary gum. Perf 14½×15..

MS4442 189×74 mm. As Nos. 4434/4441   20·00   20·00
First Day Cover (Tallents House)   22·00

The 2nd class, 1st class, £1·45, £1·70, £2·50 and £2·55 values were also issued in sheets of 20, containing 8×2nd class, 8×1st class, 1×£1·45, 1×£1·70, 1×£2·50 and 1×£2·55 values, each stamp accompanied by a *se-tenant* label.

The nine PHQ cards show the individual stamps and the complete miniature sheet.

3525 Captain James T. Kirk (William Shatner), *The Original Series*

3526 Captain Jean-Luc Picard (Patrick Stewart), *The Next Generation*

3527 Captain Benjamin Sisko (Avery Brooks), *Deep Space Nine*

3528 Captain Kathryn Janeway (Kate Mulgrew), *Voyager*

3529 Captain Jonathan Archer (Scott Bakula), *Enterprise*

3530 Captain Gabriel Lorca (Jason Isaacs), *Discovery*

3531 Spock (Leonard Nimoy), *The Original Series*

3532 Deanna Troi (Marina Sirtis), *The Next Generation*

3533 Julian Bashir (Alexander Siddig), *Deep Space Nine*

3534 Malcolm Reed (Dominic Keating), *Enterprise*

3535 Michael Burnham (Sonequa Martin-Greene), *Discovery*

3536 Ash Tyler/Voq (Shazad Latif), *Discovery*

3537 *Star Trek*. The Movies

2020 (13 Nov). *Star Trek* (1st issue). Multicoloured. Two phosphor bands.

(a) Ordinary gum. Perf 14½.

4443	**3525**	(1st) Captain James T. Kirk	1·90	1·90
		a. Horiz strip of 6. Nos. 4443/4448	11·00	11·00
4444	**3526**	(1st) Captain Jean-Luc Picard	1·90	1·90
4445	**3527**	(1st) Captain Benjamin Sisko	1·90	1·90
4446	**3528**	(1st) Captain Kathryn Janeway	1·90	1·90
4447	**3529**	(1st) Captain Jonathan Archer	1·90	1·90
4448	**3530**	(1st) Captain Gabriel Lorca	1·90	1·90
4449	**3531**	(1st) Spock	1·90	1·90
		a. Horiz strip of 6. Nos. 4449/4454	11·00	11·00
4450	**3532**	(1st) Deanna Troi	1·90	1·90
4451	**3533**	(1st) Julian Bashir	1·90	1·90
4452	**3534**	(1st) Malcolm Reed	1·90	1·90
4453	**3535**	(1st) Michael Burnham	1·90	1·90
4454	**3536**	(1st) Ash Tyler/Voq	1·90	1·90
Set of 12			20·00	20·00
Set of 2 Gutter Strips of 12			40·00	
First Day Cover (Tallents House)				22·50
Presentation Pack (PO Pack No. 594) (Nos. 4443/4454 and **MS**4455)			33·00	
PHQ Cards (set of 19) (479)			11·00	30·00

(b) Self-adhesive.

MS4455 146×74 mm. **3537** (1st) Montgomery Scott (Simon Pegg), new Movie Series (60×21 mm) (Perf 14½); (1st) Praetor Shinzon (Tom Hardy), Next Generation Movie, *Nemesis* (60×21 mm) (Perf 14½); (1st) Tolian Soran (Malcolm McDowell), Original Movie Series, *Generations* (27×37 mm) (Perf 14); (1st) Klingon Chancellor Gorkon (David Warner), Original Movie Series (27×37 mm) (Perf 14); (1st) Dr Carol Marcus (Alice Eve), new Movie Series, *Star Trek Into Darkness* (27×37 mm) (Perf 14); (1st) Krall (Idris Elba), new Movie Series (27×37 mm) (Perf 14)   11·00   11·00

First Day Cover (Tallents House)		13·50

(c) Self-adhesive. Die-cut perf 14½.

4456	**3525**	(1st) Captain James T. Kirk	2·00	2·00
4457	**3526**	(1st) Captain Jean-Luc Picard	2·00	2·00

Nos. 4443/4448 and 4449/4454 were printed together, *se-tenant*, as horizontal strips of five stamps in sheets of 60 (2 panes 6×5).

Booklet panes Nos. 4443b and 4449b come from the £18·25 Star Trek booklet, No. DY36.

Nos. 4456/4457 were issued in stamp booklets with 1st bright scarlet stamp×4, originally sold for £4·56.

A collector's sheet containing stamps as Nos. 4443/4454 but self-adhesive was originally sold for £8·70.

The 19 PHQ cards show the 18 individual stamps, including those from No. **MS**4455, and the complete miniature sheet.

3538 Montgomery Scott (Simon Pegg), New Movie Series

3539 Praetor Shinzon (Tom Hardy), Next Generation Movie. *Nemesis*

3540 Tolian Soran (Malcolm McDowell), Original Movie Series. *Generations*

3541 Klingon Chancellor Gorkon (David Warner), Original Movie Series. *The Undiscovered Country*

3542 Dr Carol Marcus (Alice Eve), New Movie Series. *Star Trek Into Darkness*

3543 Krall (Idris Elba), *Star Trek Beyond*

2020 (13 Nov). *Star Trek* (2nd issue). Multicoloured. Self-adhesive. Two phosphor bands. Perf 14½ (Nos. 4458/4459) or 14 (Nos. 4460/4463).

4458	**3538**	(1st) Montgomery Scott	2·00	2·00
4459	**3539**	(1st) Praetor Shinzon	2·00	2·00
4460	**3540**	(1st) Tolian Soran	2·00	2·00
4461	**3541**	(1st) Klingon Chancellor Gorkon	2·00	2·00
4462	**3542**	(1st) Dr Carol Marcus	2·00	2·00
4463	**3543**	(1st) Krall	2·00	2·00
Set of 6			8·00	8·00

Nos. 4458/4463 were issued in No. **MS**4455 and in booklet pane from the £18·35 *Star Trek* booklet, No. DY36.

Collectors Pack

2020 (13 Nov). Comprises Nos. 4312/**MS**4320, 4323/4330, 4332/**MS**4338, 4345/4354, 4356/**MS**4364, 4369/**MS**4377, 4380/**MS**4396, 4404/**MS**4417, 4420/4441 and 4433/**MS**4455

CP4463a	Collectors Pack (*sold for* £186) (Pack No. 595)	£300

Post Office Yearbook

2020 (13 Nov). Comprises Nos. 4312/**MS**4320, 4323/4330, 4332/**MS**4338, 4345/4354, 4356/**MS**4364, 4369/**MS**4377, 4380/**MS**4396, 4404/**MS**4417, 4420/4441 and 4433/**MS**4455

YB4463a	Yearbook (*sold for* £186)	£300

Miniature Sheet Collection

2020 (13 Nov). Comprises Nos. **MS**4320, **MS**4338, **MS**4364, **MS**4377, **MS**4396, **MS**4410, **MS**4417, **MS**4442, **MS**4455 and **MS**S180

MS4463a	Miniature Sheet Collection (*sold for* £57)	95·00

3544 Dartmoor

3545 New Forest

 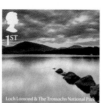

3546 Lake District

3547 Loch Lomond and The Trossachs

3548 Snowdonia

3549 North York Moors

3550 South Downs

3551 Peak District

3552 Pembrokeshire Coast

3553 Broads

2021 (14 Jan). National Parks. Multicoloured. Two phosphor bands.

(a) Ordinary gum. Perf 14×14½.

4464	**3544**	(1st) Dartmoor	1·90	1·90
		a. Horiz strip of 5. Nos. 4464/4468	9·25	9·25
4465	**3545**	(1st) New Forest	1·90	1·90
4466	**3546**	(1st) Lake District	1·90	1·90
4467	**3547**	(1st) Loch Lomond and The Trossachs	1·90	1·90
4468	**3548**	(1st) Snowdonia	1·90	1·90
4469	**3549**	(1st) North York Moors	1·90	1·90
		a. Horiz strip of 5. Nos. 4469/4473	9·25	9·25
4470	**3550**	(1st) South Downs	1·90	1·90
4471	**3551**	(1st) Peak District	1·90	1·90
4472	**3552**	(1st) Pembrokeshire Coast	1·90	1·90
4473	**3553**	(1st) Broads	1·90	1·90
Set of 10			17·50	17·50
Set of 2 Gutter Strips of 10			35·00	
First Day Cover (Tallents House)				20·00
Presentation Pack (PO Pack No. 596)			20·00	
PHQ Cards (set of 10) (480)			5·75	19·00

(b) Self-adhesive. Die-cut perf 14×14½.

4474	**3551**	(1st) Peak District	2·00	2·00
4475	**3548**	(1st) Snowdonia	2·00	2·00

Nos. 4464/4468 and 4469/4473 were each printed together, *se-tenant*, as horizontal strips of five stamps in sheets of 50 (2 panes 5×5).

Nos. 4474/4475 were issued in stamp booklets with 1st bright scarlet stamp×4, originally sold for £4·56.

3554 United Kingdom. A Celebration

2021 (26 Jan). United Kingdom, A Celebration. Multicoloured. 'All-over' phosphor. Perf 15×14½

MS4476 203×74 mm. **3554** (1st) Wheelchair athlete, cricket ball, football and racing car (Great Sport); (1st) Glass façade of office building, microphone stand silhouette, book pages and television studio (Great Creativity); £1·70 Hands making heart-shape, London Marathon, 2011, nurse reassuring patient and rainbow (Great Community); £1·70 3D illustration of binary code, London skyline, carbon fibre material and DNA (Great Industry and Innovation)

	8·50	8·50
First Day Cover (Tallents House)		11·00
Presentation Pack (PO Pack No. M26)	11·00	
PHQ Cards (set of 5) (481)	3·00	10·00

3555 'I Knew you was cheating...' (Del Boy and Boycie)

3556 'Don't worry he's house trained...' (Marlene, Del Boy and Rodney)

3557 'Play it nice and cool...' (Del Boy and Trigger)

3558 'Now brace yourself...' (Rodney and Del Boy)

3559 'Our coach has just blown up!' (Rodney and Denzel)

3560 'What have you been doing...' (Rodney and Cassandra)

3561 'It's a baby, Raquel...' (Del Boy and Raquel)

3562 'That's just over...' (Del Boy and Rodney)

3563 Del Boy, Rodney, Uncle Albert and Grandad

3564 Del Boy   **3565** Rodney

2021 (16 Feb). *Only Fools and Horses* (TV sitcom, 1981–2003) (1st issue). Multicoloured. Two phosphor bands.

(a) Ordinary gum. Perf 14.

4477	**3555**	(1st) 'I knew you was cheating...', (Del Boy and Boycie)	1·90	1·90
		a. Vert pair. Nos. 4477/4478	3·75	3·75
4478	**3556**	(1st) 'Don't worry he's house trained...' (Marlene, Del Boy and Rodney)	1·90	1·90
4479	**3557**	(1st) 'Play it nice and cool...' (Del Boy and Trigger)	1·90	1·90
		a. Vert pair. Nos. 4479/4480	3·75	3·75
4480	**3558**	(1st) 'Now brace yourself...' (Rodney and Del Boy)	1·90	1·90
4481	**3559**	£1·70 'Our coach has just blown up!' (Rodney and Denzel)	2·50	2·50
		a. Vert pair. Nos. 4481/4482	5·00	5·00
4482	**3560**	£1·70 'What have you been doing...' (Rodney and Cassandra)	2·50	2·50
4483	**3561**	£1·70 'It's a baby, Raquel...' (Del Boy and Raquel)	2·50	2·50
		a. Vert pair. Nos. 4483/4484	5·00	5·00
4484	**3562**	£1·70 'That's just over...' (Del Boy and Rodney)	2·50	2·50
Set of 8			16·00	16·00
Set of 4 Gutter Pairs (only 2 stamps in each pair)			18·00	
First Day Cover (Tallents House)				17·00
Presentation Pack (PO Pack No. 597) (Nos. 4477/4484 and **MS**4485)			26·00	
PHQ Cards (set of 13) (482)			7·50	25·00

MS4485 203×74 mm. **3563** (1st) Del Boy (David Jason); (1st) Rodney (Nicholas Lyndhurst); £1·70 Uncle Albert (Buster Merryfield); £1·70 Grandad (Lennard Pearce)   8·50   8·50

First Day Cover (Tallents House)   10·50

(b) Self-adhesive. Die-cut perf 14.

4486	**3564**	(1st) Del Boy	2·00	2·00
4487	**3565**	(1st) Rodney	2·00	2·00

Nos. 4477/4478, 4479/4480, 4481/4482 and 4483/4484 were each printed together, *se-tenant*, as vertical pairs in sheets of 60 (2 panes 5×6).

Nos. 4477/4484 also come from the £21·70 *Only Fools and Horses* premium booklet, No. DY37.

Nos. 4486/4487 were issued in stamp booklets with 1st bright scarlet stamp×4, originally sold for £5·10.

A fan souvenir folder containing excerpts from writer John Sullivan's personal *Only Fools and Horses* scripts along with first day covers for Nos. 4477/4484 and **MS**4485 was sold by Royal Mail for £19.99.

Self-adhesive designs as Types **3564/3565** perforated 14×14½ were issued in sheets of ten containing five stamps of each design with labels. These sheets were printed in Lithography and originally sold for £9·60.

The 13 PHQ cards show the 12 individual stamps, including those from No. **MS**4485, and the complete miniature sheet.

3566 Uncle Albert   **3567** Grandad

2021 (16 Feb). *Only Fools and Horses* (2nd issue). Multicoloured. Two phosphor bands. Perf 14.

4488	**3564**	(1st) Del Boy (David Jason)	2·00	2·00
4489	**3565**	(1st) Rodney (Nicholas Lyndhurst)	2·00	2·00
4490	**3566**	£1·70 Uncle Albert (Buster Merryfield)	2·75	2·75
4491	**3567**	£1·70 Grandad (Lennard Pearce)	2·75	2·75
Set of 4			9·50	9·50

Nos. 4488/4491 were issued in No. **MS**4485 and in the £21·70 *Only Fools and Horses* premium booklet, No. DY37.

3568 Merlin and the Baby Arthur   **3569** Arthur Draws the Sword from the Stone

3570 Arthur takes Excalibur   **3571** Arthur Marries Guinevere

3572 Sir Gawain and the Green Knight   **3573** Knights of the Round Table

3574 Sir Lancelot Defeats the Dragon   **3575** Sir Galahad and the Holy Grail

3576 Arthur Battles Mordred   **3577** The Death of King Arthur

2021 (16 Mar). The Legend of King Arthur. Multicoloured. Two phosphor bands. Perf 14½.

4492	**3568**	(1st) Merlin and the Baby Arthur	1·90	1·90
		a. Horiz strip of 5. Nos. 4492/4496	9·25	9·25
4493	**3569**	(1st) Arthur draws the Sword from the Stone	1·90	1·90
4494	**3570**	(1st) Arthur takes Excalibur	1·90	1·90
4495	**3571**	(1st) Arthur marries Guinevere	1·90	1·90
4496	**3572**	(1st) Sir Gawain and the Green Knight	1·90	1·90
4497	**3573**	£1·70 Knights of the Round Table	2·50	2·50
		a. Horiz strip of 5. Nos. 4497/4501	12·50	12·50
4498	**3574**	£1·70 Sir Lancelot defeats the Dragon	2·50	2·50
4499	**3575**	£1·70 Sir Galahad and the Holy Grail	2·50	2·50
4500	**3576**	£1·70 Arthur battles Mordred	2·50	2·50
4501	**3577**	£1·70 The Death of King Arthur	2·50	2·50
Set of 10			20·00	20·00
Set of 2 Gutter Strips of 10			40·00	
First Day Cover (Tallents House)				22·00
Presentation Pack (PO Pack No. 598)			22·00	
PHQ Cards (set of 10) (483)			5·75	21·00

Nos. 4492/4496 and 4497/4501 were each printed together, *se-tenant*, as horizontal strips of five in sheets of 50 (2 panes 5×5).

3486 Queen, 1974

2021 (29 Mar). Queen (Rock Band) (4th issue). As T **3486** but self-adhesive. Two phosphor bands. Die-cut perf 14½×14 (with one elliptical hole in each vert side).

4502	**3486**	(1st) Queen, 1974	2·00	2·00

No. 4502 was issued in booklets of six originally sold for £5·10.

3579 *Frankenstein* (Mary Shelley)   **3580** *The Time Machine* (H. G. Wells)

3581 *Brave New World* (Aldous Huxley)   **3582** *The Day of the Triffids* (John Wyndham)

3583 *Childhood's End* (Arthur C. Clarke)   **3584** *Shikasta* (Doris Lessing)

2021 (15 Apr). Classic Science Fiction. Multicoloured. Two phosphor bands. Perf 14½.

4503	**3579**	(1st) *Frankenstein* (Mary Shelley)	1·90	1·90
		a. Horiz pair. Nos. 4503/4504	3·75	3·75
4504	**3580**	(1st) *The Time Machine* (H. G. Wells)	1·90	1·90
4505	**3581**	£1·70 *Brave New World* (Aldous Huxley)	2·50	2·50
		a. Horiz pair. Nos. 4505/4506	5·00	5·00

4506	**3582**	£1·70 *The Day of the Triffids* (John Wyndham)	2·50	2·50
4507	**3583**	£2·55 *Childhood's End* (Arthur C. Clarke)	3·50	3·50
		a. Horiz pair. Nos. 4507/4508	7·00	7·00
4508	**3584**	£2·55 *Shikasta* (Doris Lessing)	3·50	3·50
Set of 6			14·50	14·50
Set of 3 Gutter Pairs			29·00	
First Day Cover (Tallents House)				17·00
Presentation Pack (PO Pack No. 599)			17·00	
PHQ Cards (set of 6) (484)			3·75	16·00

Nos. 4503/4504, 4505/4506 and 4507/4508 were printed together, *se-tenant*, as horizontal pairs in sheets of 60 (2 panes 6×5).

3585 Battle of Bosworth, 1485

3586 Battle of Tewkesbury, 1471

3587 Battle of Barnet, 1471

3588 Battle of Edgecote Moor, 1469

3589 Battle of Towton, 1461

3590 Battle of Wakefield, 1460

3591 Battle of Northampton, 1460

3592 First Battle of St Albans, 1455

2021 (4 May). Wars of the Roses. Multicoloured. One centre band (2nd) or two phosphor bands (others). Perf 14.

4509	**3585**	(2nd) Battle of Bosworth, 1485	1·25	1·25
		a. Horiz pair. Nos. 4509/4510	2·50	2·50
4510	**3586**	(2nd) Battle of Tewkesbury, 1471	1·25	1·25
4511	**3587**	(1st) Battle of Barnet, 1471	1·90	1·90
		a. Horiz pair. Nos. 4511/4512	3·75	3·75
4512	**3588**	(1st) Battle of Edgecote Moor, 1469	1·90	1·90
4513	**3589**	£1·70 Battle of Towton, 1461	2·50	2·50
		a. Horiz pair. Nos. 4513/4514	5·00	5·00
4514	**3590**	£1·70 Battle of Wakefield, 1460	2·50	2·50
4515	**3591**	£2·55 Battle of Northampton, 1460	3·50	3·50
		a. Horiz pair. Nos. 4515/4516	7·00	7·00
4516	**3592**	£2·55 First Battle of St Albans, 1455	3·50	3·50
Set of 8			17·50	17·50
Set of 4 Gutter Pairs			35·00	
First Day Cover (Tallents House)				20·00
Presentation Pack (PO Pack No. 600)			20·00	
PHQ Pack (set of 8) (485)			5·00	18·50

Nos. 4509/4510, 4511/4512, 4513/4514 and 4515/4516 were each printed together, *se-tenant*, as horizontal pairs in sheets of 60 (2 panes 6×5).

3593 *McCartney*

3594 *RAM*

3595 *Venus and Mars*

3596 *McCartney II*

3597 *Tug of War*

3598 *Flaming Pie*

3599 Egypt Station

3600 McCartney III

3604 McCartney II, 1980   **3605** Flaming Pie, 1997

2021 (28 May). Paul McCartney (2nd issue). Multicoloured. Two phosphor bands. Perf 14½.

4528	**3602**	(1st) McCartney, 1970	1·90	1·90
4529	**3603**	(1st) RAM, 1971	1·90	1·90
4530	**3604**	£1·70 McCartney II, 1980	2·75	2·75
4531	**3605**	£1·70 Flaming Pie, 1997	2·75	2·75
Set of 4			9·25	9·25

Nos. 4528/4531 were issued in No. **MS**4525 and in the £20·25 Paul McCartney premium booklet, No. DY38.

3601 Paul McCartney in the Studio

2021 (28 May). Paul McCartney (1st issue). Multicoloured. Two phosphor bands.

(a) Ordinary gum. Perf 14 (Nos. 4517/4524, 4526/4527) or 14½ (No. **MS**4525).

4517	**3593**	(1st) McCartney	1·90	1·90
		a. Horiz strip of 4. Nos. 4517/4520	7·50	7·50
4518	**3594**	(1st) RAM	1·90	1·90
4519	**3595**	(1st) Venus and Mars	1·90	1·90
4520	**3596**	(1st) McCartney II	1·90	1·90
4521	**3597**	£1·70 Tug of War	2·50	2·50
		a. Horiz strip of 4. Nos. 4521/4524	10·00	10·00
4522	**3598**	£1·70 Flaming Pie	2·50	2·50
4523	**3599**	£1·70 Egypt Station	2·50	2·50
4524	**3600**	£1·70 McCartney III	2·50	2·50
Set of 8			17·50	17·50
Set of 2 Gutter Strips of 8			35·00	
First Day Cover (Tallents House)				20·00
Presentation Pack (PO Pack No. 601) (Nos. 4517/4524 and **MS**4525)			29·00	
PHQ Cards (set of 13) (486)			8·25	28·00
Souvenir Folder (containing Nos. 4517/4524 and **MS**4525 plus prints of the stamps at record cover size)			40·00	

MS4525 126×89 mm. **3601** (1st) McCartney, 1970; (1st) RAM, 1971; £1·70 McCartney II, 1980; £1·70 Flaming Pie, 1997 ... 9·50 / 9·50

First Day Cover (Tallents House)				12·00

(b) Self-adhesive. Die-cut perf 14.

4526	**3593**	(1st) McCartney	2·00	2·00
4527	**3596**	(1st) McCartney II	2·00	2·00

Nos. 4517/4520 and 4521/4524 were each printed together, se-tenant, as horizontal strips of four stamps in sheets of 48 (2 panes 4×6).

Nos. 4517/4524 also come from the £20·25 Paul McCartney premium booklet, No. DY38.

Nos. 4526/4527 were issued in stamp booklets originally sold for £5·10.

A Paul McCartney Album Covers Collector's Sheet containing Nos. 4517/4518×2 and 4519/4524 with labels was originally sold for £13.

An Album cover collection fan sheet containing Nos. 4517/4524 was originally sold for £10·90.

A RAM fan sheet containing No. 4518×4 was originally sold for £7·50.

A McCartney III album fan sheet containing No. 4524×4 was originally sold for £7·50.

The 13 PHQ Cards show the 12 individual stamps, including those from No. **MS**4525 and the complete miniature sheet.

3606 Prince Philip, Duke of Edinburgh

2021 (24 June). Prince Philip, Duke of Edinburgh (1921–2021) Commemoration. Multicoloured. Phosphor band at left (2nd) or 'all-over' phosphor (others). Perf 14½×14.

MS4532 200×67 mm. **3606** (2nd) Prince Philip, Duke of Edinburgh, circa 1952; (1st) Prince Philip at passing out parade of Prince Andrew, Dartmouth Naval College, 1980; £1·70 Prince Philip at Royal Windsor Horse Show; £2·55 Prince Philip, circa 1992 ... 9·25 / 9·25

First Day Cover (Tallents House)			11·50
Presentation Pack (PO Pack No. 602)		11·50	
PHQ Cards (set of 5) (487)		3·25	11·00

3607 Dennis's First Comic Strip, 1951

3608 Dennis Adopts Gnasher, 1968

3602 McCartney, 1970

3603 RAM, 1971

3609 Dennis's Front Cover Debut, 1974

3610 Dennis Adopts Rasher the Pig, 1979

3611 Dennis Meets his Sister Bea, 1998

3612 Dennis Reveals Dad was Dennis, 2015

2021 (1 July). Dennis and Gnasher. Multicoloured. Two phosphor bands.

(a) Ordinary gum. Perf 14.

4533	**3607**	(1st) Dennis's First Comic Strip, 1951	1·90	1·90
		a. Horiz strip of 3. Nos. 4533/4535	3·50	3·50
4534	**3608**	(1st) Dennis adopts Gnasher, 1968	1·90	1·90
4535	**3609**	(1st) Dennis's Front Cover Debut, 1974	1·90	1·90
4536	**3610**	£1·70 Dennis adopts Rasher the Pig, 1979	2·50	2·50
		a. Horiz strip of 3. Nos. 4536/4538	7·50	7·50
4537	**3611**	£1·70 Dennis meets his Sister Bea, 1998	2·50	2·50
4538	**3612**	£1·70 Dennis reveals Dad was Dennis, 2015	2·50	2·50
Set of 6			12·50	12·50
Set of 2 Gutter Strips of 6			25·00	
First Day Cover (Tallents House)				15·00
Presentation Pack (PO Pack No. 603) (Nos. 4533/4538 and **MS**4539)			23·00	
PHQ Cards (*set of 11*) (488)			7·00	24·00

3613 Happy Birthday Dennis

(b) Self-adhesive. Die-cut perf 14 (Minnie the Minx) or 14½ (others).

MS4539 203×74 mm. **3613** (1st) Dennis; (1st) Gnasher; £1·70 Minnie the Minx (26×31 mm); £1·70 Dennis, his baby sister Bea and parents ... 8·50 8·50

First Day Cover (Tallents House) ... 10·50

3614 Dennis

3615 Gnasher

(c) Self-adhesive booklet stamps. Die-cut perf 14½.

4540	**3614**	(1st) Dennis	2·00	2·00
4541	**3615**	(1st) Gnasher	2·00	2·00

Nos. 4533/4535 and 4536/4538 were each printed together, *se-tenant*, as horizontal strips of three in sheets of 60 (2 panes 6×5).

Nos. 4540/4541 were issued in stamp booklets originally sold for £5·10. A Collector's Sheet containing 1st self-adhesive Dennis and Gnasher stamps×10 as Types **3614**/**3615** each×5 was originally sold for £9·70.

The 11 PHQ cards show the ten individual stamps, including those from No. **MS**4539, and the complete miniature sheet.

3616 Northern Gannet

3617 Common Cuttlefish

3618 Grey Seal

3619 Bottlenose Dolphin

3620 Spiny Spider Crab

3621 Long-snouted Seahorse

3622 Orca

3623 Fried-egg Anemone

3624 Cuckoo Wrasse

3625 Cold-water Coral Reef

3626 Marine Food Chain

2021 (22 July). Wild Coasts. Multicoloured. Two phosphor bands.

(a) Ordinary gum. Perf 14½ (Nos. 4542/4551) or 14 (No. **MS**4552).

4542	**3616**	(1st) Northern Gannet	1·90	1·90
		a. Horiz strip of 5. Nos. 4542/4546	9·25	9·25
4543	**3617**	(1st) Common Cuttlefish	1·90	1·90
4544	**3618**	(1st) Grey Seal	1·90	1·90
4545	**3619**	(1st) Bottlenose Dolphin	1·90	1·90
4546	**3620**	(1st) Spiny Spider Crab	1·90	1·90
4547	**3621**	(1st) Long-snouted Seahorse	1·90	1·90
		a. Horiz strip of 5. Nos. 4547/4551	9·25	9·25
4548	**3622**	(1st) Orca	1·90	1·90
4549	**3623**	(1st) Fried-egg Anemone	1·90	1·90
4550	**3624**	(1st) Cuckoo Wrasse	1·90	1·90
4551	**3625**	(1st) Cold-water Coral Reef	1·90	1·90
Set of 10			18·00	18·00
Set of 2 Gutter Strips of 10			36·00	
First Day Cover (Tallents House)				20·00
Presentation Pack (PO Pack No. 604) (Nos. 4542/4551 and **MS**4552)			28·00	
PHQ Cards (set of 15) (489)			9·50	29·00

MS4552 202×74 mm. **3626** (1st) Phytoplankton; (1st) Zooplankton; £1·70 Atlantic Herring; £1·70 Harbour Porpoise ... 8·50 / 8·50

First Day Cover (Tallents House) ... 10·50

(b) Self-adhesive. Die-cut perf 14½×14.

4553	**3622**	(1st) Orca	2·00	2·00
4554	**3618**	(1st) Grey Seal	2·00	2·00

Nos. 4542/4546 and 4547/4551 were each printed together, *se-tenant*, as horizontal strips of five in sheets of 50 (2 panes 5×5).

Nos. 4553/4554 were issued in stamp booklets originally sold for £5·10.

A Collector's Sheet containing designs as Nos. 4542/4551 but self-adhesive was originally sold for £9·70.

The 15 PHQ cards show the 14 individual stamps, including those from No. **MS**4552, and the complete miniature sheet.

3627 Bessemer Process, Henry Bessemer, 1856

3628 Watt's Rotative Steam Engine, James Watt, 1780s

3629 Penydarren Locomotive, Richard Trevithick, 1804

3630 Spinning Jenny, James Hargreaves, *circa* 1764

3631 Lombe's Silk Mill, Lombe Brothers, 1721

3632 Portland Cement, Joseph Aspdin, 1824

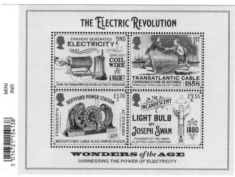

3633 The Electric Revolution

2021 (12 Aug). Industrial Revolutions (1st issue). Multicoloured. One centre band (2nd) or two bands (others). Perf 14½ (Nos. 4555/4560) or 14 (No. **MS**4561).

4555	**3627**	(2nd) Bessemer process, Henry Bessemer, 1856	1·25	1·25
		a. Vert pair. Nos. 4555/4556	2·50	2·50
4556	**3628**	(2nd) Watt's rotative steam engine, James Watt, 1780s	1·25	1·25
4557	**3629**	(1st) Penydarren locomotive, Richard Trevithick, 1804	1·90	1·90
		a. Vert pair. Nos. 4557/4558	3·75	3·75
4558	**3630**	(1st) Spinning Jenny, James Hargreaves, *circa* 1764	1·90	1·90
4559	**3631**	£1·70 Lombe's Silk Mill, Lombe Brothers, 1721	2·50	2·50
		a. Vert pair. Nos. 4559/4560	5·00	5·00
4560	**3632**	£1·70 Portland Cement, Joseph Aspdin, 1824	2·50	2·50
Set of 6			10·50	10·50
Set of 3 Gutter Strips of 4			21·00	
First Day Cover (Tallents House)				12·50
Presentation Pack (PO Pack No. 605) (Nos. 4555/4560 and **MS**4561)			22·50	
PHQ Cards (set of 11) (490)			7·00	23·00

MS4561 126×89 mm. **3633** (2nd) Michael Faraday generates electricity, 1831; (1st) First transatlantic cable, communication, 1858; £1·70 Deptford Power Station, 1889; £2·55 The incandescent light bulb by Joseph Swan, 1880 ... 10·00 / 10·00

First Day Cover (Tallents House) ... 12·00

Nos. 4555/4556, 4557/4558 and 4559/4560 were each printed together, *se-tenant*, as vertical pairs in sheets of 60 (2 panes 5×6).

Nos. 4555/4560 also come from the £18·03 Industrial Revolution premium booklet, No. DY39.

The 11 PHQ cards show the ten individual stamps, including those from No. **MS**4561, and the complete miniature sheet.

3634 Michael Faraday Generates Electricity using just Coil Wire and a Magnet, 1831

3635 First Transatlantic Cable, Communication in Seconds Through 2000 Miles of Cable, 1858

3636 AC Dynamo, Sebastian de Ferranti's Deptford Power Station, Britain's First Large-scale Power Station, 1889

3637 The Incandescent Light Bulb by Joseph Swan, Founder of the Swan Electric Light Company, 1880

2021 (12 Aug). Industrial Revolutions (2nd issue). Multicoloured. One centre band (2nd) or two bands (others). Perf 14.

4562	**3634**	(2nd) Michael Faraday generates electricity, 1831	1·25	1·25
4563	**3635**	(1st) First transatlantic cable communication, 1858	1·90	1·90
4564	**3636**	£1·70 Deptford Power Station, 1889	3·00	3·00
4565	**3637**	£2·55 The incandescent light bulb by Joseph Swan, 1880	4·00	4·00
Set of 4			10·00	10·00

Nos. 4562/4565 also come from the £18·03 Industrial Revolution premium booklet, No. DY39.

3638 Mk IV Tank

3639 Matilda Mk II (A12 Infantry Tank)

3640 Churchill AVRE (Armoured Vehicles Royal Engineers) Tank

3641 Centurion Mk 9 Tank

3642 Scorpion Tank

3643 Chieftain Mk 5 Tank

3644 Challenger 2 Tank

3645 Ajax (turreted, reconnaissance and strike vehicle)

3646 British Army Vehicles

2021 (2 Sept). British Army Vehicles. Multicoloured. Two phosphor bands. Perf 14.

4566	**3638**	(1st) Mk IV Tank	1·90	1·90
		a. Horiz strip of 4. Nos. 4566/4569	7·50	7·50
4567	**3639**	(1st) Matilda Mk II	1·90	1·90
4568	**3640**	(1st) Churchill AVRE Tank	1·90	1·90
4569	**3641**	(1st) Centurion Mk 9 Tank	1·90	1·90
4570	**3642**	£1·70 Scorpion Tank	2·50	2·50
		a. Horiz strip of 4. Nos. 4570/4573	10·00	10·00
4571	**3643**	£1·70 Chieftain Mk 5 Tank	2·50	2·50
4572	**3644**	£1·70 Challenger 2 Tank	2·50	2·50
4573	**3645**	£1·70 Ajax	2·50	2·50
Set of 8			16·50	16·50
Set of 8 Gutter Pairs			33·00	
First Day Cover (Tallents House)				19·00
Presentation Pack (PO Pack No. 606) (Nos. 4566/4573 and **MS**4574)			27·00	
PHQ Cards (set of 13) (491)			8·25	28·00

MS4574 125×89 mm. **3646** (1st) Coyote Tactical
Support Vehicle; (1st) Army Wildcat Mk 1
Reconnaissance Helicopter; £1·70 Trojan
Armoured Vehicle Royal Engineers; £1·70 Fox-
hound Light Protected Patrol Vehicle   8·50   7·25
First Day Cover (Tallents House)   11·00

The 13 PHQ cards show the 12 individual stamps, including those from
No. **MS**4574, and the complete miniature sheet.

3647 Batman

3648 Batwoman

3649 Robin

3650 Batgirl

3651 Alfred

3652 Nightwing

3653 The Joker

3654 Harley Quinn

3655 The Penguin

3656 Poison Ivy

3657 Catwoman

3658 The Riddler

3659 Justice League

3660 Wonder Woman

2021 (17 Sept). DC Collection (1st issue). Multicoloured. Two phosphor
bands.

(a) Ordinary gum. Perf 14½.

4575	**3647**	(1st) Batman	1·90	1·90
		a. Horiz strip of 6. Nos. 4575/4580	11·00	11·00
4576	**3648**	(1st) Batwoman	1·90	1·90
4577	**3649**	(1st) Robin	1·90	1·90
4578	**3650**	(1st) Batgirl	1·90	1·90
4579	**3651**	(1st) Alfred	1·90	1·90
4580	**3652**	(1st) Nightwing	1·90	1·90
4581	**3653**	(1st) The Joker	1·90	1·90
		a. Horiz strip of 6. Nos. 4581/4586	11·00	11·00
4582	**3654**	(1st) Harley Quinn	1·90	1·90
4583	**3655**	(1st) The Penguin	1·90	1·90
4584	**3656**	(1st) Poison Ivy	1·90	1·90
4585	**3657**	(1st) Catwoman	1·90	1·90
4586	**3658**	(1st) The Riddler	1·90	1·90
Set of 12			22·00	22·00
Set of 2 Gutter Strips of 12			44·00	
First Day Cover (Tallents House)				24·00
Presentation Pack (PO Pack No. 607) (Nos. 4575/4586 and **MS**4587)			35·00	
PHQ Cards (set of 19) (492)			12·00	34·00

(b) Self-adhesive.

MS4587 202×74 mm. **3659** (1st) Batman (50×30 mm)
(perf 14); (1st) Wonder Woman (35×36 mm) (perf
14); (1st) Superman (60×23 mm) (perf 14½×14);
(1st) Green Lantern and The Flash (50×30 mm)
(perf 14); (1st) Cyborg and Aquaman (35×36 mm)
(perf 14); (1st) Supergirl and Shazam! (27×36 mm)
(perf 14)   11·00   11·00
First Day Cover (Tallents House)   12·00

(c) Self-adhesive booklet stamps. Die-cut perf 14½×14.

4588	**3647**	(1st) Batman	2·00	2·00
4589	**3649**	(1st) Robin	2·00	2·00
4590	**3660**	(1st) Wonder Woman	2·00	2·00
Set of 3			6·00	6·00

Nos. 4575/4580 and 4581/4586 were each printed together, *se-tenant*,
as horizontal strips of six in sheets of 60 (2 panes 6×5).

Nos. 4575/4586 also come from the £21·20 DC Collection premium
booklet, No. DY40.

Nos. 4588/4589 were issued in stamp booklets originally sold for £5·10.
No. 4590 was issued in stamp booklets originally sold for £5·10.

A Batman Collector's Sheet containing designs as Nos. 4575/4586 but
self-adhesive was originally sold for £11·40.

The 19 PHQ cards show the 18 individual stamps, including those from
No. **MS**4587, and the complete miniature sheet.

3661 Batman

3662 Green Lantern and The Flash

3663 Superman

3664 Cyborg and Aquaman   **3665** Supergirl and Shazam!

2021 (17 Sept). DC Collection (2nd issue). Multicoloured. Self-adhesive. Two phosphor bands. Perf 14½×14 (No. 4594) or 14 (others).

4591	**3661**	(1st) Batman	1·90	1·90
4592	**3662**	(1st) Green Lantern and The Flash	1·90	1·90
4593	**3660**	(1st) Wonder Woman	1·90	1·90
4594	**3663**	(1st) Superman	1·90	1·90
4595	**3664**	(1st) Cyborg and Aquaman	1·90	1·90
4596	**3665**	(1st) Supergirl and Shazam!	1·90	1·90
Set of 6			11·00	11·00

Nos. 4591/4596 come from the £21·20 DC Collection premium booklet, No. DY40.

3666 Women's Rugby World Cup Final, 2014   **3667** Five Nations Championship, 1970

3668 Women's Six Nations Championship, 2015   **3669** Five Nations Championship, 1984

3670 Women's Home Nations Championship, 1998   **3671** Five Nations Championship, 1994

3672 Women's Six Nations Championship, 2009   **3673** Rugby World Cup Final, 2003

2021 (19 Oct). Rugby Union. Multicoloured. One phosphor band, slightly right of centre (2nd) or two bands (others). Perf 14×14½.

4597	**3666**	(2nd) Women's Rugby World Cup Final, 2014	1·25	1·25
		a. Horiz pair. Nos. 4597/4598	2·50	2·50
4598	**3667**	(2nd) Five Nations Championship, 1970	1·25	1·25
4599	**3668**	(1st) Women's Six Nations Championship, 2015	1·90	1·90
		a. Horiz pair. Nos. 4599/4600	3·75	3·75
4600	**3669**	(1st) Five Nations Championship, 1984	1·90	1·90
4601	**3670**	£1·70 Women's Home Nations Championship, 1998	2·50	2·50
		a. Horiz pair. Nos. 4601/4602	5·00	5·00
4602	**3671**	£1·70 Five Nations Championship, 1994	2·50	2·50
4603	**3672**	£2·55 Women's Six Nations Championship, 2009	3·50	3·50
		a. Horiz pair. Nos. 4603/4604	7·00	7·00
4604	**3673**	£2·55 Rugby World Cup Final, 2003	3·50	3·50
Set of 8			17·00	17·00
Set of 4 Gutter Strips of 4			34·00	
First Day Cover (Tallents House)				19·00
Presentation Pack (PO Pack No. 608)			19·00	
PHQ Cards (set of 8) (493)			5·00	18·00

Nos. 4597/4598, 4599/4600, 4601/4602 and 4603/4604 were each printed together, *se-tenant*, as horizontal pairs in sheets of 60 (2 panes 6×5).

3674 Angels   **3675** Angels

3676 Mary and Baby Jesus   **3677** Mary and Baby Jesus

3678 Joseph and Mary on Road to Bethlehem   **3679** Shepherds see Angels

3680 Wise Men Following Star of Bethlehem   **3681** Mary and Baby Jesus Visited by the Shepherds

2021 (2 Nov). Christmas. Nativity Illustrations by Jorge Cocco. Multicoloured. One centre phosphor band (Nos. 4605/4606) or two bands (others). Self-adhesive. Die-cut perf 14½×15 (Nos. 4606, 4608) or 15×14½ (others).

(a) Gravure.

4605	**3674**	(2nd) Angels	1·25	1·25
4606	**3675**	(2nd) Angels	1·25	1·25
4607	**3676**	(1st) Mary and Baby Jesus	1·90	1·90
4608	**3677**	(1st) Mary and Baby Jesus	1·90	1·90
4609	**3678**	(2nd Large) Joseph and Mary on road to Bethlehem	2·50	2·50
4610	**3679**	(1st Large) Shepherds see Angels	3·25	3·25
4611	**3680**	£1·70 Wise Men following Star of Bethlehem	2·75	2·75
4612	**3681**	£2·55 Mary and baby Jesus visited by the Shepherds	4·00	4·00
Set of 8			17·00	17·00
First Day Cover (Tallents House)				19·00
Presentation Pack (PO Pack No. 609)			19·00	
PHQ Cards (*set of* 9) (494)			5·50	18·00

(b) Litho.

MS4613 189×74 mm. As Nos. 4605/4612		17·00	17·00
First Day Cover (Tallents House)			19·50

The 2nd class and 1st class stamps with barcodes, Nos. 4605 and 4607, were each issued in counter sheets of 50.

The 2nd class with no barcode, No. 4606, was issued in booklets of 12 originally sold for £7·92

The 1st class with no barcode, No. 4608, was issued in booklets of 12 originally sold for £10·20.

The 2nd class with no barcode, 1st class with no barcode, £1·70 and £2·55 values were also issued in sheets of 20 containing 8×2nd class, 8×1st class, 2×£1·70 and 2×£2·55 values. These sheets were printed in lithography instead of gravure.

The nine PHQ cards show the individual stamps and the complete miniature sheet.

Collectors Pack

2021 (2 Nov). Comprises Nos. 4464/4473, **MS**4476/**MS**4485, 4492/4501, 4503/**MS**4525, **MS**4532/**MS**4539, 4542/**MS**4552, 4555/**MS**4561, 4566/**MS**4587 and 4597/4612

CP4613*a*	Collectors Pack (Pack No. 610) (*sold for* £180)	£325

Post Office Yearbook

2021 (2 Nov). Comprises Nos. 4464/4473, **MS**4476/**MS**4485, 4492/4501, 4503/**MS**4525, **MS**4532/**MS**4539, 4543/**MS**4552, 4555/**MS**4561, 4566/**MS**4587 and 4597/4612

YB4613*a*	Yearbook (*sold for* £199)	£350

Miniature Sheet Collection

2021 (2 Nov). Comprises Nos. **MS**4476, **MS**4485, **MS**4525, **MS**4532, **MS**4539, **MS**4552, **MS**4561, **MS**4574, **MS**4587 and **MS**4613
MS4613*a* Miniature Sheet Collection (*sold for* £59)   £100

3682 London, July 1969

3683 East Rutherford, New Jersey, USA, August 2019

3684 Rotterdam, Netherlands, August 1995

3685 Tokyo, Japan, March 1995

3686 New York, July 1972

3687 Oslo, Norway, May 2014

3688 Hertfordshire, August 1976

3689 Dusseldorf, Germany, October 2017

3690 Rolling Stones and Tour Posters

2022 (20 Jan). The Rolling Stones (1st issue). Multicoloured. Two phosphor bands. Perf 14 (No. 4614/4621) or 14½ (No. **MS**4622).

4614	**3682**	(1st) London, July 1969	1·90	1·90
		a. Horiz strip of 4. Nos. 4614/4617	7·50	7·50
4615	**3683**	(1st) East Rutherford, New Jersey, USA, August 2019	1·90	1·90

4616	**3684**	(1st) Rotterdam, Netherlands, August		
		1995	1·90	1·90
4617	**3685**	(1st) Tokyo, Japan, March 1995	1·90	1·90
4618	**3686**	£1·70 New York, July 1972	2·50	2·50
		a. Horiz strip of 4. Nos. 4618/4621	10·00	10·00
4619	**3687**	£1·70 Oslo, Norway, May 2014	2·50	2·50
4620	**3688**	£1·70 Hertfordshire, August 1976	2·50	2·50
4621	**3689**	£1·70 Dusseldorf, Germany, October		
		2017	2·50	2·50
Set of 8			16·00	16·00
Set of 2 Gutter Strips of 8			32·00	
First Day Cover (Tallents House)			18·00	
Presentation Pack (PO Pack No. 611) (Nos. 4614/4621				
and **MS**4622)			28·00	
PHQ Cards (set of 13) (495)			8·25	27·00
Souvenir Folder (Nos. 4617/4621 and **MS**4622)				
(originally *sold* for £24·99)			38·00	

MS4622 202×74 mm. **3690** (1st) The Rolling Stones;
(1st) The Rolling Stones; £1·70 Posters for Tour
of Europe, 1974 and Tour of the Americas, 1975;
£1·70 Posters for UK Tour, 1971 and American
Tour, 1981   9·50   9·50
First Day Cover (Tallents House)   12·00

Nos. 4614/4617 and 4618/4621 were each printed together, *se-tenant*,
as horizontal strips of four in sheets of 60 (2 panes 4×6).

Nos. 4614/4621 also come the Rolling Stones £20·85 premium booklet,
No. DY41.

Stamps as Nos. 4614/4621 but self-adhesive with labels were issued in
two different collector's sheets, originally sold for £11·50 each.

A Hyde Park fan sheet containing No. 4614×3 was originally sold for £7.

A Voodoo Lounge fan sheet containing No. 4617×3 was originally
sold for £7.

The 13 PHQ cards show the 12 individual stamps, including those from
No. **MS**4622, and the complete miniature sheet.

3691 The Rolling Stones

3692 The Rolling Stones

3693 Posters for Tour of Europe, 1974 and Tour
of the Americas, 1975

3694 Posters for UK Tour, 1971 and American
Tour, 1981

2022 (20 Jan). The Rolling Stones (2nd issue). Multicoloured. Two
phosphor bands. Perf 14½.

4623	**3691**	(1st) The Rolling Stones	1·90	1·90
4624	**3692**	(1st) The Rolling Stones	1·90	1·90
4625	**3693**	£1·70 Posters for Tour of Europe, 1974		
		and Tour of the Americas, 1975	3·00	3·00

4626	**3694**	£1·70 Posters for UK Tour, 1971 and		
		American Tour, 1981	3·00	3·00
Set of 4			9·50	9·50

Nos. 4623/4626 come from No. **MS**4622 and the £20·85 premium
booklet, No. DY41.

3695 Queen Elizabeth II
at Headquarters of MI5,
London, February 2020

3696 Queen Elizabeth II
and Duke of Edinburgh,
Washington, USA, October
1957

3697 Queen Elizabeth II
on Walkabout in Worcester,
April 1980

3698 Trooping the Colour,
London, June 1978

3699 Leaving Provincial
Museum of Alberta,
Edmonton, Canada, May
2005

3700 During Silver Jubilee
celebrations, Camberwell,
June 1977

3701 At Victoria Park, St
Vincent, February 1966

3702 Order of the Garter
Ceremony, Windsor, June
1999

2022 (4 Feb). Platinum Jubilee. Multicoloured. Two phosphor bands. Perf
14½.

4627	**3695**	(1st) Queen Elizabeth II at		
		headquarters of MI5, London,		
		February 2020	1·90	1·90
		a. Horiz strip of 4. Nos. 4627/4630	7·50	7·50
4628	**3696**	(1st) Queen Elizabeth II and Duke of		
		Edinburgh, Washington, USA,		
		October 1957	1·90	1·90
4629	**3697**	(1st) Queen Elizabeth II on walkabout		
		in Worcester, April 1980	1·90	1·90
4630	**3698**	(1st) Trooping the Colour, London,		
		June 1978	1·90	1·90
4631	**3699**	£1·70 Leaving Provincial Museum of		
		Alberta, Edmonton, Canada,		
		May 2005	2·50	2·50
		a. Horiz strip of 4. Nos. 4631/4634	10·00	10·00
4632	**3700**	£1·70 During Silver Jubilee celebrations,		
		Camberwell, June 1977	2·50	2·50
4633	**3701**	£1·70 At Victoria Park, St Vincent,		
		February 1966	2·50	2·50

4634 **3702** £1·70 Order of the Garter ceremony,
          Windsor, June 1999

	2·50	2·50
Set of 8	16·00	16·00
Set of 2 Gutter Strips of 8	32·00	
First Day Cover (Tallents House)		18·00
Presentation Pack (PO Pack No. 612)	18·00	
PHQ Cards (set of 8) (496)	5·00	17·00

Nos. 4627/4630 and 4631/4634 were each printed together, *se-tenant*, as horizontal strips of four in sheets of 48 (2 panes 4×6).

Nos. 4627/4634 also come from the £19·50 Platinum Jubilee premium booklet, No. DY42.

3703 The Stamp Designs of David Gentleman

2022 (18 Feb). The Stamp Designs of David Gentleman. Multicoloured. One centre band (2nd) or two bands (others). Perf 14½.
MS4635 202×74 mm. **3703** (2nd) 1962 3d. National Productivity Year; (2nd) 1969 9d. British Ships; (1st) 1973 9p. British Trees; (1st) 1976 8½p. Social Reformers; £1·70 1966 6d. 900th Anniversary of the Battle of Hastings; £1·70 4d. 1965 25th

Anniversary of the Battle of Britain	11·00	11·00
First Day Cover (Tallents House)		13·00
Presentation Pack (PO Pack No. 613)	13·00	
PHQ Cards (set of 7) (497)	4·50	12·50

The seven PHQ cards show the individual stamps and the composite miniature sheet.

No. **MS**4236 additionally inscribed 'London 2022 19 to 26 February' was only available at that exhibition (*Price* £13).

3704 Arsenal Players Charlie George and Frank McLintock Parading FA Cup, 1971

3705 Crowds on Pitch at Wembley Stadium During 1923 Cup Final

3706 West Bromwich Albion Supporters at 1968 Cup Final

3707 Keith Houchen Equalises for Coventry City Against Tottenham Hotspur, 1987 Final

3708 Lincoln City Reach Quarter Finals, 2017 (FA Cup Upsets)

3709 King George VI and Queen Elizabeth Present FA Cup to Sunderland Captain Raich Carter, 1937

3710 The FA Cup

2022 (8 Mar). The FA Cup. Multicoloured. Two phosphor bands. Perf 14½ (Nos. 4636/4641) or 14 (No. **MS**4642).

4636	**3704**	(1st) Arsenal Players Charlie George and Frank McLintock parading FA Cup, 1971	1·90	1·90
		a. Vert pair. Nos. 4636/4637	3·75	3·75
4637	**3705**	(1st) Crowds on pitch at Wembley Stadium during 1923 Cup Final	1·90	1·90
4638	**3706**	£1·70 West Bromwich Albion Supporters at 1968 Cup Final	2·50	2·50
		a. Vert pair. Nos. 4638/4639	5·00	5·00
4639	**3707**	£1·70 Keith Houchen equalises for Coventry City, 1987 Final	2·50	2·50
4640	**3708**	£2·55 Lincoln City reach Quarter Finals, 2017 (FA Cup Upsets)	3·50	3·50
		a. Vert pair. Nos. 4640/4641	7·00	7·00
4641	**3709**	£2·55 King George VI and Queen Elizabeth present FA Cup, 1937	3·50	3·50
Set of 6			15·00	15·00
Set of 3 Gutter Pairs (only 2 stamps in each pair)			17·00	
First Day Cover (Tallents House)				17·00
Presentation Pack (PO Pack No. 614) (Nos. 4636/4641 and **MS**4642)			26·00	
PHQ Cards (set of 11) (498)			6·00	24·00

MS4642 202×74 mm. **3710** (1st) Supporter's memorabilia; (1st) Winners' medal and trophy; £1·70 Official match-day items; £1·70 Cup Final

souvenirs	8·50	8·50
First Day Cover (Tallents House)		10·00

Nos. 4636/4637, 4638/4639 and 4640/4641 were each printed together, *se-tenant*, in vertical pairs in sheets of 36 (2 panes 3×6).

The 11 PHQ cards show the ten individual stamps including those from No. **MS**4642 and the complete miniature sheet.

3711 NHS Workers (Jessica Roberts)

3712 Captain Sir Tom Moore (Shachow Ali)

3713 NHS Hospital Cleaners (Raphael Valle Martin)

3714 NHS/My Mum (Alfie Craddock)

3715 Lab Technician (Logan Pearson)

3716 Delivery Driver (Isabella Grover)

3717 The NHS (Connie Stuart)

3718 Doctors, Nurses (Ishan Bains)

2022 (23 Mar). Heroes of the Covid Pandemic. Winning Entries from Schoolchildren's Stamp Design Competition. Multicoloured. Two phosphor bands. Perf 14×14½.

4643	3711	(1st) NHS Workers (Jessica Roberts)	1·90	1·90
		a. Horiz strip of 4. Nos. 4643/4646	7·50	7·50
4644	3712	(1st) Captain Sir Tom Moore (Shachow Ali)	1·90	1·90
4645	3713	(1st) NHS Hospital Cleaners (Raphael Valle Martin)	1·90	1·90
4646	3714	(1st) NHS/My Mum (Alfie Craddock)	1·90	1·90
4647	3715	(1st) Lab Technician (Logan Pearson)	1·90	1·90
		a. Horiz strip of 4. Nos. 4647/4650	7·50	7·50
4648	3716	(1st) Delivery Driver (Isabella Grover)	1·90	1·90
4649	3717	(1st) The NHS (Connie Stuart)	1·90	1·90
4650	3718	(1st) Doctors, Nurses (Ishan Bains)	1·90	1·90
Set of 8			14·00	14·00
Set of 2 Gutter Strips of 8			28·00	
First Day Cover (Tallents House)				16·00
Presentation Pack (PO Pack No. 615)			16·00	
PHQ Cards (set of 8) (499)			5·00	15·00

Nos. 4243/4246 and 4247/4250 were printed together, *se-tenant*, as horizontal strips of four in sheets of 48 (2 panes 4×6).

3722 Nightjar (*Caprimulgus europaeus*)

3723 Pied Flycatcher (*Ficedula hypoleuca*)

3724 Swift (*Apus apus*)

3725 Yellow Wagtail (*Motacilla flava*)

3726 Arctic Skua (*Stercorarius parasiticus*)

3727 Stone-curlew (*Burhinus oedicnemus*)

3728 Arctic Tern (*Sterna paradisaea*)

3729 Swallow (*Hirundo rustica*)

3730 Turtle Dove (*Streptopelia turtur*)

3731 Montagu's Harrier (*Circus pygargus*)

2022 (7 Apr). Migratory Birds. Multicoloured. Two phosphor bands. Perf 14.

4651	3722	(1st) Nightjar (*Caprimulgus europaeus*)	1·90	1·90
		a. Horiz strip of 5. Nos. 4651/4655	9·25	9·25
4652	3723	(1st) Pied Flycatcher (*Ficedula hypoleuca*)	1·90	1·90
4653	3724	(1st) Swift (*Apus apus*)	1·90	1·90
4654	3725	(1st) Yellow Wagtail (*Motacilla flava*)	1·90	1·90
4655	3726	(1st) Arctic Skua (*Stercorarius parasiticus*)	1·90	1·90
4656	3727	(1st) Stone-curlew (*Burhinus oedicnemus*)	1·90	1·90
		a. Horiz strip of 5. Nos. 4656/4660	9·25	9·25
4657	3728	(1st) Arctic Tern (*Sterna paradisaea*)	1·90	1·90
4658	3729	(1st) Swallow (*Hirundo rustica*)	1·90	1·90
4659	3730	(1st) Turtle Dove (*Streptopelia turtur*)	1·90	1·90
4660	3731	(1st) Montagu's Harrier (*Circus pygargus*)	1·90	1·90
Set of 10			17·50	17·50
Set of 2 Gutter Strips of 10			35·00	
First Day Cover (Tallents House)				20·00
Presentation Pack (PO Pack No. 616)			20·00	
PHQ Cards (set of 10) (500)			6·25	19·00

Nos. 4651/4655 and 4656/4660 were each printed together, *se-tenant*, as horizontal strips of five in sheets of 50 (2 panes 5×5).

3732 Air Raid Precautions (Protecting Civilians)

3733 Queen Alexandra's Imperial Military Nursing Service (Nursing on the front line)

3734 Auxiliary Territorial Service (Repairing Army Vehicles)

3735 Women's Royal Naval Service (Arming the Fleet)

3736 Factory Worker (Powering the War Effort)

3737 Codebreakers (Deciphering Enemy Messages)

3738 Women's Voluntary Services (Supplying Military Production)

3739 Auxiliary Territorial Service (Lighting the Way to Victory)

3740 Women's Auxiliary Air Force (Maintaining RAF Aircraft)

3741 Women's Land Army (Meeting Britain's Demand)

3742 Spitfire Women, Ferry Pilots of the Air Transport Auxiliary

2022 (5 May). Unsung Heroes. Women of World War II (1st issue). Multicoloured. Two phosphor bands. Perf 14½ (Nos. 4661/4670) or 14 (No. **MS**4671).

4661	**3732**	(1st) Air Raid Precautions (Protecting Civilians)	1·90	1·90
		a. Horiz strip of 5. Nos. 4661/4665	9·25	9·25
4662	**3733**	(1st) Queen Alexandra's Imperial Military Nursing Service (Nursing on the front line)	1·90	1·90
4663	**3734**	(1st) Auxiliary Territorial Service (Repairing Army Vehicles)	1·90	1·90
4664	**3735**	(1st) Women's Royal Naval Service (Arming the Fleet)	1·90	1·90
4665	**3736**	(1st) Factory Worker (Powering the War Effort)	1·90	1·90
4666	**3737**	(1st) Codebreakers (Deciphering Enemy Messages)	1·90	1·90
		a. Horiz strip of 5. Nos. 4666/4670	9·25	9·25
4667	**3738**	(1st) Women's Voluntary Services (Supplying Military Production)	1·90	1·90
4668	**3739**	(1st) Auxiliary Territorial Service (Lighting the Way to Victory)	1·90	1·90
4669	**3740**	(1st) Women's Auxiliary Air Force (Maintaining RAF Aircraft)	1·90	1·90
4670	**3741**	(1st) Women's Land Army (Meeting Britain's Demand)	1·90	1·90
Set of 10			17·50	17·50
Set of 2 Gutter Strips of 10			35·00	
First Day Cover (Tallents House)				20·00
Presentation Pack (Nos. 4661/**MS**4670 and **MS**4671) (PO Pack No. 617)			30·00	
PHQ Cards (set of 15) (501)			8·75	28·00

MS4671 202×74 mm. **3742** (1st) Pilots meet in their Ferry Pool briefing room; (1st) Pilot climbing into the cockpit of a Supermarine Spitfire; £1·85 Pilot completing her post-flight paperwork in a Lockheed Hudson; £1·85 Pilots of the No. 5 Ferry Pool disembarking from an Avro Anson ... 9·00 ... 9·00

First Day Cover (Tallents House) ... 11·00

Nos. 4661/4665 and 4666/4670 were each printed together, *se-tenant*, as horizontal strips of five stamps in sheets of 50 (2 panes 5×5).

Nos. 4661/4670 also come from the £20·75 Unsung Heroes: Women of World War II premium booklet, No. DY43.

The 15 PHQ cards show the 14 individual stamps including those from No. **MS**4671 and the complete miniature sheet.

3743 Pilots meet in their Ferry Pool Briefing Room

3744 Pilot climbing into the Cockpit of a Supermarine Spitfire

3745 Pilot completing her Post-Flight Paperwork in a Lockheed Hudson

3746 Pilots of the No. 5 Ferry Pool disembarking from an Avro Anson

2022 (5 May). Unsung Heroes. Women of World War II (2nd issue). Two phosphor bands. Perf 14½×14.

4672	**3743**	(1st) Pilots meet in their Ferry Pool Briefing Room	1·90	1·90
4673	**3744**	(1st) Pilot climbing into the Cockpit of a Supermarine Spitfire	1·90	1·90
4674	**3745**	£1·85 Pilot completing her Post-Flight Paperwork in a Lockheed Hudson	2·75	2·75
4675	**3746**	£1·85 Pilots of the No. 5 Ferry Pool disembarking from an Avro Anson	2·75	2·75
Set of 4			9·00	9·00

Nos. 4672/4675 were issued in No. **MS**4671 and the £20·75 Unsung Heroes. Women of World War II premium booklet, No. DY43.

3747 Siamese Cat Grooming

3748 Tabby Cat Stalking

3749 Ginger Cat Playing

3750 British Shorthair Cat Sleeping

3751 Maine Coon Cat Staring

3752 Black and White Cat on Alert

3753 Bengal Cat being Curious

3754 Tabby and White Cat Stretching

2022 (9 June). Cats. Multicoloured. One centre phosphor band (2nd) or two phosphor bands (others). Perf 14.

4676	**3747**	(2nd) Siamese cat grooming	1·25	1·25
		a. Vert pair. Nos. 4676/4677	2·50	2·50
4677	**3748**	(2nd) Tabby cat stalking	1·25	1·25
4678	**3749**	(1st) Ginger cat playing	1·90	1·90
		a. Vert pair. Nos. 4678/4679	3·75	3·75
4679	**3750**	(1st) British Shorthair cat sleeping	1·90	1·90
4680	**3751**	£1·85 Maine Coon cat staring	2·50	2·50
		a. Vert pair. Nos. 4680/4681	5·00	5·00
4681	**3752**	£1·85 Black and white cat on alert	2·50	2·50
4682	**3753**	£2·55 Bengal cat being curious	3·50	3·50
		a. Vert pair. Nos. 4682/4683	7·00	7·00
4683	**3754**	£2·55 Tabby and white cat stretching	3·50	3·50
Set of 8			17·00	17·00
Set of 4 Gutter Pairs			34·00	
First Day Cover (Tallents House)				19·00
Presentation Pack (PO Pack No. 618)			19·00	
PHQ Cards (set of 8) (502)			4·75	18·00

Nos. 4676/4677, 4678/4679, 4680/4681 and 4682/4683 were each printed together, *se-tenant*, as vertical pairs in sheets of 60 (2 panes 5×6).

A collector's sheet containing stamps as Nos. 4676/4677, 4678/4679, each×2 and Nos. 4680/4683 but self-adhesive with labels was originally sold for £15·20.

3755 Couple Kissing

3756 Marchers in Rally and 'LOVE' Slogan

3757 Three Couples and Pink, White and Blue Transgender Pride Flag

3758 Rally with Marcher Carrying Intersex Progress Pride Flag

3759 Marchers with 'GAY PRIDE' and 'LESBIANS UNITE' Banners

3760 Rally with Motorcyclist and 'GLAD TO BE GAY' Placard

3761 Couple Kissing, 'Gay Liberation' and Rainbow Flag

3762 Drag Queen, Marchers Carrying Rainbow Placard and 'LOVE ALWAYS WINS' Slogan on Flag

2022 (1 July). Pride. Multicoloured. Two phosphor bands. Perf 14.

4684	**3755**	(1st) Couple kissing	1·90	1·90
		a. Horiz pair. Nos. 4684/4685	3·75	3·75
4685	**3756**	(1st) Marchers in rally and 'LOVE' slogan	1·90	1·90
4686	**3757**	(1st) Three couples and pink, white and blue Transgender Pride flag	1·90	1·90
		a. Horiz pair. Nos. 4686/4687	3·75	3·75
4687	**3758**	(1st) Rally with marcher carrying Intersex Progress Pride flag	1·90	1·90
4688	**3759**	£1·85 Marchers with 'GAY PRIDE' and 'LESBIANS UNITE' banners	2·50	2·50
		a. Horiz pair. Nos. 4688/4689	5·00	5·00
4689	**3760**	£1·85 Rally with motorcyclist and 'GLAD TO BE GAY' placard	2·50	2·50
4690	**3761**	£1·85 Couple kissing, 'Gay Liberation' and rainbow flag	2·50	2·50
		a. Horiz pair. Nos. 4690/4691	5·00	5·00
4691	**3762**	£1·85 Drag queen, marchers carrying rainbow placard and 'LOVE ALWAYS WINS' slogan on flag	2·50	2·50
Set of 8			16·00	16·00
Set of 4 Gutter Pairs			32·00	
First Day Cover (Tallents House)				18·00
Presentation Pack (PO Pack No. 619)			18·00	
PHQ Cards (*set of 8*) (503)			4·75	17·00

Nos. 4684/4685, 4686/4687, 4688/4689 and 4690/4691 were each printed together, *se-tenant*, as horizontal pairs in sheets of 60 (2 panes 6×5).

A collector's sheet containing stamps as Nos. 4684/4691 but self-adhesive with labels was originally sold for £12·40.

3763 Diving   **3764** Boxing

3765 Para Table Tennis   **3766** Para Powerlifting

3767 Artistic Gymnastics   **3768** Mountain Biking

3769 Athletics   **3770** Wheelchair Basketball

2022 (28 July). Commonwealth Games, Birmingham. Multicoloured. Two phosphor bands. Perf 14½.

4692	**3763**	(1st) Diving	1·90	1·90
		a. Horiz strip of 4. Nos. 4692/4695	7·50	7·50
4693	**3764**	(1st) Boxing	1·90	1·90
4694	**3765**	(1st) Para table tennis	1·90	1·90

4695	**3766**	(1st) Para powerlifting	1·90	1·90
4696	**3767**	£1·85 Artistic gymnastics	2·50	2·50
		a. Horiz strip of 4. Nos. 4696/4699	10·00	10·00
4697	**3768**	£1·85 Mountain biking	2·50	2·50
4698	**3769**	£1·85 Athletics	2·50	2·50
4699	**3770**	£1·85 Wheelchair basketball	2·50	2·50
Set of 8			16·00	16·00
Set of 2 Gutter Strips of 8			32·00	
First Day Cover (Tallents House)				18·00
Presentation Pack (PO Pack No. 620)			18·00	
PHQ Cards (*set of 8*) (504)			4·75	17·00

Nos. 4692/4695 and 4696/4699 were each printed together, *se-tenant*, as horizontal strips of four in sheets of 48 (2 panes 4×6).

3771 Optimus Prime

3772 Megatron

3773 Bumblebee

3774 Starscream

3775 Grimlock

3776 Shockwave

3777 Arcee

3778 Soundwave

3779 The Dinobots

2022 (1 Sept). Transformers (1st issue). Multicoloured. One centre band (2nd) or two bands (others).

(a) Ordinary gum. Perf 14.

4700	**3771**	(1st) Optimus Prime	1·90	1·90
		a. Horiz pair. Nos. 4700/4701	3·75	3·75
4701	**3772**	(1st) Megatron	1·90	1·90
4702	**3773**	(1st) Bumblebee	1·90	1·90
		a. Horiz pair. Nos. 4702/4703	3·75	3·75
4703	**3774**	(1st) Starscream	1·90	1·90
4704	**3775**	£1·85 Grimlock	2·50	2·50
		a. Horiz pair. Nos. 4704/4705	5·00	5·00
4705	**3776**	£1·85 Shockwave	2·50	2·50
4706	**3777**	£1·85 Arcee	2·50	2·50
		a. Horiz pair. Nos. 4706/4707	5·00	5·00
4707	**3778**	£1·85 Soundwave	2·50	2·50
Set of 8			17·00	17·00
Set of 4 Gutter Pairs			34·00	
First Day Cover (Tallents House)				19·00
Presentation Pack (Nos. 4700/4707 and **MS**4708) (PO Pack No. 621)			28·00	
PHQ Cards (set of 14) (505)			8·25	18·00

(b) Self-adhesive. Die-cut perf 14.
MS4708 210×68 mm. **3779** (2nd) Swoop (27×36 mm); (1st) Slug (35×35 mm); (1st) Sludge (27×36 mm); (1st) Grimlock (35×35 mm); £1·85 Snarl (35×35 mm)

mm)	9·50	9·50
First Day Cover (Tallents House)		12·00

Nos. 4700/4701, 4702/4703, 4704/4705 and 4706/4707 were each printed together, *se-tenant*, as horizontal pairs in sheets of 60 (2 panes 6×5).

Nos. 4700/4707 also come from the £21·25 Transformers booklet, No. DY44.

A collector's sheet containing stamps as Nos. 4700/4707 but self-adhesive with labels was originally sold for £12·40.

An Optimus Prime fan sheet containing No. 4700×3 was originally sold for £7.

A Bumblebee fan sheet containing No. 4702×3 was originally sold for £7.

The 14 PHQ cards show the 13 individual stamps including those from No. **MS**4708 and the complete miniature sheet.

3780 Swoop

3781 Slug

3782 Sludge

3783 Grimlock

3784 Snarl

2022 (1 Sept). Transformers (2nd issue). Multicoloured. Self-adhesive. One centre band (2nd) or two bands (others). Die-cut perf 14.

4709	**3780**	(2nd) Swoop	1·25	1·25
4710	**3781**	(1st) Slug	1·90	1·90
4711	**3782**	(1st) Sludge	1·90	1·90
4712	**3783**	(1st) Grimlock	1·90	1·90
4713	**3784**	£1·85 Snarl	2·75	2·75
Set of 5			9·50	9·50

Nos. 4709/4713 come from the £21·25 Transformers booklet, No. DY44, and also No. **MS**4722.

3785 Aviation Operations

3786 Cold-weather Operations

3787 Mountain Operations

3788 Arid-Climate Operations

3789 Commando Training

3790 Band Service

3791 Amphibious Operations

3792 Maritime Security Operations

3793 Royal Marines Uniforms

2022 (29 Sept). Royal Marines. Multicoloured. Two phosphor bands. Perf 14½×14.

4714	**3785**	(1st) Aviation Operations	1·90	1·90
		a. Horiz strip of 4. Nos. 4714/4717	7·50	7·50
4715	**3786**	(1st) Cold-weather Operations	1·90	1·90
4716	**3787**	(1st) Mountain Operations	1·90	1·90
4717	**3788**	(1st) Arid-Climate Operations	1·90	1·90
4718	**3789**	£1·85 Commando Training	2·50	2·50
		a. Horiz strip of 4. Nos. 4718/4721	10·00	10·00
4719	**3790**	£1·85 Band Service	2·50	2·50
4720	**3791**	£1·85 Amphibious Operations	2·50	2·50
4721	**3792**	£1·85 Maritime Security Operations	2·50	2·50
Set of 8			16·00	16·00
Set of 2 Gutter Strips of 8			32·00	
First Day Cover (Tallents House)				18·00
Presentation Pack (Nos. 4714/4721 and **MS**4722) (PO Pack No. 622)			26·00	
PHQ Cards (set of 13) (506)			7·50	26·00

MS4722 115×89 mm. **3793** (1st) Sea Soldier, Duke of York and Albany's Maritime Regiment of Foot, 1664; (1st) Grenadier, Chatham Division, His Majesty's Marine Forces, 1775; £1·85 Sergeant, 4th Battalion, Royal Marines, 1918; £1·85 Officer, 48th Royal Marine Commando, 1944 ... 8·50 / 8·50
First Day Cover (Tallents House) ... 10·00

Nos. 4714/4717 and 4718/4721 were each printed together, *se-tenant*, as horizontal strips four in sheets of 24 (2 panes 4×6).

Types **3794/3798** are vacant.

The 13 PHQ cards show the 12 individual stamps including those from No. **MS**4722 and the complete miniature sheet.

3799 Rocky and Ginger (*Chicken Run*)

3800 Feathers McGraw (*The Wrong Trousers*)

3801 *Wallace and Gromit*

3802 Frank the Tortoise (*Creature Comforts*)

3803 Timmy (*Shaun the Sheep, Timmy Time*)

3804 Morph and Chas (*The Amazing Adventures of Morph & more*)

3805 Robin (*Robin Robin*, 2021)

3806 Shaun and Blitzer (*Shaun the Sheep*)

3807 Wallace and Gromit Cracking Moments

2022 (19 Oct). Aardman Classics. Multicoloured. Self-adhesive. One centre phosphor band (2nd) or 'all-over' phosphor (others). Die-cut perf 13½×14 (Nos. 4723/4730) or 14 (No. **MS**4731).

4723	**3799**	(2nd) Rocky and Ginger (*Chicken Run*)	1·25	1·25
4724	**3800**	(2nd) Feathers McGraw (*The Wrong Trousers*)	1·25	1·25
4725	**3801**	(1st) *Wallace and Gromit*	1·90	1·90
4726	**3802**	(1st) Frank the Tortoise (*Creature Comforts*)	1·90	1·90
4727	**3803**	£1·85 Timmy (*Shaun the Sheep, Timmy Time*)	2·50	2·50
4728	**3804**	£1·85 Morph and Chas (*The Amazing Adventures of Morph & more*)	2·50	2·50
4729	**3805**	£2·55 Robin (*Robin Robin*, 2021)	3·50	3·50
4730	**3806**	£2·55 Shaun and Bitzer (*Shaun the Sheep*)	3·50	3·50
Set of 8			18·00	18·00
First Day Cover (Tallents House)				20·00
Presentation Pack (Nos. 4723/4730 and **MS**4741) (PO Pack 623)			31·00	
PHQ Cards (set of 13) (507)			7·50	20·00

MS4731 192×74 mm. **3807** (1st) *A Close Shave* (vert); (1st) *A Matter of Loaf and Death*; £1·85 *The Wrong Trousers*; £1·85 *A Grand Day Out* ... 8·50 / 8·50
First Day Cover (Tallents House) ... 11·00

Nos. 4723/4724, 4725/4726, 4727/4728 and 4729/4730 were each printed together in sheets of 60 (2 panes 6×5).

A collector's sheet containing Nos. 4723/4730 with labels was originally sold for £13·25.

The 13 PHQ cards show the 12 individual stamps including those from No. **MS**4731 and the complete miniature sheet.

3808 The Annunciation

3809 Holy Family

3810 Journey to Bethlehem

3811 Angel

3812 Angel and Shepherds

3813 Magi

2022 (3 Nov). Christmas. Nativity Illustrations by Katie Ponder. Multicoloured. Self-adhesive. One centre phosphor band (No. 4732) or two bands (others). Die-cut perf 15×14½.

4732	**3808**	(2nd) The Annunciation	1·25	1·25
4733	**3809**	(1st) Holy Family	1·90	1·90
4734	**3810**	(2nd Large) Journey to Bethlehem	2·50	2·50
4735	**3811**	(1st Large) Angel	3·25	3·25
4736	**3812**	£1·85 Angel and Shepherds	2·50	2·50
4737	**3813**	£2·55 Magi	3·50	3·50
Set of 6			14·00	14·00
First Day Cover (Tallents House)				16·00
Presentation Pack (PO Pack No. 624)			16·00	
PHQ Cards (set of 7) (508)			4·25	15·00
MS4738 179×74 mm. Nos. 4732/4737			15·00	15·00
First Day Cover (Tallents House)				17·00

Nos. 4732/4737 were each issued in counter sheets of 50.

The 2nd class No. 4732 was issued in booklets of 8 originally sold for £5·44.

The 1st class No. 4733 was issued in booklets of 8 originally sold for £7·60.

The 2nd class, 1st class, £1·85 and £2·55 values were also issued in sheets of 20 containing eight 2nd class, eight 1st class and two each of the £1·85 and £2·55 values, printed in lithography and originally sold for £23·05.

The 2nd class, 1st class, £1·85 and £2·55 values were also issued in sheets of 20 containing eight 2nd class, eight 1st class, and two each of the £1·70 and £2·55 values. These sheets were printed in lithography instead of gravure.

The seven PHQ cards show the individual stamps and the complete miniature sheet.

3814 Queen Elizabeth II, 1952 (Dorothy Wilding)

3815 Queen Elizabeth II, 1968 (Cecil Beaton)

3816 Queen Elizabeth II, 1984 (Yousef Karsh)

3817 Queen Elizabeth II, 1996 (Tim Graham)

2022 (10 Nov). Queen Elizabeth II (1926–2022) Commemoration. Agate, grey and black. One phosphor band at right (2nd) or 'all-over' phosphor (others). Perf 14½×14.

4739	**3814**	(2nd) Queen Elizabeth II, 1952	1·25	1·25
4740	**3815**	(1st) Queen Elizabeth II, 1968	1·90	1·90
4741	**3816**	£1·85 Queen Elizabeth II, 1984	2·50	2·50
4742	**3817**	£2·55 Queen Elizabeth II, 1996	3·50	3·50
Set of 4			8·25	8·25
Set of 4 Gutter Pairs			16·50	
First Day Cover (Tallents House)				10·50
Presentation Pack (PO Pack No. M27)			10·50	
PHQ Cards (set of 4) (D35)			2·25	10·50

3818 Head of the King

3819 Inlaid Fan

3820 Gold Mask

3821 Falcon Pendant

3822 Lion Couch (detail)

3823 Throne (detail)

3824 Boat Model

3825 Guardian Statue

3826 Discovering Tutankhamen's Tomb

2022 (24 Nov). Tutankhamun (1st issue). Multicoloured. One phosphor band at left (2nd) or two phosphor bands (others). Perf 14×14½ (Nos. 4743/4750) or 14 (No. **MS**4751).

4743	**3818**	(2nd) Head of the King	1·25	1·25
		a. Horiz pair. Nos. 4743/4744	2·50	2·50
4744	**3819**	(2nd) Inlaid fan	1·25	1·25
4745	**3820**	(1st) Gold mask	1·90	1·90
		a. Horiz pair. Nos. 4745/4746	3·75	3·75
4746	**3821**	(1st) Falcon pendant	1·90	1·90
4747	**3822**	£1·85 Lion couch (detail)	2·50	2·50
		a. Horiz pair. Nos. 4747/4748	5·00	5·00
4748	**3823**	£1·85 Throne (detail)	2·50	2·50
4749	**3824**	£2·55 Boat model	3·50	3·50
		a. Horiz pair. Nos. 4749/4750	7·00	7·00
4750	**3825**	£2·55 Guardian statue	3·50	3·50
Set of 8			17·00	17·00
Set of 4 Gutter Strips of 4			34·00	
First Day Cover (Tallents House)				19·00
Presentation Pack (Nos. 4743/4750 and **MS**4751) (PO Pack No. 625)			28·00	
PHQ Cards (set of 13) (509)			7·50	18·00
MS4751 146×74 mm. **3826** (1st) Objects in the antechamber; (1st) Head of the outermost coffin; £1·85 Examining the innermost coffin; £1·85 Moving small shrine to laboratory			8·75	8·75
First Day Cover (Tallents House)				10·50

Nos. 4743/4744, 4745/4746, 4747/4748 and 4749/4750 were printed together, *se-tenant*, as horizontal pairs in sheets of 60 (2 panes 6×5).

Nos. 4743/4750 also come from the £21·55 Tutankhamun premium booklet, No. DY45.

The 13 PHQ cards show the 12 individual stamps including those from No. **MS**4751 and the complete miniature sheet.

3827 Objects in the Antechamber

3828 Head of the Outermost Coffin

3829 Examining the Innermost Coffin

3830 Moving Small Shrine to Laboratory

2022 (24 Nov). Tutankhamun (2nd issue). Two phosphor bands. Perf 14.

4752	**3827**	(1st) Objects in the antechamber	1·90	1·90
4753	**3828**	(1st) Head of the outermost coffin	1·90	1·90
4754	**3829**	£1·85 Examining the innermost coffin	2·50	2·50
4755	**3830**	£1·85 Moving small shrine to laboratory	2·50	2·50
Set of 4			8·75	8·75

Nos. 4752/4755 come from **MS**4751 and the £21·55 Tutankhamun premium booklet, No. DY45.

Collectors Pack

2022 (24 Nov). Comprises Nos. 4614/**MS**4622, 4627/**MS**4671, 4676/**MS**4708, 4714/4737 and 4739/**MS**4751

CP4755a	Collectors Pack (Pack No. 626) (*sold for £204*)	£300

Post Office Yearbook

2022 (24 Nov). Comprises Nos. 4614/**MS**4622, 4627/**MS**4671, 4676/**MS**4708, 4714/4737 and 4739/**MS**4751

YB4755a	Yearbook (*sold for £224*)	£325

Miniature Sheet Collection

2022 (24 Nov). Comprises Nos. **MS**4622, **MS**4635, **MS**4642, **MS**4671, **MS**4708, **MS**4722, **MS**4731, **MS**4738 and **MS**4751

MS4755a Miniature Sheet Collection (*sold for £55*)	85·00

3831 Steve Harris, Vancouver, June 2010

3832 Bruce Dickinson, Hammersmith Odeon, London, May 1983

3833 Dave Murray, Adrian Smith and Steve Harris, Pamplona, Spain, September 1988

3834 Nicko McBrain, Quito, Ecuador, March 2009

3835 Dave Murray, Bruce Dickinson and Janick Gers, Rio de Janeiro, January 2001

3836 Adrian Smith and Steve Harris, Helsinki, May 2018

3837 Iron Maiden, Twickenham Stadium, London, July 2008

3838 Bruce Dickinson sword fights with Mascot Eddie, Birmingham, August 2018

3839 Eddie the Iron Maiden Mascot

2023 (12 Jan). Iron Maiden. Multicoloured. Two phosphor bands. Perf 14 (Nos. 4756/4/63) or 14×14½ (No. **MS**4764).

4756	**3831**	(1st) Steve Harris, Vancouver, June 2010	1·90	1·90
		a. Horiz strip of 4. Nos. 4756/4759	7·50	7·50
4757	**3832**	(1st) Bruce Dickinson, Hammersmith Odeon, London, May 1983	1·90	1·90

4758	**3833**	(1st) Dave Murray, Adrian Smith and Steve Harris, Pamplona, Spain, September 1988	1·90	1·90
4759	**3834**	(1st) Nicko McBrain, Quito, Ecuador, March 2009	1·90	1·90
4760	**3835**	£1·85 Dave Murray, Bruce Dickinson and Janick Gers, Rio de Janeiro, January 2001	3·00	3·00
		a. Horiz strip of 4. Nos. 4760/4763	12·00	12·00
4761	**3836**	£1·85 Adrian Smith and Steve Harris, Helsinki, May 2018	3·00	3·00
4762	**3837**	£1·85 Iron Maiden, Twickenham Stadium, London, July 2008	3·00	3·00
4763	**3838**	£1·85 Bruce Dickinson sword fighting with Mascot Eddie, Birmingham, August 2018	3·00	3·00
Set of 8			19·50	19·50
Set of 2 Gutter Strips of 8			39·00	
First Day Cover (Tallents House)				21·00
Presentation Pack (Nos. 4756/4763 and **MS**4764) (PO. Pack No. 626)			32·00	
PHQ Cards (set of 13)			9·00	30·00
MS4764 191×74 mm. **3839** (1st) The Trooper Eddie; (1st) Aces High Eddie; £1·85 Iron Maiden Eddie, 1980; £1·85 Senjutsu Eddie			9·50	9·50
First Day Cover (Tallents House)				11·00

Nos. 4756/4759 and 4760/4763 were each printed together, *se-tenant*, as horizontal strips of four in sheets of 48 (2 panes 4×6).

An Iron Maiden Eddie fan sheet containing (1st) The Trooper Eddie; £1·85 Iron Maiden Eddie, 1980; and £1·85 Senjutsu Eddie was originally sold for £7.50. Iron Maiden 'Eddie' and an Iron Maiden 'Live Performances' Collector sheets each containing Nos. 4756/4763 were sold for £12.40 each.

The 13 PHQ cards show the 12 individual stamps, including those from No. **MS**4622, and the complete miniature sheet.

3840 Professor X

3841 Kitty Pryde

3842 Angel

3843 Colossus

3844 Jubilee

3845 Cyclops

3846 Wolverine

3847 Jean Grey

3848 Iceman

3849 Storm

3850 Beast   **3851** Rogue

3852 Enemies of the X-Men

2023 (16 Feb). X-Men (1st issue). Multicoloured. One band at right (2nd) or two bands (others).

(a) Ordinary gum. Perf 14½.

4765	**3840**	(2nd) Professor X	1·25	1·25
		a. Horiz strip of 6. Nos. 4765/4770	7·50	7·50
4766	**3841**	(2nd) Kitty Pryde	1·25	1·25
4767	**3842**	(2nd) Angel	1·25	1·25
4768	**3843**	(2nd) Colossus	1·25	1·25
4769	**3844**	(2nd) Jubilee	1·25	1·25
4770	**3845**	(2nd) Cyclops	1·25	1·25
4771	**3846**	(1st) Wolverine	1·90	1·90
		a. Horiz strip of 6. Nos. 4771/4776	11·00	11·00
4772	**3847**	(1st) Jean Grey	1·90	1·90
4773	**3848**	(1st) Iceman	1·90	1·90
4774	**3849**	(1st) Storm	1·90	1·90
4775	**3850**	(1st) Beast	1·90	1·90
4776	**3851**	(1st) Rogue	1·90	1·90
Set of 12			18·00	18·00
Set of 2 Gutter Strips of 12			36·00	
First Day Cover (Tallents House)				20·00
Presentation Pack (Nos. 4765/4776 and **MS**4777) (PO Pack No. 627)			30·00	
PHQ Cards (set of 18)			10·00	32·00

(b) Self-adhesive.

MS4777 192×74 mm. **3852** (1st) Juggernaut (p 14½); (1st) Mystique (27×37 mm) (p 14); (1st) Emma Frost (27×37 mm) (p 14); (1st) Sabretooth (p 14½); £1·85 Magneto (p 14½)	12·50	12·50
First Day Cover (Tallents House)		14·00

Nos. 4765/4770 and 4771/4776 were each printed together, *se-tenant*, as horizontal strips of six in sheets of 60 (2 panes 6×5).

Nos. 4765/4776 also come from the £19·95 X-Men premium booklet, No. DY46.

The 18 PHQ cards show the 17 individual stamps, including those from No. **MS**4777, and the complete miniature sheet.

3853 Juggernaut

3854 Mystique

3855 Emma Frost   **3856** Sabretooth

3857 Magneto

2023 (16 Feb). X-Men (2nd issue). Multicoloured. Self-adhesive. Two phosphor bands. Perf 14½ (Nos. 4778, 4781/4782) or 14 (Nos. 4779/4780).

4778	**3853**	(1st) Juggernaut	1·90	1·90
4779	**3854**	(1st) Mystique	1·90	1·90
4780	**3855**	(1st) Emma Frost	1·90	1·90
4781	**3856**	(1st) Sabretooth	1·90	1·90
4782	**3857**	£1·85 Magneto	1·90	1·90
Set of 5			11·00	11·00

Nos. 4778/4782 come from **MS**4777 and the £19·95 X-Men premium booklet, No. DY46.

A Jean Grey fan sheet containing No. 4772x4 and a Wolverine fan sheet containing No. 4771x4 was sold for £7.00 each. A Collector sheet containing Nos. 4767/4776 plus 12 labels was sold for £10.99.

A 2nd Class stamp pack containing Nos. 4765/4770 each x2 were sold for £8.46. A 1st Class stamp pack containing Nos. 4771/4776 each x2 were sold for £11.70.

3858 No. 60103, Pickering Station, North Yorkshire Moors Railway, 2016

3859 The 'Christmas Dalesman' Steam Special, Yorkshire Dales National Park, 2019

3860 The 'Cathedrals Express' crossing Ribblehead Viaduct, Yorkshire Dales National Park, 2019

3861 Steaming through Blyth, Northumberland, 2016

3862 In Blizzard, Heap Bridge, East Lancashire Railway, 2016

3863 The 'Cathedrals Express' crossing Royal Border Bridge, Berwick-upon-Tweed, 2016

3864 At Victoria Station, London, 2002

3865 Shildon, County Durham, 2019

3866 *Flying Scotsman* Posters and Advertisement

2023 (9 Mar). Centenary of the *Flying Scotsman* (steam locomotive) (1st issue). Multicoloured. Two phosphor bands. Perf 14.

4783	**3858**	(1st) No. 60103, Pickering Station, North Yorkshire Moors Railway, 2016	1·90	1·90
		a. Horiz pair. Nos. 4783/4784	3·75	3·75
4784	**3859**	(1st) The 'Christmas Dalesman' steam special, Yorkshire Dales National Park, 2019	1·90	1·90

4785	3860	(1st) The 'Cathedrals Express' crossing Ribblehead Viaduct, Yorkshire Dales National Park, 2017	1·90	1·90
		a. Horiz. pair. Nos. 4785/4786	3·75	3·75
4786	3861	(1st) Steaming through Blyth, Northumberland, 2016	1·90	1·90
4787	3862	£1·85 In blizzard, Heap Bridge, East Lancashire Railway, 2016	3·00	3·00
		a. Horiz pair. Nos. 4787/4788	6·00	6·00
4788	3863	£1·85 The 'Cathedrals Express' crossing the Royal Border Bridge, Berwick-upon-Tweed, 2016	3·00	3·00
4789	3864	£1·85 At Victoria Station, London, 2002	3·00	3·00
		a. Horiz. pair. Nos. 4789/4790	6·00	6·00
4790	3865	£1·85 At Shildon, County Durham, 2019	3·00	3·00
Set of 8			18·50	18·50
Set of 4 Gutter Pairs			37·00	
First Day Cover (Tallents House)				20·00
Presentation Pack (Nos. 4783/4790 and **MS**4791) (PO Pack No. 628)			20·00	
PHQ Cards (set of 13)			8·75	19·00
MS4791 146×74 mm. **3866** (1st) 'Scotland by the Night Scotsman' poster (Robert Bartlett), 1932; (1st) 'LNER train service to and from Scotland' advertisement (H. L. Oakley), 1923; £1·85 'Refuelling the Flying Scotsman' poster (Frank Newbould), 1932; £1·85 'Mons Meg' poster (Frank Newbould), 1935			11·50	11·50
First Day Cover (Tallents House)				13·50

Nos. 4783/4784, 4785/4786, 4787/4788 and 4789/4790 were each printed together, se-tenant, as horizontal pairs in sheets of 60 (2 panes 6×5).

Nos. 4783/4790 also come from the Flying Scotsman £21·05 premium booklet, No. DY48.

3867 'Scotland by the Night Scotsman' Poster (Robert Bartlett), 1932

3868 'LNER Train Service to and from Scotland' Advertisement (H. L. Oakley), 1923

3869 'Refuelling the Flying Scotsman" Poster (Frank Newbould), 1932

3870 'Mons Meg' Poster (Frank Newbould), 1935

2023 (9 Mar). Centenary of the Flying Scotsman (steam locomotive) (2nd issue). Multicoloured. Two phosphor bands. Perf 14½×14.

4792	3867	(1st) 'Scotland by the Night Scotsman' poster (Robert Bartlett), 1932	1·90	1·90
4793	3868	(1st) 'LNER train service to and from Scotland' advertisement (H. L. Oakley), 1923	1·90	1·90
4794	3869	£1·85 'Refuelling the Flying Scotsman' Poster (Frank Newbould), 1932	3·25	3·25
4795	3870	£1·85 'Mons Meg' Poster (Frank Newbould), 1935	3·25	3·25
Set of 4			9·50	9·50

Nos. 4292/4295 came from No. **MS**4791 and the £21·05 Flying Scotsman premium booklet, No. DY47.

Stanley Gibbons Auctions

Lot 250 - Sold for £10,200

Lot 171 - Sold for £3600

our trusted auction house with integrity, offering a tailored approach when selling your collection. Talk to our team about selling your collection today.

Decimal Machin Definitives

These are now combined into a single section to facilitate identification. The section is divided up as follows:

1. Denominated stamps, PVA, PVAD or gum arabic, 'standard' perforations

2. NVI (No Value Indicated) stamps, PVA gum, 'standard' perforations

3. NVI stamps, PVA gum, elliptical perforations

4. Denominated stamps, PVA gum, elliptical perforations

5. NVI stamps, self-adhesive gum, elliptical perforations

6. Millennium Machins

7. NVI and denominated stamps, self-adhesive gum, elliptical perforations

8. Overseas booklet stamps

9. Pricing in Proportion

10. Security Machins

DENOMINATED STAMPS, PVA, PVAD OR GUM ARABIC, 'STANDARD' PERFORATIONS

356a    **357** (Value redrawn)

1970 (17 June)–**72**. Decimal Currency. 10p. and some printings of the 50p. were issued on phosphor paper. Perf 12.

829	**356a**	10p. cerise	50	50
830		20p. olive-green	60	20
831		50p. deep ultramarine	1·25	25
831b	**357**	£1 bluish black (6.12.72)	2·25	40
Set of 4			3·25	1·20
First Day Cover (Nos. 829/831)				2·00
First Day Cover (No. 831b)				2·50
Presentation Pack No. 18 (Nos. 829/831)			8·00	
Presentation Pack No. 38 (Nos. 790 (or 831b), 830/831)			12·50	

PRINTING PROCESSES

There is a basic distinction between stamps printed by photogravure, later gravure, and those printed by lithography. Sorting the two is not as difficult as it sounds and with a little experience it should become easy to tell which method of production was employed for a particular stamp.

The tiny dots of the printing screen give uneven edges to the values on gravure stamps (right). Litho values have clean, clear outlines (left).

All you need is a reasonably good glass giving a magnification of ×4 or more (×10 is even better!).

The image on a gravure stamp is created from a pattern or 'screen' of minute dots which are not evident when looking at the stamp without a glass but show up quite clearly under magnification, especially in the Queen's face and around the margin of the stamp design where it meets the white background of the paper. Now look at the value; here also what looks to the naked eye like a straight line is in fact made up of rows of tiny little dots.

'Screens' of dots are also used in the production of litho printed stamps but they are only required where the printer is attempting to produce shades and tints as is necessary in the Queen's head portion of the stamp. Where solid colour is used, as in the background of the majority of values, there is no need to resort to a screen of dots and the background is printed as a solid mass of colour. If you look at the margins or the values of stamps produced in this way you will not see any evidence of dots, just a clear clean break between the inked portion of the stamp and the uninked white of the paper.

367    **367a**

Two types of the 3p., 10p. and 26p. (Nos. X930/X930c, X885/X886b and X971/X971b)

1971 (15 Feb)–**96**. Decimal Currency. T **367**.
(a) Photo Harrison (except for some printings of Nos. X879 and X913 in sheets produced by Enschedé and issued on 12 December 1979 (8p.) and 19 November 1991 (18p.)). With phosphor bands.

X841	½p. turquoise-blue (2 bands)	20	20
X842	½p. turquoise-blue (1 side band) (24.5.72)	45·00	25·00
X843	½p. turquoise-blue (1 centre band) (14.12.77)	20	20
X844	1p. crimson (2 bands)	20	20
X845	1p. crimson (1 centre band) (14.12.77)	20	20
X846	1p. crimson ('all-over') (10.10.79)	20	20
X847	1p. crimson (1 side band) (20.10.86)	60	60
X848	1½p. black (2 bands)	20	20
X849	2p. myrtle-green (2 bands)	20	20
X850	2p. myrtle-green ('all-over' phosphor) (10.10.79)	30	30
X851	2½p. magenta (1 centre band)	20	20
X852	2½p. magenta (1 band)	70	70
X853	2½p. magenta (2 bands) (21.5.75)	20	20
X854	2½p. rose-red (2 bands) (26.8.81)	30	30
X855	3p. ultramarine (2 bands)	20	20
X856	3p. ultramarine (1 centre band) (10.9.73)	20	20
X857	3p. bright magenta (Type I) (2 bands) (1.2.82)	35	35
X858	3½p. olive-grey (2 bands) (shades)	50	50
X859	3½p. olive-grey (1 centre band) (24.6.74)	30	30
X860	3½p. purple-brown (1 centre band) (5.4.83)	1·50	1·75
X861	4p. ochre-brown (2 bands)	20	20
X862	4p. greenish blue (2 bands) (26.8.81)	2·25	2·25
X863	4p. greenish blue (1 centre band) (3.9.84)	1·25	1·25
X864	Band at left	3·75	4·00
X865	4½p. grey-blue (2 bands) (24.10.73)	20	20
X866	5p. pale violet (2 bands)	20	20
X867	5p. claret (1 centre band) (20.10.86)	1·00	1·00
X868	5½p. violet (2 bands) (24.10.73)	30	30
X869	5½p. violet (1 centre band) (17.3.75)	25	25
X870	6p. light emerald (2 bands)	25	25
X871	6½p. greenish blue (2 bands) (4.9.74)	30	30
X872	6½p. greenish blue (1 centre band) (24.9.75)	30	30
X873	6½p. greenish blue (1 side band) (26.1.77)	60	60
X874	7p. purple-brown (2 bands) (15.1.75)	35	35
X875	7p. purple-brown (1 centre band) (13.6.77)	30	30
X876	7p. purple-brown (1 side band) (13.6.77)	40	40
X877	7½p. pale chestnut (2 bands)	25	25
X878	8p. rosine (2 bands) (24.10.73)	25	25

X879	8p. rosine (1 centre band) (20.8.79)	25	25
X880	8p. rosine (1 side band) (28.8.79)	40	50
X881	8½p. light yellowish green (2 bands)		
	(shades) (24.9.75)	30	30
X882	9p. yellow-orange and black (2 bands)	40	40
X883	9p. deep violet (2 bands) (25.2.76)	30	30
X884	9½p. purple (2 bands) (25.2.76)	30	30
X885	10p. orange-brown and chestnut (2 bands)		
	(11.8.71)	30	30
X886	10p. orange-brown (Type I) (2 bands)		
	(25.2.76)	30	30
	b. Type II (4.9.84)	12·50	12·50
X887	10p. orange-brown (Type I) ('all-over')		
	(3.10.79)	30	30
X888	10p. orange-brown (Type I) (1 centre band)		
	(4.2.80)	30	30
X889	10p. orange-brown (Type I) (1 side band)		
	(4.2.80)	30	30
X890	10½p. yellow (2 bands) (25.2.76)	35	35
X891	10½p. deep dull blue (2 bands) (26.4.78)	35	35
X892	11p. brown-red (2 bands) (25.2.76)	30	30
X893	11½p. drab (1 centre band) (14.1.81)	30	30
X894	11½p. drab (1 side band) (26.1.81)	40	40
X895	12p. yellowish green (2 bands) (4.2.80)	40	40
X896	12p. bright emerald (1 centre band)		
	(29.10.85)	40	40
X897	12p. bright emerald (1 side band) (14.1.86)	40	40
X898	12½p. light emerald (1 centre band) (27.1.82)	40	40
X899	12½p. light emerald (1 side band) (1.2.82)	40	40
X900	13p. pale chestnut (1 centre band) (28.8.84)	40	40
X901	13p. pale chestnut (1 side band) (3.9.84)	40	40
X902	14p. grey-blue (2 bands) (26.1.81)	1·00	1·00
X903	14p. deep blue (1 centre band) (23.8.88)	45	45
X904	14p. deep blue (1 side band) (5.9.88)	3·00	3·00
X905	15p. bright blue (1 centre band) (26.9.89)	40	40
X906	15p. bright blue (1 side band) (2.10.89)	2·00	2·00
X907	15½p. pale violet (2 bands) (1.2.82)	40	40
X908	16p. olive-drab (5.4.83)	70	70
X909	17p. grey-blue (2 bands) (3.9.84)	50	50
X910	17p. deep blue (1 centre band) (4.9.90)	70	70
X911	17p. deep blue (1 side band) (4.9.90)	1·25	1·25
X912	18p. deep olive-grey (2 bands) (20.10.86)	60	60
X913	18p. bright green (1 centre band) (10.9.91)	50	50
X914	19p. bright orange-red (2 bands) (5.9.88)	1·25	1·25
X915	20p. dull purple (2 bands) (25.2.76)	70	70
X916	20p. brownish black (2 bands) (2.10.89)	2·00	2·50
X917	22p. bright orange-red (2 bands) (4.9.90)	70	70
X917a	25p. rose-red (2 bands) (6.2.96)	7·50	8·50
X918	26p. rosine (Type I) (2 bands) (3.3.87)	6·50	7·50
X919	31p. purple (2 bands) (18.3.86)	8·00	9·00
X920	34p. ochre-brown (2 bands) (8.1.85)	5·50	6·00
X921	50p. ochre-brown (2 bands) (2.2.77)	1·50	1·75
X922	50p. ochre (2 bands) (20.3.90)	2·75	2·75

(b) Photo Harrison. On phosphorised paper. Perf 15×14.

X924	½p. turquoise-blue (10.12.80)	20	20
X925	1p. crimson (12.12.79)	20	20
X926	2p. myrtle-green (face value as Type **367**)		
	(12.12.79)	20	20
X927	2p. deep green (face value as Type **367a**)		
	(26.7.88)	60	60
X928	2p. myrtle-green (face value as Type **367a**)		
	(5.9.88)	7·50	8·00
X929	2½p. rose-red (14.1.81)	20	20
X930	3p. bright magenta (Type I) (22.10.80)	20	20
	c. Type II (10.10.89)	1·75	2·00
X931	3½p. purple-brown (30.3.83)	30	30
X932	4p. greenish blue (30.12.81)	25	25
X933	4p. new blue (26.7.88)	35	35
X934	5p. pale violet (10.10.79)	25	25
X935	5p. dull red-brown (26.7.88)	25	25
X936	6p. yellow-olive (10.9.91)	25	25
X937	7p. brownish red (29.10.85)	1·25	1·25
X938	8½p. yellowish green (24.3.76)	65	65
X939	10p. orange-brown (Type I) (11.79)	35	35
X940	10p. dull orange (Type II) (4.9.90)	35	35
X941	11p. brown-red (27.8.80)	1·00	1·00
X942	11½p. ochre-brown (15.8.79)	40	40
X943	12p. yellowish green (30.1.80)	35	35
X944	13p. olive-grey (15.8.79)	55	55
X945	13½p. purple-brown (30.1.80)	65	65
X946	14p. grey-blue (14.1.81)	40	40
X947	15p. ultramarine (15.8.79)	45	45
X948	15½p. pale violet (14.1.81)	45	45
X949	16p. olive-drab (30.3.83)	50	50
X950	16½p. pale chestnut (27.1.82)	50	50
X951	17p. light emerald (30.1.80)	45	45
X952	17p. grey-blue (30.3.83)	45	45
X953	17½p. pale chestnut (30.1.80)	45	45
X954	18p. deep violet (14.1.81)	45	45
X955	18p. deep olive-grey (28.8.84)	45	45
X956	19p. bright orange-red (23.8.88)	55	60
X957	19½p. olive-grey (27.1.82)	2·00	2·00

X958	20p. dull purple (10.10.79)	1·00	1·00
X959	20p. turquoise-green (23.8.88)	65	65
X960	20p. brownish black (26.9.89)	45	45
X961	20½p. ultramarine (30.3.83)	60	60
X962	22p. blue (22.10.80)	50	50
X963	22p. yellow-green (28.8.84)	55	55
X964	22p. bright orange-red (4.9.90)	55	55
X965	23p. brown-red (23.8.88)	1·50	1·75
X966	23p. bright green (23.8.88)	1·00	1·00
X967	24p. violet (28.8.84)	1·50	1·75
X968	24p. Indian red (26.9.89)	2·00	2·25
X969	24p. chestnut (10.9.91)	65	65
X970	25p. purple (14.1.81)	65	65
X971	26p. rosine (Type I) (27.1.82)	65	65
	b. Type II (4.8.87)	5·25	6·00
X972	26p. drab (4.9.90)	1·50	1·75
X973	27p. chestnut (23.8.88)	70	70
X974	27p. violet (4.9.90)	75	75
X975	28p. deep violet (30.3.83)	75	75
X976	28p. ochre (23.8.88)	75	75
X977	28p. deep bluish grey (10.9.91)	75	75
X978	29p. ochre-brown (27.1.82)	3·00	3·50
X979	29p. deep mauve (26.9.89)	2·50	3·00
X980	30p. deep olive-grey (26.9.89)	1·00	1·00
X981	31p. purple (30.3.83)	80	80
X982	31p. ultramarine (4.9.90)	1·50	2·00
X983	32p. greenish blue (23.8.88)	1·70	2·50
X984	33p. light emerald (4.9.90)	1·00	1·25
X985	34p. ochre-brown (28.8.84)	1·00	1·50
X986	34p. deep bluish grey (26.9.89)	1·00	1·50
X987	34p. deep mauve (10.9.91)	2·00	2·75
X988	35p. sepia (23.8.88)	1·75	2·25
X989	35p. yellow (10.9.91)	2·00	2·75
X990	37p. rosine (26.9.89)	2·00	2·75
X991	39p. bright mauve (10.9.91)	1·00	1·00
X991a	50p. ochre (21.1.92)	13·50	13·50

(c) Photo Harrison. On ordinary paper. Perf 15×14.

X992	50p. ochre-brown (21.5.80)	2·00	2·00
X993	50p. ochre (13.3.90)	3·50	4·00
X994	75p. grey-black (face value as Type **367a**)		
	(26.7.88)	4·50	4·75

(d) Litho J.W. Perf 14.

X996	4p. greenish blue (2 bands) (30.1.80)	20	20
X997	4p. greenish blue (phosphorised paper)		
	(11.81)	30	30
X998	20p. dull purple (2 bands) (21.5.80)	1·50	1·75
X999	20p. dull purple (phosphorised paper)		
	(11.81)	1·50	1·75

(e) Litho Questa. Perf 14 (Nos. X1000, X1003/X1004 and X1023) or
15×14 (others).

X1000	2p. emerald-green (face value as Type		
	367) (phosphorised paper) (21.5.80)	20	20
	a. Perf 15×14 (10.7.84)	25	25
X1001	2p. bright green and deep green (face		
	value as Type **367a**) (phosphorised		
	paper) (23.2.88)	45	45
X1002	4p. greenish blue (phosphorised paper)		
	(13.5.86)	45	45
X1003	5p. light violet (phosphorised paper)		
	(21.5.80)	25	25
X1004	5p. claret (phosphorised paper) (27.1.82)	45	45
	a. Perf 15×14 (21.2.84)	45	45
X1005	13p. pale chestnut (1 centre band) (9.2.88)	45	45
X1006	13p. pale chestnut (1 side band) (9.2.88)	45	45
X1007	14p. deep blue (1 centre band) (11.10.88)	2·25	2·75
X1008	17p. deep blue (1 centre band) (19.3.91)	45	45
X1009	18p. deep olive-grey (phosphorised paper)		
	(9.2.88)	40	45
X1010	18p. deep olive-grey (2 bands) (9.2.88)	5·50	6·50
X1011	18p. bright green (1 centre band) (27.10.92)	45	45
X1012	18p. bright green (1 side band) (27.10.92)	65	65
X1013	19p. bright orange-red (phosphorised		
	paper) (11.10.88)	1·10	1·10
X1014	20p. dull purple (phosphorised paper)		
	(13.5.86)	1·10	1·10
X1015	22p. yellow-green (2 bands) (9.2.88)	5·50	5·50
X1016	22p. bright orange-red (phosphorised		
	paper) (19.3.91)	65	65
X1017	24p. chestnut (phosphorised paper)		
	(27.10.92)	65	65
X1018	24p. chestnut (2 bands) (27.10.92)	1·50	2·25
X1019	33p. light emerald (phosphorised paper)		
	(19.3.91)	1·50	2·25
X1020	33p. light emerald (2 bands) (25.2.92)	1·10	1·10
X1021	34p. bistre-brown (2 bands) (9.2.88)	5·50	6·50
X1022	39p. bright mauve (2 bands) (27.10.92)	2·25	2·75
X1023	75p. black (face value as Type **367**)		
	(ordinary paper) (30.1.80)	2·25	3·00
	a. Perf 15×14 (21.2.84)	2·50	3·25
X1024	75p. brownish grey and black (face value as		
	Type **367a**) (ordinary paper) (23.2.88)	7·50	9·00

(f) Litho Walsall. Perf 14.

X1050	2p. deep green (face value as T **367a**)		
	(phosphorised paper) (9.2.93)	1·10	1·10
X1051	14p. deep blue (1 side band) (25.4.89)	2·75	2·75
X1052	19p. bright orange-red (2 bands) (25.4.89)	75	75
X1053	24p. chestnut (phosphorised paper) (9.2.93)	75	75
X1054	29p. deep mauve (2 bands) (2.10.89)	2·25	2·50
X1055	29p. deep mauve (phosphorised paper)		
	(17.4.93)	3·50	3·50
X1056	31p. ultramarine (phosphorised paper)		
	(17.9.90)	1·25	1·25
X1057	33p. light emerald (phosphorised paper)		
	(16.9.91)	2·00	1·75
X1058	39p. bright mauve (phosphorised paper)		
	(16.9.91)	1·50	1·50

First Day Covers

15.2.71	½p., 1p., 1½p., 2p., 2½p., 3p., 3½p., 4p., 5p., 6p.,	2·50
	7½p., 9p. (Nos. X841, X844, X848/X849, X851, X855,	
	X858, X861, X866, X870, X877, X882) (Covers carry	
	'POSTING DELAYED BY THE POST OFFICE STRIKE	
	1971' cachet)	
11.8.71	10p. (No. X885)	1·00
24.10.73	4½p., 5½p., 8p. (Nos. X865, X868, X878)	1·00
4.9.74	6½p. (No. X871)	1·00
15.1.75	7p. (No. X874)	1·00
24.9.75	8½p. (No. X881)	1·00
25.2.76	9p., 9½p., 10p., 10½p., 11p., 20p. (Nos. X883/X884,	2·50
	X886, X890, X892, X915)	
2.2.77	50p. (No. X921)	1·00
26.4.78	10½p. (No. X891)	1·00
15.8.79	11½p., 13p., 15p. (Nos. X942, X944, X947)	1·00
30.1.80	4p., 12p., 13½p., 17p., 17½p., 75p. (Nos. X996, X943,	2·00
	X945, X951, X953, X1023)	
22.10.80	3p., 22p. (Nos. X930, X962)	1·00
14.1.81	2½p., 11½p., 14p., 15½p., 18p., 25p. (Nos. X929, X893,	1·25
	X946, X948, X954, X970)	
27.1.82	5p., 12½p., 16½p., 19½p., 26p., 29p. (Nos. X1004,	2·00
	X898, X950, X957, X971, X978)	
30.3.83	3½p., 16p., 17p., 20½p., 23p., 28p., 31p.Nos. (X931,	2·75
	X949, X952, X961, X965, X975, X981)	
28.8.84	13p., 18p., 22p., 24p., 34p. (Nos. X900, X955, X963,	2·00
	X967, X985)	
29.10.85	7p., 12p. (X937, X896)	2·00
23.8.88	14p., 19p., 20p., 23p., 27p., 28p., 32p., 35p. (Nos.	3·50
	X903, X956, X959, X966, X973, X976, X983, X988)	
26.9.89	15p., 20p., 24p., 29p., 30p., 34p., 37p. (Nos. X905,	3·00
	X960, X968, X979/X980, X986, X990)	
4.9.90	10p., 17p., 22p., 26p., 27p., 31p., 33p. (Nos. X910,	3·00
	X940, X964, X972, X974, X982, X984)	
10.9.91	6p., 18p., 24p., 28p., 34p., 35p., 39p. (Nos. X936,	3·25
	X913, X969, X977, X987, X989, X991)	

Presentation Packs

15.2.71	No. 26 contains ½p. (No. X841), 1p. (No. X844), 1½p.	9·00
	(No. X848), 2p. (No. X849), 2½p. (No. X851), 3p. (No.	
	X855), 3½p. (No. X858), 4p. (No. X861), 5p. pale	
	violet (No. X866), 6p. (No. X870), 7½p. (No. X877),	
	9p. (No. X882)	
15.4.71	Scandinavia 71. Contents as above	25·00
25.11.71	No. 37 contains ½p. (No. X841), 1p. (No. X844), 1½p.	30·00
	(No. X848), 2p. (No. X849), 2½p. (No. X851), 3p. (No.	
	X855 or No. X856), 3½p. (No. X858 or No. X859), 4p.	
	(No. X861), 4½p. (No. X865), 5p. (No. X866), 5½p. (No.	
	X868 or No. X869), 6p. (No. X870), 7½p. (No. X877),	
	8p (No. X878), 9p. (No. X882). Later issues of this pack	
	Later issues of this pack included the 6½p. (No.	
	X871) or the 6½p. (No. X872) and 7p. (No. X874).	
2.2.77	No. 90 contains ½p. (No. X841), 1p. (No. X844), 1½p.	5·00
	(No. X848), 2p. (No. X849), 2½p. (No. X851), 3p. (No.	
	X856), 5p. (No. X866), 6½p. (No. X872), 7p. (No. X874	
	or No. X875), 7½p. (No. X877), 8p. (No. X878), 8½p.	
	(No. X881), 9p. (No. X883), 9½p. (No. X884), 10p. (No.	
	X886), 10½p. (No. X890), 11p. (No. X892), 20p. (No.	
	X915), 50p. (No. X921)	
28.10.81	No. 129a contains 2½p. (No. X929), 3p. (No. X930),	15·00
	4p. (No. X996), 10½p. (No. X891), 11½p. (No. X893),	
	11½p. (No. X942), 12p. (No. X943), 13p. (No. X944),	
	13½p. (No. X945), 14p. (No. X946), 15p. (No. X947),	
	15½p. (No. X948), 17p. (No. X951), 17½p. (No. X953),	
	18p. (No. X954), 22p. (No. X962), 25p. (No. X970),	
	75p. (No. X1023)	
3.8.83	No. 1 contains ½p. (No. X924), 1p. (No. X925), 2p.	32·00
	(No. X1000), 3p. (No. X930), 3½p. (No. X931), 4p. (No.	
	X997), 5p. (No. X1004), 10p. (No. X888), 12½p. (No.	
	X898), 16p. (No. X949), 16½p. (No. X950), 17p. (No.	
	X952), 20p. (No. X999), 20½p. (No. X961), 23p. (No.	
	X965), 26p. (No. X971), 28p. (No. X975), 31p. (No.	
	X981), 50p. (No. X992), 75p. (No. X1023)	
23.10.84	No. 5 contains ½p. (No. X924), 1p. (No. X925), 2p.	25·00
	(No. X1000a), 3p. (No. X930), 4p. (No. X997), 5p. (No.	
	X1004a), 10p. (No. X939), 13p. (No. X900), 16p. (No.	
	X949), 17p. (No. X952), 18p. (No. X955), 20p. (No.	
	X999), 22p. (No. X963), 24p. (No. X967), 26p. (No.	
	X971), 28p. (No. X975), 31p. (No. X981), 34p. (No.	
	X985), 50p. (No. X992), 75p. (No. X1023a)	
3.3.87	No. 9 contains 1p. (No. X925), 2p. (No. X1000a), 3p.	30·00
	(No. X930), 4p. (No. X997), 5p. (No. X1004a), 7p. (No.	
	X937), 10p. (No. X939), 12p. (No. X896), 13p. (No.	
	X900), 17p. (No. X952), 18p. (No. X955), 20p. (No.	
	X999), 22p. (No. X963), 24p. (No. X967), 26p. (No.	
	X971), 28p. (No. X975), 31p. (No. X981), 34p. (No.	
	X985), 50p. (No. X992), 75p. (No. X1023a)	
23.8.88	No. 15 contains 14p. (No. X903), 19p. (No. X956),	9·00
	20p. (No. X959), 23p. (No. X966), 27p. (No. X973),	
	28p. (No. X976), 32p. (No. X983), 35p. (No. X988)	
26.9.89	No. 19 contains 15p. (No. X905), 20p. (No. X960),	7·00
	24p. (No. X968), 29p. (No. X979), 30p. (No. X980),	
	34p. (No. X986), 37p. (No. X990)	
4.9.90	No. 22 contains 10p. (No. X940), 17p. (No. X910),	7·00
	22p. (No. X964), 26p. (No. X972), 27p. (No. X974),	
	31p. (No. X982), 33p. (No. X984)	
14.5.91	No. 24 contains 1p. (No. X925), 2p. (No. X927), 3p.	30·00
	(No. X930), 4p. (No. X933), 5p. (No. X935), 10p. (No.	
	X940), 17p. (No. X910), 20p. (No. X959), 22p. (No.	
	X964), 26p. (No. X972), 27p. (No. X974), 30p. (No.	
	X980), 31p. (No. X982), 32p. (No. X983), 33p. (No.	
	X984), 37p. (No. X990), 50p. (No. X993), 75p. (No.	
	X994)	
10.9.91	No. 25 contains 6p. (No. X936), 18p. (No. X913), 24p.	7·00
	(No. X969), 28p. (No. X977), 34p. (No. X987), 35p.	
	(No. X989), 39p. (No. X991)	

PHOSPHOR BANDS. See notes above No. 561. Phosphor bands are applied to the stamps, after the design has been printed, by a separate cylinder. On issues with 'all-over' phosphor the 'band' covers the entire stamp. Parts of the stamp covered by phosphor bands, or the entire surface for 'all-over' phosphor versions, appear matt. Nos. X847, X852, X864, X873, X876, X889, X894, X897, X899, X901, X906, X911, X1006 and X1012 exist with the phosphor band at left or right of the stamp.

PHOSPHORISED PAPER. First introduced as an experiment for a limited printing of the 1s.6d. value (No. 743c) in 1969, this paper has the phosphor, to activate the automatic sorting machinery, added to the paper coating before the stamps were printed. Issues on this paper have a completely shiny surface. Although not adopted after this first trial further experiments on the 8½p. in 1976 led to this paper being used for new printings of current values.

508

1977 (2 Feb)–**87**. T **508**. Ordinary paper. Perf 14×15.

1026	**508**	£1 bright yellow-green and blackish		
		olive	3·00	25
1026b		£1·30 pale drab and deep greenish blue		
		(3.8.83)	5·50	6·00
1026c		£1·33 pale mauve and grey-black		
		(28.8.84)	7·50	8·00
1026d		£1·41 pale drab and deep greenish blue		
		(17.9.85)	8·50	8·50
1026e		£1·50 pale mauve and grey-black		
		(2.9.86)	6·00	5·00
1026f		£1·60 pale drab and deep greenish blue		
		(15.9.87)	6·50	7·00
1027		£2 light emerald and purple-brown	9·00	50
1028		£5 salmon and chalky blue	22·00	32·00
Set of 8			60·00	32·00
Set of 8 Gutter Pairs			£125	
Set of 8 Traffic Light Gutter Pairs			£150	
Presentation Pack (PO Pack No. 91 (small size)) (Nos. 1026, 1027/1028)			38·00	
Presentation Pack (PO Pack No. 13 (large size)) (Nos. 1026, 1027/1028)			£170	
Presentation Pack (PO Pack No. 14) (large size) (No. 1026f)			22·00	

First Day Covers

3.2.1977	Nos. 1026, 1027/1028	10·00
3.8.1988	No. 1026b	6·50
28.8.84	No. 1026c	8·50
17.9.85	No. 1026d	9·00
2.9.86	No. 1026e	5·50
15.9.87	No. 1026f	7·50

See also No. U3920.

N.V.I. STAMPS, PVA GUM, STANDARD PERFORATIONS

913   914

1989 (22 Aug)–93. Booklet Stamps.

(a) Photo Harrison. Perf 15×14.

1445	913	(2nd) bright blue (1 centre band)	1·50	1·50
1446		(2nd) bright blue (1 side band) (20.3.90)	2·00	2·50
1447	914	(1st) brownish black (phosphorised paper)	1·60	1·60
1448		(1st) brownish black (2 phosphor bands) (20.3.90)	2·00	2·25

(b) Litho Walsall. Perf 14.

1449	913	(2nd) bright blue (1 centre band)	1·50	1·50
1450	914	(1st) blackish brown (2 phosphor bands)	1·75	1·75

(c) Litho Questa. Perf 15×14.

1451	913	(2nd) bright blue (1 centre band) (19.9.89)	1·75	1·75
1451a		(2nd) bright blue (1 side band) (25.2.92)	1·75	1·75
1452	914	(1st) brownish black (phosphorised paper) (19.9.89)	1·25	1·25

First Day Cover (Nos. 1445, 1447) 3·00

For similar stamps showing changed colours see Nos. 1511/1516, for those with elliptical perforations, Nos. 1664/1671 and for self-adhesive versions, Nos. 2039/2040, 2295, U2941/U2942, U2945, U2948, U3001/U3002 and U3271.

No. 1451a exists with the phosphor band at the left or right of the stamp.

1990 (7 Aug)–92. Booklet stamps. As Types 913/914, but colours changed.

(a) Photo Harrison. Perf 15×14.

1511	913	(2nd) deep blue (1 centre band)	1·25	1·25
1512	914	(1st) bright orange-red (phosphorised paper)	1·75	1·75

(b) Litho Questa. Perf 15×14.

1513	913	(2nd) deep blue (1 centre band)	1·75	1·75
1514	914	(1st) bright orange-red (phosphorised paper)	1·75	1·75
1514a		(1st) bright orange-red (2 bands) (25.2.92)	1·75	1·75

(c) Litho Walsall. Perf 14.

1515	913	(2nd) deep blue (1 centre band)	1·60	1·60
1516	914	(1st) bright orange-red (phosphorised paper)	1·75	1·75
		c. Perf 13	3·50	3·50

First Day Cover (Nos. 1515/1516) 3·00

For similar stamps with elliptical perforations see Nos. 1664/1672.

N.V.I. STAMPS, PVA GUM, ELLIPTICAL PERFORATIONS

1093a

1993 (6 Apr)–2017. As Types 913/914, and 1093a. Perf 14 (No. 1665) or 15×14 (others) (both with one elliptical hole in each vertical side).

(a) Photo/gravure
Harrison No. 1666
Questa Nos. 1664a, 1667a
Walsall/ISP Walsall Nos. 1665, 1668s
Harrison/De La Rue, Questa or Walsall No. 1667
Harrison/De La Rue, Enschedé, Questa or Walsall/ISP Walsall Nos. 1664, 1668, 1669.

1664	913	(2nd) bright blue (1 centre band) (7.9.93)	1·25	1·25
		a. Perf 14 (1.12.98)	1·50	1·50

1665		(2nd) bright blue (1 band at right) (13.10.98)	1·60	1·60
1666	914	(1st) bright orange-red (phosphorised paper)	1·20	1·20
1667		(1st) bright orange-red (2 phosphor bands) (4.4.95)	1·50	1·50
		a. Perf 14 (1.12.98)	1·50	1·50
1668		(1st) gold (2 phosphor bands) (21.4.97)	1·50	1·50
1668s		(1st) brownish black (2 phosphor bands) (5.6.17)	3·00	3·00
1669	1093a	(E) deep blue (2 phosphor bands) (19.1.99)	3·00	3·00

(b) Litho Questa or Walsall (No. 1670), Enschedé, Questa or Walsall (No. 1671) or De La Rue or Walsall (No. 1672).

1670	913	(2nd) bright blue (1 centre band)	1·40	1·40
1671	914	(1st) bright orange-red (2 phosphor bands)	1·50	1·50
1672		(1st) gold (2 phosphor bands) (8.1.08)	1·50	1·50

First Day Covers

21.4.97	(1st) (No. 1668), and 26p. (Y1692)	3·25
19.1.99	(E) (No. 1669)	2·75

Nos. 1664, 1667, 1669 and 1670/1671 also come from sheets.

No. 1665 exists with the phosphor band at left or right of the stamp and was only issued in booklets.

No. 1668 was issued by Harrison in booklets and Walsall in sheets and booklets for the Queen's Golden Wedding on 21 April 1997. The gold colour was later adopted for the (1st) class rate, replacing bright orange-red. As such, it appeared in a number of prestige booklets.

For No. 1668 in presentation pack see Pack No. 38 listed below No. Y1667 etc.

No. 1668s was issued on 5 June 1997 in the £15·14 50th Anniversary of the Machin Definitive Prestige booklet.

No. 1669 was valid for the basic European airmail rate, initially 30p.

No. 1672 was only issued in £7·40 or £7·15 stamp booklets.

For self-adhesive stamps in these colours see Nos. 2039/2040 and 2295/2298.

1390   1390a

1390b

1999 (16 Feb). Profile on Print. Booklet Stamps

(a) Embossed and litho Walsall. Self-adhesive. Die-cut perf 14×15.

2077	1390	(1st) grey (face value) (Queen's head in colourless relief) (phosphor background around head)	2·00	2·00

(b) Eng C. Slania. Recess Enschedé. Perf 14×14½.

2078	1390a	(1st) grey-black (2 phosphor bands)	2·00	2·00

(c) Typo Harrison. Perf 14×15.

2079	1390b	(1st) black (2 phosphor bands)	2·00	2·00
Set of 3			4·00	4·00

Nos. 2077/2079 were only issued in the £7·54 Profile on Print booklet (No. DX22).

DENOMINATED STAMPS, PVA GUM, ELLIPTICAL PERFORATIONS

II Normal figures of face value	III Open '4' and open lower curve of '5'

1993 (27 Apr)–**2017**. As Nos. X841, etc, but Perf 15×14 (with one elliptical hole in each vertical side).

Enschedé: 20p. (No. Y1684), 29p., 35p. (No. Y1698), 36p., 38p. (No. Y1706), 41p. (No. Y1712), 43p. (No. Y1716)

Harrison: 20p. (No. Y1686), 25p. (No. Y1689), 26p. (No. Y1692), 35p. (No. Y1699), 41p. (No. Y1713), 43p. (No. Y1717)

Walsall: 10p. (No. Y1676a), 19p. (No. Y1683), 38p. (No. Y1707a), 43p. (No. Y1717a).

Enschedé or Harrison/De La Rue: 4p., 5p., 6p., 25p. (No. Y1690), 31p., 39p. (No. Y1708), £1 (No. Y1743)

Enschedé, Harrison/De La Rue, Questa or ISP Walsall: 1p.

Enschedé, Harrison/De La Rue, Questa or Walsall: 2p.

Enschedé, Harrison/De La Rue or Walsall: 10p. (No. Y1676), 30p., 37p. (No. Y1703), 42p., 50p. (No. Y1726), 63p.

Harrison/De La Rue or Questa: 19p. (No. Y1682), 20p. (No. Y1685), 26p. (No. Y1691)

De La Rue or Walsall: 8p. (No. Y1707), 39p. (No. Y1709), 40p. (No. Y1710), 64p., 65p., 68p.

De La Rue: 7p., 8p., 9p., 12p., 14p., 15p., 16p., 17p., 20p. (No. Y1687), 22p., 33p., 34p., 35p. (No. Y1700), 37p. (Nos. Y1704/Y1705), 41p. (No. Y1714), 43p. (No. Y1718), 44p., 45p., 48p., 49p., 50p. (No. Y1727), 56p., 60p., 62p., 67p., 72p., 78p., 81p., 88p., 90p., 97p., £1 (No. Y1744), £1·46, £1·50, £2, £3, £5

Enschedé or De La Rue: 35p. (No. Y1701), 40p. (No. Y1711), 46p., 47p., 54p.

(a) Photo/gravure.

Y1667	**367**	1p. crimson (2 bands) (8.6.93)	20	20
Y1668		2p. deep green (2 bands) (11.4.95)	20	20
Y1669		4p. new blue (2 bands) (14.12.93)	30	30
Y1670		5p. dull red-brown (Type II) (2 bands) (8.6.93)	30	30
Y1671		6p. yellow-olive (2 bands)	40	40
Y1672		7p. grey (2 bands) (20.4.99)	2·00	2·25
Y1673		7p. bright magenta (2 bands) (1.4.04)	45	45
Y1674		8p. yellow (2 bands) (25.4.00)	45	45
Y1675		9p. yellow-orange (2 bands) (5.4.05)	45	45
Y1676		10p. dull orange (2 bands) (8.6.93)	45	45
		a. Perf 14 (13.10.98)	1·25	1·25
Y1677		12p. greenish blue (2 bands) (1.8.06)	50	60
Y1678		14p. rose-red (2 bands) (1.8.06)	50	60
Y1679		15p. bright magenta (2 bands) (1.4.08)	50	60
Y1680		16p. pale cerise (2 bands) (27.3.07)	50	60
Y1681		17p. brown-olive (2 bands) (31.3.09)	50	60
Y1682		19p. bistre (1 centre band) (26.10.93)	50	60
Y1683		19p. bistre (1 side band) (15.2.00)	60	60
Y1684		20p. turquoise-green (2 bands) (14.12.93)	60	60
Y1685		20p. bright green (1 centre band) (25.6.96)	60	70
Y1686		20p. bright green (1 side band) (23.9.97)	80	1·10
Y1687		20p. bright green (2 bands) (20.4.99)	60	70
Y1688		22p. drab (2 bands) (31.3.09)	70	70
Y1689		25p. rose-red (phosphorised paper) (26.10.93)	70	70
Y1690		25p. rose-red (2 bands) (20.12.94)	70	70
Y1691		26p. red-brown (2 bands) (25.6.96)	70	70
Y1692		26p. gold (2 bands) (21.4.97)	80	80
Y1693		29p. grey (2 bands) (26.10.93)	80	80
Y1694		30p. deep olive-grey (2 bands) (27.7.93)	80	80
Y1695		31p. deep mauve (2 bands) (25.6.96)	90	90
Y1696		33p. grey-green (2 bands) (25.4.00)	90	90
Y1697		34p. yellow-olive (2 bands) (6.5.03)	4·25	4·75
Y1698		35p. yellow (2 bands) (17.8.93)	90	90
Y1699		35p. yellow (phosphorised paper) (1.11.93)	5·25	6·00
Y1700		35p. sepia (2 bands) (1.4.04)	90	90
Y1701		35p. yellow-olive (5.4.05) (1 centre band)	90	90
Y1702		36p. bright ultramarine (2 bands) (26.10.93)	90	1·25
Y1703		37p. bright mauve (2 bands) (25.6.96)	1·00	1·00
Y1704		37p. grey-black (2 bands) (4.7.02)	1·10	1·25
Y1705		37p. brown-olive (1 centre band) (28.3.06)	1·10	1·25

Y1706	38p. rosine (2 bands) (26.10.93)	1·10	1·25
Y1707	38p. ultramarine (2 bands) (20.4.99)	1·10	1·25
	a. Perf 14 (15.2.00)	3·25	4·50
Y1708	39p. bright magenta (2 bands) (25.6.96)	1·00	1·00
Y1709	39p. grey (2 bands) (1.4.04)	1·00	1·00
Y1710	40p. deep azure (2 bands) (25.4.00)	1·00	1·10
Y1711	40p. turquoise-blue (2 bands) (1.4.04)	1·00	1·10
Y1712	41p. grey-brown (2 bands) (26.10.93)	1·00	1·10
Y1713	41p. drab (phosphorised paper) (1.11.93)	6·25	6·25
Y1714	41p. rosine (2 bands) (25.4.00)	1·25	1·25
Y1715	42p. deep olive-grey (2 bands) (4.7.02)	1·00	1·10
Y1716	43p. deep olive-brown (2 bands) (25.6.96)	1·50	2·50
Y1717	43p. sepia (2 bands) (8.7.96)	4·00	5·25
	a. Perf 14 (13.10.98)	1·75	2·50
Y1718	43p. emerald (2 bands) (1.4.04)	1·75	1·75
Y1719	44p. grey-brown (2 bands) (20.4.99)	3·25	4·00
Y1720	44p. deep bright blue (2 bands) (28.3.06)	1·25	1·25
Y1721	45p. bright mauve (2 bands) (25.4.00)	1·25	1·25
Y1722	46p. yellow (2 bands) (5.4.05)	3·00	3·25
Y1723	47p. turquoise-green (2 bands) (4.7.02)	1·25	1·25
Y1724	48p. bright mauve (2 bands) (27.3.07)	1·50	2·25
Y1725	49p. red-brown (2 bands) (28.3.06)	3·25	4·00
Y1726	50p. ochre (2 bands) (14.12.93)	1·50	1·50
Y1727	50p. grey (2 bands) (27.3.07)	1·60	1·60
Y1728	54p. red-brown (Type II) (2 bands) (27.3.07)	1·50	1·50
Y1729	56p. yellow-olive (2 bands) (1.4.08)	1·60	1·60
Y1730	60p. light emerald (2 bands) (30.3.10)	3·25	4·00
Y1731	62p. rosine (2 bands) (31.3.09)	3·25	4·00
Y1732	63p. light emerald (2 bands) (25.6.96)	1·60	1·60
Y1733	64p. turquoise-green (2 bands) (20.4.99)	1·60	1·60
Y1734	65p. greenish blue (2 bands) (25.4.00)	1·60	1·60
Y1735	67p. bright mauve (2 bands) (30.3.10)	1·75	1·75
Y1736	68p. grey-brown (2 bands) (4.7.02)	1·75	1·75
Y1737	72p. rosine (2 bands) (28.3.06)	3·50	4·00
Y1738	78p. emerald (2 bands) (27.3.07)	1·90	1·90
Y1739	81p. turquoise-green (2 bands) (1.4.08)	1·90	1·90
Y1740	88p. bright magenta (2 bands) (30.3.10)	1·90	1·90
Y1741	90p. ultramarine (2 bands) (31.3.09)	2·00	2·00
Y1742	97p. violet (2 bands) (30.3.10)	2·00	2·00
Y1743	£1 bluish violet (2 bands) (22.8.95)	2·50	2·50
Y1744	£1 magenta (2 bands) (5.6.07)	2·50	2·50
Y1745	£1·46 greenish blue (2 bands) (30.3.10)	3·00	4·25
Y1746	£1·50 brown-red (2 bands) (1.7.03)	2·50	2·50
Y1747	£2 deep blue-green (2 bands) (1.7.03)	3·00	3·00
Y1748	£3 deep mauve (2 bands) (1.7.03)	4·50	4·50
Y1749	£5 azure (2 bands) (1.7.03)	7·50	7·50

(b) Litho Cartor (1p. (No. Y1761)), 5p. (Nos. Y1763/Y1765), 10p. (No. Y1768), 16p., 17p., 20p., (No. Y1773), 22p., 50p., 54p., 60p. (No. Y1785), 62p., 67p., 90p., 97p.)
De La Rue (5p. (No. Y1762))
Questa, De La Rue or Cartor (10p. (No. Y1767))
Questa or Walsall (25p., 35p.,)
Walsall (37p., 41p. (No. Y1780) 60p. (No. Y1784), 63p.),
De La Rue (48p.)
Questa (others).

Y1760	**367**	1p. lake (2 bands) (8.7.96)	30	30
Y1761		1p. reddish purple (2 bands) (17.9.09)	2·25	3·00
Y1762		5p. chocolate (2 bands) (Type II) (12.2.09)	3·00	2·50
Y1764		5p. lake-brown (22.3.11)	2·50	3·50
Y1765		5p. red-brown (2 bands) (Type III) (7.1.10)	4·00	5·00
Y1766		6p. yellow-olive (2 bands) (26.7.94)	6·00	7·25
Y1767		10p. dull orange (*shades*) (2 bands) (25.4.95)	2·50	2·50
Y1768		10p. pale brownish orange (7.1.10)	2·50	2·50
Y1769		16p. pale cerise (2 bands) (13.1.09)	2·25	2·25
Y1770		17p. bistre (2 bands) (18.8.09)	2·25	2·25
Y1771		19p. bistre (1 band at left) (26.7.94)	80	80
Y1772		20p. bright yellow-green (1 centre band) (8.7.96)	2·50	2·50
Y1773		20p. light green (2 bands) (7.1.10)	2·50	2·50
Y1774		22p. olive-brown (2 bands) (18.8.09)	3·25	4·00
Y1775		25p. red (2 bands) (1.11.93)	75	75
Y1776		26p. chestnut (2 bands) (8.7.96)	65	75
Y1777		30p. olive-grey (2 bands) (25.4.95)	2·25	3·00
Y1778		35p. yellow (2 bands) (1.11.93)	75	90
Y1779		37p. bright mauve (2 bands) (8.7.96)	2·50	2·50
Y1780		41p. drab (2 bands) (1.11.93)	1·10	1·10
Y1781		48p. bright mauve (2 bands) (12.2.09)	2·50	3·50
Y1782		50p. grey (2 bands) (13.1.09)	3·25	4·00
Y1783		54p. chestnut (2 bands) (Type III) (7.1.10)	3·25	4·00
Y1784		60p. dull blue-grey (2 bands) (9.8.94)	1·25	1·25

Y1785	60p. emerald (2 bands) (13.5.10)	5·50	6·50
Y1786	62p. rosine (2 bands) (18.8.09)	3·50	4·25
Y1787	63p. light emerald (2 bands) (8.7.96)	3·25	4·25
Y1788	67p. bright mauve (2 bands) (22.3.11)	8·50	12·00
Y1789	90p. bright blue (2 bands) (17.9.09)	4·00	5·75
Y1790	97p. bluish violet (2 bands) (22.3.11)	8·50	12·00

(c) Eng C. Slania. Recess Enschedé (until March 2000) or De La Rue (from 11 April 2000).

Y1800	**367**	£1·50 red (9.3.99)	3·25	3·25
Y1801		£2 dull blue (9.3.99)	3·75	3·75
Y1802		£3 dull violet (9.3.99)	5·00	5·00
Y1803		£5 brown (9.3.99)	7·50	7·50
PHQ Card (D7) (No. Y1725)			50	8·00

PHQ Cards (D30) (Nos. 1664, 1668, Y1667/Y1668, Y1670, Y1675/Y1676, Y1679/Y1680, Y1687, Y1724, Y1727, Y1729, Y1739, Y1744, Y1746/Y1749, 2357a, 2652/2653, 2358/2359)   7·00

Presentation Packs

26.10.93	No. 30. contains 19p., 25p., 29p., 36p., 38p., 41p. (Nos. Y1682, Y1689, Y1693, Y1702, Y1706, Y1712)	6·00
21.11.95	No. 34. contains 1p., 2p., 4p., 5p., 6p., 10p., 19p., 20p., 25p., 29p., 30p., 35p., 36p., 38p., 41p., 50p., 60p., £1 (Nos. Y1667/Y1671, Y1676, Y1682, Y1684, Y1690, Y1693/Y1694, Y1698, Y1702, Y1706, Y1712, Y1726, Y1743, Y1784)	35·00
25.6.96	No. 35. contains 20p., 26p., 31p., 37p., 39p., 43p., 63p. (Nos. Y1685, Y1691, Y1695, Y1703, Y1708, Y1716, Y1732)	8·00
21.4.97	No. 38. contains 1st, 26p. gold (Nos. 1668, Y1692)	6·00
20.10.98	No. 41. contains 2nd, 1st, 1p., 2p., 4p., 5p., 6p., 10p., 20p., 26p., 30p., 31p., 37p., 39p., 43p., 50p., 63p., £1 (Nos. 1664, 1667, Y1667/Y1671, 1676, Y1685, Y1691, Y1694/Y1695, Y1703, Y1708, Y1717, Y1726, Y1732)	18·00
9.3.99	No. 43 or 43a. contains £1·50, £2, £3, £5 (Nos. Y1800/Y1803)	38·00
20.4.99	No. 44. contains 7p., 19p., 38p., 44p., 64p. (Nos. Y1672, Y1682, Y1707, Y1719, Y1733)	9·50
25.4.00	No. 49. contains 8p., 33p., 40p., 41p., 45p., 65p. (Nos. Y1674, Y1696, Y1710, Y1714, Y1721, Y1734)	8·50
12.3.02	No. 57. contains 2nd, 1st, E, 1p., 2p., 4p., 5p., 8p., 10p., 20p., 33p., 40p., 41p., 45p., 50p., 65p., £1 (Nos. 1664, 1667, 1669, Y1667/Y1670, Y1674, Y1696, Y1687, Y1696, Y1710, Y1714, Y1721, Y1726, Y1734, Y1743)	16·00
4.7.02	No. 58. contains 37p., 42p., 47p., 68p. (Nos. Y1704, Y1715, Y1723, Y1736)	6·50
1.7.03	No. 62. contains £1·50, £2, £3, £5 (Nos. Y1746/Y1749)	25·00
1.4.04	No. 67. contains 1st gold, 7p., 35p., 39p., 40p., 43p. Worldwide postcard (Nos. 1668, Y1673, Y1700, Y1709, Y1711, Y1718, 2357a)	10·00
6.9.05	No. 71. contains 1p., 2p., 5p., 9p., 10p., 20p., 35p., 40p., 42p., 46p., 47p., 50p., 68p., £1., 2nd, 1st, Worldwide postcard, Europe up to 40 grams, Worldwide up to 40 grams (Nos. Y1667/Y1668, Y1670, Y1675/Y1676, Y1687, Y1701, Y1711, Y1715, Y1722/Y1723, Y1726, Y1736, Y1743, 2039, 2295, 2357a, 2358, 2359)	50·00
28.3.06	No. 72. contains 37p., 44p., 49p., 72p. (Nos. Y1705, Y1720, Y1725, Y1737)	11·00
27.3.07	No. 75. contains 16p., 48p., 50p., 54p., 78p. (Nos. Y1680, Y1724, Y1727, Y1728, Y1738)	10·00
5.6.07	No. 77. contains 2nd, 1st, 1p., 2p., 5p., 10p., 14p., 16p., 20p., 46p., 48p., 50p., 54p., 78p., £1, Worldwide postcard, Europe up to 40 grams, Worldwide up to 40 grams, 2nd Large, 1st Large (Nos. 1664, 1668, Y1667/Y1668, Y1670, Y1676, Y1678/Y1679, Y1687, Y1722, Y1724, Y1727/Y1728, Y1744, 2357a, 2358, 2359, 2652/2653)	45·00
1.4.08	No. 78. contains 15p., 56p., 81p. (Nos. Y1679, Y1729, Y1739)	5·00
31.3.09	No. 84. contains 17p., 22p., 62p., 90p. (Nos. Y1681, Y1688, Y1731, Y1741)	8·50
30.3.10	No. 86. contains 60p. 67p., 88p., 97p., £1.46, Europe up to 20 grams, Worldwide up to 20 grams, 1st Recorded Signed For, 1st Large Recorded Signed For (Nos. Y1730, Y1735, Y1740, Y1742, Y1745, 2357b, 2358a, U3045/U3046)	28·00
8.5.10	No. 88. contains 2nd, 1st, 1p., 2p., 5p., 9p., 10p., 20p., 50p., 60p., 67p., 88p., 97p., £1, £1·46, Worldwide postcard, Europe up to 20 grams Worldwide up to 20 grams, Europe up to 40 grams Worldwide up to 40 grams, 2nd Large, 1st Large, 1st Recorded Signed For, 1st Large Recorded Signed For (Nos. 1664, 1668, Y1667, Y1668, Y1670, Y1675, Y1676, Y1687, Y1727, Y1730, Y1735, Y1740, Y1742, Y1744, Y1745, 2357a/2359, 2652/3265 and U2981/U2982)	50·00

First Day Covers

26.10.93	19p., 25p., 29p., 36p., 38p., 41p. (Nos. Y1682, Y1689, Y1693, Y1702, Y1706, Y1712)	6·00
9.8.94	60p. (No. Y1784)	2·00

22.8.95	£1 (No. Y1743)	3·00
25.6.96	20p., 26p., 31p., 37p., 39p., 43p., 63p. (Nos. Y1685, Y1691, Y1695, Y1703, Y1708, Y1716, Y1732)	8·00
9.3.99	£1·50, £2, £3, £5 (Nos. Y1800/Y1803) (Type G) (Philatelic Bureau or Windsor)	15·00
20.4.99	7p., 38p., 44p., 64p. (Nos. Y1672, Y1707, Y1719, Y1733) (Type G) (Philatelic Bureau or Windsor)	5·00
25.4.00	8p., 33p., 40p., 41p., 45p., 65p. (Nos. Y1674, Y1696, Y1710, Y1714, Y1721, Y1734) (Type G) (Philatelic Bureau or Windsor)	5·00
4.7.02	37p., 42p., 47p., 68p. (Nos. Y1704, Y1715, Y1723, Y1736) (Type K) (Tallents House or Windsor)	5·00
6.5.03	34p., (No. Y1697) (Type K) (Tallents House or Windsor)	4·50
1.7.03	£1·50, £2, £3, £5 (Nos. Y1746/Y1749) (Type K) (Tallents House or Windsor)	25·00
1.4.04	7p., 35p., 39p., 40p., 43p. Worldwide postcard (Nos. Y1673, Y1700, Y1709, Y1711, Y1718, 2357a) (Type K) (Tallents House or Windsor)	9·00
5.4.05	9p., 35p., 46p. (Nos. Y1675, Y1701, Y1722) (Type K) (Tallents House or Windsor)	2·25
28.3.06	37p., 44p., 49p., 72p. (Nos. Y1703, Y1720, Y1725, Y1737 (Type K) (Tallents House or Windsor)	4·25
27.3.07	16p., 48p., 50p., 54p., 78p. (Nos. Y1680, Y1724, Y1727/Y1728, Y1738) (Type K) (Tallents House or Windsor)	6·00
1.4.08	15p., 56p., 81p. (Nos. Y1679, Y1727, Y1739) (Type K) (Tallents House or Windsor)	4·50
31.3.09	17p., 22p., 62p., 90p. (Nos. Y1681, Y1688, Y1731, Y1741) (Type K) (Tallents House or Windsor)	6·00
30.3.10	60p., 67p., 88p., 97p., £1.46, Europe up to 20 grams, Worldwide up to 20 grams (Nos. Y1730, Y1735, Y1740, Y1742, Y1745, 2357b, 2358a (Type K) (Tallents House or Windsor)	20·00

For PO Pack No. 37 see below No. 1977.
For PO Pack No. 74 containing Nos. Y1677/Y1678 see below No. 2657.
For Nos. Y1677/Y1678 on first day cover see under Nos. 2650/2657.
Nos. Y1699 and Y1713 were only issued in coils and Nos. Y1676, Y1683, Y1678, Y1686, Y1707, Y1717 and Y1660/Y1689 only in booklets.
No. Y1771 exists with the phosphor band at the left or right of the stamp, but Nos. Y1683 and T1686 exist with band at right only.
See also No. **MS**2146.
For self-adhesive versions of the 42p. and 68p. see Nos. 2297/2298.

1917

2006 (31 Aug). 70th Anniversary of the Year of Three Kings. Sheet 127×72 mm containing No. Y1748. Multicoloured. Two phosphor bands. Perf 15×14 (with one elliptical hole in each vertical side).

MS2658	**1917**	£3 deep mauve	5·25	5·25
First Day Cover (Tallents House)				5·50

N.V.I. STAMPS, SELF-ADHESIVE, ELLIPTICAL PERFORATIONS

1116

1993 (19 Oct). Self-adhesive Booklet Stamp. Litho Walsall. Two phosphor bands. Die-cut Perf 14×15 (with one elliptical hole on each vertical side).

1789	**1116**	(1st) orange-red	1·50	1·50
First Day Cover (No. 1789)				2·50
Presentation Pack (PO Pack No. 29) (booklet pane of 20)			18·00	
PHQ Card (D6)			40	2·50

For similar 2nd and 1st designs printed in photogravure by Enschedé see Nos. 1976/1977.

1301   **1302**

1997 (18 Mar). Self-adhesive Coil Stamps. Gravure Enschedé. One centre phosphor band (2nd) or two phosphor bands (1st). Perf 14×15 die-cut (with one elliptical hole in each vertical side).

1976	**1301**	(2nd) bright blue	1·40	1·40
1977	**1302**	(1st) bright orange-red	1·40	1·40
Set of 2			2·75	2·75
First Day Cover				3·00
Presentation Pack (PO Pack No. 37)			3·50	

Nos. 1976/1977, which were sold at 20p. and 26p., were in rolls of 100 with the stamps separate on the backing paper.

Machin stamps printed in gold were issued on 21 April 1997 for the Royal Golden Wedding. These are listed as definitives under No. 1668 (1st) and No. Y1692 (26p.).

1998 (6 Apr)–**2006** (16 May). Self-adhesive Stamps. Gravure Enschedé, Questa or Walsall. Designs as Types **913/914**. One centre phosphor band (2nd) or two phosphor bands (1st). Perf 15×14 die-cut (with one elliptical hole in each vertical side).

2039	(2nd) bright blue	1·00	1·00
	b. Perf 14½×14 die-cut (22.6.98)	£225	
2040	(1st) bright orange-red	1·25	1·25
	b. Perf 14½×14 die-cut (22.6.98)	£225	

Nos. 2039/2040 were initially priced at 20p. and 26p. and were available in coils of 200 (Enschedé), sheets of 100 (Enschedé, Questa or Walsall) or self-adhesive booklets (Questa or Walsall).

See also Nos. 2295/2298.

'MILLENNIUM' MACHINS

1437 Queen
Elizabeth II

2000 (6 Jan–23 May). New Millennium. Photo De La Rue, Questa or Walsall (No. 2124); Questa or Walsall (No. 2124d). Two phosphor bands. Perf 15×14 (with one elliptical hole in each vertical side).

2124	**1437**	(1st) olive-brown	1·25	1·25
		d. Perf 14 (23.5.2000)	1·25	1·25
First Day Cover (Philatelic Bureau)				2·00
Presentation Pack (PO Pack No. 48)			2·50	
PHQ Card (D16) (23.5.2000)			40	2·50

No. 2124 comes from sheets or stamp booklets and No. 2124d from booklets only.

See also No. **MS**2147 for this stamp on phosphorised paper.

1459

2000 (22 May). Stamp Show 2000 International Stamp Exhibition, London. Jeffery Matthews Colour Palette. Sheet, 124×70 mm. Phosphorised paper. Perf 15×14 (with one elliptical hole in each vertical side).

MS2146 **1459** 4p. new blue; 5p. dull red-brown; 6p. yellow-olive; 10p. dull orange; 31p. deep mauve; 39p. bright magenta; 64p. turquoise-green; £1 bluish violet ... 15·00 ... 15·00

First Day Cover (Philatelic Bureau)		15·00
Exhibition Card (wallet, sold at £4·99, containing one mint sheet and one cancelled on postcard)	30·00	

The £1 value is printed in Iriodin ink which gives a shiny effect to the solid part of the background behind the Queen's head.

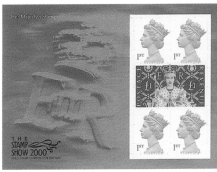

1459a

2000 (23 May). Stamp Show 2000 International Stamp Exhibition, London. Her Majesty's Stamps. Sheet 121×89 mm. Phosphorised paper. Perf 15×14 (with one elliptical hole in each vertical side of stamps as T **1437**).

MS2147 **1459a** (1st) olive-brown (Type **1437**)×4; £1 slate-green (as Type **163**) ... 9·00 ... 9·00

First Day Cover (Philatelic Bureau)		9·25
Presentation Pack (PO Pack No. M03)	40·00	
PHQ Cards (set of 2) (PSM03)	80	15·00

The £1 value is an adaptation of the 1953 Coronation 1s.3d. stamp originally designed by Edmund Dulac. It is shown on one of the PHQ cards with the other depicting the complete miniature sheet.

See also No. 2380 for T **163** from £7·46 stamp booklet.

N.V.I. AND DENOMINATED STAMPS, SELF-ADHESIVE GUM, ELLIPTICAL PERFORATIONS

2002 (5 June–4 July). Self-adhesive. Photo Questa, Walsall, De La Rue or Enschedé (No. 2295) or Walsall (others). Two phosphor bands. Perf 15×14 die-cut (with one elliptical hole in each vertical side).

2295	**914**	(1st) gold	1·50	1·50
2296	**1093a**	(E) deep blue (4.7.02)	2·25	2·25
2297	**367a**	42p. deep olive-grey (4.7.02)	4·50	4·50
2298		68p. grey-brown (4.7.02)	5·00	5·00
Set of 4			12·00	12·00
PHQ Card (D22) (No. 2295) (Walsall) (27.3.03)			40	1·10

Further printings of No. 2295 in sheets of 100 appeared on 4 July 2002 produced by Enschedé and on 18 March 2003 printed by Walsall.

OVERSEAS BOOKLET STAMPS

1655

2003 (27 Mar)–**10**. Overseas Booklet Stamps. Self-adhesive. As T **1655** Two phosphor bands. Perf 15×14 die-cut with one elliptical hole in each vertical side.

2357a		(Worldwide postcard) grey-black, rosine and ultramarine (1.4.04)	2·50	3·00
2357b		(Europe up to 20 grams) deep blue-green, new blue and rosine (30.3.10)	2·50	3·00
2358	**1655**	(Europe up to 40 grams) new blue and rosine	3·50	4·00
2358a		(Worldwide up to 20 grams) deep mauve, new blue and rosine (30.3.10)	3·50	4·00
2359		(Worldwide up to 40 grams) rosine and new blue	4·50	3·00
Set of 5			15·00	17·00
First Day Cover (Tallents House) (Nos. 2358, 2359)				6·00
Presentation Pack (PO Pack No. 60) (Nos. 2358, 2359)			5·50	
PHQ Card (D23) (No. 2358)			40	5·00

Nos. 2358 and 2359 were intended to pay postage on mail up to 40 grams to either Europe (52p.) or to Foreign destinations outside Europe (£1·12).

No. 2357a was intended to pay postcard rate to Foreign destinations (43p.)

Operationally they were only available in separate booklets of four, initially sold at £2·08, £4·48 and £1·72, with the surplus self-adhesive paper around each stamp removed.

Nos. 2357b and 2358a were intended to pay postage on mail up to 20 grams to either Europe (initially 56p., or to foreign destinations outside Europe (90p.).

Single examples of the stamps were available from philatelic outlets as sets of two or in presentation packs.

They were only available in separate booklets of four (Nos. MI3 and MJ3) initially sold at £2·24 and £3·60, increasing to £2·40 and £3·88 from 6 April 2010, with the surplus self-adhesive paper around each stamp removed.

For first day covers and presentation packs for Nos. 2357a/2357b and 2358a and PHQ cards for Nos. 2357a, 2358 and 2359 see below Nos. Y1667/Y1803.

PRICING IN PROPORTION

1915	1916

2006 (1st Aug)–**07**. Pricing in Proportion. Perf 15×14 (with one elliptical hole in each vertical side).

(a) Ordinary gum. Gravure De La Rue, ISP Walsall or Enschedé (No. 2651).

(i) As T **1915**.

2650	(2nd) bright blue (1 centre band)	1·00	1·00
2651	(1st) gold (2 bands)	1·25	1·25

(ii) As T **1916**.

2652	(2nd bright blue (2 bands)	1·50	1·50
2653	(1st Large) gold (2 bands)	1·90	1·90

(b) Self-adhesive. Gravure Walsall or Enschedé (No. 2654) or Walsall

(i) As T **1915**.

2654	(2nd) bright blue (one centre band) (12.9.06)	1·00	1·00
2655	(1st) gold (2 bands) (12.9.06)	1·25	1·25

(ii) As T **1916**.

2656	(2nd Large) bright blue (2 bands) (15.8.06)	1·50	1·50
2657	(1st Large) gold (2 bands) (15.8.06)	1·90	1·90
First Day Cover (Nos. Y1677/Y1678, 2650/2653)			5·75
Presentation Pack (PO Pack No. 74) (Nos. Y1677/Y1678, 2650/2653)			6·00

No. 2654 was issued in booklets of 12 sold at £2·76.

No. 2655 was available in booklets of six or 12, sold at £1·92 or £3·84.

Nos. 2656/2657 were issued in separate booklets of four, sold at £1·48 or £1·76.

Nos. 2650/2653 were also issued in the £7·66 The Machin. The Making of a Masterpiece booklet, No. DX39.

No. 2651 from the £15·14 50th Anniversary of the Machin Definitive Prestige booklets, DY21, issued 5 June 2017.

All these booklets had the surplus self-adhesive paper around each stamp removed.

For PHQ cards for Nos. 2652/2653, see below No. Y1803.

SECURITY MACHINS

2132a	2132b

2132c	2132d

2009 (17 Feb)–**21**. Self-adhesive. Designs as Types **367/913/914** or Types **2132a/2132d**. One centre band (Nos. U2995, U3065, U3095) or two bands (others). U-shaped slits (Nos. U2920/U3059). Die-cut perf 14½×14 (with one elliptical hole in each vertical side).

(a) Self-adhesive. As T **367**. Iridescent overprint. Printed in gravure.

U2920	1p. deep crimson (3.1.13)	40	35
U2921	2p. deep green (3.1.13)	40	35
U2922	5p. dull red-brown (3.1.13)	45	40
U2923	10p. dull orange (3.1.13)	60	50

U2924	20p. bright green (3.1.13)	70	60
U2911	50p. brownish grey	2·00	1·50
U2925	50p. slate (3.1.13)	1·75	1·50
U2926	68p. deep turquoise-green (29.3.11)	2·25	2·00
U2927	76p. bright rose (29.3.11)	2·00	1·75
U2928	78p. bright mauve (27.3.13)	2·00	1·75
U2929	81p. emerald (26.3.14)	3·75	3·50
U2930	87p. yellow-orange (25.4.12)	4·25	4·00
U2931	88p. orange-yellow (27.3.13)	2·25	2·00
U2932	97p. bluish violet (26.3.14)	2·50	2·25
U2912	£1 magenta	3·50	2·75
U2934	£1 bistre-brown (3.1.13)	3·00	2·75
U2935	£1·05 grey-olive (22.3.16)	2·75	2·50
U2936	£1·10 yellow-olive (29.3.11)	3·25	3·00
U2937	£1·17 orange-red (21.3.17)	3·00	2·75
U2938	£1·25 emerald (20.3.18)	2·75	2·50
U2939	£1·28 emerald (25.4.12)	4·00	3·75
U2940	£1·33 orange-yellow (24.3.15)	2·75	2·50
U2940a	£1·35 bright mauve (19.3.19)	3·00	2·75
U2941	£1·40 grey-green (21.3.17)	3·00	2·75
U2942	£1·42 deep rose-red (17.3.20)	3·00	2·75
U2943	£1·45 lavender-grey (20.3.18)	3·25	3·00
U2945	£1·47 lavender-grey (26.3.14)	3·50	3·25
U2913	£1·50 brown-red	3·25	3·00
U2946	£1·52 bright mauve (24.3.15)	3·00	2·75
U2947	£1·55 greenish blue (20.3.18)	3·00	2·75
U2948	£1·57 yellow-olive (21.3.17)	3·25	3·00
U2949	£1·60 orange-yellow (19.3.19)	3·00	2·75
U2949a	£1·63 orange-red (17.3.20)	3·00	2·75
U2950	£1·65 grey-olive (29.3.11)	3·75	3·50
U2951	£1·68 yellow-olive (17.3.20)	3·50	3·25
U2952	£1·70 greenish blue (23.12.20)	3·50	3·25
U2953	£1·88 dull ultramarine (27.3.13)	3·75	3·50
U2954	£1·90 bright mauve (25.4.12)	4·00	3·75
U2955	£2 deep blue-green (4.13)	3·75	3·50
U2956	£2·15 greenish blue (26.3.14)	4·25	4·00
U2957	£2·25 deep violet (24.3.15)	3·75	3·50
U2958	£2·27 bistre (21.3.17)	4·00	3·75
U2959	£2·30 grey-olive (19.3.19)	3·50	3·25
U2960	£2·42 bluish violet (17.3.20)	3·75	3·75
U2961	£2·45 bluish green (24.3.15)	4·00	3·75
U2962	£2·55 deep rose-red (21.3.17)	5·00	4·75
U2963	£2·65 bluish violet (20.3.18)	4·50	4·25
U2964	£2·80 bluish green (19.3.19)	4·25	4·00
U2965	£2·97 bright magenta (17.3.20)	4·50	4·50
U2966	£3 deep mauve (11.9.19)	4·75	4·50
U2968	£3·15 turquoise-blue (24.3.15)	5·00	4·75
U2968a	£3·25 turquoise-green (23.12.20)	4·75	4·50
U2969	£3·30 bright magenta (24.3.15)	5·25	5·00
U2970	£3·45 grey-green (19.3.19)	5·00	4·75
U2971	£3·60 yellow-orange (19.3.19)	5·25	5·00
U2972	£3·66 pale ochre (17.3.20)	5·25	5·25
U2973	£3·82 emerald (17.3.20)	5·50	5·50
U2973a	£4·20 deep violet (23.12.20)	6·25	6·00
U2974	£5 azure (11.9.19)	8·00	7·75

Presentation Packs

17.2.09	No. 82 contains Nos. U2975/U2978 and U2911/U2912	7·50
17.2.09	No, 83 contains Nos. U2913/U2916	23·50
26.10.10	No. 89 contains Nos.U3051/U3052	22·00
29.3.11	No. 90 contains Nos. U2926/U2927, U2936, U2950 and U3055/U3059	15·00
25.4.12	No. 94 contains Nos. U2930, U2939, U2954, U3271 and U3276	10·50
3.1.13	No. 96 contains Nos. U2920/U2955, U2934, U2997 and U3002	7·50
27.3.13	No. 97 contains Nos. U2928, U2931, U2953, U3049 and U3050	14·00
26.3.14	No. 99 contains Nos. U2929, U2932, U2945 and U2956	10·00
24.3.15	No. 101 contains Nos. U2940, U2946, U2957, U2961 and U2968/U2969	22·00
22.3.16	No. 103 contains No, U2935	3·00
21.3.17	No. 106 contains Nos. U2937, U2941, U2948, U2958 and U2962	17·00
20.3.18	No. 108 contains Nos. U2938, U2943, U2947 and U2963	12·50
19.3.19	No. 110 contains Nos. U2940a, U2949, U2959, U2964, U2970 and U2971	21·00
17.3.20	No. 112 contains Nos. U2942, U2949a, U2951, U2960, U2965, U2972 and U2973	25·00
23.12.20	No. 114 contains Nos. U2952, U2968a and U2973a	16·09

First Day Covers

17.2.09	Nos. U2975/U2978 and U2911/U2912	12·00
17.2.09	Nos. U 2913/U2916	20·00
29.3.11	Nos. U2926/U2927, U2936 and U2950	10·50
25.4.12	Nos. U2930, U2939, U2954, U3271 and U3276	14·00

3.1.13	Nos. 2920/U2925, U2934, U2997 and U3002	10·00
27.3.13	Nos. U2928, U2931, UU2953, U3049 and U3050	16·00
26.3.14	Nos. U2929, U2932, U2945 and U2956	14·00
24.3.15	Nos. U2940, U2946, U2957, U2961 and U2968/ U2969	25·00
22.3.16	No. U2935	3·25
21.3.17	Nos. U2937, U2941, U2948, U2958 and U2962	17·00
20.3.18	Nos. U2938, U2943, U2947 and U2963	14·00
19.3.19	Nos. U2942, U2949, U2959, U2964, U2970 and U2971	23·00
17.3.20	Nos. U2942, U2949a, U2951, U2960, U2965, U2972 and U2973	28·00
23.12.20	Nos. U2952, U2963a and U2973a	16·00

(b) Self-adhesive. As Types **913/914**, **1916** or Types **2132a/2132d**. Iridescent overprint. Printed in gravure.

U2995	(2nd) bright blue (1.7.10)	1·60	1·25
U2996	(1st) gold (20.5.10)	3·50	3·50
U3271	(1st) slate-blue	1·75	1·50
U2997	(1st) vermilion (3.1.13)	2·00	1·75
U3744	(1st) bright lilac	1·75	1·75
U2998	(1st) bright scarlet (11.4.17)	1·70	1·40
U3000	(2nd Large) bright blue (26.1.11)	1·90	1·50
U3001	(1st Large) gold (3.11.10)	6·00	6·00
U3276	(1st Large) slate-blue (25.4.12)	2·50	2·25
U3002	(1st Large) vermilion (3.1.13)	2·75	2·50
U3003	(1st Large) bright scarlet (11.4.17)	2·25	1·75
U3045	(Recorded Signed for 1st) bright orange-red and lemon	4·25	3·75
U3049	(Royal Mail Signed for 1st) bright orange-red and lemon (27.3.13)	4·50	4·00
U3046	(Recorded Signed for 1st Large) bright orange-red and lemon	4·75	4·00
U3050	(Royal Mail signed for 1st Large) red and yellow	5·00	4·25
U3051	(Special delivery up to 100g) blue and silver (26.10.10)	11·00	10·50
U3052	(Special delivery up to 500g) blue and silver (26.10.10)	12·00	11·50
Presentation Pack (PO Pack No. 89) (Nos. U3051/U3052)		13·00	11·50

First Day Covers

17.11.09	Nos. U3045/U3046	6·75
26.10.10	Nos. U3051/U3052	22·00

(c) Self-adhesive. Designs as T **367**. No iridescent overprint. Printed in gravure.

U3055	1p. crimson	80	80
U3056	2p. deep green	50	50
U3057	5p. dull red-brown	60	60
U3058	10p. dull orange	70	70
U3059	20p. bright green	1·00	1·00
Set of 5		3·25	3·25
First Day Cover (Nos. U3055/U3059)			3·50

(d) Ordinary gum. Designs as Types **367** and **913/914**. Iridescent overprint. Printed in gravure.

U3065	(2nd) bright blue (13.5.10)	7·00	7·00
U3066	(1st) gold (13.5.10)	7·25	7·25
U3279	1st slate-blue (31.5.12)	3·75	3·75
U3067	(1st) vermilion (5.6.17)	11·00	11·00
U3060	68p turquoise-green (10.1.12)	4·00	4·00
U3061	£1 magenta (5.6.17)	23·00	23·00

(e) Ordinary gum. As Types **367** and **913/914**. Iridescent overprint. Printed in litho.

U3070	1p. crimson (9.5.13)	75	75
U3071	2p. deep green (9.5.13)	85	85
U3072	5p. red-brown (26.3.13)	1·00	1·00
U3074	10p. dull orange (26.3.13)	1·25	1·25
U3075	20p. bright green (26.3.13)	1·50	1·50
U3150	(2nd) bright blue (17.12.15)	1·90	1·90
U3155	(1st) gold (9.9.11)	5·25	5·25
U3156	1st vermilion (9.5.13)	1·75	1·75
U3157	(1st) bright scarlet (15.2.17)	2·10	2·10
U3747	(1st) bright lilac (21.4.16)	3·50	3·50
U3077	50p. slate (18.6.15)	1·75	1·75
U3078	76p. bright rose (9.9.11)	9·50	9·50
U3079	81p. deep turquoise-green (19.2.15)	8·00	8·00
U3080	87p. yellow-orange (26.3.13)	6·00	6·00
U3081	97p. bluish violet (19.2.15)	3·75	3·75
U3082	£1 sepia (15.4.14)	2·25	2·25
U3083	£1·05 grey-olive (28.7.16)	2·75	2·75
U3084	£1·17 bright orange (23.1.18)	3·50	3·50
U3089	£1·25 emerald (4.12.18)	2·75	2·75
U3094	£1·33 orange-yellow (14.5.15)	3·00	3·00
U3096	£1·35 bright purple (11.2.20)	3·00	3·00
U3099	£1·40 grey-green (14.12.17)	3·00	3·00
U3104	£1·45 lavender-grey (14.3.19)	7·00	7·00
U3108	£1·50 brown-red (4.2.22)	8·50	8·50
U3109	£1·55 greenish blue (13.2.19)	8·00	8·00
U3115	£1·63 bright orange (8.5.20)	4·50	4·50
U3116	£1·70 greenish blue (12.8.21)	15·00	15·00

No. U3045 was originally sold for £1·14, U3046 for £1·36, U3047 for £5·05 and U3048 for £5·50.

No. U3049 was originally sold for £1·55 (£1·70 from 2 April 2013) and U3050 was originally sold for £2 (£2 from 2 April 2013)/

Nos. U3271, U3276 and U3279 have an iridescent overprint reading 'DIAMOND JUBILEE' and Nos. U3744 and U3747 have an iridescent overprint 'LONG TO REIGN OVER US'. The others have an iridescent overprint with the words 'ROYAL MAIL' repeated throughout.

Nos. U3070/U3086 all come from premium booklets as follows:

U3067	£15·14 50th Anniversary of the Machin Definitive
U3060	£11·47 Roald Dahl
U3061	£15·14 50th Anniversary of the Machin Definitive
U3070	£11·11 Football Heroes, £14·60 Inventive Britain, £13·96 First World War Centenary (2nd issue), £17·45 Marvel, £16·10 Visions of the Universe, £19·10 Queen (rock band)
U3071	£11·11 Football Heroes, £13·97 Classic Locomotives, £14·60 Inventive Britain, £18·69 RAF Centenary, £17·20 Queen Victoria Bicentenary, £16·10 Visions of the Universe, £16·99 James Bond, £18·35 Star Trek
U3072	£13·77 Dr Who, £11·11 Football Heroes, £11·19 Merchant Navy, £13·97 Classic Locomotives, £13·96 First World War Centenary (3rd issue), £14·47 Battle of Waterloo Bicentenary, £15·37 Beatrix Potter, £13·95 Game of Thrones, £18·69 RAF Centenary, £13·10 Leonardo da Vinci, £16·10 Visions of the Universe, £19·80 75th Anniversary of the End of the Second World War
U3074	£13·77 Dr Who, £11·11 Football Heroes, £11·39 Buckingham Palace, £11·30 First World War Centenary (1st issue), £14·47 Battle of Waterloo Bicentenary, £15·37 Beatrix Potter, £13·10 Leonardo da Vinci, £16·10 Visions of the Universe
U3075	£13·77 Dr Who, £11·39 Buckingham Palace, £11·30 First World War Centenary (1st issue), £13·95 Game of Thrones, £17·45 Marvel
U3150	£16·99 Star Wars, £16·99 James Bond, £18·35 Star Trek
U3155	£9·97 Aerial Post Centenary
U3156	£11·11 Football Heroes, £16·99 Star Wars, £15·11 90th Birthday of Queen Elizabeth, £15·99 Star Wars, £15·65 First World War Centenary (5th issue)
U3157	£14·58 Windsor Castle
U3747	£15·11 90th Birthday of Queen Elizabeth II
U3077	£11·19 Merchant Navy, £14·47 Battle of Waterloo Bicentenary, £17·20 Queen Victoria Bicentenary, £19·80 75th Anniversary of the End of the Second World War, £18·35 Star Trek
U3067	£15·59 50th Anniversary of the Machin Definitive
U3060	£11·47 Roald Dahl's Children's Stories
U3078	£9·97 Aerial Post Centenary
U3079	£14·60 Inventive Britain
U3080	£13·77 Dr Who
U3081	£14·60 Inventive Britain
U3082	£11·39 Buckingham Palace, £11·30 First World War Centenary (1st issue), £14·47 Battle of Waterloo Bicentenary
U3061	£15·59 50th Anniversary of the Machin Definitive
U3083	£15·37 Beatrix Potter
U3084	£13·95 Game of Thrones, £18·69 RAF Centenary
U3089	£15·50 Harry Potter, £17·45 Marvel
U3094	£13·96 First World War Centenary (2nd issue)
U3099	£15·99 Star Wars. The Making of the Droids, Aliens and Creatures
U3104	£17·45 Marvel
U3108	£19·50 Platinum Jubilee
U3109	£13·10 Leonardo da Vinci
U3096	£16·10 Visions of the Universe

For presentation pack containing U3045/U3046 see after Y1803.

Variations in the source and date codes incorporated into the iridescent overprint are outside the scope of this catalogue. Please refer to the Great Britain Concise Catalogue for further information.

EXHIBITION SOUVENIR

2268

2010 (8 May). London 2010 Festival of Stamps. Jeffery Matthews Colour Palette. Sheet 104×95 mm containing stamps as T **367** with a label. Two phosphor bands. Perf 15×14 (with one elliptical hole in each vertical side).

MS3073 **2268** 1p. reddish purple; 2p. deep grey-green;			
	5p. reddish-brown; 9p. bright orange; 10p. orange;		
	20p. light green; 60p. emerald; 67p. bright mauve;		
	88p. bright magenta; 97p. bluish violet; £1·46		
	turquoise-blue	50·00	50·00

In June 1967 Royal Mail introduced a new definitive stamp design. Arnold Machin's bas-relief portrait of HM The Queen has been acknowledged as a classic icon of British design.

2408

2011 (14 Sept). Birth Centenary of Arnold Machin (sculptor). Sheet 124×71 mm containing stamps as No. U3066×10. Two phosphor bands. Perf 14½×14 (with one elliptical hole in each vertical side).

MS3222 **2408** (1st) gold×10		13·00	13·50
First Day Cover (Philatelic Bureau, Edinburgh)			15·00

3041a

2017 (6 Feb). 65th Anniversary of Accession of Queen Elizabeth II. As T **3041a**. Two phosphor bands. Iridescent overprint reading '65TH ANNIVERSARY OF ACCESSION' with year code 'ACCE17ION'. Perf 14×14½.

U3920	£5 ultramarine	10·00	10·00
First Day Cover (Tallents House)			12·00
Presentation Pack (PO Pack No. 105)		11·00	

3085

2017 (5 June). 50th Anniversary of the Machin Definitive. Sheet 202×74 mm containing stamps as T **3085**. Two phosphor bands. Perf 14×14½ (T **1116** and No. U3966) or 14½×14 (others).

MS3965 **3085** No. X866; No. 1470; As No. 1789 (but			
	ordinary gum); No. 2124; No. 2651; As No. U3067		
	(but MMIL source code); As No. U3966 (but		
	gravure phosphor bands)	15·00	15·00
First Day Cover (Tallents House) (No. MS3965)			12·00
Presentation Pack (PO Pack No. 541) (Nos. **MS**3964/			
MS3865)		18·00	

On No. MS3965 only the £1 gold foil stamp is embossed.
The 5p., 20p. and £1 stamps in No. MS3965 do not have an elliptical hole in each vertical side.

3086

2017 (5 June). 50th Anniversary of the Machin Definitive Two narrow phosphor bands. Perf 14×14½.

U3966 **3086**	£1 gold	4·50	5·50

No. U3966 was issued only in No. **MS**3964 and in £15·59 booklet No. DY21.

BARCODED SECURITY MACHINS

3578	**3719**

2021 (23 Mar)–**22**. Barcoded Security Machins. Design as T **3578** or T **3719**. Self-adhesive. One centre band (Nos. V4500 and V4525) or two bands (others). U-shaped slits. Iridescent overprint . Die-cut perf 15×14½ with one elliptical hole in each vertical side).

(i) As T **3578**.

V4500	(2nd) bright blue (MBIL) (23.3.21)	2·00	2·00
V4525	(2nd) emerald (1.2.22)	1·25	1·25
V4526	(1st) deep violet (1.2.22)	1·75	1·75

(ii) As T **3719**.

V4527	(2nd Large) grey-green (1.2.22)	2·60	2·60
V4528	(1st Large) greenish blue (1.2.22)	3·25	3·25

No. V4500 came from business sheets of 50 stamps sold only through Royal Mail Philatelic Bureau, Edinburgh and through a volume retailer of business sheets. Philatelic customers could also purchase from the Philatelic Bureau, Edinburgh, a maximum of five loose single stamps.
Presentation packs were not made available for No. V4500.

3720

2022 (4 Apr). Barcoded Security Machins. Self-adhesive. Two bands. U-shaped slits. Iridescent overprint. Die-cut perf 15×14½.

Design as T **3720**.

V4600	£1·85 grey-brown	2·50	2·50
V4610	£2·55 blue	3·50	3·50
V4620	£3·25 purple	4·50	4·50
V4630	£4·20 bright green	5·75	5·75

3721

2022 (4 Apr). Barcoded Security Machins. Self-adhesive. Two bands. U-shaped slits. Iridescent overprint. Die-cut perf 15×14½.

Design as T **3721**.

V4700	1p. blue	10	10
V4702	2p. deep green	10	10
V4705	5p. dull violet-blue	10	10

V4710	10p. turquoise-green	15	15
V4720	20p. bright green	30	30
V4750	50p. slate	90	90
V4780	£1 grey-brown	1·75	1·75
V4800	£2 new blue	3·00	3·00
V4820	£3 purple	4·50	4·50
V4840	£5 emerald	7·50	7·50

First Day Covers

23.3.21	No. V4500	4·25
1.2.22	No. V4525/V4528	9·00
4.4.22	Nos. V4600, V4610, V4620, V4630	17·00
4.4.22	Nos. V4700, V4702, V4705, V4710, V4720, V4750, V4780	5·50
4.4.22	Nos. V4800, V4820, V4840	16·00

Presentation Packs

1.2.22	Nos. V4525/V4528 (PO Pack No. 116)	11·00
4.4.22	Nos. V4600, V4610, V4620, V4630 (PO Pack No. 117)	17·00
4.4.22	Nos. V4700, V4702, V4705, V4710, V4720, V4750, V4780 (PO Pack No. 118)	5·50
4.4.22	Nos. V4800, V4820, V4840 (PO Pack No. 119)	16·00

ROYAL MAIL POSTAGE LABELS

These imperforate labels were issued as an experiment by the Post Office. Special microprocessor-controlled machines were installed at post offices in Cambridge, London, Shirley (Southampton) and Windsor to provide an after-hours sales service to the public. The machines printed and dispensed the labels according to the coins inserted and the buttons operated by the customer. Values were initially available in ½p. steps to 16p. and in addition, the labels were sold at philatelic counters in two packs containing either three values (3½p., 12½p., 16p.) or 32 values (½p. to 16p.).

From 28 August 1984 the machines were adjusted to provide values up to 17p. After 31 December 1984 labels including ½p. values were withdrawn. The machines were taken out of service on 30 April 1985.

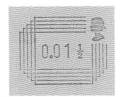

L1 Machine postage-paid impression in red on phosphorised paper with grey-green background design. No watermark. Imperforate.

1984 (1 May–28 Aug).

Set of 32 (½p. to 16p.)		15·00	22·00
Set of 3 (3½p., 12½p., 16p.)		2·50	3·00
Set of 3 on First Day Cover (1.5.84)			6·50
Set of 2 (16½p., 17p.) (28.8.84)		4·00	3·00

ROYAL MAIL POST & GO STAMPS

Following the trials of a number of self-adhesive machines capable of dispensing postage labels, Royal Mail began installing 'Post and Go' machines in larger post offices in October 2008. In addition to postage labels, the machines dispense stamps with a pre-printed background and an inkjet printed indicator of the service required, together with a four-part code.

The first machines were sited at the Galleries post office in Bristol and came into use on 8 October 2008. They dispensed five different stamps, dependent on the service; the code at the foot of the stamp referring to the branch in which the machine is sited, the machine number within the branch, and the session and transaction number.

The five original stamps were later complemented by values for 40g., 60g. and 100g. Unused stocks of earlier designs, such as Birds and Farmyard Animals also began to appear carrying the new service indicators and those seen have now been listed, although the set prices shown are generally for the values available at the time each design was released.

By the end of 2016 Post & Go machines could be found in most large post offices, nationwide.

Collectors should note that the listings are for the different values available from Post & Go machines, not the different designs provided in the special packs available from the Philatelic Bureau, Edinburgh. These packs are listed as separate items below each set.

FT1

2008 (8 Oct)–**15**. T **FT1**. Olive-brown background. Self-adhesive. Two phosphor bands. Gravure Walsall, thermally printed service indicator. Perf 14×14½.

FS1*a*	(1st Class Up to 100g)	3·25	3·25
FS2*a*	(1st Large Up to 100g)	3·50	3·50
FS3*a*	(Europe Up to 20g)	4·00	4·00
FS3*cb*	(Euro 20g World 10g)	5·50	5·50
FS3*dc*	(Europe up to 60g)	9·75	9·75
FS3*ea*	(Europe up to 100g)	9·75	9·75
FS3*f*	(Euro 100g World 20g)	13·00	13·00
FS4*a*	(Worldwide Up to 10g)	6·00	6·00
FS5*a*	(Worldwide Up to 10g)	4·75	4·75
FS5*e*	(Worldwide Up to 40g)	13·00	13·00
FS5*fc*	(Worldwide Up to 60g)	10·50	10·50
FS5*ga*	(Worldwide Up to 100g)	10·50	10·50
FS5*h*	(World 100g Zone 1-3)	14·00	14·00
FS5*i*	(World 100g Zone 2)	14·00	14·00
FS1*a*/FS3*a*, FS4*a*, FS5*a*, FS5*e* *Set of 6*		32·00	32·00
Special Pack (Nos. FS1/FS5) (31.3.09)		£100	

The special pack contains separate stamps. These are reproductions of the first 'Post & Go' stamps printed at the Galleries Post Office, Bristol. They differ from machine printed stamps in having the service indicator and branch code printed in gravure

It is possible to obtain *se-tenant* strips of mixed values from Post & Go machines but we do not list these.

See also Nos. FS77*a*/FS84*b*.

FT2 Blue Tit

2010 (17 Sept)–**14**. Birds of Britain (1st series). Garden Birds. Multicoloured. Self-adhesive. Two phosphor bands. Designs printed in gravure by Walsall, thermally printed service indicator. Perf 14×14½.

FS6	(1st Class up to 100g)	6·50	6·50
FS7	(1st Large up to 100g)	7·00	7·00
FS8	(Europe up to 20g)	8·50	8·50
FS8*a*	(Europe up to 60g) (5.14)	80·00	80·00
FS9	(Worldwide up to 10g)	14·00	14·00
FS10	(Worldwide up to 20g)	10·00	10·00
FS10*a*	(Worldwide up to 40g) (2.12)	40·00	40·00
FS10*b*	(Worldwide up to 60g) (Type II) (5.14)	80·00	80·00
FS6/FS8, FS9, FS10 *Set of 5*		40·00	40·00
First Day Cover (No. FS6 in 6 designs)			20·00
Special Pack (No. FS6 in sheet*let* of 6 gravure designs)		20·00	

Nos. FS6/FS10*b* were each available in six different designs: T **FT2**, Goldfinch, Wood Pigeon, Robin, House Sparrow and Starling.

Nos. FS6/FS10 were available from Post & Go terminals, initially in 30 post offices.

Stamps from the special pack and first day cover sold by the Philatelic Bureau Edinburgh differ from machine printed stamps in having the service indicator and branch code printed in gravure

Nos. FS8*a*, FS10*a* and FS10*b* resulted from the late use of old stock.

FT3 Blackbird

2011 (24 Jan)–**14**. Birds of Britain (2nd series). Garden Birds. Multicoloured. Self-adhesive. Two phosphor bands. Designs printed in gravure by Walsall, thermally printed service indicator. Perf 14×14½.

FS11	(1st class up to 100g)	3·50	3·50
FS12	(1st Large up to 100g)	3·75	3·75
FS13	(Europe up to 20g)	4·25	4·25
FS13*a*	(Europe up to 60g) (4.14)	20·00	20·00
FS14	(Worldwide up to 10g)	8·50	8·50
FS15	(Worldwide up to 20g)	4·25	4·25
FS15*a*	(Worldwide up to 40g) (12.11)	20·00	20·00
FS15*b*	(Worldwide up to 60g) (4.14)	20·00	20·00
FS11/FS15 FS13, FS14, FS15 *Set of 5*		20·00	20·00
First Day Cover (No. FS11 in 6 designs)			20·00
Special Pack (No. FS11 in sheet*let* of 6 gravure designs)		8·00	

Nos. FS11/FS15*b* were each available in six different designs: T **FT3**, two Magpies, Long-tailed Tit, Chaffinch, Collared Dove and Greenfinch.

Stamps from the special pack and first day cover sold by the Philatelic Bureau, Edinburgh differ from machine printed stamps in having the service indicator and branch code printed in gravure.

Nos. FS13*a*, FS15*a*, FS15*b* resulted from the late use of old stock.

FT4 Mallard

2011 (19 May)–**14**. Birds of Britain (3rd series). Water Birds. Multicoloured. Self-adhesive. Two phosphor bands. Designs printed in gravure by Walsall, thermally printed service indicator. Perf 14×14½.

FS16	(1st Class up to 100g)	2·50	2·50
FS17	(1st Large up to 100g)	3·00	3·00
FS18	(Europe up to 20g)	3·50	3·50
FS18*a*	(Europe up to 60g) (4.14)	27·00	27·00
FS19	(Worldwide up to 10g)	5·00	5·00

FS20	(Worldwide up to 20g)	4·00	4·00
FS20a	(Worldwide up to 40g) (12.11)	10·00	10·00
FS20b	(Worldwide up to 60g) (4.14)	27·00	27·00
FS16/FS18, FS19, FS20 Set of 5		15·00	15·00
Special Pack (No. FS16 in sheetlet of 6 gravure designs)		8·00	
First Day Cover (No. FS16 in 6 designs)			8·75

Nos. FS16/FS20b were each available in six different designs: T **FT4**, Greylag Goose, Kingfisher, Moorhen, Mute Swan and Great Crested Grebe.

Stamps from the special pack sold by the Philatelic Bureau, Edinburgh differ from machine printed stamps in having the service indicator and branch code printed in gravure.

Nos. FS18a, FS20a and FS20b resulted from the late use of old stock.

FT5 Puffin

2011 (16 Sept)–**14**. Birds of Britain (4th series). Sea Birds. Multicoloured. Self-adhesive. Two phosphor bands. Designs printed in gravure by Walsall, thermally printed service indicator. Perf 14×14½.

FS21	(1st class up to 100g)	2·25	2·25
FS22	(1st Large up to 100g)	2·75	2·75
FS23	(Europe up to 20g)	3·25	3·25
FS23a	(Europe up to 60g) (31.3.14)	8·00	8·00
FS24	(Worldwide up to 10g)	4·75	4·75
FS25	(Worldwide up to 20g)	3·75	3·75
FS26	(Worldwide up to 40g)	7·50	7·50
FS26a	(Worldwide up to 60g) (31.3.14)	8·50	8·50
FS21/FS23, FS24/FS26 Set of 6		20·00	20·00
First Day Cover (No. FS21 in 6 designs)			7·25
Special Pack (No. FS21 in sheetlet of 6 gravure designs)		9·00	

Nos. FS21/FS26a were each available in six different designs: T **FT5**, Gannet, Oystercatcher, Ringed Plover, Cormorant and Arctic Tern.

Stamps from the special pack and first day cover sold by the Philatelic Bureau, Edinburgh differ from machine printed stamps in having the service indicator and branch code printed in gravure.

Nos. FS23a and FS26a resulted from the late use of old stock.

FT6 Welsh Mountain Badger Face

2012 (24 Feb)–**14**. British Farm Animals (1st series). Sheep. Multicoloured. Self-adhesive. Two phosphor bands. Designs printed in gravure by Walsall, thermally printed service indicator. Perf 14×14½.

FS27	(1st Class up to 100g)	2·75	2·75
FS28	(1st Large up to 100g)	3·25	3·25
FS29	(Europe up to 20g)	3·25	3·25
FS29a	(Euro 20g World 10g) (10.14)	10·00	10·00
FS29b	(Europe up to 60g) (31.3.14)	12·00	12·00
FS30	(Worldwide up to 10g)	5·25	5·25
FS31	(Worldwide up to 20g)	4·00	4·00
FS32	(Worldwide up to 40g)	5·75	5·75
FS32b	(Worldwide up to 60g) (31.3.14)	13·00	13·00
FS27/FS29, FS30/FS32 Set of 6		22·00	22·00
First Day Cover (Philatelic Bureau, Edinburgh) (No. FS27 in 6 designs)			8·75
Special Pack (P&G 6) (No. FS27 in strip of 6 designs)		9·00	

Nos. FS27/FS32b were each available in six different designs: T **FT6**, Dalesbred, Jacob, Suffolk, Soay, Leicester Longwool.

Nos. FS29a, FS29b and FS32b resulted from the late use of old stock.

FT7 Berkshire

2012 (24 Apr)–**14**. British Farm Animals (2nd series). Pigs. Multicoloured. Self-adhesive. Two phosphor bands. Designs printed in gravure by Walsall, thermally printed service indicator. Perf 14×14½.

FS33	(1st class up to 100g)	2·75	2·75
FS34	(1st Large up to 100g)	3·25	3·25
FS35	(Europe up to 20g)	3·25	3·25

FS35a	(Euro 20g World 10g) (10.14)	8·75	8·75
FS35b	(Europe up to 60g) (31.3.14)	13·00	13·00
FS36	(Worldwide up to 10g)	5·25	5·25
FS37	(Worldwide up to 20g)	4·00	4·00
FS38	(Worldwide up to 40g)	5·75	5·75
FS38b	(Worldwide up to 60g) (31.3.14)	13·00	13·00
FS33/FS35, FS36/FS38 Set of 6		22·00	22·00
First Day Cover (Philatelic Bureau, Edinburgh) (No. FS33 in 6 designs)			8·50
Special Pack (P&G 7) (No. FS33 in strip of 6 designs)		8·00	

Nos. FS33/FS38b were each available in six different designs: T **FT7**, Gloucestershire Old Spots, Oxford Sandy and Black, Welsh, Tamworth, British Saddleback.

Nos. FS35a, FS35b and FS38b resulted from the late use of old stock.

FT8 Union Flag

2012 (21 May)–**20**. Union Flag T **FT8**. Multicoloured. Self-adhesive. Two phosphor bands. Designs printed in gravure by Walsall, thermally printed service indicator. Perf 14×14½.

FS39	(1st Class up to 100g)	2·75	2·75
FS40	(1st Large up to 100g)	3·25	3·25
FS41	(Europe up to 20g)	3·50	3·50
FS41a	(Euro 20g World 10g) (7.14)	3·50	3·50
FS41b	(Europe up to 60g) (31.3.14)	9·75	9·75
FS41c	(Europe up to 100g) (30.3.15)	9·50	9·50
FS41d	(Euro 100g World 20g) (9.20)	13·00	13·00
FS42	(Worldwide up to 10g)	5·25	5·25
FS43	(Worldwide up to 20g)	4·50	4·50
FS44	(Worldwide up to 40g)	6·00	6·00
FS44b	(Worldwide up to 60g) (31.3.14)	10·50	10·50
FS44c	(Worldwide up to 100g) (30.3.15)	10·50	10·50
FS44d	(World 100g zone 1-3) (9.20)	27·00	27·00
FS44e	(World 100g zone 2) (9.20)	35·00	35·00
FS39/FS41, FS42/FS44 Set of 6		23·00	23·00
First Day Cover (No. FS39 only)			2·50
Special Pack (P&G 8) (No. FS39 only)		3·00	

FT9 Irish Moiled

2012 (28 Sept)–**14**. British Farm Animals (3rd series). Cattle. Multicoloured. Self-adhesive. Two phosphor bands. Designs printed in gravure by Walsall, thermally printed service indicator. Perf 14×14½.

FS45	(1st Class up to 100g)	4·00	4·00
FS46	(1st Large up to 100g)	4·75	4·75
FS47	(Europe up to 20g)	5·00	5·00
FS47a	(Euro 20g World 10g) (10.14)	10·00	10·00
FS47b	(Europe up to 60g) (31.3.14)	12·00	12·00
FS48	(Worldwide up to 10g)	6·00	6·00
FS49	(Worldwide up to 20g)	5·25	5·25
FS50	(Worldwide up to 40g)	7·00	7·00
FS50b	(Worldwide up to 60g) (31.3.14)	13·00	13·00
FS45/FS47, FS48/FS50 Set of 6		29·00	29·00
First Day Cover (Philatelic Bureau, Edinburgh) (No. FS45 in 6 designs)			8·50
Special Pack (P&G 9) (No. FS45 in strip of 6 designs)		8·00	

Nos. FS45/FS50b were each available in six different designs: T **FT9**, Welsh Black, Highland, White Park, Red Poll, Aberdeen Angus.

Nos. FS47a, FS47b and FS50b resulted from the late use of old stock.

FT10 Robin

2012 (6 Nov)–**15**. Christmas Robin with year code in background. T **FT10**. Self-adhesive. Two phosphor bands. Designs printed in gravure by Walsall, thermally printed service indicator. Perf 14×14½.

FS51	(1st Class up to 100g)	2·75	2·75
FS52	(1st Large up to 100g)	3·25	3·25

FS53	(Europe up to 20g)	3·50	3·50
FS53c	(Euro 20g World 10g) (7.14)	5·00	5·00
FS53d	(Europe up to 60g) (7.14)	9·00	9·00
FS53e	(Europe up to 100g) (4.15)	13·00	13·00
FS54	(Worldwide up to 10g)	4·00	4·00
FS55	(Worldwide up to 20g)	4·50	4·50
FS56	(Worldwide up to 40g)	5·75	5·75
FS56d	(Worldwide up to 60g) (7.14)	9·75	9·75
FS56e	(Worldwide up to 100g)	14·00	14·00
FS51/FS53, FS54/FS56 Set of 6		22·00	22·00

Nos. FS53c, FS53d, FS56d resulted from the late use of old stock.

Nos. FS57 and FS58 are vacant.

FT11 Lesser Silver Water Beetle

2013 (22 Feb)–**19**. Freshwater Life (1st series). Ponds. Multicoloured. Self-adhesive. Two phosphor bands. Designs printed in gravure by Walsall, thermally printed service indicator. Perf 14×14½.

FS59	(1st Class up to 100g)	2·25	2·25
FS60	(1st Large up to 100g)	2·50	2·50
FS61	(Europe up to 20g)	4·00	4·00
FS61a	(Euro 20g World 10g) (10.14)	7·50	7·50
FS61b	(Europe up to 60g) (4.14)	9·00	9·00
FS61c	(Europe up to 100g) (5.19)	30·00	30·00
FS62	(Worldwide up to 10g)	4·00	4·00
FS63	(Worldwide up to 20g)	4·00	4·00
FS64	(Worldwide up to 40g)	5·00	5·00
FS64b	(Worldwide up to 60g) (4.14)	9·50	9·50
FS64c	(Worldwide up to 100g) (5.19)	30·00	30·00
FS59/FS61, FS62/FS64 Set of 6		20·00	20·00
First Day Cover (No. FS59 in 6 designs)			9·50
Special Pack (P&G 11) (No. FS59 in strip of 6 designs)		8·00	

Nos. FS59/FS64c were each available in six different designs: T **FT11**, Three-spined Stickleback, Smooth Newt, Fairy Shrimp, Emperor Dragonfly and Glutinous Snail.

Nos. FS61a, FS61b, FS64b and FS64c resulted from the late use of old stock.

FT12 Perch

2013 (25 June)–**19**. Freshwater Life (2nd series). Lakes. Multicoloured. Self-adhesive. Two phosphor bands. Designs printed in gravure by ISP Walsall, thermally printed service indicator. Perf 14×14½.

FS65	(1st Class up to 100g)	2·75	2·75
FS66	(1st Large up to 100g)	3·25	3·25
FS67	(Europe up to 20g)	4·25	4·25
FS67a	(Euro 20g World 10g) (10.14)	6·50	6·50
FS67b	(Europe up to 60g) (31.3.14)	8·25	8·25
FS67c	(Europe up to 100g) (5.19)	24·00	24·00
FS68	(Worldwide up to 10g)	4·25	4·25
FS69	(Worldwide up to 20g)	4·25	£425
FS70	(Worldwide up to 40g)	5·25	5·25
FS70b	(Worldwide up to 60g) (31.3.14)	8·75	8·75
FS70c	(Worldwide up to 100g) (5.19)	24·00	24·00
FS65/FS67, FS68/FS70 Set of 6		21·00	21·00
First Day Cover (No. FS65 in 6 designs)			9·50
Special Pack (P&G 12) (No. FS65 in strip of 6 designs)		8·00	

Nos. FS65/FS70c were each available in six different designs: T **FT12**, European Eel, Crucian Carp, Caddis Fly Larva, Arctic Char and Common Toad.

Nos. FS67a, FS67b, and FS70b resulted from the late use of old stock.

FT13 Minnow

2013 (20 Sept)–**19**. Freshwater Life (3rd series). Rivers. Multicoloured. Self-adhesive. Two phosphor bands. Designs printed in gravure by ISP Walsall, thermally printed service indicator. Perf 14×14½.

FS71	(1st Class up to 100g)	2·25	2·25
FS72	(1st Large up to 100g)	2·50	2·50
FS73	(Europe up to 20g)	4·00	4·00
FS73a	(Euro 20g World 10g) (10.14)	10·00	10·00
FS73b	(Europe up to 60g) (31.3.14)	7·50	7·50
FS73c	(Europe up to 100g) (5.19)	24·00	24·00
FS74	(Worldwide up to 10g)	4·00	4·00
FS75	(Worldwide up to 20g)	4·00	4·00
FS76	(Worldwide up to 40g)	5·00	5·00
FS76b	(Worldwide up to 60g) (31.3.14)	8·00	8·00
FS76c	(Worldwide up to 100g) (5.19)	24·00	24·00
FS71/FS73, FS74/FS76 Set of 6		20·00	20·00
First Day Cover (No. FS71 in 6 designs)			9·50
Special Pack (P&G 13) (No. FS71 in strip of 6 designs)		9·00	

Nos. FS71/FS76c were each available in six different designs: T **FT13**, Atlantic Salmon, White-clawed Crayfish, River Lamprey, Blue-winged Olive Mayfly Larva, Brown Trout.

Nos. FS73a, FS73b FS76b and FS76c resulted from the late issue of old stock.

NOTE: From No. FS77 onwards all Post & Go stamps incorporated a year code, unless otherwise stated.

2013 (19 Nov)–**21**. T **FT1** with year code in background. Olive-brown background. Self-adhesive. Two phosphor bands. Designs printed in gravure by Walsall, thermally printed service indicator. Perf 14×14½.

FS77	(1st Class up to 100g)	3·50	3·50
FS78	(1st Large up to 100g)	3·75	3·75
FS79	(Europe up to 20g)	5·50	5·50
FS79b	(Europe up to 20g)	3·75	3·75
FS80	(Europe up to 60g)	6·50	6·50
FS80c	(Europe up to 100g) (30.3.15)	4·00	4·00
FS80d	(Euro 100g World 20g) (1.9.20)	3·75	3·75
FS80e	(Europe Large 100g) (2.1.21)	9·50	9·50
FS81	(Worldwide up to 10g)		
FS82	(Worldwide up to 20g)	5·00	5·00
FS83	(Worldwide up to 40g)		
FS84	(Worldwide up to 60g)	7·50	7·50
FS84c	(Worldwide up to 100g) (30.3.15)	4·75	4·75
FS84d	(World 100g zone 1 & 3) (1.9.20)	9·75	9·75
FS84e	(World 100g zone 2) (1.9.20)	9·75	9·75
FS84f	(Worldwide Large 100g) (2.1.21)	10·50	10·50
FS77a, FS78a, FS79bba, FS80c, FS82a, FS84c Set of 6		20·00	20·00

2013 (17 Nov)–**16**. Union Flag T **FT8** with year code in background. Multicoloured. Self-adhesive. Two phosphor bands. Designs printed in gravure by Walsall, thermally printed service indicator. Perf 14×14½.

FS85	(1st Class up to 100g)	—	—
FS86	(1st Large up to 100g)	—	—
FS87	(Europe up to 20g)	—	—
FS87a	(Euro 20g World 10g) (10.8.16)	4·50	4·50
FS88	(Europe up to 60g)	20·00	20·00
FS88a	(Europe up to 100g) (10.8.16)	5·50	5·50
FS89	(Worldwide up to 10g)	—	—
FS90	(Worldwide up to 20g)	—	—
FS91	(Worldwide up to 40g)	—	—

FS92	(Worldwide up to 60g)	21·00	21·00
FS92a	(Worldwide up to 100g) (10.8.16)	6·75	6·75
FS85a, FS86a, FS87a, FS88a, FS90a, FS92a Set of 6		27·00	27·00

FT14

2013 (20 Nov)–**14**. T **FT14** with date code in background. New blue background. Self-adhesive. One phosphor band (over the Queen's head). Designs printed in gravure by Walsall, thermally printed service indicator. Perf 14×14½.

FS93	(2nd Class up to 100g)	2·50	2·50
FS94	(2nd Large up to 100g)	2·75	2·75
Special Pack (P&G 10) (Nos. FS93/FS94) (20.2.13)		10·00	

Post & Go stamps as T **FT14** were issued by the Philatelic Bureau, Edinburgh on 20 February 2013 in packs and on first day covers (price £7·00 per pack and £3·00 on first day cover). They were sold from Royal Mail Series I machines at Spring Stampex 2013 but were not made available through post offices until November 2013.

FT15 Primrose

2014 (19 Feb)–**15**. British Flora (1st series). Spring Blooms. Multicoloured. Self-adhesive. Two phosphor bands. Designs printed in gravure by Walsall, thermally printed service indicator. Perf 14×14½.

FS95	(1st Class up to 100g)	4·50	4·50
FS96	(1st Large up to 100g)	5·25	5·25
FS97	(Europe up to 20g)	5·50	5·50
FS97b	(Euro 20g World 10g) (5.6.14)	6·00	6·00
FS98a	(Europe up to 60g)	7·50	7·50
FS98b	(Europe up to 100g) (30.3.15)	11·50	11·50
FS99	(Worldwide up to 10g)	6·50	6·50
FS100	(Worldwide up to 20g)	5·75	5·75
FS101	(Worldwide up to 40g)	7·50	7·50
FS102	(Worldwide up to 60g)	8·50	8·50
FS102b	(Worldwide up to 100g) (30.3.15)	12·50	12·50
FS97/FS97, FS99/FS101 Set of 6		32·00	32·00
First Day Cover (No. FS95 in 6 designs)			9·50
Special Pack (P&G 14) (No. FS95 in strip of 6 designs)		8·00	

Nos. FS95/FS102b were each available in six different designs: T **FT15**, Snowdrop, Lesser Celandine, Dog Violet, Wild Daffodil, Blackthorn.

Nos. FS98b and FS102b resulted from the late use of old stock.

OPEN VALUE LABELS. In February 2014, Open Value Labels, previously dispensed from Post & Go machines printed on white self-adhesive paper began to appear on the same illustrated background designs as Post & Go stamps. These show a service indicator '1L' (1st Letter), '2SP' (2nd Small Parcel), etc and these are outside the scope of this catalogue, but on 7 July 2014 Royal Mail released a special pack (P&G 15) containing five such labels in the Machin head design, as Types **FT1** and **FT14** (Price £8)

FT16 Forget-me-not

2014 (17 Sept)–**21**. British Flora (2nd series). Symbolic Flowers. Multicoloured. Self-adhesive. Two phosphor bands. Designs printed in gravure by Walsall, thermally printed service indicator. Perf 14×14½.

FS103	(1st Class up to 100g)	3·00	3·00
FS104	(1st Large up to 100g)	3·25	3·25
FS104b	Europe up to 20g (17.9.14)	25·00	25·00
FS105	(Euro 20g World 10g)	3·50	3·50
FS106	(Europe up to 60g)	6·75	6·75
FS106b	(Europe up to 100g) (30.3.15)	10·00	10·00
FS106c	(Euro 100g World 20g) (9.20)	4·50	4·50
FS106d	(Europe Large 100g) (1.21)	10·00	10·00

FS107	(Worldwide up to 20g)	4·50	4·50
FS108	(Worldwide up to 60g)	7·25	7·25
FS108b	(Worldwide up to 100g) (30.3.15)	11·00	11·00
FS108c	(World 100g zone 1 & 3) (9.20)	14·50	14·50
FS108d	(World 100g zone 2) (9.20)	17·50	17·50
FS108e	(Worldwide Large 100g) (1.21)	11·00	11·00
FS103/FS108 Set of 6		26·00	26·00
First Day Cover (No. FS103 in 6 designs)			9·50
Special Pack (P&G 16) (No. FS103 in strip of 6 designs)		8·00	

Nos. FS103/FS108e were each available in six different designs (all with year code MA14): T **FT16**, Common Poppy, Dog Rose, Spear Thistle, Heather and Cultivated Flax.

The poppy design was released as a single design roll in the run-up to Remembrance Sunday in October 2014, October 2015, October 2016, October 2017 and October 2018.

FT17 Common Ivy

2014 (13 Nov)–**15**. British Flora (3rd series). Winter Greenery. Multicoloured. Self-adhesive. One phosphor band (Nos. FS109/FS110) or two phosphor bands (others). Designs printed in gravure by Walsall, thermally printed service indicators. Perf 14×14½.

FS109	(2nd Class up to 100g)	3·50	3·50
FS110	(2nd Large up to 100g)	4·00	4·00
FS111	(1st Class up to 100g)	3·50	3·50
FS112	(1st Large up to 100g)	4·00	4·00
FS113	(Euro 20g World 10g)	4·00	4·00
FS113c	(Europe up to 20g) (12.14)	25·00	25·00
FS114	(Europe up to 60g)	4·50	4·50
FS114c	(Europe up to 100g) (5.15)	10·00	10·00
FS115	(Worldwide up to 20g)	4·25	4·25
FS116	(Worldwide up to 60g)	5·75	5·75
FS116c	(Worldwide up to 100g) (5.15)	11·00	11·00
FS109/FS116 Set of 8		30·00	30·00
First Day Cover (Nos. FS109/FS112 in 4 designs)			9·50
Special Pack (P&G 17) (Nos. FS109/FS112 in 4 designs)		7·00	

Nos. FS109/FS110 were each available as T **FT17** or Mistletoe.

Nos. FS111/FS116 were all available as Butcher's Broom and Holly.

FT18 Falcon

2015 (18 Feb). Working Sail. Multicoloured. Self-adhesive. Two phosphor bands. Designs printed in gravure by Walsall, thermally printed service indicator. Perf 14×14½.

FS117	(1st Class up to 100g)	3·75	3·75
FS118	(1st Large up to 100g)	4·25	4·25
FS119	(Euro 20g World 10g)	4·50	4·50
FS120	(Europe up to 60g)	7·50	7·50
FS121	(Europe up to 100g)	14·00	14·00
FS122	(Worldwide up to 20g)	5·25	5·25
FS123	(Worldwide up to 60g)	8·25	8·25
FS124	(Worldwide up to 100g)	15·00	15·00
FS117/FS120, FS122, FS123 Set of 6		30·00	30·00
First Day Cover (No. FS117 in 6 designs)			9·50
Special Pack (P&G 18) (No. FS117 in strip of 6 designs)		8·00	

Nos. FS117/FS124 were each available in six different designs: T **FT18**, Briar, Harry, Margaret, Stag, Nell Morgan.

FT19 Lion

2015 (13 May). Heraldic Beasts. Multicoloured. Self-adhesive. Two phosphor bands. Designs printed in gravure by Walsall, thermally printed service indicator. Perf 14×14½.

FS125	(1st Class up to 100g)	3·75	3·75
FS126	(1st Large up to 100g)	4·25	4·25
FS127	(Euro 20g World 10g)	4·50	4·50
FS128	(Europe up to 100g)	5·50	5·50

FS129	(Worldwide up to 20g)	5·25	5·25
FS130	(Worldwide up to 100g)	6·75	6·75
FS125/FS130, Set of 6		27·00	27·00

First Day Cover (Philatelic Bureau, Edinburgh) (No.
FS125 in 6 designs)   9·50
Special Pack (P&G 19) (No. FS125 in strip of 6 designs)   8·00

Nos. FS125/FS130 were each available in six different designs: T **FT19**,
Unicorn, Yale, Dragon, Falcon and Griffin.

FT20 Dover

2015 (16 Sept). Sea Travel. Multicoloured. Self-adhesive. Two phosphor
bands. Designs printed in gravure by Walsall, thermally printed
service indicator. Perf 14×14½.

FS131	(1st Class up to 100g)	3·75	3·75
FS132	(1st Large up to 100g)	4·25	4·25
FS133	(Euro 20g World 10g)	4·50	4·50
FS134	(Europe up to 100g)	5·50	5·50
FS135	(Worldwide up to 20g)	5·25	5·25
FS136	(Worldwide up to 100g)	6·75	6·75
FS131/FS136, Set of 6		27·00	27·00

First Day Cover (No. FS131 in 6 designs)   9·50
Special Pack (P&G 20) (No. FS131 in strip of 6 designs)   8·00

Nos. FS131/FS136 were each available in six different designs: T **FT20**,
Hong Kong, Sydney, Ha Long Bay, New York City and Venice.

Nos. FS137/FS142, Poppies are omitted from this listing as they fall outside
the scope of *Collect British Stamps*, a full listing can be found in the *Great
Britain Concise Catalogue.*

FT22 Mountain Hare

2015 (16 Nov). Winter Fur and Feathers. Multicoloured. Self-adhesive. One
phosphor band at right (Nos. FS143/FS144) or two phosphor bands
(others). Designs printed in gravure by ISP Walsall, thermally printed
service indicator. Perf 14×14½.

FS143	(2nd Class up to 100g)	2·25	2·25
FS144	(2nd Large up to 100g)	3·00	3·00
FS145	(1st Class up to 100g)	3·75	3·75
FS146	(1st Large up to 100g)	4·25	4·25
FS147	(Euro 20g World 10g)	4·50	4·50
FS148	(Europe up to 100g)	5·50	5·50
FS149	(Worldwide up to 20g)	5·25	5·25
FS150	(Worldwide up to 100g)	6·75	6·75
FS143/FS150, Set of 8		28·00	28·00

First Day Cover (No. FS143/FS146 in 4 designs)   8·00
Special Pack (P&G 21) (Nos. FS143/FS146 in 4 designs)   7·25

Nos. FS143/FS144 were each available as T **FT22** or Redwing.
Nos. FS145/FS146 were each available as Red Fox or Red Squirrel.

FT23 Post Boy, 1640s

2016 (17 Feb). Royal Mail Heritage. Transport. Multicoloured. Self-
adhesive. Two phosphor bands. Designs printed in gravure by ISP
Walsall, thermally printed service indeicator. Perf 14×14½.

FS151	(1st Class up to 100g)	3·25	3·25
FS152	(1st Large up to 100g)	3·50	3·50
FS153	(Euro 20g World 10g)	3·75	3·75
FS154	(Europe up to 100g)	4·50	4·50
FS155	(Worldwide up to 20g)	4·25	4·25
FS156	(Worldwide up to 100g)	6·25	6·25
FS151/FS156, Set of 6		23·00	23·00

First Day Cover (Philatelic Bureau, Edinburgh) (No.
FS151 in 6 designs)   9·50
Special Pack (P&G 22) (No. FS151 in strip of 6 designs)   10·00

Nos. FS151/FS156 were each available in six different designs: T **FT23**;
Mail coach, 1790s; Falmouth packet ship, 1820s; Travelling Post Office,
1890s; Airmail, 1930s and Royal Mail Minivan, 1970s.

2016 (5 Aug). As T FT**14** with background text reading, alternately,
'2ndCLASS' in large lettering and 'ROYALMAIL' in small lettering,
with year code. New blue background. Self-adhesive. One phosphor
band (over the Queen's head). Designs printed in gravure by Walsall,
thermally printed service indicator. Perf 14×14½.

FS157	(2nd Class up to 100g)	2·10	2·10
FS158	(2nd Large up to 100g)	2·75	2·75

FT24 Seven-spot Ladybird

2016 (14 Sept). Ladybirds. Multicoloured. Self-adhesive. Two phosphor
bands. Designs printed in gravue by ISP Walsall, thermally printed
service indicator. Perf 14×14½.

FS159	(1st Class up to 100g)	2·50	2·50
FS160	(1st Large up to 100g)	2·75	2·75
FS161	(Euro 20g World 10g)	4·25	4·25
FS162	(Europe up to 100g)	4·25	4·25
FS163	(Worldwide up to 20g)	4·25	4·25
FS164	(Worldwide up to 100g)	5·75	5·75
FS159/FS164, Set of 6		21·00	21·00

First Day Cover (No. FS159 in 6 designs)   9·50
Special Pack (P&G 23) (No. FS159 in strip of 6 designs)   9·00

Nos. FS159/FS164a were each available in six different designs: T **FT24**,
14-spot Ladybird, Orange Ladybird, Heather Ladybird, Striped Ladybird
and Water Ladybird.

FT25 Hedgehog

2016 (14 Nov). Hibernating Animals. Multicoloured. Self-adhesive. One
phosphor band at right (Nos. FS165/FS166) or two phosphor bands
(others). Designs printed in gravure by ISP Walsall, thermally printed
service indicator. Perf 14×14½.

FS165	(2nd Class up to 100g)	2·50	2·50
FS166	(2nd Large up to 100g)	2·75	2·75
FS167	(1st Class up to 100g)	2·75	2·75
FS168	(1st Large up to 100g)	3·00	3·00
FS169	(Euro 20g World 10g)	3·25	3·25
FS170	(Europe up to 100g)	4·50	4·50
FS171	(Worldwide up to 20g)	4·25	4·25
FS172	(Worldwide up to 100g)	6·00	6·00
FS165/FS172, Set of 8		25·00	25·00

First Day Cover (FS165/FS168 in 4 designs)   8·00
Special Pack (P&G 24) (Nos. FS165/FS168 in 4 designs)   9·00

Nos. FS165/FS166 were each available as T **FT25** or Grass Snake.
Nos. FS167/FS172 were all available as Dormouse or Brown Long-
eared Bat.

FT26 Travelling Post Office: bag exchange

2017 (15 Feb). Royal Mail Heritage. Mail by Rail. Multicoloured. Self-
adhesive. Two phosphor bands. Designs printed in gravure by ISP
Walsall, thermally printed service indicator. Perf 14×14½.

FS173	(1st Class up to 100g)	2·50	2·50
FS174	(1st Large up to 100g)	2·75	2·75
FS175	(Euro 20g World 10g)	4·75	4·75
FS176	(Europe up to 100g)	4·75	4·75
FS177	(Worldwide up to 20g)	4·75	4·75
FS178	(Worldwide up to 100g)	5·75	5·75
FS173/FS178, Set of 6		23·00	23·00

First Day Cover (No. FS173 in 6 designs)   7·50
Special Pack (P&G 25) (No. FS173a in strip of 6 designs)   9·00

Nos. FS173/FS178 were each available in six different designs: T **FT26**;
Post Office (London) Railway; Night Mail: poster; Travelling Post Office:
loading; Travelling Post Office: sorting and Travelling Post Office: on
the move.

FT27 Machin Commemorative Head

2017 (5 June). Machin Anniversary 1967–2017. Design as T **FT27**. Self-adhesive. Two phosphor bands. Designs printed in gravure by ISP Walsall, thermally printed service indicator. Perf 14x14½.

FS179	(1st Class up to 100g)	3·00	3·00
FS180	(1st Large up to 100g)	3·25	3·25
FS181	(Euro 20g World 10g)	4·25	4·25
FS182	(Europe up to 100g)	4·25	4·25
FS182b	(Euro 100g World 20g) (9.20)	9·75	9·00
FS182c	(Europe Large 100g) (1.21)	12·00	10·50
FS183	(Worldwide up to 20g)	4·25	4·25
FS184	(Worldwide up to 100g)	5·75	5·75
FS184b	(World 100g zone 1-3) (9.20)	—	—
FS184c	(World 100g zone 2) (9.20)	—	—
FS184d	(Worldwide Large 100g) (1.21)	13·00	13·00
FS179/FS184, *Set of 6*		22·00	22·00

First Day Cover (No. FS179 in 6 designs) 7·50
Special Pack (P&G 26) (No. FS179 in strip of 6 designs) 17·00

Nos. FS179/FS184 were each available in six different colours: orange-brown, light olive, violet, deep sepia, bright emerald and drab.

FT28 First UK Aerial Mail, 1911

2017 (13 Sept). Royal Mail Heritage. Mail by Air. Multicoloured. Self-adhesive. Two phosphor bands. Designs printed in gravure by ISP Walsall, thermally printed service indicator. Perf 14×14½.

FS185	(1st Class up to 100g)	2·25	2·25
FS186	(1st Large up to 100g)	2·75	2·75
FS187	(Euro 20g World 10g)	4·00	4·00
FS188	(Europe up to 100g)	4·00	4·00
FS189	(Worldwide up to 20g)	4·00	4·00
FS190	(Worldwide up to 100g)	5·25	5·25
FS185/FS190, *Set of 6*		20·00	20·00

First Day Cover (No. FS185 in 6 designs) 7·50
Special Pack (P&G 27) (No. FS185 in strip of 6 designs) 9·00

Nos. FS185/FS190 were each available in six different designs: T **FT28**; Military Mail Flight, 1919; International Airmail, 1933; Domestic Airmail, 1934; Flying Boat Airmail, 1937 and Datapost Service, 1980s.

2017 (13 Nov)–**21**. British Flora (3rd series). Winter Greenery, 2017 re-issue. Nos. FS109/FS110 with blue background text reading, alternately, '2ndCLASS' in large lettering and 'ROYALMAIL' in small lettering. One phosphor band at right. Self-adhesive. Designs printed in gravure by ISP Walsall, thermally printed service indicator. Perf 14×14½.

FS191	(2nd Class up to 100g)	2·10	2·10
FS192	(2nd Large up to 100g)	2·75	2·75
FS196b	(Euro 100g World 20g) (3.11.20)	4·00	4·00
FS198b	(World 100g zone 1-3) (3.11.20)	11·00	11·00
FS198c	(World 100g zone 2) (3.22.20)	11·00	11·00
FS198d	(Worldwide Large 100g) (2.1.21)	11·50	11·50

Nos. FS191/FS192 were each available as T **FT17** or Mistletoe.
Nos. FS111/FS113, FS114c/FS115 and FS116c were also reissued (as Nos. FS193/FS198) with 'ROYALMAIL' background text in a different shade. These are outside the scope of this catalogue.

FT29 The Iron Throne–Ice

2018 (23 Jan)–**20**. Game of Thrones. Multicoloured. Self-adhesive. One phosphor band at right (Nos. FS199/FS200) or two phosphor bands (others). Designs printed in gravure by ISP Walsall, thermally printed service indicator. Perf 14×14½.

FS199	Type IIIA	5·25	5·25
FS200	Type IIIA	5·50	5·50
FS201	(1st Class up to 100g)	3·25	3·25
FS202	(1st Large up to 100g)	3·75	3·75

FS203	Type IIIA	9·00	9·00
FS204	Type IIIA	9·00	9·00
FS204b	(Euro 100g World 20g) (9.20)	16·00	16·00
FS205	Type IIIA	9·00	9·00
FS206	Type IIIA	9·00	9·00
FS206b	(World 100g zone 1-3) (9.20)	19·00	19·00
FS206c	(World 100g zone 2) (9.20)	23·00	23·00
FS199/FS206, *Set of 8*		95·00	95·00

First Day Cover (Nos. FS199 and FS201) 4·00
Special Pack (P&G 28) (Nos. FS199 and FS201) 5·00

Nos. FS201/FS206 were each available in one yellow-orange design depicting The Iron Throne–Fire.
Nos. FS199/FS200 were each available in one blue design, T **FT29**.

FT30 Packet *Antelope*, 1780

2018 (14 Feb)–**20**. Royal Mail Heritage. Mail by Sea. Multicoloured. Self-adhesive. Two phosphor bands. Designs printed in gravure, thermally printed service indicator. Perf 14×14½.

FS207	(1st Class up to 100g)	2·25	2·25
FS208	(1st Large up to 100g)	2·75	2·75
FS209	(Euro 20g World 10g)	4·00	4·00
FS210	(Europe up to 100g)	4·00	4·00
FS210b	(Euro 100g World 20g) (9.20)	13·50	13·50
FS211	(Worldwide up to 20g)	4·00	4·00
FS212	(Worldwide up to 100g)	5·25	5·25
FS212b	(World 100g zone 1-3) (9.20)	14·50	14·50
FS212c	(World 100g zone 2) (9.20)	16·50	16·50
FS207/FS212 *Set of 6*		20·00	20·00

First Day Cover (No. FS207 in 6 designs) 7·50
Special Pack (P&G 29) (No. FS207 in strip of 6 designs) 7·00

Nos. FS297/FS212 were each available in six different designs: T **FT30**; SS *Great Western*, 1838; SS *Britannia*, 1887; RMS *Olympic*, 1911; RMS *Queen Mary*, 1936; RMS *St Helena*, 1990.

FT31 Pentacycle, 1882

2018 (12 Sept)–**20**. Royal Mail Heritage. Mail by Bike. Multicoloured. Self-adhesive. Two phosphor bands. Designs printed in gravure by ISP Walsall, thermally printed service indicator. Perf 14×14½.

FS213	(1st Class up to 100g)	2·25	2·25
FS214	(1st Large up to 100g)	2·75	2·75
FS215	(Euro 20g World 10g)	4·00	4·00
FS216	(Europe up to 100g)	4·00	4·00
FS216a	(Euro 100g World 20g)	12·50	16·00
FS217	(Worldwide up to 20g)	4·00	4·00
FS218	(Worldwide up to 100g)	5·25	5·25
FS218a	(World 100g zone 1-3)	13·50	19·00
FS218b	(World 100g zone 2)	13·50	23·00
FS213/FS218 *Set of 6*		20·00	20·00

First Day Cover (No. FS213 in 6 designs) 7·50
Special Pack (P&G 30) (No. FS213 in strip of 6 designs) 9·50

Nos. FS213/FS218b were each available in six different designs: T **FT31**; Motorcycle and trailer, 1902; Tricycle and basket, 1920; Bicycle, 1949; Motorcycle, 1965; Quad bike, 2002.

REGIONAL ISSUES

PERFORATION AND WATERMARK. All the following Regional stamps are perforated 15×14, unless otherwise stated.

I. England

EN1 Three Lions of England

EN2 Crowned Lion, Supporting the Shield of St George

EN3 English Oak Tree

EN4 English Tudor Rose

2001 (23 Apr)–**02**. Printed in gravure by De La Rue or Questa (Nos. EN1/EN2), De La Rue (others). One centre phosphor band (2nd) or two phosphor bands (others). Perf 15×14 (with one elliptical hole in each vertical side).

EN1	**EN1**	(2nd) Three lions of England	1·50	1·00
EN2	**EN2**	(1st) Lion and shield	2·00	1·00
EN3	**EN3**	(E) English oak tree	3·25	2·00
EN4	**EN4**	65p. English Tudor rose	2·10	2·10
EN5	**EN4**	68p. English Tudor rose (4.7.02)	2·10	2·10

Presentation Pack (PO Pack No. 54) (Nos. EN1/EN4) 7·00
PHQ Cards (*set of 4*) (D20) (Nos. EN1/EN4) 1·25 7·00

Nos. EN1/EN3 were initially sold at 19p., 27p. and 36p., the latter representing the basic European airmail rate.

First Day Covers

23.4.01	2nd, 1st, E, 65p. (Nos. EN1/EN4) Windsor	2·00
4.7.02	68p. (No. EN5) London	1·50

Combined Presentation Pack for England, Northern Ireland, Scotland and Wales

4.7.02	PO Pack No. 59. 68p. (Nos. EN5, NI93, S99, W88)	8·50

2003 (14 Oct)–**2017**. As Nos. EN1/EN3 and EN5, and new values, but with white borders. One centre phosphor band (2nd) or two phosphor bands (others). Perf 15×14 (with one elliptical hole in each vertical side).

(a) Walsall or De La Rue (No. EN10), De La Rue (others).

EN6	**EN1**	(2nd) Three lions of England	1·50	1·00
EN7	**EN2**	(1st) Lion and shield	2·00	1·25
EN8	**EN3**	(E) English oak tree	3·25	2·00
EN9		40p. English oak tree (11.5.04)	1·25	1·25
EN10		42p. English oak tree (5.4.05)	1·75	1·75
EN11		44p. English oak tree (28.3.06)	1·25	1·25
EN12		48p. English oak tree (27.3.07)	1·00	1·00
EN13		50p. English oak tree (1.4.08)	1·25	1·25
EN14		56p. English oak tree (31.3.09)	1·25	1·25
EN15		60p. English oak tree (30.3.10)	1·50	1·50
EN16	**EN4**	68p. English Tudor rose	1·75	1·75
EN17		72p. English Tudor rose (28.3.06)	1·75	1·75
EN18		78p. English Tudor rose (27.3.07)	2·00	2·00
EN19		81p. English Tudor rose (1.4.08)	2·00	2·00
EN20		90p. English Tudor rose (31.3.09)	2·25	2·25
EN21		97p. English Tudor rose (30.3.10)	2·50	2·50

(b) Litho Enschedé or ISP Cartor (No. EN30) or ISP Cartor (others). Queen's head in grey (Nos. EN29, EN30*b* and EN36) or silver (others).

EN29	**EN1**	(2nd) Three lions of England (3.1.13)	1·50	1·00
EN30	**EN2**	(1st) Lion and shield (Queen's head silver) (20.9.07)	2·00	1·50
EN30*b*		(1st) Lion and shield (Queen's head grey) (3.1.13)	2·25	1·75
EN31	**EN3**	68p. English oak tree (29.3.11)	1·75	1·75

EN32		87p. English oak tree (25.4.12)	2·25	2·25
EN33		88p. English oak tree (27.3.13)	2·25	2·25
EN34		97p. English oak tree (26.3.14)	2·40	2·40
EN35		£1 English oak tree (24.3.15)	2·40	2·40
EN36		£1·05 English oak tree (22.3.16)	2·75	2·75
EN41	**EN4**	£1·10 English Tudor rose (29.3.11)	2·50	2·50
EN43		£1·28 English Tudor rose (25.4.12)	2·60	2·60
EN44		£1·33 English Tudor rose (24.3.15)	2·75	2·75

Presentation Pack (PO Pack No. 63) (Nos. EN6/EN8, EN16) 9·50
PHQ Cards (*set of 4*) (D24) (Nos. EN6/EN8, EN16) 1·25 6·50

Nos. EN6/EN8 were initially sold at 20p. 28p. and 38p., the latter representing the basic European airmail rate.

Stamps as No. EN30 but self-adhesive were issued on 23 April 2007 in sheets of 20 with *se-tenant* labels. These sheets were printed in lithography by Cartor and perforated 15×14 without elliptical holes. The labels show either English scenes or personal photographs.

No. EN30 was first issued in £7·66 British Army Uniforms stamp booklet, No. DX40, but was issued in sheets in January 2013.

Stamps as Nos. EN30, NI95, S131 and W122 but self-adhesive were issued on 29 September 2008 in sheets of 20 containing five of each design with *se-tenant* labels. These sheets were printed in lithography by Cartor and perforated 15×14 with one elliptical hole in each vertical side.

First Day Covers

14.10.03	2nd, 1st, E, 68p. (Nos. EN6/EN8, EN16) Tallents House	5·50
11.5.04	40p. (No. EN9) Tallents House	2·00
5.4.05	42p. (No. EN10) Tallents House	2·00
28.3.06	44p., 72p., (Nos. EN11, EN17) Tallents House	3·50
27.3.07	48p., 78p., (Nos. EN12, EN18) Tallents House	3·00
1.4.08	50p., 81p., (Nos. EN13, EN19) Tallents House	3·00
31.3.09	56p., 90p. (Nos. EN14, EN20) Tallents House	3·50
30.3.10	60p., 97p. (Nos. EN15, EN21) Tallents House	4·00
29.3.11	68p., £1·10 (Nos. EN31, EN41) Tallents House	4·50
25.4.12	87p., £1·28 (Nos. EN32, EN43) Tallents House	4·75
27.3.13	88p. (No. EN33) Tallents House	2·25
26.3.14	97p. (No. EN34) Tallents House	2·25
24.3.15	£1, £1·33 (Nos. EN35, EN44) Tallents House	5·50
22.3.16	£1·05 (No. EN36) Tallents House	2·50

Combination Presentation Packs for England, Northern Ireland, Scotland and Wales

11.5.04	PO Pack No. 68. 40p. (Nos. EN9, NI97, S112, W101)	6·50
5.4.05	PO Pack No. 70. 42p. (Nos. EN10, NI98, S113, W102)	6·25
28.3.06	PO Pack No. 73. 44p. and 72p. (Nos. EN11, EN17, NI99, NI102, S114, S120, W103, W109)	10·00
27.3.07	PO Pack No. 76. 48p. and 78p. (Nos. EN12, EN18, NI124, NI128, S115, S121, W104, and W110)	10·00
1.4.08	PO Pack No. 79. 50p. and 81p. (Nos. EN13, EN19, NI125, NI129, S116, S122, W105, W111)	10·00
29.9.08	PO Pack No. 83. 2nd, 1st, 50p. and 81p. (Nos. EN6/EN7, EN13, EN19, NI122/NI123, NI125, NI129, S109/S110, S116, S122, W98/W99, W105, W111)	40·00
31.3.09	PO Pack No. 85. 56p. and 90p. (Nos. EN14, EN20, NI126, NI130, S117, S123, W106, W112)	13·00
30.3.10	PO Pack No. 87. 60p. and 97p. (Nos. EN15, EN21, NI127, NI131, S118, S124, W107, W113)	14·00
29.3.11	PO Pack No. 91. 68p. and £1·10 (Nos. EN31, EN41, NI101, NI111, S132, S138 W123, W129)	15·00
25.4.12	PO Pack No. 95. 87p. and £1·28 (Nos. EN32, EN43, NI103, NI113, S133, S143, W124, W134)	18·00
27.3.13	PO Pack No. 98. 88p. (Nos. EN33, NI104, S134, W125)	8·50
26.3.14	PO Pack No. 100. 97p. (Nos. EN34, NI105, S135, W126)	8·50
24.3.15	PO Pack No. 102. £1 and £1·33 (Nos. EN35, EN44, NI106, NI114, S136, S144, W127, W135)	18·00
22.3.16	PO Pack No. 104. £1·05 (Nos. EN36, NI 107, S137 and W128)	10·00

EN5

2007 (23 Apr). Celebrating England. Sheet 123×70 mm. Printed in gravure by De La Rue. Two phosphor bands. Perf 15×14 (with one elliptical hole in each vertical side) (1st) or 15×14½ (78p.).

MSEN50 **EN5** (1st) No. EN7; (1st) St George's flag; 78p.
St George; 78p. Houses of Parliament, London 5·50 4·00

First Day Cover (Tallents House)		4·50	
Presentation Pack (PO Pack No. M15)		6·50	
PHQ Cards (set of 5) (CGB2)		2·00	8·00

No. **MS**EN50 was on sale at post offices throughout the UK.

Stamps as the 1st class St George's flag stamp within No. **MS**EN50 but self-adhesive were issued on 23 April 2009 in sheets of 20 with *se-tenant* labels showing English Castles.

These sheets were printed in lithography by Cartor.

The five PHQ cards show the four individual stamps and the complete miniature sheet.

EN6 St George's
Flag

2013 (9 May)–**14**. England Flag. Printed in lithography by Cartor or Enschede. Two phosphor bands. Perf 14½×14 (with one elliptical hole in each vertical side).

EN51	**EN6**	(1st) St George's Flag (Queen's head silver)	4·50	4·50
		a. St George's Flag (Queen's head grey) (20.2.14)	3·50	3·50

No. EN51 silver Queen's head was issued in £11·11 Football Heroes booklets (No. DY7) and £16.49 Centenary of the First World War (3rd issue) booklets.

No. EN51a was issued in £13·97 Classic Locomotives booklet (No. DY9).

EN7 Three
Lions of
England

EN8 Crowned
Lion, Supporting
the Shield of
St George

EN9 English
Oak Tree

EN10 English
Tudor Rose

2017 (21 Mar)–**20**. As previous set but with value indicated in revised typeface. One centre phosphor band (No. EN52) or two phosphor bands. Perf 15×14 (with one elliptical hole in each vertical side).

EN52	**EN7**	(2nd) Three Lions of England (20.3.18)	1·25	75
EN53	**EN8**	(1st) Lion and shield (Indian red) (20.3.18)	1·75	75
EN54	**EN9**	£1·17 English Oak tree (21.3.17)	2·75	2·75
EN55		£1·25 English Oak tree (20.3.18)	2·75	2·75
EN56		£1·35 English Oak tree (19.3.19)	3·00	3·00
EN60	**EN10**	£1·40 English Tudor Rose (21.3.17)	3·00	3·00
EN61	**EN9**	£1·42 English Oak tree (17.3.20)	2·50	2·50
EN62	**EN10**	£1·45 English Tudor Rose (20.3.18)	3·25	3·25
EN63		£1·55 English Tudor Rose (19.3.19)	3·25	3·25
EN64		£1·63 English Tudor Rose (17.3.20)	2·75	2·75
EN65	**EN9**	£1·70 English Oak Tree (23.12.20)	2·40	2·40

EN11 Three Lions of England

EN12 Crowned Lion,
Supporting the Shield of
St George

EN13 English Oak Tree

2022 (11 Aug). As Types **EN11**, **EN12** and **EN13** with barcoded strip at right. Self-adhesive. One centre phosphor band (2nd) or two phosphor bands (others). Die-cut perf 15×14½ (with one elliptical hole in each vertical side).

EN66	**EN11**	(2nd) Three Lions of England	1·40	1·40
EN67	**EN12**	(1st) Lion and shield	2·00	2·00
EN68	**EN13**	£1·85 English oak tree	2·50	2·50

First Day Covers

21.3.17	£1·17, £1·40. (Nos. EN54, EN60) Tallents House	6·00
20.3.18	2nd, 1st, £1·25, £1·45. (Nos. EN52/EN53, EN55, EN61) Tallents House	9·00
19.3.19	£1·35, £1·55 (Nos. EN56, EN62) Tallents House	7·00
17.3.20	£1·42, £1·63 (Nos. EN60a, EN63) Tallents House	7·00
23.12.20	£1·70 (No. EN64) Tallents House	3·75
11.8.22	2nd, 1st, £1·85 (Nos. EN66/EN68) Tallents House	7·50

Combination Presentation Packs for England, Northern Ireland, Scotland and Wales

21.3.17	PO Pack No. 107. £1·17 and £1·40 (Nos. EN54, EN60, NI159, NI165, S161, S166, W151, W156)	22·00
20.3.18	PO Pack No. 109. 2nd, 1st, £1·25 and £1·45 (Nos. EN52/EN53, EN55, EN62, NI157/NI158, NI160, NI166, S159/S160, S162, S168, W149/W150, W152, W158)	38·00
19.3.19	PO Pack No. 111. £1·35, £1·55 (Nos. EN56, EN63, NI161, NI167, S163, S169, W153, W159)	26·00
17.3.20	PO Pack No. 113. £1·42, £1·63 (Nos. EN61, EN64, NI165, NI168, S167, S170, W157, W160)	28·00
23.12.20	PO Pack No. 115. £1·70 (Nos. EN65, NI169, S171, W161)	11·00
11.8.22	PO Pack No. 120. 2nd, 1st, £1·85 (EN66/EN68, NI70/NI72, S18/S182 and W162/W164)	26·00

II. Northern Ireland

N1   N2   N3

1958–67. W **179**. Perf 15×14.

NI1	**N1**	3d. deep lilac (18.8.58)	15	15
		p. One centre phosphor band (9.6.67)	25	25
NI2		4d. ultramarine (7.2.66)	15	15
		p. Two phosphor bands (10.67)	15	15
NI3	**N2**	6d. deep claret (29.9.58)	50	50
NI4		9d. bronze-green (2 phosphor bands) (1.3.67)	40	40
NI5	**N3**	1s.3d. green (29.9.58)	50	50
NI6		1s.6d. grey-blue (2 phosphor bands) (1.3.67)	40	40

1968–69. One centre phosphor band (Nos. NI8/NI9) or two phosphor bands (others). No wmk. Perf 15×14

NI7	**N1**	4d. deep bright blue (27.6.68)	25	25
NI8		4d. olive-sepia (4.9.68)	25	25
NI9		4d. bright vermilion (26.2.69)	30	30
NI10		5d. royal blue (4.9.68)	40	40
NI11	**N3**	1s.6d. grey-blue (20.5.69)	1·50	1·50

First Day Covers

18.8.58	3d. (No. NI1)	30·00
29.9.58	6d., 1s.3d. (Nos. NI3, NI5)	35·00
7.2.66	4d. (No. NI2)	7·00
1.3.67	9d., 1s.6d. (Nos. NI4, NI6)	4·00
4.9.68	4d., 5d. (Nos. NI8, NI10)	3·00

Presentation Pack

9.12.70	PO Pack No. 25. 3d., 9d., 1s.3d., 1s.6d., 4d., 5d. (Nos. NI1p, NI4/NI6, NI8/NI10)	3·50

N4

1971–93. Decimal Currency. T **N4**. No wmk.

(a) Photo Harrison. With phosphor bands. Perf 15×14.

NI12	2½p. bright magenta (1 centre band)	45	45
NI13	3p. ultramarine (2 bands)	30	30
NI14	3p. ultramarine (1 centre band) (23.1.74)	20	20
NI15	3½p. olive-grey (2 bands) (23.1.74)	20	20
NI16	3½p. olive-grey (1 centre band) (6.11.74)	40	40
NI17	4½p. grey-blue (2 bands) (6.11.74)	30	30
NI18	5p. reddish violet (2 bands)	90	90
NI19	5½p. violet (2 bands) (23.1.74)	25	25
NI20	5½p. violet (1 centre band) (21.5.75)	25	25
NI21	6½p. greenish blue (1 centre band) (14.1.76)	20	20
NI22	7p. purple-brown (1 centre band) (18.1.78)	30	30
NI23	7½p. chestnut (2 bands)	1·25	1·25
NI24	8p. rosine (2 bands) (23.1.74)	40	40
NI25	8½p. yellow-green (2 bands) (14.1.76)	40	40
NI26	9p. deep violet (2 bands) (18.1.78)	40	40
NI27	10p. orange-brown (2 bands) (20.10.76)	40	40
NI28	10p. orange-brown (1 centre band) (23.7.80)	40	40
NI29	10½p. steel-blue (2 bands) (18.1.78)	50	50
NI30	11p. scarlet (2 bands) (20.10.76)	50	50

(b) Photo Harrison. On phosphorised paper. Perf 15×14.

NI31	12p. yellowish green (23.7.80)	50	50
NI32	13½p. purple-brown (23.7.80)	60	60
NI33	15p. ultramarine (23.7.80)	60	60

(c) Litho Questa (Type II, unless otherwise stated). Perf 14 (11½p., 12½p., 14p. (No. NI38), 15½p., 16p., 18p. (No. NI45), 19½p., 20½p., 22p. (No. NI53), 26p. (No. NI60), 28p. (No. NI62)) or 15×14 (others).

NI34	11½p. drab (1 side band) (8.4.81)	85	85
NI35	12p. bright emerald (1 side band) (7.1.86)	90	90
NI36	12½p. light emerald (1 side band) (24.2.82)	50	50
	a. Perf 15×14 (28.2.84)	3·50	3·50
NI37	13p. chestnut (Type I) (1 side band) (23.10.84)	60	60
NI38	14p. grey-blue (phosphorised paper) (8.4.81)	60	60
NI39	14p. deep blue (1 centre band) (8.11.88)	50	50
NI40	15p. bright blue (1 centre band) (28.11.89)	60	60
NI41	15½p. pale violet (phosphorised paper) (24.2.82)	80	80
NI42	16p. drab (phosphorised paper) (27.4.83)	1·00	1·00
	a. Perf 15×14 (28.2.84)	5·00	5·00
NI43	17p. grey-blue (phosphorised paper) (23.10.84)	80	80
NI44	17p. deep blue (1 centre band) (4.12.90)	60	60
NI45	18p. deep violet (phosphorised paper) (8.4.81)	80	80
NI46	18p. deep olive-grey (phosphorised paper) (6.1.87)	80	80
NI47	18p. bright green (1 centre band) (3.12.91)	80	80
	a. Perf 14 (31.12.92*)	6·00	6·00
NI48	18p. bright green (1 side band) (10.8.93)	1·50	1·50
NI49	19p. bright orange-red (phosphorised paper) (8.11.88)	80	80
NI50	19½p. olive-grey (phosphorised paper) (24.2.82)	1·50	1·50
NI51	20p. brownish black (phosphorised paper) (28.11.89)	80	80
NI52	20½p. ultramarine (phosphorised paper) (27.4.83)	2·75	2·75
NI53	22p. blue (phosphorised paper) (8.4.81)	80	80
NI54	22p. yellow-green (phosphorised paper) (23.10.84)	80	80
NI55	22p. bright orange-red (phosphorised paper) (4.12.90)	80	80
NI56	23p. bright green (phosphorised paper) (8.11.88)	80	80
NI57	24p. Indian red (phosphorised paper) (28.11.89)	90	90
NI58	24p. chestnut (phosphorised paper) (3.12.91)	80	80
NI59	24p. chestnut (2 bands) (10.8.93)	1·50	1·50
NI60	26p. rosine (phosphorised paper) (24.2.82)	90	90
	a. Perf 15×14 (27.1.87)	2·00	2·00
NI61	26p. drab (phosphorised paper) (4.12.90)	1·10	1·10
NI62	28p. deep violet-blue (phosphorised paper) (27.4.83)	1·00	1·00
	a. Perf 15×14 (27.1.87)	1·40	1·40
NI63	28p. deep bluish grey (phosphorised paper) (3.12.91)	90	90
NI64	31p. bright purple (phosphorised paper) (23.10.84)	1·40	1·40
NI65	32p. greenish blue (phosphorised paper) (8.11.88)	1·40	1·40
NI66	34p. deep bluish grey (phosphorised paper) (28.11.89)	1·40	1·40
NI67	37p. rosine (phosphorised paper) (4.12.90)	1·50	1·50
NI68	39p. bright mauve (phosphorised paper) (3.12.91)	1·50	1·50

* Earliest known date of issue.
Nos. NI48 and NI49 only come from booklets.

First Day Covers

7.7.71	2½p., 3p., 5p., 7½p. (Nos. NI12/NI13, NI18, NI23)	2·50
23.1.74	3p., 3½p., 5½p., 8p. (Nos. NI14/NI15, NI19, NI24)	2·00
6.11.74	4½p. (No. NI17)	80
14.1.76	6½p., 8½p. (Nos. NI21, NI25)	80
20.10.76	10p., 11p. (Nos. NI27, NI30)	90
18.1.78	7p., 9p., 10½p. (Nos. NI22, NI26, NI29)	90
23.7.80	12p., 13½p., 15p. (Nos. NI31/NI33)	1·50
8.4.81	11½p., 14p., 18p., 22p. (Nos. NI34, NI38, NI45, NI53)	1·25
24.2.82	12½p., 15½p., 19½p., 26p. (Nos. NI36, NI41, NI50, NI60)	2·00
27.4.83	16p., 20½p., 28p. (Nos. NI42, NI52, NI62)	2·00
23.10.84	13p., 17p., 22p., 31p. (Nos. NI37, NI43, NI54, NI64)	2·25
7.1.86	12p. (No. NI35)	90
6.1.87	18p. (No. NI46)	90
8.11.88	14p., 19p., 23p., 32p. (Nos. NI39, NI49, NI56, NI65)	2·50
28.11.89	15p., 20p., 24p., 34p. (Nos. NI40, NI51, NI57, NI66)	3·00
4.12.90	17p., 22p., 26p., 37p. (Nos. NI44, NI55, NI61, NI67)	3·00
3.12.91	18p., 24p., 28p., 39p. (Nos. NI47, NI58, NI63, NI68)	3·00

Presentation Packs

7.7.71	PO Pack No. 29. 2½p., 3p., 5p., 7½p. (Nos. NI12/NI113, NI18, NI23)	2·00
29.5.74	PO Pack No. 61. 3p., 3½p., 5½p., 8p. (Nos. NI14, NI15, NI19, NI24). 4½p. (No. NI17) added later	3·00
20.10.76	PO Pack No. 84. 6½p., 8½p., 10p., 11p. (Nos. NI21, NI25, NI27, NI30)	1·50
28.10.81	PO Pack No. 129d. 7p., 9p., 10½p., 11½p., 12p., 13½p., 14p., 15p., 18p., 22p. (Nos. NI22, NI26, NI29, NI31/NI34, NI38, NI45, NI53)	7·00
3.8.83	PO Pack No. 4. 10p., 12½p., 16p., 20½p., 26p., 28p. (Nos. NI28, NI36, NI42, NI52, NI60, NI62)	15·00
23.10.84	PO Pack No. 8. 10p., 13p., 16p., 17p., 22p., 26p., 28p., 31p. (Nos. NI28, NI37, N142a, NI43, NI54, NI60, NI62, NI64)	12·50
3.3.87	PO Pack No. 12. 12p., 13p., 17p., 18p., 22p., 26p., 28p., 31p. (Nos. NI35, NI37, NI43, NI46, NI54, NI60a, NI62a, NI64)	16·00

Combined Presentation Packs for Northern Ireland, Scotland and Wales

8.11.88	PO Pack No. 17. 14p., 19p., 23p., 32p. (Nos. NI39, NI49, NI56, NI65, S54, S62, S67, S77, W40, W50, W57, W66)	12·50
28.11.89	PO Pack No. 20. 15p., 20p., 24p., 34p. (Nos. NI44, NI55, NI61, NI67, S58, S66, S73, S79, W45, W56, W62, W68)	12·00
4.12.90	PO Pack No. 23. 17p., 22p., 26p., 37p. (Nos. NI44, NI55, NI61, NI67, S58, S66, S73, S79, W45, W56, W62, W68)	12·00
3.12.91	PO Pack No. 26. 18p., 24p., 28p., 39p. (Nos. NI47, NI58, NI63, NI68, S60, S70, S75, S80, W48, W59, W64, W69)	12·00

1993 (7 Dec)–**2000**.
(a) Litho Questa. Perf 15×14 (with one elliptical hole in each vert side).

NI69	**N4**	19p. bistre (1 centre band)	80	80
NI70		19p. bistre (1 band at left) (26.7.94)	1·25	1·25
NI71		20p. bright green (1 centre band) (23.7.96)	1·25	1·25
NI72		25p. red (2 bands)	75	75
NI73		26p. red-brown (2 bands) (23.7.96)	1·50	1·50
NI74		30p. deep olive-grey (2 bands)	1·10	1·10
NI75		37p. bright mauve (2 bands) (23.7.96)	2·25	2·25
NI76		41p. grey-brown (2 bands)	1·50	1·50
NI77		63p. light emerald (2 bands) (23.7.96)	3·50	3·50

(b) Gravure Walsall (19p., 20p., 26p. (No. NI81b), 38p., 40p., 63p., 64p., 65p.), Harrison or Walsall (26p. (No. NI81), 37p.). Perf 14 (No. NI80) or 15×14 (others) (both with one elliptical hole in each vertical side).

NI78	**N4**	19p. bistre (1 centre band) (8.6.99)	2·50	2·50
NI79		20p. bright green (1 centre band) (1.7.97)	2·50	2·50
NI80		20p. bright green (1 side band at right) (13.10.98)	3·00	3·00
NI81		26p. chestnut (2 bands) (1.7.97)	1·60	1·60
		b. Perf 14 (13.10.98)	3·00	3·00
NI82		37p. bright mauve (2 bands) (1.7.97)	1·90	1·90
NI83		38p. ultramarine (2 bands) (8.6.99)	5·50	5·50

NI84	40p. deep azure (2 bands) (25.4.2000)	3·50	3·50
NI85	63p. light emerald (2 bands) (1.7.97)	3·50	3·50
NI86	64p. turquoise-green (2 bands) (8.6.99)	6·50	6·50
NI87	65p. greenish blue (2 bands) (25.4.2000)	3·00	3·00

Nos. NI70, NI80 and NI81b were only issued in stamp booklets. No. NI70 exists with the phophor band at left or right of the stamp.

First Day Covers

7.12.93	19p., 25p., 30p., 41p. (Nos. NI69, NI72, NI74, NI76)	4·00
23.7.96	20p., 26p., 37p., 63p. (Nos. NI71, NI73, NI75, NI77)	5·00
8.6.99	38p., 64p. (Nos.NI83, NI86).	10·00
25.4.00	1st, 40p., 65p. (Nos. NI84, NI87, NI88b)	12·50

Presentation Packs

8.6.99	PO Pack No. 47. 19p., 26p., 38p., 64p. (Nos. NI78, NI81, NI83, NI86).	15·00
25.4.00	PO Pack No. 52. 1st, 40p., 65p. (Nos. NI84, NI87, NI88b)	16·00

Combined Presentation Packs for Northern Ireland, Scotland and Wales

7.12.93	PO Pack No. 31. 19p., 25p., 30p., 41p. (Nos. NI69, NI72, NI74, NI76, S81, S84, S86, S88, W70, W73, W75, W77)	20·00
23.7.96	PO Pack No. 36. 20p., 26p., 37p., 63p. (Nos. NI71, NI73, NI75, NI77, S83, S85, S87, S89, W72, W74, W76, W78)	16·00
20.10.98	PO Pack No. 42. 20p. (1 centre band), 26p., 37p., 63p. (Nos. NI79, NI81/NI82, NI85, S90/S93, W79/W82)	18·00

N5

2000 (15 Feb–25 Apr). T **N4** redrawn with '1st' face value as T **N5**. Two phosphor bands. Perf 14 (with one elliptical hole in each vertical side).

NI88	**N5**	(1st) bright orange-red	1·60	1·60
		b. Perf 15×14 (25.4.2000)	7·00	7·00

No NI88 was only issued in £7·50 Special by Design stamp booklets.
No NI88b was issued in sheets.

N6 Basalt Columns, Giant's Causeway

N7 Aerial View of Patchwork Fields

N8 Linen Pattern

N9 Vase Pattern from Belleek

2001 (6 Mar)–**03**. Printed in lithography by De La Rue (68p.), De La Rue or Walsall (E) or Enschedé (2nd) or Walsall (others). One centre phosphor band (2nd) or two phosphor bands (others). Perf 15×14 (with one elliptical hole in each vertical side).

NI89	**N6**	(2nd) Basalt columns, Giant's Causeway	1·50	1·25
NI90	**N7**	(1st) Aerial view of patchwork fields	2·00	1·50
NI91	**N8**	(E) Linen pattern	3·25	2·25
NI92	**N9**	65p. Vase pattern from Belleek	2·25	2·25
NI93		68p. Vase pattern from Belleek (4.7.2002)	2·75	2·75

PHQ Cards (set of 4) (D19) (Nos. NI89/NI92) | 1·25 | 7·50

Nos. NI89, NI90 and NI91 were initially sold at 19p., 27p. and 36p., the latter representing the basic European airmail rate.

For combined presentation packs for all four regions, see under England.

First Day Covers

6.3.01	2nd, 1st, E, 65p. (Nos. NI89/NI92) Tallents House	2·75
4.7.02	68p. (NI93) Tallents House	2·50

Presentation Pack

6.3.01	PO Pack No. 53. 2nd, 1st, E, 65p., 68p. (Nos. NI89/NI92) Tallents House	14·00

2003 (14 Oct)–**17**. As Nos. NI89/NI91 and NI93, and new values, but with white borders. One centre phosphor band (2nd) or two phosphor bands (others). Perf 15×14 (with one elliptical hole in each vertical side).

(a) (Litho Walsall (No. NI98), De La Rue or Enschedé (No. NI95), Cartor (Nos. NI101 and NI103/NI115) or De La Rue (others)).

NI94	**N6**	(2nd) Basalt columns, Giant's Causeway	1·50	1·25
NI95	**N7**	(1st) Aerial view of patchwork fields	2·00	1·50
NI96	**N8**	(E) Linen pattern	3·25	2·25
NI97		40p. Linen pattern (11.5.04)	1·60	1·60
NI98		42p. Linen pattern bluish grey and black (5.4.05)	2·25	2·25
NI99		44p. Linen pattern (28.3.06)	1·40	1·40
NI100	**N9**	68p. Vase pattern from Belleek	2·50	2·50
NI101	**N8**	68p. Linen pattern (29.3.11)	2·00	2·00
NI102	**N9**	72p. Vase pattern from Belleek (28.3.06)	2·75	2·75
NI103	**N8**	87p. Linen pattern (25.4.12)	2·25	2·25
NI104		88p. Linen pattern (27.3.13)	2·25	2·25
NI105		97p. Linen pattern (26.3.14)	2·50	2·50
NI106		£1 Linen pattern (24.3.15)	2·50	2·50
NI107		£1·05 Linen pattern (22.3.16)	2·75	2·75
NI111	**N9**	£1·10 Vase pattern from Belleek (29.3.11)	2·50	2·50
NI113		£1·28 Vase pattern from Belleek (25.4.12)	2·75	2·75
NI114		£1·33 Vase pattern from Belleek (24.3.15)	2·75	2·75

(b) Gravure De La Rue.

NI122	**N6**	(2nd) Basalt columns, Giant's Causeway (20.9.07)	1·50	1·25
NI123	**N7**	(1st) Aerial view of patchwork fields (20.9.07)	2·00	1·50
NI124	**N8**	48p. Linen pattern (27.3.07)	1·25	1·25
NI125		50p. Linen pattern (1.4.08)	1·25	1·25
NI126		56p. Linen pattern (31.3.09)	1·25	1·25
NI127		60p. Linen pattern (30.3.10)	1·40	1·40
NI128	**N9**	78p. Vase pattern from Belleek (27.3.07)	1·60	1·60
NI129		81p. Vase pattern from Belleek (1.4.08)	2·00	2·00
NI130		90p. Vase pattern from Belleek (31.3.09)	2·25	2·25
NI131		97p. Vase pattern from Belleek (30.3.10)	2·50	2·50

PHQ Cards (set of 4) (D27) (Nos. NI94/NI96, NI100) | 1·25 | 10·00

Nos. NI94/NI96 were initially sold at 20p., 28p. and 38p., the latter representing the basic European airmail rate.

The Enschedé printing of No. NI95 comes from £7·66 British Army Uniforms stamp booklet, No. DX40.

Stamps as No. NI95 but self-adhesive were issued on 11 March 2008 in sheets of 20 with *se-tenant* labels. These sheets were printed in lithography by Cartor and perforated 15×14 without the elliptical holes. The labels show either Northern Ireland scenes or personal photographs

Stamps as No. NI95 but self-adhesive were issued again on 17 March 2009 in sheets of 20 with *se-tenant* labels showing Northern Ireland castles. These sheets were printed in lithography by Cartor.

Stamps as Nos. EN30, NI95, S131 and W122 but self-adhesive were issued on 29 September 2008 in sheets of 20 containing five of each design with *se-tenant* labels.

First Day Covers

14.10.03	2nd, 1st, E, 68p. (Nos. NI94/NI96, NI100) Tallents House	3·25
11.5.04	40p. (No. NI97) Tallents House	1·75
5.4.05	42p. (No. NI98) Tallents House	2·25
28.3.06	44p., 72p. (Nos. NI99, NI102) Tallents House	3·50
27.3.07	48p., 78p. (Nos. NI124, NI128) Tallents House	2·50
1.4.08	50p., 81p. (Nos. NI125, NI129) Tallents House	3·00
31.3.09	56p., 90p. (Nos. NI126, NI130) Tallents House	3·50
30.3.10	60p., 97p. (Nos. NI127, NI131) Tallents House	4·00
29.3.11	68p., £1·10 (Nos. NI101, NI111) Tallents House	4·25
25.4.12	87p., £1·28 (Nos. NI103, NI113) Tallents House	5·00
27.3.13	88p. (No. NI104) Tallents House	2·25
26.3.14	97p. (No. NI105) Tallents House	2·25
24.3.15	£1, £1·33 (Nos. NI106, NI114) Tallents House	5·00
22.3.16	£1·05 (No. NI107) Tallents House	2·50

Presentation Pack

14.10.03	PO Pack No. 66. 2nd, 1st, E, 68p. (Nos. NI94/NI96, NI100)	9·00

N10

2008 (11 Mar). Celebrating Northern Ireland. Sheet 123×70 mm. Printed in lithography by De La Rue. Two phosphor bands. Perf 15×14½ (with one elliptical hole in each vertical side) (1st) or 15×14½ (78p).

MSNI152 **N10** (1st) Carrickfergus Castle; (1st) Giant's		
Causeway; 78p. St Patrick; 78p. Queen's Bridge and		
Angel of Thanksgiving sculpture, Belfast	5·50	4·00
First Day Cover (Tallents House)		4·75
Presentation Pack (PO Pack No. 410)	6·50	
PHQ Cards (set of 5) (CGB3)	1·50	7·00

No. **MS**NI152 was on sale at post offices throughout the UK.
The five PHQ cards depict the complete miniature sheet and the four stamps within it.

N11

2008 (29 Sept). 50th Anniversary of the Country Definitives. Sheet 124×70 mm. Containing designs as Nos. NI1, NI3, NI5, S1, S3, S5, W1, W3 and W5 (regional definitives of 1958) but inscribed 1st and printed in gravure by De La Rue on pale cream. Two phosphor bands. Perf 15×14 (with one elliptical hole in each vertical side).

MSNI153 **N11** (1st)×9 as No. W1; As No. S1; As No. W5;		
As No. S5; As No. NI1; As No. W3; As No. S3; As No.		
NI3; As No. NI5	14·00	7·00
First Day Cover (Tallents House)		9·25
Presentation Pack (PO Pack No. 80)	15·00	
PHQ Cards (set of 10)	3·00	12·50

No. **MS**NI153 was on sale at post offices throughout the UK.
The ten PHQ cards show the nine individual stamps and the complete sheet.

N11a   N11b   N11c

2008 (29 Sept). 50th Anniversary of the Country Definitives (2nd issue). As Nos. NI1, NI3 and NI5 (definitives of 1958) but inscribed 1st and printed in lithography by De La Rue. Two phosphor bands. Perf 15×14½ (with one elliptical hole in each vertical side).

NI154	**N11a**	(1st) deep lilac	2·00	1·60
NI155	**N11b**	(1st) deep claret	2·00	1·60
NI156	**N11c**	(1st) green	2·00	1·60

Nos. NI154/NI156 were only issued in the £9·72 The Regional Definitives booklet.

N12 Basalt Columns, Giant's Causeway   **N13** Aerial View of Patchwork Fields

N14 Linen Pattern   **N15** Vase Pattern from Belleek

2017 (21 Mar)–**20**. As previous set but with value indicated in revised typeface. One centre phosphor band (2nd) or two phosphor bands (others). Perf 15×14 (with one elliptical hole in each vertical side).

NI157	**N12**	(2nd) Basalt columns, Giant's Causeway		
		(20.3.18)	1·25	75
NI158	**N13**	(1st) Aerial view of patchwork fields		
		(20.3.18)	1·75	75
NI159	**N14**	£1·17 Linen pattern (21.3.17)	2·75	2·75
NI160		£1·25 Linen pattern (20.3.18)	2·75	2·75
NI161		£1·35 Linen pattern (19.3.19)	2·75	2·75
NI164	**N15**	£1·40 Vase pattern from Belleek		
		(21.3.17)	3·00	3·00
NI165	**N14**	£1·42 Linen pattern (17.3.20)	2·50	2·50
NI166	**N15**	£1·45 Vase pattern from Belleek		
		(20.3.18)	3·25	3·25
NI167		£1·55 Vase pattern from Belleek		
		(19.3.19)	3·25	3·25
NI168		£1·63 Vase pattern from Belleek		
		(17.3.20)	2·75	2·75
NI169	**N14**	£1·70 Linen pattern (23.12.20)	2·40	2·40

N16 Basalt Columns, Giant's Causeway   **N17** Aerial View of Patchwork Fields

N18 Linen Pattern

2022 (11 Aug). As Types **N16**, **N17** and **N18** with barcoded strip at right. Self-adhesive. One centre phosphor band (2nd) or two phosphor bands (others). Die-cut perf 15×14½ (with one elliptical hole in each vertical side).

NI170	**N16**	(2nd) Basalt columns, Giant's Causeway	1·40	1·40
NI171	**N17**	(1st) Aerial view of patchwork fields	2·00	2·00
NI172	**N18**	£1·85 Linen pattern	2·50	2·50

First Day Covers

21.3.17	£1·17, £1·40. (Nos. NI159, NI165) Tallents House	6·00
20.3.18	2nd, 1st, £1·25, £1·45. (Nos. NI157/NI158, NI160, NI166) Tallents House	9·00
13.9.19	2nd, 1st, £1·35, £1·55. (Nos. NI161/NI167) Tallents House	7·00
17.3.20	£1·42, £1·63 (Nos. NI164a, NI168) Tallents House	7·00
23.12.20	£1·70 (No. NI169) Tallents House	3·75
11.8.22	2nd, 1st, £1·85 (Nos. NI170/NI172) Tallents House	7·50

III. Scotland

| S1 |  S2 |  S3 |

1958–67. W **179**. Perf 15×14.

S1	**S1**	3d. deep lilac (18.8.58)	15	15
		p. Two phosphor bands (29.1.63)	7·50	6·00
		pa. One phosphor band	25	25
		pd. One centre phosphor band (9.11.67)	15	15
S2		4d. ultramarine (7.2.66)	20	20
		p. Two phosphor bands	20	20
S3	**S2**	6d. deep claret (29.9.58)	25	25
		p. Two phosphor bands (29.1.63)	25	25
S4		9d. bronze-green (2 phosphor bands) (1.3.67)	40	40
S5	**S3**	1s.3d. green (29.9.58)	40	40
		p. Two phosphor bands (29.1.63)	50	50
S6		1s.6d. grey-blue (2 phosphor bands) (1.3.67)	60	60
S1/S6 *Set of 6*			1·75	1·75

No. S1pa exists with the phosphor band at the left or right of the stamp.

1967–70. No wmk. One centre phosphor band (Nos. S7, S9/S10) or two phosphor bands (others). Perf 15×14.

S7	**S1**	3d. deep lilac (16.5.68)	15	15
S8		4d. deep bright blue (28.11.67)	30	30
S9		4d. olive-sepia (4.9.68)	15	15
S10		4d. bright vermilion (26.2.69)	15	15
S11		5d. royal blue (4.9.68)	25	25
S12	**S2**	9d. bronze-green (28.9.70)	4·00	4·00
S13	**S3**	1s.6d. grey-blue (12.12.68)	1·25	1·25
S7/S13 *Set of 7*			5·00	5·00

First Day Covers

18.8.58	3d. (No. S1)	17·00
29.9.58	6d., 1s.3d. (Nos. S3, S5)	25·00
7.2.66	4d. (No. S2)	7·00
1.3.67	9d., 1s.6d. (Nos. S4, S6)	6·00
4.9.68	4d., 5d. (Nos. S9, S11)	3·00

Presentation Pack

9.12.70	PO Pack No. 23. 6d., 3d., 4d., 5d., 9d. 1s.3d., 1s.6d. (Nos. S3, S5p, S7, S9/S13)	8·00

| S4 |

1971 (7 July)**–93.** Decimal Currency. T **S4**. No wmk.

(a) Photo Harrison. With phosphor bands. Perf 15×14.

S14		2½p. bright magenta (1 centre band)	25	20
S15		3p. ultramarine (2 bands)	25	15
S16		3p. ultramarine (1 centre band) (23.1.74)	15	15
S17		3½p. olive-grey (2 bands) (23.1.74)	20	20
S18		3½p. olive-grey (1 centre band) (6.11.74)	20	20
S19		4½p. grey-blue (2 bands) (6.11.74)	25	25
S20		5p. reddish violet (2 bands)	90	90
S21		5½p. violet (2 bands) (23.1.74)	25	25
S22		5½p. violet (1 centre band) (21.5.75)	20	25
S23		6½p. greenish blue (1 centre band) (14.1.76)	20	25
S24		7p. purple-brown (1 centre band) (18.1.78)	25	25
S25		7½p. chestnut (2 bands)	90	90
S26		8p. rosine (2 bands) (23.1.74)	35	35
S27		8½p. yellow-green (2 bands) (14.1.76)	35	35
S28		9p. deep violet (2 bands) (18.1.78)	35	35
S29		10p. orange-brown (2 bands) (20.10.76)	35	35
S30		10p. orange-brown (1 centre band) (23.7.80)	35	35
S31		10½p. steel-blue (2 bands) (18.1.78)	45	45
S32		11p. scarlet (2 bands) (20.10.76)	40	40

(b) Photo Harrison. On phosphorised paper. Perf 15×14.

S33		12p. yellowish green (23.7.80)	45	45
S34		13½p. purple-brown (23.7.80)	60	60
S35		15p. ultramarine (23.7.80)	50	50

(c) Printed in lithography by John Waddington. One side phosphor band (11½p., 12p., 12½p., 13p.) or phosphorised paper (others). Perf 14.

S36		11½p. drab (8.4.81)	55	55
S37		12p. bright emerald (7.1.86)	1·25	1·25
S38		12½p. light emerald (24.2.82)	45	45
S39		13p. pale chestnut (23.10.84)	75	75
S40		14p. grey-blue (8.4.81)	45	45
S41		15½p. pale violet (24.2.82)	50	50
S42		16p. drab (27.4.83)	50	50
S43		17p. grey-blue (23.10.84)	1·10	1·10
S44		18p. deep violet (8.4.81)	70	70
S45		19½p. olive-grey (24.2.82)	1·25	1·25
S46		20½p. ultramarine (27.4.83)	2·25	2·25
S47		22p. blue (8.4.81)	75	75
S48		22p. yellow-green (23.10.84)	2·25	2·25
S49		26p. rosine (24.2.82)	70	70
S50		28p. deep violet-blue (27.4.83)	70	70
S51		31p. bright purple (23.10.84)	1·50	1·50

(d) Litho Questa (Type II). Perf 15×14.

S52	**S4**	12p. bright emerald (1 side band) (29.4.86)	1·25	1·25
S53		13p. pale chestnut (1 side band) (4.11.86)	70	70
S54		14p. deep blue (1 centre band) (8.11.88)	45	45
S55		14p. deep blue (1 side band) (21.3.89)	50	50
S56		15p. bright blue (1 centre band) (28.11.89)	50	50
S57		17p. grey-blue (phosphorised paper) (29.4.86)	2·40	2·40
S58		17p. deep blue (1 centre band) (4.12.90)	70	70
S59		18p. deep olive-grey (phosphorised paper) (6.1.87)	70	70
S60		18p. bright green (1 centre band) (3.12.91)	60	60
		a. Perf 14 (26.9.92*)	1·00	1·00
S61		18p. bright green (1 side band) (10.8.93)	1·40	1·40
S62		19p. bright orange-red (phosphorised paper) (8.11.88)	50	50
S63		19p. bright orange-red (2 bands) (21.3.89)	1·40	1·40
S64		20p. brownish black (phosphorised paper) (28.11.89)	70	70
S65		22p. yellow-green (phosphorised paper) (27.1.87)	1·10	1·10
S66		22p. bright orange-red (phosphorised paper) (4.12.90)	60	60
S67		23p. bright green (phosphorised paper) (8.11.88)	80	80
S68		23p. bright green (2 bands) (21.3.89)	9·00	9·00
S69		24p. Indian red (phosphorised paper) (28.11.89)	1·00	1·00
S70		24p. chestnut (phosphorised paper) (3.12.91)	75	75
		a. Perf 14 (10.92*)	6·00	6·00
S71		24p. chestnut (2 bands) (10.8.93)	1·40	1·40
S72		26p. rosine (phosphorised paper) (27.1.87)	2·25	2·25
S73		26p. drab (phosphorised paper) (4.12.90)	1·00	1·00
S74		28p. deep violet-blue (phosphorised paper) (27.1.87)	1·00	1·00
S75		28p. deep bluish grey (phosphorised paper) (3.12.91)	1·00	1·00
		a. Perf 14 (18.2.93*)	9·00	9·00
S76		31p. bright purple (phosphorised paper) (29.4.86)	1·50	1·50
S77		32p. greenish blue (phosphorised paper) (8.11.88)	1·00	1·00
S78		34p. deep bluish grey (phosphorised paper) (28.11.89)	1·25	1·75
S79		37p. rosine (phosphorised paper) (4.12.90)	1·25	1·25
S80		39p. bright mauve (phosphorised paper) (3.12.91)	1·50	1·50
		a. Perf 14 (11.92)	12·50	12·50

* Earliest known date of issue.

Nos. S55, S61, S63, S68 and S71 only come from booklets.

First Day Covers

7.7.71	2½p., 3p., 5p., 7½p. (Nos. S14/S15, S20, S25)	1·50
23.1.74	3p., 3½p., 5½p., 8p. (Nos. S16/S17, S21, S26)	1·25
6.11.74	4½p. (No. S19)	1·00
14.1.76	6½p., 8½p. (Nos. S23, S27)	1·00
20.10.76	10p., 11p. (Nos. S29, S32)	1·00
18.1.78	7p., 9p., 10½p. (Nos. S24, S28, S31)	1·00
23.7.80	12p., 13½p., 15p. (Nos. S33/S35)	1·50
8.4.81	11½p., 14p., 18p., 22p. (Nos. S36, S40, S44, S47)	1·50
24.2.82	12½p., 15½p., 19½p., 26p. (Nos. S38, S41, S45, S49)	1·75
27.4.83	16p., 20½p., 28p. (Nos. S42, S46, S50)	2·00

23.10.84	13p., 17p., 22p., 31p. (Nos. S39, S43, S48, S51)	2·00	
7.1.86	12p. (No. S37)	1·00	
6.1.87	18p. (No. S59)	1·00	
8.11.88	14p., 19p., 23p., 32p. (Nos. S54, S62, S67, S77)	2·00	
28.11.89	15p., 20p., 24p., 34p. (Nos. S56, S64, S69, S78)	2·50	
4.12.90	17p., 22p., 26p., 37p. (Nos. S58, S66, S73, S79)	2·50	
3.12.91	18p., 24p., 28p., 39p. (Nos. S60, S70, S75, S80)	2·50	

Presentation Packs

7.7.71	PO Pack No. 27. 2½p., 3p., 5p., 7½p. (Nos. S14/S15, S20, S25)	2·00
29.5.74	PO Pack No. 62. 3p., 3½p., 5½p., 8p. (Nos. S16, S17 or S18, S21 or S22, S26). 4½p. (No. S19) added later	2·00
20.10.76	PO Pack No. 85. 6½p., 8½p., 10p., 11p. (Nos. S23, S27, S29, S32)	1·50
28.10.81	PO Pack No. 129b. 7p., 9p., 10½p., 12p., 13½p., 15p., 11½p., 14p., 18p., 22p. (Nos. S24, S28, S31, S33/S36, S40, S44, S47)	6·00
3.8.83	PO Pack No. 2. 10p., 12½p., 16p., 20½p., 26p., 28p., (Nos. S30, S38, S42, S46, S49/S50)	14·00
23.10.84	PO Pack No. 6. 10p., 13p., 16p., 17p., 22p., 26p., 28p., 31p., (Nos. S30, S39, S42/S43, S48/S51)	12·00
3.3.87	PO Pack No. 10. 12p., 13p., 17p. (grey-blue), 18p., 22p., 26p., 28p., 31p. (Nos. S52/S53, S57, S59, S65, S72, S74, S76)	15·00

Presentation Packs containing stamps of Northern Ireland, Scotland and Wales are listed after those for Northern Ireland.

1993 (7 Dec)–**98**.
(a) Litho Questa. Perf 15×14 (with one elliptical hole in each vert side).

S81	**S4**	19p. bistre (1 centre band)	70	70
S82		19p. bistre (1 band at right) (25.4.95)	2·00	2·00
S83		20p. bright green (1 centre band) (23.7.96)	1·25	1·25
S84		25p. red (2 bands)	80	80
S85		26p. red-brown (2 bands) (23.7.96)	1·40	1·40
S86		30p. deep olive-grey (2 bands)	1·25	1·25
S87		37p. bright mauve (2 bands) (23.7.96)	1·75	1·75
S88		41p. grey-brown (2 bands)	1·25	1·25
S89		63p. light emerald (2 bands) (23.7.96)	2·50	2·50

(b) Gravure Walsall (20p., 26p. (No. S91a), 63p.), Harrison or Walsall (26p. (No. S91), 37p.). Perf 14 (No. S90a) or 15×14 (others) (both with one elliptical hole in each vertical side).

S90	**S4**	20p. bright green (1 centre band) (1.7.97)	1·00	1·00
S90a		20p. bright green (1 side band at right) (13.10.98)	3·00	3·00
S91		26p. chestnut (2 bands) (1.7.97)	1·40	1·40
		a. Perf 14 (13.10.98)	3·00	3·00
S92		37p. bright mauve (2 bands) (1.7.97)	1·60	1·60
S93		63p. light emerald (2 bands) (1.7.97)	3·50	3·50

Nos. S82, S90a and S91a only come from booklets. The Harrison printings of Nos. S91/S92 come from booklet pane No. NI81l.

First Day Covers

7.12.93	19p., 25p., 30p., 41p. (Nos. S81, S84, S86, S88)	3·50
23.7.96	20p. 26p., 37p., 63p. (Nos. S83, S85, S87, S89)	4·00

For Presentation Pack containing stamps of Northern Ireland, Scotland and Wales see after No. NI87 of Northern Ireland.

S5 Saltire   **S6** Lion
Rampant of
Scotland

S7 Thistle   **S8** Tartan

1999 (8 June)–**2002**. Printed in gravure by De La Rue (68p.), De La Rue, Questa or Walsall (2nd, 1st) or Walsall (others). One centre phosphor band (2nd) or two phosphor bands (others). Perf 15×14 (with one elliptical hole in each vertical side).

S94	**S5**	(2nd) Saltire	1·50	1·25
S95	**S6**	(1st) Lion Rampant of Scotland	2·00	1·50
S96	**S7**	(E) Thistle	2·25	2·25
S97	**S8**	64p. Tartan	5·50	5·50

S98		65p. Tartan (25.4.00)	2·00	2·00
S99		68p. Tartan (4.7.02)	2·25	2·25
PHQ Cards (set of 4) (D12) (Nos. S94/S97)			1·25	10·00

Nos. S94, S95 and S96 were initially sold at 19p., 26p. and 30p., the latter representing the basic European airmail rate.
For combined presentation pack for all four Regions, see under England.

First Day Covers

8.6.99	2nd, 1st, E, 64p. (Nos. S94/S97) Tallents House	3·50
25.4.00	65p. (No. S98) Tallents House	2·50
4.7.02	68p. (No. S99) Tallents House	2·00

Presentation Packs

08.06.99	PO Pack No. 45. 2nd, 1st, E, 64p. (Nos. S94/S97)	9·50
25.04.00	PO Pack No. 50. 65p. (No. S98)	10·00
12.03.02	PO Pack No. 55. 2nd, 1st, E, 65p. (Nos. S94/S96, S98)	15·00

S9

2000 (15 Feb). T **S4** redrawn with '1st' face value as T **S9**. Two phosphor bands. Perf 14 (with one elliptical hole in each vertical side).

S108	**S9**	(1st) bright orange-red	1·60	1·60

No. S108 was only issued in £7·50 stamp booklet (No. DX24).

2003 (14 Oct)–**17**. As Nos. S94/S96 and S99, and new values, but with white borders. One centre phosphor band (2nd) or two phosphor bands (others). Perf 15×14 (with one elliptical hole in each vertical side).
(a) Gravure Walsall or De La Rue (42p.) or De La Rue (others).

S109	**S5**	(2nd) Saltire	1·50	1·25
S110	**S6**	(1st) Lion Rampant of Scotland	2·00	1·50
S111	**S7**	(E) Thistle	3·25	2·10
S112		40p. Thistle (11.5.04)	1·40	1·40
S113		42p. Thistle (5.4.05)	1·75	1·75
S114		44p. Thistle (28.3.06)	1·40	1·40
S115		48p. Thistle (27.3.07)	1·25	1·25
S116		50p. Thistle (1.4.08)	1·25	1·25
S117		56p. Thistle (31.3.09)	1·40	1·40
S118		60p. Thistle (30.3.10)	1·50	1·50
S119	**S8**	68p. Tartan	1·60	1·60
S120		72p. Tartan (28.3.06)	1·75	1·75
S121		78p. Tartan (27.3.07)	1·75	1·75
S122		81p. Tartan (1.4.08)	2·00	2·00
S123		90p. Tartan (31.3.09)	2·25	2·25
S124		97p. Tartan (30.3.10)	2·40	2·40

(b) Litho Enschedé, De La Rue or ISP Cartor (1st) or ISP Cartor (others). Queen's head in grey (Nos. S130a and S131a) or silver (others).

S130	**S5**	(2nd) Saltire (27.6.12)	1·50	1·25
		a. Saltire (Queen's head grey) (5.16)	2·00	1·50
S131	**S6**	(1st) Lion Rampant of Scotland (20.9.07)	2·00	1·50
		a. Lion Rampant of Scotland (Queen's head grey) (19.5.16)	2·50	2·00
S132	**S7**	68p. Thistle (29.3.11)	1·90	1·90
S133		87p Thistle (25.4.12)	2·25	2·25
S134		88p. Thistle (27.3.13)	2·25	2·25
S135		97p. Thistle (26.3.14)	2·40	2·40
S136		£1 Thistle (24.3.15)	2·40	2·40
S137		£1·05 Thistle (22.3.16)	2·60	2·60
S138	**S8**	£1·10 Tartan (29.3.11)	2·40	2·40
S143		£1·28 Tartan (25.4.12)	2·60	2·60
S144		£1·33 Tartan (24.3.15)	2·75	2·75
PHQ Cards (set of 4) (D25) (Nos. S109/S111, S119)			1·25	6·50

Nos. S109/S111 were initially sold at 20p., 28p. and 38p., the latter representing the basic European airmail rate.
No. S131 was issued in £7·66 British Army Uniforms stamp booklet, No. DX40, printed by Enschedé and also on 27 June 2012 in sheets.
Stamps as No. S131 but self-adhesive were issued on 30 November 2007 in sheets of 20 with se-tenant labels. Theses sheets were printed by Cartor in lithography, and perforated 15×14 without elliptical holes. The labels show either Scottish scenes or personal photographs.
Numbers have be left for possible additions to this definitive series.

First Day Covers

14.10.03	2nd, 1st, E, 68p. (Nos. S109/S111, S119) Tallents House	2·00
11.5.04	40p. (No. S112) Tallents House	1·50
5.4.05	42p. (No. S113) Tallents House	1·75
28.3.06	44p., 72p. (Nos. S114, S120) Tallents House	3·00
27.3.07	48p., 78p. (Nos. S115, S121) Tallents House	3·00
1.4.08	50p., 81p. (S116, S122) Tallents House	3·25
31.3.09	56p., 90p. (Nos. S117, S123) Tallents House	3·50

30.3.10	60p., 97p. (Nos. S118, S124) Tallents House	3·75
29.3.11	68p., £1·10 (Nos. S132, S138) Tallents House	4·25
25.4.12	87p., £1·28 (Nos. S133, S143) Tallents House	4·50
27.3.13	88p. (No. S134) Tallents House	2·00
26.3.14	97p. (No. S135) Tallents House	2·25
24.3.15	£1, £1·33 (Nos. S136, S144) Tallents House	5·25
22.3.16	£1·05 (No. S137) Tallents House	2·50

Presentation Pack

14.10.03	PO Pack No. 64. 2nd, 1st, E, 68p. (Nos. S109/S111, S119)	9·00

S9a

2004 (5 Oct). Opening of New Scottish Parliament. Sheet 123×70 mm. Printed in gravure by De La Rue. One centre phosphor band (2nd) or two phosphor bands (others). Perf 15×14 (with one elliptical hole on each vertical side).

MSS152 **S9a** Nos. S109, S110×2 and S112×2	6·00	5·00
First Day Cover (Tallents House)		5·50

S10

2006 (30 Nov). Celebrating Scotland. Sheet 124×71 mm. Printed in gravure by De La Rue. Two phosphor bands. Perf 15×14 (with one elliptical hole in each vertical side) (1st) or 14½×14 (72p).

MSS153 **S10** (1st) As No. S110; (1st) Saltire; 72p. St Andrew; 72p. Edinburgh Castle	5·50	4·00
First Day Cover (Tallents House)		4·25
Presentation Pack (PO Pack No. M14)	6·50	
PHQ Cards (set of 5) (CGB1)	1·50	4·00

No. **MS**S153 was on sale at post offices throughout the UK.

Stamps as the 1st class Saltire stamp within No. **MS**S153 but self-adhesive were issued on 30 November 2009 in sheets of 20 with *se-tenant* labels showing Scottish Castles. These sheets were printed in lithography by Cartor and sold for £8·35 each.

The five PHQ cards depict the complete miniature sheet and the four stamps within it.

S10a	S10b	S10c

2008 (29 Sept). 50th Anniversary of the Country Definitives. As Nos. S1, S3 and S5 (definitive of 1958) but inscribed 1st and printed in lithography by De La Rue. Two phosphor bands. Perf 15×14½ (with one elliptical hole in each vertical side).

S154	**S10a**	(1st) deep lilac	2·00	1·60
S155	**S10b**	(1st) deep claret	2·00	1·60
S156	**S10c**	(1st) green	2·00	1·60

Nos. S154/S156 come from £9·72 The Regional Definitives stamp booklets.

S11

2009 (22 Jan). 250th Birth Anniversary of Robert Burns (poet). Sheet 145×74 mm. Printed in gravure by Enschedé. One centre phosphor band (2nd) or two phosphor bands (others). Perf 14½ (size 34×34 mm) or 15×14 (with one elliptical hole in each vertical side) (others).

MSS157 **S11** (2nd) No. S109; (1st) 'A Man's a Man for a' that' and Burns ploughing (detail) (James Sargent Storer) (34×34 mm); (1st) No. S110; (1st) Portrait of Burns (Alexander Nasmyth) (34×34 mm); 50p. No. S116; 81p. S122	8·00	5·00
First Day Cover (Tallents House)		5·50
Presentation Pack (PO Pack No. 422)	9·50	
PHQ Cards (set of 3) (319)	90	7·00

No. **MS**S157 was on sale at post offices throughout the UK.

The three PHQ cards show the two 34×34 mm Robert Burns stamps and the complete miniature sheet.

S12 Saltire

2013 (9 May)–**14**. Scotland Flag. Printed in lithography by Cartor or Enschedé. Two phosphor bands. Perf 14½×14 (with one elliptical hole in each vertical side).

S158	**S12**	(1st) Saltire (Queen's head silver)	4·75	4·75
		a. Saltire (Queen's head grey)		
		(20.2.14)	3·50	3·50

No. S158 was only issued in £11·11 Football Heroes and £13·97 Classic Locomotives booklets, Nos. DY7 and DY9.

No. S158a was issued in £13·97 Classic Locomotives and £16·49 Centenary of the First World War (3rd issue) booklets.

S13 Saltire	S14 Lion Rampant of Scotland

S15 Thistle	S16 Tartan

2017 (21 Mar)–**2020**. As previous set but with value indicated in revised typeface. One centre phosphor band (2nd) or two phosphor bands (others). Perf 15×14 (with one elliptical hole in each vertical side).

S159	**S13**	(2nd) Saltire (20.3.18)	1·25	75
S160	**S14**	(1st) Lion of Scotland (20.3.18)	1·75	75
S161	**S15**	£1·17 Thistle (21.3.17)	2·75	2·75
S162		£1·25 Thistle (20.3.18)	2·75	2·75
S163		£1·35 Thistle (19.3.19)	2·75	2·75
S166	**S16**	£1·40 Tartan (21.3.17)	3·00	3·00
S167	**S15**	£1·42 Thistle (17.3.20)	2·50	2·50
S168	**S16**	£1·45 Tartan (20.3.18)	3·25	3·25
S169		£1·55 Tartan (19.3.19)	3·25	3·25
S170		£1·63 Tartan (17.3.20)	2·75	2·75
S171		£1·70 Thistle (23.12.20)	2·40	2·40

S17

2020 (6 Apr). 700th Anniversary of the Declaration of Arbroath. Sheet 133×70 mm. Printed in lithography by ISP Cartor. One centre phosphor band (2nd) or two phosphor bands (others). Perf 15×14 (with one elliptical hole in each vertical side).

MSS180 **S17** Nos. S159/S160, S167 and S170		7·00
First Day Cover (Tallents House)		9·00

S18 Saltire  **S19** Lion Rampant of Scotland

S20 Thistle

2022 (11 Aug). As Types **S18**, **S19** and **S20** with barcoded strip at right. Self-adhesive. One centre phosphor band (2nd) or two phosphor bands (others). Die-cut perf 15×14½ (with one elliptical hole in each vertical side).

S181	**S18**	(2nd) Saltire	1·40	1·40
S182	**S19**	(1st) Lion of Scotland	2·00	2·00
S183	**S20**	£1·85 Thistle	2·50	2·50

First Day Covers

21.3.17	£1·17, £1·40 (Nos. S161, S166) Tallents House	5·00
20.3.18	2nd, 1st, £1·25, £1·45 (S159/S160, S162, S168) Tallents House	9·00
19.3.19	£1·35, £1·55 (Nos. S163/S169) Tallents House	7·00
17.3.20	£1·42, £1·63 (Nos. S167, S170) Tallents House	7·00
23.12.20	£1·70 (No. S171) Tallents House	3·75
11.8.22	2nd, 1st, £1·85 (Nos. S181/S183) Tallents House	7·50

IV. Wales

W1 W2 W3

1958–67. W **179**. Perf 15×14.

W1	**W1**	3d. deep lilac (18.8.58)	15	15
		p. One centre phosphor band (16.5.67)	20	15
W2		4d. ultramarine (7.2.66)	20	20
		p. Two phosphor bands (10.67)	20	20
W3	**W2**	6d. deep claret (29.9.58)	35	35
W4		9d. bronze-green (2 phosphor bands) (1.3.67)	35	35
W5	**W3**	1s.3d. green (29.9.58)	40	40
W6		1s.6d. grey-blue (2 phosphor bands) (1.3.67)	40	40

1967–69. One centre phosphor band (Nos. W7, W9/W10) or two phosphor bands (others). No wmk. Perf 15×14.

W7	**W1**	3d. deep lilac (6.12.67)	15	15
W8		4d. ultramarine (21.6.68)	15	15
W9		4d. olive-sepia (4.9.68)	15	15
W10		4d. bright vermilion (26.2.69)	15	15
W11		5d. royal blue (4.9.68)	15	15
W12	**W3**	1s.6d. grey-blue (1.8.69)	2·75	2·75

First Day Covers

18.8.58	3d. (W1)	12·00
29.9.58	6d., 1s.3d. (W3, W5)	25·00
7.2.66	4d. (W2)	7·00
1.3.67	9d., 1s.6d. (W4, W6)	4·00
4.9.68	4d., 5d. (Nos. W9, W11)	3·00

Presentation Pack

9.12.70	PO Pack No. 24. 3d., 4d., 5d., 9d., 1s.6d. (Nos. W4, W6/W7, W9/W11)	5·50

W4 With 'p'  **W5** Without 'p'

1971–92. Decimal Currency. T **W4**.

(a) Gravure Harrison. With phosphor bands. Perf 15×14.

W13	2½p. bright magenta (1 centre band)	20	20
W14	3p. ultramarine (2 bands)	25	20
W15	3p. ultramarine (1 centre band) (23.1.74)	25	25
W16	3½p. olive-grey (2 bands) (23.1.74)	20	30
W17	3½p. olive-grey (1 centre band) (6.11.74)	20	20
W18	4½p. grey-blue (2 bands) (6.11.74)	25	25
W19	5p. reddish violet (2 bands)	80	80
W20	5½p. violet (2 bands) (23.1.74)	25	25
W21	5½p. violet (1 centre band) (21.5.75)	25	25
W22	6½p. greenish blue (1 centre band) (14.1.76)	20	25
W23	7p. purple-brown (1 centre band) (18.1.78)	25	25
W24	7½p. chestnut (2 bands)	1·25	1·25
W25	8p. rosine (2 bands) (23.1.74)	30	30
W26	8½p. yellow-green (2 bands) (14.1.76)	35	35
W27	9p. deep violet (2 bands) (18.1.78)	35	35
W28	10p. orange-brown (2 bands) (20.10.76)	35	35
W29	10p. orange-brown (1 centre band) (23.7.80)	35	35
W30	10½p. steel-blue (2 bands) (18.1.78)	45	45
W31	11p. scarlet (2 bands) (20.10.76)	40	40

(b) Gravure Harrison. On phosphorised paper. Perf 15×14.

W32	12p. yellowish green (23.7.80)	45	45
W33	13½p. purple-brown (23.7.80)	55	55
W34	15p. ultramarine (23.7.80)	55	55

(c) Litho Questa. Perf 14 (11½p., 12½p., 14p. (No. W39), 15½p., 16p., 18p. (No. W46), 19½p., 20½p., 22p. (No. W54), 26p. (No. W61), 28p. (No. W63)) or 15×14 (others).

W35	11½p. drab (1 side band) (8.4.81)	70	70
W36	12p. bright emerald (1 side band) (7.1.86)	1·00	1·00
W37	12½p. light emerald (1 side band) (24.2.82)	50	50
	a. Perf 15×14 (10.1.84)	2·75	2·75
W38	13p. pale chestnut (1 side band) (23.10.84)	50	50
W39	14p. grey-blue (phosphorised paper) (8.4.81)	55	55
W40	14p. deep blue (1 centre band) (8.11.88)	55	55
W41	15p. bright blue (1 centre band) (28.11.89)	60	60
W42	15½p. pale violet (phosphorised paper) (24.2.82)	70	70
W43	16p. drab (phosphorised paper) (27.4.83)	1·10	1·10
	a. Perf 15×14 (10.1.84)	1·10	1·10
W44	17p. grey-blue (phosphorised paper) (23.10.84)	80	80
W45	17p. deep blue (1 centre band) (4.12.90)	60	60
W46	18p. deep violet (8.4.81)	80	80
W47	18p. deep olive-grey (phosphorised paper) (6.1.87)	80	80
W48	18p. bright green (1 centre band) (3.12.91)	55	55
	b. Perf 14 (12.1.93*)	7·50	7·50
W49	18p. bright green (1 side band) (25.2.92)	1·75	1·75
W50	19p. bright orange-red (phosphorised paper) (8.11.88)	70	70
W52	20p. brownish black (phosphorised paper) (28.11.89)	70	70
W51	19½p. olive-grey (phosphorised paper) (24.2.82)	1·25	1·25
W53	20½p. ultramarine (phosphorised paper) (27.4.83)	2·50	2·50

W54		22p. blue (phosphorised paper) (8.4.81)	80	80
W55		22p. yellow-green (phosphorised paper) (23.10.84)	80	80
W56		22p. bright orange-red (phosphorised paper) (4.12.90)	80	80
W57		23p. bright green (phosphorised paper) (8.11.88)	80	80
W58		24p. Indian red (phosphorised paper) (28.11.89)	90	90
W59		24p. chestnut (phosphorised paper) (3.12.91)	70	70
		b. Perf 14 (14.9.92*)	6·00	6·00
W60		24p. chestnut (2 bands) (25.2.92)	90	90
W61		26p. rosine (phosphorised paper) (24.2.82)	80	80
		a. Perf 15×14 (27.1.87)	3·00	3·00
W62		26p. drab (phosphorised paper) (4.12.90)	1·25	1·25
W63		28p. deep violet-blue (phosphorised paper) (27.4.83)	90	90
		a. Perf 15×14 (27.1.87)	1·25	1·25
W64		28p. deep bluish grey (phosphorised paper) (3.12.91)	80	80
W65		31p. bright purple (phosphorised paper) (23.10.84)	1·00	1·00
W66		32p. greenish blue (phosphorised paper) (8.11.88)	1·25	1·25
W67		34p. deep bluish grey (phosphorised paper) (28.11.89)	1·25	1·25
W68		37p. rosine (phosphorised paper) (4.12.90)	1·25	1·25
W69		39p. bright mauve (phosphorised paper) (3.12.91)	1·25	1·25

* Earliest known date of issue.

Nos. W49 and W60 were only issued in stamp booklets. The former exists with the phosphor band at left or right of the stamp.

First Day Covers

7.7.71	2½p., 3p., 5p., 7½p., (Nos. W13/W14, W19, W24)	2·00
23.1.74	3p., 3½p., 5½p., 8p. (Nos. W15/W16, W20, W25)	1·50
6.11.74	4½p. (No. W18)	80
14.1.76	6½p., 8½p. (Nos. W22, W26)	80
20.10.76	10p., 11p. (Nos. W28, W31)	80
18.1.78	7p., 9p., 10½p. (Nos. W23, W27, W30)	1·00
23.7.80	12p., 13½p., 15p. (Nos. W32/W34)	2·00
8.4.81	11½p., 14p., 18p., 22p. (Nos. W35, W39, W46, W54)	2·00
24.2.82	12½p., 15½p., 19½p., 26p. (Nos. W37, W42, W51, W61)	2·50
27.4.83	16p., 20½p., 28p. (Nos. W43, W53, W63)	2·50
23.10.84	13p., 17p., 22p., 31p. (Nos. W38, W44, W55, W65)	3·00
7.1.86	12p. (No. W36)	1·00
6.1.87	18p. (No. W47)	1·00
8.11.88	14p., 19p., 23p., 32p. (Nos. W40, W50, W57, W66)	3·00
28.11.89	15p., 20p., 24p., 34p. (Nos. W41, W52, W58, W67)	4·00
4.12.90	17p., 22p., 26p., 37p (Nos. W45, W56, W62, W68)	4·00
3.12.91	18p., 24p., 28p., 39p. (Nos. W48, W59, W64, W69)	4·25

Presentation Packs

7.7.71	PO Pack No. 28. 2½p., 3p., 5p., 7½p. (Nos. W13/W14, W19, W24)	2·00
29.5.74	PO Pack No. 63. 3p., 3½p., 5½p., 8p. (Nos. W15, W16, W20, W25). 4½p. (No. W18) added later	2·25
20.10.76	PO Pack No. 86. 6½p., 8½p., 10p., 11p. (Nos. W22, W26, W28, W31)	1·40
28.10.81	PO Pack No. 129c. 7p., 9p., 10½p., 11½p., 12p., 13½p., 14p., 15p., 18p., 22p. blue (Nos. W23, W27, W30, W32/W35, W39, W46, W54)	6·00
3.8.83	PO Pack No. 3. 10p., 12½p., 16p., 20½p., 26p., 28p. (Nos. W29, W37, W43, W53, W61, W63)	14·00
23.10.84	PO Pack No. 7. 10p., 13p., 16p., 17p., 22p., 26p., 28p., 31p. (Nos. W29, W38, W43a, W44, W55, W61, W63, W65)	12·00
3.3.87	PO Pack No. 11. 12p., 13p., 17p., 18p., 22p., 26p., 28p., 31p. (Nos. W36, W38, W44, W47, W55, W61a, W63a, W65)	15·00

1993 (7 Dec)–**96**. Printed in lithography by Questa. Perf 15×14 (with one elliptical hole in each vertical side).

W70	**W4**	19p. bistre (1 centre band)	60	60
W71		19p. bistre (1 band at right) (25.4.95)	1·90	1·90
W72		20p. bright green (1 centre band) (23.7.96)	1·00	1·00
W73		25p. red (2 bands)	75	75
W74		26p. red-brown (2 bands) (23.7.96)	1·20	1·20
W75		30p. deep olive-grey (2 bands)	80	80
W76		37p. bright mauve (2 bands) (23.7.96)	1·60	1·60
W77		41p. grey-brown (2 bands)	1·40	1·40
W78		63p. light emerald (2 bands) (23.7.96)	3·50	3·50

No. W71 only comes from booklets.

For combined presentation packs for all three Regions see under Northern Ireland.

First Day Covers

7.12.93	19p., 25p., 30p., 41p. (Nos. W70, W73, W75, W77)	3·75
23.7.96	20p., 26p., 37p., 63p. (Nos. W72, W74, W76, W78)	6·00

1997 (1 July)–**98**. Printed in photogravure by Walsall (20p., 26p. (No. W80), 63p.), Harrison or Walsall (26p., (No. W80), 37p.). Perf 14 (No. W79a) or 15×14 (others) (both with one elliptical hole in each vertical side).

W79	**W5**	20p. bright green (1 centre band)	80	80
W79a		20p. bright green (1 side band at right) (13.10.98)	3·25	3·25
W80		26p. chestnut (2 bands)	1·40	1·40
		a. Perf 14 (13.10.98)	3·25	3·25
W81		37p. bright mauve (2 bands)	1·75	1·75
W82		63p. light emerald (2 bands)	3·50	3·50

Presentation Pack (PO Pack No. 39) (Nos. W79 and W80/W82) — 12·00

Nos. W79a and W80a were only issued in booklets.

First Day Cover

1.7.97	20p., 26p., 37p., 63p. (Nos. W79, W80/W82)	6·00

Presentation Pack

1.7.97	PO Pack No. 39. 20p., 26p., 37p., 63p. (Nos. W79, W80/W82)	12·00

W6 Leek    **W7** Welsh Dragon

W8 Daffodil    **W9** Prince of Wales' Feathers

1999 (8 June)–**2002**. Printed in gravure by De La Rue (68p.), Walsall or De La Rue (1st), (2nd), (No. W83) or Walsall (others). One phosphor band (2nd) or two phosphor bands (others). Perf 14 (No. W83a) or 15×14 (others) (both with one elliptical hole in each vertical side).

W83	**W6**	(2nd) Leek (1 centre band)	1·50	1·10
W83a		(2nd) Leek (1 band at right) (Perf 14) (18.9.2000)	2·25	2·25
W84	**W7**	(1st) Welsh dragon	2·00	1·75
W85	**W8**	(E) Daffodil	3·75	2·10
W86	**W9**	64p. Prince of Wales' Feathers	5·50	5·50
W87		65p. Prince of Wales' Feathers (25.4.2000)	2·50	2·50
W88		68p. Prince of Wales' Feathers (4.7.2002)	2·25	2·25

PHQ Cards (set of 4) (D13) (Nos. W83, W84/W86) — 1·25 — 10·00

Nos. W83, W84 and W85 were initially sold at 19p., 26p. and 30p., the latter representing the basic European airmail rate.

No. W83a comes from the £7 Treasury of Trees booklet (No. DX26).

For combined presentation pack for all four Regions, see under England.

First Day Covers

8.6.99	2nd (centre band), 1st, E, 64p. (Nos. W83, W84/W86) Tallents House	3·00
25.4.00	65p. (No. W87) Tallents House	3·00
4.7.02	68p. (Nos. W88) Tallents House	2·50

Presentation Packs

08.06.99	PO Pack No. 46. 2nd, 1st E, 64p. (Nos. W83, W84/W86)	9·00
25.04.00	PO Pack No. 51. 65p. (No. W87)	10·00
12.03.02	PO Pack No. 56. 2nd, 1st, E. 65p. (Nos. W83, W84/W85, W87)	16·00

W10

2000 (15 Feb). T **W4** redrawn with 1af/st face value as T **W10**. Two phosphor bands. Perf 14 (with one elliptical hole in each vertical side).

W97	**W10**	(1st) bright orange-red	1·60	1·60

No. W97 was only issued in £7·50 Special by Design stamp booklets.

2003 (14 Oct)–**17**. As Nos. W83, W84/W85 and W88, but with white borders. One centre phosphor band (2nd) or two phosphor bands (others). Perf 15×14 (with one elliptical hole in each vertical side).
(a) (Gravure Walsall or De La Rue (42p.) or De La Rue (others)).

W98	**W6**	(2nd) Leek	1·50	1·10
W99	**W7**	(1st) Welsh Dragon	2·00	1·60
W100	**W8**	(E) Daffodil	3·25	2·25
W101		40p. Daffodil (11.5.04)	1·40	1·40
W102		42p. Daffodil (5.4.05)	2·00	2·00
W103		44p. Daffodil (28.3.06)	1·60	1·60
W104		48p. Daffodil (27.3.07)	1·10	1·10
W105		50p. Daffodil (1.4.08)	1·40	1·40
W106		56p. Daffodil (31.3.09)	1·50	1·50
W107		60p. Daffodil (30.3.10)	1·70	1·70
W108	**W9**	68p. Prince of Wales' Feathers	1·60	1·60
W109		72p. Prince of Wales' Feathers (28.3.06)	1·60	1·60
W110		78p. Prince of Wales' Feathers (27.3.07)	2·00	2·00
W111		81p. Prince of Wales' Feathers (1.4.08)	2·25	2·25
W112		90p. Prince of Wales' Feathers (31.3.09)	2·40	2·40
W113		97p. Prince of Wales' Feathers (30.3.10)	2·50	2·50

(b) (Litho Enschedé, De La Rue or ISP Cartor (1st) or ISP Cartor (others)).

W121	**W6**	(2nd) Leek (1.13)	1·75	1·40
W122	**W7**	(1st) Welsh Dragon (20.9.07)	2·00	1·60
W123	**W8**	68p. Daffodil (29.3.11)	1·75	1·75
W124		87p Daffodil (25.4.12)	2·25	2·25
W125		88p. Daffodil (27.3.13)	2·25	2·25
W126		97p. Daffodil (26.3.14)	2·50	2·50
W127		£1 Daffodil (24.3.15)	2·50	2·50
W128		£1·05 Daffodil (22.3.16)	2·75	2·75
W129	**W9**	£1·10 Prince of Wales' Feathers (29.3.11)	2·50	2·50
W134		£1·28 Prince of Wales' Feathers (25.4.12)	2·75	2·75
W135		£1·33 Prince of Wales' Feathers (24.3.15)	2·75	2·75
PHQ Cards (set of 4) (D26) (Nos. W98/W100, W108)				5·00

The Walsall printing of No. W102 was issued on 5 April 2005 and the De La Rue on 24 May 2005.

Nos. W98/W100 were initially sold at 20p., 28p. and 38p., the latter representing the basic European airmail rate.

No. W122 was first issued in the £7·66 British Army Uniforms stamp booklet, No. DX40, and No. **MS**W125. It was issued in sheets in January 2013.

Stamps as W122 but self-adhesive were issued on 1 March 2007 in sheets of 20 with *se-tenant* labels. These sheets were printed in lithography and perforated 15×14 without elliptical holes. The labels show either Welsh scenes or personal photographs.

Stamps as Nos. EN30, NI95, S131 and W122 but self-adhesive were issued on 29 September 2008 in sheets of 20 containing five of each design with *se-tenant* labels.

First Day Covers

14.10.03	2nd, 1st, E, 68p. (Nos. W98/W100, W108) Tallents House		3·25
11.5.04	40p. (No. W101) Tallents House		1·75
5.4.05	42p. (No. W102) Tallents House		2·00
28.3.06	44p., 72p. (Nos. W103, W109) Tallents House		3·25
27.3.07	48p., 78p. (Nos. W104, W110) Tallents House		3·50
1.4.08	50p., 81p. (Nos. W105, W111) Tallents House		3·75
31.3.09	56p., 90p. (Nos. W106, W112) Tallents House		4·00
30.3.10	60p., 97p. (Nos. W107, W113) Tallents House		4·00
29.3.11	68p., £1·10 (Nos. W123, W129) Tallents House		4·25
25.4.12	87p. £1·28 (Nos. W124, W134) Tallents House		5·00
27.3.13	88p. (No. W125) Tallents House		2·25
26.3.14	97p. (No. W126) Tallents House		2·50
24.3.15	£1, £1·33 (Nos. W127, W135) Tallents House		5·25
22.3.16	£1·05 (No. W128) Tallents House		2·75

Presentation Pack

14.10.03	PO Pack No. 65. 2nd, 1st, E, 68p. (Nos. W98/W100, W108)	9·00

W10a

2006 (1 Mar). Opening of New Welsh Assembly Building, Cardiff. Sheet 123×70 mm. Printed in gravure by De La Rue. One centre phosphor band (2nd) or two phosphor bands (others). Perf 15×14 (with one elliptical hole in each vertical side).

MSW143	**W10a**	Nos. W98, W99×2 and W108×2	6·50	4·50
First Day Cover (Tallents House)				5·00

W10b	W10c	W10d

2008 (29 Sept). 50th Anniversary of the Country Definitives. As Nos. W1, W3 and W5 (definitives of 1958) but inscribed 1st and printed in lithography by De La Rue. Two phosphor bands. Perf 15×14½ (with one elliptical hole in each vertical side).

W144	**W10b**	(1st) deep lilac	2·00	1·60
W145	**W10c**	(1st) deep claret	2·00	1·60
W146	**W10d**	(1st) green	2·00	1·60

Nos. W144/W146 were only issued in the £9·72 The Regional Definitive stamp booklet.

DATHLU CYMRU · CELEBRATING WALES

W11

2009 (26 Feb). Celebrating Wales. Sheet 123×70 mm. Printed in lithography by De La Rue. Two phosphor bands. Perf 15×14 (with one elliptical hole in each vertical side (1st) or 14½×14 (81p.)).

MSW147	**W11**	(1st) Red Dragon; (1st) No. W122; 81p. St David; 81p. National Assembly for Wales, Cardiff	5·50	4·25
First Day Cover (Tallents House)				5·25
Presentation Pack (PO Pack No. 424)			6·50	
PHQ Cards (set of 5) (CGB4)			1·50	8·00

No. **MS**W147 was on sale at post offices throughout the UK.

Stamps as the 1st class Red Dragon stamp from No. **MS**W147 but self-adhesive were issued on 1 March 2010 in sheets of 20 with *se-tenant* labels showing Welsh Castles. These sheets were printed in lithography by Cartor.

The five PHQ cards show the four individual stamps and the complete miniature sheet.

W12 Red Dragon

2013 (9 May). Wales Flag. Printed in lithography by Cartor or Enschedé. Two phosphor bands. Perf 14½×14 (with one elliptical hole in each vertical side).

W148	**W12**	(1st) Red Dragon	4·00	4·00

No. W148 was issued in £11·11 Football Heroes, £13·97 Classic Locomotives and £16·49 Centenary of the First World War (3rd issue) booklets.

W13 Leek	W14 Dragon	W15 Daffodil	W16 Prince of Wales' Feathers

2017 (21 Mar)–**20**. As previous set but with value indicated in revised typeface. One centre band (2nd) or two phosphor bands. Perf 15×14 (with one elliptical hole in each vertical side).

W149	**W13**	(2nd) Leek (20.3.18)	1·25	75
W150	**W14**	(1st) Dragon (20.3.18)	1·75	75
W151	**W15**	£1·17 Daffodil (21.3.17)	2·75	2·75
W152		£1·25 Daffodil (20.3.18)	2·75	2·75
W153		£1·35 Daffodil (19.3.19)	2·75	2·75

W156	**W16**	£1·40 Prince of Wales Feathers (21.3.17)	3·00	3·00
W157	**W15**	£1·42 Daffodil (17.3.20)	2·50	2·50
W158	**W16**	£1·45 Prince of Wales Feathers (20.3.18)	3·25	3·25
W159		£1·55 Prince of Wales' Feathers (19.3.19)	3·25	3·25
W160		£1·63 Prince of Wales Feathers (17.3.20)	2·75	2·75
W161	**W15**	£1·70 Daffodil (23.12.20)	2·40	2·40

W17 Leek　　　　　**W18** Dragon

W19 Daffodil

2022 (11 Aug). As Types **W17**, **W18** and **W19** with barcoded strip at right. Self-adhesive. One centre phosphor band (2nd) or two phosphor bands (others). Die-cut perf 15×14½ (with one elliptical hole in each vertical side).

W162	**W17**	(2nd) Leek	1·40	1·40
W163	**W18**	(1st) Dragon	2·00	2·00
W164	**W19**	£1·85 Daffodil	2·50	2·50

First Day Covers

21.3.17	£1·17, £1·40 (Nos. W151, W156) Tallents House	6·00
20.3.18	2nd, 1st, £1·25, £1·45. (Nos. W149/W150, W152, W158) Tallents House	9·00
19.3.19	£1·35, £1·55. (Nos. W153, W159) Tallents House	7·00
17.3.20	£1·42, £1·63 (Nos. W157, W160) Tallents House	7·00
23.12.20	£1·70 (W61) Tallents House	3·75
11.8.22	2nd, 1st, £1·85 (Nos. W162/W164) Tallents House	7·50

V. Isle of Man

1　　　　2

1958 (18 Aug)–**68**. W **179**. Perf 15×14. W **179**. Perf 15×14.

1	1	2½d. carmine-red (8.6.64)	70	70
2	2	3d. deep lilac (18.8.58)	50	50
		p. One centre phosphor band (27.6.68)	20	20
3		4d. ultramarine (7.2.66)	1·00	1·00
		p. Two phosphor bands (5.7.67)	30	30

First Day Covers

18.8.58	No. 2 (3d.)	32·00
8.6.64	No. 1 (2½d.)	45·00
7.2.66	No. 3 (4d.)	15·00

1968–69. No wmk, One centre phosphor band (Nos. 5/6) or two phosphor bands (others). Perf 15×14.

4	2	4d. blue (24.6.68)	25	25
5		4d. olive-sepia (4.9.68)	30	30
6		4d. bright vermilion (26.2.69)	45	45
7		5d. royal blue (4.9.68)	45	45
4/7 *Set of 4*			1·25	1·25

First Day Cover

4.9.68	Nos. 5 and 7 (4d., 5d.)	4·00

3

1971 (7 July). Decimal Currency. One centre phosphor band (2½p.) or two phosphor bands (others). Perf 15×14.

8	3	2½p. bright magenta	30	30
9		3p. ultramarine	30	30
10		5p. reddish violet	70	70
11		7½p. chestnut	80	80
8/11 *Set of 4*			1·90	1·90
Presentation Pack (PO Pack No. 30)			2·50	

For comprehensive listings of the Independent Administration issues of the Isle of Man, see Stanley Gibbons *Channel Islands and Isle of Man stamps*.

First Day Cover

7.7.71	Nos. 8/11 (2½p., 3p., 5p., 7½p.)	3·50

VI. Channel Islands General Issues

C1 Gathering Vraic (seaweed)　　　**C2** Islanders gathering Vraic

1948 (10 May). Third Anniversary of Liberation. W **127** of Great Britain. Perf 15×14.

C1	**C1**	1d. scarlet	25	55
C2	**C2**	2½d. ultramarine	25	60

First Day Cover

10.05.48	Nos. C1/C2 (1d., 2½d.)	35·00

VII. Guernsey

(a) War Occupation Issues

Stamps issued under the authority of the Guernsey States during the German Occupation.

1 Arms of Guernsey

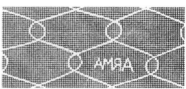

1a Loops (*half actual size*)

1941–44. Rouletted.

		(a) White paper. No wmk.		
1	1	½d. light green (7.4.41)	6·00	3·50
2		1d. scarlet (18.2.41)	3·25	2·00
3		2½d. ultramarine (12.4.44)	18·00	15·00
1/3 *Set of 3*			22·00	14·00
		(b) Bluish French banknote paper. W **1a** (sideways).		
4	1	½d. bright green (11.3.42)	32·00	25·00
5		1d. scarlet (9.4.42)	18·00	25·00

First Day Covers

18.2.1941	No. 2 (1d.)	15.00
7.4.1941	No. 1 (½d.)	10.00
12.4.1941	No. 3 (2½d.)	20.00
11.3.1942	No. 4 (½d.)	£325
9.4.1942	No. 5 (1d.)	£125

(b) Regional Issues

2   **3**

1958 (18 Aug)–**67**. W **179** of Great Britain. Perf 15×14.

6	**2**	2½d. rose-red (8.6.64)	40	40
7	**3**	3d. deep lilac	30	30
		p. One centre phosphor band (24.5.67)	30	30
8		4d. ultramarine (7.2.66)	40	40
		p. Two phosphor bands (24.10.67)	20	20
6/8p Set of 3			1·00	1·00

First Day Covers

18.8.1958	No. 7 (3d.)	20.00
8.6.1964	No. 6 (2½d.)	30.00
7.2.1966	No. 8 (4d.)	8.00

1968–69. No wmk. One centre phosphor band (Nos. 10/11) or two phosphor bands (others). Perf 15×14.

9	**3**	4d. pale ultramarine (16.4.68)	20	20
10		4d. olive-sepia (4.9.68)	20	20
11		4d. bright vermilion (26.2.69)	20	20
12		5d. royal blue (4.9.68)	30	30
9/12 Set of 4			80	80

First Day Cover

4.9.1971	4d. (No. 10), 5d. (No. 12)	3.00

For comprehensive listings of the Independent Postal Administration of Guernsey, see Stanley Gibbons *Collect Channel Islands and Isle of Man Stamps*.

VIII. Jersey

(a) War Occupation Issues

Stamps issued under the authority of the Jersey States during the German Occupation.

5 Arms of Jersey

1941–43. Stamps issued during the German Occupation White paper. No wmk. Perf 11 (line).

1	**5**	½d. bright green (29.1.42)	8·00	6·00
2		1d. scarlet (1.4.41)	8·00	5·00

First Day Covers

1.4.41	1d. (No. S2)	8·00
29.1.42	½d. (No. S1)	7·50

6 Old Jersey Farm   **7** Portelet Bay

8 Corbière Lighthouse   **9** Elizabeth Castle

10 Mont Orgueil Castle   **11** Gathering Vraic (seaweed)

1943 (1 June)–**44**. Pictorial Issue. Perf 13½.

3	**6**	½d. Old Jersey Farm (1.6.43)	12·00	12·00
4	**7**	1d. Portelet Bay (1.6.43)	3·00	50
5	**8**	1½d. Corbière Lighthouse (8.6.43)	8·00	5·75
6	**9**	2d. Elizabeth Castle (8.6.43)	7·50	2·00
7	**10**	2½d. Mont Orgueil Castle (29.6.43)	3·00	1·00
8	**11**	3d. Gathering Vraic (seaweed) (29.6.43)	3·00	2·75
3/8 Set of 6			30·00	21·00

First Day Covers

01.06.43	Nos. 3/4 (½d., 1d.)	10·00
08.06.43	Nos. 5/6 (1½d., 2d.)	10·00
20.06.43	Nos. 7/8 (2½d., 3d.)	16·00

12   **13**

1958 (18 Aug)–**67**. W **179**. Perf 15×14.

9	**12**	2½d. carmine-red (8.6.64)	45	45
10	**13**	3d. deep lilac (18.8.58)	30	30
		p. One centre phosphor band (9.6.67)	20	20
11		4d. ultramarine (7.2.66)	25	25
		p. Two phosphor bands (5.9.67)	25	25
9/11 Set of 3			80	80

First Day Covers

18.5.58	3d. (No. S10)	20·00
8.6.64	2½d. (No. S9)	30·00
7.2.66	4d. (No. S11)	10·00

1968–69. No wmk. One centre phosphor band (4d. values) or two phosphor bands (5d.). Perf 15×14.

12	**13**	4d. olive-sepia (4.9.68)	20	20
13		4d. bright vermilion (26.2.69)	20	20
14		5d. royal blue (4.9.68)	20	20
12/14 Set of 3			50	50

For comprehensive listings of the Independent Postal Administration issues for Jersey, see Stanley Gibbons *Collect Channel Islands and Isle of Man Stamps*.

First Day Cover

4.9.68	4d., 5d. (Nos. 12, 14)	3·00

POSTAGE DUE STAMPS

PERFORATIONS. All postage due stamps to No. D101 are perf 14×15.

| | D1 | | | D2 |

1914–22. W **100** (Simple Cypher) sideways.

D1	**D1**	½d. emerald	50	25
D2		1d. carmine	50	25
D3		1½d. chestnut	48·00	20·00
D4		2d. agate	50	25
D5		3d. violet	9·00	75
D6		4d. dull grey-green (wmk. sideways inverted)	40·00	5·00
D7		5d. brownish cinnamon	7·00	3·50
D8		1s. bright blue	40·00	5·00
D1/D8 *Set of 8*			£130	32·00

1924–31. W **111** (Block Cypher) sideways.

D10	**D1**	½d. emerald	1·25	75
D11		1d. carmine	60	25
D12		1½d. chestnut	48·00	22·00
D13		2d. agate	1·00	25
D14		3d. dull violet	1·50	25
D15		4d. dull grey-green	15·00	4·25
D16		5d. brownish cinnamon	65·00	45·00
D17		1s. deep blue	8·50	50
D18	**D2**	2s.6d. purple/*yellow*	85·00	1·75
D10/D18 *Set of 9*			£200	70·00

1936–37. W **125** (E 8 R) sideways.

D19	**D1**	½d. emerald	15·00	11·00
D20		1d. carmine	2·00	1·75
D21		2d. agate	15·00	12·00
D22		3d. dull violet	2·00	2·00
		Wi. Watermark sideways-inverted	—	
D23		4d. dull grey-green	65·00	35·00
D24		5d. Yellow-brown (1937)	40·00	28·00
D25		1s. deep blue	25·00	8·50
D26	**D2**	2s.6d. purple/*yellow*	£325	12·00
D19/D26 *Set of 8*			£450	£100

1937–38. W **127** (G VI R) sideways.

D27	**D1**	½d. emerald	13·00	3·75
D28		1d. carmine	3·00	50
D29		2d. agate	2·75	30
D30		3d. violet	11·00	30
D31		4d. dull grey-green	£110	10·00
D32		5d. yellow-brown	17·00	75
D33		1s. deep blue	80·00	75
D34	**D2**	2s.6d. purple/*yellow*	85·00	1·25
D27/D34 *Set of 8*			£300	16·00

1951–54. Colours changed and new value (1½d.). W **127** (G VI R) sideways.

D35	**D1**	½d. yellow-orange	3·50	3·50
D36		1d. violet-blue	1·50	75
D37		1½d. green	2·00	2·00
D38		4d. blue	50·00	22·00
D39		1s. ochre	28·00	5·25
D35/D39 *Set of 5*			75·00	30·00

1954–55. W **153** (Tudor Crown) sideways.

D40	**D1**	½d. bright orange	7·00	5·25
D41		2d. agate	26·00	23·00
D42		3d. violet	75·00	60·00
D43		4d. blue	26·00	32·00
D44		5d. yellow-brown	20·00	20·00
D45	**D2**	2s.6d. purple/*yellow*	£150	5·75
D40/D45 *Set of 6*			£250	£130

1955–57. W **165** (St Edward's Crown) sideways.

D46	**D1**	½d. bright orange	2·75	3·25
D47		1d. violet-blue	5·00	1·50
D48		1½d. green	8·50	7·00
D49		2d. agate	45·00	3·50
D50		3d. violet	6·00	1·50
D51		4d. blue	25·00	6·00
D52		5d. brown-ochre	26·00	20·00
D53		1s. ochre	65·00	2·25
D54	**D2**	2s.6d. purple/*yellow*	£200	8·25
D55		5s. scarlet/*yellow*	£150	32·00
D46/D55 *Set of 10*			£475	75·00

1959–63. W **179** (Multiple Crowns) sideways.

D56	**D1**	½d. bright orange	15	1·25
D57		1d. violet-blue	15	50
D58		1½d. green	2·50	2·50
D59		2d. agate	1·10	50
D60		3d. violet	30	30
D61		4d. blue	30	30
D62		5d. yellow-brown	45	60
D63		6d. purple	50	30
D64		1s. ochre	90	30
D65	**D2**	2s.6d. purple/*yellow*	3·00	50
D66		5s. scarlet/*yellow*	8·25	1·00
D67		10s. blue/*yellow*	11·50	5·75
D68		£1 black/*yellow*	45·00	8·25
D56/D68 *Set of 13*			65·00	20·00

1968–69. Design size 22½×19 mm. No wmk.

D69	**D1**	2d. agate	75	1·00
D70		3d. violet	1·00	1·00
D71		4d. blue	1·00	1·00
D72		5d. orange-brown	8·00	11·00
D73		6d. purple	2·25	1·75
D74		1s. ochre	4·00	2·50
D69/D74 *Set of 6*			15·00	16·00

1968–69. Design size 22½×17½ mm. No wmk.

D75	**D1**	4d. blue	7·00	6·75
D76		8d. red	50	1·00

| | D3 | | | D4 |

1970–75. Decimal Currency.

D77	**D3**	½p. turquoise-blue	15	2·50
D78		1p. deep reddish purple	15	15
D79		2p. myrtle-green	20	15
D80		3p. ultramarine	20	15
D81		4p. yellow-brown	25	15
D82		5p. violet	25	15
D83		7p. red-brown	35	1·00
D84	**D4**	10p. carmine	30	30
D85		11p. slate-green	50	1·00
D86		20p. olive-brown	60	25
D87		50p. ultramarine	2·00	1·25
D88		£1 black	4·00	1·00
D89		£5 orange-yellow and black	25·00	1·50
D77/D89 *Set of 13*			30·00	7·75

| | D5 | | | D6 |

1982 (9 June).

D90	**D5**	1p. lake	10	30
D91		2p. bright blue	30	30
D92		3p. deep mauve	15	30
D93		4p. deep blue	15	25
D94		5p. sepia	20	25
D95	**D6**	10p. light brown	30	40
D96		20p. olive-green	50	60
D97		25p. deep greenish blue	80	90
D98		50p. grey-black	1·75	1·75
D99		£1 red	3·00	1·25
D100		£2 turquoise-blue	5·00	4·25
D101		£5 dull orange	10·00	2·25
D90/D101 *Set of 12*			19·00	10·00
D90/D101 *Set of 12 Gutter Pairs*			38·00	
Presentation Pack (PO Pack No.135)			24·00	

| | D7 |

1994 (15 Feb). Perf 15×14 (with one elliptical hole in each vertical side).

D102	**D7**	1p. red, yellow and black	10	75
D103		2p. magenta, purple and black	10	75
D104		5p. yellow, red-brown and black	15	50
D105		10p. yellow, emerald and black	30	75
D106		20p. blue-green, violet and black	75	1·50
D107		25p. cerise, rosine and black	1·50	2·00
D108		£1 violet, magenta and black	7·00	7·00
D109		£1·20 greenish blue, blue-green and black	8·00	9·00
D110		£5 greenish black, blue-green and black	20·00	20·00
D102/D110 *Set of 9*			35·00	35·00
First Day Cover				45·00
Presentation Pack (PO Pack No.32)			38·00	

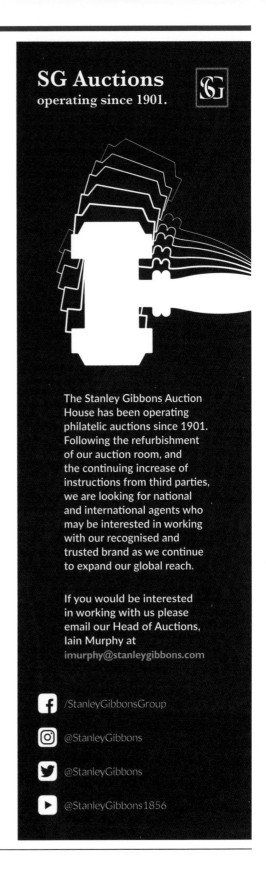

King Charles III

8 September 2022

5002	**5002**	(1st) Lily	1·90	1·90
5003	**5003**	(1st) Sunflower	1·90	1·90
5004	**5004**	(1st) Fuschia	1·90	1·90
5005	**5005**	(1st) Tulip	1·90	1·90
		a. Horiz strip of 5. Nos. 5005/5009	9·25	9·25
5006	**5006**	(1st) Peony	1·90	1·90
5007	**5007**	(1st) Nasturtium	1·90	1·90
5008	**5008**	(1st) Rose	1·90	1·90
5009	**5009**	(1st) Dahlia	1·90	1·90
Set of 10			18·50	18·50
Set of 2 Gutter Strips of 10			37·00	
First Day Cover (Tallents House)				20·00
Presentation Pack (PO Pack No. 519)			20·00	
PHQ Cards (set of 10) (335)			6·50	20·00

Nos. 5000/5004 and 5005/5009 were each printed together, *se-tenant*, as horizontal strips of five stamps in sheets of 50 (2 panes 5×5).

5000 Sweet Pea — SWEET PEA

5001 Iris — IRIS

5002 Lily — LILY

5003 Sunflower — SUNFLOWER

5004 Fuschia — FUCHSIA

5005 Tulip — TULIP

5006 Peony — PEONY

5007 Nasturtium — NASTURTIUM

5008 Rose — ROSE

5009 Dahlia — DAHLIA

2023 (22 Mar). Flowers. Self-adhesive. Multicoloured. Two phosphor bands. Die-cut perf 14½.

5000	**5000**	(1st) Sweet Pea	1·90	1·90
		a. Horiz strip of 5. Nos. 5000/5004	9·25	9·25
5001	**5001**	(1st) Iris	1·90	1·90

5013 Robin Hood is Declared an Outlaw

5014 Robin Hood Meets Little John

5015 Friar Tuck Carries Robin Hood

5016 Robin Hood Robs the Rich

5017 Robin Hood Wins the Archery Contest

5018 Robin Hood Captures the Sheriff

5019 Robin Hood Helps Maid Marian Escape

5020 Robin Hood Marries Maid Marian

5021 King Richard Removes His Disguise

5022 Robin Hood Shoots His Last Arrow

2023 (13 Apr). The Legend of Robin Hood. Multicoloured. Two phosphor bands. Perf 14½.

5010	5013	(1st) Robin Hood is declared an outlaw	1·90	1·90
		a. Horiz strip of 5. Nos. 5010/5014	9·25	9·25
5011	5014	(1st) Robin Hood meets Little John	1·90	1·90
5012	5015	(1st) Friar Tuck carries Robin Hood	1·90	1·90
5013	5016	(1st) Robin Hood robs the rich	1·90	1·90
5014	5017	(1st) Robin Hood wins the archery contest	1·90	1·90
5015	5018	(1st) Robin Hood captures the Sheriff	1·90	1·90
		a. Horiz strip of 5. Nos. 5015/5019	9·25	9·25
5016	5019	(1st) Robin Hood helps Maid Marian escape	1·90	1·90
5017	5020	(1st) Robin Hood marries Maid Marian	1·90	1·90
5018	5021	(1st) King Richard removes his disguise	1·90	1·90
5019	5022	(1st) Robin Hood shoots his last arrow	1·90	1·90
Set of 10			18·50	18·50
Set of 2 Gutter strips of 10			38·00	
First Day Cover (Tallents House)				20·00
Presentation Pack (PO Pack No. 520)			20·00	
PHQ Cards (set of 10) (336)			6·50	20·00

Nos. 5010/5014 and 5015/5019 were each printed together, *se-tenant*, as horizontal strips of five in sheets of 50 (2 panes 5×5).

5023 The Coronation

2023 (6 May). King Charles III, A New Reign. Perf 14½.
MS5020 126×88 mm. **5023** (1st) The Coronation (dull purple, blackish purple); (1st) Diversity and Community (azure, deep dull blue); £2·20 The Commonwealth (rose-red and deep rose-red); £2·20 Sustainability and Biodiversity (green, deep green)

		11·00	11·00
First Day Cover (Tallents House)			12·50
Presentation Pack (PO Pack No. 521)		12·50	
PHQ Cards (set of 5) (337)		4·50	22·00

A collector's sheet containing the stamps from No. **MS**5020 but self-adhesive with labels was originally sold for £14.40.

The 5 PHQ cards show the four individual stamps from No. **MS**5020 and the complete miniature sheet.

5024 Blackadder the Third, episode 3 (Hugh Laurie, Tony Robinson, Rowan Atkinson)

5025 Blackadder the Third, episode 6 (Rowan Atkinson, Stephen Fry)

5026 Blackadder Goes Forth, episode 6 (Tim McInnerny, Hugh Laurie, Rowan Atkinson, Tony Robinson)

5027 Blackadder Goes Forth, episode 6 (Stephen Fry, Rowan Atkinson, Tim McInnerny, Tony Robinson)

5028 The Black Adder, episode 3 (Rowan Atkinson, Brian Blessed)

5029 The Black Adder, episode 2 (Rowan Atkinson, Tim McInnerny, Tony Robinson)

5030 Blackadder II, episode 1 (Miranda Richardson, Patsy Byrne)

5031 Blackadder II, episode 4 (Rowan Atkinson, Tim McInnerny, Tony Robinson)

5032 Blackadder, Portraits

2023 (17 May). Blackadder. Multicoloured. One centre phosphor band (2nd) or two phosphor bands (others).

(a) Ordinary gum. Perf 14½×14.

5021	5024	(2nd) Blackadder the Third, episode 3 (Hugh Laurie, Tony Robinson, Rowan Atkinson)	1·25	1·25
		a. Horiz pair. Nos. 5021/5022	2·50	2·50
5022	5025	(2nd) Blackadder the Third, episode 6 (Rowan Atkinson, Stephen Fry)	1·25	1·25
5023	5026	(1st) Blackadder Goes Forth, episode 6 (Tim McInnerny, Hugh Laurie, Rowan Atkinson, Tony Robinson)	1·90	1·90
		a. Horiz pair. Nos. 5023/5024	3·75	3·75
5024	5027	(1st) Blackadder Goes Forth, episode 6 (Stephen Fry, Rowan Atkinson, Tim McInnerny, Tony Robinson)	1·90	1·90
5025	5028	£2 The Black Adder, episode 3 (Rowan Atkinson, Brian Blessed)	3·25	3·25
		a. Horiz pair. Nos. 5025/5026	6·50	6·50
5026	5029	£2 The Black Adder, episode 2 (Rowan Atkinson, Tim McInnerny, Tony Robinson)	3·25	3·25
5027	5030	£2·20 Blackadder II, episode 1 (Miranda Richardson, Patsy Byrne)	3·50	3·50
		a. Horiz pair. Nos. 5027/5028	7·00	7·00
5028	5031	£2·20 Blackadder II, episode 4 (Rowan Atkinson, Tim McInnerny, Tony Robinson)	3·50	3·50
Set of 8			18·50	18·50
Set of 2 Gutter Strips of 8			37·00	
First Day Cover (Tallents House)				20·00
Presentation Pack (Nos. 5021/5028 and **MS**5029) (PO Pack No. 522)			32·00	
PHQ Cards (set of 13) (338)			9·00	30·00

(b) Self-adhesive. Die-cut perf 14.

MS5029 157×74 mm. **5032** (1st) Blackadder II; (1st) Blackadder Goes Forth; £2·20 The Black Adder; £2·20 Blackadder the Third

		11·00	11·00
First Day Cover (Tallents House)			12·50

Nos. 5021/5022, 5023/5024, 5025/5026 and 5027/5028 were each printed together, *se-tenant*, as horizontal pairs in sheets of 60 (2 panes 6×5).

A collector's sheet containing Nos. 5021/5028 but self-adhesive with labels was originally sold for £15.40.

The 13 PHQ cards show the 12 individual stamps including those from No. **MS**5029 and the complete miniature sheet.

5033 Space Marines

5034 Orks

5035 Stormcast Eternals

5036 Slaves to Darkness

5037 High Elves

5038 Dwarfs

5039 Illustrations from Codexes and Rule Books

2023 (8 June). Warhammer. Multicoloured. Two phosphor bands.

(a) Ordinary gum. Perf 14½.

5030	**5033**	(1st) Space Marines	1·90	1·90
		a. Vert pair. Nos. 5030/5031	3·75	3·75
5031	**5034**	(1st) Orks	1·90	1·90
5032	**5035**	£2 Stormcast Eternals	3·25	3·25
		a. Vert pair. Nos. 5032/5033	6·50	6·50
5033	**5036**	£2 Slaves to Darkness	3·25	3·25

5034	**5037**	£2·20 High Elves	3·50	3·50
		a. Vert pair. Nos. 5034/5035	7·00	7·00
5035	**5038**	£2·20 Dwarfs	3·50	3·50
	Set of 6		17·00	17·00
	Set of 2 Gutter Strips of 6		34·00	
	First Day Cover (Tallents House)			19·00
	Presentation Pack (Nos. 5030/5035 and **MS**5036) (PO Pack No. 523)		30·00	
	PHQ Cards (set of 11) (339)		6·50	29·00

(b) Self-adhesive. Die-cut perf 14½.

MS5036 203×74 mm. **5039** (1st) Rogue Trader; (1st) The Old World, Battle for Skull Pass; £2·20 The Horus Heresy, The Emperor of Mankind; £2·20 Age of Sigmar, Yndrasta, the celestial spear 11·00 11·00

First Day Cover (Tallents House) 12·50

Nos. 5030/5031, 5032/5033 and 5034/5035 were each printed together, *se-tenant*, as vertical pairs in sheets of 32 (2 panes 6×3).

A collector's sheet containing stamps as Nos. 5030/5035, but self-adhesive, as well as the individual stamps from **MS**5036 with labels was originally sold for £18.30.

A Space Marines fan sheet containing No. 5030×3 was originally sold for £7.50.

A Stormcast Eternals fan sheet containing No. 5032×3 was originally sold for £7.50.

The 11 PHQ cards show the 10 individual stamps including those from No. **MS**5036 and the complete miniature sheet.

5040 *Carnival Come Thru!!* by Bokiba

5041 *Basking in the Sun After a Hard Day Work* by Emma Premoeh

5042 *From Small Island Life to Big Island Dreams* by Kareen Cox

5043 *Ode to Saturday Schools* by Tomekah George

5044 *The March* by Emma Prempeh

5045 *Here We Come* by Bokiba

5046 *Taste the Caribbean* by Kareen Cox

5047 *Dancehall Rhythms* by Alvin Kofi

2023 (22 June). 75th Anniversary of Windrush. Multicoloured. Two phosphor bands. Perf 14½×14.

5037	**5040**	£1 *Carnival Come Thru!* by Bokiba	1·60	1·60
		a. Horiz pair. Nos. 5037/5038	3·25	3·25
5038	**5041**	£1 *Basking in the Sun After a Hard Work Day* by Emma Premoeh	1·60	1·60
5039	**5042**	(1st) *From Small Island Life to Big Island Dreams* by Kareen Cox	1·90	1·90
		a. Horiz pair. Nos. 5039/5040	3·75	3·75
5040	**5043**	(1st) *Ode to Saturday Schools* by Tomekah George	1·90	1·90
5041	**5044**	£2 *The March* by Emma Prempeh	3·25	3·25
		a. Horiz pair. Nos. 5041/5042	6·50	6·50

5042	5045	£2 Here We Come by Bokiba	3·25	3·25
5043	5046	£2·20 Taste the Caribbean by Kareen Cox	3·50	3·50
		a. Horiz pair. Nos. 5043/5044	7·00	7·00
5044	5047	£2·20 Dancehall Rhythms by Alvin Kofi	3·50	3·50
Set of 8			20·00	20·00
Set of 2 Gutter Strips of 8			40·00	
First Day Cover (Tallents House)				22·00
Presentation Pack (PO Pack No. 524)			22·00	
PHQ Cards (set of 8) (340)			5·00	21·00

Nos. 5037/5038, 5039/5040, 5041/5042 and 5043/5044 were each printed together, *se-tenant*, as horizontal pairs in sheets of 60 (2 panes 6×5).

5048 Beaver (*Castoreum*)

5049 Atlantic Salmon (*Salmo salar*)

5050 Kingfisher (*Alcedo atthis*)

5051 Beautiful Demoiselle (*Calopteryx virgo*)

5052 Water Vole (*Arvicola amphibius*)

5053 Grey Wagtail (*Motacilla cinerea*)

5054 Common Mayfly (*Ephemera vulgata*)

5055 Otter (*Lutrinae*)

5056 Brown Trout (*Salmo trutta*)

5057 Dipper (*Cinclus*)

2023 (13-27 July). Wildlife. Multicoloured. One centre phosphor band (Nos. 5045/5054) or two phosphor bands (Nos. 5050b/5054b). Perf 14½×14.

5045	5048	(2nd) Beaver (*Castoreum*)	1·25	1·25
		a. Horiz strip of 5. Nos. 5045/5049	6·25	6·25
5046	5049	(2nd) Atlantic salmon (*Salmo salar*)	1·25	1·25
5047	5050	(2nd) Kingfisher (*Alcedo atthis*)	1·25	1·25
5048	5051	(2nd) Beautiful Demoiselle (*Calopteryx virgo*)	1·25	1·25
5049	5052	(2nd) Water vole (*Arvicola amphibius*)	1·25	1·25
5050	5053	(1st) Grey wagtail (*Motacilla cinerea*)	1·90	1·90
		a. Horiz strip of 5. Nos. 5050/5054	9·25	9·25
		b. Two phosphor bands	1·90	1·90
5051	5054	(1st) Common mayfly (*Ephemera vulgata*)	1·90	1·90
		b. Two phosphor bands	1·90	1·90
5052	5055	(1st) Otter (*Lutrinae*)	1·90	1·90
		b. Two phosphor bands	1·90	1·90

5053	5056	(1st) Brown trout (*Salmo trutta*)	1·90	1·90
		b. Two phosphor bands	1·90	1·90
5054	5057	(1st) Dipper (*Cinclus*)	1·90	1·90
		b. Two phosphor bands	1·90	1·90
Set of 10			15·00	15·00
Set of 2 Gutter Strips of 10			30·00	
First Day Cover (Tallents House)				25·00
Presentation Pack (PO Pack No. 525)			55·00	
PHQ Cards (set of 10) (341)			6·50	25·00

Nos. 5045/5049 and 5050/5054 were each printed together, *se-tenant*, as horizontal strips of five in sheets of 50 (2 panes 5×5).

Nos. 5045/5054 were originally sold in error with one phosphor band, and it is in this format they appear on First Day Covers and in Presentation Packs. They were subsequently re-printed and issued (27.7.23) with the correct two phosphor bands (Nos. 5050b/5054b).

There were no new First Day Cover arrangements for the reissued first class stamps.

A collector's sheet containing stamps as Nos. 5045/5054 but self-adhesive with labels was originally sold for £10.45.

5058 The Libarian

5059 Granny Weatherfax

5060 Rincewind

5061 Moist Von Lipwig

5062 Sam Vimes

5063 Death and Mort

5064 Tiffany Aching

6065 Great A'Tuin

2023 (10 Aug). Discworld. Multicoloured. Two phosphor bands. Perf 14½.

5055	5058	£1 The Librarian	1·60	1·60
		a. Horiz pair. Nos. 5055/5056	3·25	3·25
5056	5059	£1 Granny Weatherfax	1·60	1·60
5057	5060	(1st) Rincewind	1·90	1·90
		a. Horiz pair. Nos. 5057/5058	3·75	3·75
5058	5061	(1st) Moist Von Lipwing	1·90	1·90
5059	5062	£2 Sam Vimes	3·25	3·25
		a. Horiz pair. Nos. 5059/5060	6·50	6·50
5060	5063	£2 Death and Mort	3·25	3·25
5061	5064	£2·20 Tiffany Aching	3·50	3·50
		a. Horiz pair. Nos. 5061/5062	7·00	7·00
5062	6065	£2·20 Great A'Tuin	3·50	3·50
Set of 8			20·00	20·00
Set of 2 Gutter Strips of 8			40·00	
First Day Cover (Tallents House)				22·00
Presentation Pack (PO Pack No. 526)			22·00	
PHQ Cards (set of 8) (342)			5·00	21·00

Nos. 5055/5056, 5057/5058, 5059/5060 and 5061/5062 were each printed together, *se-tenant*, as horizontal pairs in sheets of 60 (2 panes 6×5).

A collector's sheet containing Nos. 5055/5062 but self-adhesive with labels was originally sold for £16.

5067 Paddington With a Jar of Marmalade

5068 Paddington Sawing Wood

5069 Paddington Pushing a Shopping Trolley

5070 Paddington Holding an Ice Cream

5071 Paddington Carrying Presents

5072 Paddington and a Crab

5073 Paddington

2023 (5 Sept). Paddington. Multicoloured. Two phosphor bands. Perf 14½.

5063	**5067**	(1st) Paddington with a jar of marmalade	1·90	1·90
		a. Horiz pair. Nos. 5063/5064	3·75	3·75
5064	**5068**	(1st) Paddington sawing wood	1·90	1·90
5065	**5069**	£2 Paddington pushing a shopping trolley	3·25	3·25
		a. Horiz pair. Nos. 5065/5066	6·50	6·50
5066	**5070**	£2 Paddington holding an ice cream	3·25	3·25
5067	**5071**	£2·20 Paddington carrying presents	3·50	3·50
		a. Horiz pair. Nos. 5067/5068	7·00	7·00
5068	**5072**	£2·20 Paddington and a crab	3·50	3·50
Set of 6			17·00	17·00
Set of 2 Gutter Strips of 6			35·00	
First Day Cover (Tallents House)				19·00
Presentation Pack (Nos. 5063/5068 and **MS**5069) (PO Pack No. 527)			30·00	
PHQ Cards (set of 11) (343)			6·50	30·00

MS5069 192×74 mm. **5073** (1st) Paddington reaching for a marmalade sandwich; (1st) Paddington and Mr. Gruber having elevenses; £2 Paddington and the Brown family having breakfast; £2 Paddington baking.   11·00   11·00

First Day Cover (Tallents House)   12·50

Nos. 5063/5064, 5065/5066 and 5067/5068 were each printed together, *se-tenant*, as horizontal pairs in sheets of 60 (2 panes 6×5).

A collector's sheet containing stamps as Nos. 5063/6064 each ×5 but self-adhesive with labels was originally sold for £12.

The 11 PHQ cards show the 10 individual stamps including those from No. **MS**5069 and the complete miniature sheet.

5074 Performing at the Pigalle Nightclub, London, 13 September 1965

5075 Performing in Bournemouth, October 1974

5076 Performing at the BBC Electric Proms, The Roundhouse, London, 23 October 2009

5077 Performing at the Safeway Picnic in the Park 2002

5078 Hyde Park, London, 29 June 2002

5079 Performing in Brighton

5080 Singing 'World in Union' (with Bryn Terfel) during the Opening Ceremony of the Rugby World Cup, Cardiff, 1 October 1999

5081 Performing during the Oscars held at the Dolby Theatre, Hollywood, California, 24 February 2013

5082 Dame Shirley Bassey

2023 (21 Sept). Dame Shirley Bassey (1st issue). Multicoloured. Two phosphor bands. Perf 14½.

(a) Ordinary gum. Perf 14½.

5070	**5074**	(1st) Performing at the Pigalle nightclub, London, 1965	1·90	1·90
		a. Horiz strip of 4. Nos. 5070/5073	7·50	7·50
5071	**5075**	(1st) Performing in Bournemouth, October 1974	1·90	1·90
5072	**5076**	(1st) Performing at the BBC Electric Proms, London, 2009	1·90	1·90

5073	**5077**	(1st) Performing at the Safeway Picnic in the Park 2002	1·90	1·90
5074	**5078**	£2 Hyde Park, London, 29 June 2002	3·25	3·25
		a. Horiz strip of 4. Nos. 5074/5077	14·00	14·00
5075	**5079**	£2 Performing in Brighton	3·25	3·25
5076	**5080**	£2 Singing 'World in Union' (with Bryn Terfel), Cardiff, 1999	3·25	3·25
5077	**5081**	£2 Performing during the Oscars, Hollywood, California, 2013	3·25	3·25

Set of 8	21·00	21·00
Set of 2 Gutter Strips of 8	42·00	
First Day Cover (Tallents House)		23·00
Presentation Pack (Nos. 5070/5077 and **MS**5078) (PO Pack No. 528)	32·00	
PHQ Cards (set of 13) (344)	7·50	35·00

(b) Self-adhesive. Die-cut perf 14½×14.
MS5078 146×74 mm. **5082** (1st) Rehearsing before a concert at the Royal Albert Hall to celebrate her 25 years in show business, March 1978; (1st) During rehearsals before the opening of her season at the Talk of the Town theatre in London, 26 September 1962; £2 In the recording studio, 1961; £2 At Grouse Lodge Studios, Ireland, 2009.

	11·00	11·00
First Day Cover (Tallents House)		13·00

Nos. 5070/5073 and 5074/5077 were each printed together, *se-tenant*, as horizontal strips of four in sheets of 48 (2 panes 4×6).

Nos. 5070/5073 and 5074/5077 also from the £22.50 Dame Shirley Bassey premium booklet, No. CY1.

A collector's sheet containing stamps as Nos. 5070/5077 but self-adhesive with labels was originally sold for £13.60.

A Dame Shirley Bassey fan sheet containing Nos. 5070/5077 was originally sold for £13.50.

The 13 PHQ cards show the 12 individual stamps including those from No. **MS**5078 and the complete miniature sheet.

5083 Rehearsing Before a Concert at the Royal Albert Hall to Celebrate Her 25 Years in Show Business, March 1978

5084 During Rehearsals Before the Opening of Her Season at the Talk of the Town Theatre in London, 26 September 1962

5085 In the Recording Studio, 1961

5086 At Grouse Lodge Studios, Ireland, 2009

2023 (21 Sept). Dame Shirley Bassey (2nd issue). Self-adhesive. Two phosphor bands. Die-cut perf 14½×14.

5079	**5083**	(1st) Rehearsing before a concert at the Royal Albert Hall, 1978	2·00	2·00
5080	**5084**	(1st) During rehearsals London, 1962	2·00	2·00
5081	**5085**	£2 In the recording studio, 1961	3·50	3·50
5082	**5086**	£2 At Grouse Lodge Studios, Ireland, 2009	3·50	3·50
5079/5082		*Set of 4*	11·00	11·00

Nos. 5079/5082 come from No. **MS**5078 and from the £22·50 Dame Shirley Bassey premium booklet, No. CY1.

5087 Ron Weasley and the Weasley Twins

5088 Minerva McGonagall and Kingsley Shacklebolt

5089 Harry Potter and Ginny Weasley

5090 Neville Longbottom and Luna Lovegood

5091 Hermione Granger and Molly Weasley

5092 Bellatrix Lestrange and Narcissa Malfoy

5093 Fenrir Greyback and Scabior

5094 Lord Voldemort and A Death Eater

5095 Severus Snape and Alecto Carrow

5096 Draco Malfoy and Gregory Goyle

5097 Harry Potter

2023 (19 Oct). Harry Potter (1st issue). Multicoloured. Two phosphor bands (Nos. 5083/5092) or 'all-over' phosphor (**MS**5093).

(a) Ordinary gum. Perf 14×14½.

5083	**5087**	(1st) Ron Weasley and the Weasley twins	1·90	1·90
		a. Horiz strip of 5. Nos. 5083/5087	9·25	9·25
5084	**5088**	(1st) Minerva McGonagall and Kingsley Shacklebolt	1·90	1·90
5085	**5089**	(1st) Harry Potter and Ginny Weasley	1·90	1·90
5086	**5090**	(1st) Neville Longbottom and Luna Lovegood	1·90	1·90
5087	**5091**	(1st) Hermione Granger and Molly Weasley	1·90	1·90
5088	**5092**	(1st) Bellatrix Lestrange and Narcissa Malfoy	1·90	1·90
		a. Horiz strip of 5. Nos. 5088/5092	9·25	9·25
5089	**5093**	(1st) Fenrir Greyback and Scabior	1·90	1·90
5090	**5094**	(1st) Lord Voldemort and A Death Eater	1·90	1·90

5091	**5095**	(1st) Severus Snape and Alecto Carrow	1·90	1·90
5092	**5096**	(1st) Draco Malfoy and Gregory Goyle	1·90	1·90
Set of 10			18·50	18·50
Set of 2 Gutter strips of 10			37·00	
First Day Cover (Tallents House)				21·00
Presentation Pack (PO Pack No. 529)			32·00	
PHQ Cards (*set of 17*) (345)			10·00	30·00

(b) Self-adhesive.

MS5093 220×74 mm. **5097** (1st) Hedwig (p 14½); (1st)
Aragog (p 14½); (1st) Dobby (p 14); (1st) Crook-
shanks (p 14½×14); (1st) Fawkes (p 14½); (1st)
Buckbeak (p 14½×14). 12·00 12·00

First Day Cover (Tallents House) 14·00

Nos. 5083/5087 and 5088/5092 were each printed together, *se-tenant*, as horizontal strips of five in sheets of 50 (2 panes 5×5).

Nos. 5083/5087 and 5088/5092 also come from the £25·25 Harry Potter premium booklet, No. CY2.

A collector's sheet containing stamps as Nos. 5083/5092 but self-adhesive with labels was orginially sold for £13.70.

A Harry Potter fan sheet containing No. 5085×3 was originally sold for £7.50.

A Lord Voldemort fan sheet containing No. 5090×3 was originally sold for £7.50.

A Dobby fan sheet containing the 1st class 'Dobby' stamp from No. **MS**5093 was originally sold for £7.50.

The 17 PHQ cards show the 16 individual stamps including those from No. **MS**5093 and the complete miniature sheet.

5098 Hedwig

5099 Aragog

5100 Dobby   **5101** Crookshanks

5102 Fawkes   **5103** Buckbeak

2023 (19 Oct). Harry Potter (2nd issue). Each steel-blue, lemon and stone. Self-adhesive. 'All-over' phosphor. Die-cut perf 14½.

5094	**5098**	(1st) Hedwig	2·00	2·00
5095	**5099**	(1st) Aragog	2·00	2·00
5096	**5100**	(1st) Dobby	2·00	2·00
5097	**5101**	(1st) Crookshanks	2·00	2·00
5098	**5102**	(1st) Fawkes	2·00	2·00
5099	**5103**	(1st) Buckbeak	2·00	2·00
Set of 6			12·00	12·00

Nos. 5094/5099 come from No. **MS**5093 and the £25·25 Harry Potter premium booklet, No. CY2.

5104 Angel   **5105** Mary and Baby Jesus

5106 Bethlehem   **5107** Baby Jesus

5108 Three Kings

2023 (2 Nov). Christmas. Nativity Illustrations by Tom Duxbury. Multicoloured. Self-adhesive. One centre phosphor band (No. 5100) or two bands (others). Die-cut perf 15×14½.

5100	**5104**	(2nd) Angel	1·25	1·25
5101	**5105**	(1st) Mary and Baby Jesus	1·90	1·90
5102	**5106**	(2nd Large) Bethlehem	2·50	2·50
5103	**5107**	(1st Large) Baby Jesus	3·25	3·25
5104	**5108**	£2·20 Three Kings	3·50	3·50
Set of 5			12·00	12·00
First Day Cover (Tallents House)				14·00
Presentation Pack (PO Pack No. 530)			14·00	
PHQ Cards (*set of 6*) (346)			4·00	25·00
MS5105 190×75 mm. Nos. 5100/5104			12·00	12·00
First Day Cover (Tallents House)				14·00

Nos. 5100/5104 were each issued in counter sheets of 50.

The 2nd class, 1st class and £2.20 values were also issued in sheets of 20 containing eight 2nd class, eight 1st class and four £2.20 values. These sheets were printed in lithography instead of gravure and originally sold for £26.

The 6 PHQ cards show the 5 individual stamps and the complete miniature sheet.

Post Office Yearbook

2023 (7 Dec). Comprises Nos. 4756/4795, 5000/5049, 5050b/5054b and 5055/**MS**5105.

YB5101a	Yearbook (*sold for £250*)	£375

Collectors Pack

2023 (7 Dec). Comprises Nos. 4756/4795, 5000/5049, 5050b/5054b and 5055/**MS**5105.

CP5105a	Collectors Pack (Pack No. 531) (*sold for £230*)	£345

Miniature Sheet Collection

2023 (7 Dec). Comprises Nos. **MS**4764, **MS**4777, **MS**4791, **MS**5020, **MS**5029, **MS**5036, **MS**5069, **MS**5078, **MS**5093 and **MS**5105.

MS5105a Miniature Sheet Collection (*sold for £64*)   £100

King Charles III Definitives

BARCODED SECURITY DEFINITIVES

Please note that the 'V' numbers in this section are temporary and subject to change.

Like the Queen Elizabeth II barcoded definitives they have the usual security features of U-shaped slits, an overall iridescent overprint, sometimes with source codes, year codes, and self-adhesive backing paper with 'ROYALMAIL' printed backing. Barcoded definitives are nearly 50% larger than a traditional definitive, partly due to the adjacent barcode. The main features, such as the value, iridescent overprint and U-shaped slits, are scaled up accordingly.

Each stamp's (2D) barcode (also known as a data matrix) is unique and printed alongside the stamp design's main body, and a simulated perforation line separates the two elements. The simulated perforation line and 2D barcode are printed in the same colour as the stamp. Barcode stamps are a two-process printing, the main design and simulated perforation in gravure, and each stamp's barcode is separately digitally printed. The barcode enables tracking and further helps combat counterfeiting.

USED STAMPS. Because the self-adhesive stamps in this section do not include a water-soluable layer of gum, we recommend that used stamps are retained on their backing paper and trimmed with a uniform border of 1-2 mm around all sides, taking care not to cut into the perforations.

'ROYALMAIL' printed backing paper. Barcoded stamps' self-adhesive backing paper has the repeating 'ROYALMAIL' wording, first introduced as an additional security measure in 2016. It is described at the beginning of the non-barcoded Security Machin section.

Barcoded stamps from counter sheets have the 'ROYALMAIL' backing at 90 degrees to the stamp design. With the stamp design positioned upright (as a stamp is intended to be used), reading the backing from the left, the pairs of lines can appear with the Large lettering before (as opposed to over) the small (Type PB(L)-Ls), or with the small before the Large (Type PB(L)-sL). These differences are not listed in this catalogue unless the barcoded stamps themselves are different.

| 5010 | 5011 |

2023 (4 Apr). Barcoded Security Definitives. Design as T **5010** or T **5011**. Self-adhesive. One centre band (Nos. V5000, V5010) or two bands (others). U-shaped slits. Iridescent overprint. Die-cut perf 15×14½ (with one elliptical hole in each vertical side).

(i) Gravure and digital Cartor SP as Type **5010**.

V5000	(2nd) emerald (4.4.23)	1·25	1·25
V5001	(1st) deep violet (4.4.23)	1·75	1·75

(ii) As Type **5011**.

V5002	(2nd Large) grey-green (4.4.23)	2·60	2·60
V5003	(1st Large) greenish blue (4.4.23)	3·25	3·25

| 5012 |

2023 (4 Apr). Barcoded Security Definitives. Design as T **5012**. Self-adhesive. Two bands. U-shaped slits. Iridescent overprint. Die-cut perf 14½×15.

(a) Without source code, with year code, gravure and digital Cartor ISP.

V5025	£2.20 dark green (4.4.23)	3·75	3·75

| 5066 |

2023 (29 Aug). Barcoded Security Definitives. Design as T **5066**. Self-adhesive. Two bands. U-shaped slits. Iridescent overprint. Die-cut perf 14½×15.

(a) Without source code, with year code, gravure and digital Cartor ISP.

V5100	1p. blue	10	10
V5101	2p. deep green	10	10
V5105	5p. dull violet-blue	10	10
V5110	10p. turquoise-green	15	15
V5120	20p. bright green	30	30
V5150	50p. slate	90	90
V5180	£1 grey-brown	1·75	1·75
V5200	£2 new blue	3·00	3·00
V5240	£5 emerald	7·50	7·50

First Day Covers

4.4.23	Nos. V5000/V5003, V5025	12·00
29.8.23	Nos. V5100/V5191, V5105, V5110, V5120, V5150, V5180	5·50
29.8.23	Nos. V5200, V5240	13·50

Presentation Packs

4.4.23	Nos. V5000/V5003, V5025 (PO Pack No. 120)	12·00
29.8.23	Nos. V5100/V5101, V5105, V5110, V5120, V5150, V5180 (PO Pack No. 121)	5·50
29.8.23	Nos. V5200, V5240 (PO Pack No. 122)	13·50

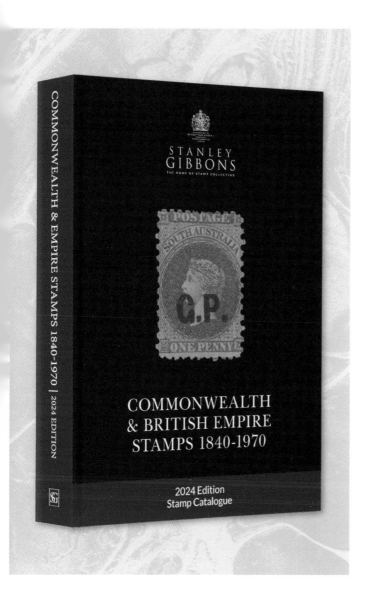

Prestige and Sponsored Booklets – a Simplified listing

On 1 December 1969 a new style of large-size booklet was issued, entitled Stamps for Cooks, sponsored by the Milk Marketing Board and containing recipes and stamps to a value of £1. The booklet contained one pane in a *se-tenant* combination that was not available from any other source, ensuring that sales to stamp collectors were high, even if those to cooks were probably rather limited!

In spite of this success, however, it was 1972 before a second sponsored booklet, The Story of Wedgwood was issued, providing the only source of the ½p. Machin definitive with one phosphor band at left. Nearly eight years were to pass before the same company sponsored a second Story of Wedgwood booklet, followed two years later by Stanley Gibbons with Story of Stanley Gibbons.

From then on, sponsored large-size booklets became an annual event, generally containing at least one stamp which was not available from any other source. In 1989 Royal Mail themselves became the 'sponsors' of each new booklet, which were by then widely known among collectors simply as 'Prestige Booklets'. Their frequency of issue increased steadily, until in 2009 four such booklets were issued.

In 2011, with the issue of the Morris & Co booklet, Royal Mail introduced an additional charge, over and above the face value of the stamps contained in them to cover the costs of manufacturing these booklets and with this change the Stanley Gibbons catalogue number prefix was altered from 'DX' to 'DY'.

This simplified checklist provides a complete listing of the Prestige and Sponsored booklets issued to date.

DX3

ZP1a	£1	Stamps for Cooks (1.2.69)	6·50
DX1	£1	The Story of Wedgwood (24.5.72)	45·00
DX2	£3	The Story of Wedgwood (16.4.80)	3·50
DX3	£4	Story of Stanley Gibbons (19.5.82)	4·50
DX4	£4	Story of the Royal Mint (14.9.83)	4·50
DX5	£4	The Story of our Christian Heritage (4.9.84)	13·00
DX6	£5	The Story of The Times (8.1.85)	8·50
DX7	£5	The Story of British Rail (18.3.86)	10·00
DX8	£5	The Story of P&O (3.3.87)	9·50
DX9	£5	The Story of The Financial Times (9.2.88)	16·00
DX10	£5	The Scots Connection (21.3.89)	10·00
DX11	£5	London Life (20.3.90)	12·50
DX12	£6	Alias Agatha Christie (19.3.91)	8·50
DX13	£6	Cymru-Wales (25.2.92)	9·00
DX14	£6	Tolkien, the Centenary (27.10.92)	9·00
DX15	£5·64	The Story of Beatrix Potter (10.8.93)	18·00
DX16	£6·04	Northern Ireland (26.7.94)	10·50
DX17	£6	The National Trust (25.4.95)	10·00
DX18	£6·48	European Football Championship (14.5.96)	8·50

DX19	£6·15	Celebrating 75 years of the BBC (23.9.97)	10·00
DX20	£7·49	The Wilding Definitives (10.3.98)	10·50
DX21	£6·16	Breaking Barriers (13.10.98)	17·50
DX22	£7·54	Profile on Print (16.2.99)	30·00
DX23	£6·99	World Changers (21.9.99)	13·50
DX24	£7·50	Special by Design (15.2.00)	25·00
DX25	£7·03	The Life of the Century (4.8.00)	20·00
DX26	£7·00	A Treasury of Trees (18.9.00)	17·00
DX27	£6·76	Unseen & Unheard (22.10.01)	25·00
DX28	£7·29	A Gracious Accession (6.2.02)	30·00
DX29	£6·83	Across the Universe (24.9.02)	32·00
DX30	£6·99	Microcosmos (25.2.03)	20·00
DX31	£7·46	A Perfect Coronation (2.6.03)	32·00
DX32	£7·44	Letters by Night (16.3.04)	20·00
DX33	£7·23	The Glory of the Garden (25.5.04)	18·50
DX34	£7·43	The Brontë Sisters (24.2.05)	15·00
DX35	£7·26	Battle of Trafalgar (18.10.05)	16·00
DX36	£7·40	Isambard Kingdom Brunel (23.2.06)	14·00
DX37	£7·44	Victoria Cross (21.9.06)	14·00
DX38	£7·49	World of Invention (1.3.07)	18·00
DX39	£7·66	The Machin, the Making of a Masterpiece (5.6.07)	18·50
DX40	£7·66	British Army Uniforms (20.9.07)	14·00
DX41	£7·40	Ian Fleming's James Bond (8.1.08)	19·00
DX42	£7·15	Pilot to Plane, RAF Uniforms (18.9.08)	17·00
DX43	£9·72	50th Anniversary of Country Definitives (29.9.08)	27·50
DX44	£7·68	British Design Classics (13.1.09)	20·00
DX45	£7·75	Charles Darwin (12.2.09)	35·00
DX46	£8·18	Treasures of the Archive (18.8.09)	14·00
DX47	£7·93	Royal Navy Uniforms (17.9.09)	16·00
DX48	£8·06	Classic Album Covers (7.1.10)	27·00
DX49	£7·72	The Royal Society (25.2.10)	18·00
DX50	£11·15	King George V (8.5.10)	25·00
DX51	£9·76	Britain Alone (13.5.10)	15·00
DX52	£9·05	WWF, For a Living Planet (22.3.11)	24·00
DY1	£9·99	Morris & Co (5.5.11)	14·50
DY2	£9·97	First United Kingdom Aerial Post (9.9.11)	40·00
DY3	£11·47	Roald Dahl (10.1.12)	18·00
DY4	£12·77	The Diamond Jubilee (31.5.12)	19·00
DY5	£10·71	Olympic and Paralympic Games (27.7.12)	35·00
DY6	£13·77	50 Years of *Doctor Who* (26.3.13)	24·00
DY7	£11·11	Football Heroes (9.5.13)	25·00
DY8	£11·19	Merchant Navy (19.9.13)	16·00
DY9	£13·97	Classic Locomotives (20.2.14)	32·50
DY10	£11·39	Buckingham Palace (15.4.14)	19·00
DY11	£11·30	Centenary of the First World War (28.7.14)	17·50
DY12	£14·50	Inventive Britain (19.2.15)	21·50
DY13	£13·96	Centenary of the First World War (2nd issue) (14.5.15)	18·50
DY14	£14·47	Bicentenary of the Battle of Waterloo (18.6.15)	27·00
DY15	£16·99	The Making of *Star Wars* The British Story (17.12.15)	28·00
DY16	£16·36	500 Years of Royal Mail (18.2.16)	27·00
DY17	£15·11	90th Birthday of Queen Elizabeth II (21.4.16)	32·50
DY18	£16·49	Centenary of the First World War (3rd issue) (21.6.16)	25·00
DY19	£15·37	The Tale of Beatrix Potter (28.7.16)	22·50
DY20	£14·58	Windsor Castle (15.2.17)	22·50
DY21	£15·14	50th Anniversary of the Machin Definitive (5.6.17)	38·00
DY22	£15·41	Centenary of the First World War (4th issue) (31.7.17)	24·50
DY23	£15·99	*Star Wars*. The Making of the Droids, Aliens and Creatures (14.12.17)	24·50
DY24	£13·95	Game of Thrones (23.1.18)	24·00
DY25	£18·69	Centenary of the RAF (20.3.18)	28·00
DY26	£15·65	Centenary of the First World War (5th issue) (13.9.18)	25·00
DY27	£15·50	Harry Potter (4.12.18)	25·00
DY28	£13·10	500th Death Anniversary of Leonardo da Vinci (13.2.19)	33·00
DY29	£17·45	Marvel (14.3.19)	27·00

DY30	£17·20	Birth Bicentenary of Queen Victoria *(24.5.19)*	50·00
DY31	£17·65	*Star Wars* the Making of the Vehicles *(26.11.19)*	27·00
DY32	£16·10	Visions of the Universe. Bicentenary of the Royal Astronomical Society *(11.2.20)*	38·00
DY33	£16·99	James Bond *(17.3.20)*	38·00
DY34	£19·80	75th Anniversary of the Second World War *(8.5.20)*	39·50
DY35	£19·10	Queen (rock band) *(9.7.20)*	27·00
DY36	£18·35	*Star Trek (13.11.20)*	26·00
DY37	£21·70	Only Fools and Horses *(16.2.21)*	30·00
DY38	£20·25	Paul McCartney *(28.5.21)*	30·00
DY39	£18·03	Industrial Revolutions *(12.8.21)*	35·00
DY40	£21·20	DC Collection *(17.9.21)*	32·00
DY41	£20·85	The Rolling Stones *(20.1.22)*	30·00
DY42	£19·50	Platinum Jubilee *(4.2.22)*	29·00
DY43	£20·75	Unsung Heroes: Women of World War II *(5.5.22)*	31·00
DY44	£21·75	Transformers *(1.9.22)*	32·00
DY45	£21·55	Tutankhamun *(24.11.22)*	32·00
DY46	£19·95	X-Men *(16.2.23)*	34·00
DY47	£21·05	*Flying Scotsman (9.3.23)*	35·00
CY1	£22·50	Shirley Bassey *(21.9.23)*	36·00
CY2	£25·25	Harry Potter *(19.10.23)*	36·00

Philatelic, Numismatic and Philatelic Medallic Covers

On 2 June 1993 Royal Mail and the Royal Mint prepared a commemorative cover to celebrate the 40th anniversary of the Coronation of Her Majesty The Queen. The cover bore the Royal Mint's Coronation Anniversary Crown and the £10 'Britannia' stamp, issued on 2 March 1993 (No. 1658).

On 1 March 1994 a similar cover was produced for the 25th Anniversary of the Investiture of HRH The Prince of Wales. The cover bore the set of five stamps issued on that date (Nos. 1810/1814), showing paintings by Prince Charles, and a commemorative medal struck by the Royal Mint.

So began a series of Philatelic Numismatic Covers (PNC) and Philatelic Medallic Covers (PMC) produced by Royal Mail and the Royal Mint.

This listing comprises only those jointly produced covers sold by the Philatelic Bureau. Privately sponsored covers incorporating coins or medals including those sponsored by the Royal Mint alone, are outside its scope.

No.	Date	Issue	Stamps	Coin/Medal	Price
RMC1	2.6.93	Coronation 40th Anniversary	1658	£5 Coin	18·00
RMC2	1.3.94	Prince of Wales Investiture 25th Anniversary	1810/1814	Medal	22·00
RMC3	27.7.94	Bank of England 300th Anniversary	1671×4 + label	£2 Coin	18·00
RMC4	20.5.95	R. J. Mitchell Birth Centenary	1671×4 + label	Medal	14·00
RMC5	15.8.95	End of Second World War 50th Anniversary	1873, 1875	£2 Coin	14·00
RMC6	29.10.95	William Wyon Birth Bicentenary	Y1743	Medal	14·00
RMC7	21.4.96	Queen's 70th Birthday	1671×4 + label	£5 Coin	17·00
RMC8	8.6.96	European Football Championship	1925/1929	£2 Coin	18·00
RMC9	1.10/3.11.96	Classic Sports Cars	1945/1949	Medal	17·00
RMC10	28.1.97	King Henry VIII 450th Death Anniversary	1965/1971	£1 Coin	14·00
RMC11	30.6.97	Transfer of Hong Kong to Chinese Rule	1671×4 + label	Hong Kong $5 Coin	22·00
RMC12	23.8.97	British Aircraft Designers	1984/1988	£2 Coin	14·00
RMC13	20.11.97	Royal Golden Wedding	2011/2014	£5 Coin	17·00
RMC14	24.2.98	Order of the Garter 650th Anniversary	2026/2030	£1 Coin	£100
RMC15	5.7.98	NHS 50th Anniversary	2046/2049	50p. Coin	25·00
RMC16	25.8.98	Notting Hill Carnival	2055/2058	50p. Coin	14·00
RMC17	14.11.98	HRH Prince of Wales 50th Birthday	1671×4 + label	£5 Coin	17·00
RMC18	12.5.99	Berlin Airlift 50th Anniversary	1671×4 + label	Medal	14·00
RMC19	1.7.99	New Scottish Parliament Building	S94/S97	£1 Coin	35·00
RMC20	1.10.99	Rugby World Cup, Wales	1671×4 + label	£2 Coin	14·00
RMC21	31.12.99	Millennium	**MS**2123	£5 Coin	12·00
RMC22	4.4.00	National Botanic Garden of Wales	2124×4 + label	£1 Coin	16·00
RMC23	14.8.00	150 Years of Public Libraries	2116, 2121, 2100	50p. Coin	14·00
RMC24	4.8.00	Queen Mother's 100th Birthday	**MS**2161	£5 Coin	17·00
RMC25	1.1.01	*Archers* Radio Programme 50th Anniversary	2107/2108, 2110	Medal	14·00
RMC26	24.5.01	RN Submarine Service Centenary	2202/2205	Medal	17·00
RMC27	20.6.01	Queen Victoria Death Centenary	2133a×2 + label	£5 Coin	17·00
RMC28	2.10.01	Northern Ireland	NI89/NI92	£1 Coin	10·00
RMC29	6.2.02	Golden Jubilee	2253/2257	£5 Coin	15·00
RMC29a	6.2.02	Golden Jubilee	2258/2259	£5 Coin and £5 note	40·00
RMC30	31.5.02	World Cup Football, Japan & Korea	2291, **MS**2292	£1 Coin	11·00
RMC31	16.7.02	17th Commonwealth Games, Manchester	2299/2303	4×£2 Coins	£160
RMC32	11.12.02	Queen Mother Commemoration	2280/2283	£5 Coin	17·00
RMC33	25.2.03	Discovery of DNA 50th Anniversary	2343/2347	£2 Coin	14·00
RMC34	2.6.03	Coronation 50th Anniversary	2368/2377	£5 Coin	17·00
RMC35	27.8.03	Extreme Endeavours	2360/2365	£1 Coin	14·00
RMC36	7.10.03	British Museum 250th Anniversary	2404/2409	Medal	14·00
RMC37	13.1.04	Classic Locomotives	2417/2422	£2 Coin	14·00
RMC38	6.4.04	Entente Cordiale Centenary	2446/2447 + France 50c., 75c.	£5 Coin	20·00
RMC39	13.4.04	Ocean Liners	2448/2453	Medal	14·00
RMC40	25.5.04	RHS Bicentenary	2456/2461	Medal	14·00
RMC41	30.11.04	Scotland Definitive	S109/S110, S112/S119	£1 Coin	25·00
RMC42	24.2.05	Charlotte Brontë 150th Death Anniversary	2518/2523	50p. Coin	15·00
RMC43	1.3.05	Wales Definitive	W98/W9, W101/W108	£1 Coin	16·00
RMC44	21.4.05	World Heritage Sites	2532/2535 + Australia 2×50c. & 2×$1	50p. Coin + Australia 50c.	40·00
RMC45	5.7.05	End of the War 60th Anniversary	**MS**2547	Medal and £2 Coin	22·50
RMC46	18.10.05	Battle of Trafalgar Bicentenary	2574/2579	2×£5 Coins	40·00
RMC47	23.2.06	Brunel Birth Bicentenary	2607/2612	2×£2 Coins	17·00
RMC48	17.3.06	Northern Ireland Definitive	NI94/NI95, NI98, NI100	£1 Coin	18·00
RMC49	21.4.06	Queen's 80th Birthday	2620/2627	£5 Coin	19·00
RMC50	6.6.06	World Cup Football	2628/2633	Medal	16·00
RMC51	18.7.06	National Portrait Gallery 150th Anniversary	2640/2649	Medal	16·00
RMC52	21.9.06	Victoria Cross 150th Anniversary	2659/2664	2×50p. Coins	20·00
RMC53	16.1.07	Act of Union 300th Anniversary	6×1st as 2570 but litho	£2 Coin	16·00
RMC54	13.2.07	*The Sky at Night* 50th Anniversary	2709/2714	Medal	16·00
RMC55	22.3.07	Abolition of the Slave Trade Bicentenary	2728/2733	£2 Coin	35·00
RMC56	23.4.07	England Definitive	EN6/EN7, EN12, EN18	£1 Coin	21·00
RMC57	5.6.07	First Machin Stamps 40th Anniversary	2741	Medal	16·00
RMC58	3.7.07	British Motor Racing	2744/2749	Medal	16·00

No.	Date	Issue	Stamps	Coin/Medal	Price
RMC59	26.7.07	Scouting Centenary	2758/2763	50p. Coin	20·00
RMC60	20.11.07	Diamond Wedding	2780/2786	£5 Coin	28·00
RMC61	1.4.08	Territorial Army Centenary	2774/2776	Medal	16·00
RMC62	13.5.08	St Paul's Cathedral 300th Anniversary	**MS**2847	Medal	16·00
RMC63	5.6.08	First Machin Coin 40th Anniversary	2741	Medal	16·00
RMC64	17.7.08	Farnborough A Celebration of Aviation	2855/2860	Medal	16·00
RMC65	24.7.08	1908 Olympic Games, London Centenary	1668x4	£2 Coin	28·00
RMC66	29.9.08	Country Definitives 50th Anniversary and £1 Coin 25th Anniversary	**MS**NI153	£1 Coin	18·00
RMC67	6.11.08	Armistice 90th Anniversary	2883/2885	Medal	16·00
RMC68	13.1.09	Mini car 50th Anniversary	2889×2	Medal	17·00
RMC69	22.1.09	Robert Burns 250th Birth Anniversary	**MS**S157	£2 Coin	32·00
RMC70	12.2.09	Charles Darwin Birth Bicentenary	2898/2903	£2 Coin	35·00
RMC71	2.3.09	First Concorde Test Flight 40th Anniversary	2891×2	Medal	17·00
RMC72	21.4.09	Accession of Henry VIII 500th Anniversary and Accession of Elizabeth I 450th Anniversary	2925, 2929 2×£5	Coins	35·00
RMC73	19.5.09	Royal Botanic Gardens, Kew 250th Anniversary	**MS**2941	50p. Coin	£275
RMC74	1.9.09	Fire and Rescue Service	2958/2963	Medal	17·00
RMC75	18.9.09	Big Ben 150th Anniversary	2805 + label	Medal	17·00
RMC76	22.10.09	Countdown to London 2012 Olympic Games I The countdown begins...	2981/2990	£5 Coin	20·00
RMC77	1.12.09	High value Security Definitives	U2913/U2916	£1 Coin	24·00
RMC78	2.2.10	Girlguiding Centenary	**MS**3025	50p. Coin	20·00
RMC79	25.2.10	Royal Society 350th Anniversary	3026/3035	Medal	20·00
RMC80	11.3.10	Battersea Cats and Dogs Home 150th Anniversary	3036/3045	Medal	20·00
RMC81	21.4.10	City of London	As 1st St George's flag stamp from **MS**EN50 but self-adhesive+label	£1 Coin	27·00
RMC82	13.5.10	Dunkirk	**MS**3086	Medal	20·00
RMC83	27.7.10	Countdown to London 2012 Olympic Games II The Games spring to life...	3097/3106	£5 Coin	24·00
RMC84	1.8.10	Florence Nightingale	2805 + label	£2 Coin	32·00
RMC85	12.10.10	Olympic and Paralympic Sports I. Athletics – Track	2983	50p. Coin	13·00
RMC86	12.10.10	Olympic and Paralympic Sports II Cycling	3101	50p. Coin	13·00
RMC87	30.11.10	Olympic and Paralympic Sports III Football	3104	50p. Coin	13·00
RMC88	30.11.10	Olympic and Paralympic Sports IV Boccia	2985	50p. Coin	13·00
RMC89	11.1.11	F.A.B. The Genius of Gerry Anderson	**MS**3142	Medal	20·00
RMC90	1.2.11	Olympic and Paralympic Sports V Weightlifting	2989	50p. Coin	13·00
RMC91	1.2.11	Olympic and Paralympic Sports VI Hockey	3103	50p. Coin	13·00
RMC92	17.3.11	City of Belfast	NI123	£1 Coin	28·00
RMC93	22.3.11	WWF 50th Anniversary	**MS**3172	50p. Coin	22·00
RMC94	24.3.11	Olympic and Paralympic Sports VII Shooting	3098	50p. Coin	13·00
RMC95	24.3.11	Olympic and Paralympic Sports VIII Goalball	3105	50p. Coin	13·00
RMC96	21.4.11	Royal Wedding	**MS**3180	£5 Coin	32·00
RMC97	26.5.11	Olympic and Paralympic Sports IX Taekwondo	3100	50p. Coin	13·00
RMC98	26.5.11	Olympic and Paralympic Sports X Boxing	3106	50p. Coin	13·00
RMC99	14.6.11	Thomas the Tank Engine	3187/3192	Medal	20·00
RMC100	27.7.11	Countdown to London 2012 Olympic Games IV The final push to the line	3195/3204	£5 Coin	22·00
RMC101	27.7.11	Olympic and Paralympic Sports XI Wrestling	3199	50p. Coin	13·00
RMC102	27.7.11	Olympic and Paralympic Sports XII Handball	3204	50p. Coin	13·00
RMC103	23.8.11	Restoration of the Monarchy	3207/3214	£5 Coin	22·00
RMC104	22.9.11	Olympic and Paralympic Sports XIII Basketball	2990	50p. Coin	13·00
RMC105	22.9.11	Olympic and Paralympic Sports XIV Modern Pentathlon	3099	50p. Coin	13·00
RMC106	6.10.11	500th Anniversary of Launch of *Mary Rose*	2925 and *Mary Rose* stamp from **MS**2930	£2 Coin	60·00
RMC107	8.11.11	Christmas 400th Anniversary of the King James Bible	3237/3243	£2 coin	60·00
RMC108	29.11.11	Olympic and Paralympic Sports XV Canoeing	2981	50p. coin	13·00
RMC109	29.11.11	Olympic and Paralympic Sports XVI Archery	2982	50p. coin	13·00
RMC110	30.11.11	City of Edinburgh	S110 + label	£1 coin	22·00
RMC111	5.1.12	Olympic and Paralympic Games	3250/3253	£2 coin	24·00
RMC112	12.1.12	Olympic and Paralympic Sports XVII Aquatics	2984	50p. coin	13·00
RMC113	12.1.12	Olympic and Paralympic Sports XVIII Rowing	3097	50p. coin	13·00
RMC114	28.2.12	Olympic and Paralympic Sports XIX Sailing	3195	50p. coin	13·00
RMC115	28.2.12	Olympic and Paralympic Sports XX Badminton	2988	50p. coin	13·00
RMC116	1.3.12	City of Cardiff	W99+label	£1 coin	22·00
RMC117	1.4.12	Olympic and Paralympic Sports XXI Judo	2986	50p. coin	13·00
RMC118	1.4.12	Olympic and Paralympic Sports XXII Triathlon	3203	50p. coin	13·00
RMC119	6.5.12	Olympic and Paralympic Sports XXIII Wheelchair rugby	3198	50p. coin	13·00
RMC120	6.5.12	Olympic and Paralympic Sports XXIV Volleyball	3197	50p. coin	13·00
RMC121	31.5.12	Diamond Jubilee	3319/3326	£5 coin	20·00
RMC122	12.6.12	Olympic and Paralympic Sports XXV Equestrian	2987	50p. coin	13·00
RMC123	12.6.12	Olympic and Paralympic Sports XXVI Table Tennis	3102	50p. coin	13·00
RMC124	19.6.12	Charles Dickens Birth Bicentenary	3330/3335	£2 coin	28·00

No.	Date	Issue	Stamps	Coin/Medal	Price
RMC125	27.7.12	Olympic and Paralympic Sports XXVII Wheelchair Tennis	3200	50p. coin	13·00
RMC126	27.7.12	Olympic and Paralympic Sports XXVIII Fencing	3201	50p. coin	13·00
RMC127	27.7.12	Countdown to London 2012 Olympic Games IV. Crossing the Finishing Line	MS3341	£5 coin and £5 silver proof coin	20·00
RMC128	28.8.12	Olympic and Paralympic Sports XXIX Gymnastics	3202	50p. coin	13·00
RMC129	28.8.12	Olympic and Paralympic Sports XXX Athletics – Field	3196	50p. coin	13·00
RMC130	9.1.13	150th Anniversary of the London Underground	3423/3428	2×£2 Coins	40·00
RMC131	30.5.13	60th Anniversary of the Coronation. Six Decades of Royal Portraits	3491/3496	£2 Coin	26·00
RMC132	10.10.13	Dinosaurs	3532/3541	Medal	38·00
RMC133	22.11.13	Birth Centenary of Benjamin Britten	3459	50p. Coin	40·00
RMC134	7.1.14	Classic Children's TV	3552/3563	Medal	30·00
RMC135	15.4.14	Buckingham Palace	3589/3594	Medal	26·00
RMC136	17.7.14	Commonwealth Games, Glasgow	3619/3624	50p. coin	26·00
RMC137	28.7.14	Centenary of the First World War	3626/3631	£2 coin	26·00
RMC138	23.9.14	Ryder Cup, Gleneagles	S158	Medal	22·00
RMC139	18.9.14	500th Anniversary of Trinity House	3638	£2 coin	22·00
RMC140	24.1.15	50th Death Anniversary of Winston Churchill	3645	£5 Coin	26·00
RMC141	5.3.15	Alice in Wonderland	3658/3667	Medal	22·00
RMC142	6.5.15	175th Anniversary of the Penny Black	MS3710	Medal	22·00
RMC143	14.5.15	Centenary of the First World War (2nd issue)	3711/3716	£2 Coin	26·00
RMC144	2.6.15	800th Anniversary of the Magna Carta	3718/3723	£2 coin	22·00
RMC145	18.6.15	Centenary of the Battle of Waterloo (1st issue)	3724/3729	£5 Coin	26·00
RMC146	9.9.15	Long to Reign Over Us	MS3747	£5 Coin	32·00
RMC147	15.9.15	75th Anniversary of the Battle of Britain	MS3735	50p. Coin	32·00
RMC148	20.10.15	Star Wars. Battles	3758/3762, 3764/3767	Medal	23·00
RMC149	20.10.15	Star Wars. Vehicles	MS3770	Medal	23·00
RMC150	17.12.15	Star Wars. Characters	3758/3769	Medal	42·00
RMC151	5.4.16	400th Death Anniversary of William Shakespeare	3816/3825	3×£2 Coins	45·00
RMC152	21.4.16	90th Birthday of Queen Elizabeth II	MS3832	£5 Coin	30·00
RMC153	21.6.16	Centenary of the First World War (3rd issue)	3838/3843	£2 Coin	32·00
RMC154	28.7.16	The Tale of Peter Rabbit	MS3868	50p. Coin	32·00
RMC155	2.9.16	350th Anniversary of the Great Fire of London	3879/3884	£2 Coin	32·00
RMC156	14.10.16	950th Anniversary of the Battle of Hastings	EN51×4+label	50p. Coin	24·00
RMC157	6.2.17	65th Anniversary of Accession of Queen Elizabeth II	U3920	£5 Coin	30·00
RMC158	15.2.17	Windsor Castle	3920/3925	Medal	23·00
RMC159	6.4.17	Racehorse Legends	3940/3947	Medal	23·00
RMC160	5.6.17	50th Anniversary of the Machin definitive	MS3964	Medal	23·00
RMC161	31.7.17	Centenary of the First World War (4th issue)	3983/3988	Coin	23·00
RMC162	12.10.17	Star Wars. BB 8	4007/4014	Medal	23·00
RMC163	12.10.17	Star Wars. R2-D2	4007/4014	Medal	23·00
RMC164	20.11.17	Royal Platinum Wedding Anniversary	MS4031	Coin	23·00
RMC165	14.12.17	Star Wars. C3-PO	4007/4014	Medal	23·00
RMC166	23.1.18	Game of Thrones	4033/4042	Medal	30·00
RMC167	23.1.18	Game of Thrones	MS4043	Medal	30·00
RMC168	15.2.18	Votes for Women	4050/4057	50p. coin	26·00
RMC169	19.5.18	Royal Wedding	MS4092	£5 coin	30·00
RMC170	16.8.18	Captain Cook and the Endeavour Voyage	4118/4123	£2 coin	26·00
RMC171	13.9.18	Centenary of the First World War (5th issue)	4133/4138	£2 coin	26·00
RMC172	17.9.18	Centenary of the RAF	4058/4063	4×£2 coins	70·00
RMC173	17.9.18	Centenary of the RAF – Red Arrows	MS4064	£2 coin	26·00
RMC174	16.10.18	Harry Potter Dragon Alley	4041/4050	Medal	30·00
RMC175	16.10.18	Harry Potter Hogwarts	MS4153	Medal	30·00
RMC176	14.11.18	70th Birthday of the Prince of Wales	MS4163	£5 coin	30·00
RMC177	14.3.19	Marvel Spider-man	4182/4191	Medal	25·00
RMC178	14.3.19	Marvel Hulk	4182/4191	Medal	25·00
RMC179	26.4.19	Marvel Avengers	MS4192	Medal	25·00
RMC180	2.5.19	50th Anniversary of Introduction of the Harrier Jump Jet to RAF Service	MS4218	Medal	17·00
RMC181	24.5.19	Birth Bicentenary of Queen Victoria	4219/4224	£5 coin	20·00
RMC182	6.6.19	75th Anniversary of D-Day	4230/4235	£2 coin	17·50
RMC183	9.9.19	Centenary of Remembrance	3626, 3711, 3838, 3983, 4133	£5 coin	30·00
RMC184	10.10.19	The Gruffalo	MS4282	50p. coin	17·50
RMC185	26.11.19	Star Wars. The Skywalker Family	4292/4301	Medal	30·00
RMC186	26.11.19	Star Wars. A Galaxy of Vehicles	MS4303	Medal	30·00
RMC187	11.2.20	Professor Stephen Hawking	4323/4330	50p coin	26·00
RMC188	17.3.20	James Bond. Q Branch	MS4338	£5 coin	30·00
RMC189	27.4.20	The Design of James Bond	4332/4337	£5 coin	30·00
RMC190	7.4.20	William Wordsworth	4345/4354	£5 coin	30·00
RMC191	8.5.20	75th Anniversary of the End of the Second World War	4356/4363	£2 coin	26·00
RMC192	9.7.20	Queen Live	MS4396	£5 coin	30·00
RMC193	15.8.20	75th Anniversary of the End of the Second World War	MS4364	£5 coin	30·00
RMC194	18.8.20	Sherlock and Moriarty	4411/4416	Medal	30·00
RMC195	18.8.20	The Genius of Sherlock Holmes	MS4417	Medal	30·00

No.	Date	Issue	Stamps	Coin/Medal	Price
RMC196	13.11.20	*Star Trek* The Original Series	4443/4454	Medal	30·00
RMC197	13.11.20	*Star Trek* Movies	**MS**4455	Medal	30·00
RMC198	16.2.21	*Only Fools and Horses* (TV sitcom, 1981-2003)	4477/4484	Medal	30·00
RMC199	21.4.21	95th Birthday of Queen Elizabeth II	U2998x4,EN53, NI158, S160, W150+label	£5 coin	30·00
RMC200	28.5.21	Paul McCartney Albums	4517/4524	Medal	30·00
RMC201	28.5.21	Paul McCartney In the Studio	**MS**4525	Medal	30·00
RMC202	13.8.21	H. G. Wells	4504x3	£2 coin	26·00
RMC203	19.8.21	Prince Phillip, Duke of Edinburgh (1921-2021) Commemoration	**MS**4532	£5 coin	30·00
RMC204	17.9.21	DC Collection. Batman	4575/4586	Medal	30·00
RMC205	17.9.21	DC Collection. Wonder Woman	**MS**4587	Medal	30·00
RMC206	20.1.22	The Rolling Stones. Bridges to Babylon Tour 1997/1998	4614/4621	Medal	30·00
RMC207	20.1.22	The Rolling Stones. Licks Tour 2002/2003	**MS**4622	Medal	30·00
RMC208	4.2.22	Platinum Jubilee	4627/4634	£5 coin	30·00
RMC209	8.3.22	The FA Cup	4636/4641	£2 coin	30·00
RMC210	1.6.22	Platinum Jubilee	U3071, U3074, U3077, U3108, each x 2+label	50p coin	26·00
RMC211	1.7.22	Pride	4684/4691	50p coin	26·00
RMC212	28.7.22	Commonweath Games, Birmingham	4692/4699	50p coin	26·00
RMC213	1.9.22	Transformers	4700/4707	Medal	30·00
RMC214	1.9.22	Transformers: The Dinobots	**MS**4708	Medal	30·00
RMC215	29.9.22	Royal Marines Uniforms	**MS**4722	Medal	30·00
RMC216	19.10.22	Aardman Classics. Wallace and Gromit Cracking Moments	**MS**4731	Medal	30·00
RMC217	10.11.22	Queen Elizabeth II (1926-2022) Commemoration	4739/4742	50p coin	26·00
RMC218	10.11.22	Queen Elizabeth II (1926-2022) Commemoration	4739/4742	£5 coin	30·00
RMC219	24.11.22	Tutankhamun	4743/4750	£5 coin	30·00
RMC220	12.1.23	Iron Maiden	4756/4763	Medal	30·00
RMC221	12.1.12	Iron Maiden	**MS**4764	Medal	30·00
RMC222	16.2.23	X-Men	4765/4776	Medal	30·00
RMC223	16.2.23	X-Men	**MS**4777	Medal	30·00
RMC224	9.3.23	*Flying Scotsman*	4783/4790	£2 coin	28·00
RMC225	6.5.23	King Charles III, A New Reign	**MS**5020	£5 coin	30·00
RMC226	8.6.23	Warhammer	5030/5035	Medal	30·00
RMC227	8.6.23	Warhammer	**MS**5036	Medal	30·00
RMC228	22.6.23	Windrush	5037/5044	50p coin	28·00
RMC229	5.9.23	Paddington	5063/5068	Medal	30·00
RMC230	21.9.23	Shirley Bassey	5070/5077	£5 coin	30·00
RMC231	19.10.23	Harry Potter	5083/5092	Medal	30·00
RMC232	19.10.23	Harry Potter	**MS**5093	Medal	30·00
RMC233	14.11.23	King Charles III, 75th Birthday	V5240	£5 Coin	30·00

This index gives an easy reference to the inscriptions and designs of the Special Stamps of Queen Elizabeth II from 1953 to March 2023. Where a complete set shares an inscription or type of design, then only the catalogue number of the first stamp is given in addition to separate entries for stamps depicting popular thematic subjects. Paintings, inventions, etc., are indexed under the name of the artist or inventor, where this is shown on the stamp.

Subscribe &
Save Money
on the cover price*

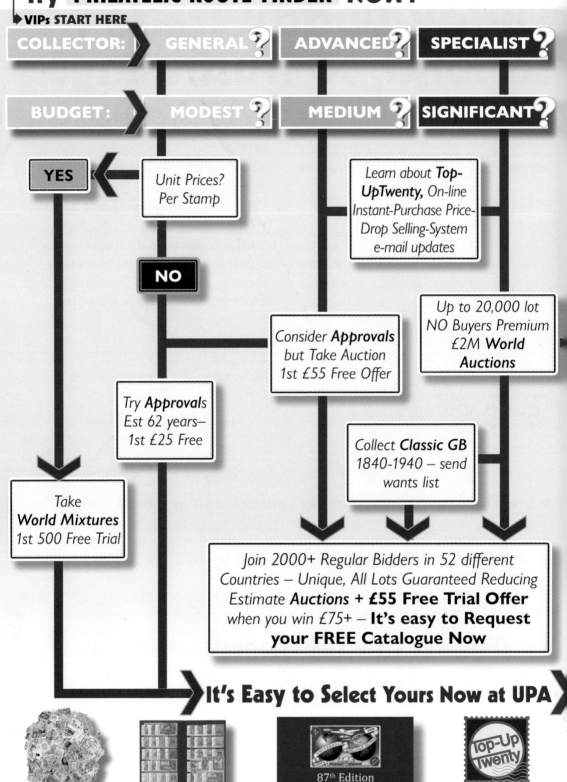